# THE RAMAYANA
# ARANYA KANDAM

Owing to the antiquity and rarity of this book, certain pages are regrettably absent, and readability is compromised due to the blurring of the original text. If you possess any insights regarding the availability of these missing sections, kindly inform us. Your assistance is crucial in ensuring the completion of this significant work for the benefit of future generations.

# THE RAMAYANA
# ARANYA KANDAM

EDITED BY

**MANMATHA NATH DUTT**

GYAN

*Published by*

Gyan Publishing House
5, Ansari Road
Daryaganj, New Delhi-110002
Phone: 011-47034999, 9811692060
E-mail: books@gyanbooks.com

*Distribution Network*
gyanbooks.com
India, USA, Canada, UK, Australia



ISBN: 978-93-7169-211-3 (HB)

First Published, 1892

2nd Impression 2025

*Printed at:* Gyan Press, Delhi.



**THE RAMAYANA ARANYA KANDAM**
Editor: MANMATHA NATH DUTT

VOL. III. PARTS X—XII.

THE

# RAMAYANA.

TRANSLATED INTO ENGLISH PROSE FROM THE ORIGINAL SANSKRIT OF VALMIKI.

## ĀRANYA KĀNDAM.

*EDITED AND PUBLISHED BY*

**MANMATHA NATH DUTT, M. A.**

*Rector, Keshub Academy.*

PRINTED BY

GIRISH CHANDRA CHACKRAVARTI,

DEVA PRESS, 65/2, BEADON STREET,

CALCUTTA.

THE

# RAMAYANA.

TRANSLATED INTO ENGLISH PROSE FROM THE ORIGINAL

SANSKRIT OF VALMIKI.

# ĀRANYA KĀNDAM.

*EDITED AND PUBLISHED BY*

**MANMATHA NATH DUTT, M. A.**

*Rector, Keshub Academy.*

PRINTED BY

GIRISH CHANDRA CHACKRAVARTI,

DEVA PRESS, 65/2, BEADON STREET,

CALCUTTA.

1892.

# ĀRANYA KANDAM.

## SECTION I.

ENTERING the extensive forest of Dandaka, the irrepressible and self-composed Rāma saw the collection of asylums belonging unto the ascetics, strewn with Kuça and bark, and environed by spiritual energy; incapable of being beheld; like the solar disc in the heavens,—the refuge of all creatures—with their ornamented yards; filled with a great many deer, and abounding in multitudes of birds; in which Apsarās always danced and which they held in respect; (asylums) beauteous with spacious rooms for fire-sacrifice, with sacrificial necessaries, deer-skins, Kuça, faggots, water-pitchers, fruits and roots; surrounded by mighty and sacred forest-trees; crowned with lucious fruits; honored with Vāli* and Homa†; holy; resounding with the sounds of Vedic recitations; scattered with divers blossoms; and containing tanks filled with lotuses; with ancient ascetics living on fruits and roots, having their senses under control, wearing bark and black deer-skins, and possessing the splendour of the sun or fire; and adorned by great and holy sages living upon regulated fare. Beholding that

* Offerings to the spirits of air.—T.

† Burnt offerings, or oblations of clarified butter into the sacred fire, as an offering to the gods, accompanied with prayers or invocations.—T.

collection of asylums belonging unto the ascetics, resembling the regions of Brahmā, resonant with the voices of Vedic recitations; and grateful; with highly pious Brāhmanas versed in the Vedas,—the exceedingly energetic and graceful Rāghava entered the same, having first unstrung his mighty bow. Thereupon, seeing the righteous Rāma resembling the moon risen, as well as Lakshmana and the illustrious Vaidehi, those Maharshis endued with spiritual intuition, came forward (to meet the incomers); and, having uttered benedictions, those persons of rigid vows, received them. And those dwellers of the wood, struck with wonder, beheld Rāma's tender grace and loveliness and elegance of dress. And struck with astonishment, those inhabitants of the woods of pre-eminent piety saw Vaidehi, Lakshmana and Rāma, with winkless eyes. And those persons of exalted virtue, engaged in the welfare of all creatures, made Rāghava, their guest, sit down in their thatched cottage. Then having received Rāma respectfully according to scriptural prescription, those virtuous ones of eminent piety, resembling fire, procured water (for Rāma). And, experiencing great delight, those high-souled ones, uttering benedictions, procured wild fruits, flowers and roots; and, having assigned an asylum (unto Rāma), those persons cognizant of righteousness, said with joined hands. Possessed of high fame, thou, the protector of righteousness, art the refuge of these people. Thou shouldst be honored and worshipped, being their king, holding the rod, and their superior. O Rāghava, it is because he that governs his subjects, is a fourth part of Indra himself, that the king, being bowed down unto by all, enjoys the choicest things. And we, being in thy dominions, ought to be protected by thee. Whether living in the city or in the woods, thou, lord of men, art our sovereign. We have renounced chastising others; and, O monarch, we have conquered our anger, and subdued our passions. Therefore, evenas a child in its mother's womb (should be protected by her), should we be protected by thee." Having said this, they entertained Rāghava, along with Lakshmana, with fruits and roots and flowers and diverse other edibles procurable in the woods. In the same way, other ascetics of accomplished purposes, living lives of integrity, duly pleased that lord, Rāma, resembling Vaiçyānara.

## SECTION II.

HAVING received the homage of the ascetics, Rāma about sun-rise, having greeted them all, entered into the forest. And Rāma, followed by Lakshmana, saw the heart of the forest abounding in various kinds of beasts,—ranged by bears and tigers, with its trees and shrubs torn and trampled, its pools turbid, and its birds crying. And, having in company with Sitā arrived at that forest abounding in terrible beasts, Kākutstha saw a man-eater, resembling a mountain-summit, emitting tremendous roars, with hollow eyes, a huge face, frightful, having a deformed belly, disgusting, dreadful, Cyclopean, mis-shapen,of a horrible sight, clad in a tiger-skin, besmeared with fat, covered with blood, capable of frightening all creatures, with his mouth widely extended, like unto the Destroyer himself, and uttering loud shouts,—who stood piercing with his iron dart three lions, four tigers, two leopards, four Prishatas, and the huge tusked head of an elephant dripping fat. Having seen Rāma and Lakshmana as well as Sitā the daughter of Mithilā, he growing angry, rushed (against them), like the Destroyer himself rushing against creatures at the universal dissolution. Uttering a dreadful yell, and, as if making the earth tremble, he took Vaidehi on his waist, and, going a little distance, said, "O ye wearing bark and matted locks, O ye of feeble strength, that accompanied by your (common) wife, have entered the forest of Dandaka, bearing bows and arrows and scimitars, why, being ascetics, do ye wish to associate with a (single) woman? Ye wicked wretches, ye impious wights, who are ye that bring disgrace upon ascetics? I am a Rākshasa, Virādha by name. This forest is my fastness. Accoutred in arms, I range (here), feeding on the flesh or ascetics. This transcendentally beauteous one shall be my wife. And in battle I shall drink your blood, wretches that ye are." Hearing the wicked and vaunting speech of the impious Virādha, as he said this, Janaka's daughter, Sitā, began to tremble from fear, like a plantain tree shaken by the wind. Seeing the graceful Sitā on the waist of Virādha, Rāghava with a blank countenance said unto Lakshmana, "O amiable one, behold the daughter of king Janaka, my wife of pure ways, an illustrious princess brought up in luxury—on Virādha's waist. O Lakshmana, what had been wished for by Kaikeyi with reference to us, (hath taken place), and the dear boon (that she had asked) hath borne fruit. That far-sighted lady—my second mother—who had not been satisfied with having secured the kingdom in the interest of her son, and by whom I that was dear unto her above all other creatures, had been banished to the woods hath to-day her wishes crowned with success. O Sumitrā's son, nothing can impart unto me greater anguish than the touching of Vaidehi by another—which surpasses my father's demise and my having been deprived of the kingdom." As Kākutstha with his eyes flooded with tears was speaking thus, Lakshmana flying into a rage, spoke like unto a confined elephant: "Why dost thou, O Kākutstha, being the lord of all creatures and resembling Vāsava himself,—and also backed by myself, thy servant,—grieve like one forlorn? The earth shall drink the gore of this Rākshasa, Virādha, when deprived of life, after he hath been slain with a shaft by my angry self. That ire of mine which I had conceived against Bharata hankering after the kingdom, will I discharge on Virādha; even as the wielder of the thunder bolt hurls his weapon at a hill. Let my mighty arrow acquiring velocity from the speed imparted to it through the energy of my arms, light on his huge breast, and force his life from forth his body ; and let him whirling (at length, fall down to the earth.

---

## SECTION III.

THEN* Virādha again spoke filling the forest, "Do ye tell me who ask you,—who are ye and whither are ye going ?" Thereupon, the highly energetic Rāma answered the Rākshasa with a flaming face, when he had thus asked (Rāma)—that he belonged to the Ikshwāku race. "Know us that are in the forest, for Kshatriyas of respectable character. I also am anxious of knowing who thou art, that goest about the Dandakas." Virādha answered Ramā having truth for his prowess, "Ah ! I will tell thee, O king. Do thou, O Rāghava understand ! I am son unto Java, and my mother is Satarhadā. All the Rākshasas of the earth have called me Virādha. Having gratified Brahmā by my asceticism, I received (this boon) that none in the world would be able to slay me by mangling my body with weapons. Forsaking this fair one, do ye renouncing all hope (of either recovering her or vanquishing me), speedily flee away to that place whence ye had come ;—else I shall deprive you of your lives." Thereat, Rāma with his eyes reddened through wrath replied unto that Rākshasa of a deformed shape, the wicked Virādha—saying, "Little ! shame on thee of base purposes ! Thou surely seekest thy own death ; and (death) thou shalt get in battle. Stay ! Thou escapest

---

The North-West Provinces text has an additional *Sloka ;—Haviug said this, the graceful Lakshmana spoke unto Virādha as if jestingly, "Who art thou that coming to the forest, art ranging it pleasantly ?"—T.*

me not with life." Then stringing his bow, Rāma, speedily aiming at the Rākshasa, pierced him with sharpened shafts; and (then) from his bow-string let go seven shafts, having their feathered parts plated with gold. furnished with great velocity, and coursing like Suparna or the wind. Thereat, resembling flames, those arrows furnished with peacocks' feathers, pierced Virādha's body, and fell to the earth, covered with blood. On being thus pierced, the Rākshasa set Vaidehi down, and, upraising a dart, rushed in wrath towards Rāma and Lakshmana. And sending forth a mighty roar, he took up a dart resembling the banner of Sakra; and he then appeared like the Destroyer* with opening mouth. Then the brothers showered a blazing volley of shafts on the Rākshasa, resembling the Destroyer himself. And stationing himself at a spot, the Rākshasa, laughing terribly, yawned, and as he yawned the fleet-coursing shafts fell off from his person. And by virtue of the bestowal of the boon (by Brahmā), the Rākshasa Virādha drew up his vital energies, and, lifting up a pike, darted at the descendants of Raghu. That best of those bearing arms cut off with two arrows that dart resembling the thunder-bolt and flaming in the sky. And the dart severed by the shafts of Rāma, fell to the earth, as falls a crag severed by the thunder-bolt. Thereat, swiftly raising up a sword, resembling a black snake, each (of the Rāghavas) approached his antagonist, and began to assail him hastily. Thus hard beset, that terrible one, seizing them both with his arms, attempted to make away with those foremost of men, who, however, retained their calmness. Reading his purpose, Rāma spake unto Lakshmana, "Let the Rākshasa bear us by this way.

* The text has, *Kālāntakayamopame—abl.*—resembling *Kāla*, *Antaka*, or *Yama*. The commentator cites a *sloka*, which assigns three several functions to the three,—*Kāla* executes his office on the occasion of the separation of life from the body; *Antaka* compasses the end; and *Yama* finally sits in judgment upon the departed soul. But this strikes me as misplaced erudition. I, however, give the commonsense rendering.—T.

No use of letting him. O Sumitrā's son, let the Rākshasa bear us wherever he likes. Even this, by which the ranger of the night is proceeding, is our way." And lifting up (Rāma and Lakshmana) by his might and prowess, as if they were striplings, that haughty ranger of the night laid them on his shoulders. And having deposited the Raghavas on his shoulders, Virādha—ranger* of night—sending up dreadful shouts, directed his course towards the forest. And he at length entered the forest resembling a mighty mass of clouds, furnished with various kinds of trees, picturesque with diverse species of birds, and abounding in jackals, serpents and beasts.

## SECTION IV.

SEEING those foremost of Raghus, the Kākutsthas, carried away, Sitā cried in a loud voice, raising up her arms,† "Rāma, the son of Daçaratha, the strong, the truthful and the pure, is, along with Lakshmana, being carried away by you, Rākshasa of a terrible appearance. Me bears will devour and tigers and panthers. Renouncing the Kākutsthas, do thou carry me away. I bow unto thee, O best of Rākshasas." Hearing these words of Vaidehi, Rāma and Lakshmana bestirred themselves for compassing the death of that wicked one. And Sumitrā's son broke his left arm; while Rāma at once broke the Rākshasa's right one. On his arms being broken, the Rākshasa resembling a mass of clouds, growing weak, sank down on the ground in a swoon like a hill riven by the thunder-bolt. Thereupon, they assailed the Rākshasa with

* Another reading is:—*That ranger of the night laid on his shoulders, those ones, who were puffed up with their exceeding prowess.*—T.

† Another reading is *Subhuyabhuyan*—*That one of elegant arms (raising) them up.*—T.

their fists, arms and feet; and lifting him up once and again, and pressing him, they trod on him over the ground. Although he was sore pierced by full many an arrow and cut sorryly by scimitars, and pressed down on the earth in various ways, yet the Rākshasa expired not. Seeing him utterly incapable of being killed, and resembling a hill, that inspirer of hope in times of peril, the graceful (Rāma), said, "O foremost of men, in consequence of his austerities, yon Rākshasa cannot be vanquished with weapons in conflict. Therefore, let us cast him into a pit. O Lakshmana, dig a capacious pit in this forest* for this Rākshasa resembling an elephant, teribile, and of a grim presence." Having said this unto Lakshmana,—"Do thou dig a pit," the powerful Rāma remained planting his foot on Virādha's throat. Having heard Rāghava's words, the Rākshasa spake gently, "Slain am I, O chief of men, by thee possessed of strength equal to that of Sakra. Through ignorance, O foremost of men, I could not before know thee. Now I know thee that art Rāma, the worthy Son of Kauçalyā, my child; as well as the highly virtuous Vaidehi and the renowned Lakshmana. By virtue of a curse, I entered this dreadful Rākshasa form, I a Gandharba, having been cursed by Vaiçravana. Being propitiated by me, that greatly famous one said,—'When Rāma the son of Daçaratha, shall slay thee in encounter, thou, attaining thy natural condition, shalt repair to the celestial regions.' Getting wroth, he cursed me, who had been absent; and thus did king Vaiçravana address me, who had conceived love for Rambhā. Through thy grace have I been freed from this fearful curse, I shall (now) repair to heaven. Hail, O repressor of foes! Half a Yoyana hence, my child, dwells the righteous and potent Maharshi, Sarabhanga, resembling the Sun. Seek him speedily: he will bring about thy good. Casting me (into this pit) in the wood, do thou, O Rāma, peacefully go thy way. Even this is the eternal usage of the Rākshasas.

* The reading slightly varies in some texts.—T.

Those that die in the forest, attain eternal regions." Having said this unto Kākutstha, the mighty Virādha, afflicted with arrows, having his body deposited (in the pit), attained heaven. Having heard that speech of Virādha, Rāghava ordered Lakshmana, saying, "O Lakshmana, do thou in this forest dig a capacious pit for this Rākshasa resembling an elephant, dreadful, and of terrible acts." Having said unto Lakshmana, "Dig a pit,"—Rāma possessed of prowess remained fixing his foot on Virādha's throat. Then taking a hoe, Lakshmana dug a spacious pit by the side of the huge-bodied* Virādha. Then when his throat had been freed, (Lakshmana) cast into the pit Virādha having ears resembling javelins, sending loud and dreadful sounds. Having vanquished him in fight, Rāma and Lakshmana possessed of activity and steady in fight, being exceedingly delighted, raising up the dreadful Rākshasa by main force, cast him howling (into the pit). Reflecting that he was incapable of being slain (by sharpened weapons), those foremost of men, exceedingly well versed (in arms), compassed the death of that mighty Asura, Virādha, in the pit, after they had dug it. Virādha had himself sincerely wished for his death at the hands of Rāma; and that ranger of the woods had accordingly told (Rāma),—"My death cannot be effected by means of weapons." Having heard these words, Rāma decided upon casting him into a pit. And when the excessively strong Rākshasa entered the cavity, he made the forest resound with his cries. Having thrown him into the hole, Rāma and Lakshmana, their fears removed, appeared with joyful looks, and rejoiced in that forest like the sun and the moon seated in the heavens.†

---

* *Mahatmanam—lit—high-souled.* The poet may have applied the epithet in this sense in view of Virādha being really a Gandharba. I have, however, preferred the other sense, as being more in harmony with the character of Virādha as a Rākshasa; and have accordingly rendered the word *huge-bodied.—T.*

† Another reading of this line is:—*And buried him under stones.* The North-West Provinces text has four additional lines:—*Having slain the*

## SECTION V.

HAVING in the forest slain the Rākshasa Virādha possessed of tremendous strength, Rāma endued with prowess, embracing and cheering Sitā, spoke unto his brother Lakshmana of flaming energy, saying, "This dense forest is hard to live in; nor are we acquainted with the ways of the wood. Therefore will we speedily repair to the ascetic Sarabhanga." Thereupon Rāghava set out for the hermitage of Sarabhanga. And Rāma beheld a mighty wonder near that one of celestial virtue, who had purified his soul through asceticism. He saw the lord of the celestials, possessed of a resplendent person, resembling in effulgence the sun or Vaicwānara—mounted on a superb car—(saw) him that is followed by all the celestials, stationed in the sky, not touching the earth, adorned in luminous ornaments—the god dressed in a clean apparel; worshipped by many a high-souled personage dressed in the same way. And from a distance, (Rāma) saw the car stationed in the sky yoked with green steeds—resembling the infant sun; and he saw the spotless umbrella possessing the beauty of a mass of white clouds, resembling the lunar disc,—and graced with variegated wreaths. And his (Indra's) head was being fanned by two chowris, costly and furnished with golden handles, held by two manificent damsels; and innumerable Gandharbas and Siddhas and prime sages were hymning the celestial stationed in the welkin. And seeing Sarabhanga engaged in converse with Satakratu, Rāma said unto Lakshmana (the following words). And pointing out the car, Rāma showed the wonder unto his brother. "Behold, O Lakshmana, yonder car stationed in the sky, splendid, furnished with exceeding

*Rákshasa and taken Mithilá's daughter, those ones having bows decked in gold, being delighted, rejoiced in that mighty forest, like the sun and the moon seated in the sky.—T.*

grace, wonderful, and seeming as if the sun had fallen from the heavens. The steeds standing in the sky are for certain those of which we had formerly heard as belonging unto Sakra of many sacrifices. And, thou foremost of men, these youths environing (the celestial) by hundreds, wearing ear-rings, and bearing swords in their hands, are broad of chest, have arms resembling bludgeons in size, and are clad in crimson vesture, like unto tigers incapable of being approached. Over the breasts of all appear chains of blazing sheen ; and, O son of Sumitrā, their beauty appears that of five and twenty. And even this is the ever-enduring age of the celestials, as these foremost of men of sweet looks appear. O Lakshmana, stay here awhile with Vaidehi, so long as I do not gather who it is that is in the effulgent car." Saying unto Sumitrās son, "Stay here," Kākutstha bent his steps towards Sarabhanga's asylum. And seeing Rāma approach, Sachi's lord, taking Sarabhanga's permission, addressed the celestials, saying, "Rāma is coming hither. Do ye set out for another place, ere he yet addresses me. He is not fit to behold me (now). When he shall have vanquished (his foe in fight) and won success, shall I readily show myself unto him. He shall have to achieve an act incapable of being achieved by others." Then rendering homage unto that anchoret and conversing with him, the wielder of the thunderbolt—subduer of enemies—repaired to heaven in a car yoked with steeds. When the thousand-eyed one had gone away, Rāghava accompanied by his companions appeared before Sarabhanga in the *Agni-hotra* chamber. Taking his feet, Rāma, Sitā and Lakshmana sat down with the permission of the ascetic, who received them and set apart quarters for them. Then Rāghava questioned (the sage)concerning the visit of Sakra ; and Sarabhanga related everything unto Rāghava. "O Rāma, this bestower of boons wishes to take me to the regions of Brahmā. I have conquered them, incapable of being attained by persons that have not schooled themselves,—by virtue of fierce austerities. O chief of men, knowing that thou wert near, I became anxious to go to the minor celestial regions and the supreme heaven (of Brahmā), after I had seen thee, righteous and high-souled, who art my dear guest now. O foremost of men, I have for aye attained the excellent regions of Brahmā and Nākaprishtha. Do thou receive them as pertaining to me." Thus adressed by the sage, Sarabhanga, that best of men, Rāghava, versed in every branch of learning, said, "O mighty anchoret, I shall acquire all those regions myself. I now wish that thou mayst direct me as to my abode in this forest." Thus occosted by Rāghava resembling Sakra in strength, the eminently wise Sarabhanga again said, "O Rāma, here in this forest lives a pious and self-restrained ascetic of mighty energy, named Sutikshna. He will bring about thy good. O Rāma, follow this Mandākini flowing among flowers, which (here) runs in an opposite direction to her usual course; and then wilt thou reach there. This is thy course, thou best of men. Do thou now, my child, for a space look at me; while I leave off my limbs, even as a serpent renounces its slough." Then preparing a fire and with Mantras offering oblations into it, the exceedingly energetic Sarabhanga entered into the fire. The fire consumed the down, hair, old skin, bones, flesh and blood of that high-souled one. (Anon) Sarabhanga became a youth resembling fire; and rising from the flame, he appeared splendid. And proceeding past the regions of high souled sages sacrificing with fire, as well as of the celestials, he ascended those of Brahmā. And that one of pious acts done on earth—that best of the twice-born race—saw the grand-father, in company with his followers. And the grand-father also, beholding that Brāhmana, rejoiced greatly, and said,—"Hail!"

## SECTION VI.

After Sarabhanga had ascended heaven, ascetics in bodies, assembled together, presented themselves before Kākutstha, Rāma of flaming energy. And Vaikhānasas, and Vālakhilyas, and Sanprakhālas, Marichipas, Açmwakuttas in numbers, and those ascetics, Patrāhāras, and Dantolukhalas, Unmajjakas next, and Gātracayyās, and Açayyās and Anavakāçikas, those ascetics, Salilāhāras, Vāyubhakshas after them, Akāçanilayas, Sthandilaçāyis, Urddhavāsis of controlled senses, and Ardrapattavāsas given to *Japa*, practising penances, and engaged in performing the five kinds of austerities—all furnished with the grace that comes of spiritual energy, and all firmly concentrated in Yoga—these ascetics presented themselves before Rāma in the asylum of Sarabhanga. And coming before Rāma, the foremost of those practising righteousness,those sages conversant with morality, —met in a body, said unto that pre-eminently virtuous one, "A mighty car-warrior, thou art the foremost person of the Ikshwāku race and the world ; as well as their lord,—even as Maghavān is the lord of the celestials. Famous over the three worlds in high worth and prowess, in thee are found the truth and virtue in profusion and obedience unto the mandate of thy sire. O lord, it behoves thee cognizant of virtue and attached unto it, to forgive us for what we as suiters say unto thee. The sin, O lord, of that monarch is mighty that taketh a sixth part of the subjects' incomes,but doth not protect them as sons. But he that, setting his heart on protecting the people, doth ever carefully protect all the inhabitants of his dominions, like his own life or like his son dearer unto him than life itself, reapeth, O Rāma, enduring renown extending over many years, and (at length) attaining the regions of Brahmā is glorified there. The king that protects his subjects righteously, is entitled to a fourth part of the great religious merit that is reaped by an ascetic subsisting on fruits and roots. O Rāma, this many Brāhmanas—this great body of men that have assumed the Vānaprastha mode of life, although having thee for their lord, are being sorely troubled by Rākshasas, as if they had none. Come and behold the bodies of innumerable ascetics of pure hearts that have in various ways been slaughtered by Rākshasas in the forest. And great is the worry that is experienced by the dwellers on the river Pampā and the Mandākini as well as those that reside in Chitrakuta. We cannot bear the terrible affliction of the ascetics in the forest at the hands of Rākshasas of dreadful deeds. Therefore, for obtaining refuge, have we come before thee who art the refuge (of all). Do thou, O Rāma, deliver us all, who are being exceedingly afflicted by the rangers of the night. O hero, we have no greater refuge on earth than thyself. Do thou, O king's son, rescue us all from Rākshasas." Hearing these words of the sages and ascetics, that righteous-souled one addressed them, saying, "It doth not behove you to speak thus. I should be commanded by the anchorets. I have entered the forest solely with a view to my own purpose. I have entered this forest in obedience to the mandate of my father, with the object (at the same time) of putting an end to these ravages of the Rākshasas on you. I have at my own will come hither for securing your interest. Then shall my stay in the woods be crowned with mighty fruit. I wish to slay in battle the enemies of the ascetics. Let the sages and ascetics behold my prowess as well as that of my brother." Having been conferred a boon by the ascetics, that hero entered upon a noble undertaking, and accompanied by the ascetics, in company with Lakshmana directed his course to (the hermitage of) Sutikshna.

---

## SECTION VII.

And Rāma accompanied by his brother as well as Sitā went to the asylum of Sutikshna in company with the twice-born ones. And having proceeded far, and crossed many a stream of copious waters, Rāma saw a holy peak towering high like the mighty Meru. Then those worthy scions of the Ikshwāku race—descendants of Raghu—with Sitā entered the forest ever furnished with various kinds of trees. And having entered the dense forest abounding in blossoms and ruits and trees, Rāma saw in a recess an asylum glittering with bark and garlands. There Rāma duly addressed an ascetic seated in the lotus-attitude* for warding off evil, even Sutikshna, "O thou coversant with righteousness, speak to me, O Maharshi, O thou that hast truth for thy prowess." Thereupon, eying Rāma keenly, that calm (ascetic)—the foremost of those practising righteousnes, embracing him with his arms, said, "Welcome, thou foremost of the Raghus, O Rāma, thou the best of those practising righteousness. This asylum now hath been furnished with its master in consequence of thy visit. O illustrious one, O hero, expecting thee, I have not yet ascended heaven, renouncing on earth this body of mine. I had (already) heard that, coming to Chitrakuta, (thou hadst been staying there), having been deprived of the kingdom. Here came, O Kākutstha, the Sovereign of the celestials of an hundred sacrifices. Coming to me, that mighty deity, the Sovereign of the celestials, said that I had acquired all the worlds by my pious acts. Do thou, by my grace, in company with thy wife and Lakshmana, dwell delightfully in those regions won by my asceticism, containing Devarshis." Thereupon the self-possessed Rāma answered that blazing and truth-telling Brāhmana of fiery austerities, like Vāsava answering Brahmā, saying, "O

* The *yoga* system has many positions for concentrating thought.—T.

mighty ascetic, I myself will win those regions. I wish to be directed to a dwelling in this forest. Thou art possessed of ability in respect of everything, and art (at the same time) engaged in the welfare of all beings,—this hath been told unto me by the high-souled Sarabhanga of the Gautama race." Thus addressed by Rāma, that Maharshi known over all the worlds, spoke sweet words in great joy, "O meritorious Rāma, even this is the asylum (for thee. Do thou live here pleasantly. It is inhabited by numbers of saints and is always provided with fruits and roots. This forest is haunted by herds of deer that range here without doing harm to any one, although they possess great energy; and go away, having bewitched people (by their beauty). Save what comes from these deer, there is no other evil to be encountered here." Hearing those words of the Maharshi, the placid elder brother of Lakshmana, taking up his bow with the arrow set, said "O exalted one, if by means of sharpened shafts blazing like lightning, I slay those herds of deer when they come, it shall impart pain unto thee,—and what can be more unfortunate than this? Therefore I shall not be able to dwell long in this asylum." Having said this, Rāma ceased and became engaged in his evening adorations, and, having finished them, along with Sitā and Lakshmana fixed his quarters in the asylum of Sutikshna. Then, when the evening had passed away and night fell, Sutikshna, having done homage unto those chiefs of men, offered them excellent fare, suitable to ascetics.

## SECTION VIII.

Having been well entertained by Sutikshna, Rāma in company with Sumitrā's son, having passed away the night there, awoke in the morning. And arising in due time,

Rāma along with Sitā, bathed in cool waters odorous with the aroma of lotuses; and having in proper time duly worshipped Fire as well as the deities, in that forest containing abodes of ascetics, Rāma, Lakshmana and Videha's daughter, their sins purged off, seeing the sun risen, approached Sutikshna and spoke unto him these mild words, saying,—"O Reverend sir, we have stayed here pleasantly, being excellently ministered unto by thee. We greet thee, and go away. The ascetics urge speed upon us. We hasten to view the collections of asylums that belong unto the holy sages inhabiting the forest of Dandaka. Now we crave thy permission along with that of these foremost of anchorites, steady in virtue, crowned with asceticism and self-controled, resembling smokeless flames. And we intend to set out ere the sun, like unto a low-sprung one that hath attained to auspicious fortune through evil ways, with rays incapable of being borne, shines too fiercely." Having said this, Rāghava along with Sitā and Sumitrā's son bowed down unto the ascetic's feet. And as they touched his feet, that best of ascetics, raising Rāma and Laāshmana up, embraced them closely and said, "O Rāma, go thy way safely, in company with Sumitrā's son and this Sitā that followeth thee like a shadow. Behold the beauteous asylums, O hero, of these pure-spirited ascetics inhabiting the forest of Dandaka. Thou wilt see blossoming woods garnished with fruits and roots, containing goodly deer, and mild feathered tribes; tanks and pools laughing with blown lotuses, containing pleasant waters, and abounding in Kārandavas; charming mountain-springs; and romantic forests picturesque with pea cocks. Go, O child; and go thou also, O Sumitrā's son. And come again to my asylum after having seen these." Thus addressed, Kākutstha along with Lakshmana, having gone round the ascetic, prepared for departing. Then Sitā of expansive eyes handed to the brothers excellent quivers, bows and shining swords. Then fastening the graceful quivers, and taking the sweet-sounding bows, both Rāma and Lakshmana issued from the hermitage. And permitted by the Maharshi, the Rāghavas furnished with grace, equipped with bows and scimitars, swiftly set out along with Sitā.

## SECTION IX.

WHEN the son of Raghu had set out with Sutikshna's permission, Sitā addressed him in affectionate words and convincing speech, saying,—"Although thou art great and followest the narrow way (of righteousness), yet thou art on the eve of entering into unrighteousness. But thou couldst by refraining from action, eschew this unrighteousness that springs from an evil begot of desire. This evil begot of desire is threefold. One prominent evil is falsehood, and both the others are of weightier significance,—association with others' wives, and vindictiveness without any (basis of) hostility. Falsehood, O Rāghava, hath never been thine, nor can it ever be thine (in the future). Nor yet, O foremost of men, canst thou ever even in fancy be (guilty of) going after others' wives, which marreth all religious merit. These, O Rāma, are by no means in thee. O King's son, thou ever and a day directest thy attentions unto thy own wife. And thou art righteous and truthful and doest the will of thy sire. In thee are established virtue and truth—and every thing; and by help of thy conquered senses, thou, O mighty-armed one, art capable of bearing everything. And, O thou of a gracious presence, thine is control over sense. The third evil that leads men through ignorance to bear hostility towards others without any (cause of) hostility, is now present (unto thee). Thou hast, O hero, for the protection of the saints dwelling in the forest of Dandaka, promised the slaughter of Rākshasas in battle. And it is for this reason that equipped with bows and arrows, thou hast along with thy brother set out for the forest known as Dandaka. Seeing thee set out,my mind reflecting on thy truthfulness as well as thy happiness in this world and welfare in the next, is wrought up with anxiety. And,O hero,I do not relish this journey to Dandaka. Thereof I will tell thee the reason. Do thou listen to me as I tell thee. Bearing bows and arrows in thy hands, thou hast come to the wood along with thy brother ; and (it may well happen) that seeing grim rangers of the forest, thou mayst discharge thy shafts And even as the vicinity of faggots increases the energy of fire, the proximity of (the bow) enhances the strength and energy of the Kshatriya. Formerly, O long-armed one, in a sacred wood haunted by beasts and birds,there lived a truthful ascetic of a pure person. Intending to disturb his auterities, Sachi's lord, Indra, bearing a sword in his hand, came to the asylum in the guise of a warrior. And in that asylum, that excellent scimitar was deposited as a trust with that righteous person practising asceticism. Receiving that weapon, that ascetic intent upon preserving his trust, rangeth the forest, maintaining his faith. And intent upon preserving his trust, he goeth nowhere for procuring fruits and roots without that sword deposited with him as a trust. Constantly carrying the sword, by degrees, the ascetic, foregoing all thoughts about asceticism, had his mind involved in fierce sentiments. Thus in consequence of bearing that weapon, that ascetic taken up with fierce thoughts,losing his sobriety and led astray from righteousness, went to hell. This ancient story anent the carrying of arms, asserts that even as fire worketh change in a piece of wood, the presence of arms worketh alteration in the mind of him bearing them. From affection and the high honor in which I hold thee, I merely remind thee of this matter. I do not teach thee. Equipped with bows as thou art, thou shouldst renounce all thoughts of slaying without hostility the Rākshasas residing in Dandaka. Without offence none should be slain.—It is the duty of Kshatriya heroes by means of their bows to protect persons of subdued souls, come by any calamity. Where are arms? And where is the forest? Where is Kshatriya virtue? And where is asceticism? These are opposed to each other,—let us, therefore, honor the morality that pertains to this place. From following arms, one's sense gets befouled and deformed. Again going to Ayodhyâ, thou wilt observe the duties of Kshatriyas. Then my mother-in-law and father-in-law shall experience enduring delight, if, having renounced the kingdom, thou lead the life of an ascetic. Interest springs from righteousness; and happiness also results therefrom. One attains everything through righteousness—in this world the only substantial thing. Repressing self by diverse restrictions, intelligent people attain righteousness; but virtue crowned with felicity, is incapable of being attained by following pleasure. O mild one, ever cherishing thy heart in purity, do thou practise piety, in the wood of asceticism. Everything—the three worlds—are truly known unto thee. I have spoken this through feminine fickleness. Who can speak of righteousness unto thee? Reflecting on and understanding things, do thou along with thy younger brother speedily do what thou likest."

---

## SECTION X.

HEARING Vaidehi's words spoken through high regard (for her husband), Râma with his energy enhanced, answered Janaka's daughter, saying, "O noble lady, thou hast spoken mild words fraught with worth and profit; and, O Janaka's daughter versed in virtue, thou hast expounded the duties of Kshatriyas. What, O exalted one, shall I say? Thou hast thyself by thy words (furnished an answer to what thou hadst said). Kshatriyas wear bows in order that the word 'distressed' may not exist (on earth). O Sitā, those ascetics of severe vows that are beset with perils in Dandaka, having personally come unto me, who am their refuge, have sought protection at my hands. Always dwelling in the forest, subsisting on fruits and roots, they on account of Rākshasas of cruel deeds, do not O timid one, attain ease. These ascetics are devoured by (terrible Rākshasas) living on human flesh. Being eaten up (by the Rākshasas), the anchorites living in the forest of Dandaka—those best of the twice born ones—said unto us—'Be thou gracious unto us.' Hearing those words of theirs which fell from their lips, I, resolving to act in accordance with their request, said,—'Be ye propitious.' This is surpassing shame unto me that such Vipras who themselves are worthy of being sought, seek me. What shall I do? I said this in the presence of those twice-born ones. Thereat all those that had come, said, 'We have been, O Rāma, immensely harassed in the forest of Dandaka by Rākshasas wearing shapes at will. Do thou deliver us. These irrepressible Rākshasas living on human flesh vanquish us at the time of *Homa*, and on the occasions of Parvas, O sinless one. Of the saints and ascetics afflicted by the Rākshasas, who are on the search for their refuge, thou art our best refuge. We can by virtue of the energy of our asceticism easily destroy the rangers of the night; but we are loath to lose our asceticism earned in a long time. O Rāghava, our austerities are constantly disturbed, and we can hardly perform them. Therefore, although sore afflicted and devoured by the Rākshasas dwelling in the forest of Dandaka, we do not cast our curse on them. Thou along with thy brother art our protector: thou art our master in this forest.' Having heard these words, I promised my perfect protection unto the saints in the forest of Dandaka, O daughter of Janaka. Having promised, I living cannot violate my vow concerning the ascetics; verily truth is ever dear unto me.

I had rather renounce my life, or thee, O Sitā, along with Lakshmana,—but by no means my promise made, especially unto Brāhmanas. O Videha's daughter, the protection of the saints is incumbent on me even without any representation,—and what (shall I say) when I have promised the same ? Thou hast spoken this unto me through affection and friendship. I have been well pleased with thee, O Sitā. One doth not instruct another that one doth not bear affection to. O beauteous damsel, (what thou hast said) is worthy of both thy love and thy race." Having said these words unto Mithilā's princess, the beloved Sitā, the high-souled Rāma, equipped with bows, along with Lakshmana, directed his steps towards the inviting woods of asceticism.

## SECTION XI.

RAMA went first; in the middle, Sitā; and bearing a bow in his hand, Lakshmana went in their wake. And they went with Sitā, seeing many mountain-peaks, and forest, and delightful streams, and Chakravākas haunting river islets, and tanks with lotuses containing aquatic birds, and herds of deer, and horned buffaloes maddened with juices, and boars, and elephants—foes to trees. Having proceeded a long way, when the sun was aslant, they together saw a delightful tank measuring a *yoyana*, filled with red and pale lotuses, graced with herds of elephants, and abounding in aquatic cranes, swans and *Kadamvas*. And in that tank containing charming and pleasant waters, they heard sounds of song and instrumental music; but no one was seen there. Thereat, from curiosity, Rāma and Lakshmana—mighty car-warrior—asked an ascetic named Dharmabhrit, saying,

"Hearing* this mighty wonder, we have been worked up with intense curiosity. Do thou tell us what this is. Thus accosted by Rāghava, the ascetic then at once began to expatiate over the potency of the pool. "This tank goes by the name of Panchāpsarā, and is always filled with water. It was made, O Rāma, by the ascetic Māndakarni, by virtue of his asceticism. In yonder tank, the mighty ascetic, living on air, performed signal austerities for ten thousand years. Thereat, exceedingly agitated, all the deities with Agni at their head, assembled together, said, 'This ascetic wishes to have the position of one of us.' Thus all the deities present there were filled with anxiety. Then with the view of disturbing his austerities, the deities ordered five principal Apsarās, possessed of the splendour of live lightning. And for compasssing the end of the celestials, that ascetic conversant with the morality and otherwise as well of this life as that to come, was brought by those Apsarās under the sway of Madana. And those five Apsarās (ultimately) became the wives of the ascetic; and their hidden residence was reared in the pool. And there the five Apsarās living happily, pleased the anchorite, established in youth through asceticism and *yoga*. As thy sport, we hear the sounds of their musical instruments, and the sweet voice of their song mixed with the tinklings of their instruments." (Hearing this), the illustrious Rāghava along with his brother declared the story narrated by that one of a pure heart to be wonderful. Thus conversing, Rāma saw the collection of asylums, strewn with Kuça and bark, and be-girt with energy derived from Brahma lore. Entering (the place) along with Vaidehi and Lakshmana, the highly famous Rāghava dwelt there respected by all the ascetics. Having happily dwelt in those collections of graceful asylums, honored of the Maharshis, Kākutstha by turns went to the hermitage of those ascetics with whom that one well versed in arms had

* Some texts :—*Seeing*.

dwelt before. And Rāghava happily passed his days somewhere for ten months, somewhere for one year, somewhere for four months somewhere for five or six months, somewhere for many months, somewhere for a month and a half,—somewhere for more, somewhere for three months, and somewhere for eight. And as Rāma lived in the assylums of the ascetics and amused himself through their good graces, ten years were passed away (in this way). Having gone round the asylums of all the ascetics, Rāghava cognizant of righteousness returned to the hermitage of Sutikshna. Coming to this asylum, respected by the ascetics, that subduer of enemies, Rāma, stayed there for a time. Once upon a time, as Kākutstha dwelling in that asylum was seated, he humbly observed unto that great ascetic. "I have always heard from men speaking on the subject that that foremost of ascetics, the reverend Agastya, lives in this forest. On account of the vastness of this forest, I do not know that place. Where is the hermitage of that intelligent Maharshi ? For propitiating that revered one, I, accompanied by my brother and Sitā, will go to Agastya for paying our respects unto the ascetic. This great desire is burning in my heart, that I should myself minister unto that best of anchorets." Hearing these words of the righteous-souled Rāma, Sutikshna, well pleased, answered Daçaratha's son, saying, "I also am desirous of telling thee this along with Lakshmana. Repair unto Agastya in company with Sitā, O Rāghava. By luck thou hast thyself said this unto me as to thy purpose. I will, O Rāma, tell thee where that mighty ascetic, Agastya, is. My child, go four miles from the hermitage in a southerly direction ; and thou wilt come to the hermitage of the brother of the auspicious Agastya situated on a land covered with trees, graced with *Pippali* woods, abounding in fruits and flowers, charming, and resonant with the notes of various birds. There are many tanks containing delightful waters, swarming with swans and Kārandavas, and beauteous with Chakravākas.

Passing a night there, do thou, O Rāma, in the morning, taking a southerly course, go by the skirts of the forest tract. Passing a *yojana*, thou shalt come upon Agastya's asylum, located at a charming woodland graced with many a tree. There Videha's daughter and Lakshmana shall experience delight in thy company. O magnanimous one, if thou intend to see the mighty ascetic, Agastya, in that charming woodland, containing a great many trees, then do thou make up thy mind to set out this very day." Hearing these words of the anchoret, Rāma, saluting him, along with his brother, set off for Agastya's (place) with his younger brother and Sitā. And, pleasantly proceeding by the way directed by Sutikshna, seeing picturesque woods, hills resembling clouds, watery expanses and streams flowing by their path; Rāma filled with delight said these words unto Lakshmana, "Surely we see the asylum of that high-souled one, the ascetic, Agastya's brother of pious acts. These trees standing by thousands on the way bending beneath the weight of fruits and flowers, bear the signs that had been mentioned to me as belonging to this wood. And from the wood is wafted by the wind the pungent odour of ripe *pippalis*. And here and there are found heaps of fire-wood, and torn *Darva* are seen, of the lustre of lapises. And the top of the column of smoke belonging unto the fire lit in the asylum in this wood, appears like the peak of a dark mountain. And twice-born ones, having performed their ablutions in sacred and retired bathing places, are offering flowers gathered by themselves. O placid one, from what I had heard from Sutikshna, this would appear to be the asylum of Agastya's brother. The righteous Agastya it is who, wishing for the welfare of the worlds, destroying by virtue of his austerities a Daitya resembling Death, hath rendered this quarter habitable. Once on a time here dwelt together two mighty Asuras, brothers, given to slaughtering Brāhmanas—the wily Vātāpi and Ilwala. Wearing the form of a Brāhmana, and speaking Sanskrit, the cruel one used to invite Vipras to a *Srâddha*. And, cooking his brother wearing the shape of a sheep, he used to feed the twice-born ones according to the rites prescribed for *Srâddhas*. Then when the Vipras had fed, Ilwala said,—"O Vâtâpi, come out, uttering a loud sound." Hearing his brother's words, Vâtâpi, bleating like a sheep, came out, riving their bodies. In this way, thousands of Brâhmanas gathered together, were destroyed by flesh-eating ones wearing shapes at will. (And it came to pass that once upon a time) the Maharshi Agastya, having been invited to a Srâddha, fed on the mighty Asura. Thereupon uttering—'Finished' and offering water to wash hands with, Ilwala said unto his brother, 'Come out'! And, as that brother of Vâtâpi, given to slaughtering Vipras was speaking thus, that foremost of ascetics, the intelligent Agastya, said with a laugh, 'Where is the power of coming out, of the Râkshasa, thy brother wearing the shape of a sheep, who hath gone to Yama's abode?' Hearing his words, from wrath the ranger of the night prepared to assail the ascetic, and he rushed against that foremost of the twice-born ones And, being consumed by that ascetic of flaming energy with his eyes resembling fire, the Râkshasa met his end. This asylum graced with pools and groves belongs to the brother of him who hath performed this arduous feat from compassion for the Vipras." As Râma was thus conversing with Sumitrâ's son, the sun set and evening approached. Then, duly performing his afternoon adorations along with his brother, Râma entered the hermitage, and saluted the ascetic. Well received by the ascetic, Râghava spent there a night, eating fruits and roots. When the night had passed away, and the solar disc arose, Râghava greeted Agastya's brother, saying, "O reverend Sir, I salute thee. I have pleasantly passed the night. I greet thee; I shall go to behold my preceptor, thy elder brother." Thereat, on the ascetic's saying, 'Go thou,' the descendant of Raghu went away by the prescribed route. And Râma viewed the forest, and Nihāras, and Panaças, and Sālas, Vanjulas and Tinisas, and Chirivilwas, and Madhukas, and Vilvas, and Tindukas,—all in full flower, and graced with blossoming creepers, and trees in the wood by hundreds, roughly handled by elephants with their trunks, and graced by monkeys, and resounding with the voices of an hundred maddened warblers. Then the lotus-eyed Rāma said unto that enhancer of auspiciousness, the heroic Lakshmana, who was by him, and was following him at his back. "The leaves of these trees are glossy, and the beasts and birds are mild, even as (we had been told). The asylum of the pure-hearted Maharshi must not be far. This asylum capable of removing the fatigue, of the weary, belonging to him that is known among men as Agastya by his own acts, is seen, with the (neighbouring woods) filled with smoke, and itself decorated with bark and wreaths, containing herds of mild deer, and ringing with the notes of various birds. This is the asylum of that pious one, who destroying (the Asura resembling) Death, hath, desirous of the welfare of mankind, rendered the Southern quarter habitable, and through whose potency the Rākshasas from fear barely cast their eyes in this direction, but do not approach. Ever since that one of pious ways possessed himself of this quarter, the rangers of the night have foregone their hostility, and assumed a peaceful attitude. This Southern quarter rendered safe (by Agastya), and incapable of being harassed by those ones of tortuous ways, is celebrated over the three worlds in connection with the name of the reverend ascetic. And this graceful asylum ranged by mild beasts belongs to that long-lived one of renowned achievements—Agastya—in obedience to whose command, the Vindhya mountain—foremost of its kind—which had always obstructed the way of the Sun, doth not increase. This pious one honored of men, ever engaged in the welfare of the righteous, shall do good unto us, who have come to him. I shall adore the mighty ascetic, Agastya, anb, O mild one, O master, here pass away the remainder of the term of my banishment. Here celestials with the Gandharbas, and Siddhas and eminent saints, observing restrictions in respect of food, aye adore Agastya. And the ascetic is such that a liar cannot live here, nor a cunning or a crafty person, nor a wicked wight, nor one that is given to unrighteousness. And adoring righteousness, celestials, and Yakshas, and Nāgas, and birds, live here restricting their fare. And high-souled Siddhas and eminent saints, renouncing their bodies, repair to the celestial regions in cars resembling the sun. And adored by auspicious individuals, the deities here confer on them the states of Yakshas and celestials, and divers kingdoms. O Sumitrā's son, entering the asylum before us, do thou announce unto the saints that I along with Sitā, have arrived here."

## SECTION XII.

HAVING entered the asylum, Rāghava's younger brother, Lakshmana, coming to a disciple of Agastya, spoke unto him, saying, "There was a king, named Daçaratha. His eldest son, the strong Rāma, hath come (to this asylum) along with his wife, Sitā for seeing the ascetic.—Named Lakshmana, I am his younger brother, obedient and devoted to him.—Thou mayst have heard of it. Having entered this horrid forest, in consonance with the mandate of our sire, we desire to see the reverend one. Tell this unto him." Hearing Lakshmana's words, that ascetic, saying, "So be it," entered the chamber of the sacrificial fire, for the purpose of communicating (the news unto Agastya). Entering in, Agastya's beloved disciple, with joined hands communicated unto that foremost of ascetics, incapable of being repressed,*

* Some texts :—*Effulgent.*

exactly what Lakshmana had told him,—"For seeing the reverend one, and serving him as well, those subduers of their foes, Daçaratha's sons, Rāma and Laāshmana accompanied by Sitā, have entered this asylum. It now behoves thee to command what is to be done next." Hearing from his disciple that Rāma had come along with Lakshmana and the highly virtuous Vaidehi, Agastya said, "By luck it is that after a long time, Rāma hath come to see me. I had mentally wished for his arrival. Go thou; and let Rāma, having been respectfully received, come before me. Why hast thou not brought him thyself?" Thus addressed by the high-souled and righteous ascetic, the disciple saluting him, with joined hands, said, "So be it." Then issuing out, the disciple said unto Lakshmana, "Where is Rāma? Let him come and enter in." Thereat, going to the asylum in company with the disciple (of Agastya) Lakshmana showed unto him Kākutstha and the daughter of Janaka, Sita. Then joyfully communicating unto Rāma the words of the reverend one, the disciple (of Agastya) duly took in that one worthy of being honored. And seeing the asylum teeming with mild deer, Rāma entered in with Lakshmana and Sitā. And there Rāma beheld the place of Brahmā, and that of Agni,—that of Vishnu, and that of the great Indra, the place of Vivaswat, and that of Soma, and that of Bhaga, and that of Dhātā and Vidhātā, and that of Vāyu, and that of the high-souled Vāruna having the noose in his hand, and that of Gāyatri and that of the Vasus, and that of the monarch of the *Nâgas*, and that of Garura, and that of Kārtikeya, and that of Dharma. And it came to pass that, surrounded by his disciples, the ascetic came (before Rāma). And Rāma saw that one of flaming energy at the head of the ascetics; and the hero said unto Lakshmana, enhancer of auspiciousness, "O Lakshmana, the revered saint, Agastya, is coming out. I recognize that mass of asceticism by a certain kind of majesty (that characterizes him)." Having said this touching Agastya of the splendour of the sun, that son of Raghu took hold of his feet. Then, having paid him homage, Rāma with joined hands stood there in company with Videha's daughter, Sitā, and Lakshmana. Thereat, embracing Rāma and honoring him with water and a seat, and asking him questions anent his welfare, the saint said, "Welcome!" Offering oblations unto the fire, and presenting Arghya unto the guests, and paying them homage, that ascetic entertained them with food in accordance with the Vānasprastha mode of life; and then first sitting down, that foremost of ascetics, the pious Agastya, addressed Rāma cognizant of righteousness, staying with joined hands, "O Kākutstha, if an ascetic acts otherwise (in respect of guest), he in the next world feeds on his own flesh, like a false witness. The sovereign of all the worlds, righteous, a mighty car warrior, worthy of being honored and worshipped, thou hast become our beloved guest." Having said this, Agastya, according to his desire, worshipping Rāghava with fruits, roots and flowers, said unto him, "O foremost of men, this mighty, celestial bow belonging unto Vishnu and constructed Viçwakarmā, and this best of arrows (named) Brahmadatta, infallible and resembling the sun, and this inexhaustible couple of quivers filled with sharpened shafts, like unto flaming fire, were granted unto me by the mighty Indra. And here is this mighty golden scabbard, and this sword decked in gold. Having, O Rāma, slain the mighty Asuras with this bow, Vishnu in days of yore in battle secured the effulgent Fortune of the celestials. O bestower of honor, do thou for securing victory, take this bow, these quivers, this arrow, and this scimitar, like the holder of the thunder-bolt, taking the same." Having said this, that highly energetic one, the reverend Agastya, consigning unto Rāma all those weapons, again said.

## SECTION XIII

"O RAMA, I am pleased with thee ; good betide thee ! And, O Lakshmana, I am gratified by thee. Ye are in trouble in consequence of the great fatigue that ye have undergone on the way. And Janaka's daughter, the noble Maithili, is evidently eager (for rest). Of tender years and unknown to hardship, she hath come to the forest rife with troubles, being urged by the love she bears unto her lord. Do thou, O Rāma, conduct thyself so, that Sitā may find a pleasant time of it. By following thee to the forest, it is a hard task that she is performing. O son of Raghu, this hath been the nature of the fair sex from the commencement of creation, that they gladden him that is well off, and forsake a person in adversity. And women imitate the instability of lightning, the sharpness of weapons,and the celerity of Garura and the wind.* But this wife of thine is absolutely free from all these defects ; she is worthy of being extolled and the foremost of those devoted to their lord, like Arundhati among the gods. This region, O Rāma, will be adorned, since, O subduer of enemies, thou along with Vaidehi and Sumitrā's son, wilt dwell here." Thus addressed by the ascetic, Rāghava, joining his hands, humbly observed unto that saint resembling flaming fire, "Blessed and beholden am I, since the foremost of ascetics is gratified with my merits as well as with those of my brother and wife. Do thou now direct me to a country well watered, and abounding in woods, where rearing an asylum, I may dwell delightfully and pleasantly." Hearing Rāms's words, that best of ascetics, reflecting for a while, spoke these excellent words, "Two Yojanas hence, my child, is a region abounding in fruits and roots, containing

* The commentator explains :—*They imitate the lightning in changing their residence, the sharpness of weapons in severing affection, and the celerity of Garura or the wind in doing wrong.—T.*

countless deer, and beautiful—known by the name of Panchavati. Repairing thither, do thou, rearing an asylum, pass thy time pleasantly in company with Sumitrā's son, duly doing the mandate of thy sire. O sinless one, all this news relating to thyself, has from affection been known to me through the potency of my asceticism, as also that relating to Daçaratha. Although thou hast promised to dwell with me in this ascetic grove, yet by virtue of my asceticism I know the desire that is in thy heart. I therefore tell thee, repair to Panchavati. That is a charming woodland, and there Mithila's daughter shall dwell with delight. And that tract is worthy of all praise, and, O Rāghava, it is not distant from here.—It is in the vicinity of the Godāvari. Mithilā's daughter shall live there agreeably. And that spot abounds in fruits, and roots, is frequented by various fowls, is retired, O mighty-armed one, and is sacred and beautiful. And thou of pure ways, and competent to protect the ascetics, shall, O Rāma, protect them. O hero, yonder is the mighty wood of Madhukas. Directing thy course to the asylum of Nagrodha trees, go by the north of this Madhuka wood. Then arriving at a spot hard by a hill, (thou wilt) come upon the celebrated Panchavati, crowned with blossoming woods." Thus accosted by Agastya, Rāma along with Sumitrā's son honouring the truth-speaking saint, greeted him. Then, having saluted his feet, they, taking the saint's permission, set out along with Sitā for the hermitage of Panchavati. And, taking their bows and quivers those sons of the king, of undiminished martial virtue, with intent minds bent their course to Panchavati by the way laid down by the Maharshi.

## SECTION XIV.

As he was proceeding to Panchavati, Raghu's son saw a huge-bodied vulture of terrible powess. And seeing him in the forest, the exalted Rāma and Lakshmana, as they were conversing with each other, knowing the bird to be (in reality) a Rākshasa, asked him, saying, "Who art thou?" Thereupon, in soft and sweet words, he, pleasing them, said, "My child, know me for a friend of thy father." Knowing him to be a friend of his sire, Rāghava paid him homage, and enquired for his name and lineage. Hearing Rāma's words, he mentioned his own lineage, and related the origin of all beings. "O mighty-armed one, I shall describe (unto thee) from the very beginning the (history of) those that were Prajāpatis in days of yore. Listen, O Rāghava. Of these, the first is Kardamā, then Vikrita, and then Sesha, Sancraya, the powerful Vahuputra, Sthānu, Mārichi, Atri, the mighty Kratu, Pulastya, Angira, Pracheta, Pulaha, Daksha, Vivaswat, Arishtanemi, O Rāghava, and the exceedingly energetic Kaçyapa. These had the west. The Prajāpati Daksha, it hath been heard by us, O Rāma, had sixty famous and illustrious daughters. Of these Kaçyapa wed eight, with elegant waists;—Aditi, Diti, Danu, Kālikā,* Tamrā, Krodhavasā, Manu and Analā. Then, well pleased, Kaçyapa again said unto those damsels, "Do thou bring forth sons like unto myself, who shall be lords of the three worlds." Thereat, Aditi, O Rāma, Diti, Danu, and Kālikā, O mighty-armed one, consented,—the rest were of another mind. And of Aditi were born thirty-three deities, O repressor of thy foes, *viz.*, the Adityas, the Vasus, the Rudras, and the Açwinas, O subduer of enemies. And, my child, Diti gave birth to those sons, the renowned Daityas. Formerly, this earth girt with seas was in the possession of these. And, O vanquisher of

* Some texts:—*Kalaka.*—*T.*

thy foes, Danu gave birth to a son, named, Açwagriva. And Kālikā brought forth Naraka and Kālaka. And Tāmra gave birth to these five daughters celebrated in the world,—Kraunchi, Bhāsi, Syeni, Dhritarashtri, and Suki. And Kraunchi gave birth to the Ulukas, and Bhāsi, to Bhāsas, and Syeni to hawks and vultures possessed of energy; and Dhritarashtri to swans, all kinds of Kalahansas, and Chakravākas, and that damsel, Suki, to Natā. And Vinatā was Natā's daughter. And Krodhavasā, O Rāma, brought forth ten daughters, *viz.*, Mrigi, Mrigamandā, Hari, Bhadramadā, Mātangi, Sārduli, Swetā, Surabhi crowned with every (auspicious mark), Surasā and Kadrukā. And, thou foremost of the best of men, Mrigi's sons were all the deer, and those of Mrigamandā were bears, Srimāras and Chamaras. And Bhadramadā bore one daughter, Irāvati. And Irāvati's son is the mighty elephant, who is the lord of the worlds. And Hari's sons are lions and the nimble monkeys. And Sārduli brought forth as her sons, Golāngulas, and tigers; and the offspring of Mātangi were mad elephants, O best of men. And Swetā O Kākutstha, gave birth to the elephants of the cardinal points. And, O Rāma, Surabhi gave birth unto two daughters—the famous Rohini, and Gandharbi. Rohini produced kine, and the sons of Gandharbi are horses. And Surasā, O Rāma, gave birth to Nāgas, and Kadru, to Pannagas. And Kāçyapa's other wife Manu begot mankind—Brāhmanas, Kshatriyas, Vaiçyas, and Sudras. From the mouth, it is known, sprang Brāhmanas, from the breast, Kshatriyas, from the thighs, Vaiçyas, and from the feet, Sudras. And Analā produced all trees bearing sacred fruits. Vinatā (was) Suki's grand-daughter, and Kadru, Surasā's aunt. And Kadru gave birth to a thousand Nāgas with the holder of the Earth. And Vinatā brought forth two sons,—Garura, and Aruna. And from Aruna sprang myself and my elder brother Sampāti. O subduer of enemies, know me for Jatāyu, the son of Syeni.

If thou wilt, I shall become thy help during thy abode (in the woods). And, O child, I shall protect Sitā when thou shalt go out along with Lakshmana." There Rāghava paying homage unto Jatāyu, and embracing him joyfully, bent low; and that self-possessed one listened to the story of Jatāyu's friendship with his father, as related by him repeatedly. Then consigning unto that bird of exceeding strength, Mithilā's daughter, Sitā, Rāma accompanied by Lakshmana went to Panchavati, destroying his foes and protecting the worlds.

## SECTION XV.

THEN repairing to Panchavati filled with various animals and beasts of prey, Rāma remarked unto his brother of flaming energy, "(Now) we have come to the place to which we had been directed by the ascetic. This, O amiable one, is Panchavati furnished with blossoming woods. Do thou cast thy eyes around this forest, and (ascertain) what spot shall suit our asylum. Do thou find out such a place in the vicinity of a tank where thyself Sitā and I may dwell happily, which is graced with the garniture of woods and delightful with liquid lapses, and whose neighbourhood yields fuel, flowers, Kuça and water." Thus addressed by Rāma, Lakshmana with joined hands, said unto Kākutstha in the presence of Sitā, "O Kākutstha, even if I were to stay with thee for an hundred years, I shall remain thy servant. Thyself selecting some beauteous spot, do thou tell me,—'Construct (an asylum).'" Well pleased with the words of Lakshmana, that highly effulgent one, after due reflection, selected a site having every recommendation. Going to that romantic spot for rearing an asylum, Rāma, taking the hand of Sumitrā's son in his, said unto him, "This place is level, graceful, and surrounded with blossoming trees. Do thou duly construct an asylum at this spot. Hard by is seen a beautiful pool, embellished with lotuses, resembling the sun, and breathing balmy perfume. And, as told by that pure-hearted ascetic, Agastya, this is the graceful Godâvari, bordered by flowering trees;—swarming with swans and Kârandavas, delighted with Chakravâkas; thronged with herds of deer,* not far, yet not so very near. And resounding with the cries of peacocks; charming; elevated; containing full many a cave; do thou, O amiable one, behold these hills, covered with trees in full flower; and they are shining like elephants painted with divers colors by persons with the utmost care; adorned with Sâlas, palmyras, Tamâlas, dates, Panasas, Nivâras, Tinisas, and Punnâgas. And covered with mangoes, and Tilakas, and Ketakas, and Champakas, and trees entwined by flowers and herbs and plants; and containing Syandanas, sandals, Nipas, Panasas, Lakuchas, Dhavas, Açwakarnas, Khadiras, Samis, Kinçukas and Pâtalas. This spot is sacred —this spot is charming—this spot abounds in beasts and birds. Here will I dwell, O Sumitrâ's son, in company with this bird."† Thus addressed by Râma, the exceedingly powerful Lakshmana, slayer of hostile heroes, in a short time raised an asylum for his brother. And the exceedingly stout Lakshmana created there for Râghava a spacious hut thatched with leaves made of clay, furnished with pillars, constructed with long bamboos, graceful,—spread with Sami boughs; tightly fastened with strong cords; covered with Kuçâ, reeds, and leaves; with its floor well leveled; and charming; beautiful to look at, and exceedingly excellent. And then going to the river Godâvari, the lovely Lakshmana, performing his bath, and securing lotuses and fruits, came back (to the asylum). Then offering flowers, and duly performing rites for the peace (of the habitation), Lakshmana showed the asylum which he had made unto Râma. Seeing the

* *Come to slake their thirst.*—Râmâyana.—T.

† Jatâyu.

beautiful asylum along with Sitā, Rāghava experienced high raptures. And joyfully embracing Lākshmana with his arms, Rāma said these exceedingly calm and solemn words, "Pleased am I with thee. Thou hast done a great deed, my brother; for which I have granted thee my embrace by way of reward. While thou, his son, skilled in reading thought, grateful, and cognizant of righteousness art alive, O Lākshmana, my father is not dead." Having said this unto Lākshmana, Rāghava—the enhancer of auspiciousness—experiencing felicity, began to dwell happily in that region filled with fruits. And ministered unto by Sitā and Lākshmana, that righteous one lived there, like the immortals in heaven.

## SECTION XVI.

As the high-souled Rāghava was dwelling there peacefully, after autumn had departed, the welcome winter commenced. And it came to pass that once on a time, when the night had passed away and day broke, that son of Raghu went to the romantic river Godāvari for performing his bath. And as the humble son of Sumitrā Rāma's puissant brother bearing a water pitcher in his hand was following Rāma along with Sitā at his back, the former said unto Rāma, "O sweet-speeched one, now is come that season which thou hast ever held dear; and as if decorated by which comes on the entire auspicious year. Now people have their persons rendered rough from dew; the earth is replenished with corn; water is difficult of being used; and fire becomes enjoyable. And men having worshipped the gods and the Pitris by celebrating Agrahāyana on the occasion of prataking new rice, have at this season, their sins purged off. The provinces overflow with food, and abound in milk and articles prepared therefrom; and kings bent on conquest, range about for surveying them. And on the sun having veered steadily to the quarter presided over by the Destroyer*, the north appears like a female without her *tilaka*†. Naturally abounding in snow, and now having the sun at a great distance, the mountain Himavān‡ justly beareth that name. At mid-day the days are delightful to a degree to range in, feel highly agreeable, and have pleasant suns; while shade and water are uncomfortable. And the days now have mild suns, are covered with dew, severely cold, with the forests remaining idle§, and the lotuses destroyed by frost. And now at night people cannot lie down in unsheltered places; and the nights are inferred from the presence of Pushyā. And at night the atmosphere (being covered with vapour) looks brown; and it is bitter cold then; and the hours are long. And the good fortune of the Moon hath fallen to the Sun; and the disc of the former is reddish with vapour; and like unto a glass breathed upon, it doth not shine clearly. And the moonlight furnished by vapour doth not appear pleasant; and Sitā pallid because of (exposure to) sunshine, is perceptible, but doth not look beauteous. And at this season the western wind naturally of gelid feel, being permeated at present with cold, blows with double coldness. And the forests enveloped in mist, and stocked with wheat and barley, look brilliant at sunrise, with Kraunchas and cranes crying (in chorus). Golden-hued paddy slightly inclined, appear graceful, with their heads like unto date-flowers filled with rice. And the sun although high advanced, yet having its rays covered with thick mist, appeareth like the moon. And feeble at the first part of the day, and of agreeable touch at mid-day,

---

* *i. e.*—The South.—T.

† A mark made with colored earths or unguents upon the forehead and between the eye-brows either by way of ornament or a sectarial distinction.—T.

‡ *Himavān* means *having snow*.—T.

§ 'Of antres vast and deserts *idle*.' *Othello*. Although not in common use, the word is very picturesque, and hence the adoption.—T.

the sunshine, being surcharged with mist, appeareth palish over the face of the earth. And in the woods, swards covered with green grass, and with dew-drops on it, look handsome on the morning sun brightening it up. And wild elephants waxing exceedingly thirsty, draw away their trunks, just as they touch beautifully clear and cold water. And those aquatic fowls seated by, do not dip themselves in the water, like unto cravens shunning fight. And the rows of trees, shorn of their blossoms, on being enveloped with dew at night and mist at morn, look as if they were fast asleep. And the streams appear with their waters enveloped in vapour, and the cranes, perceived through their cries, and their banks having their sands wet. And what on account of the snow-fall, what of the mildness of the sun, and what through the cold, water even when it is on a mountain top, tastes sweet. And lotuses afflicted by the cold, with the stalks only left, and with their petals dropping down and their pericarps and filaments shrivelled up, do not appear beautiful. And, O foremost of men, at this season, influenced by regard for thee, Bharata undergoing affliction of spirit, is performing mortifications in the city. And forsaking kingdom, and dignity, and the many and various enjoyments, Bharata practising asceticism and restraining himself in respect of food, in this winter lieth down on the bare earth. And he also, for certain, at this hour of the day, surrounded by his subjects, daily wendeth to the river Sarayu for performing his ablutions. Brought up in luxury, and exceedingly tender, how can he, afflicted with cold, perform his ablutions during the latter part of the night? Of eyes resembling lotus petals, grey-hued, endued with grace, with a navel depressed, and mighty, Bharata understandeth righteousness, is truth-speaking, of restrained senses (in respect of others' wives) and also of subdued senses. And he speaketh fair, and is sweet-tempered, and long-armed and the vanquisher of foes. And renouncing various pleasures, he hath devoted himself unto the noble one. Thy high-souled brother hath secured heaven, since he, resorting to asceticism, is imitating thee that resident in the woods. The saying that people follow their mother and not their father, is falsified in the case of Bharata. How can mother Kaikeyi, whose husband is Daçaratha and son the righteous Bharata, have such crooked way ?" As the virtuous Lakshmana was speaking thus from affection, Rāghava, not bearing the blame cast upon his mother (Kaikeyi), said, "My brother, thou shouldst by no means, tax our second mother. Do thou talk of that lord of the Ikshwāku race, Bharata. Albeit my mind is firm as regards my sojourn in the woods, yet is my mind unsteady, being inflamed with affection for Bharata. I remember his dear sweet words, taking the heart, resembling ambrosia, filling the soul with delight. When shall I, O son of Raghu meet with the high-souled Bharata, and the heroic Satrughna, and thyself."* Having bewailed thus, Kākutstha, coming to the river Godāvari, there performed his ablutions in company with his younger brother and Sitā. Then having offered his adorations with water unto the gods and the Pitris, those sinless ones hymned the risen sun as well as the celestials. Having with Sitā as the second and Lakshmana,performed his bath. Rāma looked beautiful like that lord the reverend Rudra in company with Nandi and the daughter of the king of mountains.

## SECTION XVII.

HAVING bathed, Rāma, Sitā and Sumitrā's son went to their own asylum from the banks of the Godāvari. Arriving at the asylum, Rāghava along with Lākshmana, performing his morning devotions, entered the cottage. And honored of the Maharshis Rāma happily dwelt in that cottage ; and

* *Thyself,* the meaning is evident *when shall we all meet together.—T.*

seated with Sitā that mighty-armed one looked like the Moon in conjunction with Chitra. And he carried on various con verse with his brother Lākshmana. As Rāma was thus seated with his mind engrossed in that talk. A Rākshasi came to that region at her will. And that one named Surpanakhā, sister unto the ten-necked Rākshasa, coming upon Rāma, saw him like a celestial, having a leonine chest, mighty-arms, and expansive eyes resembling lotus leaves, with the powerful gait of the elephant, wearing a head of matted locks, with a resplendent countenance, bearing regal marks. And beholding Rāma dark-blue like the lotus, and becoming like Kandarpa himself,and resembling Indra, the Rākshasi was maddened with desire. Rāma was graced with a beauteous countenance, that Rākshas had a hideous face; Rāma had a slender waist, she had a huge abdomen; he had expansive eyes, she had terrible eyes; he was gifted with an elegant head of hair, she had coppery hair; Rāma was of a dear presence, she was of an unsightly presence; Rāma had a sonorous voice, she had a hideous voice; Rāma was youthful, the Rākshasi was an old hag; Rāma had mellifluous accents, she had harsh accents; Rāma was ever abiding by justice, she was unruly; Rāma was handsome, she was ugly. That Rākshasi being wrought up with passion addressed Rāma saying, "Wearing matted locks, and equipped with bows and arrows, why hast thou along with thy wife come to this region haunted by Rākshasas? It behoveth thee to say what the object of thy visit is." Thus accosted by the Rākshasi, Surpanakhā, that subduer of his foes from sincerity of disposition began to relate everything:—"There was a king named Daçaratha endued with the prowess of a celestial. I am his eldest son known among men by the name of Rāma. This is my younger brother (named) Lākshmana, (ever) serving me. This is my wife, known by the name of Sitā. Commanded by my father and mother, I in obedience to their mandate, desirous of acquiring religious merits, have for the purpose of securing righteousness, come to the forest for dwelling here. I also am anxious to know thee. Whose daughter art thou? And what is thy name, and what thy lineage? Possessed of a captivating form, thou appearest to me as a Rākshasi. Tell me truly why thou hast come here." Hearing these words the Rākshasi, afflicted with lust said, "Listen, O Rāma. I will relate everything truly. I am a Rākshasi, capable of wearing shapes at will. My name is Surpanakhā. Striking terror into the hearts of all, I range this forest alone. My brother is named Rāvana.* Thou mayst have heard of him. And he that is given to long sleep—the mighty Kumbhakarna, the righteous Bibhishana, who never serves the Rākshasas, and the brothers Khara and Dushana renowned in conflict (are also my brothers). O Rāma, I have surpassed them all (in prowess). At first sight of thee, I approach thee, thou best of men, as my husband, with (feelings of) love. I am endued with power, and range about at will by virtue of my strength. Become my husband for ever and a day. What wilt thou do with Sitā? Deformed and unsightly, she is not worthy of thee. I am fit for thee. Do thou look upon me as a wife. This unsightly, grim unchaste and human one with a lean abdomen, will I devour up, along with this brother of thine. Then having thy wish, in company with me, thou wilt range the Dandakas, surveying the various mountain summits and forests." Thus addressed, Kākutstha having charming eyes, well skilled in speech, with a smile, began to speak thus.

---

* Another reading is: *my brother is named Rávana—a Rákshasa, and the lord of Rákshasas. He is the son of Viasavan. Thou mayst have heard of him.—T.*

## SECTION XVIII.

With a smile, Râma jestingly addressed Surpanakhâ who had been ensnared in the noose of love, in soft words, saying, "Gentle one, I am already wedded; this is my beloved wife. To females like unto thee co-wife-hood is exceedingly miserable. This young brother of mine is good-looking, and is of an excellent character; he is graceful, and is still unmarried. The powerful one is named Lakshmana. He hath not yet tested the pleasures of a wife's company, and is desirous of having a spouse. And he is youthful and of an inviting presence. He will become a fit husband for thee, considering this thy beauty. O thou of expansive eyes, seek this brother of mine as thy husband, even as the solar beam seeks Meru. (By doing so),thou O supremely beautiful damsel, wilt not have to fear a co-wife." Having been thus addressed by Râma, the Râkshasi intoxicated with lust, at once leaving Râma, spake unto Lakshmana, saying, "I am fit to be thy wife possessed of transcendental grace, having regard to this beauty of thine. And with me thou wilt happily range these Dandaka's." Thus accosted by the Râkshasi, Sumitrâ's son, Lakshmana versed in speech, with a smile appropriately observed unto Surpanakhâ, "Why wishest thou to be the servant of me who am a servant myself?* O lotus-hued one, I am dependent on my noble brother, O thou of expansive eyes, be thou securing the *summum bonum*, with a joyful heart, become, O superbly beautiful wench, the younger wife of the noble one of great good fortune. Renouncing this frightful, unchaste, hideous, old wife possessed of a lean abdomen; he will devote himself unto thee. O paragon among damsels, O supremely charming lady, what man possessed of discernment, passing by such grace, would bear

* The text is difficult to render literally:—*Why wishest thou to be the female servant of me who am myself a male servant.—T.*

affection to a human female ?" Thus accosted by Lakshmana, that hideous one having a lean abdomen being incapable of understanding jest, took his words as true. Thereupon as that subduer of enemies, the irrepressible Rāma, was seated in the cottage in company with Sitā, the Rākshasi, transported with lust, said unto him, "Forsaking this deformed, unchaste, horrible old wife of thine possessed of a lean abdomen, thou dost not regard me. To-day, thou looking on, I shall eat up this human female. And I shall, rid of a co-wife, happily range with thee." Having said this, even as a mighty meteor striketh Rohini, that one having eyes resembling live coals, waxing exceedingly enraged, rushed towards that (damsel) with the eyes of a doe. Thereupon, hindering the Rākshasi resembling the noose of death, as she was rushing on, the mighty Rāma, growing wroth, said unto Lakshmana, "O Saumitri,* what is the good of jesting with a base and wicked one ? No use of doing it. Look, O amiable one, Vaidehi† is well nigh dead. It behoves thee, O foremost of men, to deform this frightful, unchaste Rākshasi of a huge abdomen, transported with lust." Thus desired the exceedingly strong Lakshmana, fired with wrath, taking out his sword, in the sight of Rāma, cut off her nose and ears. Her ears and nose cut off, the terrible Surpanakhā, uttering frightful cries, fled amain into the forest whence she had come. And being deformed, and covered with gore, the dreadful Rākshasi sent up many a roar, like clouds rumbling in the rains. And bleeding profusely, the grim-visaged Rākshasi, lifting up her arms, and roaring, entered the mighty forest. Then, having been deformed, (the Rākshasi) approaching, her brother of fierce energy, Khara, come to Janasthāna, seated surrounded by numbers of Rākshasas), fell down to the

---

* We are obliged to use this epithet as it is in order to prevent the too frequent recurrence of *Sumitrā's son*.—*T*.

† *Videha's daughter*. We retain this epithet also for the reason assigned above.—T.

earth, even as the thunder-bolt bursts from the sky. Then that sister of Khara, bathed in blood, and deprived of her senses through fright, related all about Râma's arrival at the forest along with Lakshmana and his own wife, as well as the circumstances connected with her being deformed.

## SECTION XIX.

Seeing his sister deformed, and covered with blood, fallen on the ground, the Râkshasa, Khara, fired with wrath asked her, saying, "Arise! Leave off fear and amazement. Tell me plainly by whom thou hast been thus deformed. Who is it that with his finger-end hath by way of sport hurt a black venomous snake that was innocent? He that coming in contact with thee hath to-day drunk virulent poison, winding a fatal noose round about his neck, knoweth it not through ignorance. Endowed with strength and prowess, ranging about at will, wearing shapes at pleasure, and resembling the destroyer himself, going to whom hast thou come by this condition? Who among the gods, Gandharbas or creatures or the high-souled saints is of such mighty energy as to have deformed thee? In this world I do not see him that would do me wrong. Even as a crane afflicted with thirst appropriateth milk mixed in water (leaving the latter out), so by means of fleet and life-destroying shafts will I among the immortals take the life of that chastiser of Pâka, the thousand-eyed mighty Indra. The forthy blood of whom, having his marrow pierced (by me) and slain by me in battle, doth the Earth wish to drink? Tearing off flesh from the cropse of whom slain by me in conflict, shall the birds so joyfully feed on it? Him, whom I shall wrong mightily, neither the gods, nor the Gandharbas, nor the Piçâchas,* nor the Râkshasas, will be able to rescue in fierce encounter. Recovering by degrees

* A kind of foul spirits.

thy sense, it behoves thee to tell me what individual it was of execrable character, who by his prowess, hath humbled thee in the forest." Hearing these words of his brother, who was under the influence of extreme rage Surpanakhā with tears in her eyes, said, "Tender, and endowed with beauty, possessed of youth and gifted with great strength, with expansive eyes resembling white lotuses; clad in bark and dark dear-skins; subsisting on fruits and roots, having their senses under control; leading an ascetic life and a Brahmacharya mode of existence; there are two sons of Daçaratha the brothers Rāma and Lakshmana resembling the Sovereign of the Gandharbas, and marked with signs betokening royalty. I cannot ascertain whether they be celestials, or human beings. And between them I saw there a youthful female furnished with grace, and having a dainty waist; adorned with every kind of ornament. And it is on account of this female that I have like one unchaste and uncared for, have come by this condition at their hands. Nor I wish in the midst of encounter to drink the forthy blood of that crooked one as well as those two slain (in battle). Let this my prime wish be crowned there with fruition. Her and their blood will I drink in dreadful conflict." As she said this, Khara wrought up with boundless passion, said, "Two human beings accoutred in arms, and wearing bark and dark deer-skins have in company with a female entered this deep Dandaka forest. Do ye return, after slaying them, as well as that wicked one. And this sister of mine will drink their blood. Ye Rākshasas, even this is my sister's dear desire. Repairing thither, speedily accomplish this, bearing them down by your native might. Seeing those two brothers slain by you, this one, exceedingly rejoiced, will drink their blood in the field." Thus commissioned, those fourteen Rākshasas set out there like clouds driven by the winds, accompanied by Surpanakhā.

---

## SECTION XX.

THEN the grim Surpanakhā, coming to Rāghava's asylum pointed out to the Rākshasas those brothers in company with Sitā. And they saw the mighty Rāma seated in the cottage in company with Sitā, and ministered unto by Lākshmana. And seeing her, as well as the Rākshasas who had come, Rāma remarked unto his brother, Lākshmana of flaming energy, saying, "O Sumitrā's son, do thou for a while guard Sitā. I shall slay these that have come to this asylum here." Hearing these words of Rāma versed in the knowledge of self, Lākshmana honored his speech by saying, "So be it." And the righteous Rāghava strung his mighty bow decked with gold; and addressed the Rākshasas, saying, "We that have entered into this untractable forest of Dandaka in company with Sitā are the sons of Daçaratha, the brothers, Rāma and Lākshmana. Why do you intend to do injury unto us. Subsisting on fruits and roots, having our senses under control, carrying on asceticism and leading a Brahmacharya life, we are passing our days in the forest of Dandaka. It is to destroy you, wicked, and troublesome that I equipped with the bow have come here at the desire of the saints. Stay there content you should not move further. If you have a care for your lives, desist, ye rangers of the night." Hearing those words of his, those fourteen grim Rākshasas bearing darts in their hands, exceedingly enraged, with their eyes reddened, breathing high spirits, harshly said unto the sweet-speeched Rāma, having his eyes reddened, whose prowess they had not seen before, "Having excited there our lord, the high-souled Khara, it is thou that shalt lose thy life no later than this day, being slain by us in battle. What power hast thou, being one, to stay before us many, in the field,—what shall I say of thy coping with us in conflict?

in consequence of the *parighas*, darts, and *pathifas* discharged by our arms, thou wilt surely lose thy life, along with thy prowess, and this bow which thou pressest with thy hand." Having said this in wrath, those fourteen Rākshasas, uplifting their weapons and daggers rushed towards Rāma; and discharged darts at the invincible Rāghava. Thereupon Kākutstha by means of shafts decked with gold, cut off those fourteen darts of theirs. Seeing this, that exceedingly energetic one, waxing highly enraged, took out fourteen *nârâchas*, whetted on stone, resembling the sun. And even as Satakratu hurls the thunder-bolt, Rāghava drawing his bow and taking his aim at the Rākshasas, let go those shafts. And those Rākshasas, their breasts pierced with vehemence, and themselves bathed in blood, fell down to the earth, like snakes dropping down from an ant hill. And with their breasts pierced, they dripping with blood, deformed and deprived of their lives, lay on the ground like trees whose roots have been severed. Seeing them fallen on the ground, the Rākshasi, beyond herself in wrath, approaching Khara, with her blood a little dried up, again in distressful guise threw herself on the earth, like a plant exuding gum. And in presence of her brother, she set up a mighty roar; and then her face grown pallid, she dropped tears, emitting cries. Seeing those Rākshasas slain in battle, Surpanakhā again hastened (to his brother), and the sister of Khara, related in detail the slaughter of those Rākshasas.

## SECTION XXI.

SEEING Surpanakhā again lying on the ground, Khara in anger spake out unto that one, who had come to bring on evil, saying, "I had but recently commissioned for thy behoof those heroic Rākshasas living on flesh. Why then dost thou again weep? Bearing regard and attached unto me, and ever engaged in my welfare, they, assailed by others, are incapable of being slain; nor do they not obey my orders. What can it be? I would hear of the occasion owing to which again, crying 'Ah lord,' thou rollest on the earth like a serpent. Why dost thou beweep like one forlorn, while I thy lord, am living? Arise! Arise! Do not fear, cast off thy stupor." Thus addressed, and consoled by Khara, that irrepressible one, wiping her eyes, spoke unto Khara, "Having had my nose and ears cut off, I had come hither, covered with blood; and thou hadst consoled me. And thou also hadst despatched fourteen heroic Rākshasas, for my behoof, for slaying the terrific Rāghava along with Lākshmana. But all those, bearing ill will (towards Rāma), bearing darts and *pathsas* in their hands, have been slain in conflict by means of weapons penetrating into the vitals. Seeing those possessed of great speed, in a moment laid low on the ground,—as well as (witnessing) Rāma's mighty deed, great fear hath taken possession of me. O ranger of the night, I am afraid, and agitated, and cast down. I have (at length) found in thee a refuge, seeing fear on all sides. Wilt thou not rescue me who am sinking in this ocean of grief having sorrow for its alligators and affright for billows? And these Rākshasas, living on flesh who had arrived at that place, have been slain by Rāma with sharpened shafts. If thou hast any kindness for me as well as those sons of Rākshasas and, O ranger of night, if thou hast strength and energy to cope with Rāma do thou kill this thorn of the Rākshasas, who hath set up his dwelling in the forest of Dandaka. If thou do not to-day slay that destroyer of foes,* Rāma, I shall banishing shame, give up my life in thy very presence. Meseems, thou backed by thy forces† art incapable of staying in battle before Rāma in high encounter. Thou plumest thyself on being a hero; but

* Another reading is *that enemy of mine*.—*T*.

† Some texts—(Rāma) *equipped with the bow*.—*T*.

art really none such. Prowess hath been falsely attributed unto thee. Go off from Janasthâna without delay, along with thy friends. O stainer of thy line, do thou in battle slay those fool-hardy ones. But if thou fail in slaying those human beings, Râma and Lakshmana, then how canst thou void of strength and of slender prowess, stay here? Overcome by the energy of Râma, thou shalt speedily meet with destruction. Daçaratha's son, Râma, is endued with energy. His brother is possessed of high vigour by whom I have come to be deformed." Having thus bewailed long, that Râkshasi, possessed of a spacious abdomen, through sorrow, became bereft of her senses before her brother, and exercised with great grief cried, striking her abdomen with her hands.

## SECTION XXII.

On being thus taunted by Surpanakhâ, Khara spoke these sharp words in the midst of the Râkshasas, "Arising from this thy humiliating censure, my wrath is beyond compare. I can not bear it, like salt-water cast on a sore. From my prowess I count not Râma who is a human being possessed of a frail life—him who slain by me shall to-day in consequence of his misdeed give up existence. Restrain thy tears, and remove thy fear. I shall despatch Râma along with his brother to the abode of Yama. Thou shalt O Râkshasi, quaff on the ground the hot blood of Râma of evil life, slain by my axe." Overjoyed on hearing the words that dropped from Khara's mouth, she again through fickleness extolled that foremost of Râkshasas, brother. At first reprimanded by her and then praised, Khara spoke unto his general, named Dushana, saying, "Do thou, O gentle one, array fourteen thousand of those Rākshasas, gifted with furious vehemence, ever following my wish, who never turn away from the field; who are hued like unto purple clouds, who revel in cruelty,* and who are elated (in consequence of their prowess). And thou gentle one, do thou at once bring my car as well as my bows, and pasty colored arrows and scimitars, and darts, and various whetted javelins. O thou versed in warfare, for slaying this haughty Rāma, I go in the very fore-front of the high-souled Paulastyas.† As he said this, Dushana brought his great cas hued like the sun, yoked with excellent steeds of various colors. And thereupon in a passion Khara ascended that car resembling a peak of Meru, embellished with burnished-gold, furnished with golden wheels, open; having its pole studded with lapises; surrounded with fishes and flowers and trees and stones, and the sun and the moon and gold, and auspicious articles; and swarms of birds, and stars; having streamers and swords; garnished with bells; and yoked wite superb coursers. And beholding that mighty army consisting of cars and arms and pennons, Khara as well as Dushana, said unto that multitude of Rākshasas, "March forth!" And then uttering tremendous roars, rushed out with great vehemence four and ten thousands of those terrible Rākshasas equipped with clubs and *pattisas* and darts and sharpened axes, and scimitars and discuses,—shining beautifully in their hands and *saktis* and dreadful *parighas* and innumerable bows, and maces, and *mushalas* and *vajras* fearful to behold, griped fast. And those following the will of Khara issued out of Janasthāna. Seeing those Rākshasas of dreadful forms rushing out, Khara's car remaining a little away (from the press), proceeded after a short space. Then

* The North-West Province's text has some additional *sloka*:—*Dreadful, wearing forms at will, possessing the pride of the lion, having large mouth, high-souled, revelling in cruelty, endued with strength, of fierce energy.—T.*

† *Lit.—pulastya's sons.* The Rakshasas were commouly descended from *Pulastya.—T.*

taking the permission of Khara, the charioteer drove at speed those powerful steeds decked in shining gold. And driven with speed. the car of Khara—slayer of foes—filled all directions with its rattle. And Khara, fired with wrath, and having piercing voice, hastening to destroy his enemy like the Destroyer himself, again urged his charioteer with roars, like a mighty cloud showering down stones.

## SECTION XXIII.

As those terrible and inauspicious forces were marching on, a mighty sable cloud with dreadful sounds began to shower down blood. And the steeds yoked to his (Khara's) car, gifted with great celerity, dropped down all of a sudden on the level high ways strewn with blossoms. A dark circle bordered with red, resembling that of charcoal, appeared in the vicinity of the sun. And a frightful vulture, having a huge body, approaching the banner, sat upon the upraised golden flagstaff. And beasts and birds having shrill voices, living on flesh, remaining near Janasthāna, emitted various dissonant notes. And in the quarter lighted up by the sun, fierce jackals having mighty voices, in dreadful cries presaged evil unto the Rākshasas. And terrific clouds surcharged with water and blood, and resembling elephants with rent temples, enveloped the sky. And a dense darkness appeared, capable on making one's hair stand on end, and no quarter was distinctly visible. And out of season, there appeared evening hued like a cloth soaked in blood. And facing Khara, terrible beasts and birds set up cries. Kankas, Gomayas and vultures, portending fear, began to cry. Ever inauspicious in war, jackals presaging evil, with their mouths belching forth flame, howled in the face of the forces. And comets, resembling *parighas* appeared beside the sun,

That mighty planet Swarbhānu seized the sun when there was no *parva*. And the winds blew violently; and the sun was without lustre. And when there was no night, stars wearing the sheen of fireflies, began to fall. And in the tanks fishes and fowls were inert, and the lotuses were withered. And at that hour the trees were shorn of fruits and flowers; and without wind there arose dust dusky like clouds. And the parrots uttered wild notes—*chichikuchi*. And meteors of terrific aspects fell with loud noises. And the earth with her mountains, woods, and forests, shook. And as the intelligent Khara was roaring from his car, his left arm shook, and his voice fell, and as he surveyed around, his eyes moistened, and his head ached; yet through ignorance, he did not desist. Witnessing these mighty portents capable of making one's hair stand on end, Khara with a laugh, addressed the whole body of Rākshasas, saying, "Even as a strong person from prowess counts not a weak one, I do not dwell upon all these mighty portents, dreadful to behold, that have appeared. Even the stars will I bring down from heaven with my sharp shafts; and even Death will I engaged, bring to mortality. Without slaying Rāghava puffed up with pride as well as Lakshmana, by means of sharp weapons, I return not (from the conflict). Let that sister of mine, for whom Rāma and Lakshmana have had sense perverted, attain her desire, by drinking their blood. I had never before met with defeat in conflict. Ye have witnessed it. I do not speak a falsehood. Wrought up with rage, I shall slay in fight the sovereign of the celestials himself, going on his mad Airāvata, with the thunder-bolt in his hand,—what shall I say of those two, who are human beings? Entangled in the noose of death, that mighty army of the Rākshasas, hearing his challenge, experienced boundless enthusiasm. And anxious to see the encounter, there came high-souled saints, and celestials, and Gandharbas, and Siddhas, with the Chāranas. And these pious ones assembled, spoke unto one another, "Welfare unto those cows, and Brāhmanas, and those that are prized by the worlds! As the discus-handed Vishnu vanquished the foremost Asuras, may Rāghava rout in battle those rangers of the night, the progeny of Pulastya! And saying this as well as various other things, the supreme saints and the celestials stationed in the sky conceiving curiosity (as to the issue of the conflict), beheld the host of those Rākshasas, whose days had been numbered. Then impetuously Khara issued in his car from the van of the army.* And these twelve endowed with exceeding prowess, *viz.*, Synagāmi, Prithuçyāma, Yaynaçatru, Vihangama, Duryyaya, Karavirāksha, Purusha, Kālakānuka, Maghamāli, Mahāmāli, Sarpasya, and Rudhirāçana posted themselves around Khara. And Mahākapāla, Slhulāksha Hramāthi and Triçiras†—[these four going before the forces, went at the back of Dushana]. Then as the planets dart towards the sun and moon, that heroic and dreadful army of Rākshasas, eager for victory suddenly rushed towards the princes with great vehemence.

## SECTION XXIV.

When Khara of fierce prowess had come to the asylum Rāma in company with his brother saw all those evil prognostics. And beholding those dreadful portents, Rāma exceedingly distressed, apprehending some calamity to the Rākshasas, observed unto Lakshmana, "O mighty armed one, behold these great presages that have taken place, capable of annihilating all beings, and which have for their object the utter extermination of the Rākhasas! Yonder

* The N. W. P. text has a different *sloka*. *And seeing him come out on the ground, they themselves came out.—T.*

† The *sloka* in the text is incomplete: The part within brackets, taken from the N. W. P. recension completes it.—T.

threatening clouds of assinine sable, showering down blood and uttering loud sounds are ranging the welkin. And, O discerning one, rejoicing at the prospect of my fight, all these arrows emit smoke, and my bows plated on the back with gold, are restless. Meseems from the noise of the wild birds that impending on us is danger and uncertainty to life. Without doubt, there shall take place a mighty conflict. At this critical time, my arm shaking momentarily, betokens, O hero, victory unto us, and defeat unto the enemy. And thy face appeareth pleasant with a delightful lustre. O Lakshmana, the pallid face of those that prepare for conflict, auger shortening of life. We can hear the shouts of the Rākshasas as they roar, as also the blasts of the trumpets of those doomed to be wounded blown by Rākshasas of remorseless deeds. A considerate person that wisheth for his welfare, apprehending peril, should prevent disaster ere it arrives. Therefore bearing arrows in thy hand, and equipped with thy bow, do thou, taking Videha's daughter, take refuge in the mountain cavern, covered with trees and difficult of access. That thou shouldst act contrary to my words, is what I do not wish. Swearing by my feet, go thou without delay, my brother. Thou art both strong and a hero: Thou canst, without doubt, slay these (Rākshasas). But I wish to slay all these rangers of the night myself." Thus accosted by Rāma, Lākshmana, taking arrows and a bow, took refuge in an inaccessible cave along with Sitā. Thereupon, saying, "Ah! we have spoken it sharp," Rāma put on his mail. And adorned with that mail resembling fire Rāma appeared in the dark like a mighty flame streaming up. And uplifting his bow, and taking his arrows, that powerful one stood there, feeling all directions with the twangs of his bow-string. Then the high-souled gods and Gandharbas, Siddhas and Chāranas came there, with the intention of witnessing the fight. And high-souled saints of the world, and the foremost Brahmarshis, of pious acts, coming together, spoke unto one another, saying, "Hail to cows and Brahmanas, and all those in whom are established the worlds! May Rāghava vanquish in fight those rangers of the night, the progeny of Pulastya, even as the discus-handed Vishnu routed in battle the foremost Asuras!" Having said this, they again spoke, eying one another, "There are fourteen thousand of the Rākshasas of dreadful deeds, while the righteous Rāma is single. How can fight take place (between two such parties)?" Having said this, the Rājarshis, Siddhas, multitudes of the best of the twice-born ones, and celestials stationed in the sky were moved with curiosity (as to the issue of the conflct). Then seeing Rāma filled with energy, remaining in the field, all beings from fear experienced great pain. And the peerless grace of Rāma of energetic deeds became like unto that of the high-souled infuriated Rudra.* While the gods, Gandharbas and Chāranas were thus conversing, the forces of the Rākshasas sending up solemn sounds, furnished with horrible armour, arms and flags, conversing in heroic parlance, roaring at each other, stretching bows, momentarily yawning,† sending forth shouts, and blowing trumpets. The universal uproar filled that (entire) forest. Scared and terrified at the hubbub the rangers of the wood fled to quarters free from noise; nor did they cast their eyes backward. And that army resembling the ocean, and rife with sounds, equipped with various weapons, with furious speed came towards Rāma. And Rāma also versed in warfare, casting his eyes around, found the forces of Khara ready for fight.‡ Then stretching his dreadful bow, and swiftly taking out shafts, (Rāma) for compassing the destruction of the entire body of the Rākshasas, waxed furiously enraged. And like

* There is a variation in reading here; the sense, however, is the same.

† The commentator says the yawning was in consequence of the soldiers having during the conflict indulged in liquor.—T.

‡ Another text:—The holder of *pinaka*.—T.

unto the flaming fire at the universal dissolution, he. growing wroth, was incapable of being looked at. And seeing him filled with energy, the sylvan deities were extremely pained.* And the aspect of the enraged Rāma appeared like that of the holder of Pināka, intent upon destroying Daksha's sacrifice. Furnished with bows and ornaments and cars and mail hued like fire, that army of those subsisting on flesh, appeared like masses of blue clouds at sunrise.

## SECTION XXV.

Coming to the asylum, Khara in company with those that went before him, saw that slayer of foes, the enraged Rāma, holding his bow. And seeing him, Khara possessing a shrill voice, raising his bow, commanded unto the charioteer to drive towards Rāma,—"Drive on!" At Khara's command, the charioteer drove the steeds to where the mighty-armed Rāma stood alone, holding his bow. And seeing him (Khara) entered the field, all those rangers of the night—the counsellors—uttering mighty shouts, environed him round. And Khara stationed on his car in the midst of Rākshasas appeared like red bodied one risen in the midst of the stars. Then in battle Khara, afflicting Rāma of incomparable energy with a thousand shafts, uttered a tremendous roar. Then all the rangers of the night, waxing exceeding wroth, showered various weapons on that terrible bowmen, the invicible Rāma. And wrought up with rage, the Rākshasas in battle assailed him with iron clubs, and darts, and *prâsas*, and swords, and axes. And resembling clouds (in hue), the exceedingly strong Rākshasas, having huge bodies, darted towards Kākutstha by means of steeds and cars. And mounted on elephants resembling mountain-

* Another reading is :—The sylvan deities fled away.

peaks, numbers of Rākshasas, intent upon slaying Rāma in battle, showered arrows on him, as mighty clouds pour down showers on the monarch of mountains. And Rāma was hemmed in by all those fierce-looking Rākshasas, even as in the evening Mahādeva is surrounded by his courtiers. And as the ocean resisteth the tide of a river, Rāghava by means of arrows resisted the weapons discharged by the Yatudhānas. As a mighty mountain, assailed by the thunder-bolt, doth not feel pain, Rāma, having his person pierced by terrible flaming weapons, did not feel pain. And pierced, and with his person covered with blood, Rāma, the descendant of Raghu, resembled the sun enveloped in evening clouds. And seeing him single, surrounded by many thousands, the Gods, Gandharbas, Siddhas, and supreme saints became sorrowful. Then Rāma getting enraged, bringing his bow to a circle, discharged sharpened shafts by hundreds and by thousands. And as if in sport, Rāma in the conflict shot irrisistible (shafts) furnished with Kanka feathers, and decked with gold, irrisistible, capable of inflicting extreme pain, and resembling the noose of Death. And sportively discharged by Rāma, those arrows deprived the Rākshasas of their lives, like the noose forged by death. And piercing the persons of the Rākshasas, those arrows, soaked in blood, going up to the sky, appeared with the splendour of flaming fire. And innumerable shafts, exceedingly fierce, capable of depriving the Rākshasas of their lives, were let go from the circle of his bow. And with those Rāma severed bows, in battle by hundreds and by thousands and flag ends, and shields, and mail, and many arms with embellished hands, resembling the trunks of elephants. And the arrows of Rāma discharged from the string pierced and cut off steeds mailed in gold, yoked unto cars, together with the charioteer; and elephants with their riders; and horsemen with horses. And slaying foot-soldiers, he despatched them to the abode of Yama.

And cut off with *nâlikas* and *nârâchas*, and sharp-pointed *vikirnas*, the rangers of the night uttered dreadful howls of distress. And like a withered wood afflicted by fire, that host harassed by the various marrow-piercing* shafts shot by Râma, did not attain ease. And some heroic rangers of the night possessed of great strength, waxing furious, threw† at Râma *prasas*, and darts and axes. Thereupon resisting by means of shafts those weapons of theirs, the mighty-armed Râma endued with prowess, took their lives in the conflict, and cut off the heads (of warriors). And having their heads, and shields and bow-strings, severed, they fell as fall on the earth trees thrown down by blasts from the wings of Suparna.‡ Those rangers of the night that remained there, wounded by arrows, and losing heart, fled with speed to Khara, to seek his protection. Thereat, encouraging them, Dushana, taking his bow, ran furiously in high rage against Râma, like the enraged Destroyer himself. And rallied again (by Dushana) and, their fear dispelled through their having found refuge with him, they armed with *sâlas*, *tâlas*, and crags, darted against Râma. And bearing in their hands darts, and clubs, and nooses, those exceedingly strong ones showered in battle shafts and weapons. And the Râkshasas discharged vollies of trees and crags. And capable of making one's hair stand on end, that battle was dreadful and furious and now on the side of Râma and now again on that of the Râkshasas. And waxing exceedingly wroth, they bore on him hard from all sides. Then finding all directions entirely covered with Râkshasas, and showers of shafts, that one gifted with mighty strength, sending up a terrific shout, fixed (on the bow-string) the exceedingly effulgent Gandharba, weapon (for discharging it) among the Râkshasas. Then thousands of shafts went forth from the circle of his bow;

* Another reading is, *sharpened.*—*T.*

† Another reading: *remaining before Râma, threw powerful weapons.*—*T.*

‡ *Lit.*—Of *fair feathers.* A name of Garura.

and all directions were covered with thronging arrows. And those Rākshasas, afflicted with arrrows could not see Rāma how he took out his dread shafts, nor how he discharged those excellent shafts ; they only saw him drawing his bow. And the darkness spread by the arrows enveloped the sky with the sun. And Rāma stationed there continued pouring in shafts And the earth was covered with shafts shot, and alighting, and alighted simultaneously. And at places were seen Rākshasas by thousands slain, falling, enfeebled, torn and riven. And cut off by Rāma with arrows, darts and *patticas* in that battle the fearful field was scattered heads with turbans, arms with finger-fences ; torn thighs and arms, and various ornaments, horses, excellent elephants and cars, shattered in numbers, chouris, fans, and umbrellas, and pennons of various descriptions. Beholding all those stain, the (remaining) Rākshasas, sore distressed, could not (again) advance before that captor of hostile capitals Rāma.

## SECTION XXVI.

FINDING his own forces slaughtered, the mighty-armed Dushana speedily ordered five thousand Rākshasas, gifted with tremendous velocity, difficult of being approached,—who never turned from the field. And from all sides they incessantly showered darts and *patticas*, and scimitars, and stones, and trees, and shafts. Thereupon by means of shafts the righteous Rāghava resisted that mighty destructive shower of trees and stones. Resisting that shower, Rāma with his eyes staring, and resembling a bull, flew into a great rage, for the purpose of slaying the whole body of Rākshasas. Then influenced by wrath, and flaming in energy he on all sides covered the army along with Dushana with arrows. Then the general, Dushana, destroyer of enemies, getting wroth, opposed Rāghava with arrows resembling thunderbolts. Then heroic Rāma highly angered, severed his (Dushana's) mighty bow with shafts sharp as razors, and slew his four horses by means of as many shafts. And having slain the steeds, he (Rāma) cut off the head of the charioteer by means of a crescent shaped weapon, and pierced the (Rākshasa Dushana) in the breast with a brace of shafts. His bow cut off, his steeds together with the charioteer slain, and himself deprived of his car, he (Dushana) took a *parigha* resembling a mountain peak, able to make one's down stand on end plated with gold, capable of afflicting celestial hosts, studded with sharp iron *sankus*, and graced with the fat of foes ;—of the touch of a thunderbolt, able to pierce the persons of enemies.* And taking up in that encounter the *parigha* resembling a mighty snake, that ranger of the night of cruel deeds Dushana, rushed towards Rāma. And as Dushana was rushing forward, Rāghava by means of a couple of shafts cut off his two arms with the ornaments. And the huge *parigha* escaping from (Dushana's grasp) fell forward on the field like the banner of Sakra. And like a mighty elephant whose husks have fallen off, Dushana, on his arms having been severed, fell down to the earth. Seeing Dushana down on the ground, and slain in battle, all creatures, saying, "well done !" "well done !" paid homage unto Kākutstha. In the meantime, three generals, getting wroth, being entrapped in the noose of death, rushed against Rāma in a body—viz ; Mahākapāla, Sthulākshya, and the mighty Pramāthi the Rākshasa, Mahakapala, upraising a large dart, and Sthulākshya, taking a *pathica*, and Pramāthi, an axe. And as soon as Rāghava beheld them advance, he resisted them by means of sharp and keen-edged shafts, even as one receives guests that have come. And Raghu's son split Mahākapāla's head,—afflicted Pramāthi with countless shafts, and lodged the eyes of Sthulākshya with sharp shafts. And they fell down to the earth like mighty

---

* The text may also mean—*able to rend the cities of foes.*—T.

trees of many boughs. Thereat instantly inflamed with wrath, Rāma by means of five thousand shafts, sent as many thousands of Dushana's followers to Yama's abode. Hearing that Dushana had been slain, Khara, waxing wroth, commanded his mighty generals, saying, "Fighting with that vile man, Rāma, along with his mighty forces Dushana hath been slain in battle, together with his followers. Let all the Rākshasas slay him with weapons of various shapes." Having said this in wrath, Khara darted towards Rāma. And discharging choice shafts, Syenagāmi Prithugriva, Jajnasatru, Vihangama, Durjaya, Paravirāksha, Parusha, Kālakāmuka, Hemamāli, Mahāmāli, Sarpāsya, and Rudhirāçana,—these twelve generals endued with mighty prowess accompanied with their forces, proceeded vehemently against Rāma, discharging excellent shafts. Thereat with shafts resembling fire,and decked with diamonds and with gold, (Rāma) possessed of energy destroyed the rest of his (Khara's) forces. And as the thunderbolt slayeth the mighty, Asuras, those shafts studded with gold, and like unto smoking fire, slew those Rākshasas. And in the field Rāma slew an hundred Rākshasa with an hundred Karnis, and a thousand (again) with a thousand. And, their armour and ornaments severed, and their bows broken in shivers, those rangers of the night fell down on the earth, bathed in blood. And as a spacious dais is covered with Kuça, the entire field was scattered with the Rākshasas fallen in battle with hair dishevelled, and covered with blood. And at that time that fearful forest, with the Rākshasas slaughtered, and with its clay mired with flesh and blood, resembled hell itself. Fourteen thousand Rākshasas of dreadful deeds were slain by Rāma single, a human being, fighting, (moreover) on foot. And the remnant of his (Khara's) forces were that mighty car-warrior, Khara himself, and the Rākshasa, Triçira ; and (on the other side) was that destroyer of foes—Rāma. The rest of the Rākshasas, gifted with great prowess, terrible, and difficult of being withstood, were all slain in battle by the elder brother of Lakshmana. Then seeing that dreadful army destroyed in teribble conflict by the mighty Rāma, Khara ascending a great car, advanced before Rāma, like Indra with the upraised thunder-bolt.

## SECTION XXVII.

As Khara was advancing before Rāma, that leader of the army named Triçira, approaching him, said, "Do thou employ me, who am possessed of prowess; and thyself desist from this rashness. Behold the mighty-armed Rāma brought down in battle. I swear (unto thee) truly; I touch this weapon, (to say) that I will slay Rāma, who deserves to be slain by all the Rākshasas. Either I shall prove his death in battle, or he shall prove mine. Restraining thy martial ardour, do thou for a while become a witness. Either, joyed in consequence of Rāma being slain, thou shalt repair unto Janasthāna; or I being slain, thou shalt enter the field (against him)." Thus satisfied by Triçira, from his desire to meet with death, the latter, on being permitted with "Go," proceeded towards Rāma. And like a hill with three summits, Triçira rushed towards Rāma on an effulgent car yoked with steeds. And as a mighty cloud pours down shower, (Triçira) discharging vollies of shafts, uttered a roar resembling the sounds of a wet kettledrum. And seeing that the Rākshasa Triçira was advancing, Rāghava resisted (his attack) by discharging sharpened shafts. And that encounter of those exceedingly powerful ones, Rāma and Triçira was fierce, like unto that between a lion and an elephant. Then struck on the forehead by a brace of shafts shot by Triçira, the wrathful Rāma enraged, and inflamed with anger, said, "Ah! such is the strength of the heroic Rākshasas! I have been wounded in the forehead with shafts resembling flowers. Do thou also take the arrows shot from my bow." Saying this, (Rāma) enraged, and influenced by wrath, wounded Triçira in the breast with fourteen arrows. And that energetic one by means of four shafts having their joints bent, brought down his four steeds. And by means of eight arrows (Rāma) laid low the charioteer from the front of the car. And Rāma with a shaft severed his upraised standard. Then as that ranger of the night was descending from his broken car, Rāma pierced his breast with arrows,—and thereat he was stupified. Thereupon, that one of immeasurable prowess, out of anger by means of three shafts possessed of celerity, brought down Triçira's three heads. And that ranger of the night present in the field, afflicted by the shafts of Rāma, after his heads had fallen first, fell, vomitting smoking gore. And the Rākshasas remaining after the rest had been slain, belonging unto Khara's original forces losing heart, began to flee like deer terrified at a hunter. And seeing them fly, Khara waxing wroth, swiftly making them desist, darted towards Rāma, like Rāhu darting towards the moon.

## SECTION XXVIII.

SEEING Dushana slain in fight along with Triçira, Khara, witnessing Rāma's prowess, was filled with fear. And seeing that irrisistible Rākshasa host—even Dushana and Triçira—slain by the mighty Rāma alone, and seeing the great courage that was made in the army, that Rākshasa, Khara, was seized with despondency. Then as Namuchi advances against Vāsava, Khara stretching his powerful bow, advanced against Rāma. And Khara hurled at Rāma *nārāchas* reveling in blood, resembling infuriated venomous snakes. And repeatedly twanging his bow, Khara, mounted on his car, began to range the field, displaying his weapons through his acquired skill. And that mighty car-warrior covered all sides with his shafts. And seeing this, Rāma of a tremendous bow with shafts incapable of being borne, and resembling tongues of flaming fire, entirely enveloped the welkin, even as a cloud poureth down showers. And with the sharpened shafts shot by Khara and Rāma, the entire firmament on all sides was thronged. And as each enraged was engaged in coping with the other, the sun, enveloped in a net-work of shafts, did not appear. And as a mighty elephant is struck with the goad, Rāma in the conflict attacked (his opponent) with *nâlikas* and *nârâchas* and sharp-pointed *vikirna*. And as that Rākshasa sat on his car, bow in hand, all creatures saw him, as if he were the very Destroyer with the noose in his hand. And at this time Khara thought that Destroyer of all his forces, established in his manliness, the exceedingly powerful Rāma to be overcome with fatigue. And seeing that one powerful like the lion, and gifted with the vigorous gait of the lion, Rāma was not moved, as a lion seeing a pony deer (is not moved). And then as an insect falls into a flame, Khara mounting a mighty car, resembling the sun, approached Rāma. And, displaying his lightness of hand, Khara severed the bow of the magnanimous Rāma, with the arrow (fixed on it) at the place where it is grasped. Then taking up seven other shafts, resplendent like the thunder-bolt of Sakra, Khara, enraged, sent them into (Rāma's) main-joints, and then afflicting Rāma of unparalleled energy with a thousand shafts, Khara sent up in that conflict a loud shout. And riven by the shafts discharged by Khara, Rāma's mail resembling the sun fell to the ground. And pierced with those arrows, all over his body, and inflamed with rage, Rāghava appeared in the field, like a smokeless flaming fire. Then that destroyer of foes, Rāma, for compassing the end of his enemy, stringed another mighty bow, sending forth solemn sounds,—the redoubtable Vaishnava bow that had been conferred on him by the Maharshi. And uplifting that superior bow, Rāma rushed against Khara. Then with shafts having bent knots and golden feathers, Rāma, wrought up with rage, severed in battle Khara's standard. And on that exceedingly graceful golden standard being hewn down it seemed as if the sun dropped to the earth at the behest of the celestials. And thereat Khara, understanding the import of things, fired with wrath, pierced Rāma's breast with five arrows, like one striking an elephant with a goad. And Rāma on being pierced with a good many shafts discharged from Khara's bow, and having his body bathed in blood, was highly wroth. Thereupon that foremost of bowmen, and wielder of a mighty bow, taking six shafts, let them go, after aiming at them. And with one shaft he pierced Khara's head, with two his arms; and with three arrows headed like half-moon, Rāma wounded Khara in the chest. Then that highly energetic one, influenced by anger, assailed the Rākshasa with thirteen *nârâchas* whetted on stone and with one that exceedingly powerful one, cut the yoke of the car, with four the four steeds, with the sixth the head of Khara's charioteer, with three the stout *trivenu* of the car, with two the wheel, and with the twelfth, severing as if in sport Khara's bow with his hand,* with the thirteenth, resembling the thunder-bolt pierced Khara in the encounter. Then with his bow shattered, deprived of his car, (Khara) having his horses slain as well as his charioteer killed, taking a mace in his hand leaped to the ground, and stood there. And the celestials and Maharshis exceedingly rejoiced assembled in the welkin in a body, and with joined hands extolled that feat of that mighty car-warrior Rāma.

---

* Another text reads: *with the arrow set.*

## SECTION XXIX.

AND to Khara deprived of his car standing with a mace in his hand, that exceedingly energetic one, Rāma, preluding his speech with mildness, spake, "Backed by this mighty host abounding in elephants and horses and cars, thou hast done an exceedingly wicked deed, execrated by all the worlds. Even if one happen to be the lord of the three worlds, one given to troubling creatures, and who is cruel and engaged in wicked acts, can not exist. All persons destroy, like a snake that hath intruded itself, him that doth cruel deeds, hostile to the interests of every one. People delightedly behold the end of him that doing an action either from covetuousness or desire, doth not like a Brāhmana swallowing a Karakā, see the consequence thereof. What, O Rākshasa, dost thou gain by slaughtering exceedingly pious ascetics engaged in righteous acts, living in the forest of Dandaka? Like unto trees whose roots have been reduced, cruel persons, execrated of men, who perpetrate iniquitous acts, do not exist long. And as a tree puts forth blossoms is season, the doer of sinful deeds, at the hour (of repentance) inevitably reaps their fruit in the shape of dreadful anguish (of the spirit). And, O ranger of night, as the effect of having taken rice mixed with poison, appears without delay, even so also people readily reap the fruit of their own acts. O ranger of the night,it is to take the lives of the perpetrators of dreadful sins, who wish ill unto men, that I the king have come. To-day the gold-decked arrows discharged by me, piercing (thy body), shall enter into the earth, cleaving it, like serpents falling into an ant-hill. Slain in battle, thou shalt in company with thy army,follow those people practising piety, whom thou hast devoured in the Dandaka forest. To-day let those great saints, who had formerly been slain by thee, stationed in the sky, behold thee slain (in turn) with my arrows, and inhabiting hell. Do thou strike as thou likest. And thou that art of an odious race, do thou put forth thy energy. To-day I will bring down thy head, even as a palm falls to the ground." Thus addressed by Rāma, Khara enraged and beyond himself with passion, with eyes reddened, replied, "O son of Daçaratha, why having slain inferior Rākshasas in battle, dost thou praise thyself without reason? Those foremost of men that are puissant and powerful, do not, inflated with their energy, mouth (their own consequence). It is the mean-minded Kshatriyas of impure hearts that magnify themselves among men, even as thou O Rāma, dost. What hero, when the hour of his death hath approached, publishes in the field his own lofty lineage and sings his own hymn. As brass wearing the semblance of gold, displays its own defect on being heated,* with a fire lit with Kuça,† so thou hast betrayed thy own lightness by this speech of thine. Thou dost not see me staying here mace in hand, like a moveless mountain dyed in metals, bearing mobile and immobile things. I can, mace in hand, deprive thee and the three worlds to boot clean of your lives, like the very Destroyer with the noose in his hand. But I will not parley much with thee as much as I could wish: the sun is going to set, and our fight shall be interrupted. Fourteen thousand Rākshasas have been slaughtered by thee. I will for their deaths wipe their tears to-day." Saying this, Khara, highly enraged, hurled his mace‡ provided with golden rings at Rāma, like unto the blazing thunder-bolt. Thereat, reducing to ashes trees and shrubs, that mighty flaming mace, discharged by Khara's arm, fell before Rāma. And Rāma severed in many fragments that mighty mace, resembling the noose of Death, as ascending the welkin, it was coming down. Thereupon, like a she-serpent

* *i. e. becomes dusky*, as Rāmanuya intelligently remarks.—T.

† Another reading is, *lit with husks.*

‡ Another reading is, *plated with gold.*

brought down by force of incantations, the mace fell to the earth shattered and riven.

## SECTION XXX.

Cutting off the mace with his shafts, Rāghava attached unto righteousness with a smile said unto Khara these angry words, "Thou vilest of Rākshasas, this is the utmost of thy might, which thou hast displayed. Rendered more nerveless at my hands, in vain dost thou storm. Riven by my shafts, thy mace, belonging unto thee who art prolix in the matter of vocabulary, destroying thy confidence, hath saught the earth. And what thou hadst said,—"I will wipe the tears of the Rākshasas that have been slain," hath also proved false. As Garura stole ambrosia, will I deprive thee, O Rākshasa, who art base, of a mean disposition and a false character, of thy life. To-day the earth shall drink the blood vitiated with foamy bubbles, of thee, having thy throat severed, and riven by my shafts. Having all thy body covered with dust, and thy two arms lopped off, thou shalt, difficult to win, take thy nap, embracing the earth, like a damsel difficult to win. On thee, disgrace of Rākshasas, lying down, and being fast asleep, this Dandaka shall be refuge of those that shall resort to it for shelter. O Rakshasa, in thy Janasthāna, with its (Rākshasas slain by my shafts, ascetics shall fearlessly go about in the wood. To-day Rākshasas, capable of exciting fear in others, rendered forlorn and with their friends slain, shall from fear, with their faces wet with tears, fly (this place). To-day thy wives whose husband art thou of such a nature,—and who art of a like lineage (with thyself),—shall experience the sentiment of sorrow, and be deprived of their all. Thou of a cruel disposition, thou of ignoble soul, thou that art aye a thorn (in the side) of Brāhmanas, it is for thee that ascetics, frightened and dispirited, have so long been pouring the clarified butter." As Rāghava, influenced by anger, said this in the field, Khara from wrath, with accents rendered harsher, fell to censuring (Rāma), "Thou art wondrous proud ; and thou art fearless albeit fear is present unto thee. And come under the sway of death, thou dost not understand what should be said and what left unspoken. Those persons that have been fast bound by the noose of death, do not in consequence of their senses having ceased to perform their functions, discern what is proper and what improper." Saying this unto Rāma, that ranger of the night (Khara), pursing his brows, espied a mighty *sâla* hard by. And looking about him on all sides in the field for a weapon, he uprooted it, biting his nether lip. And raising up the tree with his arms, and uttering a roar, that exceedingly powerful one aiming at Rāma discharged it, exclaiming,—"Dead thou art." And as it descended, the puissant Râma cut it off by means yf a multitude of shafts, got into a mighty rage for the purpose of slaying Khara in battle. Then Rāma perspiring, with eyes reddened in wrath, pierced Khara in battle with a thousand shafts. And blood mixed with froth gushed by the sides of the shafts, like torrents flowing from fountain in a hill* stupified in battle by the shafts shot by Rāma, and maddened by the smell of blood, Khara furiously made for Rāma. And as he (Khara) was rushing on, bathed with blood, Rāma equipped with arms, suddenly summoning his strength walked backward two or three paces. Then with the view of bringing about (Khara's end) Rāma took up in the conflict an arrow resembling fire or another weapon of Brahmā himself. And that righteous one shot at Khara, that (arrow), which had been conferred on him by the intelligent Maghavān. And discharged by Rāma from his bent bow, that mighty arrow with the roaring of the thunder-

* The text varies slightly in other texts.—T

bolt fell at Khara's breast. And burning in the fire of the arrow, Khara fell down on the earth, like the giant Andhaka* in the forest of Sweta, consumed by Rudra. And thereat Khara slain fell down like Vritra slain by the thunder-bolt, or Namuchi by foam,† or Vala by Indra's *Acani*. After this, the celestials, assembled with the Chāranas, struck with wonder joyfully sounded kettle-drums and showered blossoms on Rāma. "In over half a moment Rāma by means of sharpened shafts hath slain in mighty encounter fourteen thousand Rākshasas, wearing shapes at will, headed by Khara and Dushana. Ah! mighty is the feat achieved by Rāma knowing self. Ah! this mighty prowess, this mighty firmness, show like unto those of Vishnu himself." Saying this all the deities went to from where they had come. Then the Rājarshis in company with supreme saints, with Agastya (at their head), gladly paying homage unto Rāma, said the following words, "It is for this that the chastiser of Paka, the great Indra, Purandra, had paid a visit to the sacred asylum of Sarabhanga. And the Maharshis had dexterously brought thee to this place, for compassing the destruction of those foes—the wicked Rākshasas. And it is owing to this, that, O son of Daçaratha, thou hast performed this mighty deed. (Now) the Maharshis will carry on their proper pious offices in the Dandaka." After this, that hero, Lakshmana, accompanied with Sitā came out of the mountain cavern, and joyfully entered the asylum. Then the victorious and heroic, Rāma, honored by the Maharshis, entered the asylum, worshipped by Lakshmana. And seeing that destroyer of foes, and bringer of comfort unto the Maharshis, her husband,

* The Asura Andhaka was slain in the forest of *Sweta* by Rudra. This is related in the Puranas. Another reading is *Swetarayga yathantaka like the Destroyer in the forest of Sweta*. Swa, according to the *Kurma Purana Uttra Khanda*, in the Kalanyara hill, by a kick with his left leg, slew the Destroyer, engaged in pennances, who had come to kill the Rajarshi Sweta, who was a great votary of Siva.—T.

† Namuchi was slain by a thunder-bolt laid over with foam.—T.

Vaidehi embraced him. And seeing the multitudes of Rākshasas slain, Janaka's daughter, beholding the undeteriorating Rāma, ministered unto him with supreme joy. And with a delightful countenance again embracing that destroyer of foes, who had been honored by the delighted Maharshis, Janaka's daughter became exceedingly happy.

## SECTION XXXI.

Then Akampana bestiring himself, speedily issuing out of Janasthāna, spake unto Rāvana, "O king, a great many Rākshasas living in Janasthāna, have been slain, and Khara also hath been slain in battle. I alone have with much difficulty managed to come here." Thus addressed, the ten-necked one, flaming up in energy, with his eyes reddened in wrath, said this unto Akampana, "Who, having his days numbered, hath ravaged the dreadful Janasthāna? Who shall no more wend the way of all beings? Doing me a bad turn, Maghavān himself, or Vaiçravana, or Yama, or Vishnu, cannot attain happiness. I am the destroyer of the Destroyer himself; and I burn even very Fire. And I can bring Death itself to mortality. I can by my impetus resist the force of the wind. And when enraged, I can by my energy consume the Sun and Fire." Thereat, Akampana, with joined hands, from fear replied to the ten-necked Rāvana, in faltering words, beseeching courage. Thereat that foremost of Rākshasas, the ten-necked one, granted him courage. Then inspired with confidence, Akampana without fear spoke, "There is a son of Daçaratha, youthful, resembling a lion,* named Rāma, of broad shoulders, and possessed of excellent beauty of long and mighty-arms. (He) is sable-hued, of high fame, and

* Another reading is *Viranga* : *rupopeta* : *possessed of handsome person.*—*T.*

of matchless prowess and vigor. It is he that in Janasthāna hath slain Khara with Dushana" Hearing Akampana's words, that lord of the Rākshasas, Rāvana, breathing like a mighty serpent, said these words, "Tell me, O Akampana, hath Rāma come to Janasthāna, accompanied with the sovereign of the celestials and the body of the immortals ? Again hearing Rāvana's words, Akampana described the strength and energy of that high souled one. (He) is named Rāma, and is exceedingly energetic ; the foremost of all bowmen— furnished with celestial panoply ; and is possessed of pre-eminent prowess in warfare. Like unto him in strength, of red eyes, and gifted with a voice like the sound of a kettledrum, his younger brother, Lākshmana has a countenance resembling the full-moon. He hath met with him (Rāma) as the wind meeteth with a flame. He is endued with grace, and is the foremost of monarchs. It is he who hath ravaged Janasthāna. The magnanimous gods did not come there. No doubts need be entertained on this head. The feathered shafts, plated with gold near the plumed part, becoming five-mouthed serpents ate up the Rākshasas. Wherever oppressed with fear the Rākshasas go, they see Rāma stationed before them. In this way, O sinless one, hath Janasthāna been exterminated by him." Hearing Akampana's words, Rāvana said, "I will go to Janasthāna for slaying Rāma with Lākshmana." When he had said this, Akampana said, "Hear, O king, the true report of Rāma's prowess and manliness. Enraged, the highly famous Rāma cannot by putting forth vigor be checked. And by means of his shafts, he can make river in full flood turn its course. And he can bring down from the sky its stars and planets, and that graceful one can recover the depressed Earth. And that lord can submerge all creatures by riving the continents of the sea, and with his shafts can resist the onset of the ocean, and the wind ; and that illustrious one that foremost of persons by virtue of his vigor, destroying the worlds, can again create all creatures. O ten-necked one, forsooth, Rāma cannot be subdued in conflict, either by thee or the world of Rākshasas, as heaven is incapable of being attained by a sinner. I deem him incapable of being slain by all the Gods and Asuras together. This alone is the means of slaying. Do thou heedfully listen to it! He has a wife of sterling worth in the world, and that slender-waisted one is known by the name of Sitā. She is in the full bloom of youth, and hath a symmetrical person—a jewel among womankind embellished with jewels. And neither a goddess, nor a Gandharbi, nor yet an Apsari, nor a Pannagi is equal to her; and what is a human female? Thrashing him, do thou in the mighty forest, carry away his wife. Without Sitā, Rāma shall cease to exist." Thereupon, the lord of the Rākshasas, Rāvana, happened to relish those words; and reflecting (a while), that mighty-armed one addressed Akampana, saying, "Excellent well. I will go there alone, accompanied by my charioteer only. I will this very morning with a glad heart bring Vaidehi to this spacious palace." Saying this, Rāvana departed, lighting up all sides, on a sun-shiny car, yoked with mules. And coursing the firmament, that mighty car of that foremost of Rākshasas looked like the Moon among clouds. And proceeding far, he, approaching the asylum (of Tāraka's son), presented himself before him. And Māricha entertained the king with meats and drinks passing human. And having entertained him personally with a seat and water (to wash the feet), Māricha spoke these pregnant words, "O king, O lord of the Rākshasas, is it well with the worlds? I am filled with fear: I apprehend that all is not right, since thou hast come hither (alone) in such post-haste speed." Thus addressed by Māricha, the highly energetic Rāvana, versed in speech, said, "My child, the guards (of Janasthāna) have been slain by Rāma of untiring energy; and all Janasthāna, incapable of being slain, hath (by him) been brought down in battle. Do thou, therefore, assist me in carrying away his wife." Hearing these words of the lord of Rākshasas, Māricha said, "What enemy of thine in the guise of a friend, hath spoken of Sitā unto thee ? And,O foremost of monarchs, who, having been, entertained by thee, doth not bear thee good will ?* Tell me, who is it that hath told thee, 'Bring Sitā hither ?' Who is it that hath set his heart on severing the summit of the entire Rākshasa world ? He must be thy enemy that excites thee to this. Of this there is not the least doubt. He wishes to extract through thy agency the fangs of a venomous snake. Who (intends) to lead thee astray by imposing on thee such a deed ? Who, O king, hath struck in the head, thee that wast slumbering in peace ? Rāghava in war is like a mad elephant, having an unblemished ancestry for his trunk, perspiration for his temporal exudation ; and arms resting well beside him for his tusks. O Rāvana, thou art not competent even to look at him. Thou ought not to rouse up the sleeping man-lion, that slayer of skilful Rākshasas resembling deer, with his sport in the field, for his joints and down ; arrows for his body and sharp scimitar for his teeth. O Sovereign of the Rākshasas, thou ought not to plunge thyself into this dreadful, and abyssless ocean, having the bow for its alligators, activity of arms for its shine, arrows for its billows, and engagement for its waters. Be propitious,O lord of Lankā ! O foremost of Rākshasas, with a contented heart, thou hadst better go thy way to Lankā. Do thou ever sport with thy own wives : let Rāma in company with his wife,sport in the woods." Thus addressed by Māricha, the ten-throated Rāvana desisted, and entered Lankā the best of capitals.

* Another reading is—*ko na nandati ninditi ; who having been insulted by thee, doth not rejoice (in thy prosperity)*, and, therefore, in the garb of friendship hath done thee this wrong ?—T.

## SECTION XXXII.

SEEING fourteen thousands of Rākshasas of dreadful deeds, together with Dushana, and Khara, and Triçira, slain in battle by Rāma single-handed, that one resembling clouds, Surpanakhā, again fell to send up mighty sounds. And witnessing Rāma's deeds, incapable of being performed by others, she, extremely agitated, went to Lankā, ruled by Rāvana. And she saw the effulgent Rāvana in front of his palace, surrounded by his counsellors, like Vāsava surrounded by the Maruts ; seated on a supreme golden seat resembling the sun, and like unto a flaming fire on a golden dais kept alive by sacrificial offerings ; unconquerable by high-souled saints, celestials, Gandharbas and all creatures ; terrible like the Destroyer with his mouth wide open ; his persons containing scars* of wounds inflicted by the thunder-bolt and the lightnings, in the war between the gods and Asuras ; his breast bearing marks of attacks made by Airāvata with the ends of his tusks ;—having twenty hands, and ten heads,—wearing elegant attire ; broad-breasted ; heroic ; marked with royal signs ; (in hue) resembling cool lapises ; embellished in ornaments of burnished gold ; having goodly hands, white teeth, and a huge face resembling a hill ;—even him who in the war of the gods had been assailed an hundred ways with the descent of Vishnu's discus ; whose body had been cut with all the weapons of the celestials ; (him) who furiously disturbs the deep incapable of being disturbed ; uproots mountain summits, and tramples over gods,—the destroyer of righteousness, and the violater of other's wives ;—the employer of all celestial arms, and the disturber of sacrifices ;—who going to the city of Bhagabati,

* This reminds one of Milton : of Beelzebub, he says,—

"————————His person
Deep scars of thunder had intrenched—*Par. Lost*,—Book I.

and vanquishing Vāsuki, had carried off Takshaka's beloved wife; who, going to Kailaça, and defeating him having for his vehicle a human being, had carried off the car Pushpaka coursing everywhere at will; who endued with prowess had devastated the divine Chaitraratha grove, the tank (situated there) and the Nandana wood,—as well as the gardens of the gods; and, who, himself resembling a mountain summit, had by means of his upraised arms, obstructed the rising of these repressor of foes the exalted Sun and Moon; who, possessed of calmness, having formerly for ten thousand years carried on asceticism in the mighty forest, offered his own heads unto the self create one; who in conflict fears not death from either gods or Dānavas or Gandharbas, or Piçāchas or birds or serpents, from none save human beings; who, possessed of prodigious strength, forcibly takes away the clarified butter sanctified with *mantras* from the sacrifical ground; the destroyer of sacrifices about to be completed; of villainous nature; the slaughterer of Brāhmanas; of cruel deeds; harsh and kindless, and ever bent on doing evil unto all creatures; and railing furiously at all creatures; the inspirer of fear in all beings. And the Rākshasi beheld her exceedingly powerful and cruel brother, wearing gorgeous apparel and ornaments, and decked in a glorious garland,—seated, like the Destroyer at the time (of dissolution) ready (to destroy); the exalted chief of Rākshasas; the delight of the race of Paulastya. Stupified with fear, the Rākshasi, approaching that destroyer of foes; Rāvana, surrounded by his counsellors, said these words. And transported with fear and desire, Surpanakhā, given to fearlessly ranging every where, who had been deformed by that high-souled one, showing (her mutilation), addressed these harsh words unto Rāvana of flaming and expansive eyes.

## SECTION XXXIII.

Then the woe begone Surpanakhā, in high wrath spoke harshly in the midst of the courtiers, unto Rāvana, given to railing loudly against all creatures, "Intoxicated with enjoyments, acting as thou wilt, and without any control whatever, thou dost not see that a dreadful disaster is impending. The subjects do not esteem a monarch that is given to sensual enjoyments, is intent upon satisfying his lust and is covetous like the fire in a cemetery. The king that doth not act at the proper time, finds destruction along with his kingdom and acts. Even as elephants shun the muddy river, do people shun from a distance, the ruler that doth not send out spies, who showeth not himself (unto his subjects), and who hath lost his independence. Like unto rocks in the sea, those monarchs that do not administer their dominions, that are not dependent, do not prosper. Having incurred the hostility of the gods, the Dānavas and the Gandharbas of subdued souls and senses, how canst thou, who art fickle, and hast not employed spies, become the king? And, O Rākshasa, thou art childish and foolish; and doth not know what thou shouldst. How canst thou then become the king? O thou best of conquerers, those kings whose spies, exchequer and morality are not free, are like the common herd. It is because kings know distant dangers through spies, therefore they are styled far-sighted. I believe thou hast no spies, and that thy counsellors are common folks, since although Janasthāna with thy kinsmen is destroyed, yet thou takest it not to heart. Fourteen thousands of Rākshasas of dreadful deeds, with Khara and Dushana, have all been slain by Rāma single-handed; Rāma of untiring energy hath inspired the saints with courage; the Dandakas have been benefitted; and Janasthāna hath been harassed. But thou, covetous and intoxicated and in the power of.

others, dost not understand that a great danger is overhanging (thee). People do not in times of peril assist a sovereign that is wrathful, stingy, intoxicated, haughty and deceitful. Even his own kindred slay a sovereign that sets immense store by his own self, is of light worth, regards himself highly, and irascible. They do not serve him ; nor do they fear when he intimidates them. Such an one is speedily dethroned ; and reduced to poverty and becomes like a straw. Even dry wood may serve a purpose ; or stone, or dust ; but no purpose is capable of being served by a sovereign that hath been cast off his place. Like a cloth that hath been worn, like a garland that hath been trodden, a king that hath been dethroned, although able, is of no consequence. But a king that keeps his wits about him, understands everything, is of controlled senses, and grateful, and of virtuous character, endureth for ever. That king is honored by men, that sleeping with his eyes, is awake as respects his eye of duty, and (the effects of) whose anger and favor, are seen (by all). But, thou Rāvana, who hast not by means of spies, acquainted thyself with the slaughter of Rākshasas, art of evil understanding and bereft of all these virtues. Given to disgracing others, ignorant of the proper distribution of time and place,* and never taking care to distinguish merits and defects, thou, thy kingdom being in danger, wilt speedily meet with disaster." On his vices having been thus celebrated by her (Surpanakhā), that lord of the rangers of night, Rāvana, musing a while, was long plunged in thought.

* The commentator, is silent here. The meaning evidently is, *thou dost not discern the where and when of things.*—T.

## SECTION XXXIV.

SEEING Surpanakhā speak harsh words in the midst of the courtiers, Rāvana, being enraged, asked her, saying, "Who is Rāma? And what is his prowess? And what his form? And what his power? And why hath he entered the forest of Dandaka, difficult to range? And what Rāma's weapons, by means of which he hath slain the Rākshasas? And Khara hath been slain in battle, and Dushana and Triçira. Do thou, O thou of a pleasing person, tell me the truth. And who hath deformed thee?" Thus addressed by the lord of the Rākshasas, the Rākshasi, transported with rage, commenced to duly narrate all about Rāma. "Rāma the son of Daçaratha is long-armed, of expansive eyes, clad in bark and dark deer-skin, and like Kandarpa in grace. And drawing a bow resembling that of Sakra, decked with golden rings, he discharges blazing *nârâchas*, like unto serpents of virulent poison. I do not see in the field, Rāma drawing his bow: I only see the host being slaughtered by a shower of shafts. And as Indra destroys (a field of) goodly crops, by pouring down hail stones, fourteen thousand Rākshasas of dreadful prowess, as well as Khara and Dushana were in a little over a moment slain with sharp shafts by Rāma alone fighting on foot. And he hath reassured the saints, and after having been deformed, I alone from fear of slaying a woman, have been let off by the high-souled Rāma knowing self. His brother is endued with mighty energy, and in merit, is of equal prowess; and he is devoted to his brother, and beareth him regard; the puissant one is named Lakshmana. And wrathful and invincible and victorious, and powerful, and intelligent and mighty, (he) is Rāma's right-arm—his life ranging externally. And Rāma's virtuously wedded beloved wife, having expansive eyes, and a face resembling the full-moon, is ever to the welfare of her lord.

And that fair-haired, fair-nosed, and fair-thighed illustrious one possessed of beauty, graceth the forest like a goddess,—as if a goddess of wealth herself. Of the lustre of burnished gold, with her finger nails reddish and projecting, and graceful, that surpassingly lovely wench is named Sitā—the slender waisted daughter of Videha. And neither a goddess, nor a Gandharbi, nor a Yakshi, nor a Kinnari, had I seen before on earth, possessed of such beauty. He that shall have Sitā for his spouse, and who shall be warmly embraced by her, shall live longer in the world than the Lord of celestials himself. That good-natured girl, unparalleled on earth in loveliness, who can well pride herself on her person, is a worthy wife for thee; and thou too art a fit husband for her. It is to bring over for thee that one of spacious hips, and a high and well-developed bust, that I had put forth my endeavours. But, O mighty-armed one I have been disfigured by the wicked Lakshmana. As soon as thou hast seen Vaidehi having a countenance resembling the full-moon, thou shalt be afflicted with the shafts of Cupid. If it is thy purpose to have her for thy wife, at once stretch forth thy right leg, for attaining success. If, O lord of Rākshasas, thou relishest my speech, do thou then, O Rāvana, without fear, do as I tell thee. Understanding their incapacity, do thou, O lord of Rākshasas, for making her thy wife, by force carry away the frail Sitā of a blameless person. Hearing that Rāma by means of straight coursing shafts hath slain the Rākshasas that had gone to Janasthāna, and seeing Khara and Dushana, killed, do thou ascertaining thy course, adopt it.

## SECTION XXXV.

HEARING those words of Surpanakhā, able to make one's hair stand on end, (Rāvana) ascertaining his course after issuing his orders to his councillors, departed. And proposing to himself that act, weighing its good and evil, considering his capacity or otherwise, and (finally) determining his purpose, Rāvana with a fixed mind went to the handsome stable. And going to the stable in disguise, the lord of the Rākshasas commanded the charioteer, saying, "Yoke the car." Thus asked, the charioteer possessed of fleet vigor, in a trice, yoked an excellent car after his heart. And ascending the car coursing at will, made of gold and garnished with spectral faces as well as arrow decked with gold,—resembling a mass of clouds, the graceful ruler of the Rākshasas—younger brother to the Lord of wealth—proceeded in that noiseless (vehicle), past the lord of rivers and streams. And with chouris of white hair, and a white umbrella, having ten-faces, resembling (in hue) cool lapises, wearing ornaments of polished gold, possessed of ten mouths, and twenty arms, clad in elegant apparel,—the foe of the celestials, and slayer of the foremost ascetics—having huge heads like unto the monarch of mountains, the lord of the Rākshasas, mounted on that chariot coursing at will, appeared beautiful like a mass of clouds in the sky, with cranes, in the midst of lightning. And that one possessed of prowess beheld the shore of the sea, containing crags, scattered with trees bearing fruits and flowers of various kinds by thousands, bordered all around with pools furnished with cool and delightful waters, ornamented with spacious asylums having daises, graced with woods of plantain, beauteous with cocoanuts, and blossoming *sâla* and palmyra, and *tamâla*, trees, grateful with supreme saints rigidly restraining their fear, and with serpents and fowls of fair feathers and Gandharbas and Kinnaras by thousands ; and pleasant with Siddhas and Chāranas, that have controlled their lust ; with those descendants of Brahmā—the Vaikhanas, the Māshas, the Vālakhilyas, and the Marichipas ; swarming with females,divinely beautiful, dight with gorgeous ornaments and garlands, and Apsarās skilled in sport, by thousands ; frequented by the wives of the celestials,and honored by graceful girls ; ranged by multitudes of deities and Dānavas, feeding on ambrosia ; abounding with swans, Krauncbas, and frogs, echoing to (the cries of) cranes ; containing stones resembling the lapis, and mild and cool by the influence of the ocean. And as he proceeded,the younger brother of the Lord of wealth, saw on all sides spacious cars capable of coursing at will, sable,furnished with fair garlands, and resounding with trumpet notes,—and Gandharbas and Apsarās. And surveying by thousands woods of sandal exuding gum at their roots,* and of choice *aguru*, grateful unto the sense of smell ; and woods and groves of excellent and odorous takkola fruits ; blossoms of the Tamāla, and thickets of black pepper ; heaps of pearls drying on the shore ; rocks ; the best corals in masses ;† summits of gold and silver ;‡ charming pellucid rills at places ; and cities filled with corn and wealth, abounding in gems of women, and thronged with horses, elephants and cars—Rāvana on the shore of the ocean beheld around a level and soft scene, resembling heaven itself—where breezes of delicate feel kept breathing. And there he saw a fig tree, hued like clouds, surrounded by ascetics ; its branches stretched around an hundred Yoyanas, and the exceedingly powerful Garura had ascended one of its boughs, taking an elephant and a huge tortoise, for the purpose of devouring them. And that best of birds, the powerful Suparna by his weight suddenly broke

---

* *Niryydsurasamutanam, gen, (sandal), which forms the principal ingredient in perfumes, containing odorous gums.—T.*

† Another reading is : *heaps of conch,—T.*

‡ Some texts read *sailam—hills.—T.*

a branch containing full many leaves. And it came to pass that Vaikhānas, Māshas, Vālakhilyas, Marichipas, Ayas, and Dhumras,—saints of the highest order—had assembled there. Thereat, moved by commisseration (for the ascetics), the virtuous Garura, taking with promptitude the broken bough measuring an hundred Yoyanas as well as the elephant and the tortoise, by one leg, at length eating up the animals, and by means of the bough, exterminating the country of the Nishādas—that best of birds attained unequalled delight in consequence of having rescued the mighty ascetics. Thereat, attaining double energy by virtue of that delight, that intelligent one set his heart on bringing ambrosia. And tearing off the iron links of the network, and bursting into the repository of gem,he carried away secreted ambrosia from the residence of the great Indra. Kuvera's younger brother beheld this fig tree, named Subhadra, graced with the Maharshi, on which Suparna had left his mark. Then repairing to the other shore of that lord of rivers, the ocean, Rāvana saw an asylum lying in the forest in a charming and sacred recess. And there he saw a Rākshasa,named Māricha, clad in a dark deer-skin, bearing a head of matted locks, subsisting on restricted fare. And approaching Rāvana duly, the Rākshasa, Māricha, received the king with every hospitality passing human. And having entertained him personally with meats and drinks, Māricha addressed him in weighty words, saying, "O lord of the Rākshasas, O king is it well with thee in Lankā ? And what for hast thou again come hither so speedily ?" Thus addressed by Māricha, that highly powerful one, skilled in speech, Rāvana said.

## SECTION XXXVI.

"O MARICHA, hearken unto me, my child, as I relate (everything unto thee). I am distressed; and in this distress of mine, thou art certainly my great refuge. Thou knowest Janasthāna, where lives my brother Khara, and the mighty-armed Dushana, and my sister, Surpanakhā; as also that Rākshasa subsisting on (human) flesh, the long armed Triçira, many other heroic night-rangers besides, of high enthusiasm in battles—Rākshasas, who had been living there at my command, troubling in the mighty forest the ascetics carrying on their pious offices. And fourteen thousands of Rākshasas of dreadful deeds, heroic, high-spirited,—Rākshasas possessed of exceeding prowess; while residing in Janasthāna of late,—clad in mail and equipped with various weapons, headed by Khara, met with Rāma in the field. Getting enraged, Rāma in conflict without returning any harsh speech, by means of his shafts shot from his bow,—hath, a human being, and fighting on foot, with his flaming arrows slaughtered fourteen thousand Rākshasas of fierce energy. And Khara hath been slain in battle, and Dushana also hath been brought down. And having slain Triçira too, (Rāma) hath rid the Dandaka of all fear. Having been expelled by his enraged sire, that disgrace of Kshatriyas, the weak Rāma, living in company with his wife hath effected the destruction of this army. He is of a vile character, crabbed, foolish, covetous, of uncontrolled senses, bereft of morality, sinful, and ever engaged in the evil of all creatures,—by whom, violently without hostility my sister hath been deformed in the forest by having her nose and ears cut off. Of him will I carry off by force from Janasthāna, his wife, Sitā, resembling the daughter of a celestial. Be thou my help in it. For certain, O exceedingly strong one, if thou help me at my side, if my brothers also back me, I do not think much of all the celestials. Therefore, be thou my help ; for, thou art capable, O Rākshasa. In prowess in battle, and in indomitableness, there is none like thee. Thou art a mighty hero commanding resources and conversant with potentillusory displays. Taking this to my heart, I have come to thee, O ranger of the night. Do thou listen as to the business in which by my command thou art to help me. Becoming a golden deer, marked with silver spots, do thou range about in Rāma's asylum in presence of Sitā. Seeing thee helpless, in the shape of a deer, Sitā will say unto her lord and Lakshmana also,—"Do ye catch it." And when they shall have departed, I shall carry off from the empty asylum, Sitā without let, like Rāhu depriving the Moon of his splendour. Then when Rāma shall be sore afflicted because of the carrying off of his wife, I shall easily, crowning my soul with success, safely bear away Sitā. Hearing Rāma's words, the face of the high-souled Māricha became blank and he was seized with apprehension. And licking up his dried lips, with winkless eyes,(Māricha) as if dead, and exceedingly distressed, eyed Rāvana, steadily. And alarmed because of Rāvana, with his mind depressed, Māricha who well knew Rāma's prowess in the forest, with joined-hands in agitation spoke words lending to his own as well as Rāvana's welfare.

## SECTION XXXVII.

HEARING the words of that sovereign of the Rākshasas, the highly energetic Māricha, skilled in speech, answered the Rākshasa chief, saying,"O king, the speaker of soft words is common, but the speaker and the listener of unwelcome though beneficial words are rarities. Volatile, and employing no spies, thou surely dost not understand the exceedingly powerful Rāma towering high in virtues, and resembling the illustrious Indra or Varuna himself. I shall be well, my child, if Rāma fired with rage, do not render all the world bereft of Rākshasas ; if Janaka's daughter hath not sprung to compass thy destruction, if a dreadful disaster do not befall thee because of Sitā, and if having obtained for her lord thee that art wilful and wicked, the city of Lānka with thee and the Rākshasas do not meet with utter extermination. The sovereign who is wicked, whimsical and of evil intent like thee, bringeth about his own destruction as well as that of his kingdom and relatives. Rāma, the enhancer of Kauçalya's delight hath not been abandoned by his father, nor is he devoid of propriety of conduct ; he is not avaricious, wicked nor the destroyer of Kshatriya race. He does not lack religious merits or accomplishments, nor is he of a harsh temperament and intent on causing misery unto creatures. Finding his truthful sire imposed on by Kaikeyi he has sojourned unto woods. For compassing the welfare of his father Daçaratha and Kaikeyi he hath entered the forest of Dandaka. Rāma, O my child is not harsh or foolish ; nor has he not control over his senses. Far from speaking untruth he does not know false stories even. It doth not behove thee therefore to use such improper language towards him. He is an incarnation of virtue, pious and truthful, and lord of all men as Bāsava of all celestials. How dost thou then wish to carry away by force his Vaidehi, protected by virtue of her own chastity, like unto the rays of Sun ? It doth not behove thee to enter that fire of Rāma who hath arrows for rays and bow and scimitar for fuel. It doth not behove thee, O Rāvana, to approach Rāma renouncing thy kingdom, happiness and love of life, who is like unto death itself and has bow for his widened and flaming mouth, and arrows for his rays and who is irrepressible, of mighty prowess, holding bows and arrows and repulsing the forces of the enemy. Incomparable is his power ; daughter of

Janaka is his wife and lives in the forest confiding in the mighty strength of his bow; thou shalt not be able to carry her away. She is the beloved wife of that best of men having a leonine chest—and he holds his wife dearer than his life and is ever attached unto her. And young Sitā beloved of the mighty Rāma, and like unto the rays of flaming fire is ever incapable of being carried away by thee. Of what avail is this vain attempt O Rākshasa chief? No sooner Rāma shall see you in the battle thou shalt meet with thy end. Hard it is to attain life, happiness and kingdom, so it behoveth thee to act properly, after consulting with thy ministers headed by Bivishana. judging Rāma's merits and demerits and ascertaining his and thy own strength and as well as thy welfare. Methinks thy approaching conflict with the son of the Koçala chief forebodes no good unto thee; hear again therefore O prince of the night-rangers, words sensible and lending to thy welfare.

## SECTION XXXVIII.

ONCE on a time I was engaged in travelling all over the earth. I had in my body, resembling a huge mountain, the strength of a thousand Nagas. I had *parigha* in my hands, crown on my head and golden ear-rings on my ears and my body was of a dark blue colour like that of a cloud. Causing fright unto the people I used to wander through the forest of Dandaka and live upon the flesh of the *Rishis*. The pious ascetic Viswamitra being afraid of me went in person to the king Daçaratha and said, "When I shall remain absorbed in meditation on the occasion of *parva*, let Rāma protect me O king, Truly am I afraid of this Māricha." Being thus addressed by the ascetic the virtuous-souled king Daçaratha replied, saying "Rāghava is still under twelve years of age and hath not been well disciplined in military arts. But I have soldiers enough, and if permitted by thee, O thou best of ascetics, I shall with my four-fold forces kill thy enemies, the rangers of the night." Being thus addressed that ascetic spoke unto the monarch, saying, "True it is that thou wert the protector of the celestials in the War and thy exploits are well known to the world, but no one shall be able to withstand the Rākshasas but Rāma. The highly energetic Rāma, though a boy is sufficiently qualified to defeat the enemies; therefore, O Destroyer of foes, let thy soldiery remain here and let me proceed along with Rāma. May God bless thee." Saying this the ascetic Viswāmitra being pleased went to his asylum along with Rāma. Afterwards having been initiated for the sacrifice in the forest of Dandaka Rāma having unstrung his mighty bow came to the ascetic to protect the sacrifice. He had a gold chain round his neck. a crest on his head and a bow in his hands; he had a pair of beautiful eyes, and only one piece of cloth; his countenance was of green hue and exquisite beauty and even then mustaches or other signs of manhood did not appear on his face. Beautifying the entire forest of Dandaka with his own splendour Rāma appeared like the newly risen moon. Thereupon I resembling a cloud and having golden ear locks entered the asylum being proud of power on account of the boons offered unto me by Brahmā. Seeing me enter he took up his dart and attached string unto his bow with proper care. Being under the influence of sheer foolishness I passed by him as a child and darted towards the sacrificial altar of Viswamitra. Thereupon he wounded me with a sharpened sword capable of doing away with the enemies and threw me away into the ocean situated at a distance of hundred *yoyanas*. He had no mind of killing me then and for this he saved my life. I was thrown however into the deep ocean being hindered by the velocity of his arrows and having lost my consciousness. Regaining my sense after a long while I returned to the city of Lankā. Myself saved thus, my followers however were all killed by Rāma of unwearied activity though a mere child and a novice in the art of warfare. It is for this that I do prevent thee; thou shalt be overwhelmed with calamities and meet with destruction if dost thou engage thyself in battle with him. In vain shalt thou bring about the affliction of the mirthful and sportive Rākshasas ever witnessing social festivities. And in vain shalt thou for Sitā compass the destruction of the city of Lankā, adorned with diverse jewels and filled with golden edifices. Pious men living with a vicious man, meet with destruction for his sins, though they themselves do not commit any misdeed, like unto fish (devoured by Garura) living in a lake where snakes dwell. Thus shalt thou witness that for thy own folly the rangers of the night, adorned with celestial ornaments and having their body pasted with sandal, have been killed and brought down to the earth. And they deprived of shelter have fled away to different directions, some with their wives and some alone, having their wives carried away (by the enemies). Thou shalt further observe that all edifices of Lankā being enveloped with arrows and flaming fire have been burnt down to ashes. There is no greater sin on earth than carrying away another's wife. There are thousand ladies in thy seraglio O king. Being attached unto thy wives do thou preserve the race of the Rākshasas, thy own line, thy wished-for life, kingdom, wealth and dignity. Do not bring about Rāma's mischief if thou dost wish to live happily with thy wives and friends. I am thy friend and ask thee again and again to desist (from thy evil intention); if thou dost encroach upon Sitā surely thou shalt along with thy kinsmen go to the abode of Yama being enfeebled by the arrows of Rāma."

## SECTION XXXIX.

I WAS however somehow saved by Rāma in that conflict. Listen what happened afterwards. I was not humbled even by the danger of my life. Once again I entered the forest of Dandaka accompanied by two Rākshasas assuming the the shape of deer. I had a flaming tongue, huge teeth, pointed horns and lived on the flesh of ascetics. Assuming such a terrible appearance I began to traverse with great vehemence the *Tirtha*, *Agnihotri* and the place of worship; eating the flesh and drinking the blood of the ascetics after killing them I began to hinder all religious services. I had a most ugly figure and was maddened with drinking blood, and all the animals of the forest were exceedingly frightened at me. While I was thus traversing the forest of Dandaka throwing obstacles in the way of religious services I saw the pious ascetic Rāma living on restricted fare, the honored Sitā and the mighty Lakshmana, taking recourse to asceticism, moderate in eating and ever engaged in the welfare of created beings. Remembering his former enmity and aggrandisement, I, being extremely wrathful, in my deer shape and with my pointed horns, darted towards him with a view to kill him, thinking through my ignorance the effulgent Rāma as none other than an ascetic living in the forest. Then stringing his huge bow he darted three sharpened arrows at me. Those three terrible arrows with bent knots resembling thunder-bolts, killing enemies and drinking blood and having the motion of Garura and air, coalescing with each other came before us. Wicked as I am, I was fully aware of his prowess, having been frightened by him on a former occasion, and so I saved myself by escaping, but those two Rākshasas were killed. O Rāvana, any how saved from the arrows of Rāma and having got my life back I have adopted the life of an ascetic and have been carrying on asceticism here being absorbed in *Yoga*.

From that very day I see Rāma wearing bark and deer-skin even in the very trees before me like unto Death with the noose in his hands. Terrified as I am I always see thousands of Rāma around me. Meseems the entire forest is inhabited by Rāma only. O king of Rākshasas, I see Rāma even in the quarter where there is no Rāma. Seeing him in my dreams even I look around like one awaken. O Rāvana what more shall I speak unto thee, I am so much afraid of Rāma that such words as *Ratna* (jewel), *Ratha* (chariot) which begin with the letter *Ra* impart consternation unto me. I am fully apprised of the prowess of that descendant of Raghu; it doth not behove thee to enter into conflict with him; he can destroy Vali and Namuchi. O Rāvana, whether thou dost fight with Rāma or not, do not mention him unto me if thou dost wish to see me. Many persons pious and devoted to asceticism on this earth have met with destruction for another's misdeeds. And I shall meet with similar fate for thy sins. O ranger of the night do whatever thou likest, I shall not follow thee. Truely is that highly intelligent and effulgent Rāma of mighty prowess like Death himself unto the rangers of night. Though the wicked Khara of Janasthāna hath been slain by him on Surpanakhā's account, yet how is he to blame for it? Do thou truly speak. Thou art my friend; it is for this and for thy welfare that I speak this truth unto thee. If thou dost not follow my words, thyself with all thy kinsmen, shall be slain in battle by Rāma.

## SECTION XL.

As a person desirous of meeting with his end doth not take medicine, Rāvana, the king of night-rangers paid no heed to the appropriate and sound words of Māricha skilled in speech, foreboding good unto him. Moreover he addressed him with the following harsh words. "O Māricha, what thou hast spoken unto me, shall bear no fruit like unto seeds sown into a desert-land. I shall not be frightened thereby to fight with that foolish Rāma—a human being of vicious deeds. Surely shall I before thee take away from that Rāma the destroyer of Khara, his favourite wife, at whose words he has sojourned into woods renouncing his father mother, kingdom and friends. I have made this firm resolution in my mind O Māricha; even Indra, with the celestials and Ashuras shall not be able to shake it. It would have been proper for thee to give vent to these expressions had I but asked thee for advice to ascertain my duty, the propriety or impropriety of my action, its way or losses. A wise counsellor who wishes prosperity unto himself should always communicate unto his master his desire with joined-hands whenever asked to do so. It is always proper to speak before monarchs such pleasant and favourable words as are intended for the welfare of the master and are sanctioned by the royal etiquette. A respectable king doth not receive with good grace friendly words even when they are expressed disrespectfully. Sovereigns of superb prowess assume the semblance of five deities—Agni, Indra, Moon, Yama, and Varuna. Powerful kings, O Ranger of the night, assume haughtiness, power, a placid look and contentment and administer punishment unto the wicked. They are to be adored and honored therefore on all occasions. Thou art ignorant of kingly morality and fully absorbed in illusion. It is for this that thou dost out of thy wickedness of heart address me thy guest with these harsh words. I do not ask thee, O Rākshasa, about the propriety (of my conduct) or about my welfare. I did only ask thee for thy help. Listen what thou shalt have to do at my request in my aid; assuming the shape of a deer having golden skin painted with silvery drops do thou proceed to the asylum of Rāma, and ranging at large before Vaidehi do thou after captivating her take thy wished-for way. Vaidehi, being struck with wonder seeing thee a golden deer capable of illusions, shall request Rāma to get thee soon for her. Kākuthstha issuing out of the asylum, thou shalt, at a great distance utter such cries as "O Sitā, O Lākshmana" imitating his (Rāma's) voice. Hearing those cries Lākshmana also, at the behest of Sitā, shall proceed to Rāma. When both Rāma and Lākshmana shall go elsewhere in this way, I shall to my felicity carry away Vaidehi like unto the thousand-eyed deity earrying away Sachi. O Rākshasa, do thou go wherever thou likest after doing this. I shall confer on thee, O Māricha, half of my kingdom. O thou of auspicious look, do thou proceed towards the forest of Dandaka to compass this end of mine; I shall follow thee in my chariot. Acquiring Sitā without any conflict, after imposing upon Rāma I shall return to Lankā successful along with thee. I shall kill thee, O Māricha, if thou dost not obey my behest. I shall compell thee to do this. No body can attain to prosperity and happiness, actiug against his sovereign's will. Truly thou shalt risk thy life if thou approachest Rāma, but thou shalt meet with sure destruction if thou dost act against my will. Consider about it, and do what thou thinkest proper.

## SECTION XLI.

Being thus commanded by Rāvana like a king to act against his will Māricha fearlessly addressed the lord of the Rākshasas with the following bold words, "What person of impious deeds hath advised thee O ranger of the night thus inorder to exterminate thee with thy kingdom, counsellors and children? Who of a vicious heart, O King, doth not feel himself happy at thy welfare? Who hath pointed out unto thee the way of thy death under the cover of thy means? O Ranger of night surely do thy weak enemies wish to bring about thy destruction by making thee enter into a conflict with a powerful man. What little-minded man of eveil intent hath counselled thee thus? O Ranger of night, really do they desire that thou dost bring destruction upon thyself by thy own actions. Thou dost not exterminate thy counsellors O Rāvana, albeit they are worthy of being destroyed. For they do not prevent thee entirely from thy evil course. Wise counsellors do always restrain a king who wends a vicious track being guided by his impulses and passions; but about thee they are quite unmindful, though thou shouldst by every means be brought under restraint. O thou the best of conquerors, O thou the ranger of night, ministers by the grace of their sovereign attain virtue, wealth, desire and fame. But those objects are never attained O Rāvana when they are not in good odour with their sovereign; moreover the subjects meet with dangers when he is devoid of all qualities. O thou the best of conquerors, the king is the root of virtue and fame unto the subjects; he should therefore be always protected by them. O Ranger of night, proud kings of cruel temperament, acting against the subjects can never administer their kingdoms. So do the ministers of cruel counsel meet with their end like unto a chariot driven into a wild track by an unskilled charioteer. Many a pious person, on this earth, ever engaged in the performance of religious services, have, for the folly of other persons, met with destruction along with their relatives. Verily the subjects, O Rāvana, can never expect to prosper under the regime of hot-natured sovereigns acting against their subjects like unto deer under the protection of a jackal. All the Rākshasas shall surely die, O Rāvana whose lord art thou, foolish, cruel and under the control of thy passions. I shall not be the least sorry if I do meet with a sudden accident—what I do deplore most is that thou shalt meet in no time with destruction along with thy soldiery. Compassing my end Rāma shall exterminate thee in no time—and blessed I shall be being killed by an enemy in the conflict. Surely thou dost know that no sooner shall I see Rāma I shall be done away with; thou shalt carrying away Sitā meet with thy end along with thy kinsmen. And if thou dost bring Sitā with me from the asylum, none shall be saved,—me, thyself, the city of Lankā and the Rākshasas. Thou dost not relish my words O ranger of the night though prevented by me, who wishes thee welfare; those men who range on the verge of death, well-nigh finishing the term of their existence do not receive with good grace the counsels of friends.

## SECTION XLII.

SPEAKING these harsh words unto Rāvana, Māricha being afraid of him said, "We shall both go. Surely shall I be deprived of my life by him (Rāma) taking up his scimitar and having a bow and arrows in his hands, if I go before him again. Meeting with his prowess thou shalt never return with thy life; he is like the noose of Death unto thee though thou hadst baffled its power. Thou art vicious-souled, what can I do for thee? Be thou crowned with success O ranger of the night, I shall go." The Lord of Rākshasas being pleased with Māricha's words embraced him warmly and said, "This is worthy of thy heroism that thou hast addressed thyself to act after my desire. Thou wert another Rākshasa before and hast now become true Māricha. Do thou now with me ascend this chariot coursing in the air, crested with jewels and driven by asses having faces of a demon. Enchanting Vaidehi thou shalt wend thy way and away shall I carry the daughter of the king of Mithilā by force (when there shall be neither Rāma nor Lakshmana by her.)" Thereupon Tārakā's son assented to Rāvana's words, and both of them ascending the chariot like unto a heavenly car set out for the hermitage. And beholding diverse towns, forests, mountains, rivers, kingdoms and cities they reached the forest of Dandaka and the asylum of Rāma. And descending now from the golden car the lord of Rākshasas together with Māricha beheld Rāma's asylum. Taking him (Māricha) by the hand Rāvana spake saying, "There stands the asylum of Rāma surrounded by palm trees. Do thou do that for which we have come here." Hearing the words of Rāvana, the Rākshasa Māricha assuming the wonderful shape of a (golden) deer began to range at large before Rāma's hermitage. The points of its horns were like unto (two) excellent jewels, its countenance was diversified with white and black colour, its face was like a red lotus, its ears were like unto two blue lotuses, its neck was little raised, its belly was like a saphire, its sides were like unto Madhuka flowers, its colour was like that of a filament of a lotus, its hoops were like unto *Baidurjas* (a gem of a dark colour); of lean thighs; of firm joints; its tail having the diversified colour of a rainbow was upraised. It was of a pleasant and cool hue and crested with various jewels.

And in no time the Rākshasa assumed the shape of a beautiful deer. To tempt Vaidehi that ranger of the night, assuming a beautiful countenance painted with diverse metals, illumining the beautiful forest and Rāma's asylum with its beauty, and ranging at large on the green field and living on grass, began to proceed. That one of lively presence having its body painted with hundreds of silver drops and living on twigs of trees began to range in the forest. Sometimes walking into the plantain house, sometimes walking around the forest of *Karnikā*, sometimes coming within the compass of Sitā's vision, that best of deer having its back painted with gold began to range slowly around the hermitage. It began to walk at pleasure near Rāma's asylum. Sometimes going, sometimes stopping, at one time running very swiftly and receding the next moment, that best of deer began to range at large. Some times playing around, sometimes lying on earth and sometimes following the deer-herd having come within the threshhold of the asylum and then followed again by them that Rākshasa assuming the form of a deer came back to see Sitā. He then began to range at large in the beautiful forest (extending far and wide). Seeing him other forest-deer came (by him) and smelling him fled away into different quarters. That Rākshasa, though expert in killing deer, did not eat them up, though touching, inorder to hide his real self. In the meantime Vaidehi, of auspicious looks whose eyes inebriate like wine, being engaged in plucking flowers, was going sometimes to the *Karnikā* grove and sometimes to the mangoe grove. That best of women, ever inured to living in the forest and possessed of a graceful countenance, walking and plucking flowers, saw that jewelled deer, having its body deversified with pearls and diamonds. It had beautiful teeth and lips and had its down resembling silver. She began to behold with affection and with her eyes expanded with surprise. That illusive deer seeing Rāma's wife began to move around as if lighting up that forest (with the fire of its beauty). Beholding that deer ornamented with diverse jewels, and the like of which she had never seen before, the daughter of Janaka was struck with immense wonder.

---

## SECTION XLIII.

BEHOLDING that deer with its sides painted with gold and silver, while collecting flowers, Sitā, having blameless limbs and beautiful hips and having the color of her body like that of pure gold became immensely pleased and called aloud her husband and Lakshmana with scimitars in their hands. "Do thou come soon, do thou come soon, O son of the worshipful Sire, along with thy younger brother"—having called (her husband) again and again in this strain she continued beholding that deer. Being thus called by the daughter of the king of Videha those two best of men Rāma and Lakshmana, casting their looks around beheld that deer. Seeing him Lakshmana, struck with fear, said "Methinks, this deer is the Rākshasa Mārich. This vicious Māricha, O Rāma, assuming the shape of a deer oftentimes kills at pleasure the kings who come here a-hunting. He is cognizant of illusions, by virtue of which he has assumed this shape, O best of men; its countenance is perfectly fine like the abode of Gandharbas and resplendent like the Sun; there is no such jewelled deer on earth. O Rāghava, O Lord of earth, there is no doubt that this is nothing but illusion." When Lakshmana spake thus Sitā with a pure smile being under the influence of enchantment contradicted him, and being pleased said "O son of the worshipful Sire, this deer hath attracted my mind, get it for me, pray, O thou of mighty arms; it shall be an object of sport for us. Many a beautiful deer range at large in the vicinity of our hermitage such as *Chamara*, *Srimara*, *Rik*, *Prishata*, *Bānara*, and *Kinnara*. They are all very beautiful and of mighty strength; but O

Prince, I have never seen before the like of this deer. In energy, strength and beauty it stands above all deer. Its entire body is diversified with various colors, nay, it is a jewel itself. It moves before me, beautifying the forest with its resplendance, like unto Moon himself. Ah ! what beauty, what beautiful a lustre, how musical a voice, this wonderful deer of variegated countenance, hath indeed captivated my heart ! If canst thou get by this deer alive, O what wonder, what surprise ! When shall we regain our kingdom after the expiry of the term of our banishment, this deer shall beautify the interior of our palace. O Lord, truly shall this celestial deer create surprise in Bharata, yourself, me and my mothers-in-law. O best of men, if canst thou not get hold of it alive its skin shall also look very beautiful (to us). Spreading on Kuça the skin of this golden deer when killed do I wish to invoke the Almighty. It looks (no doubt) unseemly and terrible and smacks of wilfulness on the part of a wife to command her husband in this way, but I am sunk in surprise seeing the countenance of the deer." Rāma's heart was struck with surprise beholding that wonderful deer having its down resembling gold, horns resembling exquisitely fine diamonds, color like that of the newly risen Sun, and resplendance like that of the orbit of the planets. Being enchanted by its beauty and spurred on by Sitā's words, Rāghava pleased, spake unto his younger brother saying "Behold, O Lakshmana, it has immensely excited Vaidehi's desire. On account of its exquisite beauty it shall lose its life to-day. It has its equal no where on the earth—neither in the celestial garden nor in the Chaittraratha forest. The hairs of its body being arranged in regular and contrary courses and being painted with golden drops do indeed look very beautiful. Do thou see, while expanding its mouth, its tongue comes out resembling flaming fire like unto a thunder-bolt reaving the mass of clouds. Its face is like a glass made of the best blue saphire, its belly resembling a conch and pearl, and it is very difficult to ascertain its shapes. Beholding it who is there (on earth) whose heart is not enamoured? Its beauty resembles the rays of gold and is variegated with diverse hues of jewels. Whose heart is not enveloped with surprise beholding such a celestial beauty, O Lakshmana? Princes, with bows in their hands, while a-hunting in a deep forest destroy deer either for flesh or for sport. Moreover while engaged in sporting they collect many a jewel and various metals as gold and silver, in the woods. There is not the least doubt that these wild riches filling up their coffers are comparatively far better (than the wealth acquired by other sources) like unto the objects of enjoyment, enjoyed at their fancy by the people inhabiting the celestial region. The object which persons desirous of acquiring wealth follow without any discretion in their actions, is the true definition of wealth given by the political economists. Vaidehi of slender waist desireth to sit with me on the exquisitely fine golden skin of this gem of a deer, meseems no deer skin is so comfortable to touch as this—neither the skin of *Kâdali*, *Priaki*, *Prabeni* nor of *Abiki*. Truly handsome is this deer and the one that rangeth in the welkin, indeed these two deer only are celestial—the one that rangeth in the sky* (Mrigashirā) and this that rangeth on earth. And if it be a Rakshasa's illusion as thou sayest, O Lakshmana, then it must be killed by me. This cruel vicious-souled Māricha made away with many eminent ascetics, while travelling in the forest; and this Rākshasa assuming the shape of an illusive deer destroyed many kings—mighty archers while a-hunting in this forest; it is for this that this deer must be killed. Formerly this *Bâtâpi*† entering into the womb of twice-born ones used to come out reaving them like unto

* This refers to *Mrigashirâ*, the fifth lunar constellation which resembles a deer.—T.

† The name of an *Asur* devoured by Agastya.—T.

the embryo of a mule. Once on a time this Bātāpi approached the eminent saint Agastya and was devoured by him. After the *Srâdha* ceremony had been over, finding that Bātāpi desirous of assuming the shape of a Rākshasa the great saint Agastya said smiling "Being blinded with thy prowess O Bātāpi, thou hast destroyed many eminent twice-born ones on this earth and for this that I do digest thee. Truly that Rākshasa, O Lakshmana, who wisheth to surpass one like me who hath controlled his senses and is ever engaged in pious offices shall meet with his end like unto this Bātāpi. Therefore this Māricha approaching me shall be killed by me like nnto Bātāpi devoured by Agastya. Do thou therefore vigilantly protect Vaidehi with mail and armours on. It is our prime duty, O descendant of Raghu, to protect Jānaki. I shall either kill this deer or shall get hold of it. Look, O Lakshmana, Vaidehi is extremely anxious to get the skin of this deer, I shall therefore proceed at once, O son of Sumitrā, to catch this deer. The skin of this deer is the best of its kind ; for certain shall it lose its life to-day. As long as I do not kill this deer, O Lakshmana, do thou with Sitā remain with vigilance in this asylum. I shall in no time come back with its skin after killing it with one arrow. Do thou stay here, O Lakshmana, with Jānaki in constant fear and vigilance, along with the mighty Yatayu, intelligent and ever engaged in pious offices.

## SECTION XLIV.

HAVING thus directed his brother, the highly energetic son of Raghu equipped himself with his gold-hilted scimitar. And girting himself with his bow bent at three places, which served him as an ornament,—as well as a couple of quivers, that one of fierce energy sallied out. Seeing that foremost of monarchs approach, that best of beasts from fear disappeared ; and then again showed himself. Thereat girt with the bow and sword, (Rāma) rushed where the deer was ; and beheld him illumining all before him with his beauty,—and bow in hand (Rāma beheld) him in that vast forest, darting away after gazing at him,—and sometimes seeming to have got beyond arrow range, and at others tempting Rāma (by his vicinity). And sometimes influenced by fear and bewildered, (the deer) seemed to course the welkin ; and in the forest now he became visible and now vanished from sight. And like the autumnal lunar disc enveloped by indented clouds, he momentarily showed himself, and anon discovered himself at a distance. And Māricha wearing the shape of a deer, showing himself and disappearing from sight, drew Rāghava a long way from the hermitage. Thereat Rāma, eagerly anxious to secure the deer, being foiled by the deer, and in consequence growing enraged, wearied out, rested under a shadow, on a sward. And that ranger of the night, wearing the form of a deer, maddening Rāma, discovered himself (again) at a distance surrounded by (other) deer. And Rāma desirous of taking (the beast), seeing him again, set off at speed. At the very moment the deer disappeared from fear ; and again showed himself at a distance behind a tree. And seeing him, the exceedingly energetic and strong Rāghava, determined to slay him, growing wroth, taking out a flaming shaft, resembling the rays of the sun, powerfully drew his bow, and firmly setting the shaft, and aiming it at the deer, let go the blazing and burning weapon forged by Brahmā, resembling a flaming serpent. And that best of arrows, like unto a thunder-bolt, deeply pierced the breast of Māricha, wearing the shape of a deer. Thereat bounding up high as a palmyra palm, that one whose saws had almost run out, uttered terrible sounds, lying on the earth. And while on the point of death, Māricha renounced his counterfeit shape. And remembering the words of Rāvana, the Rākshasa reflected, "By what means can Sitā send away Lakshmana, and Rāvana carry off Sitā staying in solitude?" And pierced to the marrow by that peerless shaft, Māricha, renouncing his deer form, resumed his Rākshasas lineaments; and giving up his life attaining a huge person, considering the time had come (for availing himself of the advice tendered by Rāvana), began to cry with the voice of Rāghava, "Ah Sitā! Ah Lakshmana!" And seeing that grim-visaged Rākshasa lying low on the ground, with his person bathed in blood, and rolling hither and thither, Rāma proceeded towards the asylum, thinking of Sitā and revolving within himself Lakshmana's words. While returning he thought aside "Lakshmana said before that this was Māricha's illusion!" His words have been verified now. Truly have I killed Māricha. Māricha has given up his ghost exclaiming aloud Ah! Sitā, Ah! Lakshmana. I do not know what shall Sitā do hearing the cry? And what shall the mighty-armed Lakshmana do?" While pondering thus the hairs of the virtuous souled Rāma stood on their end. Killing that Rākshasa assuming the shape of a deer and hearing his terrible cry Rāma was overwhelmed with fear arising out of sorrow. Thereupon killing a deer and taking its flesh he hastened towards Janasthāna.

## SECTION XLV.

HEARING that cry in the forest resembling her husband's voice Sitā spake unto Lakshmana saying, "Do thou go and learn what has befallen Rāghava. He is crying aloud in pitiable accents; hearing them my life and soul are incapable of remaining any longer in their proper places. It behoveth thee to save tho brother why is crying aloud in the forest; do thou immediately repair hence to save him, who is in need of thy help. He hath been over-powered by the Rākshasas like unto a bullock brought under the power of a lion." Remembering the behest of Rāma, Lakshmana did not go, though accosted thus by Sitā. Extremely mortified, the daughter of Janaka spake unto him saying, "O Son of Sumitrā, thou art an enemy unto Rāma, in the garb of a brother. Thou dost not proceed for the relief of thy brother who hath been reduced to such a plight. Dost thou desire, for me, O Lakshmana, Rāma's destruction? Truely being under the influence of lust for me thou dost not follow Rāghava! For this thou dost welcome Rāma's disaster; thou hast no affection for him. For this it is that thou dost sit here without anxiety not seeing the highly effulgent (Rāma). Rāma, following whom thou hast repaired unto this forest, being in danger, of what avail is life unto me?" Vaidehi speaking thus being influenced by sorrow, and with tears in her eyes, like unto a deer, Lakshmana spake unto her saying, "O Vaidehi, celestials, Dānavas, Gandharbas, Rākshasas, Asuras, or Pannagas, there is none who can defeat thy husband. There is not the least doubt in this. Worshipful madam! Celestials, Dānavas, Gandharbas, Rākshasas, Piçāchas, men, Kinnaras, animals or birds, there is none among them, who can withstand Rāghava, who equals the lord of celestials in warfare. In fact there is none who can do away with Rāma in battle. It doth not behove thee therefore to accost me thus. Nor do I dare leave thee here alone in this forest without Rāma. Even the mighty heroes, as the Lord of celestials, cannot subdue his prowess with all their strength. Even the Almighty Himself, with the celestials and the three worlds, cannot defeat him. Do thou therefore renounce grief and console thyself. Sooner shall thy husband return killing the best of deer. It is not his voice nor one sent by any deity. It is but an illusion of that

Rākshasa (Māricha). O Vaidehi, thou hast been left unto my charge by the high-souled (Rāma)—I therefore do not dare leave thee behind, O thou the jewel of a damsel. We have made these night-rangers our enemies. For compassing the destruction of Khara, O worshipful one, and devastating Janasthāna, Rākshasas oftentimes use improper words unto us in this extensive forest. O Vaidehi, to create mischief unto the pious is the only amusement of these Rākshasas—thou shouldst not therefore be anxious for this." Being thus addressed by him her eyes were reddened with ire, and she spake these harsh words unto the truthful Lakshmana saying "O cruel one! O thou the destroyer of thy line! it is a disgrace unto thee that thou wishest to protect me (killing Rāma). Methinks, this mighty disaster of Rāma is welcome unto thee, or else why shouldst thou seeing this, speak thus, O Lakshmana. It is not a wonder that an evil desire lurks in thee who art a hypocrite and a cruel-hearted enemy. Verily art thou a monster of wickedness, that Rāma repairing unto woods, thou hast, being lustful for me, followed him alone. Or hast thou been engaged by Bharata to act thus? But thy or Bharata's intention shall not be satisfied, O Saumitri. How shall I desire another man after serving the lotus-eyed Rāma of dark-blue hue as my husband? I shall renounce my life before thee, therefore, O Lakshmana; without Rāma I shall not maintain my being for a moment on this earth." Hearing these brazen words of Sitā, capable of making one's down stand on end, the self-controlled Lakshmana with joined hands spake unto her saying, "Thou art a very Goddess unto me, I therefore dare not answer thee. What thou hast spoken, O Maithili, is nothing surprising for females. Such is the nature of womankind on this earth. Women by nature are crooked, fickle, devoid of religious knowledge, and bring about difference between father and sons. O Vaidehi, O daughter of Janaka, truly am I incapable of putting up with these words of thine. They have pierced through both of my ears like a heated *Nârâcha*. However the deities ranging in this woodland are my witnesses—may they hear thee. I spoke what was fair and have been thus addressed by thee with these harsh words. I do always obey my superior's commands. Fie on thee! Thy destruction is near at hand that thou dost suspect me, being influenced by this womanish nature. I shall go where Kākuthstha is, may good betide thee, O thou the best of damsels! May the deities of the forest protect thee, O thou of expansive eyes! Many a bad omen appear before me. May I see thee again when I shall come back with Rāma." Being thus accosted by Lakshmana the daughter of Jānaka replied weeping and being bathed in tears. "Without Rāma, O Lakshmana, I shall drink virulent poison, enter fire or dive into the Godāveri. I shall destory this body either by hanging or by falling down from the top of a high object. I shall never be able to touch another man but Rāma." Speaking thus unto Lakshmana, Sita, being enveloped with grief, weeping, struck her belly* with her hands. Seeing the daughter of Janaka of expansive eyes weep thus in pitiable accents, Lakshmana losing his attention began to console her. Afterwards the pure-hearted Lakshmana, having control over his senses, saluting Sitā with clasped palms and bending low a little proceeded where Rāma was, casting again and again his glance upon her as he went.

* Properly it should be "struck her breast." But it has a special significance here, i. e.—she would not be satisfied until her belly be filled with all the Râkshasas.—T.

## SECTION XLVI.

HAVING been addressed with those harsh words the younger brother of Rāghava, enraged, proceeded at once, being anxious to see Rāma. Thereupon the ten-necked one, availing of this opportunity came before Vaidehi assuming the semblance of a mendicant. Wearing a soft silken cloth, with a lock of hair on his head with an umbrella and shoes and having on his left shoulder a rod and *Kamandalu*, the highly powerful one assuming the appearance of a wandering devotee carrying three long bamboo staves appeared before Vaidehi in the forest when there was none of the brothers by her. He saw there the young and pious daughter of the king like unto an evening void of both sun and moon and as the highly terrible Rāhu eyes Rohini forsaken by Moon. Seeing that terrible one the doer of evil deeds, the trees of Janasthāna did not move nor the wind did blow. Seeing him eye Sitā with his blood-red eyes, the fast streaming river Godāvari even slackened its course out of fear. In the mean time the Ten-necked Rāvana, enquiring about Rāma's weak points appeared before Vaidehi in the guise of a mendicant. Like unto *Sani* approaching *chitra*, that impious one, assuming the appearance of a pious man like a well covered with grass, approached Vaidehi who was bewailing her husband. And seeing that pious spouse of Rāma—Vaidehi, Rāvana stood before her. Her lips and teeth were extremely fine, her face resembled the full moon and her eyes were like lotus-petals. She had a yellow silken cloth on and sat in the thatched cottage, overwhelmed with grief and bathed in tears. And that ranger of the night with a pleased heart approached Vaidehi. Seeing her that Lord of Rākshasas was pierced with the shafts of passion. And speaking highly of her, surpassing in beauty the three worlds and resembling by the excellence of her own person the very goddess of wealth herself Rāvana uttering the name of God spake unto her saying, "O thou having the color of gold and silver, O thou wearing silken cloth, O thou appearing like a lotus wearing a garland of lotus-petals, O thou of beautiful countenance! Art thou Bashfulness, Beauty, Fame, Wealth, Apsara, Dignity or Rati herself who is ranging at will in this forest? All thy teeth are equal having their tops like unto the buds of *Kunda* flower, beautiful and yellow. Thy eyes are expansive, clear, of bloody hue, and having black pupils. Thy hip is fleshy and spacious. Thy thighs are like those of elephants, round, fleshy and perfectly strong. Thy nipples are bulky, pointed, highly captivating like cold palm fruits, beautiful and ornamented with diverse jewels. O thou of beautiful smile! O thou of beautiful teeth! O thou of beautiful eyes! O fine damsel, thou dost carry away my heart like unto a river carrying away its banks by its stream. The lock of thy hair is exquisitely fine, thy breast very close and thy waist is so thin that they may be got round even by fingers. There is none so beautiful like thee—a Goddess, a Gandharbhi, a Yakshi or a Kinnari. I had never seen before on this earth a damsel so beautiful as thou. This thy beauty the best on earth, thy youth, thy grace and thy abode in the forest do agitate my mind. So it is well for thee to come (with me); it doth not behove thee to remain here. This is the abode of terrible Rākshasas wearing shapes at will. Picturesque palaces, prosperous cities and sweet-smelling gardens are worthy of thy abode. O thou of dark-blue eyes, fine is thy garland, fine is the smell of thy person and fine is thy apparel—methinks fine is thy husband too. O thou of pure smile! whom dost thou belong to?—Rudras, Marutas, or Vasus—Meseems, O fine damsel thou art a very goddess. No one comes here—the Gandharbas, the celestials or Kinnaras; this is an abode of the Rākshasa; how dost thou come here? Art thou not afraid of these monkeys, lions, tigers, wolves, bears, herons and hyenas? Alone in this forest, art thou not afraid of these terrible elephants of fierce motion and maddened with the exuding of their temporal juice? Who art thou? Whose wife? What for dost thou range alone in this forest of Dandaka frequented by terrible Rākshasas?" Thus addressed was Vaidehi by the vicious-souled Rāvana. Seeing him come under the guise of a twice-born one, Maithili worshipped him with diverse articles necessary for serving a guest. Offering him a seat first and afterwards inviting him to wash his feet she said unto that one of placid look "cooked rice is ready." Seeing Rāvana approach with *Kamandalu* and wearing a red cloth under the guise of a Brāhmana, Maithili could not pass by him any way, and considering him a twice-born one by various signs invited him as if a Brāhmana saying, "O Brāhmana, do thou sit on this seat facing the right; do thou take this water (to wash thy feet); do thou enjoy these well-cooked eatables growing in the forest and intended for thee." Jānaki the wife of Lord of men inviting him thus, Rāvana, casting a look upon her, addressed himself for his own destruction, to carry her away. She was anxiously expecting the return of Rāma who had gone a-hunting with Lakshmana; she looked around and beheld but on all sides the spacious yellow forest-land—there was neither Rāma nor Lakshmana.

## SECTION XLVII.

Being thus addressed by Rāvana under the guise of a mendicant, desirous of carrying her away, Vaidehi thought within herself—"This person is my guest and a Brāhmana ; he may curse me if I do not speak to him." Thinking this for a moment Sitā said "May good betide thee ! I am the daughter of the high-souled Janaka, the king of Mithilā, the beloved Queen of Rāma and my name is Sitā. Dwelling in the palace of Ikshakus for twelve years, I enjoyed many things passing human and had all my desires satisfied. On the thirteenth year king (Daçaratha) counselled with his ministers about the installation of Rāma. Accordingly everything necessary for the installation being made ready, Kaikeyi, one of my mothers-in-law, begged of her husband a boon. Bringing my father-in-law under control by means of her virtuous deeds, Kāikeyi begged, of that truthful, best of monarchs, two boons namely the exile of my husband into woods and the installation of Bharata, and said "I shall never eat, drink or sleep and (if Rāma be installed) I shall end my life." Kaikeyi speaking thus, that lord of earth, my father-in-law begged her to accept diverse riches ; but Kaikeyi did not agree. Then the highly effulgent Rāma, my husband was twenty-five years old, and myself was eighteen only counting from my birth. My husband is known all over the world under the name of Rāma. He is truthful, good-natured, of pure character, ever engaged in the welfare of all created beings, of mighty-arms and expansive eyes. Our father the king Daçaratha was entirely under the control of passions, and hence for the satisfaction of Kaikeyi did not install Rāma. When Rāma came to his father for being installed Kaikeyi spoke unto my husband the following cruel words, "Do thou hear, O Rāghava, how I have been ordered by thy Sire. This kingdom, rid of thorns is to be conferred on Bharata, and thou shalt have to sojourn into the woods for years nine and five. Do thou therefore repair unto forest, O Kākuthstha and save thy Sire from untruth." Whereto Rāma fearlessly replied 'So be it !' Hearing her words my husband of firm vows acted accordingly. He always maketh gifts and taketh none. He always speaketh truth and never telleth an untruth. This is his best observance, O Brāhmana.. His half-brother named Lakshmana is of mighty prowess. That best of men is Rāma's help and the destroyer of foes in battle. That brother of his named Lakshmana is of firm resolution and given to asceticism. With a bow in hand he hath followed (Rāma) flying as an exile unto the woods along with me. Thus that one (Rāma) of firm resolution and ever engaged in pious offices wearing matted hairs and assuming the semblance of an ascetic hath entered this forest of Dandaka along with myself and his younger brother. O thou the best of twice-born ones, we three being deprived of our kingdom by Kaikeyi have been living in this dense forest by virtue of our effulgence. Do thou take heart for a moment and live here. Instantly shall my husband return with good many wild fruits and roots and with sufficient meat after killing many a deer, hog and *Gosamp*. Truly do thou relate unto me thy name, *Gotra* and leneage. O thou twice-born one, why dost thou range alone in this forest of Dandaka ?" Sitā the wife of Rāma speaking thus, the mighty Lord of Rākshasas—Rāvana replied with these harsh words—"O Sitā I am that Rāvana, the lord of Rākshasas, whom fear the celestials, Asuras and human beings. O thou of blameless beauty, seeing thee of golden hue and wearing silk cloth I do not relish my own wives. I have brought many a beautiful damsel from various quarters, do thou become my foremost Queen amongst them. That great city in the midst of the ocean, Lankā, encircled on all sides by the sea and situated on the summit of a hill, is my capital. There shalt thou with me, O Sitā, walk in gardens, and thus thou shalt no more long for living in the forest. If thou dost become my wife, O Sitā, five thousand maid-servants decorated with divers ornaments shall serve thee." That blameless daughter of Janaka, being thus addressed by Rāvana, was highly enraged, and, passing by him, replied, "I am a dependant of Rāma, who is incapable of being shaken, like unto a mighty mountain, incapable of being agitated, like unto a vast ocean, and resembling Mahendra in effulgence. I am a dependant of that great and truthful Rāma who is gifted with auspicious marks and like unto a fig tree. I am dependant of that lion among men, Rāma, of mighty-arms, of a spacious breast and treading like a lion. I am a dependant of that son of a king, Rāma, of mighty-arms,having control over his passions, whose face resembles the full moon and whose fame hath spread far and wide over the earth. Why dost thou being a tiger wish for a she-lion ? Thou shalt not be able to touch me like unto the rays of the sun. O thou wretched Rākshasa, when thou hast desired to steal away Rāghava's beloved spouse, surely dost thou see these trees (before thee) as made of gold. Dost thou wish to uproot the teeth from the mouth of a lion, that enemy of deer, or from that of a serpent ? Dost thou wish to clasp with thy hands the Mandara hill, or dost thou wish to walk in peace after drinking poison ? Dost thou wish to rub thy eyes with pins and lick a razor with thy tongue ? Thou dost wish to swim ascross an ocean, having a rock tied unto thy neck. Thou dost wish to get at the Sun and Moon, to bind a flaming fire with a piece of cloth and walk through iron-spikes, as thou hast wished to come by the worthy spouse of Rāma. Mighty is the difference between Rāma and thee, like unto that between a lion and a jackal, a sea and a rivulet, nectar and gruel, gold and iron, sandal and mud, an elephant and a cat, a crow and Garura, a peacock and a *madgie* (an acquatic bird), or a duck and a vulture. Even if thou dost steal me, that mighty archer Rāma, gifted with the prowess of the lord of celestials, living, surely shall I die, like unto a gnat sucking clarified butter." Addressing those words unto that wicked ranger of the night, that innocent (Sitā) shook like a plantain tree shaken by the wind. Thereupon Rāvana, like unto Death in prowess, trembling, began to relate unto her with a view to frighten (her) his race, power, name and actions.

---

## SECTION XLVIII.

After Sitā had spoken these harsh words, Rāvana, enraged, with a frown, replied, "O thou of a beautiful countenance, I am the step-brother of the Lord of wealth and my name is the mighty Ten-necked Rāvana. May good betide thee! Like unto people fearing Death, the celestials, Gandharbas, Pisāchas, Pannagas and Serpents fly in diverse directions being frightened by me. I have subdued by my prowess, my step-brother, the Lord of wealth in a conflict, quarrelling with him for some reason. Thereat, that one carried by men, renouncing out of my fear this wealthy abode of Lankā, hath been living on that Lord of mountains, Kailāça. O thou auspicious one, by virtue of my prowess I have taken away that beautiful chariot of his called Puspaka. Ascending that chariot thou shalt travel by the etherial route. O Maithili, when I am excited with ire, Indra and other celestials at the mere sight of my countenance fly away in divers directions out of fear. Wherever I live, the Wind bloweth cautiously and the Sun (of piercing rays) out of fear for me appeareth in the welkin like the Moon. What shall I say more? Wherever I live, even the leaves of the trees do not flutter and the currents of the rivers are stopped. Beyond the ocean stands my beautiful capital

Lankā like unto Indra's Amarāvati, (the capital of the Lord of celestials),guarded on all sides by the terrible night-rangers and encircled by yellow walls. That beautiful city hath gate-ways of ornamented and jewelled arches and golden apartments. It is filled with elephants, horses and chariots, always resounds with the sounds of bugles, and is beautified with gardens having divers trees of wished for fruits. O Sitā, O thou the daughter of a king, in this city shalt thou dwell with me. O large-minded damsel, thou shalt never think of earthly women. O thou of an exquisite countenance, enjoying these many things passing human, thou shalt not any more think of Rāma—a human being of brief existence. Placing his beloved son on the throne, king Daçaratha hath sent away his eldest son of weak prowess into the woods. O thou of expansive eyes, what shalt thou do with that wretched ascetic Rāma who hath been deprived of his kingdom ? I am the lord of the whole world of Rākshasas ; being pierced by the shafts of Kāma have I come by thee. It doth not behove thee therefore to pass by me. O timid damsel, truly shalt thou repent afterwards if thou dost disregard me, like unto Urvashee kicking Puraravā. Rāma is a human being and is not even equal to a finger of mine in battle. By thy good luck have I come unto thee—do thou give thyself up unto me, O thou of a beautiful countenance." Being thus addressed by him, Vaidehi exceedingly wroth and with blood-red eyes spoke unto that Lord of Rākshasas in the lonely forest these bold words. "How dost thou wish to perpetrate such an impious deed after introducing as thy brother that highly worshipful Kuvera adored by all the deities. O Rāvana, surely shall all the Rākshasas meet with death, who have such a stupid, harsh and lustful person like thee for their king. One can breathe on this earth carrying away Indra's wife, Sachi—but stealing me, the wife of Rāma, no body shall be able to live in peace. O Rākshasa, it might be possible for one to live on this earth treating contemptuously the wife of the holder of thunder-bolt but insulting me none shall escape the hands of Death even if he drinketh nectar.

---

## SECTION XLIX.

HEARING those words of Sitâ the highly powerful Ten-necked one striking his hands together, increased his body too high. Thereupon, that one skilled in speech again spake unto Maithili, "Methinks thou hast run mad. Hast thou not heard of my valour and prowess? Stationing myself in the welkin I can with my hands raise up the earth. I can drink up the waters of the ocean. And engaged in conflict I can destroy Death itself. With my sharpened shafts I can pierce the Sun and cut asunder the earth. Thou art mad with thy beauty. Do thou look upon me, who am capable of illusions." When he had spoken thus, his yellow eyes became blood-red with rage and assumed the semblance of flaming fire. Thereat Râvana, the younger brother of the Lord of wealth, changing his placid countenance, instantly assumed his own terrible shape resembling that of Yama. Highly exercised with ire, that ranger of the night became of ten countenances and twenty arms; his eyes were bloody and he appeared beautiful like unto blue clouds, being dressed in gold-hued apparel. Leaving aside the semblance of a mendicant, that lord of Râkshasas, Râvana, increasing in bulk, assumed his own shape. And wearing a blood-red cloth he stood there fixing his look upon that jewel of a damsel—Maithili. Thereupon Râvana spake unto Maithili like unto the rays of the sun, having a head of black hair and wearing apparel and ornaments, saying, "O thou fine damsel, if thou dost wish to have a husband known all over the world, do thou surrender thyself unto me. I am a worthy husband for thee. Do thou serve me for ever, thy praiseworthy husband. O fine lady, I shall never do what thou dost not like. Renouncing thy attachment for a man, do thou place thy love in me. O foolish girl, worthy of being adored by the learned, for what quality art thou attached unto Rāma of a limited life. who hath been deprived of his kingdom and hath his desire frustrated, and who of an evil intent, hath, at the words of his wife, renouncing his kingdom and kinsmen, been living in this forest—the abode of voracious animals." Speaking thus unto Maithili, sweet-speeched and worthy of being sweetly addressed, that highly wicked Rākshasa, Rāvana, being exercised with lust, approached towards Sitā and got hold of her, like unto Budha holding Rohini in the sky. With his left hand he held her, having eyes like unto lotus-petals, by the hair, and with his right hand got hold of her thighs. Seeing Rāvana of sharpened teeth, and mighty arms, resembling the summit of a mountain and like unto Death himself, the deities of the forest became highly terrified and fled in different directions. Instantly appeared there the celestial car of Rāvana, decked in gold, drawn by asses and making a terrible sound. Thereupon, that one emmiting terrible accents, remonstrated with Vaidehi in harsh words and clasping her ascended the car. The virtuous Sitā, being thus caught by Rāvana, began to cry aloud, addressing Rāma, who had gone away to a distant forest. Rāvana, racked with lust, rose high up with her like unto the wife of a *Pannaga*, though she tried her best (to get rid of him), for she was not in the least attached unto him. Being thus carried away by the ethereal track by that Lord of Rākshasas, Sitā began to cry aloud, like one mad, distressed and of deranged senses. "Ah! mighty Lakshmana, ever ministering unto the satisfaction of thy superiors, dost thou not know that I have been stolen away by a Rākshasa assuming shapes at will? O Rāghava, for virtue hast thou renounced thy life, happiness and wealth,—dost thou not see that I have been carried away by one of mighty iniquity? O thou the subduer of foes, thou dost always control the rebellious,—why dost thou not punish such a vicious Rākshasa? The vicious do not instantaneously meet with the fruits of their actions; as for corn to ripen requires the assistance of time. For this iniquitous deed, which thou hast perpetrated, availing of the time and losing thy sense, thou shalt meet with a mighty disaster from Rāma, bringing about thy end. Ah! being the virtuous wife of the virtuous and far-famed Rāma, I have been stolen away. Now hath the desire of Kaikeyi and other relations been fulfilled. I invoke this Janasthāna and these flowery Karnikās to tell Rāma that Rāvana hath stolen away Sitā. I invoke thee, O Godāvari, having swans and cranes sporting in thy stream, to tell Rāma that Rāvana hath stolen away Sitā. I salute and invoke the deities that live in this forest of many trees to tell my husband of my being stolen away (by Rāvana). I do seek the refuge of all deer, birds and other animals that live in this forest, and may they all communicate unto Rāma the news of his dear spouse being carried away, and tell him that Sitā, losing her control, hath been stolen away by Rāvana. Even if I am taken away by Yama, and if the mighty-armed Rāma is apprised of it, surely shall he bring me back by the display of his prowess." Racked with sorrow that one of expansive eyes, while thus bewailing in piteous accents, she espied Yatāyu, the king of vultures, seated on a tree. Thereat the daughter of Janaka, brought under the control of Rāvana and terrified, began to cry and utter those piteous words,—"O worshipful Yatāyu, do thou see that this vicious lord of Rākshasas hath ruthlessly carried me away like one having no husband. Thou wilt not be able to withstand this mighty, wicked and cruel night-ranger wearing emblems of conquest and having a scimitar in his hand. Do thou relate unto Rāma and to

Lakshmana everything about my being carried away from the beginning to the end.

---

## SECTION L.

HEARING these words Yatāyu, who lay burried in a deep slumber, awoke and beheld both Rāvana and Jānaki. Thereat the lord of birds resting on the tree, having a big sharp beak like unto the summit of a hill, addressed these soft words unto Rāvana, "O brother Ten-necked one, I am coversant with Purānas, of truthful vows and abide by religion. It doth not behove thee to perpetrate such an iniquitous deed before me. I am Yatāyu, the mighty lord of vultures. Daçaratha's son Rāma is the lord of all men like unto Mahendra and Varuna. He is ever engaged in the welfare of all men. This exquisitely beautiful and far-famed Sitā whom thou art about to steal away, is the married wife of that lord of men. And how dost thou thyself being a monarch and engaged in the royal office of maintaining subjects, carry away by stealth another's wife? O thou of mighty prowess, thou shouldst specially protect the wives of kings. Do thou therefore control thy base inclination of oppressing another's wife. A hero doth never perform what bringeth calumny upon himself. It becometh every individual to save another's wife from the touch of a second man like unto his own wife. O son of Paulastya, at the instance of the king mild subjects perform many an action conducing to virtue, wealth and desire, though not mentioned in the *Sâstras*. The king is the virtue, the king is the desire and the king is the prime jewel of all subjects. Virtue, desire or sin—every thing ariseth from the king. O thou the best of Rākshasas, thou art vicious and unsteady; how hast thou come by riches like unto a sinner attaining to the abode of celestials ? A vicious person can never relinquish his sinful habits—virtue doth never reside in the abodes of impious persons.

The mighty and the virtuous-souled Rāma hath committed nothing wrong in thy city or thy dominions. Why dost thou then commit wrong by him ? Khara of Janasthāna is highly wicked and if Rāma of blameless actions hath killed him on Surpanakha's account how is he to blame ? Why dost thou then carry away the wife of that lord of men ? Do thou soon leave off Vaidehi. Like unto Indra burning down Vitrasura, Rāma, looking with his terrible eyes like flaming fire, shall reduce thee to ashes. Dost thou not understand that thou hast tied with cloth a virulent serpent ? Dost thou not see that thou hast placed around thy neck the noose of death ? It is always proper to carry such a weight as doth not exhaust (him who carries) ; it is always proper to take such a food as doth not cause illness. Who engageth himself in such an action as doth not confer virtue, fame or glory, but bringeth about physical affliction only ? O Rāvana, I am sixty thousand years old and have been administering regularly my ancestral kingdom. Old though I am, thou shalt not be able to carry away with safety Jānaki in my presence, young, accoutered in mails as thou art with bow and arrows in thy hands and ascending a car. As it is not easy to destroy, by the reasonings of Logic, Vedas and Sruties containing eternal and immutable truths, so thou shalt not be able to carry away Vaidehi by force before me. If thou art a hero do thou fight. Or do thou wait for a moment, O Rāvana, thou shalt also embrace the earth like unto Khara. Soon shall Rāma clad in bark destroy thee in the battle field, who hadst many a time and oft destroyed in conflict the celestials and Dānavas. These two princes Rāma and Lakshmana are at a distance, what shall I do now ? O vile being, undoubtedly shalt thou, terrified, be destroyed by them. Myself drawing my breath thou shalt not be able to carry away this beloved queen of Rāma, the pure-natured Sitā having eyes resembling lotuses. It is my duty to do good unto the high-souled Rāma and Daçaratha even at the sacrifice of my life. Do thou stand,O Ten-necked one. Behold for a moment. O Rāvana, I shall throw thee headlong from this car, like unto a fruit from its stalk. O ranger of the night, even to my utmost might I will render thee hospitality in encounter.

---

## SECTION LI.

WHILE Yatāyu, the king of birds, spake thus, Rāvana, the lord of Rākshasas, wearing pendants made of pure gold, having his eyes reddened with ire, darted towards him. Thereupon they began a terrible conflict in the welkin, like unto clouds driven by wind. There occurred a mighty conflict between Yatāyu, the lord of vultures, and Rāvana, the lord of Rākshasas, like unto two *Malyavān** hills supplied with wings. Thereat Rāvana began to shower continually terrible and sharpened pikes, iron arrows and *Vikarnis* upon the mighty lord of vultures. Yatāyu, the king of birds, began to withstand in conflict the arrows and weapons darted by Rāvana, and wounded Rāvana's persons with his feet supplied with sharpened talons. Thereupon, to destroy his enemy, that mighty hero, the Ten-necked Rāvana, being exercised with ire, took up ten terrible arrows like unto the sceptre of Death, and stretching the bow to the full he shot those straight-coursing sharpened shafts at Yatāyu, the king of birds. Beholding Jānaki with tears in her eyes in that Rākshasa's car, Yatāyu, the king of birds, disregarding those arrows, darted towards Rāvana, and with his feet

* A mountainous range described as one of the smaller mountains of *India* proper, lying eastward of mount *Meru*.—*T*.

broke asunder his bow with the arrows, adorned with pearls and diamonds. Thereat Rāvana, almost beside himself with wrath, taking up another bow, began to shower arrows by hundreds and thousands. Being covered with those arrows, the lord of birds appeared like a bird lying in his nest. Pushing away these arrows by the wind of his wings, he again snapped that mighty bow with his feet, and with a stroke of his wings shattered Rāvana's flaming shield like unto burning fire. Thereupon, moving away with the wind of his wings Rāvana's blazing cuirass resembling flaming fire, Yatāyu, in that conflict made away with his fleet-coursing asses having the faces of demons. Next crumbling into pieces with his impetus the mighty chariot of Rāvana, coursing at will, flaming like fire, having steps studded with jewels, and a wooden pole, and throwing down the umbrella and *chowris* like unto the full moon along with the Rākshasas engaged in carrying them,the effulgent and mighty lord of birds shattered the head of the charioteer with the strokes of his beak. Having his bow snapped and deprived of his car, horses and charioteer, Rāvana fell down to the earth, taking Vaidehi on his lap. Beholding Rāvana fallen on the ground and of broken conveyance, all creatures praised the king of vultures again and again and worshipped him.

Thereupon, finding the lord of birds worn out on account of his old age, Rāvanana, highly encouraged, again rose high up in the welkin, taking Maithili with him. He had all his weapons broken in the conflict, and had but his dagger left to him. Beholding him proceed thus pleased, taking the daughter of Janaka on his lap,—all his weapons having been lost, with his sword alone left,—the mighty and powerful lord of vultures, Yatāyu, rose up and, darting towards Rāvana, resisted him and said,—"O Rāvana of feeble sense, it is for the destruction of the whole line of Rākshasas that thou carriest away this spouse of Rāma, having arrows like unto thunderbolts. Like one thirsty drinking water, thou dost address thyself to drinking poison along with thy friends, courtiers, four-fold forces, servants and relatives. Foolish persons unaware of the fruit of their actions, meet in a short time with their own destruction,—so shalt thou very soon meet with thy own end. Thou hast been bound up by the noose of Death ; and, proceeding whither, shalt thou save thyself, like unto fish eating up baits with hooks for their own destruction ? O Rāvana, it is beyond thy power to defeat the Kākutsthas. They shall not forgive thee for this thy encroachment upon their asylum. What hath been perpetrated by thee, coward, is blamed by all, and is the way taken recourse to by thieves and not by heroes. Do thou fight, O Rāvana, if thou art a hero, or wait for a moment and thou shalt lie down on the earth like unto thy brother Khara. Truly hast thou for thy own destruction engaged thyself in these impious acts, which are perpetrated by men on the eve of their death. What person doth that which leadeth solely into sin ? Neither the lord of celestials nor the self-create Deity doth engage in such an action." Addressing these moral words, the mighty Yatāyu swooped on the back of that Ten-necked Rākshasa. Like unto the rider of a mad elephant, the lord of vultures began to tear Rāvana with his sharpened claws, and that one having for his weapons his beak, talons, and wings, began to rive Rāvana's back with his beak and claws, and to uproot his hair. Being thus afflicted again and again by the king of vultures, the Rākshasa shook, with his lips quivering in anger. Beside himself with anger, Rāvana, holding Jānaki fast by her left flank, struck Yatāyu with his palms. Yatāyu, the subduer of foes, bearing the strokes, tore into pieces his ten left arms with his beak. His arms cut off, instantly sprang up as many others, like unto serpents issuing out of ant-hills, being exercised with the pangs of poison. The mighty Ten-necked one, leaving aside Sitā, out of anger bore down Yatāyu with his fists and feet. Thereupon arose a mighty conflict between the lord of vultures and the lord of Rākshasas of incomparable prowess. Yatāyu addressing himself to displaying his prowess for the benefit of Rāma, Rāvana taking out his dagger, cut off his two wings, two legs and two sides. The ranger of the night of cruel deeds having sundered his wings, the king of vultures approaching wellnigh the verge of death, fell down on the earth. Beholding him fallen on the ground with his person bathed in blood, Sitā became exceedingly aggrieved and darted towards him like unto a friend. The lord of Lankā beheld Yatāyu, fallen on the ground, resembling sable clouds, having a yellow breast and of exceeding prowess,—like unto an extinguished forest-fire. Then Sitā the daughter of Janaka, having a moon-like countenance began lamenting, clasping with her hands Yatāyu, crushed and fallen on the ground by the vehemence of Rāvana's prowess.

## SECTION LII.

Beholding the king of vultures slain by Rāvana, that one possessed of a face fair as the moon, striken with grief, broke out into lamentations, saying, "Throbbings of the eyes or other parts of the body, dreams, seeing birds or hearing their voices, are found to augur happiness or misery to men. And, O Rāma, although birds and beasts are scampering away before thee on my account, thou understandest not the mighty mishap that has befallen thee. O Rāma, this bird, who, moved by kindness, had come to rescue me, owing to my (ill) luck, lies slain on the ground. O Kākutstha, O Lākshmana, save me!" Thus did that best of females, afflicted with fear, bewail; and those near (her) heard her lamentations. Thereat, that lord of the Rākshasas,

Rāvana, darted towards Vaidehi, who, with a faded wreath for her ornament, was bewailing in forlorn guise. Exclaiming repeatedly, "Leave off !" "Leave off," the lord of the Rākshasas got at her, as she was clasping a mighty tree as if it were a creeper. And as she, bereft of the company of Rāma in the wilderness, was wailing, saying, "O Rāma," "O Rāma," that one resembling the Destroyer himself, with the view of compassing his own end, seized her by her hair. On Vaidehi being thus outraged, this entire world consisting of mobile and immobile objects, had its nature altered. A dense darkness enveloped (everything). And the air did not not breathe there ; and the sun grew dim. Espying with his divine vision that Sitā was overcome, that Deity, the graceful Great-father exclaimed, "Our work is accomplished." And seeing Sitā overpowered, the supreme saints inhabiting the Dandaka forest, concluding the destruction of Rāvana to be as good as accomplished without much ado, became at once delighted and aggrieved. As she went on weeping with "O Rāma," "O Lakshmana," Rāvana—lord of Rākshasas —taking her, coursed through the sky. And then the king's daughter hued like molten gold, clad in a yellow silken cloth, looked exceedingly beautiful like unto lightning. And on her yellow cloth streaming up, Rāvana looked surpassingly graceful like a hill aflame with fire. And coppery fragrant lotus-leaves belonging to the eminently auspicious Vaidehi showered upon Rāvana. And her gold-glowing silken cloth, flying in the air, appeared like clouds coloured by the sunken sun. And her blameless countenance on Rāvana's lap in the sky did not appear beauteous without Rāma,—like a lotus without its stalk ; it appeared like the moon risen tearing away dark clouds. And in the aerial regions her countenance on Rāvana's lap furnished with a fair forehead and graceful hair glowing like the inferior of a lotus, without scars, graced with white, shining, stainless teeth, having excellent eyes,—lovely like the moon, having a shapely nose, a rubeous upper lip,—wearing the splendour of gold in the sky,—that captivating countenance of hers in consequence of her weeping, and of being stained with tears, as also owing to the violence it had undergone at the hands of the lord of Rākshasas,—did not appear beautiful without Rāma ; like the moon risen during the day. And furnished with the hue of gold, Mithilā's daughter beside the dark-bodied lord of the Rākshasas, looked like a golden girth round a sable elephant. And Janaka's daughter, yellow-hued like lotus, having the lustre of gold,—and adorned with shining ornaments, coming in contact with Rāvana, appeared like lightning embosomed among clouds. And in consequence of Vaidehi's ornaments sending sounds, the lord of Rākshasas resembled an entirely dark rumbling cloud. And as Sitā was being borne away, showers of blossoms, falling off from her head, were scattered all around on the earth beneath. And that blossomy shower all around, drawn up by the vehemence of the ten-headed Rāvana, again alighted beside him. And the showers of blossoms scattered around Vaiçravana's younger brother, looked like rows of burning stars round the foremost of mountains.* And the bangles studded with gems, loosened from Vaidehi's feet, fell on the earth, like the lightning circle.† Of hue like the light red of tender twigs, Vaidehi set off the dark-bodied lord of Rākshasas, as does a golden cover an elephant. Vaiçravana's younger brother carried away Sitā, who, like a mighty meteor, filled the heavens with her splendour. And like stars of exhausted religious merit dropping down from the sky, her fiery ornaments began to fall to the earth with sounds. And the chain of the splendour of the moon, removed from Vaidehi's breast, falling down, shone like the Gangā dropping from the sky. The trees filled with various fowls, with their tops waving because of the wind blowing on high

* Sumeru.—T

† Instead of *On the earth*—some texts have [bangles] *sweet-sounding.—T.*

and swaying them, seemed to say, "No fear," [unto Sitâ.] And the pools with their lotuses faded and their fishes agitated, seemed to sorrow for the desponding daughter of Mithilâ as for their friend. And following Sitâ's shadow, lions, and tigers, and other beasts and birds, rushed from all sides in wrath. And the mountains, with their faces washed with water-falls representing tears, and their summits resembling uplifted arms, seemed to lament for Sitâ, as she was being carried away. And beholding Vaidehi carried away, the glorious Sun, oppressed with sadness, had his rays dimmed and his disc darkened. "Virtue is not; and where is truth? And there is neither sincerity nor kindness,—in a case in which Râvana is carrying away Râma's Vaidehi;" thus did all creatures lament in numbers. And the young of deer, afflicted with fear, wept with woe-begone faces. And the sylvan deities, looking up now and again with eyes betokening fear, had their persons all in a tremble. For compassing his own destruction, the Ten headed one carried away the intelligent Vaidehi, bewailing bitterly, Sitâ, who had come by such misfortune, sweet-voiced, crying, "O Lakshmana," "O Râma," and casting glances on the ground many a time and oft,—the ends of her hair waving and her *tilaka* wiped out. Then oppressed with the load of fear, Sitâ of luminous smiles,—Mithilâ's daughter, bereft of her friends —not beholding either Râma or Lakshmana, became pale of countenance.

## SECTION LIII.

SEEING him fly up into the air, Janaka's daughter, Maithili, became aggrieved and exceedingly agitated, and great was the fear that possessed her. Her eyes expressing rage, weeping and fright, Sitâ, as she was being carried away, weeping piteously, spoke to the grim-eyed lord of the Rākshasas, saying, "Dost thou not, O base wretch, O Rāvana, feel shame on account of this act—thou, who, knowing that I was alone, fliest away, carrying me? Coward that thou art, thou it was, who, desirous of carrying me off, by the shape of a deer, hadst, by thy [powers of] illusion taken away my lord. And he also that endeavoured to rescue me, has been slain by thee—the ancient king of vultures, who was the friend of my father-in-law. Great, forsooth, is found to be thy might, thou vilest of Rākshasas; in that thou hast carried me off by simply declaring thy name, but hast not won me in war. Why dost thou not, O execrable one, take shame unto thyself, having perpetrated such a heinous act—having carried off another's wife in the absence of her husband? This fell and foul act of thine fraught with unrighteousness, heroic persons shall bruit about the world. Fie on thy heroism and thy truth,—of which thou didst speak at that time; and fie also on this character of thine, calculated to sully thy line in this world. What can I do (unto thee), as thou proceedest with speed? But stay thou for a moment; and thou shalt not return with life. Shouldst thou come within the range of the vision of those sons of the king, thou couldst not, although thou shouldst happen to be accompanied with thy army, live for a moment. Even as a bird cannot bear the touch of a flaming fire in a forest, thou canst never bear the touch of their arrows. Effecting thy own welfare, do thou, O Rāvana, leave me. If thou do not let me go, my husband along with his brother would strive for thy destruction. As intent upon sensual enjoyment, thou endeavourest to ravish me, this very endeavour of thine, O mean wight, shall come to naught. Not beholding my lord resembling a celestial, I cannot, come under the sway of my enemy, bear to live long. As one dwelling on earth perceives objects in their reversed relations at the time of one's death, so thou dost not perceive what is for thy good or profit. Those moribund do not relish what would do them good. I see thee with the noose of Death wound round thy neck. As, O ranger of night, thou art not affected with fear, albeit the situation is one calculated to raise one's apprehensions, it is clear that thou wilt see the golden trees, the dreadful river Vaitarani flowing with blood, the terrible wood, O Rāvana, rife with leaves in the shape of swords, and a sharp Sālmali containing blossoms of shining gold, having lapises for its leaves, and bearing iron thorns. But, O shameless one, like a person that hath drunk poison, having done this wrong unto that high-souled one, thou wilt not be able to save thyself. O Rāvana, thou art fast fettered in the noose of Death. Having done this foul turn unto that high-souled one, repairing whither, shalt thou obtain respite? Shall not that strong and heroic Rāghava, skilled in all weapons, who without his brother, in the twinkling of an eye, in battle slew fourteen thousand Rākshasas, slay thee, who carriest away his beloved wife?" Thus and in other ways, Videha's daughter, lying on the lap of Rāvana, overwhelmed with fear and grief, indulged in piteous lamentations. And the wicked (Rāvana) with a shaking frame carried away the daughter of the king extremely distressed, speaking much, and speaking piteously, uttering lamentations, and putting forth endeavours (to free herself).

## SECTION LIV.

CARRIED away (by Rāvana), Vaidehi, not finding any defender, saw five principal monkeys stationed on the top of a hill. Thereat, that lady of expansive eyes and surpassing charms, in the hope that they might convey the intelligence unto Rāma, flung off in their midst her gold-gleaming silken sheet, and elegant ornaments. But the Ten-headed one owing to hurry did not observe the throwing of the cloth along with the ornaments. Those foremost of monkeys having tawny eyes observed with winkless eyes the large-eyed Sitā as she was giving way to grief. And the lord of Rākshasas, passing beyond Pampā, directed his course towards the city of Lankā, taking Mithilā's daughter along with him, indulging in lamentations. Experiencing the height of delight, Rāvana ravished her, taking her, on his lap, like a sharp-toothed serpent of virulent poison. And speedily, like an arrow shot from a bow, he, coursing the welkin, left behind woods and streams and mountains and pieces of water. And coming to the abode of Varuna, that refuge of rivers, the exhaustless ocean—the home of whales and alligators, he crossed over it. In consequence of the carrying away of Vaidehi, Varuna's abode, from grief, had all its waves stilled and its fishes and mighty snakes inert.—And the Chāranas uttered in the heavens these words, "O Ten-headed one, this is thy end." Thus did the Siddhas then say. And taking Sitā on his lap, representing his own Death,—who endeavoured (to liberate herself), Rāvana entered the city or Lankā. And entering the city of Lankā, vast, with all its highways well-arranged, and with people thronging its gates, he entered his own inner apartment. Then Rāvana set Sitā there, having eyes with dark outer corners, exercised with grief and dole ; as if Maya had set his own Asura illusion (in his own palace). Then the Ten-headed one spoke unto some female friends of terrible visages, "Let no man or woman behold Sitā without my permission. And I command that, should she ask for pearls, or rubies, or gold, or apparel, or ornaments, the same should be rendered unto her. She that, whether knowingly or unknowingly should say anything unpleasant to Vaidehi, would hold her life cheap." Having said this unto the Rākshasis, the puissant lord of the Rākshasas, went out of the inner apartment, and thought within himself as to what was to be done (next). And he saw eight flesh-eating Rākshasas of wondrous prowess. And seeing them, the exceedingly powerful (Rāvana), blinded by the bestowal of the boon, after extolling their strength and heroism, addressed them, saying, "Equipped with various weapons, do ye speedily take yourself to Janasthāna,—that field of carnage—which ere this contained the abode of Khara; and casting off fear at a distance, do ye sojourn in vacant Janasthāna with all its Rākshasas slain (by Rāma). A great many troops endued with exceeding prowess, who had been posted in Janasthāna, have, along with Dushana and Khara, been slain by the shafts of Rāma. Hence unprecedented is my wrath, towering above my patience; and great and fierce also is the hostility I have conceived against Rāma. I wish to avenge myself on my mighty enemy. Sleep find I none without slaying my foe in fight. Slaying that slayer of Khara and Dushana, Rāma, I shall attain delight like unto that attained by a pauper on gaining riches. Staying in Janasthāna, ye shall gather true information touching Rāma as to what he is about. Repair all ye rangers of the night carefully, and strive yourselves always for slaying Rāma. I have been well acquainted with your strength in many a field, and it is for this that I set ye in Janasthāna." Hearing these agreeable and weighty words of Rāvana, those Rākshasas, bowing down unto Rāvana, left Lankā, and in a body invisibly proceeded in the direction of Janasthāna. Having obtained Mithilā's daughter, Rāvana experienced great joy in establishing her (in his own house); and having created high hostility with Rāma, Rāvana through blindness rejoiced greatly.

## SECTION LV.

HAVING commissioned those eight terrible and mighty Rākshasas, Rāvana, in consequence of perversion of sense, considered himself as crowned with success. And brooding over Vaidehi, he, sore pierced by the shafts of Kāma, hastily entered his charming mansion, with the intention of seeing Sitā. And entering that apartment, Rāvana—lord of Rākshasas—saw the distressed Sitā in the midst of the Rākshasas, with a tearful countenance, oppressed with a load of grief, like unto a bark sinking in the ocean through the violence of the winds; like unto a doe separated from the herd of deer, and surrounded by dogs. Coming to Sitā disconsolate in consequence of stress of sorrow, remaining with her head bent down, that ranger of the night, the lord of the Rākshasas, forcibly shewed unto her that mansion resembling the mansion of the celestials, thick with palaces and lordly piles, inhabited by thousands of females; containing birds of various kinds; furnished with various gems; with beautiful pillars of ivory gold and crystal and silver, studded with diamonds and lapises. Rāvana in company with Sitā ascended the beautiful golden stairs, resounding with the sounds of kettle-drums and embellished with ornaments of burnished gold. And those lofty edifices had excellent windows made of ivory and silver, and covered with golden nets. The ground all over was decorated with ambrosia and gems. The Ten-headed one in his own mansion shewed unto Maithili large tanks and pools covered with various kinds of flowers. (All this) Rāvana shewed unto Sitā overmastered by sorrow. And after having shewed unto Vaidehi the whole of that goodliest of mansions, that wicked one, with the intention of tempting Sitā, spoke unto her, saying "O Sitā, leaving out old men and boys, I am the lord of thirty-two *kotis* of night-rangers of terrible deeds. And a thousand come forward whenever required for any service.—If such is my sovereignty, all this is established in thee, O large-eyed lady, as well as my life. Thou art dearer unto me than life. O Sitā, be thou the mistress of those numerous excellent women who are my wives. Dear, be thou my wife. This is for thy good. Why shouldst thou act otherwise ? Do thou relish my speech. Do thou bend thy mind towards me. It behoves thee to favour me, who am burning (in the heat of desire). This Lankā measuring an hundred Yoyanas girt round by the ocean, is incapable of being harassed by the celestials themselves headed by Indra. Neither among the celestials nor Yakshas nor Gandharbas nor Serpents, find I any one that can match me in prowess. What wilt thou do with Rāma a human being of short life, poor, of small prowess, practising mendicancy ? O Sitā, bend thy mind unto me. I am a fit husband for thee. O timid one, youth is uncertain. Sport with me here. And, O thou of a handsome countenance, do not wish for the sight of Rāghava. O Sitā, what power hath he to come hither even in thought ? None can fetter the exceedingly fleet wind in the sky, or hold the bright flame of a burning fire. O beauteous one, in these three worlds I find no one that can by his might carry thee away, who art protected by my arms. Do thou govern at Lankā this extensive kingdom. The like of me and celestials and all that are mobile and immobile shall be thy servants. Laving thy limbs with water, do thou gratify me. The evil that thou hadst done, hath been expiated by thy life in the forest : now do thou reap the fruit of thy good deeds. Here are garlands furnished with divine fragrance, and, O Maithili, superb ornaments. Enjoy thou all these along with me. O thou of shapely hips, the car called Pushpaka, resembling the sun, which (formerly) belonged to my brother Vaiçravana, was through my prowess won by me in fight. And vast and beautiful is that car furnished with the speed of the mind. Do thou, O Sitā, at thy pleasure sport on it along with me. Thy face stainless and lovely to look at resembling the lotus, doth not, O thou of a comely countenance, O magnificent damsel, appear beautiful in consequence of thy being exercised with grief." When Rāvana had spoken thus, that best of females Sitā muffling up her moon-like countenance with the ends of her cloth, began to shed gentle tears. Thereat the heroic ranger of the night, Rāvana said unto Sitā, distressed, sunk in thought, and deprived of her splendour through anxiety, "O Vaidehi, banish bashfulness, which stands in the way of one's duty. The yearning I feel after thee is in consonance with what the sages prescribe. These tender feet of thine I press upon my heads. Do thou speedily shew thy favour unto me. I am thy slave (ever) obedient unto thee. Let not these words of mine spoken by me under the withering influence of love prove fruitless. Rāvana hath never bowed his head to any female." Having said this, the Ten-headed one, come under the subjection of the Destroyer, looked upon Maithili, Janaka's daughter (as his own) saying, "She is mine."

## SECTION LVI.

HAVING been thus addressed, Vaidehi unaffected by fear, although exercised with grief, placing a blade of grass between herself and Rāvana, answered, him, saying, "There was a king named Daçaratha, the bridge of righteousness, like unto a mountain, ever bearing regard towards the truth and renowned among men, whose son is Rāghava. He is named Rāma and is righteous-souled and celebrated over the three worlds. He is long-armed, of expansive eyes,—like unto a celestial—he is my husband. Born in the race of the Ikshwākus, he hath the shoulders of a lion and is possessed of exceeding effulgence—the same that along with his brother, Lakshmana, shall take thy life. If thou hadst wronged me forcibly in his presence, thou wouldst have lain in battle in Janasthâna even as Khara. All the mighty Râkshasas of grim visages, whom thou hast extolled (before me), shall be deprived of their venom before Râma, as serpents are before Suparna. The shafts decorated with gold shot by the bow-string of Râghava, shall pierce their bodies, as the waves of the Gangâ (beat against) her banks. Although, O Râvana, thou mayst be incapable of being slain either by the gods or the Asuras, yet having roused the high hostility of Râghava, thou wilt not be able to liberate thy life. The strong Râghava will compass the end of what remains of thy life. Like the life of a beast tied to the sacrificial stake, thy own is incapable of being reclaimed. Should Râma look at thee with eyes aglow with anger, thou, O Râkshasa, wouldst be consumed even as Manmatha was by Rudra. He who is able to bring down the Moon or destroy him, and to drink up the ocean dry, will surely liberate Sitâ from here. Thy days are numbered, and auspiciousness hath bidden thee adieu. Thou art shorn of strength, and thy senses have been dulled. And it is owing to thee that Lankâ shall be subject to widowhood. That thou by force hast for naught carried me away from the side of my husband —this sinful act can never conduce to thy felicity. That exceedingly effulgent lord of mine along with my husband's younger brother, summoning up their energy, is fearlessly dwelling in the vacant Dandaka. By means of an arrowy shower in conflict, he will take thy prowess and strength, thy hauteur and wickedness out of thy person. When urged by the Destroyer, the destruction of creatures is perceptible, then, coming under the sway of the Destroyer, men become careless in their actions. Having outraged me, thou, O worst of Râkshasas, thy time come; for compassing thy own destruction as well as that of the Râkshasas and those dwelling in thy inner apartment. A Chandâla cannot tread the dais reared in the midst of a sacrifice beauteous with ladles, and vessels, and sanctified by the twice-born ones. So I, the religiously wedded wife of that one, ever intent on virtue, and (always) firm in my vows, is incapable, thou vilest of Rākshasas, of being touched by thee, a sinner. How can the female that hath always sported with her mate amidst lotuses, cast her eyes on a shag staying among rushes. Do thou either bind or destroy this body deprived of sensation. This body will I not protect, nor yet this life, O Rāvana; and I shall not be able to bring blame on myself in this world." Having said these harsh words in wrath, Videha's daughter, Jānaki, did not there again say anything unto Rāvana. Hearing Sitā's words, harsh and calculated to make one's down stand on end, Rāvana answered her in words tending to excite one's apprehension, "Hear, O Maithili, my words. O damsel if, O thou of sweet smiles, within this thou do not turn thyself unto me, the cooks shall cut thee off in pieces to serve my morning meal." Having herself spoken thus, Rāvana,—challenger of foes—growing exceedingly wroth, addressed the Rākshasis in these words, "Ye frightful Rākshasis terrible to behold, subsisting on flesh and gore, do ye at once crush her pride." As soon as he had said this, those frightful and terrible Rākshasis with joined hands encircled Maithili. Then the grim-visaged king Rāvana, as if riving the earth by his tread, proceeding a pace or two, said, "Do ye take Maithili to the wood of *Asoka*. There surrounding her, do ye secretly guard her; and there (sometimes) by storming, and (at others) by means of soft speech, do ye all strive to bring Mithilā's daughter, like a wild female elephant, under your sway." Thus commanded by Rāvana, those Rākshasis taking Māithili along with them, went to the *Asoka* wood, abounding with trees granting every desire, and filled with various kinds of fruits and flowers; and frequented by fowls fraught with juices at all seasons. And as a doe comes under the subjection of tigresses, Janaka's daughter, Maithili, her frame worked up with grief, came under the sway of the Rākshasis. And like a female deer fast bound by a trap, Janaka's timid daughter Maithili, agitated by the mighty grief, did not attain respite. And greatly up-braided by the fierce eyes (of the Rākshasis), Maithili did not know repose; and, afflicted with grief and fear, she, remembering her beloved lord along with Lakshmana swooned away.

---

The passage included within the brackets are wanting in some texts :—

(ON Sitā having entered Lankā, the Great father addressed the gratified Devendra of an hundred sacrifices, "For bringing about the weal of the three worlds, and the woe of the Rākshasas, Sitā hath been taken into Lankā by the wicked-minded, Rāvana. Devoted unto her husband, the exalted lady always brought up in happiness, not seeing her husband, and seeing (on the other hand) environed by numbers of Rākshasis,—is hungering after the sight of her lord. The city of Lankā is situated on the shores of the lord of rivers and streams. How can Rāma get a knowledge of that blameless one, staying there? Brooding over the various ills she hath undergone, that exceedingly rare damsel is passing her days. Surely she will resign her existence. Great is the doubt that hath arisen as to Sitā putting a period to her existence. Having thyself from here, do thou see the fair-faced Sitā. Having entered the city of Lankā, offer excellent clarified butter." Thus addressed by the reverend chastiser of Pāka, Devendra in company with sleep, approached the city ruled by Rāvana. He then addressed sleep, saying, "Go thou; and stupify the Rākshasas." Thus accosted by Maghavat, that goddess, exceedingly delighted, for securing success to the work of the celestials, covered the Rākshasas with stupor. In the meanwhile, that god, the thousand-eyed lord of Sachi went to (Sitā) staying in the woods, and spoke unto her these words, "I am the sovereign of the celestials. Good betide thee! I am here, O thou of luminous smiles! For securing success unto the work of the magnanimous Rāghava, I will lend my aid unto thee. Do not, O daughter of Janaka, grieve. Through my grace, he shall along with his forces cross over the ocean. And, O excellent wench, I have by my supernal power, stupified the Rākshasis. And, O Sitā, for this reason, I along with sleep, taking these rice,—rice boiled in clarified butter, have, O Vaidehi, come unto thee. If thou partake of these from my hand, thou shalt never, O beauteous one, be afflicted either with hunger or thirst, O thou of thighs resembling *rambhā* (trunks), for years." Thus addressed, Sitā, alarmed, said, "How can I know thee for Devendra, Sachi's husband, staying here? By the side of Rāma and Lakshmana, I had beheld the signs of the celestials. If, O Devendra, thou art thyself the sovereign of the celestials, show those unto me." Hearing Sitā's words, the lord of Sachi did accordingly. He did not touch the earth with his feet, and his eyes remained winkless. He bloomed in youth, and the blossoms did not fade on his attire. Thereupon knowing him for Vāsava, Sitā was overjoyed. And weeping, she spoke regarding Rāghava, "By luck it is that I had heard of that mighty-armed one along with his brother. As is my father in-law, the king, as is the master of Mithilā, so art thou (unto me), thou whom I behold to-day; my husband hath now found a protector.—And by thy command, O Devendra, will I partake of this *pāyasa* cooked with milk, which hath been offered unto me, and which shall enhance (the prosperity) of our race." Thereupon taking the *pâyasa* from Indra's hands, that Maithili of luminous smiles (mentally) offered it unto her husband as well as Lakshmana. "If my mighty lord live along with his brother, let this through my reverence for them, be theirs." She then partook of the *pâyasa* herself. Hav.ᵹg thus eaten it, that one of excellent countenance, had her hunger and rising sorrow removed; and attaining a mental tendency from Indra, Jānaki grew glad with reference to the Kākutsthas. And Sakra also for bringing about the success of Rāghava's work, with a pleased mind, went to the abode of celestials. And greeting Sitā again and again, that high-souled celestial, in company with sleep went back to his own abode.")

## SECTION LVII.

KILLING the Rākshasa, Māricha assuming shapes at will and ranging in the shape of a deer, Rāma wended speedily his way. And as he hurried himself, eager to behold Maithili, jackals began to howl hideously at his back. Hearing their harsh cries, capable of making one's hair stand on end, Rāma struck with fear at the voices of the jackals, became filled with alarm. "Ah! I consider this as inauspicious—that these jackals are crying. Escaping being devoured by the Rākshasas, may fair fortune befall Vaidehi! If Lakshmana should have heard the cries which Māricha, knowing my voice, and fixing on the means of harming me, uttered in the form of a deer, Saumitri, hearing that voice, leaving Mithilā's daughter and commissioned by herself, must have come near me. Surely, the Rākshasas in a body are desirous of slaying Sitā. Becoming a golden deer, Māricha, having alluredme far, transformed himselfinto a Rākshasa, as soon as he had been struck with my shafts; and exclaimed, 'Ah Lakshmana, slain am I.' It is doubtless, we having left (Sitā), whether all is well with her. I having raised the hostility of the Rākshasas for the sake of Janasthāna; and many and dreadful are the omens I see (around me)." Thus reflecting as he heard the howlings of the jackals, the self-possessed Rāma with hasty steps returned to the asylum. Rāghava went back to Janasthāna, alarmed in consequence of his having been drawn away by the Rākshasa in the form of a deer. And birds and beasts approached that high-souled one distressed and depressed in spirit; and staying on his left set up frightful cries. As he was witnessing the exceedingly dreadful signs, Rāghava saw Lakshmana coming with a lacklustre (countenance); and Lakshmana came up to Rāma. And depressed in spirit, he was rendred still more sad by that one who, afflicted with depression shared his sorrow. And, seeing that (Lakshmana) had come, leaving Sitā in that solitary wood frequented by Rakshasas, his brother fell to reprimanding him. And taking Lakshmana's left hand, the son of Raghu in extreme distress sweetly spake these rough words, "Alas! Lakshmana, thou hast committed a censurable act; leaving Sitā, O mild one, thou hast come hither. Is it well with her? I make no doubt, O hero, but that Janaka's daughter hath either been slain or devoured by Rākshasas ranging the forest. And, considering the many omens that take place before me, O Lakshmana, I do not know whether we shall light upon welfare of Janaka's daughter Sitā being alive, O best of men. And as these multitudes of beasts and these jackals are crying frightfully in the flaming direction,* I do not know, O thou of mighty strength, whether it is well with that daughter of the king. This Rākshasa, who, wearing the shape of a deer, and, alluring me, had drawn me far, hath in some sort been slain by me with much ado;

* *i. e.* The quarter presided over by the sun, *viz.*, the East.—T.

and he became a Râkshasa at the time of his death. Yet my mind is poor and cheerless ; and my left eye throbs. Doubtless, O Lakshmana, Sitâ is not,—she is either carried away, or dead, or is wandering on the way.

## SECTION LVIII.

SEEING Lakshmana cast down, cheerless, and come without Vaidehi, the righteous son of Daçaratha, asked him, saying, "Where, O Lakshmana is that Vaidehi, who hath followed me unto the Dandaka forest, and leaving whom thou hast come hither ? Where is that one of a slender waist, who is my help in trouble, deprived of my kingdom, dispirited, and running about the Dandakas ? Without whom, O hero, I cannot live for a moment—where is that help of my life, Sitâ, resembling the daughter of a celestial ? O Lakshmana, without Janaka's daughter (hued) like burning gold, I covet not the sovereignty of the celestials or the earth. Liveth Vaidehi, dearer unto me than life ? Shall this exile of mine be of no avail ? O Sumitrâ's son, on my dying for Sitâ and thy returning (to the city), shall Kaikeyi have her desire, and attain felicity ; and shall Kauçalyâ,—her son dead, and herself wearing the guise of a female mendicant, humbly wait upon Kaikeyi when she shall have succeeded in obtaining the kingdom for her son ? If Vaidehi live, I will then return to the asylum ; but O Lakshmana, if that one of excellent character should happen to be dead, I will also renounce my life. If, O Lakshmana, Vaidehi ever preluding her speech with a smile should not speak to me when I arrive at the asylum, I shall give up my life. Do thou tell me, O Lakshmana, whether Videha's daughter liveth or not ; or whether, in consequence of thy acting heedlessly, that forlorn wench hath been devoured by Râkshasas.

Of a tender frame, and a mere girl, Vaidehi, never having experienced unhappiness being cast down, surely weepeth for my separation. When that exceedingly wicked Rākshasa cried, "Lakshmana" at the top of his voice, wast thou also seized with fear? And I apprehend that voice resembling mine was heard by Vaidehi; and, despatched by her from fear, thou mayst have come hither swiftly to see* me. Thou hast every way acted unwisely in having left Sita alone in the wood. By this thou hast afforded opportunity to the cruel Rākshasas to repair the mischief (I have done them). The Rākshasas subsisting on flesh are aggrieved because of Khara having been slain; and now, without doubt, those terrible ones have slain Sitā. Alas! absolutely sunk am I in peril, O destroyer of foes. What shall I do now? I fear such an event was appointed for me." Thus thinking of Sitā, paragon among women, Rāghava hastily went to Janasthāna in company with Lākshmana. Taking to task his yonger brother of distressed visage, Rāma, afflicted with hunger and thirst, and dejected in spirits, sighing heavily with a countenance turned pale, entered the asylum and found it vacant. And entering his own asylum, that hero went to the play-grounds (of Sitā) and remembering the sporting ground (of Sitā) in that abode, he was filled with grief and his down stood on end.

## SECTION LIX.

THEN coming out of the hermitage, Raghu's descendant, Rāma, after a while, from grief, spake these words to the son of Sumitrā, "When confiding myself in thee, I had left Maithili with thee in the wood, why then didst thou go out, leaving her behind? O Lakshmana, directly I saw thee

* Some texts—*to rescue me.*—*T.*

approach, renouncing Maithili, my mind, apprehending great wrong, became really aggrieved. O Lakshmana, seeing thee coming at a distance, renouncing her, my left eye and arm as well as my heart keep throbbing." Thus accosted, Lakshmana having auspicious signs, afflicted with great grief, said unto the aggrieved Rāma, "I have not come hither, of my own accord, renouncing Sitā ; but I have come to thee having been urged thereto by herself with rudeness. The cries of "O Lakshmana, save me," as if uttered by the master, came to the ears of Maithili. Hearing those distressful accents, Maithili from affection (for thee), breaking out into lamentations, and overwhelmed with fear, spoke unto me, "Off," "off." On being repeatedly urged, with "Go," I answered Maithili in these words, tending to inspire her confidence, 'I do not see such a Rākshasa, as can excite his fear. Do thou desist. These cries do not come from him; but must have been uttered by some one else. How can he that can rescue the celestials themselves, utter, O Sitā, such blame-worthy and base word as—save (me)? Some one for some purpose, assuming my brother's voice, is crying—O Lakshmana, save me. O beauteous lady, these words, Save me—must have been uttered by some Rākshasa from fear. Thou shouldst not act like a mean woman. Do not be overwhelmed ; and banish thy anxiety. There breathes no person, nor yet shall there be born any one in these three worlds who in the field shall vanquish Rāghava in fight. Rāghava is incapable of being beaten in battle by the very gods headed by Indra.' Thus addressed (by me) Vaidehi, deprived of her sense, shedding tears, spake unto me these cruel words, 'Thou cherishest the vile idea that on thy brother perishing, thou shalt come by me ; but me thou shalt never have. As thou dost not go to him albeit he is crying loudly (for help), thou followest Rāma in consonance with a hint from Bharata. A foe going about in disguise, thou followest Rāma for my sake, prying into Rāghava's draw-backs ; and is it for this that thou dost not go (to him)?' Thus accosted by Vaidehi, I, with eyes reddened in wrath, and my nether lip swollen in ire, rushed out of the asylum." When Saumitri had spoken thus, Rāma transported by grief, said unto Lakshmana, "O gentle one, thou hast done wrong in having come out hither without her. Although thou knewest (full well) that I was able to withstand the Rākshasas, yet didst thou sally out at the angry words of Mithilā's daughter. I am not pleased with thee that hearing her harsh speech spoken in wrath, thou hast come hither, leaving Vaidehi behind. Thou hast every way done wrong in not acting out my mandate in consequence of being urged by Sitā, and under the influence of indignation. That Rākshasa lieth low, being wounded by my shafts—that had drawn me away from the asylum wearing the from of a deer. I hit him stretching my bow slightly and fixing the shaft on it; when, renouncing his deer-form he became a Rākshasa wearing a bracelet and began to emit distressful shrieks. Wounded by my shaft, he, assuming my voice, and in accents capable of being heard from far, uttered those dreadful words fraught with dole, hearing which, thou hast come hither, renouncing Mithilā's daughter."

## SECTION LX.

As Rāma went on, his feet failed him, his left eye began to beat, and a trembling came over his frame. Seeing again and again all these signs, he continually kept on asking (Lakshmana), "Is it well with Sitā?" Eager to behold Sitā, he proceeded fast; but finding the abode empty, he was filled with anxiety. And proceeding with swiftness, throwing about his limbs, Raghu's son began to survey all around the hut. He then found it empty of Sitā, like unto a tank in evil plight and bereft of lotuses—during the winter. And seeing the cottage empty, with its trees as if sorrowing and its flowers faded, and its beasts and birds sunk in gloom,—shorn of grace, worn out, forsaken by the sylvan deities, strewn with deer-skins and Kuça, and twists of Kāsa, he wept again and again—"Hath the timid one been carried off, or is she dead, or hath any one eaten her up, or hath she vanished (from the earth), or hath she gone to the wood, or hath she gone to cull flowers and fruits, or hath she gone to the pool for procuring water, or hath she repaired to the river?" Although he searched his beloved one carefully, yet he failed to find her out in the wood-land. And that graceful one with his eyes reddened with grief, seemed like a maniac. And he rushed from tree to tree, and bewailing being sunk in an occean of grief traversed all the rivers and mountains. "O *Kadamba*, hast thou seen where is that one fond of Kadamba groves? If knowest thou this do thou tell me of Sitā having an auspicious countenance. O *Bilya*, tell me pray, if thou hast seen her, wearing silken cloth, resembling cool leaves and having breast like unto *Bilya* fruits. Or, O Aryunā, she was very fond of thee, tell me if liveth that daughter of Janaka of slender frame. This *Kakuva* knoweth for certain about Maithilee having thighs like unto *Kakuva*. Yon stands beautifully that *Banaspati* being enveloped with creepers, flowers and leaves and filled with the hum of *Vramaras*. Surely doth this *Tilaka* know about her who was fond of her. O *Asoka*, who doth remove sorrows, do thou make good thy name by making me, who am exercised with grief, see instantly my beloved (spouse). O *Tâla*, if thou hast any pity on me do thou tell me whether thou hast beheld that fair damsel having breast resembling ripe *Tâla* fruits. Do thou tell me without fear, O Jāmbhu, if thou hast seen my dear one resembling in hue the river Jāmbhu. O *Karnikar*, thou appearest very beautiful with this blossoming flowers, tell me if thou hast seen my dear devoted wife who was fond of thee." Thus the highly famous Rāma asking about Sitā, nearing the various trees such as mangoe, Nipa, Mahāsāla, Panaça, Kurava, Pomegranate, Vakula, Pumnaga, Sandal and Ketaka began to traverse the forest like a maniac. Again addressed he the diverse animals—"O deer, knowest thou for certain about Jānaki having the eyes of a doe ; is she engaged in play with the does ? O elephant, methinks thou dost know about the daughter of Janaka having thighs resembling thy trunk ; pray tell me if thou hast beheld her. O tiger, fearlessly do thou relate unto me if thou hast seen my beloved Maithilee, having a countenance resembling Moon. O dear ! O thou having eyes like unto lotuses ! why dost thou fly away ? Surely have I seen thee. Why dost thou not address me hiding thyself behind the tree ? Wait, wait, O thou fair damsel, thou hast no compassion for me ! Never hadst thou mock me before in this way ! Why dost thou neglect me now ? O exquisitely fair damsel, truly have I found thee out from this thy yellow silken cloth. I have seen thee flying away. Stand if thou hast any love for me. Or, O thou having a sweet smile, thou art not she ; truly thou hast been killed or else thou wouldst not have neglected me at this time of dire affliction. True it is that she hath been devoured in my absence by the Rākshasas living on flesh having torn into pieces her limbs. Truly hath her face, resembling the full-moon, having beautiful teeth a fine nose and white Kundalas, become of pale countenance being brought under the possession of the Rākshasas. Her neck had the hue of sandal and was adorned with necklace—that beautiful tender neck was eaten up by the Rākshasas, my beloved wife wailing. Her arms were tender like leaves and adorned with various ornaments ; truly have the Rākshasas eaten them up, shaken as they were, by throwing them here and there. Alas ! did I leave her alone only to be devoured by the Rākshasas ? And she hath been eaten up like one weak and helpless albeit she has many friends. O Lakshmana, O thou of mighty-arms, hast thou seen where my dear wife is ? O dear ! O Sitā ! where hast thou gone ?" Bewailing again and again in this strain Rāma began to range the forest. Sometimes leaping, sometimes walking in an uncertain direction, again and again he looked like one void of sense. And again intent on searching Sitā he furiously engaged in traversing the rivers,mountains,fountains and the woods. He could not wait patiently anywhere. Entering a vast forest he searched every nook and corner for Maithili; his desire was not satisfied and he again engaged with great labour in the finding out of his dear spouse.

## SECTION LXI.

Beholding the hermitage and cottage desolate and the seats strewn here and there, Rāma the son of Daçaratha looked around. And finding Sitā nowhere he raised up his beautiful arm and broke out into lamentations saying, "O Lakshmana where is Sitā ? Where has she gone hence ? O Saumitri, who hath carried away my dear one or who hath devoured her ? O Sitā, if wishest thou to mock me, hiding thyself behind the tree, enough—enough it is—console me who am exercised with grief. O pleasant Sitā, without thee these faithful little deer have engaged in meditation being bathed in tears. Without Sitā I shall not breathe, O Lakshmana. A mighty grief hath overtaken me in consequence of her being carried away. My father the monarch shall surely behold me in the next world and ask me 'I engaged thee in the observance of a vow ; without fulfilling that, why hast thou come here ? O shame on thee !' For certain shall my father address me with these words relating to my passionate, false and base conduct. All my desires have now been baffled and I have lost all control over myself and have been exercised with grief. O fine damsel, O thou of slender waist, where dost thou repair leaving me behind like unto fame renouncing a person of vicious nature? Without thee I shall renounce my own life." Being desirous of seeing Sitā, Rāma afflicted with grief began to bewail in this strain, but did not behold the daughter of Janaka. Being sunk in grief on Sitā's account he became worn out like unto an elephant fallen in mud. Thereat for his well being, Lakshmana spoke unto him saying, "O thou of mighty intellect—do not grieve. Do thou put forth thy endeavours along with me. There is that high hill, O hero, containing many a cave. Maithili who is fond of ranging the forest and ever delighteth in beholding the flowery woods, must have entered therein or have gone to the watering-place blooming with flowerets and lotuses. She has gone to the river abounding in fish and *Banjulas* or has hidden herself somewhere in the forest to frighten us and to know, O best of men, how we can search her out. O thou of great beauty, let us soon engage in quest of her. O Kākutstha, if thinkest thou that she is somewhere in this forest, we shall leave no quarter untried. Do thou not grieve." After Lakshmana had spoken thus out of fraternal affection, Rāma, with a composed heart, set out along with him in quest of Sitā. And searching every nook and corner of the mountains, rivers, ponds, table-lands, hills and summits they found Sitā nowhere. And searching thus all the mountains Rāma spake unto Lakshmana saying, "Behold not I the auspicious Vaidehi on this mountain, O Saumitri." Ranging the entire forest of Dandaka, Lakshmana, sore distressed, spake unto his brother of flaming energy, saying, "Surely shalt thou come by Maithili the daughter of Janaka like unto the mighty-armed Vishnu obtaining this earth after having bound Vāli." Being thus addressed by the heroic Lakshmana, Rāghava, greatly afflicted with sorrow, replied in piteous accents,—"O thou of mighty intellect I have searched every nook of this forest, this pool abounding in blown lotuses, and this mountain containing many a cave and fountain; but nowhere have I seen Vaidehi dearer than my life. Thus bewailing Rāma, racked with sorrow consequent on Sitā being carried away, became poorly and afflicted with grief and swooned away for sometime. He lost his sense and his whole frame was worked with grief. Being greatly anxious and breathless he sighed hot and fast and began to lament. And sobbing again and again the lotus-eyed Rāma bewailed with his voice choked with the vapour of grief, exclaiming "Ah Sitā!" Thereat his dear brother Lakshmana, aggrieved, consoled him with joined hands. But passing by the words dropping from Lakshmana's lips Rāma again and again bewailed not beholding his dear Sitā.

## SECTION LXII.

NOT beholding Sitā the virtuous-souled Rāma, of mighty arms, having eyes resembling lotuses, beside himself with grief, lamented (in many a way). Pierced with the shafts of Manmatha, Rāghava, as if beholding Sitā though he actually did not see her, uttered the following piteous accents—"O my dear, thou delightest greatly in flowers. Covering thy own person with *Asoka* twigs thou art increasing my grief. Thy thighs are like unto the trunks of plantain trees and thou hast hidden thyself behind the plantain grove. But I percieve thee, O fair one, thou art incapable of keeping thyself hidden. O auspicious one, thou hast entered smiling the *Karnikar* grove. No more with thy pastime, O dear one, leading to my death. Moreover it is not proper to sport in this way in a hermitage. I know it full well, O my dear, that thou art by nature fond of pastimes. But O thou of expansive eyes, this cottage lieth desolate, do thou come here. Evident it is that Sitā hath either been devoured by the Rākshasas or carried away by them, and therefore she doth not approach me, O Lakshmama, who am thus bewailing. These deer, O Lakshmana, with tearful eyes have been as if declaring that Sitā hath been devoured by the night-rangers. O chaste one, O thou of exquisitely fine hue, O worshipful madam, whither hast thou repaired ? O Sitā, truly hath the desire of Kaikeyi been fulfilled to-day. I came out with Sitā and shall return home without her. How shall I enter again that inner apartment void of Sitā ? Surely shall the people blame me as being cruel and destitute of energy. That I have no prowess hath already been manifested in the destruction of Sitā. When the king Janaka shall come to me after my return home from exile, to ask me of my welfare how shall I meet him ? And surely shall he be overwhelmed with grief on his daughter's account when he shall find me without Sitā. Blessed is my father since he is in heaven now. I shall not repair to that city protected by Bharata. Without her even the heaven itself appears to me as desolate. Do thou therefore repair to the city of Ayodhya leaving me in this forest. By no means shall I breathe without her. Embracing him warmly do thou tell Bharata, as instructed by me—'Rāma hath given thee permission to administer this kingdom.' As ordered by me do thou with proper respect salute all my mothers Kauçalya, Kaikeyi and Sumitrā and protect them all with great care and respectful compliments. O destroyer of foes, do thou relate at length unto my mother the story of Sitā's destruction." Rāma bewailing thus, being overwhelmed with grief on account of his separation from Sitā having a head of fine hair, Lakshmana became of pale countenance and was greatly distressed at heart.

## SECTION LXIII.

THAT son of a king, stricken as he was with grief consequent upon separation from his dear one, was again overwhelmed with a terrible grief after causing sorrow unto his brother. Sunk in the abyss of grief, Rāma, sighing hot and weeping piteously, spoke unto Lakshmana who was equally aggrieved, words worthy of being said on that occasion. "Methinks there is none other on this earth like me, the perpetrator of vicious crimes. My heart or soul is not riven though crushed again and again without respite with a multitude of doleful events. Surely did I perpetrate many a vicious deed in my previous birth, the fruit of which I do now suffer and in consequence whereof misfortune after misfortune hath befallen me. Coming within the compass of my remembrance, the loss of my kingdom, the death of my father, the separation of my mother and other kinsmen culminates my grief. Repairing unto woods, O Lakshmana, in Sitā's company my grief was assuaged, nay I did not suffer physical affliction even. Without Sitā these sorrows have grown anew like unto fire flaming again by means of fuel. Truly my wife, timid as she is, hath been carried away by a Rākshasa by the etherial track. Alas! doubtless it is, that one of pleasant accents, wept piteously out of fear many a time and oft. For certain my dear wife's breast round and sprinkled as it was with red sandal paste, was bathed in blood (while devoured by the Rākshasas)—but there is no death for me. That countenance the beauty of which was enhanced by a head of curly hair and which used to emit forth tender, soft and clear accents, hath become pale, being taken possession of by the Rākshasas like unto the Moon almost devoured by Rāhu. Surely have the Rākshasas subsisting on gore drunk her blood in the sky tearing off the neck of my dear one ever devoted to pious observances. Surely did that one of beautifully expansive eyes cry aloud poorly like unto a hind when she was drawn hither and thither by the Rākshasas encircling her in the forest in my absence. O Lakshmana, sitting at the foot of this hill with me that large-hearted, pious Sitā, of smiling countenance, used to address thee on many a topic. This is Godāvari the best of rivers, my dear wife took delight in her—has she gone there ?—But she never goes there alone. Or has Jānaki having eyes resembling lotus-petals hath gone to bring lotuses ? But how is that possible, she never goes without me to bring lotuses. Hath she entered at her pleasure this forest filled with many flowery trees and diverse birds ? But that is not possible too—she is timid and feareth much to enter alone in this forest. O Āditya, knowest thou the pious and vicious actions of men ; bearest thou testimony to the truth and untruth of their actions—do thou tell me, pray, who am striken with grief, whither hath my dear one repaired, or whether hath she been killed ? O Air, there is nothing on earth which is not within the compass of thy vision, do thou relate unto me whether Sitā preserving the fame of my ancestry, hath been killed or carried away or if she waiteth on the way." After Rāma had bewailed thus being beside himself with grief, Saumitri, ever treading the right path and not of poorly mind spoke words worthy of being said on that occasion.—"Do thou take heart renouncing thy grief and engage with energy in quest of Sitā. Persons of high energy are never exhausted on the earth even in the face of arduous works." The highly powerful Lakshmana having spoken thus being afflicted with grief, Rāma, the best of Raghu's descendants, did not consider that worth pondering over. Renouncing patience he again indulged in excessive grief.

---

## SECTION LXIV.

RAMA striken with grief spake unto Lakshmana the following piteous words saying, "O Lakshmana, do thou speedily repair to the river Godāvari and learn if Sitā hath gone there to fetch lotuses." Being thus addressed by Rāma, the quick-paced Lakshmana went to the pleasant stream Godāveri. Reconnoitering full well the river containing many a watering-place Lakshmana spake unto Rāma saying, "Searched have I all the watering-places but have found her nowhere—anon I cried aloud but she did not hear. I cannot trace whither hath Vaidehi of slender waist repaired ever assuaging our mental affliction." Hearing Lakshmana's words, Rāma, aggrieved and overwhelmed with sorrow repaired in person to the river Godāvari. Arriving there cried he "Where is Sitā ?" Neither did the world of creatures nor the river Godāvari apprise Rāma of Sitā's being carried away by the Lord of Rākshaśas worthy of being slain. Thinking of the terrible figure and monstrous actions of that vicious souled Rāvana, that river did not dare relate unto him anything about Sitā, albeit appointed by the creatures to relate the story concerning her and accosted by Rāma in piteous accents. Being thus disappointed by the river in beholding Sitā, Rāma racked with her separation spake unto Lakshmana saying, "O thou of auspicious looks, this river Godāvari doth give no reply. But, O Lakshmana, returning without her what shall I say unto Janaka and Vaidehi's mother ? Where hath that Vaidehi gone who used to assuage my grief who had been deprived of kingdom and living in this forest on wild fruits and vegetables ? Nights shall appear too long unto me, keeping late hours being deprived of my kinsmen and relatives and not beholding Vaidehi. I can range this

Mandâkini, this Janasthâna and this Prasrabana hill if I can find Sitâ there. Behold, O hero, the high deer have been casting their looks again and again at men ; methinks from their gestures, they intend speaking something unto me." Beholding them, Râghava, the best of men, looked at them and said in accents choked with vapour—"Where is Sitâ ?" Being thus addressed by that Lord of men the deer rose up all on a sudden and looked up to the sky facing the south and proceeded to the direction by which Maithili had been carried away. And moving by that way these deer eyed the Lord of men and again and again fixed their looks upon that way and earth and passed along emitting cries which was marked by Lakshmana. He marked with attention their movements and cries and spake unto his elder brother like one aggrieved saying—"Being accosted by thee with—'Where is Sitâ ?' these deer have stood up all on a sudden and have been pointing to the south and earth—let us therefore proceed in this direction—it may be that we shall either meet with that worshipful madam or find some momentos concerning her." Thereat Kâkutstha, gifted with supreme beauty, proceeded towards the south being followed by Lakshmana and casting his look upon the earth. While proceeding thus, conversing with each other the two brothers beheld some flowers scattered on the high-way.

Beholding a collection of flowers scattered on earth,Râma, exceedingly sorry, spake unto Lakshmana in piteous accents saying, 'O Lakshmana,I have come to know that these are the flowers of the forest I gave Vaidehi ; with these she decorated her hair. Me-thinks the sun, the air and the famed earth have preserved them for my well-being." Having spoken these words unto Lakshmana, the best of men, the virtuous-souled Râma, of mighty-arms, addressed the mountain in front of him containing many fountains, saying—"O thou the best of mountains, hast thou beheld in this picturesque forest-land, that exquisitely fine damsel racked with my separation ?" Exceedingly wroth he accosted the mountain like unto a lion addressing a little deer, saying "Show me my graceful Sitā hued like gold before I crush down thy summits." Being thus addressed by Rāma on Maithili's account the mountain did not show him Sitā. Again addressed him Rāma—"Thou shalt by the fire of my arrows, be reduced to ashes—thy twigs and leaves shall be totally destroyed and no one shall resort to thee. O Lakshmana, I shall dry up this river Godāvari if it telleth me not about Sita having a moon-like countenance." Rāma, exceedingly wroth, cast his looks around as if desiring to burn everything with his eyes and beheld footprints of the Rakshasas on the earth as well as those of Sitā moving wildly hither and thither, terrified and desirous to see Rāma, while pursued by the Rākshasas. Beholding these footmarks, the snapped bow, the quiver and the chariot broken into many pieces, Rāma, terrified spake unto his dear brother. "Behold O, Lakshmana, the remnants of Vaidehi's golden ornaments, strewn hither and thither, and diverse garlands. Behold O Saumitri, the earth covered with drops of blood resembling golden drops. Methinks, O Lakshmana, Vaidehi hath been devoured by the Rākshasas assuming shapes at will, having sundered her in pieces. O Saumitri, there took place a terrible conflict between the Rākshasas, fighting with each other on Sitā's account. O gentle one, whose is this snapped bow lying on the breast of the earth adorned and crested with pearls and diamonds ? O brother, this belongs either to the celestials or to the Rākshasas. Whose is this golden armour lying shattered on earth, resembling the newly risen sun, in color and adorned with sapphire ? Whose is this umbrella lying broken on earth, containing a hundred rod and adorned with celestial garlands ? In whose conflict have these terrible asses, of large proportions, having faces of demon and with breast plates, been killed ? Whose is this shattered war-car lying upset on the ground and broken flag resembling in lustre the burning gold? Whose are these terrible arrows feathered in gold, measuring four-hundred fingers, lying without blades on earth? Behold, O Lakshmana, these two quivers have been totally spoiled though filled with arrows. Whose charioteer is this who hath been killed with reins and lash in hands? These foot-marks must be some Rākshasa's. I made these Rākshasas my fatal enemies, assuming shapes at will and of crooked hearts. Poor Sitā must have been either dead, carried away by them or devoured. Virtue did not save her from being carried away in this mighty forest. O Lakshmana, while virtue did not protect Janaki being devoured or taken away by stealth, what person else gifted with heavenly power, on this earth shall bring about my well-being? For this it is that people through ignorance disregard the ever kind Almighty—the lord of creatures and the best of the celestials. Truly shall the celestials regard me as one devoid of prowess, who am mild-tempered, kind, ever engaged in the welfare of the humanity, and have controlled all my senses. Observe, O Lakshmana, obtaining me as the stay these accomplishments have been turned into so many blemishes. Truly shall my prowess manifest itself to-day overshadowing all my other accomplishments for the destruction of the Rākshasas and all created beings like unto the rising of the Sun casting the Moon into shade on the day of dissolution. None shall enjoy felicity, O Lakshmana,—Yakshas, Gandharbas, Piçachas, Rākshasas, Kinnaras, or human beings. To-day shall the welkin be filled up with my arrows. Motionless shall I make all the animals inhabiting the three worlds. I shall arrest the movement of the planets and overshadow the Moon. Stopping the course of the wind and destroying the rays of the Sun and fire I shall envelope the earth with darkness, crush down the summits of the mountains, dry up the pools, blow up the creepers, demolish the Ocean and erradicate the trees. If the celestials do not give me back my Sitā I shall bring about the dissolution of the three worlds which would else have been wrought by time. O son of Sumitrā, instantly shall the celestials headed by Indra, meet with my prowess, if they do not give back my Sitā, ever advancing my welfare. None shall be able to range the welkin. Behold O Lakshmana, being perpetually crushed down by my arrows shot off my bow, the world shall be disturbed and dislodged and the animals and birds shall be confused and destroyed. Stretching the bow to my ears I shall make the world, for Sitā's sake, void of *Pisâchas* and Rākshasas with my arrows incapable of being withstood by created beings. To-day shall the celestials behold the power of my arrows coursing a long distance shot through my ire. Three worlds destroyed on account of my wrath, celestials, Dānavas, Piçachas or Rākshasas,—none shall be saved. The dwellings of the celestials, Asuras, Yakshas and Rākshasas shall fall down sundered by my arrows into diverse pieces. I shall dislodge the whole world by my arrows. If the celestials do not give me back my Vaidehi dead or carried away or as she was before, I shall destroy the whole world mobile or immobile and disturb all with my arrows until I see her." Having spoken thus, Rāma, with his eyes reddened with ire and lips swollen, tying fast his bark and deer-skin, braided his matted locks. Having done this, being exceedingly wroth he looked like Rudra about to destroy Tripura. Thereat taking his bow from Lakshmana and holding it fast, the effulgent Rāma, the conqueror of foes, fixed flaming arrows to it like so many serpents and said being exercised with ire like unto fire on the eve of dissolution.—"O Lakshmana none shall be able to withstand me, who am inflamed with rage, as debility consequent on old age, death, time, duty are incapable of being averted from their destined ends by the animals. I shall bring about a mighty revolution in the world containing the celestials Gandharbas, human beings, Pannagas and the mountains, if I do not get back, in her pristine beauty, my Sitā, the daughter of the King of Mithilā."

## SECTION LXV.

RAMA highly aggrieved on account of Sitā's being carried away, addressing himself to destroy the world like unto the fire of dissolution and casting his look, sighing again and again, upon the stringed bow like unto Mahadev desirous of burning down the whole world at the time of dissolution, Lakshmana, having his countenance dried up, beholding his rage not seen before, began with folded hands—"Ere this thou hadst been gentle, self-controlled and engaged in the welfare of all beings. It doth not behove thee now to renounce thy natural temper being influenced by ire. Ever manifested itself in thee, glory *par excellence* like unto splendour in the Moon, lustre in the Sun, motion in the wind and forgiveness in the Earth. It becometh thee not to devastate the whole world for the crime of an individual being. Methinks for certain, this shattered car must be the property of an individual person, not of many. But I do not know whose is this car with yokes and dresses and what for it hath been shattered? Behold, O thou the son of a King, this terrible spot bathed in blood and raked with hoofs and wheels. Surely here took place a conflict. O thou the foremóst of those skilled in speech, it appeareth from these signs that this skrimish did take place with one, not with two. Here are not to be seen the foot-marks of a large army. It therefore doth not behove thee to destroy the whole world for one's individual offence. Kings, gentle and mild by nature, do always administer punishment,proportionate to the amount of offence. Thou art always the stay and the best refuge of all animals. Who shall think well, O Rāghava, of the destruction of thy wife? The celestials, Dānavas, Gandharbas, rivers, seas, and mountains—none can act unfriendly by thee as the learned priests cannot act improperly towards those initiated by them. It is thy duty, O king, with bow in hand to search out the person who hath carried away Sitā, along with me and the devotees. Explore shall we, with great care,the seas,the forest,the mountains, the fearful caves, the pools and the abodes of the celestials and Gandharbas until we find out the person who hath carried away thy wife. If the celestials do not return thee peacefully thy wife, O Lord of Koçala, thou shalt adopt measures, befitting the occasion. Thou shalt then uproot the whole world, O lord of men, with thy gold-feathered arrows resembling the thunderbolt of Mahendra, if thou dost not come by thy wife by resorting to good conduct, self-control, lowliness and polity."

## SECTION LXVI.

RAMA bewailing thus like one helpless being stricken with grief, overwhelmed with sorrow and losing control over himself, Lakshmana touched his feet and consoling him instantly began :—"By constant asceticism and manifold pious observances king Daçaratha obtained thee like unto the celestials obtaining ambrosia. As I have heard from Bharata, king Daçaratha died for thy separation, attached as he was unto thee for thy accomplishments. O Kākutstha, if dost thou not bear patiently this impending peril what little-minded person else shall bear it? Compose thyself, O thou best of men. Peril overtaketh everybody like unto fire but vanisheth in no time. This is the nature of men. Yayati, the son of king Nahusha, though attained to the state of celestials, was however thrown down for an iniquitous deed. The hundred sons, that had been born unto our ancestral priest Vasishtha, were all killed in one day. O lord of Koçala, even Vasumati, the mother of the world, adored of all beings, meeteth with misery consequent upon earth-quake. Even the mighty Sun and Moon witness eclipse who are the eyes of the world and the very images of virtue and in whom the whole world is stationed. O thou best of men, what of insignificant beings cased in this frail body, even the mighty creatures and celestials are subject to the influence of destiny. I have heard, O best of men, even the celestials headed by Indra are subject to happiness or misery. So it doth not behove thee to bewail thus. O descendant of Raghu, it becometh thee not to lament like an ordinary person even if Jânaki is dead or hath been carried away. O Râma, persons, highly experienced and ascertaining right or wrong without being moved, do not lament even in the face of mighty perils. O thou best of men, do thou, after due consideration, ascertain what is proper or improper; persons of thy vast wisdom are cognizant of the right or wrong by dint of their understanding. Without proper exercise, actions, of unknown merit and uncertain issue do not bear fruits. O hero, many a time and oft ere this, thou hadst given me the self-same counsel. Who is capable of counselling thee who art the very preceptor of the gods? O thou of great intellect even the celestials cannot measure thy mental acumen. Greatly benumbed is thy wisdom with the slumber of grief, and I am to rouse it. O thou the best of Ikshwâkus, do thou engage in the destruction of thy foes considering well thy celestial and human prowess. O thou best of men, what necessity hast thou to destroy the whole world? Do thou rescue Sitâ after finding out thy vicious enemy."

---

## SECTION LXVII.

After Lakshmana had spoken these highly sound and pleasant words, Rāma, ever taking to what is sound, accepted them. Thereupon that one, of mighty-arms, slaking his flaming ire and reclining himself upon his beautiful bow, addressed Lakshmana, saying, "Do thou ponder over, O brother, where shall we repair, what shall we do and by what means shall we come by Sitā ?" Whereto Lakshmana replied saying unto the highly aggrieved Rāma, "It is proper for thee to search this Janasthāna filled with a multitude of Rākshasas and covered with diverse trees and creepers. Here are many strongholds in the midst of mountains, clefts of rocks, many caves and numerous cavities filled with various animals. Many are the abodes here belonging to the Kinnaras and Gandharbas. Do thou, along with me, search all these places. Great men, of thy calibre, do remain unagitated even in the midst of difficulties like unto mountains never shaken by the velocity of the wind." Hearing these words, Rāma, enraged, fixing sharp and terrible arrows to his bow, began to range the forest with Lakshmana. Thereupon he beheld, fallen on ground, having his person bathed in blood, the king of birds—Yatāyu, resembling a mountain-peak, and spake unto Lakshmana, saying, "It is clear and beyond all doubt that Vaidehi hath been devoured by this Rākshasa, assuming the shape of a vulture and ranging the forest. This Rākshasa hath been reposing at ease after devouring that one of expansive eyes ; I shall kill him with terrible straight-coursing arrows, having flaming points." Fixing sharpened shafts to his bow, Rāma, enraged, darted towards the vulture, as if moving the sea-girt earth. Vomitting frothy blood Yatāyu, the king of vultures, spoke unto Rāma, the son of Daçaratha, saying, "O thou of long life, that goddess, whom thou hast been searching in this vast forest like unto *Oshadhi*, and my life have been carried away by Râvana. I saw her, O Râghava, carried away stealthily by the powerful Râvana, in thy absence as well as that of Lakshmana. Myself nearing Sitâ, for her rescue,O Lord,Râvana was thrown down on earth by me in conflict having his car and unbrella shattered. This is his snapped bow and these are his broken shafts. And this is his war-car, O Râma, shattered in fight. This is his charioteer lying on earth being killed by the velocity of my wings. Having sundered my wings with his dagger, who had been exhausted, Râvana taking Sitâ, rose high up in the welkin. It behoveth thee not to kill me who had been wounded before by the Râkshasa." Hearing from him pleasant words relating to Sitâ, Râma, leaving aside, instantly, his mighty bow, embraced him, and rolling on earth having lost self-control through grief, began to lament with Lakshmana. Though highly composed by nature, he was overwhelmed with doubled grief. And beholding Yatâyu, sigh again and again and breathing with difficulty in a helpless plight, Râma,highly aggrieved,spake unto Lakshmana saying, "I have lost my kingdom and have been living in this forest. My Sitâ hath been carried away and this bird hath been killed (on my account)—This misfortune of mine can burn even the very fire. If for assuaging my grief I do enter the mighty ocean, verily shall that misfortune dry up even that lord of rivers. There is none so unfortunate as I, throughout this earth, mobile or immobile, and it is for this bad luck that I have confronted this mighty disaster. This mighty king of vultures is our father's friend and he lieth on earth killed through the evil turn of my fortune." Uttering these and various other words, Râghava, along with Lakshmana touched his body manifesting his paternal affection. Embracing the king of vultures, bathed in blood, having its wings cut off, Râghava, fell on the ground, exclaiming 'where hath Maithili gone like unto my life?'

## SECTION LXVIII.

BEHOLDING Yatāyu fallen on the ground by the terrible Rākshasa, Rāma spoke unto Lakshmana, having compassion for all, saying "Verily for my service this bird hath breathed its last, being killed by the Rākshasa. O Lakshmana, its voice hath been enfeebled, its vision weakened and its life, greatly exhausted, lieth in a very little proportion in its body. May good betide thee, O Yatāyu ; if thou art capable of speaking again, do thou relate how Sitā hath been carried away and thou hast been killed. Why hath Rāvana taken away by stealth the worshipful Jānaki ? What offence did I commit by him that he hath carried away my dear one ? O thou best of birds, how looked the moon-like, pleasant countenance of Sitā at the time of her being carried away ? What did she speak then ? What is the prowess, appearance and action of that Rākshasa ? Where doth he live, O reverend Sir ? Pray tell me, I do ask thee." Beholding Rāma, lament like one helpless, the virtuous-souled Yatāyu spake in faltering accents—"Sitā hath been carried away by Rāvana, the lord of Rākshasas, creating a mighty illusion producing wind and showers. O darling, myself being worn out that night-ranger, having sundered my wings, fled away with Sitā to the southerly direction. O Rāghava, my life is about to expire, my eye-sight hath grown of mistaken perception, I see trees before me made of gold having hair resembling *Ushira.** Rāvana hath taken away Sita at a moment when a person regains soon his lost property. O Kakuthstha, this moment is called *Vindya,*† which Rāvana

* Andropogon muricatum—(Lat). The root of a fragrant grass. This alludes to a terrible vision which is generally seen by a person on the eve of death—a golden tree having hair.—T.

† This refers to *Yatāyu's* astrological knowledge. *Vindya* is derived from the root *Vid*—to gain. Thus this moment is favourable to the loser and un-

hath not been able to perceive. (At this moment) the person who taketh away (a thing) is soon destroyed like unto a fish devouring a hook. Do not therefore entertain the least doubt about thy coming by Jānaki. Destroying him at the head of the battle thou shalt soon sport with Vaidehi." Thereupon flesh and gore began to come out of the mouth of Yatāyu, the king of vultures, not loosing his sense even while treading the verge of death. Thereupon the king of birds gave up his dear life uttering only.—"Rāvana is the son of Vishravā and brother to Vaishravana (the lord of wealth)." Rāma again and again addressed him with joined palms saying, "Do thou speak! Do thou speak." And instantly Yatāyu's vital spark rose up in the sky, leaving his bodily frame. Thereupon the king of vultures fell down on the earth by stretching forth his legs, body and head on the ground. Beholding the vulture dead, of huge proportions, resembling a hill and having red eyes, Rāma, aggrieved, spoke piteously unto Saumitri, saying—"Living happily, for years, in this forest of Dandaka inhabited by the Rākshasas, Yatayu hath, at last, given up his life. He lived for a long time, of an uplifted person, and hath now laid low on the earth. None can withstand the course of destiny. Observe, O Lakshmana, this vulture for my benefaction, hath been killed by the powerful Rāvana in his attempt to rescue Sitā. For me, hath this lord of birds, breathed his last, renouncing his large ancestral kingdom. In every status of animal creation, the heroic, the righteous and the honest, affording refuge unto all, are to be found, even amongst the birds. I do not feel so much affliction, O hero, for Sitā's ravishment as I do for this vulture, who hath been killed for me. Like unto the highly famous, effulgent king Daçaratha, this King of birds is worthy of being adored and worshipped by me. O Saumitri, do thou bring fuels; I shall produce fire there-

---

favourable to the taker. Hence Ravana carrying away Sita at this moment shall meet with destruction.—T.

with and burn the dead body of this king of birds who hath been killed on my account. Placing on a funeral pile, I shall cremate, O Saumitri, the dead body of this king of birds who hath been destroyed by the grim-visaged Rākshasas. Being consecrated and commanded by me, do thou, O highly powerful king of birds, attain to that excellent state of existence, which is reached by persons ever performing pious observances, by *Ahitagnis** by heroes who are not afraid of entering a battle-field and by persons who confer grants of land." Saying this the virtuous-souled Rāma, afflicted with sorrow, burned the body of the king of birds, placing it on the funeral pile, like unto his own kinsman. Entering the forest with Saumitri, Rāma gifted with prowess, killed plump high deer and stretched forth grass and twigs for offering oblation to that bird. Taking off the flesh of those high deer and clustering it, Rāma, of great renown, offered it to the vultures in that pleasant forest-land, abounding in green grass. Thereupon for his speedy arrival at the abode of celestials, Rāma recited those *Mantras* which are being uttered by the twice-born ones. Afterwards repairing to the river Gadāveri the two princes offered water unto that kingly vulture. And offering water unto him according to the prescribed rites of the *Sastras*, those two descendants of Raghu, after bathing, performed the *Udaka*† ceremony for that king of vultures. Having been killed in battle for an arduous but glorious work, that king of vultures, consecrated by the ascetic-like Rāma, attained to an excellent state. Having performed the *Udaka* ceremony for that best of birds and considering him in the light of a father they went away and entered the forest in quest of Sitā like unto the two best of celestials—Visnu and Vāsava.

---

* A *Brāhmana* who has preserved a sacred fire kept alive perpetually in a family, &c.,—from *ahita*—placed, *agni*—fire.—T.

† Presentation of water specially to the manes as a religious or obsequal rite.—T.

## SECTION LXIX.

HAVING offered him the gift of water, those two descendants of Raghu wended their way in that forest in quest of Sitā and proceeded towards the south west.* Then turning to the south, with bow and arrows in hand, they reached a track not wended by the people. It was a ghastly, impenetrable forest, covered on all sides with groves, trees and creepers. Proceeding by the southerly direction, those two mighty ones, passed hastily by that terrible, dreary forest. Thereupon, the highly effulgent descendants of Raghu entered the dense forest of *Krauncha*, situated at a distance of six miles from *Janasthāna*. It was a dense forest like unto a collection of clouds, as if smiling on all sides blooming with charming flowers of diverse hues and frequented by various animals and birds. Waiting for sometime here and there they, exercised with Sitā's ravishment, explored the entire forest in quest of Vaidehi. Proceeding three *Krosas* towards the East and passing by the forest of *Krauncha* the two brothers described on their way the asylum of Mātanga. Having seen that dreary forest frequented by various animals and birds and covered with diverse trees and dense groves, the two sons of Daçaratha beheld a cave in the mountain, deep as the region under the earth and ever enveloped with darkness. Arriving there they espied hard by a grim-visaged Rākshasi, having a formidable figure, ever causing fright unto persons of feeble courage, loathesome, terrible looking, having a huge belly, sharpened teeth, a high person and rough skin, devouring voracious animals and looking fearful with dishevelled hair. Beholding there the two brothers, Rāma and Lakshmana, she neared the heroes and saying, 'come, we shall sport' assailed

* In this Sloka *west* is mentioned and in the next one there is reference to their turning to the *south* and hence *west* here refers to south-west.—T.

Lakshmana who had been going before his brother. And embracing him she spake unto Saumitri the following words :—"My name is Ayomukhee ; it is a great gain to thee that thou hast become my beloved one, O my lord. Do thou sport with me, for ever, O hero, in these mountainous strongholds and on the banks of the rivers." Thereat, exercised with ire, Lakshmana, the subduer of foes, uplifting his dagger, chopped off her nose, ears and breast. Having her nose and ears cut off, that terrible-looking Rākshasi, emitting fearful cries, fled away whence she had come. On her departure, proceeding quickly, the two brothers, Rāma and Lakshmana, the conquerors of foes, reached a dense forest. Thereupon the highly effulgent and truthful Lakshmana, possessing a pure character, spake, with folded hands, unto his brother of flaming energy—"My left arm is throbbing, my mind is filled with anxiety and I perceive before me many a bad omen. Do thou put on thy habiliments, O worshipful one, and act by what I say for thy well-being. Methinks from these bad omens some calamity shall soon befall us. O Rāma, this terrible bird *Banchulaka* is emiting fearful cries as if announcing our victory in the conflict." Thereupon while they began to explore the entire forest with their prowess there arose a terribe sound as if breaking down the wood. The forest was enveloped on all sides with a mighty wind and everywhere was audible a roar filling the wood-land. With a view to ascertain whence the sound proceeded, Rāma, with a dagger in hand, along with his yonger brother, espied a Rākshasha of huge proportions, having big thighs. The two brothers behold that Rākshasa stationed before them, having a huge body, devoid of head and neck and therefore a headless demon and having its mouth on its belly. Its body resembled a huge mountain and was covered with sharpened down ; its look was terrible like unto sable could and its roar resembled the muttering whereof. Its one terrible, expansive eye, seeing all, was on the forehead placed on its breast and shone forth like unto the flaming fire and it had huge yellow eye-lashes. Its mouth was greatly widened and covered with rows of huge teeth and it was again and again licking that terrible mouth. And stretching forth its two huge arms extending over a *yoyana* it was devouring bears, lions and deer. It was catching and throwing with its huge hands many an animal, bird and bear. Hindering the way-fare it was awaiting those two brothers. And proceeding a *Krosa*, they espied that fearful, grim-visaged, headless demon, hindering all creatures with its arms, terrible-looking and appearing like a *kavanda* from its very situation. Thereupon that one, of huge arms, stretching them forth, got hold of those two descendants of Raghu crushing them with its strength. Those two highly powerful brothers, of mighty-arms, with daggers and bows in their hands, were assailed and got hold of by that Rākshasa. Rāma was heroic and patient by nature and consequently was not much afflicted ; but Lakshmana was a mere boy and impatient by nature and was consequently greatly afflicted. Being greatly distressed, the younger brother of Rāghava spake unto him, saying "Do thou behold me, O hero, brought under the hold of this Rākshasa, and renouncing me only, O Rāghava, do thou get thyself off. And offering me as sacrifice, do thou escape at thy ease. Methinks for certain, O Kākutstha, thou shalt soon come by Vaidehi and regain thy anscestral kingdom. But remember me always, O Rāma when thou shalt fiind thyself placed on the throne." Being thus addressed by Lakshmana, Rāma, spake unto Saumitri—"Fear not in vain, O hero ; persons of thy prowess are never afflicted (with fear)." Meanwhile the wicked headless, demon, of huge arms, the foremost of Dānavas, addressed the two brothers Rāma and Lakshmana —"Who are ye two youthful figures having the neck of a bull and with mighty daggers and bows in your hands ? Arriving in this fearful place ye have by chance come within the compass of my vision. Tell me now what have ye to do here, and what for have ye come? I have been waiting here being hungry, and ye have come here having daggers and bows with arrows in your hands like unto two oxen having sharpened horns. Nearing me quickly, it will be hard for ye to draw your vital breath." Hearing those words of the vicious-souled *Kavandha*, Rāma having his countenance dried up, bespake Lakshmana,—"O thou, having truth for thy prowess, again and again, greater and worse calamities have been threatening us. We have already met with a dire disaster leading to our death, consequent on my separation from my dear one. Mighty is the course of Destiny in all creatures, O Lakshmana. Do thou O best of men, behold even thyself and me stricken with calamity. But O Lakshmana it is not very difficult for destiny to afflict all creatures. Under the influence of destiny even the mighty heroes, well habited in armours are distressed like unto a bridge of sands." Addressing these words unto Saumitri, the resolute, powerful and highly famous son of Daçaratha, having truth for his prowess, composed himself by dint of his own understanding.

## SECTION LXX.

BEHOLDING both the brothers, Rāma and Lakshaman, clasping each other with their arms, the headless demon spake:—"O two best of Kshatryas, are ye waiting here beholding me hungry? O ye having lost your sense, ye have been chosen by Destiny as my food." Hearing those words Lakshmana, sore distressed and determined to display his valour, addressed Rāma with words worthy of being said on that occasion. "This vile Rākshasa shall seize both of us; let us sunder soon its two huge arms with our daggers.

This grim-visaged Rākshasa, of huge proportions, gifted only with the strength of arms, defeating all other persons, hath addressed itself at last to destroy us. It is odious for the Kshatryas to make away with those who cannot defend themselves like unto animals brought for sacrifice."* Hearing their conversation, the Rākshasa, inflamed with rage, widening its terrible mouth, prepared to devour them up.† Thereat Rāma and Lakshmana, cognizant of time and place, pleased,‡ sundered its arms off its shoulders with their daggers. Rāma, stationed on the right side§ cut off in no time its right arm with his dagger and the heroic Lakshmana, the left one. Having got its arms dissevered, the terrible-voiced, *Kavandha*, of huge arms, roaring like unto the muttering of clouds and resounding the heaven earth and all the quarters, fell flat on the ground. Beholding both its arms cut off, the demon, with its person bathed in blood, asked them poorly—"Who are ye ?" Being thus accosted by *Kavandha*, the mighty Lakshmana, gifted with auspicious marks, spake unto it, about Kākutstha. "He is a descendant of the Ikshwakus known on earth by the name of Rāma, and know me as his younger brother, by name—Lakshmana. Being thwarted by mother (Kaikeyi) in his accession of kingdom, he, renouncing all, hath fled as an exile unto woods, and hath, along with me and his spouse, been ranging this forest. While living in the dense forest the wife of Rāma, effulgent like unto the celestials hath been ravished by a Rākshasa. Searching her, have we come here. Who art

---

* The purport is:—"Lakshmana wanted to chop off the arms of *Kavandha* and not to put an end to its life as it was not capable of fighting, being a headless demon. And it is not proper for the Kshatryas to destroy those who cannot fight.—T.

† This has a special significance here—meaning to get hold of them by stretching forth its arms.—T.

‡ They were pleased because they cut off its arms with ease like unto the trunk of a plantain tree.—T.

§ It may mean also *expert*.—*T*.

thou? And what for art thou ranging this forest like unto a headless demon, having thy thighs broken and thy flaming face placed on thy breast?" Being thus addressed by Lakshmana with these goodly words, *Kavandha*, pleased, recollecting the words of Indra, bespake him,—"O two best of men, ye are welcome! By my good luck it is that I do behold you. By my good fortune ye have dissevered my shoulders to-day. Do ye hear, I shall relate truly unto you how have I, by my haughtiness,come by this unsightly shape."

## SECTION LXXI.

"O MIGHTY-ARMED Rāma of great prowess, formerly my beauty, beyond conception, was known all over the three worlds, like unto the beauty of the Sun, the Moon and Indra. I used to frighten everywhere the ascetics living in the forest by turning this my beauty into a terrific form. Once on a time assuming this terrible shape I assailed and enraged the great ascetic *Sthulashira* collecting diverse wild fruits. Thereupon he imprecated curses upon me, saying, "Do thou retain this ghastly shape hated of all mankind." Upon my praying unto that angry ascetic for my relief from that curse, he said—"Thou shalt regain thy stalwart and beautiful shape when thou shalt be burnt by Rāma in a dense forest having got thy arms disevered by him. O Lakshmana, know me to be the beautiful son of Danu. Through Indra's curse in the battle field I have been metamorphosed into my present shape. After I had pleased him with hard austerities, the Grand-Father of the celestials conferred on me a long life.And therefore I was inflamed with pride and assailed Indra in a conflict, thinking within me, 'I have gained a long life—what can Indra do me?' Thereupon by his thunder-bolt, having hundred edges, hurled off his hands, my thighs were shattered and my head thrusted into my body. Myself praying for the close of my life, he did not despatch me to the abode of Yama. He only said, "May the words of the Grand-Sire prove true." Whereto I replied 'How shall I live long without any food, being smitten by thee having a thunder-bolt in thy hand,and having my head, thighs and mouth crushed down ?' Thereat Indra made my hands extending over a *yoyana* and placed my mouth, having sharpened teeth, on my belly. Thenceforth, stretching out my long arms I used to devour all lions, tigers, wolves and deer ranging the forest. Indra said to me, 'Thou shalt attain to heaven when Rāma, along with Lakshmana, shall cut off thy arms in a battle.' Acting under the conviction that Rāma, resolved to destroy my person, shall surely come within the compass of my arms, I do always assail with relish, O worshipful one, O thou best of kings, every animal I meet with in this forest. Thou art that Rāma. May good betide thee, O Rāghava. Verily did the great ascetic speak unto me that none should be able to assail me but Rāma. Being cremated by you, I shall counsel you best and tell you with whom you should contract friendship." Being thus addressed by Danu, the virtuous-souled Rāghava spake before listening Lakshmana, "My renowned spouse Sitā was easily ravished by Rāvana after I had gone out of Janasthāna along with my brother. I know that Rākshasa's name only—but do not know his whereabouts, his figure and his prowess. It behoveth thee to show proper compassion for us, who have been stricken with grief, who are helpless, have been ranging this forest in this way and are ever engaged in the well being of others.* O, hero, we shall burn thee after collecting all the

* This Sloka may be rendered in another way :—Do thou continue benifitting us by showing proper compassion for us, who are stricken with grief helpless and ranging the forest in this way. We have however adopted here the commentator Rāmanuya's explanation.—T.

branches that have been broken down by the elephants and dried up in time, and digging a big trench. Do thou tell us who hath carried away Sitā ? And where ? If dost thou know it truly do thou perform us this good service." Thereat the Rākshasa, skilled in speech, spake unto Raghava, addressing him thus—"I am not gifted with divine fore-sight and therefore do not know where Maithilee is. I shall let you know of him who shall be able to tell you all about her, after I resume my original shape, being burnt (by thee). I shall furthermore tell thee, O Rāma, who knows that Rākshasa. Without being burnt I am incapable of being cognizant of that highly powerful Rākshasa who hath carried away thy Sitā. By the influence of curse, I have lost my fore-sight and by my own improper actions I have been transformed into this ugly figure. Do thou cremate me according to the prescribed rites after throwing me into the ditch before the sun, with his worn out carriers descends into the western horizon. Being burnt by thee in the ditch, with due ceremonials, O descendant of Raghu, I shall mention, unto thee, one who knows that Rākshasa. O Rāghava, O fleet-footed hero, do thou contract friendship with him gifted with good qualities and he shall assist thee. There is nothing unknown to him, O Rāghava in the three worlds. Formerly for some reasons he had travelled all over them."

---

## SECTION LXXII.

AFTER *Kavandha* had spoken thus, the two best of men, Rāma and Lakshmana took him to a mountain-cave and placed on fire. Lakshmana kindled the funeral pile, which was ablaze on all sides. Thereupon the fire began to burn down slowly the huge and corpulent body of

*Kavandha* like unto a lump of clarified butter. Afterwards the highly powerful demon, shaking the funeral pile, rose up quickly like a smokeless flame of fire, wearing a clean cloth and a celestial garland. And the graceful demon, wearing an unsullied cloth and having all its limbs crested with diverse ornaments, rose from the pile high up in the welkin with a delighted heart. Thereupon mounting on a famed car, brilliant and drawn by swans* and lighting up all the quarters with the effulgence of his person, that highly powerful one, stationing himself in the heaven, addressed Rāma, saying:—"Do thou hear truly, O Rāghava, of the means by which thou shalt come by Sitā. There are six expedients.† O Rāma, by virtue of which kings acquire all objects. He, in whom misfortune hath culminated, should seek the company of one such.‡ Thou hast, O Rāma along with Lakshmana, met with the culmination of misfortune and for which thou hast been assailed with such a disaster as the ravishment of thy spouse. O thou best of my friends, it behoveth thee, therefore to make friends with such a person. Or else I do not find any means for thy success. Do thou hear, O Rāma, what I relate. There liveth with four monkeys a heroic, self-controlled monkey by name Sugriva, on that best of mountains *Rishyamuka,* situated on the banks of the lake Pampa, being driven by his enraged brother Vāli, the son of Indra. That mighty, powerful effulgent lord of monkeys, of immeasurable prowess and truthful vows, humble, patient, intelligent, great, expert, bold, graceful

* By virtue of the pious observances preformed by him in his previous existence and for his being burnt by Rama that celestial car appeared there.—T.

† The six expedients are as follow—(1) *Sandhi*, peace. (2) *Vigraha* war-fare. (3) *Yána*, military expedition against an enemy. (4) *Ashana*—halting. (5) *Daidhibhava*—sowing dissension. (6) *Samashraya* seeking protection.—T.

‡ This is a moral law referring to the sixth expedient, to be resorted to by the kings—namely *Samashrarya* or seeking protection.—T.

and puissant, hath been banished by his brother, O hero, for kingdom. Surely he shall be friend and assist thee in thy search for Sitā. Do thou not plunge thy soul in grief. O thou best of Ikshwakus, none can withstand destiny on this earth, truly unavoidable is its course. Do thou proceed soon, O hero, to Sugriva of mighty prowess, and repairing hence even to-day do thou contract friendship with him, taking vow in the presence of flaming fire* that ye shall not envy each other. Despise not that kingly monkey Sugriva, because he is grateful, capable of assuming shapes at will, seeking protection and powerful. Ye too are able to accomplish his wished-for object. Benefitted by thee or not, he shall engage in thy service. He was begotten of the Sun unto the wife of *Riksharaja*. He hath been roaming the bank of Pampā being in constant fear of Vāli after creating enmity with him. Do thou make friends with that monkey ranging the wood and and inhabiting the Rishyamuka mountain after placing thy weapon in the very presence of fire as a witness, because that best of monkeys knoweth minutely all the abodes of Rākshasas, living on human flesh. There is no place under the sun of many rays, O Rāghava, O slayer of foes, unknown to him. Exploring, with all his monkeys, the rivers, huge mountains, strongholds and caves, he shall learn about thy spouse. He shall search that exquisitely fine damsel Maithili in Rāvana's abode, bewailing on thy separation ; and to find her out he shall despatch, O Rāghava, many a monkey of huge proportions to various quarters. Whether on the summit of the mount Meru or in the region under the earth, that lord of monkeys, shall give thee back thy blameless spouse, killing all the Rākshasas."

* This refers to the oriental custom of performing every sacred rite in the presence of fire as witness. The Hindus regard the fire with sacred reverence and for this in all their social and religious ceremonials fire plays a very prominent and sacred part.—T.

## SECTION LXXIII.

HAVING pointed out unto Râma the expedient for finding out Sitâ the wise *Kavandha* began with the following significant words:—"This is the way, O Râma, leading to the mount Rishyamuka, where stand, beautifying the West, the *Jambu,*[a] *Priâla,*[b] *Panaca,*[c] *Nagrodha,*[d] *Plaksha,*[e] *Tinduka.*[f] *Ashathya,*[g] *Karnikâr,*[h] *Chuta,*[i] *Nâga,*[j] *Tilaka,*[k] *Naktamal,*[l] *Neelashok,*[m] *Cadamva.*[n] *Karavira,*[o] *Agnimukhya,*[p] *Asoka, Raktachandan,*[q] *Pâribhadraka,*[r] and many other trees. Ascending those trees or lowering them by force on earth, do thou proceed living on those fruits like unto ambrosia. Passing by this forest, O Kâkutstha, thou shalt reach another abounding in trees blooming with flowers like unto the garden of celestials and *Uttarkuru* where in all the months of the year the trees produce fruits and honey and where all the seasons dwell as in the forest

a—A fruit-tree, the rose apple—*Lat.* (*Eugenia Jambolana*).—T.

b—A tree commonly *Piyal*—*Lat.* (*Buchanania latifolia*).—T.

c—The bread fruit of *Jaka* tree—*Lat.* (*Artocarpus integrifolia*).—T.

d—The Indian fig-tree—*Lat.* (*Ficus Indica*).—T.

e—Waved leaf fig-tree—*Lat.* (*Ficus infectoria*).—T.

f—A sort of ebony—*Lat.* (*Diospyros glutinosa*).—T.

g—A holy fig-tree—Lat. (*Ficus religiosa*).—T.

h—The name of a tree commonly *Kaniyar*—*Lat.* (*Pterospermum acerifolium*).—T.

i—The mango—*Lat.* (*Mangifera Indica*).—T.

j—A small tree—*Lat.* (*Mesua ferrea*).—T.

k—A kind of tree commonly *Tila.*—T.

l—A tree—*Lat.* (*Galedupaarborea, Rox*).—T.

m—Blue *Asoka*—*Lat.* (*Jonesia Asock*).—T.

n—A plant commonly *Kadamva*—*Lat.* (*Nauclea Kadamba*).—T.

o—A fragrant plant *Lat.*—(*Oleander or Nerium Odorum*).—T.

p—The marking nut plant—*Lat.* (*Semecarpius anacardium*).—T.

q—Red Sandal.—T.

r—The coral tree—*Lat.* (*Erythrina fulgens*).—T.

of *Chitraratha*.* There stand beautifully many a tree lowered down with the burden of fruits, containing towering branches, dense as a collection of clouds or a mountain. Ascending those trees and lowering them, Lakshmana shall offer thee, fruits like unto ambrosia. O heroes, ranging from forest to forest, from high mountains to hillocks, ye shall get at the lake Pampā, void of gravels and acquatic plants and hence there is no danger of falling down to the people, having level watering-places, covered with sands and blooming with red and white lotuses. There emit forth musical notes, swans, frogs, cranes and ospreys sporting in the lake Pampā. They are not filled with terror in view of human beings, inexperienced as they are in the matter of destruction. O Rāghava, do ye fare on those plump birds like unto a lump of clarified butter and diverse fishes such as *Rohita*,† *Chakratunda*,‡ and *Nala*.§ O Rāma, the devoted Lakshmana, shall offer unto thee, various other best fishes, devoid of scale and fins, plump, filled with bones, having destroyed them with shafts and roasted them in fire. And after thou hadst feasted on them, Lakshmana shall bring thee water for drinking on a lotus leaf, smelling like a lotus, coming in contact with flowers, delicious, pleasantly cold, wholesome, void of impurities, transparent like silver and crystal. And while roaming in the evening he shall point out unto thee fat monkeys ranging in the wood and lying in the hollows of mountains. And thou too, O best of men, shalt behold those fat monkeys, who had drunk water, roaring like unto oxen appearing on the banks of a river to drink water. And rambling in the evening, thou shalt assuage thy grief beholding the pleasant water of Pampā and blossoming

* The garden of the deity *Kuvera*. It is derived from *Chitraratha*—a *Gandharba* in charge of the garden.

† The *Rohi* fish—Lat. *(cyprinus Rohita Ham)*.—*T*.

‡ A kind of fish resembling a wheel in appearance.—T.

§ A kind of sprat, according to some, a shrimp or prawn.—T.

trees. There, O Rāghava, the *Tilakas* and *Naktamalakas*, crested with flowers and full blown white and red lotuses shall mitigate thy sorrows. There liveth no person who wears garlands of those flowers. Garlands strung with those flowers never wither away, O Rāghava, because the disciples of the great ascetic Mātanga lived there with concentrated hearts. Drops of perspiration, falling on the earth from the persons of those ascetics worn out with the burden of the wild fruits collected by them for their spiritual guide, have been transformed by virtue of their asceticism unto these garlands. These garlands do never wither, O Rāghava, because of their origination from those drops of perspiration. Even at the present day, O Kākutstha, there liveth an immortal mendicant woman, by name *Savari*, who had waited in attendance upon those departed ones. Beholding thee, O Rāma, who art adored of all creatures like unto the Deity Himself, that mendicant woman, ever engaged in pious observances, shall attain to the abode of celestials. O Rāma, turning to the western bank of Pampā, thou shalt, O Kākutstha, behold the incomparable and secret asylum of Mātanga. Fearing the divine authority of that great ascetic Mātanga, the elephants, though there are many, dare not cross the threshold of his asylum. O Rāghava, this forest is widely known as Mātanga. wood. Thou shalt sport, O Rāma, with a delighted heart in that forest resembling the celestial garden—*Nandana* and filled with various birds. There stands in front of Pampā the highly inaccessible mount *Rishyamuka*, ornamented with many a blossoming tree and guarded on all sides by little serpents. That mount is highly munificent. It was created by Brahmā in the days of yore. A person, sleeping on the summit of that hill and dreaming of an accession of wealth, really gets at it after the dream is over. A perpetrator of iniquitous deeds and engaged in impious observances ascending that hill, the Rākshasas seize upon him, asleep, and bruise him. Thou shalt hear the terrible roar of the young elephants ranging in the asylum of Mātanga, situated on the banks of Pampā. Thou shalt furthermore observe many a quickly moving, infuriated elephant, resembling clouds in hue and with red temporal juice oozing out of their heads, roaming here and there sometimes separately and again in a band. Those mighty elephants, roaming the forest, return to their woody homes, drinking the pleasant, pure and sweet smelling water of Pampā. And do thou assuage thy grief, beholding there the bears, wolves and *Rurus* of a tender countenance like unto sapphire, who are harmless and never afraid of human beings. There is a huge cave, O Rāma, in that mountain, covered on all sides with rocks and where it is very hard to enter At the entrance of that cave lies a beautiful, wide lake of cool water, hedged on all sides with trees abounding in fruits. There liveth with other monkeys the virtuous souled *Sugriva*, who sometimes resideth on the summit of the hill." Having thus addressed Rāma and Lakshmana, *Kavandha*, highly powerful resembling the sun in effulgence and wearing garlands appeared beautiful in the sky. Thereupon Rāma and Lakshmana, preparing to proceed spoke unto that great one stationed in the sky, saying, "Do thou go." Whereto *Kavandha* replied, saying "Do ye proceed to make good your end" and bidding them adieu, who were well pleased, departed. Regaining his pristine beauty and shining in grace and effulgence that *Kavandha*, who was in the sky, fixing his looks upon Rāma, and pointing out unto him his way, said "Do thou make friends with (Sugriva)."

## SECTION LXXIV.

THEREUPON Rāma and Lakshmana, sons of a kingly father, passing along the way, pointed out by *Kavandha*, leading to the lake Pampā, proceeded towards the West. They wending their way desirous of seeing Sugriva, there came within the compass of their vision many trees, grown on the summits of the mountains, blossoming with flowers and abounding in fruits tasting sweet like unto honey. Passing the night on the summit of a hill those two descendants of Rāghu arrived at the western bank of Pampā and espied the pleasant asylum of *Savari*. Getting at that charming hermitage covered on all sides with trees and castiug their looks around they beheld that female mendicant—*Savari*. No sooner had that one of perfect asceticism beheld those highly intelligent Rāma and Lakshmana than she rose up with folded hands and touching their feet offered them duly water for washing their feet and mouth. Thereupon Rāma spake unto that female ascetic, engaged in religious services, saying, "O thou of sweet accents, hast thou got all hindrances to asceticism removed ? Is thy asceticism growing stronger every day ? O thou having asceticism for thy wealth, hast thou restricted thy anger and fare ? Hast thou observed the commandments and attained to mental felicity ? Hast thy attendance upon thy spiritual guide borne fruits ?" Being thus accosted by Rāma that old *Savari*, of accomplished asceticism and recognised by the *Sidhas*, approaching Rāma spake :—"Favoured with thy presence my asceticism hath attained to its consummation. Blessed is my birth, fruitful is my service unto my spiritual guides and accomplished is my asceticism. O best of men, thou art the foremost of celestials ; worshipping thee I attain to the abode of deities. O gentle one, O slayer of foes, O thou that dost confer honors on men, thyself casting thy auspicious looks upon me, consecrated I, by thy favour, shall attain to the imperishable land of celestials. On thy setting foot on the mount *Chitrakuta*, the ascetics whom I served, ascending celestial cars of incomparable lustre, departed to heaven. Those great ascetics, cognizant of virtue, said to me, 'Rāma shall come to thy holy asylum. Do thou receive with great reverence that guest together with Lakshmana. On beholding him, thou shalt attain to that best land of the celestials whence none returneth.' O best of men, I was thus told by those great ascetics, and for thee I have collected various wild fruits growing on the banks of Pampā. Being thus addressed by *Savari*, the virtuous-souled Rāghava spake unto her conversant with the knowledge of past and future, saying, "I have heard from Danu, in truth, about thy divine authority as well as that of thy spiritual guides. If thou purposest so I wish to witness it with my own eyes." Hearing those accents dropping from Rāma's lips, *Savari* showing unto them the vast forest said, "Do thou behold, O Rāghava, this forest, crowded with deer and birds resembling a dense cloud. This forest is known as Mātanga's wood. Here in this forest the pure-souled preceptors sacrificed unto fire their persons consecrated by the *Mantras* as Mantra itself. This is that altar *Pratyaksthali*, ascending which my worshipful preceptors used to offer flowers unto the deities with hands trembling with toil. Behold, O best of Raghus, this altar of incomparable beauty, by virtue of their asceticism, hath been still shedding its lustre on all the sides. Behold, again, the seven seas have appeared here in conjunction, at their very thought, worn out with fasts and therefore incapable of moving on. Even those barks, which they used to place on these trees after ablution have not yet been dried up. These flowers, of blue colour which they offered unto the deities, being engaged in divine services, have not yet been withered away. Thou hast observed this entire forest and heard every thing worth hearing. I purpose now to renounce my body being commanded by thee. I wish to approach those pure-souled ascetics, whom I used to wait upon, and whom these asylums belong to. Hearing with Lakshmana the speech of that pious one, Rāma gained an excess of joy and exclaiming, "Wonderful it is!" again spake unto *Savari* of keen austerities,—"O gentle one, I have been worshipped by thee. Do thou repair at thy ease and pleasure." Being thus addressed and ordered by Rāma, *Savari*, wearing matted locks, rags and the skin of an antelope, surrendered herself unto fire and rose high up in the welkin like unto blazing fire. Adorned with celestial ornaments, wreathed with celestial garlands, sprinkled with sandal-paste and wearing celestial cloth she appeared of exqisite grace and lighted up the quarters like unto lightning. By virtue of her devout meditation, *Savari* repaired to that holy region where dwelt her spiritual preceptors—the pure-hearted ascetics.

---

## SECTION LXXV.

AFTER Savari had repaired unto heaven by virtue of her divine prowess, Rāma with his brother Lakshmana began to ponder over the pious influence of those great ascetics. Thinking within himself about the divine authority of those great ones, the virtuous-souled Rāma spake unto Lakshmana, devoted and ever engaged in his well-being.—"Beheld have I, O gentle one, the wondrous asylum of the pure-souled ascetics filled with diverse birds and tigers rambling friendly with antelopes. O Lakshmana, we have performed ablutions in the sacred waters of these seven seas and offered oblations unto our manes Our misfortunes have ended and prosperity hath appeared and my mind is now filled with ecstacy of delight. Methinks, O best of men, auspiciousness shall soon appear unto us ; do thou come, therefore, we shall proceed towards the picturesque lake Pampā. Yon appeareth in view, at no distance, the mount Rishyamuka. Here dwells with four monkeys, the virtuous souled Sugriva—Suryya's son, in constant fear of Vāli. I am in a hurry to behold Sugriva the best of monkeys, for my business—Sitā's quest—is entirely at his hands."Unto the heroic Rāma, speaking thus, Saumitri said,—"Let us depart soon, I am in haste too." Issuing out of Mātanga's asylum, the mighty Rāma, lord of men, repaired with Lakshmana to the lake Pampā. Exercised with grief, he arrived at the bank of that best of lakes, beholding (as he passed along), various trees and pools, the mighty forest covered on all sides with huge trees and flowers and resounding with the noise of lapwings, peacocks, woodpeckers and various other birds and rattling of the bamboos. Beholding, from distance, Pampā of sweet, cool and pure water, Rāma performed ablution at the *Mâtanga sara* (a portion of Pampā) and paced slowly towards the lake. Thereupon Daçaratha's son, stricken with grief, bathed in Pampā covered with lotuses. It was adorned on all sides with *Tilakas*, *Asokas*, *Punnagas*, *Uddalas* and *Vakulas*. It was a lake girt on all sides with picturesque gardens, having its waters undulating beautifully and transparent like unto crystal, and covered all around with soft sands. It was filled with fish and tortoise, adorned with trees on its banks, encircled with creepers embracing her like companions and frequented *Gandharbas*, *Kinnaras*, serpents, *Yakshas* and Rākshasas. It was covered with trees and creepers of various kind, of cool water, and enveloped with beauty. It was, somewhere, of red hue, in contact with water lillies, somewhere white with *kumudas*, somewhere blue with blue lotuses like unto a blanket of diverse hues. It was filled with white and red lotuses and encircled with blossoming mangoe groves and resounding with the music of the peacocks. Beholding

Pampā, ornamented like a damsel with *Tilakas*, *Bijapuras*,(a) fig-trees, *Sukladrumas*,(b) flowery *Karavis*, blossoming *Punnagas*, groves of *Mâlati*(c) *and Kunda*,(d) *Vandhiras*,(e) *Nichulas*,(f) *Asokas*, *Saptaparuas*,(g) *Ketakas*,(h) *Atimuktas*,(i) and various others trees, Rāma the mighty son of Daçaratha began to lament with Lakshmana. "There stands on its bank the mount Rishyamuka, abounding in various metals and covered with trees of variegated flowers as mentioned before (by *Kavandha*). There dwelleth the famous lord of monkeys, Sugriva, the heroic son of the great Rikshyaraja. O best of men, do thou approach the chief of monkeys." Rāma, having truth for his prowess, again spake unto Lakshmana, saying, "O Lakshmana, how shall I live without Sitā, who have been deprived of my kingdom, who am poorly and have Sitā for my life?" Having said this unto Lakshmana, who had nothing else in view, that best of Raghus, racked with sorrow and grief and oppressed by Cupid, entered the lake Pampā graced with lotuses. Proceeding slowly, observing the forest, Rāma beheld and entered with Lakshmana Pampā, girt on all sides with beautiful woods and filled with a multitude of diverse birds.

---

*a*—Common citron—*Lat. (Citrus-medica)*.—T.

*b*—*Lat. (Symplocos racemosa)*.—T.

*c*—Great-flowered Jasmine—*Lat.* (*Jasminum Grandiflorum*).—T.

*d*—A kind of Jasmine—*Lat.* (*J. Multiflorum*).—T.

*e*—*Lat.* (*Memisa Sirisha*).—*T.*

*f*—*Lat.* (*Barringtonia Açutangula*).—*T.*

*g*—*Lat.* (*Alstonia-Scholaris*).—*T.*

*h*—(*Pandanus Odoratissiumus*).—*T.*

*i*—*Lat.* (*Gaertnera Racemosa*).—*T.*

END OF THE ARANYAKANDAM.

THE

# RAMAYANA.

TRANSLATED INTO ENGLISH PROSE FROM THE ORIGINAL SANSKRIT OF VALMIKI.

## YUDDHA KĀNDAM.

*EDITED AND PUBLISED BY*

**MANMATHA NATH DUTT, M. A.**

*Rector, Keshub Academy.*

PRINTED BY

GIRISH CHANDRA CHACKRAVARTI,

DEVA PRESS, 65/2. BEADON STREET,

CALCUTTA.

1893.

# YUDDHAKĀNDAM.

## SECTION I.

HEARING the words of Hanumān rehearsed properly, Rāma, exceedingly delighted, said,—"By Hanumān hath been performed a very great deed, rare on earth, and one incapable of being even conceived by any other in the world. Save Garuda and the Wind-god, and save also Hanumān, him find I not who crosseth the wide ocean. Entering by main force the city of Lankā, incapable of being subjugated by the gods and Danavas and Yakshas, the Gandharbas, serpents or Rakhas, and well protected by Rāvana,—who, living, cometh out (of it)? And who that is not the compeer of Hanumān in strength and prowess, even entereth into (Lankā), hard to subdue, and carefully guarded by the Rākshasas? And having so put forth his strength commensurate with his prowess, Hanumān hath also performed a great act befitting a servant on behalf of Sugriva.* That servant who, being entrusted with a hard task,—after having accomplished it, doeth another work in pursuance of (the prescribed business), is the best of men. That servant is middling, who, deputed to any task,† doth not, albeit capable, perform any other work which may be dear to the

* Having seen Sitâ—which was all that he had been commissioned to do by Sugriva, Hanumán has destroyed Râkshasas and burnt Lanká; and this he did of himself like a good servant.—T.

† i. e. *performing the entrusted work.—T.*

king. And that servant who, entrusted with any work of the king, doth not, although competent, heedfully accomplish the same, hath been called the worst. Anent the order (which he had received), Hanumān hath done the work (and more). He hath not been humbled,*—and, further, he hath pleased Sugriva. And by seeing Vaidehi, (Hanumān) hath, while reaping righteousness, saved me, the Raghu race, and the highly powerful Lakshmana. And this paineth my mind sore, that I cannot do a like benefit, returning this dear office of his. Embrace expresseth the all (of the Deity),† and, finding this occasion, I extend my embrace unto the high-souled Hanumān." Having said this, Rāma, with his down standing on end in joy, embraced the self-controlled Hanumān, who was present after having finished his speech. Then reflecting for a while, the best of the Raghus again spoke in the presence of Sugriva, lord of monkeys,—"Complete success hath been attained anent the search of Sitā. But when I think of the ocean, my mind is again sunk in dejection. How can the assembled monkeys go over to the southern shore of the vasty deep, difficult to cross? This tidings thou hast related unto me touching Vadehi; but what are the monkeys to do next about crossing the sea?" Having said this unto Hanumān, that slayer of foes, the mighty-armed Rāma, agitated by anxiety, was then plunged in thought.

---

* *By the Rákshasas.—T.*

† The commentator explains this obscure passage after his own orthodox fashion. The gist is this. Delight is the essence of the Deity, and all His incernations body forth this. Embrace is typical of this emotion.—T.

## SECTION II.

THEN the graceful Sugriva spake words capable of soothing sorrow, unto Daçaratha's son, Rāma, who was wrought up with grief,—"Why, O hero, dost thou grieve, like one that is base? Let not this be so. Chase away thy grief, even as an ingrate resigneth amity. Nor, O Rāghava, when the whe eabouts of Sitā hath been discovered, and when too the abode itself of the foe hath been known, do I perceive the reason of thy sorrow. Thou, O Rāghava, art intelligent, conversant with learning, wise, and judicious. Do thou cast away this sorry way of thinking, even as a self-controlled (ascetic) casteth away any course of thought interfering with the attainment of his purpose. Crossing over the ocean swarming with gigantic alligators, we shall enter Lankā and slay thy enemy. Of a person that is dispirited and poor in pluck and that hath his soul overwhelmed with grief, every interest droopeth, and he cometh by misfortunes (one after another). All these heroes, these leaders of monkey-hordes, who are ardent for thy welfare, are competent to enter into fire itself. From their cheerful attitude I know this, and firm is my faith. It behoveth thee so to arrange things that, slaying the foe, Rāvana of impious acts, we may bring hither Sitā by our own prowess. Do thou, O Rāghava, so order matters that a bridge may be constructed (over the main), and that we may behold the palace of the Rākshasa monarch. We having seen the city of Lankā, established on the summit of Trikuta, do thou for certain conclude Rāvana as slain in battle immediately after (we see her). Without throwing a bridge over the ocean—the dread abode of Varuna—even the Asuras and celestials with Indra (at their head) are unequal to subduing Lankā. When the bridge over the ocean hath been constructed up to near Lankā, and when my forces have crossed (over the sea), consider victory as secured. As these monkeys are heroic in fight, and able to wear forms at will, O king, do not let thy intellect get stupified and thus mar all interests. In this world, sorrow berefts people of their prowess. Do thou do even what should be done by a man—summon thy manliness ; for what an actor doeth promptly, conduceth to his success. At this time, O eminently wise one, do thou realise goodness through thy energy.* Of heroic, high-souled, men like thyself, on their sustaining an entire or a partial loss, grief undoeth every interest. Therefore, the foremost of intelligent persons, and conversant with every lore, thou shouldst along with councilors like me, strive to beat thy foe. Find I none in the three worlds, O Rāghava, who can stay in fight before thee equipped with thy bow. Thy business entrusted to these monkeys shall not (anyway) suffer. And soon, crossing over the boundless main, thou shalt behold Sitā. Therefore, O king, renounce thy sorrow, and call up wrath. Those Kshatriyas that conceive no anger in respect of their enemies, have their activity annulled ; and all fear furious persons. Drawing nigh unto us, do thou, gifted with acute intelligence, cast about for crossing over the dreadful deep—lord of streams—along with us. On these forces getting beyond the ocean, do thou take it for certain that we have won ; and when my whole host hath reached the further shore, do thou indubitably conclude that we have obtained victory. These monkeys, heroic and capable of assuming in fight forms at will, shall slaughter those foes by showering rocks and trees. If I see any means of crossing the ocean, Varuna's abode, I shall, O destroyer of foes, deem him as slain in battle. And what is the use of dilating ? Every way thou shalt prove victorious. And I see omens, and my mind is filled with delight."

---

* *i. e.* as I understand this rather obscure passage, *prove thou good through thy vigor—secure victory to the cause of goodness through thy might.*—T

## SECTION III.

HEARING Sugriva's speech, reasonable and fraught with high sense, Kākutstha accorded his assent to it and spoke unto Hanumān, saying,—"By asceticism, or constructing a a bridge, or drying up the ocean,—competent every way am I for crossing over this ocean. Of impracticable places, tell me how many there are in (Lankā), which are incapable of being come at. O monkey, as thou hast seen personally, I wish to get acquainted with all this. And thou hast at thy leisure duly noticed in Lankā the number of the army, the inaccessibility (or otherwise) of the gates, the defence of Lankā, and the dwellings of the Rākshasas. Do thou faithfully relate this unto me, for thou art observant." Hearing Rāma's speech, Hanumān, offspring of the Wind-god, foremost of those conversant with speech, again spake unto Rāma,—"Hearken! I will describe unto thee by what method is the city of Lankā guarded and protected by the Rākshasas, how loyal the Rakshasas are, the surpassing prosperity of Lankā, the dreadfulness of the deep, the divisions of the forces, and the number of the elephants, horses, cars, *etc.*," Having said this, that best of monkeys, knowing the nature of things, went on,—"Lankā, filled with mad elephants, ever rejoiceth. She is great, thronging with cars and inhabited by Rākshasas. Her doors are firmly established and furnished with massy bolts. And she hath four wide and giant gates. (At those gates) are powerful and large arms, stones, and engines, whereby a hostile host approaching, is opposed. At the entrances are arrayed and set in order by bands of heroic Rākshasas, hundreds of dreadful sharp iron *sataghnis*.* She hath a mighty impassable golden wall,

* A kind of fire-arms, or ancient Hindu rocket; or a stone set round with sharp iron spikes.—According to Râmânuya, a sort of mace about two yards in length, with spikes.—T.

having its side emblazoned in the centre with costly stones, coral, lapises and pearls. Round about is a moat, exceedingly dreadful, with cool water, eminently grand, fathomless, containing ferocious aquatic animals, and inhabited by fishes. At the gates are four broad bridges, furnished with machines and many rows of grand structures. On the approach of hostile forces, their attack is repulsed by these machines,and they are thrown into the ditch. One among these bridges is immovable, strong and fast established; adorned with golden pillars and daises. O Rāma, albeit Rāvana hungereth for fight, yet is he calm; and he is vigilant and ever engaged in superintending his army. And dreadful and resembling a celestial citadel, Lankā cannot be ascended by means of any support. She hath fortresses composed of streams, those of hills, and artificial ones of four kinds. And, O Rāghava, she is situated on the other shore of the ocean having its limit far away. And way there is none even for barks,—and all sides are destitute of division. And that citadel is built on the mountain's brow; and, resembling the metropolis of the immortals, the exceedingly invincible Lankā is filled with horses and elephants. And a moat and *sataghnis* and various engines adorn the city of Lankā, belonging to the wicked Rāvana. And an *ayuta* of Rākshasas, dart-handed, hard to subdue,—and all fighting at the front with their swords—protect the Eastern gate. And a *niyuta* of Rakshasas with a fourfold force, and with the flower of the soldiery—protect the Southern gate. And a *prayuta* of Rakshasas, bearing swords and shields, and skilled in all arms, protect the Western gate. And an *arvuda* of Rakhas protect the Northern gate. And car-warriors and horsemen—persons honored and sprung from noble lines—by hundreds and thousands,—and irrepressible goblins and *kotis* of Rākshasas, protect the garrison. I have broken down the bridges and filled up the entrenchment. I have burnt the city of Lankā and laid the wall low. Let us by any way whatever cross over Varuna's abode. Do thou take it for certain that the city of Lankā is subdued by the monkeys. What is the use of thy reckoning the rest? Angada, Dwivida, Mainda, Jāmbavān, Panasa, Nala, and the general, Nila, bounding and reaching Rāvana's abode, and riving the same consisting of woods and hills, moat and gateway, walls and dwellings, shall, O Rāghava, bring (hither) Sitā. If this be so,* do thou order the entire body of the army to be brought; and do thou set out at the proper hour."

## SECTION IV.

HEARING Hanumān's speech duly from the beginning, the exceedingly energetic Rāma having truth for his prowess, said,—"What thou sayest—'I shall speedily destroy the city of this dreadful Raksha,'—is true, I tell thee. Therefore, at this very moment arrange for Sugriva's march. The Sun hath attained his meridian at this proper moment, capable of conferring victory.† Let Rāvana carry away Sitā (to his own country),—whither shall Rāvana, living, repair? Like a dying person who hath taken a death-dispelling drug and drunk ambrosia, Sitā, hearing of my preparations for war, shall inspire hope of life. To-day the Northern Phālguni (is in the ascendant); and to-morrow the moon shall be in conjunction with Hastā.‡ O Sugriva, shall we set

* *Ebam ājnāpaya*: Rāmānuja reads sense into this passage. *If thou wishest the principal monkeys to go, bring them; if thou wish the whole host to march, call it hither, and march at the auspicious moment.—T.*

† The moment is named *abhijit.—T.*

‡ Hastā sprung from Punarvasu is the star of doom, portending death to Rāvana. The Northern Phālguni is Sitā's natal star. The expedition begun during the influence of this star, augurs deliverance to Vaidehi.—T.

out, surrounded by the entire host? The omens I witness, augur, that, having slain Rāvana, I shall bring back Jānaki. The upper lid of my eye throbbeth; and it betokeneth that my desire hath indeed been had." Then, honored by the monkey-king as well as Lakshmana, the righteous Rāma, understanding the import of things, again said,—"Surrounded by hundreds and thousands of fast-speeding monkeys, let Nila go ahead of this force, for surveying the route. O Nila, do thou, O general, expeditiously take the army by a path furnished with fruits and roots, having cool waters of the woods, and replenished with honey. The wicked Rākshasas vitiate* fruits, roots and water along the way. Thou, ever on the alert, shouldst preserve these from the Rakshas. And, bounding down into hollow places, mountain-fastnesses, and woods, let the rangers of the wilds, spy the posted detachments of the enemy. Let those that are incompetent, stay here. This business is dreadful, and we should apply our best strength in conducting the same. Therefore let the foremost monkeys gifted with prodigious prowess lead forth the choice portion of the army, numbering hundreds and thousands. And let Gaja resembling a hill, and the exceedingly powerful Gavaya, and that monkey, Gavāksha, master of the leaping ones,† like a haughty bull among kine, go in the van of the monkey-host. And let that foremost of monkeys, Rishava, go, protecting the right wing (of the army); and let Gandha, irrisistible like an elephant with the fragrant temporal juice trickling down, and the vehement Gandhamādana, go,‡ protecting the left wing (of the monkey-army). And, cheering the army, I myself, mounted on Hanumān, like the Lord (mounted) on Airāvata, shall march in the midst of the forces. And like

---

* By means of poison, *etc.*—*T.*

† *i.e.* monkeys.—T.

‡ The verb is singular, instead of dual, as also the qualifying epithet, *Párçamadishthita*. But the sense is clear.—T.

the lord of wealth and master of riches, mounted on Sārvabhauma, let Lakshmana resembling the Destroyer, march forth, mounted on Angada. And let that king of bears, the long-armed Jāmbavān, Sushena, and the monkey, Vegadarçi, protect the rear (of the forces)." Hearing Rāghava's words, that foremost of monkeys and lord of the army, the exceedingly energetic Sugriva, issued his orders. And anon those highly powerful monkeys issuing up from caves and mountain-summits, began to bound (on all sides). Thereafter, honored by the king of monkeys and also Lakshmana, the righteous Rāma, accompanied by his forces, set out in a southerly direction. And he marched,surrounded by hundreds and thousands, Kotis and Ayutas of monkeys resembling elephants. And he marching was followed by the mighty host of monkeys ; and all those maintained by Sugriva were filled with joy and betrayed demonstrations of delight. And bounding by way of guarding the flanks of the forces, and leaping in front of the army for pioneering, blustering, emitting leonine roars, and uttering cries, the monkeys made towards the south. And some partook of perfumed honey and fruits, and some bore mighty trees, holding the sprouts. And some in pride (of strength) suddenly raised others and threw them down. And some fell and were anon up, and some brought others down. 'We shall slay Rāvana, as also all the rangers of the night' ; thus did the monkeys roar out in the presence of Rāghava. Before (the army), Rhrishabha, the heroic Nila, and Kumuda, along with many monkeys, went on clearing the route. In the middle were king Sugriva, Rāma and Lakshamana, environed by innumerable powerful and terrible monkeys. And the heroic monkey, Satavali, surrounded by ten Kotis (of troops), alone on all sides protected that monkey host. And accompanied by an hundred Kotis, Kesari, Panasa, Gaja* and Arka, by means of many protected that host on

* Some other than the first-mentioned Gaja.—T.

every side. And taking Sugriva before them, Sushena, and Jāmbavān, surrounded by innumerable bears, protected the rear (of the army.) And that foremost of rangers possessed of excellence, and of restrained senses, the heroic Nila, general (of the army), kept going round the ranks. And Valimukha, and Prajangha, Jambha and the monkey Rabhasa, went everywhere, urging on the monkeys. While thus marching, breathing pride of strength, those tiger-like monkeys saw that foremost of mountains *Sahya* crowned with hundreds of trees, and watery expanses laughing with flowers, and beautiful tanks. And knowing the order of Rāma of dreadful wrath, that terrible and mighty host, exceedingly terrific and resembling the bosom of the deep, cowed down through fear, leaving behind cities and villages and provinces, went like the deep-sounding sea. And at the side of Daçaratha's son those heroic monkeys resembling elephants, proceeded by bounds, like noble horses, spurred on. And those foremost of men, mounted on the monkeys, looked beautiful like the Sun and the Moon half eclipsed by the two mighty planets, *viz.*, Rāhu and Ketu. And (thus) did the righteous Rāma proceed towards the South, accompanied by his army. Then Lakshmana, furnished with consummate sense and promptitude, who was mounted on Angada, spoke unto Rāma, inviting words, fraught with import. "Speedily recovering Vaidehi, who hath been carried away, and slaying Rāvana, thou wilt, thy end attained, return to Ayodhyā, who shall also have her desire. O Rāghava, I see all the great auspicious omens on earth and in the sky, signifying success unto thee. Mildly and grateful doth the blessed breeze blow behind the army, inspiring pleasure. And the birds and beasts are crying in sonorous voices. And all the points (of the compass) appear pleasant; and the lord of day is cloudless. Bhrigu's son, Uçanas, also weareth for thee an auspicious aspect, and Dhruva is without blemish. And all the *rishis*, pure and furnished with lustre, go round Dhruba. And before us shineth the grandfather of the high-souled Ikshwākus; the spotless Rājarshi Triçanku, with his priest.—And stainless and free from disturbances appeareth Visākhā. This is the racial star of us, the high-souled Ikshwākus. And Nairita, the radical star of the Nairitas, is sore afflicted and, touched by the rod-bearing Dhumketu is in trouble. All this is for the destruction of the Rākshasas. At the fated time, those that are in the clutches of Death, have their stars afflicted by the planets. And the water is dear and tastes sweet; and the woods are stocked with fruit. And the odorous gale doth not blow strongly; and the trees are furnished with all blossoms of of the season. And, O lord, this host of monkeys appeareth splendid to the height, as did the celestial host on the occasion of the destruction of Tāraka. Seeing all this, thou shouldst, O noble one, feel delighted." Having thus consoled his brother, Sumitrā's son, feeling enlivened, said this. The monkey-host went on, covering the earth. And the mighty dust raised by bears, monkeys, and tigers, having for their weapons nails and teeth,—with the foreparts of their feet and hands, enveloped the world, and the splendour of the sun was obscured. And as clouds envelope the sky, the mighty monkey-host went on, covering up the Southern quarter with its mountains, woods, and sky. And as they marched covering many a *yoyana*, the streams seemed as if they flowed in an opposite direction.* And they, while proceeding, took rest by pools of clear water, on mountains covered with trees, on plains and in forests teeming with fruits. Some moving straight, some moving askance, and some moving on the earth, that enormous

* Kataka remarks :—"As when clouds drift past, the Moon it is that seems to scud accross the sky, as the monkey-army marched on, the rivers seemed to flow in an opposite direction". Râmânuya says that the waters of the streams dashed by the monkeys, held an opposite course. The former interpretation is hardly satisfactory, and Râmânuya seems to be right.—T.

monkey-host went on covering the entire earth. And they were all of delighted countenances and gifted with the velocity of the wind. And these monkeys devoted all their energy to the accomplishment of Rāghava's work. And they were displaying unto each other their joy, prowess and energy. And influenced with the vanity of youth they set up diverse cries. Some proceeded with speed,some leaped, some set up cries expressing joy, some were uplifting their tails, and some were striking the ground with their feet. Some, stretching forth their arms, were breaking the hills, and others the trees. And others were ascending the tops of the hills. Some began to make terrible sounds, and others made a tingling noise. And many others blasted the creepers with the velocity of their thighs. And some were engaged in sporting with trees and rocks. And thus was the earth enveloped with millions and *kotis* of fearful monkeys. And thus the enormous monkey host went on day and night. And all those monkeys, delighted, guided by Sugriva, and taking delight in battle, went on speedily. And they did not take rest even for a moment, desirous of rescuing Sitā. Thereupon, getting at the mount *Sahya* covered with various trees and forests, those monkeys ascended it. And Rāma went on beholding the variegated forest, rivers and fountains of the mount *Sahya and Malaya*. And those monkeys broke down various trees—*Champakas, Tilakâs*, mangos, *Prasekas, Sindubarakas, Tiniças and Karaviras, Asokas, Karanjas, Plakshas, Nyagrodhas, Jambukas* and *Amalakas*. And seated on picturesque rocks, various forest trees, shaken by the wind, showered flowers on them. And there blew in those forests filled with the smell of honey, a wind of pleasant touch, cool as the Moon, accompanied by the hummings of the bees. And that mount was richly embellished with diverse metals. And dust issuing from these metals and thickened by the air, enveloped on all sides the huge monkey-host. There blossomed in that picturesque mountain-vale *Ketakas, Sindubaras,* beautiful *Vasantees, Mâdhabis, Gandhapurnas, Kandas, Chiravilyas, Mahikas, Vanjulas, Vakulas, Ranjakas, Tilakâs, Nagas, Chutas, Patalikas, Kobidaras, Muchlindas, Arjunas, Singsapas, Kutajas, Pintalas, Tiniças, Churnkas, Neepakas, Neela-Sokas, Saralas, Ankolas* and lotuses. And all these trees were greatly disturbed by those monkeys, delighted with their view. There were in that mountain many a picturesque lake and pond filled with *Chakravakas* and *Karandavas,* ducks, *Chraunchas* and the mount abounded on all sides with boars, deer, and terrible bears, lions and tigers and various other fearful animals, and it was beautified with full blown lotuses, lilies, *Utpalas* and various other fragrant trees growing in the water. And various birds set up their musical choir on the summit of that mount. And bathing and drinking, these monkeys sported in the water. And ascending the mount these monkeys continually bounded. And excited with drink, they crumbled into pieces the ambrosia-smelling fruits, roots and flowers of the trees. And those monkeys yellow as honey, delighted, feasted on mangoes, long and measuring a *drona.* Breaking down the trees, blasting the creepers, bounding from one tree to another and making the mount *Sahya* echo, those leading monkeys went on delighted and excited with drink. Some ascending the trees, and others drinking, the whole earth was enveloped with those monkeys, and seemed as if beautified with ripe paddy crops. And reaching the mount Mahendra, the large-armed Rāma, having eyes like lotuses, ascended the summit adorned with diverse trees. And getting at the top, Daçaratha's son espied the vast deep filled with tortoises and fishes. Thereupon, passing by the mounts *Sahya* and *Malaya* and arranging their enormous host, they* by and by reached the roaring deep. And descending therefrom, Rāma, the foremost of those who minister happiness unto all, accompanied by Lakshmana and

* The monkey leaders.—T.

Sugriva, entered the forest situate on the banks of the ocean. And reaching the expansive banks having rocks thereon and continually washed by the rising billows, Rāma spoke saying,—"O Sugriva we have arrived at the abode of Varuna. Now hath arisen in my mind what I had not thought of before. And this ocean, the lord of the streams, whose other side is not seen, cannot be crossed over without some excellent measure. Let the monkey-host be encamped here therefore, and then concert a plan by means of which they might get at the other side. And reaching the shores of the ocean, the large-armed Rāma, stricken with grief for Sitā, ordered their encampment, saying,—"O foremost of monkeys, do thou encamp thy host on the brink of the ocean. Now hath arrived the hour for counsel, when we should devise some plan for crossing over the main. I fear the Rākshasas at every step, for they are greatly illusion creating—let the leaders therefore go to their own hosts and let them not proceed anywhere else, renouncing them." Hearing the words of Rāma, Sugriva along with Lakshmana, encamped the army on the brink of the ocean, covered with trees. And stationed near the main, the monkey-host in consequence of their resemblance in colour with the blue contents of the deep, looked like a second ocean. Thereupon, reaching the shore, those leading monkeys engaged in concerting a plan to cross over the vasty deep. And the tumult of that monkey-host encamped there, was heard above the roaring of the deep. And that huge army of the monkeys commanded by Sugriva, and set up in three divisions, were deeply concerned with the accomplishment of Rāma's work. And reaching the shore of the vasty deep, that monkey host, delighted, beheld the ocean moved by the Wind. And they waited there beholding the deep of unimpeded expanse, having its distant shore inhabited by the demons, and thronged with various aquatic animals. While upheaving its foam on the approach of eve, it appeared laughing and setting up its surges, it appeared to dance. It increased with the rising of the Moon and he reflected himself on its breast. That abode of Varuna was infested with gigantic sharks, whales and *Timingalas**, disturbed with the fury of the Wind, filled with serpents having flaming frames, and various aquatic animals and rocks, and was fathomless deep. It had picturesque fortresses on its marge and its other shore was hard to get at. And the *Makaras*† and serpents living therein were moved by the Wind. The waters, as if delighted, were rising and falling. And having serpents of flaming frames underneath, it appeared as if sprinkled with scintillations of fire. And that terrible abode of the demons extended down to the regions inhabited by the *Nagas* or serpents. The deep resembled the welkin and the welkin the deep, and there appeared no difference between them. The sky crested with stars and the deep filled with gems resembled each other. The sky enveloped with clouds and the ocean overflowing with surges presented no contrast whatsoever. The waves of the mighty deep beating at each other continually, set up a sound resembling that of a trumpet in the sky. It was filled with diverse gems and its water was poisoned by means of the air. It was filled with various aquatic animals, and upheaving its billows, it appeared as if excited with ire. And there beheld those high-souled monkeys the mighty main agitated by the Wind and muttering as if with the upheaval of the waves. Thereupon, overwhelmed wth surprise, those monkeys, stationed there, espied the main brimming with rolling waters and moving as if (off its place).

* A large fabulous fish.—T.

† A marine monster confounded usually with the crocodile and shark.—T.

## SECTION V.

THERE on the northern shore of the ocean the army was encamped and arranged in order by Nila. And the two leading monkeys Mainda and Divida patrolled about on all sides to protect the monkey host. And the army being encamped on the shore of the lord of streams and rivers, Rāma, beholding Lakshmana by his side, spoke, saying—"I know that grief abates as time passes by, but my sorrow arising from the separation of my spouse, is increasing day by day. I am not sorry that she hath been stealthily taken away by the demon—but my sorrow is that her end is drawing nigh. O Wind, do thou go there where my dear spouse is, and touching her person, do thou touch me, for I shall then be happy stationing my looks in the Moon and being touched by thee. Alas! my dear one cried 'O lord, O lord' when she was taken away. Those words, revolving burn me like poison. I am now being burnt down day and night by the fire of desire,having separation from her for its fuel and her thoughts for its flame. Leaving thee, O Son of Sumitrā, I shall jump into the deep and then shall not this fire burn me any more. This is my only consolation,for which I draw my vital breath—that myself and she breathe on the same earth. Like unto a dry land drawing water from a watered ground, I do live, hearing that Jānaki still survives. When shall I, discomfitting my enemies, behold Sitā, having a beautiful waist and eyes resembling lotus-petals, as a victorious hero beholdeth the royal Grace. Like unto the sick drinking the *elixir* of life, when shall I, raising a little her lotus-like countenance having graceful teeth and lips, imprint kisses thereon? And when shall she, laughing, embrace me with her rising breast resembling the palm fruit? Alas that chaste dame having scarlet corners of the eye, being encircled by the demons, is wishing for a protector like unto one having no husband, albeit having a husband in me. How fareth in the midst of the she-demons, that daughter of the king Janaka, my beloved spouse, and the daughter-in-law of king Daçaratha? And having those Rākshasas, hard to repress, slain by me, truly shall she appear like unto the rays of the Moon extricated from sable autumnal clouds. Sitā is constitutionally slender, and forsooth, she has been greatly reduced by sorrow, fasting and calamities touching time and place. When shall I, piercing with my shafts the breast of the lord of Rākshasas, renounce my mind's grief? And when shall my devoted Sitā resembling the daughter of a celestial, fling herself anxiously around my neck and shed tears of joy? And when shall I renounce this my sorrow arising out of Maithili's separation, like unto one casting off his soiled clothes?" The highly intelligent Rāma bewailing thus, the day passed away and the Sun, decreasing gradually, disappeared at last. And consoled by Lakshmana, Rāma, stricken with thought touching Sitā having eyes like lotus-petals, engaged in rites relating to the worship of Eve.

## SECTION VI.

Beholding in Lankā that dreadful and awe-inspiring work performed by Hanumān like unto the high-souled Sakra, the lord of Rākshaṣas, looking down with shame, addressed them all, saying—"That monkey alone hath invaded and entered the city of Lankā hard to reach and hath espied Sitā, the daughter of king Janaka. He hath shattered the palace, and the altar of sacrifice, slain the leading

Rākshasas, and, in short, agitated the whole city of Lankā. What shall I do now? And what should you all do on this occasion? It behoveth you all to give me such counsel as becometh me and will conduce to my glory." 'Victory is the outcome of consultation'—this do the sages* say. Let us, therefore, O mighty ones, engage in counsel, relating to the measures we should adopt towards Rāma. There are three orders of men on this earth—the superior the middling and the inferior. This distinction cannot be perceived without a knowledge of the signs, and so I shall relate unto you their merits and demerits. He is said to belong to the superior order, whose counsel contains the three signs (mentioned below), or who engages in works after consulting duly with friends capable or with persons having the same end in view, and some times with others, and who serveth Providence. He belongs to the middle order who consults his own self only,depends on the Providence, and engages alone in works. And he belongs to the inferior order who engageth in works without ascertaining their merits or demerits, disregarding the will of the Providence and saying, 'I will do this', and is inactive (at last). And counsels are also divided into three divisions like unto the three orders of men (mentioned). That counsel belongs to the superior order in which the counsellors with their judgment reinforced by a knowledge of political ethics, are unanimous. That one belongs to the middle order in which the counsellors after varied discussion, arrive at unanimity in the long run. And that one is the worst in which the counsellors differ from each other and agree a little in the long run, with no good result. You are all gifted with good intellects: do you all unanimously settle as to what becometh me and conduceth to my well-being. Environed by a thousand of patient monkeys, Rāma, with a view to capture our city, is approaching towards Lankā. Forsooth, shall he cross over the main along

---

* *Manaswina*, according to Râmânuya, means, hero.—T.

with his younger brother and a mighty host. He can by his prowess dry up the ocean and do the other.* Rāma approaching thus with a hostile intention along with the monkeys, it behoveth you to devise such means as might protect my city and army.

---

## SECTION VII.

BEING thus accosted by their lord, the highly powerful Rākshasas, devoid of good sense and ignorant of sound counsel, replied with folded palms, saying,—"Thou hast, O king, enough of soldiers and weapons. Why art thou smitten with sorrow then? Repairing to Bhagavati, thou didst discomfit the serpents in battle. The God of Death, living on mount Kailaça, encircled by *Yakshas*, was subjugated by thee in a great battle. And that mighty lord of men, proud of his friendship with Siva, was defeated by thee wrathfully in battle. Discomfitting and slaying the band of Yakshas, thou didst bring this flowery car from the mount Kailāça. O lord of Rākshasas, desiring thy friendship out of fear, Maya, the king of Dānavas, offered thee his daughter† for thy spouse. O thou of mighty arms, thou didst bring under thy subjection the powerful and irrepressible Dānava‡ for the pleasure of *Kumbhinasi.*§ And entering the region under the earth, thou didst defeat the serpents—and thus bring under thy subjection Vāsuki, Takshaka, Sankha, and Jati. Those heroic Dānavas, the *Kalakeyas*, were greatly powerful,

* *i. e.* bridge over the ocean.—T.

† This refers to Mandodari, Ravana's favourite queen.—T.

‡ This refers to Madhu.—T.

§ Ravana's sister, who was married to Madhu.—T.

irrepressible, and proud of the boons conferred on them. And fighting with them perpetually for a year, thou didst bring them under thy control, O lord, O slayer of foes, and learn from them the science of varied illusions, O king of the Rākshasas. O great hero, by thee were defeated in battle, the heroic and powerful sons of Varuna, followed by a fourfold division of their army. The dominion of Death is like the mighty main, having his rod for aquatic animals, agonies for the trees that cover its islands, the noose for the billows, his attendants for the serpents and his terrible fever for the dreadful attitude of the deep. And diving into this terrible deep, thou didst, O king, discomfit Death himself and win glorious victory. And every one was pleased there with thy successful fight. The Earth was filled with various heroic Kshetriyas, resembling Sakra in prowess as she is adorned now with various trees. Rāghava is not their equal either in strength or prowess. And all those heroes, hard to repress in battle, were slain by thee, O king. Do thou wait here, O great king; thou needst not take any trouble. Indrajit alone shall slay all these monkeys. And this one, O mighty monarch, having celebrated the Māheçwara* sacrifice, hath obtained a noble boon, rarely (attained by persons). Having agitated the ocean of celestial hosts, having darts and lances for its fishes, showering arms for its moss, elephants for its tortoises, steeds for its frogs, Rudra and Aditya for its ferocious animals, the Maruts and Vasus for its mighty serpents, cars, horses, and elephants for its volume of waters, and infantry for its spacious shore, this one (Indrajit), taking captive the lord of the celestials himself, had brought him into Lankā. Then, O king, liberated agreeably to the injunction of the Great-father, the slayer of Samvara and Vritra, worshipped of all the celestials, went (back) to heaven. Do thou, O great king, entrust Indrajit with this business,—until he bringeth to destruction the

* Relating to Mahaçwara—the great Lord, a designation of Siva.—T.

monkey-host along with Rāma. O king, thou must not think that this calamity, coming from an ignoble person is not insignificant. Thou shalt slay Rāghava."

## SECTION VIII.

THEN that heroic general, the Rākshasa named Prahasta, possessing the splendour of sable clouds, submitted with joined hands,—"I am competent to baffle in battle gods and Dānavas and Gandharbas, ghosts, birds and serpents,—what then is a couple of human beings? Having been negligent and confident (in our power), we have all been deceived by Hanumān. But, I living, that ranger of woods shall not (again) go hence with his life. All the earth down to the ocean, containing hills, forests and woods, shall be rendered free from monkeys. Do thou command me. And, O ranger of the night, I shall deliver (the Rākshasas) from the monkeys; and thou shalt not have to suffer in the least in consequence of thy transgression."* Then the Rākshasa named Durmukha, growing enraged, said,—"This overpowering of all of us must not be forgiven—this flagrant discomfiture of the metropolis of the auspicious lord of the Rākshasas as well as of his inner appartment by the foremost of monkeys. This moment marching alone (from hence) will I exterminate the monkeys, even if they shall have entered the dreadful deep, or the sky, or the subterranean regions." Then the exceedingly powerful Vajradanshtra, weilding up a terrific bludgeon, stained with flesh and gore, wrathfully observed,—"Rāma the irrepressible existing, and also Sugriva with Lakshmana, what have we to do with the weak and

* *i. e.* the ravishment of Sitâ.—T.

wretched Hanumân ? This very day, slaying single-handed Râma with Sugriva and with Lakshmana, with this bludgeon, shall I return, after having sorely troubled the monkey-host. And, O monarch, if thou art minded, hear this other word of mine ! Verily he that is fertile in resources and ever ready, compasseth success. Let thousands of Râkshasas, heroic, terrible, fearful to behold, and wearing forms at will, appointed by the lord of Râkshasas, presenting themselves before Kâkutstha in palpably human shapes, calmly say unto that foremost of the Raghus,—'Despatched have we been by thy younger brother.' Hearing this, he (Râma), summoning his forces without delay, shall come hither. Then, equipped with darts, javelins and maces, and bearing bows, arrows and scimitars in our hands, we shall swiftly and summoning speed* set out (from hence) ; and stationing ourselves in the sky in bands, and slaughtering the monkey-army with mighty showers of rocks and weapons, we shall lead it to Death's door. Let us in this wise decoy Râma and Lakshmana ; and if they fall into our design, they shall, without doubt, lose their lives." Then that hero, Kumbhakarna's son, named Nikumbha, endowed with exceeding prowess, in high wrath remarked unto Râvana, destroyer of worlds,—"Do ye, all of you, stay here along with the great king. I alone shall slay Râghava together with Lakshmana, and Sugriva with Hanumân, and all the monkeys." Then a Râkshasa, named Vajrahanu, resembling a hill, in wrath lapping the corners of his mouth with his tongue, said,—"Do ye,casting off anxiety, engage yourself as ye list. I alone shall swallow up that entire monkey-host. Do ye,remaining at ease and without anxiety, drink *Varuna*† wine. I single-handed shall slay Sugriva with Lakshmana, as well as Hanumân with Angada,—and all the monkeys.

* *Twarita*—summoning speed—redundant.—T.

† *Váruna* wine, otherwise named *Várnni* is prepared from hog-weed, ground with the juice of the date or palm, and then distilled.—T.

## SECTION IX.

THEN, in fierce wrath seizing bludgeons, and *pattiças*, lances and bearded darts and javelins, and axes, bows and excellent shafts and swords, resembling crystelline water, sprung up the Rākshasas, Rabhasa, and the mighty Suryyaçatru, and Saptaghna,and Yajnakopa, and Mahāpārçwa and Mahodara, Agniketu the irrepressible, and the Rākshasa Raçmiketu, and the lusty Indraçatru, son unto Rāvana—and Prahasta, Virupāksha, and the exceedingly strong Vajradanshtrā,—and Dhumrāksha, and Nikumbha, and the Raksha Durmukha. And, flaming in energy, they all addressed Rāvana, saying,—"To-day shall we slay Rāma, and Sugriva along with Lakshmana, and the helpless Hanumān, who hath damaged Lankā. Then, preventing them, who had (thus) equipped themselves with all kinds of weapons, and making them sit down, Vibhishana, with joined hands, again spoke unto them, saying,—"The wise have asserted that an appeal to prowess should be resorted to anent a business *then* only when the end sought cannot be attained through the three (other) means.* Prowess produceth fruit only in respect of well-advised action directed while carefully watching(enemies) that are negligent, or captive,† or under Divine affliction. But why do ye intend to discomfit (Rāma), who is vigilant, who desireth victory, who is strong in the Divine strength, who hath subdued passion, and who is hard to subdue ? Who had in this world ever thought of or reasoned about Hanumān's career over the dreadful deep, the lord of streams and rivers ? O rangers of the night, the strength and prowess (of the foe) being immeasurable, ye should by no means recklessly disregard him. And what was the wrong that formerly

* *Viz.*, conciliation, gift, and creating division.—T.

† In the hands of other enemies.—T.

had been done by Rāma unto the king of the Rākshasas, that he hath carried off from Janasthāna the spouse of that illustrious one? If Khara, who had trespassed into regions not his own, hath been slain in battle by Rāma, surely a creature should to the best of his might preserve his life. It is for this great fear that exerciseth us on the score of Vaidehi owing its existence to this,* that she, having been ravished, should (now) be given up. What is the use of acting so that quarrel may be the consequence? And (Rāma), possessed of prowess, yet ever abiding by morality, is incapable of initiating hostilities for no purpose. Therefore, do ye give him his Maithili. And before, he by means of his shafts riveth this city together with her elephants and steeds, overflowing with countless gems, do ye give him his Maithili. And before the dreadful, irrepressible and mighty monkey-host blocketh up this Lankā of ours, do ye give (back) Sitā. This city of Lankā shall perish as also all the heroic Rākshasas, if thou dost not thyself make over Rāma's spouse unto him. I exert myself to pleasure thee, because of the fraternity (that subsisteth between us). Do what I say. I say what is truth and what also is for thy good. Do thou render (back) Rāma's Maithili. Ere yet the king's son, for compassing thy destruction, showereth sure shafts resembling the rays of the autumnal Sun, having shining heads and feathered parts, and exceedingly hard, do thou render Maithili unto Dāçarathi. Forsake thy wrath at once, which destroyeth happiness and virtue; and follow righteousness, which enhanceth enjoyment and fame. Be thou propitious,—so that we may live (at ease) along with our sons and relatives. Render (back) Maithili unto Daçaratha's son." Having heard Vibhishana's speech, Rāvana—lord of Rākshasas—leaving all of them, entered his own chamber.

* The feeling of revenge for the slaughter of Khara and the rest.—T.

## SECTION X.

THEN early in the morning, like the fiery and refulgent sun entering a mighty mass of clouds, Vibhishana, fast to virtue and interest, heroic and possessed of exceeding splendour, playing a perilous part,* entered the apartment of his elder brother, resembling an assemblage of mountain-summits and elevated like the peak of a mountain, orderly, divided into spacious rooms,—the resort of the great—inhabited by august and intelligent persons attached (to Rāvana); guarded around by lusty Rākshasas in limited numbers; having the air agitated by the breath of mad elephants; with loud blares of conchs, and resounding with trumpets; embosoming numbers of beautiful damsels, with its high-ways (overflowing with talk); furnished with doors of polished gold; embellished with excellent ornaments; resembling the abode of the Gandharbas, or the mansion of the Maruts; containing heaps of gems; like unto the dwelling of serpents. And that one of exceeding energy heard sacred and holy sounds uttered by Veda-versed Brāhmanas celebrating the victory of his brother; and that highly powerful (hero) acquainted with Mantras and the Vedas saw Vipras worshipped with vessels of curds, clarified butter, flowers and fried paddy. And the mighty-armed (Vibhishana) saluted the younger brother of the bestower of riches,† seated there. And that one acquainted with manners, after proper courtesy, sat him down on a seat decked in gold, which was pointed out (by a royal glance). And in retirement as also in presence only of his counsellors,

* The project he had conceived, *viz.*, converting Râvana to his own policy of pacification, was fraught with peril to himself, considering his brother's fierce temperament.—T.

† Kuvera.—Rávana was Kuvera's younger brother.—T.

Vibhishana spoke unto the high souled Râvana words backed by reason, and greatly fraught with his welfare. And having, with soothing speech, pacified his elder brother and extended towards him the due civilities, that one, who through height of sentiment had noted excellence and the want of it, addressed (Vibhishana) in words befitting the occasion and the place,—"Ever since, O subduer of enemies, Vaidehi hath come hither, are seen inauspicious omens. Fire, enveloped in smoke at the time of its being ignited, and thereafter throwing out scintillations, with its brightness obscured by vapour, doth not increase adequately even on oblations being poured into it with Mantras. Reptiles are discovered in kitchens, sacrificial fire-chambers, and the places of Vaidika recitations ; and ants (are found) in clarified butter. The milk of the kine hath been dried up ; and the nobler elephants are without the temporal juice. And horses, albiet they have feasted on fresh grass, neigh distressfully.* And asses, camels and mules, O king, with their hair standing erect, shed tears ; and although they are ministered unto medically, they do not return to nature. And crows in numbers emit harsh cries on all sides, and are seen in swarms at the tops of edifices. Vultures sit sadly and distressed upon the roofs of houses. During the two twilights, the jackals, coming in sight, utter ominous howls. And wolves and other (ferocious) animals, as well as deer, approaching the gate of the palace in swarms, are heard to set up loud roars resembling the thunder. Things having come to this pass, even this expiation, I fancy, is capable of removing the evil omens. Do thou render back Vaidehi unto Râghava. If I have said this through ignorance or covetuousness, thou ought not, O mighty monarch, criminate me. All Râkshasas and Râkshasis, as well as those belonging to palace and the inner apartment—shall have to

* The commentator remarks, evidently with justice—"That is, the horses, having eaten their fill, still hunger."—T.

experience the evil consequence (of this act of thine). All the counsellors have refrained from tendering this counsel unto thee; but surely I must tell thee what I have seen or heard; and adopting proper measures, it behoveth thee to act so."* (Rāvana's) brother, Bibhishana, thus spoke, unto his brother, the chief of Rakshas, in the midst of counsellors, these words fraught with his good. Hearing this beneficial, mild and pregnant speech, fortified by reasons and capable of compassing (his welfare) for the present, past and the future, (Rāvana) who had conceived a passion (for Sitā), getting into a rage, replied,—"Fear find I none whatever. Rāghava never shall have Mithilā's daughter. Even if Lakshmana's elder brother should be supported in battle by the celestials with Indra (at their head), how can he stay before me (in the field)?" Having said this, that destroyer of celestial hosts, the Ten-necked one, possessed of mighty strength and of terrific prowess in battle, then dismissed his brother Vibhishana, who had spoken truth.

## SECTION XI.

THE unrighteous king, overmastered by his passion (for Sitā), in consequence of his sinful act as well as the loss of honor he sustained at the hands of his friends, became reduced. And the occasion for war was wanting. Rāvana, possessed by lust, and continually thinking of Vaidehi, conceived along with his counsellors that the time for entering into hostilities had arrived. And sallying forth, he ascended a mighty car furnished with golden network, adorned with pearls and coral, and yoked with trained steeds. And having

* In accordance with my suggestion.—T.

ascended that excellent vechicle, having sounds resembling those of mighty clouds, that foremost of Rakshas, the Ten-necked one, drove towards the court. And as he coursed on, Rākshasas, bearing swords and shields, and carrying all kinds of weapons, went before the lord of the Rākshasas. And (some of) these, wearing various frightful suits, and decked with diverse ornaments, went, surrounding his rear and flanks. And *atirathas* went with cars, and superb mad elephants, and sportive steeds; and bearing in their hands maces and bludgeons; and darts and clubs. And as Rāvana marched towards the court, there arose the loud blares of a thousand trumpet, and the uproarious sounds of conchs. And that redoubtable and mighty car-warrior held his course, suddenly making sides resound, and beautifying the high ways. And the spotless white umbrella of the lord of Rākshasas, being raised up, looked beautiful like the Moon at her full. On his right and left graced two crystal white chowris furnished with threads of gold. And all those Rākshasas standing on the ground with joined hands, bowed down their heads to the foremost of Rākshasas who was seated on his car. Hymned by the Rākshasas with blessings of victory, that exceedingly energetic chastiser of enemies arrived at the court constructed (by Viçwakarmā). And that highly energetic one in person entered that court paved with silver and gold, having its heart decorated with crystal, and gracefully covered with silk, embroidered with gold; excellently constructed by Viçwakarmā, and guarded by six hundred ghosts. And Rāvana sat down on a superb and august seat consisting of lapises, furnished with a pillow; and covered with a soft dear-skin. And lord-like he commanded the envoys possessed of fleet vigor, saying,—"Do ye speedily summon hither the Rākshasas. I fancy some mighty effort hath to be put forth against our foes." Hearing his words, the envoys began to range Lankā; and going to every house, they fearlessly collected the Rākshasas from places of sport, bed-rooms, and gardens. Then some set out, mounting cars, and some mounting proud coursers, and some on foot. And like the welkin filled with fowls, the city thronged with approaching cars, elephants and steeds. And leaving their various vehicles and cars behind, they entered the court on foot, like lions entering mountain caverns. And taking the feet of the sovereign, and honored by him (in turn), they sat them down, some on raised seats, some on cushions of Kuça, and some on the floor. And presenting themselves agreeably to the command of the monarch, they sat them down each according to his position, before the lord of Rākshasas, Rāvana. And there came also the learned and competent to arrive at infallible decisions, and they sat them down in order of merit. And there also came courtiers endowed with virtues, versed in every thing, and having intelligence for their eye-sight,—and innumerable heroes by hundreds also (arrived) at that court for ascertaining the course that would prove beneficial. And then mounting a large, noble and splendid car, having its parts decked with gold, and yoked with horses, the magnanimous and renowned Vibhishana went to the court of his elder brother. And that younger brother (of Rāvana), announcing his name, bowed down at the feet of his elder brother. And Suka and Prahasta were employed in giving to each a separate seat befitting his rank. And from all sides in the court there began to spread the odour of excellent *agura* and sandal and wreaths belonging to the Rākshasas, decked in gold and various gems, and clad in costly attires. And no one among these present at court uttered any thing, or spoke any falsehood, or conversed in loud accents. And having completely attained their desire, all of fierce prowess, gazed at the face of their lord. And in the assembly of those intelligent, and exceedingly powerful persons, equipped with arms, the intelligent Rāvana appeared splendid like the Vajra-handed Indra among the Vasus.

## SECTION XII.

Then surveying that entire assembly, that conqueror in battle delivered himself unto Prahasta,—general of the forces, saying,—"O general, it behoveth thee so to order the disciplined fourfold forces that they may successfully protect the city." Thereat, Prahasta, carefully carrying out the royal behest, stationed all the forces within and without the city. And having posted the army for the defence of the city, Prahasta sitting down before the king, said,—"I have stationed the forces belonging to thee who art possessed of strength, inside as well as outside. (Now), without suffering thy mind to be agitated with anxiety, speedily, do what is in thy heart. Hearing the speech of Prahasta seeking the welfare of the kingdom, Rāvana craving for enjoyment, spoke in the midst of his aderents,—"When virtue, or happiness, or interest is in straits, it behoveth you to (know your course) in relation to pleasant and unpleasant, happiness and misery, profitable and unprofitable, and good and evil. No business of mine which ye have set about after taking counsel, hath ever miscarried. And like Vāsava environed by the moon, stars and plannets, and the Maruts, I surrounded by you, have attained to plenitude of prosperity. I am, for certain, going to employ you all. In consequence of his sleep, I could not inform him of this matter. After having slept for six months that one of prodigious strength—foremost of those bearing arms—hath just risen. Janaka's daughter and Rāma's beloved wife hath been brought hither from the forest of Dandaka, the region ranged by Rakshas. That indolent damsel wisheth not to ascend my bed; nor is there any in the three spheres, that to me is like unto Sitā. She is slender-waisted, and high-hipped, and her face is as the autumnal Moon resembling a golden image. She is meek and looketh like the hand work of Maya himself gifted with an infinite variety of fascinations.* And beholding her dainty and tender feet with roseate soles, and having coppery nails, my mind burneth (with desire). And seeing her resembling the flame of a sacrificial fire and the splendour of the Sun himself; and her fair face furnished with a prominent nose and elegant eyes, I, having lost control over self, have come under the sway of desire. And my passion, uninfluenced by anger and joy, capable of producing pallor, and constantly causing anguish and sorrow, hath rendered me pale. Expecting her lord, Rāma, the beautiful one having expansive eyes, hath solicited for a year's space; and I have pledged my fair woods to her of graceful eyes. But tired am I on account of my passion,—like a horse spent on the way. How can the rangers of the woods, or the sons of Daçaratha cross over the sea ungovernable and swarming with countless creatures and fishes? On the other hand, a single month hath troubled us grievously. Hard it is therefore to understand the course of events. Do ye act, each as he thinks proper. And although no fear can come from mortals, yet ye should deliberate (as to what ye should do). Formerly I had gained victory with the help given by you; do ye in the same way stand by me now. The king's son, having learnt that Sitā is on the other shore of the ocean, taking before them monkey headed by Sugriva, reached Varuna's abode. Do ye so counsel that Sitā may be with-holden by me and the sons of Daçaratha may be slain; but ye must prefer certain counsel. No other† person in this world hath the power to cross the sea along with the monkeys,—victory, therefore, is undubitably mine." Hearing the sorrowful

* This reminds one irrisistibly of Cleopatra's. The Bengali translators evidently failing to understand *Mayava Mayanirmita*, have conveniently—trasferred the phrase in tact to their versions.—T.

† I fail to understand *anyasya*, "*no other* person";—nor does the commentator helps me anyway.—T.

speech of (Rāvana) afflicted with lust, Kumbhakarna grew enraged, and said,—"When just on seeing (Sitā) of Rāma along with Lakshmana, thou didst by main force carry her away, it plainly appeareth that thy mind, like the Yamunā filling her bed, hath been possessed (by her).* O great king all this (that thou hast done) is not worthy of thee. If thou hadst at the outset consulted us in this matter, we would have done what was proper.† O ten-faced one, the king, that arriving at certain conclusions, carrieth on his regal affairs agreeably to justice, hath not to repent afterwards. But those actions that are done without deliberation, like unto clarified butter poured in an impure sacrifice, conduceth only to harm. He doth not know what is proper and what not, that performs prior actions afterwards, and posterior actions first. Others spy holes in the actions of the volatile, the latter may be possessed of great power,—like swans passing Krauncha through the hole.‡ By luck it is that Rāma hath not yet slain thee, who hath done this tremendous thing, without reflection, resembling food mixed with poison. But as thou hast entered upon a course of action which is improper even in repect of foes, I will, O sinless one, perform thy work by slaying thy enemies. And, O ranger of the night, I will exterminate thy foe. Even if Sakra and the sun, even if fire and the War-god, even if Kuvera and Varuna, should range themselves against me, I will fight them. Purandara himself shall be afflicted with fright when I having my body measuring a mountain, and furnished with sharp teeth, shall, setting up roars, fight with my huge bludgeon. Before Rāma shooteth a second shaft, to slay me, I shall drink his life-blood. Be thou comforted by slaying Daçaratha's son, I will exert to secure blessed victory for thee. Having

---

* This passage is very obscure, and the commentator's gloss does not at all serve.—T.

† i. e. *we would have prevented thee.—T.*

‡ The hole made by the dart of Kumara.—T.

killed Rāma along with Lakshmana, I shall devour all the principal monkeys. Do thou make merry at thy will, drink the Varuni, and, with thy mind set at rest, conduct affairs fraught with thy welfare. On Rāma being despatched to the mansion of Yama, Sitā shall come under thy subjection for ever and a day.".

---

## SECTION XIII.

SEEING Rāvana wrought up with wrath, the exceedingly strong Mahāpārcwa, reflecting for a moment, observed with joined hands,—"The man that, entering the forest, abounding with deer and ferocious animals, doth not drink honey, maketh a fool of himself. O destroyer of foes, who is the lord of thee, that art lord thyself? Enjoy with Vaidehi, taking thy enemy by the hand. And, O thou endowed with prodigious power, do thou exerting thy might lead thy life, after the manner of hens, and invading Sitā again and again, do thou enjoy her and derive pleasure (therefrom). And when thou hast attained thy purpose; what fear can succeed? Alike when on thy guard, and off it, thou shalt provide against all exigencies. Kumbhakarna along with us, as well the exceedingly powerful Indrajit, are competent to chastise the thunder-bearing (Deity) equipped with his thunder. Passing by gift, conciliation, and dissension, which have been assigned by the wise as the means of success, I relish the success in business which is attained through chastisement. O highly powerful one, we shall, without doubt, by the prowess of our arms, subdue all these enemies

143

of thine that have come hither." Thus addressed by Mahāpārcwa, king Rāvana, honoring his speech, said,—"O Mahāpārcwa, I will relate unto thee, who hast spoken (thus), a secret matter relating to myself, which befell me long since I saw Panjikasthalā, like a flame in the sky, coursing to the Great-father's mansion. Her pace slackened, as soon as she saw me, (turn) I feasted on her and deprived her of her attire. Then she went to the Great-father's place, like a crumpled lotus. That high-souled one received information of all that I had done; and thereat, waxing enraged, the Deity spoke unto me,—"If from this day, thou ravish a female by force, thy head certainly shall be driven in an hundred pieces. It is for this, that with my mind afflicted with fear, I do not violently force, Videha's daughter Sitā, anent lying with her fair self. My rush is like that of the sea, and my motion that of the wind. Dācaratha's son doth not know this, and therefore doth he approach sea. Who wisheth to address a lion that is lying asleep in a cave, resembling Death wrought up by wrath? Rāma hath not seen shafts shot by me, resembling two-tongued serpents,—and therefore, it is that he approacheth me. Like a meteor burning an elephant, I shall, with shafts shot from bow in hundreds, resembling the thunder-bolt, consume Rāma. And as at the proper hour the risen Sun defeateth the splendour of the stars, will I, surrounded by a mighty army, overpower his strength. Neither the thousand-eyed Vāsava, nor yet Varuna, is capable of fighting me. By the might of this arm did I formerly conquer this city, governed by Vaiçravana."

---

## SECTION XIV.

HEARING the words of the lord of Rākshasas, as well as the thundering of Kumbhakarna, Vibhishana addressed the Rākshasa chief, in a pregnant speech, fraught with his welfare,—"Thou hast been bound about thy neck by the mighty and huge serpent, Sitā, having her breast for its body anxiety for its venom, smile for its sharp fangs, and her five fingers for its hood. Therefore before the monkeys, resembling mountain-peaks, having teeth for their arms and nails for their weapons,—subjugate Lankā, do thou render Maithili unto Daçaratha's son. And before the shafts shot by Rāma, resembling the thunder-bolt and having impetuosity of the wind, cut off the heads of the foremost of the Rākshasas, do thou render Mithilā's daughter unto the son of Daçaratha. Neither Kumbhakarna nor Indrajit, neither Mahāparçwa nor Mahodara, neither Nikumbha nor Kumbha nor yet Atikaya, O king, can stay in the field against Rāghava. Living, thou, whether thou art protected by the Sun or the winds, or throwest thyself into the lap itself of Vāsava, or enterest the sky or the nether spheres, shall not escape death." Hearing Vibhishana's words, Prahasta said,—"Fear know we none whatever from the celestials, or Dānavas, or Yakshas, or Gandharbas, or huge snakes ; fear know we none in battle with birds and serpents. How can fear at all afflict us proceeding from the king's son, Rāma ? Hearing Prahasta's speech, Vibhishana, seeking the welfare of the king, and having his intellect grounded in virtue, interest and profit, said words enfolding high sense,—"O Prahasta, like a sinful person being unable to ascend heaven, what the king, Mahodara, thou, and Kumbhakarna, are saying with reference to Rāma, shall not prove true. As one without a raft cannot cross over the mighty main, how can I, or thou, or all the

Rākshas combined, cause death unto Rāma, who, O Prahasta, is versed in the sense of things. Even the gods become stolid before the sovereign of the Ikshwāku race, having righteousness for his principle quality, and being a mighty car-warrior and of such a character, and who is competent in action. As yet the Kanka-feathered, terrible and sharp shafts shot by Rāghava, have not pierced into thy body; and therefore thou dost speak so. And, O Prahasta, as yet the sharpened shafts, capable of destroying life and having the impetuosity of the thunder-bolt, have not entered into thy body, and therefore thou dost speak thus, neither Rāvana, nor the exceedingly powerful Triçirsha. Neither Kumbhakarna's son Nikumbha nor Indrajit, is capable of bearing in battle the son of Daçaratha, resembling Sakra himself. And neither Devantaka* nor Narantaka,† neither Atikāya,‡ nor the magnanimous Atiratha, nor the equally strong Akampana, is competent to stay Rāghava in fight. And the king, naturally of fierce temper and thoughtless, through the instrumentality of ye who appearing to be his friends are in reality his foes, seeketh to destroy the Rākshasas. Do ye take out and deliver the monarch, who hath through force become subject to a dreadful and mighty, and thousand-headed serpent bursting with immeasurable prowess. As a person possessed by fearfully strong ghosts, is saved by his friends pulling him by his hair, attaining your desire ye should, assembling together, rescue the king. This one is sunk in the Rāghava sea having excellent waters. Do ye speedily coming together deliver him. He (the king) hath fallen into the Kākutstha nether regions, I tell thee my full mind,—fraught with the welfare of this city together with the Rākshasas, as well of the king with his adherents. Do thou make over Maithili unto the son of the king. He is a true

---

* *Lit.*—destroyer of the Deity.—T.

† *Lit.*—destroyer of men.—T.

‡ *Lit.*—huge-bodied.—T.

counsellor who adviseth his master, after duly ascertaining the strength, position, increase or destruction of the enemies as well as of their own party.

---

## SECTION XV.

HEARING carefully the words of Bibhisana, gifted with the intelligence of the lord of speech, the high-souled Indrajit, the leader of demons, spake, saying,—"Why art thou, O uncle, speaking these useless words like one terrified? He even, who is not born in this race, cannot speak or act in this wise. Only one man in this family, my uncle Bibhisana, is weak in energy, strength, prowess, patience, heroism and vigor. Why art thou O timid one, afraid of them since any one of these Rākshasas is capable of slaying those two princes, human beings as they are? The master of the three worlds, the lord of the celestials, has been brought down by me as captive on this earth. And all the celestials smitten with fear fled to different quarters. I brought down on earth the loud-roaring celestial elephant Airavata and uprooted by force its tusks. And all the celestials were terrified at this. Am I not, who have shattered the pride of the celestials, afflicted the leading Daityas, and am gifted with excellent prowess, capable of discomfitting these two princess—very ordinary mortals as they are?" Hearing the words of (Indrajit) gifted with high energy, irrepressible and resembling the lord of celestials, Bibhisana, the foremost of those using weapons,addressed him with words, fraught with high import,—"O my son, thou art a mere child and of unripe intellect and hence thou art not capable of ascertaining the propriety and impropriety of counsels. Thou art therefore speaking thus like a maniac for thy own destruction. Thou art known as a son unto Râvana, O Indrajit, but in sooth, thou art his foe in disguise, since knowing of his destruction from Rāghava, thou dost not prevent him. Thou art brave, childish and hast been impelled by thy silly understanding. Thou shalt be slain along with him who hath brought thee in this counsel chamber. Thou art, O Indrajit, foolish, imprudent, devoid of humility, of an irritable temper, of feeble sense, vicious-minded and of a silly understanding. And thou dost speak so, being impelled by childishness. Who shall withstand in battle, the shafts, shot by Rāghava, resembling the rod of Death, the stick of Brahman, flaming like the Fire of Dissolution. Do thou render back Sitā, O king, unto Rāma, with riches, jewels, excellent ornaments, clothes and jems and we shall then be able to live here void of grief."

## SECTION XVI.

Bibhishana addressing him with these excellent and auspicious words, fraught with high sense, Râvana, impelled by Death, again spake in harsh accents.—"It is better to live with open enemies or enraged serpents than with those who pass for friends but are in reality foes. I know well the nature of kinsmen, in all the worlds, O Rākhasa,—one takes delight in another's misfortune. The kinsmen, O Rākshasa, generally disregard him who is their king,* protecteth the kingdom, educated and pious—and they always try to discomfit him, if he be a heroe. These terrible enemies—the kinsmen, hypocrite as they are, always take delight in one another's

* On account of the priority of his birth—T.

calamity. Hear, I shall relate what the elephants, in yore, spoke beholding some persons with noose in hand—"We do not fear, fire, weapons, or even the terrible noose—we fear only the dreadful kinsmen, blinded with selfishness. They alone unfold the means of our detection—there is not the least doubt about it. Fear from kinsmen is therefore known as the worst of all fears. In kine there is milk, in kinsmen, there is fear, in women there is fickleness, and in Brahmanas, there is asceticism. It doth not please thee, I fancy, O gentle one, that I am honored of the three worlds, the lord of riches, and the subduer of my foes. As the drops of water do not last long on the leaves of lotuses, so is the friendship with unworthy persons. As the autumnal clouds, albeit muttering, do not pour forth water, so is the friendship with unworthy persons. As a bee flies away after sucking up the honey so is the friendship with unworthy persons. As a bee, after feeding upon the Kāça flowers, doth not get honey so is (fruitless) the friendship with unworthy persons. As an elephant, after being bathed, covers its body again with dust, taking it with its trunk, so is the friendship with unworthy persons.* Fie thee, O monkey, O thou that bringest disgrace on the family. Had any one else spoken thus he would have ceased to live by this time." Being thus accosted harshly, Bibhisana, speaking truth, rose up along with four Rākshasas having maces in their hands. "Thereupon, rising up in the welkin, the graceful brother Bibhisana, worked up with ire, addressed the lord of Rākshasas—Thou art mistaken, O king. Do thou speak what thou wishest—thou art my elder brother, adorable like unto father—thou dost not follow the track of virtue. I cannot tolerate the harsh accents of thine, my elder brother.—For thy welfare I spoke those well-meaning words, O Ten-necked one, but thou didst not pay heed to them being brought under the control of Death. O king, many are the persons who speak sweet words, but rare are they

* They afterwards forsake their former friends.—T.

who can speak and hear unpalatable but well-meaning words. How can I disregard thy death like unto a burning house bound as thou art by the noose of Death, the destroyer of all creatures. I do not wish to behold thee slain by the well-sharpened shafts of Rāma, feathered in gold and resembling the flaming fire. Even the heroic and powerful persons, well versed in the use of weapons, wear away like sands in battle, being attracted by Death. Thou art worshipful unto me, do thou forgive me for what I have said for thy welfare. Do thou protect thyself and this city, abounding in Rākshasas. May good betide thee! I am going away and do thou be happy without me. What, I spoke unto thee, O ranger of the night, to prevent thee, for thy welfare, did not please thee. Persons, whose lease of life is well-nigh expired, do not pay heed to the well-meaning words of their friends."

## SECTION XVII.

HAVING addressed Rāvana with these harsh words, his younger brother, reached in no time, where Rāma along with Lakshmana was. The leading monkeys, stationed on earth, espied him on the welkin, resembling in size the summit of the mount Meru, and burning like lightning in the effulgence of his own person. And his four attendants of terrible prowess were adorned with excellent ornaments and armed with armours and maces. He was like unto a collection of clouds, powerful as the thunder-bolt, holding an excellent mace, heroic and embellished with excellent ornaments. And beholding him along with four counsellors, the highly intelligent Sugriva, the lord of monkeys, engaged in meditation along with them. And meditating for a while, he spoke unto the monkeys headed by Hanumān the following excellent words—"Behold, there comes a Rākshasa, armed with various weapons and followed by four demons to slay us and there is not the least doubt about it." And hearing the words of Sugriva, the excellent monkeys, taking up huge trees and crags, bespoke him,—"Do thou order us, O king, to destroy these vicious-souled demons. These shall crush them to death, limited as is the tenure of their life." They addressing each other in this wise, Bibhisana descended from the sky on the northern shore. And beholding Sugriva and all others stationed near him, the highly intelligent Bibhisana accosted them, at the highest pitch of his voice, saying,—"Liveth there the Rākshasa, Rāvana, the lord of demons, and perpetrator of many iniquitous deeds. I am his younger brother known as Bibhisana. By him, slaying the vulture Yatāyu, was carried away Sitā from Janasthāna. She is imprisoned, brought under his sway, poorly, and being well guarded by the Rākshasees. With various well meaning words and reasonings I pointed out unto him, the necessity of rendering back Sitā unto Rāma. And Rāvana, possessed by Death, paid no heed to my well-meaning words, like unto one, lying on the brink of death, neglecting the administration of medicine. Being reviled by him and treated harshly like a menial, I have come to seek Rāghava's shelter, renouncing my children and wives. Do ye soon mention unto the high-souled Rāghava, the refuge of all creatures, that Bibhisana hath arrived." Hearing those words the quick-paced Sugriva, excited with ire, spake unto Rāma, before Lakshmana, saying,—"Forsooth hath an enemy entered secretly in our midst and he shall slay us getting an opportunity like unto an owl killing the crows. O slayer of foes, it now behoveth thee to be particularly careful about the counsels, arrangement of soldiers, polity—civil and military and spies of our own party as well as those of the enemies. These Rākshasas are heroic; they assume shapes at will, always lie in ambush and secretly bring about others' ruin—we should not therefore place confidence in them. This must be the emissary of Rāvana—the lord of Rākshasas. Entering in our midst, he shall, in sooth, sow dissensions in our camp, or he shall slay us when we are careless, confiding in them. Avoiding the enemies, we should now collect the forest-rangers our friends and servants. O lord, this man is a Rākshasa by birth and the brother of our foe and so is he our enemy, how can we trust him? Rāvana's younger brother, known as Bibhishana, hath come here with four Rākshasas, to seek thy shelter. O thou the foremost of forgiving persons, I consider this Bibhishana, who hath been despatched by Rāvana, worthy of being slain. Being impelled by his wicked intention and commissioned by Rāvana, this Rākshasa hath come here and secretly by virtue of his illussive powers he shall slay thee, O innocent one, when thou shalt place confidence in him." Having thus accosted Rāma, skilled in the art of speech, that lord of the army, Sugriva, well versed in speech, became silent. And hearing the words of Sugriva, the mighty Rāma spake unto the monkeys, near him, headed by Hanumān, saying,—"Ye have all heard, the words well grounded in reason, the lord of monkeys hath said, regarding Rāvana's younger brother. It behoveth him, who desireth for perpetual wealth, and is intelligent and capable of giving sound counsels, to advise his friends in difficult matters." Being thus addressed by Rāma (to minister unto him best counsels) all those monkeys, intent upon encompassing his well-being, gave out their respective opinions. "O Rāghava, there is nothing beyond thy knowledge in the three worlds. It is only to show thy respect towards us, O Rāma, that thou dost accost us in this wise. Thou art of truthful vows, heroic, pious, of firm prowess, discriminating, recollecting and having implicit confidence in thy friends. Let the intelligent and capable counsellors deliver their reasonable opinions unto thee." They speaking thus unto Rāghava, the intelligent monkey Angada, spoke as follows for sounding the intention of Bibhishana,—"We should always suspect him since he has come from the side of our enemies, and should not, all on a sudden, place confidence in him. The wicked-minded always move about hiding their real self, and bring about peoples' calamity, taking advantage of their weak points. And great is the disaster thereof. It is always proper to engage in actions, considering what is right and what is wrong. Virtues should always be gathered and vices abondoned. Do thou renounce him unhesitatingly, if dost thou find in him a source of a great calamity and do thou embrace him if dost thou find him crowned with many virtues." Thereupon followed Sarava with words fraught with high import,—"O best of men, do thou speedily despatch emissaries to sound Bibhishana. If dost thou, sounding him well through the instrumentality of sharp spies, find him friendly, do thou win him over to thy side." Thereupon the wise Jāmbhaban, arriving at conclusions by virtue of his knowledge of *Sastras*, began with words, void of defects,—"Surely doth Bibhishana come from the vicious lord of Rākshasas, dead set against us and hath arrived at such a bad place and in such a bad hour. We should always fear him." And thereupon followed Mainda, conversant with what is right and wrong, after due deliberation, with words pregnant with reason,—"He is Rāvana's younger brother, by name Bibhishana. Let the lord of men ask him every thing at first in sweet words. Do thou first ascertain, O foremost of men, with what intention he hath come—evil or good—and then settle what course to adopt." Thereupon spake Hanumān, the foremost of the counsellors and well versed in *Sastras*, in accents sweet, glorious and fraught with a high value,—"Even Vrihaspati, (the lord of speech) cannot excell thee, capable,* gifted with the best of intellect and foremost of those skilled in the art

* Capable to ascertain the truth of all Sastras.—T.

of speech, as thou art. And what I know I speak, O king. I do so, in the interest of Rāma's work and not impelled by my skill in the art of speech, by the pride of being a counsellor, by the vanity of being gifted with a high intellect or by the desire of speaking for its own sake. What thy counsellors have said for ascertaining the good or evil intention of Bibhishana appeareth to me as most defective and productive of no consequence whatever. It is impossible to sound him without any command.* And even to command him now for the same appears to me as improper. And as regards the despatch of spies, anent what thou hast been advised by thy ministers, I do not observe any utility. And what little I have thought of, I have something to say (regarding Jāmbabān's proposal) that Bibhishana hath arrived at such a bad place and in such an evil hour. He has really come to a very good place and in a very good hour. And truly has he performed a becoming and sensible action by coming here after duly ascertaining that Rāvana is a vicious wight and thou art a pious person—he is full of vices—thou art gifted with many virtues—he is tyrranical and thou art powerful. And what they have said, O king, as regards sounding him through secret spies, appears to me as one requiring great wisdom. An intelligent man, when questioned by any suddenly, suspects many things. And if the new-comer be a friend and has come here for his own happiness, how greatly shall his mind be changed by such a course? Besides by a sudden questioning it is impossible to ascertain the intention of a foreigner. Do thou therefore thyself accost him and determine, by his voice, his secret motive. I did not however mark anything of his wickedness while he spoke; rather I did observe signs of gladness on his countenance. So I do not suspect him. The wily can never come fearless and undisturbed. Nor were his words cunning. So I do not suspect him. It is not very easy to hide one's real nature. It manifests itself by force.

* To command to relate for what he has come.—T.

So this action of Bibhishana is not out of place or season. When accomplished it shall redound to his own interest. Considering well thy preparations for war and Râvana's vain conduct, hearing of Vali's destruction and Sugriva's installation on the throne, he hath, impelled by his good sense, come here, desirous of gaining the kingdom. Taking these into account, it seems prudent to take him to our side. O thou the foremost of the intelligent, I have spoken thus considering him sincere. It now behoveth thee to perform what thou thinkest proper."

## SECTION XVIII.

HEARING those words of the Wind-god's son, the irrepressible Râma, conversant with all the Sâstras, replied, with words expressing his own opinion—"I have also thought of some thing regarding Bibhishana. I wish you all, interested in my well-being, to hear that. (Bibhishana) hath come here as a friend so I cannot forsake him by any means. And even if he has come with any evil intent it is not culpable for the pious to afford him shelter." Thereupon hearing his words and considering them well, Sugriva, the lord of the monkeys, replied in more auspicious* words,—"Whether this ranger of the night is sincere or wicked, he should never be offered any shelter, since he hath forsaken his brother in the midst of these calamities. What reason is there to believe that he shall not renounce us in our difficulty ?" Hearing the words of the lord of monkeys and casting his looks towards them, Kâkutstha, having truth for his prowess, smiling a little, spake, unto Lakshmana,

* More reasonable words.—T.

crowned with all the marks of piety, saying—"Without being conversant with *Sastras*, and living in the company of old men, none can speak such words as have been uttered by the king of the monkeys. There appear unto me, however two subtler reasons anent the difference between brothers, amongst the kings—one is evident and another mundane. There are two classes of foes—one consisting of the members of the same line the other of the neighbours. And these generally bring about our misfortune whenever any opportunity presents itself. And it is for this that he hath come here. Those kinsmen, who do not think of one another's mischief, generally long for their respective well-being. But even such well-meaning relatives are feared by the kings. And hear, I shall relate, what the *Sastras* say regarding the weak points thou hast mentioned as to the advisability of taking the enemies to our side. We are not his kinsmen and this Rākshasa hath come here with a view to gain the kingdom. Even the Rākshasas are wise enough to ascertain the proper course—so we must take Bibhishana. If the brothers are confident and satisfied with each other they generally live together, or else they fear each other and ultimately engage in a tumultuous war. And there hath sprung up some difference with Rāvana and therefore Bibhishana hath come here. Nor are, O friend, all brothers like Bharata, all sons like me unto their father, all friends like thee." Being thus addressed by Rāma, the highly wise Sugriva, along with Lakshmana, rose up and bending low his head, said—"O thou the best of all forgiving persons, this night-ranger hath been despatched by Rāvana. I therefore think it better to kill him. Being impelled by his vicious sense that Rākshasa hath come here to slay us, O innocent one, when myself, thou and Lakshmana shall consider ourselves secure. Therefore the large-armed Bibhisana, the younger brother of the ruthless Rāvana, deserves to be slain along with his counsellors." Hāving thus addressed (Rāma) the foremost of Raghu's race, skilled in art of speech, Sugriva, the lord of monkey host, equally versed in the art of speech, became silent. And hearing the words of Sugriva, and weighing them, Rāma again addressed the foremost of monkeys with more reasonable accents—"Wicked or otherwise, whatever this night-ranger may be, he shall not be able to do me the least mischief. Pisāchas, Dānavas, Yakshas or all the Rākshasas on earth,—I can slay them all, if I like, with the tips of my fingers, O thou the lord of monkeys. I have heard of a pigeon adoring and entertaining with its own flesh, an enemy who took its shelter. While a pigeon received so friendly its enemy, the slayer of its mate, how can I then act otherwise, O foremost of the monkeys? Do thou hear, I shall relate, a sacred story, narrated by the great ascetic, the truthful Kandu, son of the ascetic Kanya. O slayer of foes, even a wicked-minded enemy, if he, with folded palms and a poor heart, craveth for thy shelter, should not be slain. If an enemy, proud or terrified, seeketh shelter in affright, he should be saved by a great man even at the risk of his own life. One, who from fear, ignorance or wilfully doth not protect him who seeketh his shelter, perpetrateth a mighty iniquity, blamed of all. When a person is slain before him whose shelter he hath taken he taketh away all the virtues of his protector. So great is the sin in not affording shelter unto those who seek for it; it standeth in the way of going to heaven, bringeth in calumny and destroyeth the strength and prowess. I shall therefore follow the excellent words of Kandu—leading to piety, fame and the attainment of the abode of the celestials. I always declare 'no fear' unto all creatures, whenever any, approaching me, says, 'I am thine' and seeketh my shelter. Even this is my pious observance. O Sugriva, O foremost of monkeys, do thou soon bring him here, whether he be Rāvana or Bibhishana and I shall declare unto him 'no fear.' Hearing the words of Rāma, Sugriva, the lords of those who go bounding, over-flowing with friendliness, bespake Kākutstha.—"What wonder is there that thou wouldst speak these auspicious words, O thou the foremost of kings, conversant with morality, gifted with prowess and ever treading the pious track as thou art. Truly doth my inner self regard Bibhisana as devoid of any wicked intention. He has been well sounded by signs and gestures. And let the greatly wise Bibhisana, O Rāghava, be placed on an equal footing with us and gain our friendship." Hearing the words of Sugriva, the lord of monkeys, the king of men (Rāma) made instantly friends with Bibhisana, like unto the conqueror of enemies' cities making friends with the king of birds.

## SECTION XIX.

RAGHAVA thus declaring unto him 'no fear', Rāvana's younger brother, the greatly wise Bibhisana, bending low his head, cast his looks on the earth. And descending from the welkin with his devoted attendants the virtuous-souled Bibhisana, delighted, bowed unto Rāma. And thereupon touching his feet along with four Rākshasas, Bibhisana addressed Rāma,—with words, fraught with piety, befitting the occasion and conducing to pleasure. "I am Rāvana's younger brother and have been greatly insulted by him. I have therefore come to seek thy shelter, the refuge of all creatures, abandoning Lankā and renouncing my friends and riches. My kingdom, life and happiness are all at thy disposal." Hearing his words Rāma replied,—comforting him with words and favouring him as if with looks. "Do thou relate unto me truly the strength and weakness of the enemies." Being thus accosted by Rāma of unwearied actions, the Raksha, began to describe the strength of Râvana. "O prince, by virtue of the boon acquired from the Self-Create, the Ten-necked one is incapable of being slain by all creatures—Gandharbas, serpents, or birds. My elder brother—the one next to Râvana—is the heroic and highly effulgent *Kumbhakarna*—Sakra's equal in battle. Thou mayst have heard, O Râma, his commander is Prahasta, by whom was defeated Manibhadra on the mount Kailâça. (His son) Indrajit, equipped with invincible armour, bow and finger-protector made of the skin of iguana, becomes invisible in fight. And, worshipping Fire and becoming invisible, that graceful hero, O Râghava, slayeth the enemies in conflict, having the contending parties vast and well arranged. Mahodara, Mahâpârçwa and the Râkshasa, Akampana, are his lieutenants, who equal the Lokapâlas* in battle. His army consists of ten thousand *kotis* of Râkshasas, wearing shapes at will, inhabiting the city of Lankâ, and living on flesh and gore. And with the *Lokpâlas* and the celestials, they were all defeated by the vicious-souled Râvana." Hearing the words of Bibhisana and weighing them in his mind, that foremost of Raghu's race said—"I understand well the strength and prowess of Râvana, which thou hast depicted truly, O Bibhisana. Do thou hear truly that I shall slay the Ten-necked one together with Prahasta and his sons, and I shall make thee king. Whether he entereth the *Rasâtala*† or the regions under the earth, or seeketh shelter of the Grand-father of the celestials, he shall not be able to save his life from me. I do swear by my three brethern that I shall enter the city of Ayodhyâ, after slaying in battle Râvana with his sons, kinsmen and friends." Hearing these words of Râma of unwearied action, the virtuous-souled

* Divinities who protect the regions, or the Sun, Moon, Fire, Wind, Indra, Yama, Varuna and Kuvera.—T.

† The seven infernal regions under the earth and the residence of the *Nâgas*, *Asuras* and *Daityas*. This is the lowest of the seven divisions of Pâtâla.—T.

(Bibhisana), bowing his head unto him, began—"I shall lend thee my might in slaying the Râkshasas and devastating the city of Lankâ, and shall be in the midst of Râvana's army." Thereupon, embracing Bibhisana, who spoke thus, Râma, delighted, said unto Lakshmana,—"O my brother, do thou bring water from the ocean. Sprinkling the greatly wise Bibhisana, I shall make him at once the king of the Râkshasas, O conferer of honor; for I am greatly pleased with him." Being thus addressed, Saumitri, at the command of the king, annointed Bibhisana and made him the king of the Râkshasas in the presence of the monkey-host. Beholding Râma's kindness (towards Bibhisana), the monkeys eulogized the high-souled one, exclaiming "Excellent! Excellent!" Thereupon, Hanumân and Sugriva addressed Bibhisana, saying, "Do thou tell us how we shall cross over the main—the abode of Varuna, along with the host of the highly powerful monkeys. Do thou inform us of the means by which we may cross over, along with our army, the lord of rivers and streams—the abode of Varuna." Being thus addressed, the virtuous-souled Bibhisana replied,—"It behoveth the king, Râghava, to seek refuge from the Ocean. This measureless deep was dug out by (the king) Sagara.* And the great Ocean shall surely help Râma belonging to Sagara's race." Being thus accosted by the wise Râkshasa, Bibhishana, Sugriva reached where Râma with Lakshmana was. Thereupon, the broad-necked Sugriva began to explain the well-meaning words of Bibhishana, requesting Râma to seek the shelter of the Ocean. And those words pleased Râma, pious by nature. And the highly effulgent (hero) requested, smiling, the active Lakshmana and the monkey-chief Sugriva to collect necessaries for his adoration. "O Lakshmana, this counsel of Bibhisana appeareth to me as most sound. Sugriva is always greatly

* *Sagara* was a sovereign of Ayodhyâ, belonging to the same family with Râma.—T.

wise, and thou art greatly proficient in counsel. Do ye, holding a conference, intimate to me what you think becoming." Thus addressed, those two heroes—Lakshmana and Sugriva, spoke respectfully the following words fraught with propriety,—"Why shall not the well-meaning words of Bibhisana expressed now, please us, O Rāghava, O thou best of men? Without constructing a bridge over the deep, the terrible abode of Varuna, even the celestials and their lord (Indra) cannot get at the city of Lankā. Do thou act on the genuine counsel of the heroic Bibhisana, and without losing time, do thou engage the Ocean for this work, so that we may with our army proceed to the city of Rāvana." Being thus addressed Rāma reached the shore of the lord of rivers and streams, covered with Kuça, like unto fire getting into the sacrificial dais.

## SECTION XX.

THEREUPON the greatly powerful Rākshasa, by name *Sârdula,* beheld the army of Sugriva arranged on the shore of the ocean. And, beholding the army all busy, the emissary of the vicious-souled Rākshasa—Rāvana, entered the city of Lankā and, approaching his lord, said,—"The army of monkeys and bears hath approached Lankā. It is immeasurably deep as the ocean. And those two sons of the king Daçaratha—the brothers Rāma and Lakshmana, gifted with great beauty, coming to rescue Sitā, have stationed themselves on the shore of the ocean, O thou of great effulgence. The army of Rāma extends over the sky and ten *yoyanas.* I have come, O great king, to acquaint thee with the real truth. And, knowing everything, it behoveth thy emissaries, O king, to settle whether to render back Sitā, to adopt measures of conciliation, or to sow dissensions in the enemy's camp." Hearing the words of *Sârdula*, Rāvana, the lord of Rākshasas, being anxious to ascertain his duty, addressed a Rākshasa by name Suka, the most sensible of his counsellors, with the following pregnant words, —"Do thou go and communicate unto king Sugriva my behest, in becoming and excellent accents. 'Thou art born of a great family and art the mighty son of the king of bears. I have no dissension with thee. In fact I consider thee as my brother, O king of monkeys. Though I have stolen the spouse of the high-souled prince (Rāma), yet what is that to thee, O Sugriva? Do thou return to Kishkindhā. The monkeys shall not by any means be able to attack the city of Lankā. Even the celestials and Gandharbas could not— what of these men and monkeys?" And being thus commissioned by the lord of Rākshasas, that night-ranger assumed the shape of a bird and, bounding, speedily reached the sky. And, proceeding far over the deep and stationing himself at the welkin, he spoke unto Sugriva all the words with which he was addressed by the vicious-souled Rāvana. Hearing him speak thus, the monkeys leaped up quickly and reached there with a view to chop off his wings or to slay him with their clenched fists. On being seized vehemently by all these monkeys, that night-ranger was brought down speedily from the sky to the earth. And being assailed by the monkeys, Suka said,—"O Kākutstha, it doth not behove (people) to slay an emissary. Do thou therefore prevent the monkeys. He who passing by his master's behest, giveth out his own intention, is not faithful; and he therefore deserveth to be slain." Hearing the piteous accents of Suka, Rāma spake unto the monkeys, who were about to kill him, saying, "Do not kill him." And again stationing himself on the welkin, that night-ranger said,—"O Sugriva, O thou gifted with great energy, O thou of great prowess, what shall I speak unto

Rāvana, dreaded by all people ?" Being thus addressed, that mighty king of monkeys, the bull among them, of unwearied energy, spake unto that emissary—the night-ranger, Suka, saying—"O Rāvana, thou art not my friend or an object of pity. Thou art not my benefactor, nor art liked by me. Thou art Rāma's enemy, and thou dost therefore deserve to be slain by him like Vāli along with thy friends and relatives. I shall therefore slay thee, O king of night-rangers, together with thy sons, friends and relatives. And I shall have the whole city of Lankā reduced to ashes by my mighty force. Thou shalt not be able to escape Rāghava, O Rāvana, O thou who hast lost thy sense, even if thou art protected by the celestials. And thou shalt with thy brother be slain by Rāma, even if thou dost fly into the sky, enter into the regions under the earth, or seek shelter of Mahādeva. I do not behold any in these three worlds—Pisācha, Rākshasa, Gandharba, or Asura, who can protect thee. Thou hast slain the monarch of vultures, who had grown decrepit through age.* Thou hast carried off the large-eyed Sitā from the vicinity of Rāma and the neighbourhood of Lakshmana ; but, having captured her, thou understandest not (thy native strength). Nor dost thou understand that foremost of Rāghus, high-souled, possessed of great strength, and incapable of being repressed even by the celestials,—who shall take thy life." Then spake that best of monkeys, Angada, son of Vāli,—"O highly wise one, this is no emissary. This one clearly appeareth to me as a spy. He hath come to form an estimate of thy entire army. Take him. Let him not go (back) to Lankā. This is indeed what I would." Thereat, commanded by the king, the monkeys, springing up, seized (Suka) and bound him, as he burst out bewailing like one forlorn. On being sorely handled by the

---

* The commentator has a queer and characteristic note on *Jarāvriddha—decrepit through age. One that is old, may stave off decrepitude through some drug, while a youthful person may come by the same in consequence of some curse.—T.*

relentless monkeys, Suka cried unto the high-souled Rāma, son of Daçaratha,—"They by main force sever my wings, and they pierce my eyes. If I lose my life, may all the evil deeds that I have committed between the night when I was born and the night when I shall die, be thine!" Hearing this pitiful cry, Rāma prevented (the monkeys); and he said unto them,—"Let go this envoy, who hath come here."

---

## SECTION XXI.

Then on the shore of the sea, Rāghava, spreading *darbha*, with his hands joined towards the great deep, laid him down, with his face to the East. And that slayer of foes (lay down), making his pillow his arm resembling the shining form of a serpent; always dight with golden ornaments; full many a time pressed with the palms of beauteous damsels,* decked with jewelled golden *Keyuras* and superb ornaments studded with pearls; smeared from above with sandal and *aguru*; (his arm) which formerly had been graced in bed with the head of Sitā; like unto the body of Takshaka under the waters of the Gangā; resembling a yoke; in battle increasing the sorrow of foes and enhancing for long the delight of friends;—his left arm having its skin destroyed by the strokes of the bow-string; which was the refuge of the entire earth;—his right arm resembling a mighty bludgeon,—the donor of thousands of kine,—making this great arm his pillow (he laid him down). "To-day either I shall die, or shall the Ocean."—Having thus formed his

* The commentator appropriately remarks: *As Rāma was wedded to a single wife, these damsels must mean nurses attending on him.*—T.

resolution in respect of the great deep, Rāma, restraining his speech, with a concentrated mind lay down there agreeably to rule. And as Rāma slept on the earth on Kuça spread over, without ever swerving from the rule, three nights passed away. And while spending three nights, Rāma, learned in polity and attached to virtue, prayed unto that lord of streams—the Ocean. Yet the wicked Ocean, albeit adored according to his deserts by Rāma with his mind concentrated, did not show himself. Thereat Rāma grew enraged and had the corners of his eyes crimsoned; and he spake unto Lakshmana of auspicious marks, saying,—"Behold the hauteur of the Ocean in not presenting himself before me. Calmness,forbearance, candour, and soft speech—these virtues of the good are by the insolent taken for the effects of incompetency. The person* that is self-laudatory, wicked, and badly-bold, publisheth his own praise,and meteth out chastisement everywhere,† is honored in the world. By moderation one cannot attain celebrity, by moderation one cannot attain fame,—and, O Lakshmana, in this world by moderation one cannot attain victory on 'the edge of battle.'‡ See, O Sumitrā's son, the abode of Makaras, with his waters obstructed all around with Makaras destroyed by my shafts. And, O Lakshmana, see the bodies here of serpents, and the huge bodies of mighty fishes, and the trunks of elephants,—torn by my arrows. And to-day in terrible battle will I dry up the Ocean with conchs and oysters, and fishes and Makaras. This abode of Makaras taketh me, who is forbearing, to be incompetent. Fie on forbearance towards such as he! In consequence of my moderation, Ocean showeth not his own form. O Saumitri, bring thou my bow, my arrows resembling venomous snakes. I will dry up the Ocean, and

---

* The word, however, is *naram (ac.), man.*—T.

† i. e. *indiscriminately.*—*T.*

‡ *Rana murddhani,*—'The perilous *edge of battle* when it raged.'

*Par. Lost.*, Bk. I.

the monkeys shall go over on foot. And, being angered, to-day, albeit incapable of being agitated, will I agitate the deep. And by means of my shafts will I make Varuna's abode, surging with a thousand billows and having his dignity maintained by his shores,—overleap his continents. And I will agitate the deep harbouring numbers of mighty Dānavas." Having spoken thus, Rāma, equipped with his bow, with his eyes dilated in wrath, became exceedingly irrepressible, like unto the flaming fire at the final dissolution. And straining his dreadful bow, making the earth shake, tremulously, he let fly fierce shafts like him of an hundred sacrifices hurling his thunder-bolt. Thereat, flaming up, those vehement choice shafts surcharged with energy, enter into the waters of the sea, with its serpents afflicted with fear. And then great and exceedingly dreadful was the motion of the sea, with fishes and Makaras, and with the roar of the winds (blowing there). And on a sudden the mighty deep was heaving with mighty surges, with conchs scattered about, and a smoke (enveloped) the ocean ; and the billows became visible on all sides. And the serpents were distressed, with their faces flaming and their eyes aglow ; as well as the Dānavas of terrific energy, and the dwellers of the nether spheres. And billows of the sovran Ocean, resembling Vindhya or Mandara, containing crocodiles and Makaras, sprang up by thousands. And Varuna's abode had its surges whirling, its serpents and Rākshasas seized with affright, and its ferocious aquatic animals borne all around ; and it sent forth sounds. Then Sumitrā's son, springing up, said unto Rāghava of fiery vehemence, as he sighed and kept stretching his matchless bow.—"This must not be." And he took away his (Rāma's) bow. "Without doing this unto the Ocean, thou, supreme of heroes, mayst have thy work accomplished. Personages like thee do not come under the influence of passion. Do thou deliberately look about for some worthy means (for compassing thy end.)" Then remaining invisible in the sky, Brahmarshis and Surarshis,* exclaiming,—"Well-a-day !" and "Do'nt," in loud accents ejaculated,—(Oh ! and alas !)

---

## SECTION XXII.

THEN the foremost of Raghus addressed Ocean in stern words, saying,—"To-day will I dry up the Ocean along with the nether regions. And, O Ocean, thy waters being burnt up by my shafts, and thou being dried up, with thy (aquatic) animals slaughtered, a mighty volume of dust shall arise (from thy bed). And, O Ocean, in consequence of the arrowy shower discharged from my bow, the monkeys shall go over to the further shore on foot. Having attained dimensions in consequence of access of waters, thou knowest not my manliness or my prowess. But, O abode of Dānavas, grief shalt thou reap at my hands." Then fixing an arrow resembling the rod of Brahmā with a Brahma Mantra, on the best of bows, that exceedingly strong on drew it. And as Rāghava suddenly stretched his bow, heaven and earth seemed to be riven, and the mountains trembled. And darkness covered the world, and the cardinal points became invisible. And at once the watery expanses and rivers were agitated. And the stars appeared simultaneously with the Sun and Moon.† And the sky was illumined with the rays of the Sun, and yet it was overspread with darkness; and it burned with an hundred meteors. And thunder-bolts sending forth sounds surpassing all others, dropped from the firmament. And the

---

* Celestial saints.

† The phenomenon, remarks the commentator, was owing to the heavenly bodies obstructing each other's orbit.—T.

winds began to blow violently; breaking down trees and momentarily scattering clouds; damaging mountain-tops and shattering summits. And then the dread and mighty thunders possessing impetuous speed and emitting tremendous roars,—coming together, produced lightning flashes. And those creatures that could be seen, uttered sounds resembling the thunder; and those that were invisible gave forth frightful cries. And overwhelmed with fright, and quaking (for fear), the creatures began to measure their lengths,—and they were sore affiicted, and bereft of motion through terror. And then the mighty deep with its animals, and with its waters and waves, and with its serpents and Rākshasas, was suddenly wrought up with a violent motion. And albeit it was not the occasion of the universal dissolution, the Ocean passed beyond his shores for a full hundred *yoyanas*. And seeing the elated Ocean—lord of streams and rivers—thus overpass his bounds, that destroyer of enemies, Raghu's son, Rāma, was not moved.* Then from forth the mid-sea arose Ocean himself, even as the maker of day riseth from the mighty ascending-hill, Meru. And accompanied by Pannagas† of flaming faces, the Ocean showed himself, appearing like cool lapises, adorned with golden ornaments,—wearing a wreath of gems and a jewelled vesture, with his eyes resembling lotus-leaves, bearing on his head a noble garland containing all flowers; decked with ornaments of polished gold; as well with excellent ornaments of gems originating in himself, like the mountain Himavān embellished with metals (sprung in himself),—(the Ocean arose) with wave on wave whirling around, and rife with winds blowing among clouds,—surrounded by streams, Gangā, Sindhu (and others). And approaching the arrow-showering Rāma, and greeting him fair, Ocean spoke unto him with joined hands,—"O Rāghava, earth, air,

---

* *Nātichakrāma* may also mean, (*Rāma*) did not discharge any more arrows.—T.

† Semi-divine serpents.—T.

sky, water and light,—these, O mild one, retaining their eternal course, maintain their (respective) natures. Mine also is that nature whereby I am fathomless and incapable of being crossed. The reverse of this is the having a bottom. And for this reason I speak to thee (concerning the means). O king's son, not from desire, or covetuousness, or fear, or anger, can I anywise deprive my waters abounding in alligators of their (perpetual) motion. I will tell thee how thou wilt pass (over me); and I will bear it. And no ferocious aquatic animals shall do wrong so long as thy forces have not crossed. And, O Rāma, I will make as it were firm land for the crossing over of the monkeys." Then Rāma said,—"O Varuna's abode, listen to me! This arrow (of mine) must accomplish the end (intended). Where shall I let it light?" Hearing Rāma's speech, and looking at the mighty arrow, that exceedingly energetic one, the great Deep, addressed Rāghava, saying,—"There is a certain spot of mine in the North, which is more sacred (than the rest). It is famed as Drumakulya, even as thou art famed in the world. There are there many robbers of ferocious forms and actions, —wicked wights, headed by cow-herds,—who drink of my water. These persons of unrighteous acts touch me, and I cannot bear this sin. O Rāma, do thou at that place render this best of arrows successful.'' Hearing the words of the high-souled Ocean, (Rāma) immediately after,* let fly that flaming shaft. And the place where the arrow resembling the thunder-bolt and *vajra* in splendour, alighted, hath been celebrated on earth as Marukāntāra. And hurt with the dart, the Earth emitted roars; and in consequence of this, water began to gush out at the mouth of the wound from the subterranean regions. And this then became well-known as Vrana; and there are seen the waters of the Ocean spring up. And there arose a terrific report of riving. And owing

* *Sāgaradarçanāt*—may also mean, agreeably to the Ocean's instruction.—T.

to this,* as well as the incident of the arrow, the water that existed in the tanks, was dried up. Having dried up Marukāntāra famous throughout the three regions, as well as the reservoirs of water, Rāma the son of Daçaratha, learned and of god-like prowess, conferred a boon on the desert, saying,—"This place shall be filled with food nourishing beasts; and ailments shall be rare here. And the fruits and roots shall be replete with relish; and it shall abound in oil and overflow with milk; and it shall contain various odorous drugs." Thus did the desert come to possess these attributes; and from Rāma's bestowal of a boon, it attained a pleasant aspect. On that place being burnt up, that lord of streams, the Ocean, thus spake unto Rāghava, versed in every branch of learning,—"O mild one, this one is named Nala, son unto Viçwakarmā. He hath received a boon from his sire. Viçwakarmā's son is well pleased with thee. Let this monkey, surcharged with exhuberant spirits, build a bridge over me. I will hold that up. This one is as his sire." Having delivered himself thus, Ocean disappeared. Then that foremost of monkeys, Nala, arising, spoke unto the mighty Rāma,—"Resorting to my sire's skill, I will build a bridge over the spacious abode of Makaras. The mighty Ocean hath spoken justly. In respect of the ingrate even chastisement is supreme in this world,—this is my conviction. Down with forbearance, or moderation, or gift! This dreadful Ocean, this mighty deep, expecting to see a bridge (thrown over him), hath granted depth unto Rāghava.—(Formerly) in Mandara, Viçwakarmā had conferred a boon on my mother: 'O exalted one, thy son shall be like me.' I am a son of his, sprung from his loins, and I am like unto Viçwakarmā. Not having been asked by thee, I had not unfolded my qualifications. I also am capable of constructing a bridge over Varuna's abode. Therefore this very day let the foremost monkeys construct the bridge." Then directed by Rāma, the

* i. e. *the sound.*

principal monkeys with alacrity entered the mighty forest in hundreds and thousands. And themselves resembling mountains, the foremost of the monkeys began to break down trees and draw them towards the Ocean. And the monkeys filled the Ocean with *sâlas*, and *açwakarnas*, *dhavas*, bamboos and *kutajas*, *arjunas*, palms, *tilakas*, *tiniças*, *billakas*, *saptaparnas*, and blossoming *karnikâras*, mangoes, and *açoka* trees. And those monkeys—the foremost of their species—began to gather the trees, some with their roots, and some without them,—carrying them like Indra's ensign. And those huge-bodied monkeys possessed of prodigious strength, procured palms and pomegranates, cocoanuts and Vibhitakas, Kariras, Vakulas, and Nimbas,—as well as rocks, measuring elephants' dimensions; and uprooting crags, they carried them by means of machines. And on rocks being plunged into the waters, the latter, suddenly swelling up, mounted to the welkin, and again subsided.—And (the trees) dropping (into the deep), vexed it all around. And some took lines (for insuring straightness unto the bridge). And at the middle of the lord of rivers and streams, Nala made a grand bridge measuring an hundred *yoyanas*. And then he set about constructing the bridge with the assistance of monkeys of dreadful deeds. And some took the measuring rod, and others bore (timber to the sea). And by help of hundreds of monkeys following Rāma's mandate, hued like clouds or mountains, (they) constructed a bridge with grass, and wood. And the monkeys made the bridge of trees with blossoming tops. And (monkeys) resembling Dānavas were seen rushing all around with rocks resembling hills, and mountain-summits. And tremendous was the tumult that arose of crags thrown and rocks toppled down into the mighty deep. And on the first day the elephant-like monkeys full of spirits and exerting themselves vigorously, finished fourteen *yoyanas*. And the exceedingly strong and huge-bodied monkeys on the second day speedily disposed of twenty *yoyanas*. And on the third day the huge-bodied active monkeys did one and twenty *yoyanas* on the sea. And on the fourth day the exceedingly impetuous monkeys, bestirring themselves vigorously, did two and twenty *yoyanas*. And on the fifth day the fast-speeding monkeys accomplished three and twenty *yoyanas* reaching unto the fair shore. And resembling his sire, that best of monkeys, the lusty and graceful offspring of Viçwakarmā, (thus) constructed the bridge over the sea. And that bridge built by force over the abode of *makaras*, looked graceful and splendid like the Milky way in the firmament. And then the deities and Gandharbas, the Siddhas and the prime saints, appearing in the heavens, stood there, eager to behold this wonder. And the gods and Gandharbas saw that bridge of Nala, difficult of being made, having an area of ten *yoyanas* and measuring an hundred in length. And the monkeys, leaping and bounding and roaring, as well as all creatures, beheld that building of the bridge on the ocean, inconceivable, and marvellous, displaying skill past thought and capable of making one's hair stand on end. And those thousands of Kotis of exceeding vigor, having constructed the bridge over the ocean, went over to the other shore of the mighty main. And spacious, skillfully constructed, graceful, well-paved and nicely finished, the great bridge appeared like the line where the hair hath been parted on the Ocean's head. Then on the other shore of the ocean, Bibhishana, with the view of opposing foes (that might advance), stationed himself mace in hand, along with some councilors. Then Sugriva spoke unto Rāma having truth for his prowess,—"Do thou get upon Hanumān, and let Laskhmana get upon Angada. O hero, vast is this Ocean—abode of Makaras. These monkeys, rangers of the sky, shall hold you up both." Thereat the graceful and righteous Rāma along with Lakshmana, equipped with his bow, set out in the van of the army in company with Sugriva. And some monkeys proceeded along the middle, and some plunged into the deep, and some went by the road. And some coursed through the air, bounding up bird-like. And that dreadful array of monkeys crossing over, with its mighty uproar drowned the dreadful roar of the deep, which had been arising. On the monkey-host having crossed by the bridge of Nala, the king stationed it on the shore abounding in fruits, roots and water. Beholding that work of Râghava incapable of being performed,the deities together with the Siddhas and Chāranas, and the Maharshis, suddenly presenting themselves before Rāma, sprinkled him one by one with sacred water, and said,—"Mayst thou be victorious, O human-divine one! Rule thou the Earth eternally!" Thus in various auspicious words, did they pay homage unto that one honored by the Brāhmanas, Rāma.

## SECTION XXIII.

HAVING seen omens, that one, Lakshmana's elder brother, conversant with them, embracing the son of Sumitrā, said these words,—"O Lakshmana, occupying (this tract) of cool waters and woods affluent with fruits, will we, dividing and arranging our forces, stay here. Mighty is the fear that I see at hand,—boding destruction to people and the slaughter of the foremost heroes of bears, monkeys and Rākshasas. The wind bloweth darkly, and the Earth shaketh. The tops of the mountains tremble, and trees topple down. And the clouds are ashen and roistering, and roar roughly. And lowering, they shower portentous drops of blood. And the twilight is terrible and looketh like the red sandal. And a fiery circle droppeth from the flaming sun. And on all sides birds and beasts, distressed, uttering woe-begone notes, and grim-visaged, set up cries against the sun, arousing great fear. And the Moon, although not appearing* in the night, burneth, and with dark and red rays riseth, as if it intended to exterminate people. And the aspect (of the sun) is slight, rough, and good;† and, O Lakshmana, a blue mark is visible on the unclouded Sun. And the stars seem erased by a mighty volume of dust. O Lakshmana, behold this sight disastrous to people like unto the universal dissolution. Crows, and hawks, and the inferior vultures, wheel all round. And jackals are sending inauspicious yells, exciting great fear. The earth shall be covered with darts and javelins, and swords discharged by monkeys and Rākshasas, and be turned into mire with flesh and gore. Surrounded by all the monkeys, will we, using speed, this very day rapidly enter into the city ruled by Rāvana, incapable of being subdued." Having said this, that subduer in conflict, that lord, that enchanter of men, Rāma,‡ equipped with his bow, proceeded in the direction of Lankā. And all the principal monkeys—Sugriva with Bibhishana—went on, setting up roars, for the destruction of foes, who were determined to battle with them. And consequently Raghu's son was well pleased with the fortitude and exertions of the powerful monkeys, for bringing about what was dear unto Rāghava.

---

* The moon, it seems, *doth* appear, but does not look out clearly.—T.

† *Praçasta*—I do not see the propriety of this epithet in this connection. This may be a mistake.—T.

‡ The word *Râma* occurs twice, one being the cognomen of the solar hero. The other means, *the enchanter of men.—T.*

## SECTION XXIV.

AND with the presence of the king* that assembly of heroes looked beautiful, as doth the autumnal night, garnished with beauteous stars, with the Moon. And oppressed with the bursting energy of the host resembling the ocean, the Earth trembled. And then the rangers of the forest heard a hubbub in Lankā, as well as the sounds of trumpets and Mridangas, mighty and capable of making people's down stand on end. And at those sounds, the leaders of monkey-bands were delighted beyond measure, and, resenting the same, set up cries louder than those sounds. And the Rākshasas also heard the roars of the monkeys, resembling the rumbling of haughty clouds in the sky. Beholding Lankā with variegated standards, and streamers, Daçaratha's son went† to Sitā with an aggrieved heart. "Here that one having eyes resembling those of a young deer, is confined by Rāvana, like unto Rohini overpowered by the red-bodied planet."‡ And, sighing hot and long, and looking at Lakshmana, that hero spoke words fraught with his good at that time,—"Behold, O Lakshmana, Lankā towering up as if piercing the heavens; and, built by Viçwakarmā on the brow of the mountain, she seems to have been made by the Mind. Constructed in time past with edifices thronging her, Lankā looks like the all-encasing air, covered with pale clouds. Lankā is embellished with groves resembling Chitraratha, fair, and eloquent with the notes of various birds, and fraught with fruits and flowers. Behold the intoxicated birds, and the black bees blending (with the blossoms). And the blessed breeze swayeth the trees vocal

* Râma.—T.

† *i.e.* mentally.—T.

‡ Angâraka.—T.

with the coels." Having divided his forces there agreeably to the directions of the scriptures, Daçaratha's son, Rāma, thus spoke unto Lakshmana. And he ordered that monkey-army, saying,—"Taking his own forces, let the puissant and invincible Angada along with Nila, station himself in the centre of the forces. And let the monkey, named Rishabha, surrounded by numbers of monkeys, post himself at the right of the monkey-army. And let the active and irrepressible Gandhamādana, resembling an elephant fragrant with the temporal exudation, stay, occupying the left of the forces. I myself along with Lakshmana, shall heedfully stay in the fore-front. And the monkeys, Jāmvabān, Sushena and Vagadarçi, the three high-souled, foremost bears,*—shall protect the interior (of the forces). And as the Sun, surcharged with energy, protects the hind half of the globe, let the monkey-monarch protect the rear of the monkey-army." And that army being skilfully divided into parts and protected by great monkeys, resembled the welkin covered with clouds. Then, taking up mountain-peaks and mighty trees, the monkeys began to proceed towards Lankā, burning to crush Lankā in battle. "We shall demolish Lankā by hurling mountain-peaks, or with our clenched fists." Thus did the foremost of monkeys think in their minds. Then the exceedingly energetic Rāma addressed Sugriva, saying,—"Our forces have been rightly marshalled,—let go (now) Suka." Hearing Rāma's words, the lord of monkeys possessed of great strength, liberated the envoy, Suka, at the command of Rāma. Liberated at the word of Rāma, Suka, who had been sore tormented by the monkeys, oppressed with exceeding great fear, went to the lord of Rākshasas. Thereat, Rāvana, laughing, said unto Suka,—"Are thy wings fettered? And thou seemst as if thy wings had been

---

* The epithet 'bears' coming after 'monkeys' may look incongruous; but, I fancy, 'monkeys' is used in the general sense of *being connected with the monkey-host.*—*T.*

severed. Why? Didst thou come under the control of the volatile (monkeys)?" Thereat, exercised with fear, Suka, commanded by the monarch, answered the lord of Rākshasas in this excellent speech, saying,—"Repairing to the northern shore of the sea, I, pacifying (the monkeys) with mild speech, communicated thy tidings clearly (unto Sugriva). Thereat, as soon as they saw me, the monkeys flying into a wrath, captured me, and attempted to clip my wings and slay me with their clenched fists. They are insuseptible of being spoken to. No doubt whatever can exist that, O lord of Rākshasas, the monkeys are by nature wrathful and fierce. The same Rāma that hath slain Virādha and Kavandha and Khara, hath arrived (here) along with Sugriva, searching for the whereabouts of Sitā. Having thrown a bridge across the brine and crossed the salt sea, Rāghava, equipped with his bow, stayeth here, setting the Rakshas at naught. And the hosts consisting of thousands of bears and monkeys, resembling hills and clouds, envelope the Earth. And peace there can be none between the forces of the Rākshasas and the hosts of the sovereign of monkeys, like unto the deities and the Dānavas. And they advance before the wall. Speedily do one of these things—make over Sitā without delay, or give (him) battle." Hearing Suka's speech, Rāvana with his eyes reddened in wrath, spoke, as if burning (Suka) with them,—"Even if gods, and Gandharbas, and Dānavas should array themselves against me, I will not from fear of all creatures, render (back) Sitā. When shall my shafts pursue Rāghava, like maddened Bhramaras making towards blossomy trees in spring? When by means of flaming shafts shot from my bow shall I burn (Rāghava) with his body bathed in blood, even as a meteor (burneth) an elephant? And when, surrounded by a mighty host, shall I confound his ranks, even as the Sun arising, (vanquisheth) the light of the stellar spheres? My impetuosity like the Ocean's, my strength like the Wind's, Dācarathi doth not know,—and therefore it is that he desireth to fight with me. Rāma hath not seen my shafts resting in the quiver, resembling venomous serpents,—and therefore it is that he seeketh to fight with me. Rāghava hath not in conflict formerly known my bow representing my Vinā sounded with my shafts; having tremendous sounds proceeding from the strings; dreadful; with the cries of distressed people for its mighty strains of music; and resonant with the reports of Nārāchas and palms. And, having bathed in the great field of battle representing the river of hostile forces, I will in the encounter strike (this Vinā). Neither the thousand-eyed Vāsava, nor Varuna himself, can (cope) with me in battle; nor can Yama, or Vaicravana's self vanquish me in mighty conflict with the fire of arrows."

---

## SECTION XXV.

On Daçaratha's son, Rāma, having crossed the Ocean with his forces, the graceful Rāvana addressed his two counsellors, Suka and Sārana, saying,—"The crossing the entire ocean incapable of being crossed, by the monkey-forces, and the building over the sea of the bridge by Rāma—all this had never happened before. The construction of a bridge over the ocean cannot at all command credence. But (however it be),I must enumerate the monkey-hosts. Entering the monkey-army unobserved, it behoveth you to ascertain the magnitude thereof, its strength, who are the foremost monkeys, who are the councilors assembled there of Rāma, and who of Sugriva, who range at the head, who among the monkeys are heroic; how they have constructed the bridge over the water of the ocean; how the high-souled monkeys stay there; Rāma's, as well as Lakshmana's purpose, prowess and the arms (they fight with). And who is the commander of those magnanimous monkeys? Having learnt all this truly, ye ought to return speedily." Being thus commissioned, these heroes, the Rākshasas, Suka and Sārana, assuming monkey-shapes, entered into the hosts of monkeys. But Suka and Sārana could not number that army of monkeys, incomprehensible and capable of making people's hair stand on end. The forces were on mountain-tops, by fountains and in caves. And those rangers of the night beheld those forces, some having already crossed, and some crossing, and some intent on doing so; and some having sat down and some sitting—that mighty army sending terrific roars,—that ocean of hosts incapable of being disturbed. As they remained thus disguised, they were discovered by Vibhishana. Thereat, taking them captive, he unfolded (the fact) unto Rāma, saying,—"These are the counsellors of the lord of Rākshasas—Suka and Sārana. O captor of hostile capitals, they have come as spies from Lankā." Seeing Rāma, they were greatly afflicted, and, despairing of their lives and exercised with fear, with joined hands, said,—"O placid one, cammanded by Rāvana, we have come here, O son of Raghu, for the purpose of gathering information concerning this army." Hearing their speech, Rāma—son unto Daçaratha—ever engaged in the welfare of all beings, laughing, remarked,—"If you have heedfully noted this entire array, or if you have done what ye had been commanded to do, return in peace. If aught remaineth unseen, do ye see it anew. Or Vibhishana will again fully show it unto you. Having been taken, ye need not fear on the score of your lives. Even if envoys happen to be taken who are equipped with weapons, they should not be slain. And albeit these night-rangers have come as spies in disguise, with the view of creating division among their foes, yet, O Vibhishana, let them off. Entering the extensive Lankā, ye should say unto the king—younger brother unto the Dispenser of riches—the words which I utter,—'That force relying on which thou hast carried away my Sitā, do thou as thou wishest, along with thy forces and friends, display the same. On the morning of the morrow behold the city of Lankā with her wall and gates, as well as the hosts of Rākshasas, destroyed by me with my shafts. And as Vāsava equipped with the thunder-bolt hurleth the same amidst the Dānavas, will I, O Rāvana, on the morning of the morrow pour down my dreadful ire upon thee along with thy forces.'" Thus directed (by Rāma), those Rākshasas, Suka and Sārana, having saluted the righteous Rāghava with 'Victory !,' came (back) to Lankā and spoke unto the lord of Rākshasas, saying,—"O lord of Rākshasas, having been taken by Vibhishana for the purpose of being slain, we came to be seen by the righteous-souled Rāma of immeasurable energy, and (finally) were liberated (by him). As these four persons have combined—like unto the Lokapālas, heroic, accomplished in arms, and of steady prowess—viz., Daçaratha's son, Rāma, the graceful Lakshmana, Vibhishana, and the highly powerful Sugriva, resembling the great Indra, these are capable of uprooting the city of Lankā—walls and gateways—and replacing her (on her former site),—leave thou the monkeys aside. Such is Rāma's figure and arms that he shall alone demolish Lankā,—leave the other three alone. And that host protected by Rāma, Lakshmana and Sugriva, shall become exceedingly hard to combat even by the Asuras and gods.—And the army of the high-souled rangers of the woods, eager for encounter, contains warriors bursting with high spirits. No use of dispute. Be thou intent on pacification. Do thou render back Maithili unto Daçaratha's son."

## SECTION XXVI.

HEARING Sārana's words, pregnant and truthful, king Rāvana addressed him, saying,—"Even if the gods, Gandharvas and Dānavas should attack me, Sitā will I not part with from fear of all creatures. O amiable one, thou, having been hard handled by the monkeys and distressed in consequence, deemst it fit that Sitā should be rendered back this very day. What foe of mine is there who is competent to conquer me in battle?" Having uttered this rough speech, the graceful Rāvana—lord of the Rākhasas—desirous of surveying (the monkey-hosts), ascended an edifice white like snow, and elevated like many palms (placed one upon another). And transported with passion, Rāvana in company with those spies, saw the sea, mountains and forests. And they beheld the Earth enveloped with monkeys, and the mighty host of monkeys, boundless and irresistible. And having seen this, king Rāvana asked Sārana,—"Who among these monkeys are the foremost, who are the heroes, and who possessed of great strength? Who, bursting with spirits, stay all about the fore? Whom doth Sugriva listen to? And who are the leaders of the monkey-leaders? O Sārana, relate thou all this unto me. And what is the prowess of the monkeys?" Thereat, Sārana, knowing the chiefs (of the monkey-army), spoke unto the sovereign of Rākshasas, who had asked (him), as to who were the heads of the rangers of the woods. "This monkey, that, setting up roars, stayeth in front of Lankā, surrounded by hundreds and thousands of monkey-leaders, by whose tremendous shouts Lankā trembleth with her wall, gateways, hills, woods and forests, and who is posted in front of the forces of the high-souled Sugriva—master of all the monkeys—is the heroic leader of monkey-bands named Nilā. And that one, possessed of prowess, who, folding up his arms, paceth the gound on foot, who, facing Lankâ, from wrath is frequently yawning, who resembles a mountain-peak and is like the filaments of a lotus, who, enraged again and again, soundeth his tail,and the ten cardinal points resound with the sounds of whose tail,—is he who hath been sprinkled by Sugriva—king of monkeys—the heir apparent,named Angada. He challengeth thee to the fight. The worthy son of Vâli and ever dear unto Sugriva, he putteth forth his prowess, as Varuna doth for Sakra. That that well-wisher of Râghava,the vehement Hanumân,hath seen Janaka's daughter, was owing to the advice of this one. That powerful (hero) is proceeding, taking innumerable bands belonging to the lord of monkeys, for the purpose of beating thee by means of his soldiery. Following Vâli's son, and surrounded by a mighty force, stayeth in the field the heroic Nala, the builder of the bridge. Those that with their limbs lying inactive, and setting up roars and ululations, are following this one,* are heroes dwelling in *Chandana*.† With his own army alone, the silver-hued Sweta of dreadful prowess hopes to subdue Lankâ. Marshalling his monkey-forces and cheering up his soldiers, that intelligent monkey, famed over the three regions, having speedily met with Sugriva, is retracing his steps. From days of yore on the banks of the Gomati there is a mountain, (named) Ramya, (otherwise) called Sanrochana. The mount abounds with various trees. There that leader of bands, named Kumuda, governs his kingdom. And he that cheerfully draweth after him hundreds and thousands of monkeys, and the long grim hairs of whose tail, coppery, yellow, sable and white, are cast about, is the energetic monkey, Chanda, eager for encounter. And he hopes to conquer Lankâ by help of his own forces.

---

* The reference is prospective. It means the monkey, Sweta, in the next *sloka*.—*T*.

† This may mean some *wood of sandals*; but the commentator is silent over it.—T.

And this one, resembling a lion, tawny and furnished with a long mane, who, remaining apart, vieweth all Lankā as if consuming her with his eyes, dwelleth for ever and a day in Vindhya, the mountain Krisha, Sahya, and the mount Sudarçana, and, a leader of bands, is named Rambha. Three hundred Kotis of the foremost of monkeys, dreadful and fierce and possessed of terrific prowess, surrounding (him) go in his wake for the purpose of demolishing Lankā by their (native) might. And he that expandeth his ears and yawneth again and again, who defieth the fear of death and doth not move his forces, who trembleth for wrath and eyeth frequently askance,—and behold the lashing of his tail!—and who setteth up leonine shouts, O king, with great energy and with fear cast off,—resideth in the romantic mount, Sālweya, and, a leader of companies, is named Sarabha. To him, O king, belong forty hundred thousands of powerful leaders. And he that stayeth, like unto a mighty mass of clouds covering up the sky, in the midst of the monkey-heroes, as doth Vāsava in the centre of the celestials, whose lofty shout is heard (mingled with) the uproar set up by the foremost monkeys, burning for battle, dwelleth in the excellent hill Pārijātra; and, ever irrepressible in fight, is named Panaça, a leader of (monkey)-bands. Fifty *lacs* of leaders with their forces arranged, environ this commander of monkeys. He that stayeth gracing the dreadful array overflowing with talk, stationed on the shore of the ocean,—resembling a second sea and like unto Durdara*—is the leader named Vitata. And he rangeth, drinking of (the waters of) the Venā,—best among streams—and his forces are sixty lacs of monkeys. And the monkey, named Krathana, challengeth thee to conflict. He hath (under him) powerful and vigorous generals, and forces well divided. And the monkey owning that person of the hue of red chalk, and, who, elated with strength, disregardeth all the monkeys,—is

* Name of a celebrated monkey-leader.—T.

named Gavaya, who approacheth thee wrathfully. Seventy lacs (of troops) girt him round ; and by their means he hopes to bring down Lankā. These are the heroes, incapable of being borne, whose numbers cannot be enumerated. These are the leaders and the heads thereof, as well as the forces set in order of battle."

## SECTION XXVII.

As thou lookest on, I shall describe unto thee those leaders who shall put forth their prowess for Rāghava, and lay down their lives (in his behalf.) That one of dreadful deeds the long hairs on whose long tail, coppery, and yellow, and black, and white, thrown up, look like the rays of the Sun, and are trailing over the ground, is the monkey, named Hara ; whom follow hundreds and thousands (of monkeys) desperately upraising trees, intent upon (scaling) Lankā—the leaders of the monkey-king and his servants present (in this conflict.) And these whom thou beholdest present,resembling mighty masses of sable clouds, like unto black collyrium, of genuine prowess,countless and incapable of enumeration,—dwelling in mountains, provinces, and rivers,—terrible bears —approach thee, O king. In their amidst is their king, grim-eyed and of fierce appearance, like unto Parjanya* encompassed by clouds,—who dwelleth in that best of mountains, Rikkhavān, drinking of the Narmadā.—Behold this one resembling a hill—younger brother of Dhumra, lord of all the bears. He is equal to his brother in beauty, and of superior prowess. This leader of redoubtable leaders is named Jāmbavān. He is mild, obedient to his superiors and

* Indra.

fierce in fight. The intelligent Jāmbavān assisted Sakra signally in the war of the gods and Asuras, and he hath won many boons (in consequence). Ascending the tops of mountains, these hurl down gigantic crags huge as colossal clouds, nor doth (the fear of) death (ever) disquiet them. And their bodies covered with hair, they resemble Rākshasas and ghosts (in their conduct). This one of immeasurable energy hath innumerable troops going about, who behold this leader of leaders under unusual excitement leaping and resting (by turns). This lord of monkeys dwelleth near the thousand-eyed Deity ; and this leader of bands, gifted with strength, is named Rambha. And he that going, toucheth with his side a mountain situated at the distance of a Yoyana, and, rising up, measureth the same length,—and whose beauty is surpassed by none among quadrupeds,—is known under the name of Sannādana, the grand-father of the monkeys ;—this intelligent one battled with Sakra,*—nor did he meet with discomfiture. This is that general of the forces. And he whose prowess is like that of Sakra, is this one begot by Fire on a Gandharva's daughter, for assisting the celestials on the occasion of the war of the gods and the Asuras. And this graceful and powerful one—best of monkeys—disporteth in that sovereign of mountains inhabited by numbers of Kinnaras, where king Vaiçravana eateth rose apples, and which, O lord of Rakshas, ever conduceth to the pleasure of thy brother. And this one who never extolleth himself in battle, is named Krathana—leader of hosts. Surrounded by a thousand Koti (of troops), and stationed in the midst of the monkeys, he hopeth to subjugate Lankā with his own troops alone. And he that roameth about the Gangā, terrifying leaders of elephant-herds, remembering the former hostility of the monkeys and the

---

* There is a word—*rane, in battle*—in this line, left out on the ground of pleonasm.—T.

elephants, is this leader of bands, who, roaring, opposeth wild elephants in mountain-caverns and crusheth trees, —and foremost of monkeys, and chief of the monkey-forces—like Sakra himself in heaven, sporteth, resorting to Uçiravija pertaining to Mandara, best of mountains, on the golden river.* A thousand lacs of monkeys, elated with vigor and prowess, setting up roars and furnished with (long) arms follow him; and this one is the leader of those high-souled monkeys. And, O king, he whom thou seest resembling clouds uplifted by the winds, is a leader named Pramâthi. And his fleet-coursing soldiery are fiery, and volumes of red-hued dust are scattered about him profusely on all sides. And these wondrous strong and dreadful Golângulas† numbering hundreds and hundred thousands, seeing the building of the bridge, surrounding, O mighty monarch, the leader named Gavāksha—a Golāngula—set up shouts, intending to demolish Lankā with their prowess. Where the trees bring forth fruits of every season and the black bees resort,—in the mountain furnished with solar splendour, which the Sun circumambulates, by whose radiance ever beam beasts and birds with a like hue,—whose table-lands are never forsaken by magnanimous Maharshis; where the trees yield every object of desire and all are fraught with fruits; in which best of mountains excellent honey is found,—there in the charming Golden hill, O king, sporteth this one—the foremost of the principal monkeys, Kaçari by name, a leader of bands. There are sixty thousand charming Golden hills. In their midst is that best of mountains,‡ even as thou, O sinless one, art among the Rakshas. There in the inmost hill dwell (monkeys) tawny-hued; and white,—with coppery faces; yellowish like honey; sharp-toothed; having nails for their weapons; and four teeth like lions; irresistible like tigers

---

* Gangâ.—T.

† *Vide antè.*

‡ Sâvarni Meru.—T.

all equal to Vaiçwānara, and resembling flaming venomous snakes; furnished with long tails; like unto mad elephants; seeming like gigantic hills; roaring like mighty clouds; with eyes tawny and round; of terrific mein; and emitting sounds,—and these are gazing at Lankā, as if devastating her. And this powerful one staying in their midst, is their leader, eager for victory; and the puissant (monkey) always looketh like the Sun himself; and this one, O king, is famed on earth by the name of Satavali. And this heroic one, powerful and mighty, established in his own prowess, hopeth to devastate Lankā with his own forces. And for compassing Rāma's desire, the monkey doth not cherish any kindness for his life. Gaya, Gavāksha, Nala, and the monkey Nila—each of these is encompassed by ten *kotis* of warriors. (Besides these), there are other choice monkeys dwelling in the Vindhya mountain, but I cannot enumerate these (monkeys) possessed of fleet vigor, in consequence of their vast number. All these, O mighty monarch, are of exceeding prowess,—all possess persons resembling mighty mountains; and all are competent in a moment to remove mountains and scatter the Earth with them."

## SECTION XXVIII.

HAVING heard the words of Sārana, who had described the forces (of the monkeys), Suka, addressed Rāvana, lord of Rākshasas, saying,—"Those, O king, whom thou seest stationed, resembling mad elephants, like unto *nyagrodhas** belonging to the Gangā,—like unto Sālas in the Himavān,—are incapable of being borne,—they are possessed of

* Banians.

strength, and able to wear forms at will; resembling deities and Dānavas, and like the gods in conflict. These, numbering nine, five, and seven thousand *kotis* and thousand *sankus* and an hundred *vrindas*, are the ministers of Sugriva, residing in Kishkindhā—monkeys begot by gods and Gandharvas, capable of assuming shapes at will. And those two whom thou beholdest, staying there, of equal proportions and endowed with god-like shapes, are Mainda and Dwivida,—who have no equals in fight. Permitted by Brahmā, they had partaken of ambrosia. They hope to humble Lankā by their prowess. And he whom thou seest staying like a mad elephant, the monkey who, being enraged, can by his strength agitate the deep itself, who, searching for Vaidehi, had presented himself before thee, lord,—behold this monkey come again!—whom thou hadst seen before!*—is the eldest son of Kaçari, known as the offspring of the Wind-god—celebrated as Hanumān, who had bounded over the deep. Capable of wearing forms at pleasure, that first of monkeys is endeued with grace and strength,—and is of irresistible impetuosity even as that lord, the Wind. Seeing the Sun risen, (he) while a boy, resolving in his mind,—'Coursing a way measuring three thousand *yoyanas*, I will bring the Sun,—my hunger is not appeased;' and he sprang up, elated with strength. And, not getting that god, incapable of being subdued by the deities, saints and Rākshasas, he dropped down on the Ascending-hill. And thereat a jaw of that strong-jawed one was a little fractured on the rock,—and he is called Hanumān in consequence. I know this monkey and all his previous history. I cannot describe his strength, beauty or prowess. And this one alone hopes to lay Lankā low by his energy. And why dost thou today forget the monkey, who had flung flaming fire into Lankā? And next to him is the hero of dark-blue hue, having eyes like lotuses, the

* This dislocation occurs in the original. These descriptions generally are hardly amenable to a sound syntax.—T.

Atiratha among the Ikshwākus—of prowess celebrated in the world—in whom virtue never wavereth and who never swerveth from righteousness; who knoweth the Brāhma Mantra and the Vedas,—the best of those versed in them—who pierceth the sky with his shafts and cleaveth the Earth, whose ire is like death, and whose prowess is like that of Sakra,—whose wife, Sitā, hath been carried away by thee from Janasthāna. And this is Rāma, who, O king, advanceth to encounter thee in conflict. And on his right side is one of the splendour of pure gold, broad-breasted, having dark curled hair—this one is named Lakshmana, ever mindful of his brother's welfare. He is versed in polity as well as warfare—the foremost of those learned in all the branches of knowledge; wrathful, invincible, victorious, powerful, conquering and strong,—the right arm of Rāma and his own life going about. For Rāghava he careth not for his life. He hopeth to exterminate all the Rākshasas in battle. He that stayeth occupying the left side of Rāma, and surrounded by Rākshasas, is the king, Bibhishana, sprinkled as the king of Lankā by the auspicious king of kings,—he, filled with wrath, approacheth thee (for battle). And he whom thou seest staying in the middle like a firm-based mountain, the lord of all monkeys, of inmeasurable prowess,—and who in energy fame, intelligence, strength, and lineage, is as superior to the monkeys as the mountain Himavān overtoppeth all the mountains, who in company with the principal monkey-leaders dwelleth in inaccessible Kishkindhā hard to penetrate, and dense with trees, and difficult of access, and denying approach on account of rocks; and whose golden garland consisting of an hundred lotuses looks exceedingly elegant, which is the desire of men and gods, and where is established Lakshmi—(is Sugriva). And Rāma, having slain Vāli, hath conferred this garland, Tārā, and the eternal monkey-kingdom on Sugriva. An hundred of an hundred thousand is called a *koti* by the wise. An hundred of a thousand *koti* is called a Sanku.

An hundred of a thousand Sanku is known as a Mahâçanku. An hundred of a thousand Mahâçanku is here termed a Vrinda. An hundred of a thousand Vrinda is known as a Mahâvrinda. A thousand Mahâvrinda is called here a Padma. An hundred of a thousand Padma is known as a Mahâpadma. An hundred of a thousand Mahâpadma is termed a Kharva. An hundred of a thousand Kharva is termed a Samudra. An hundred of a thousand Samudra is known as a Mahaugha. Thus backed by a thousand *koti*, and an hundred Sanku, and a thousand Mahaçanku, and an hundred Vrinda, and a thousand Mahâvrinda, and an hundred Padma, and a thousand Mahâpadma and an hundred *kharva*, and an equal Samaudra and an equal Mahaugha,—by *kotis* of Mahaughas—resembling the sea,—and surrounded by the heroic Bibhishana as well as his counsellors,—that Lord of monkeys, always engirt by a mighty force, and possessed of exceeding strength and prowess, will encounter thee in battle. Observing this host, that hath presented itself, resembling a flaming planet, do thou, O mighty monarch, prepare thyself to the uttermost, —so that victory may be thine, and that thou mayst not come by discomfiture at the hands of the foe."

## SECTION XXIX.

SEEING the leaders of monkeys as pointed out by Suka,—the exceedingly puissant Lakshmana—Râma's right arm—and his* brother Bibhishana staying near Râma, and Sugriva of dreadful prowess—sovereign of all the monkeys,—and the strong Angada, grandson unto the thunder-handed one,†

* *i. e.* Râvana's

† Indra.—T.

and the powerful Hanumān; and the unconquerable Jāmbavān; and Sushena; and Nila; and Nala—best of monkeys,—and Gaya; and Gavāksha; and Sarabha; and Mainda; and Dwivida,—Rāvana, with his heart agitated a little, and his wrath aroused,—when their talk had ended, rebuked those heroes, Suka and Sārana. And he wrathfully spoke unto them, standing in humble guise with their heads hung down, harsh words faltering with passion,—"That counsellors subsisting (on the wealth of their master and sovereign), should say aught disagreeable to him, whether they meet with his favor or disfavor—is not meet. Without being questioned, it is (proper) for you both to hymn the praises of a foe that is opposed and that hath advanced for encounter! Ye have in vain worshipped your preceptors, aged people, and spiritual guides, for ye have failed to appropriate the cream of Political Science, which should be availed of. Or if ye had appropriated the same, you have forgotten it afterwards; and ye bear the burden of ignorance. And it is owing to my good fortune that, having such stupid counsellors, I have as yet held my kingdom. Have ye no fear of death that ye use harsh speech towards me, who am the ruler and whose tongue dispenseth good and evil? Even trees may exist in the forest, coming in contact with burning fire; but transgressors cannot exist, visited with the chastisement of the monarch. I shall slay these wicked wights, who praise the side of the enemy, if my anger be not moderated, remembering their former good offices. Avaunt! Go hence from near me! I do not wish to slay you, remembering your good acts. Slain ye (already) are, who are ingrate and cherish no affection for me." Thus accosted, Suka and Sārana, seeing (how things stood), covered with bashfulness, went out, saluting Rāvana by uttering 'Victory!' Then that ranger of night, the Ten-necked one, said unto Mahodara, who was present, to summon some spies. Thus accosted, Mahodara speedily ordered some spies (to present themselves). Thereat, the spies, hurriedly arriving there at the mandate of the monarch, and, presenting themselves, stood with joined hands, uttering blessings of victory. Then the lord of Rākshasas, Rāvana, addressed the spies, who were heroic, faithful, calm, and courageous,—"Go hence, and acquaint yourselves with the exertions of Rāma; as well as with those who, being the custodians of Rāma's closest counsels, have gladly joined him (here). How he sleepeth and how he waketh, and what he engageth himself in,—having deftly acquainted yourselves with all this thoroughly, do you come (back here). The wise king that gathers (a knowledge of) his enemy through spies, can, putting forth a modicum of effort in conflict, neutralise (his exertions)." Thereat the spies, saying,—"So it is", taking Sardula to the fore, with delighted hearts went round the sovereign of the Rākshasas. And, having gone round the high-souled Rākshasa-chief, the spies set out for where Rāma with Lakshmana was. And repairing secretly to the vicinity of the mountain bordering on the fair shore,* they saw Rāma and Lakshmana with Sugriva and Bibhishana. And seeing that host, they were overwhelmed with fear. And, while staying there, they, discovered by the righteous lord of Rākshasas, Bibhisana, were sore harassed (by the monkeys). And that wicked Rākshasa, Sārdula, alone was taken (before Rāma). But Rāma liberated him, who was assailed by the monkeys. And Rāma also, entertaining no enmity against them, also liberated the others, (who accompanied Sārdula). And, on having been put to straits by the powerful monkeys of fleet vigor, they,† breathing hard, and with their consciousness lost, again arrived at Lankā. Then those exceedingly strong spies, always ranging outside, presenting themselves before the Ten-necked one, informed him of the forces of Rāma, stationed near mount Suvela.

---

* *Suvelasya Sailasya*—may also mean, of the mount *Suvela*.—T.

† The spies, that is.—T.

## SECTION XXX.

THEN the spies communicated unto Lankā's lord news concerning Rāghava and his host stationed at the mount Suvela. Hearing the words of the spies, that Rāma, accompanied by a mighty army, had arrived (there), Rāvana was a little agitated and spoke unto Sārdula,—"Thy color hath changed its natural aspect, and, O ranger of the night, thou lookest poorly. Didst not come under the control of the wrathful foes?" Thus ordered by him, then (Sārdula), bewildered by fear, addressed that tiger of a Rākshasa, saying,—"Those powerful monkeys, O king, puissant, strong, and protected by Rāghava, are incapable of being ranged (by us). And they cannot be conversed with or interrogated. All around, the courses are kept by monkeys resembling hills. As soon as I entered, and was scanning that host, I was discovered. And forcibly taken by the Rakshas, I was pulled by them hither and thither. And furiously assailed by the monkeys with thighs, clenched fists, teeth, and palms, I was dragged in the midst of the army by the enraged monkeys. And, after having been taken all about, I was (at length) taken before Rāma, bleeding, with my limbs showing sorry work, and my senses swimming and paralysed. And, having been belabored by the monkeys, I, on craving his kindness with joined hands, was, at his pleasure, rescued by Rāghava, with, "Don't, don't"! Having filled up the deep with rocks and crags, Rāma equipped with weapons, stayeth, occupying the gate of Lankā. And, letting me off, that one of suspassing vigor, surrounded by monkeys, and, arranging his forces in the Garura fashion, advanceth upon Lankā. And he draweth nigh to the wall. Therefore, do one of these things in preference to the other,—either render back Sitā, or give him battle." Hearing this, Rāvana, lord of Rākshasas, then reflecting in his mind, spoke unto Sārdula these pregnant words,—"Even if the gods, Gandharvas, and Dānavas should array themselves against me, Sitā I shall not give, from fear of all creatures." Having said this, that exceedingly energetic one again said,—"Thou hast ranged this army. Who here among the monkeys are heroic? And, O amiable one, what is their potency? And what are those monkeys that are hard to approach, like? And, O thou of fair vows, whose sons and grandsons are they? Truly relate all this (to me). Having ascertained their strength and weakness, I shall in this matter adopt my course. Those who wish for fight, certainly take account of all this." Thus addressed by Rāvana, Sārdula—best of spies—thus began to speak in the presence of Rāvana,—"O king, that unconquerable one in fight, Jāmbavān, is well known as the son Gadgada, king of bears. The other son of Gadgada is the son of Sakra's preceptor. By which son, single-handed, was done immense oppression to the Rakshas. And the righteous and puissant Sushena is the son of Dharma.* And the mild monkey, Dadhimukha, O king, is the son of Soma.† And Sumukha, Durmukha and the monkey, Vegadarçin (resembling) Death himself, were for certain begot by the Self-create in the shape of a monkey.‡ And Nila himself is the son of the bearer of sacrificial oblations;§ and Hanumān is famed as the son of the Wind-god. And the irrepressible and youthful Angada is the grandson of Sakra. And the lusty Mainda and Dwivida are sprung from Açwi. And five are the sons of Vaivaswata, resembling the Reaper himself—Gaya, Gavāksha, Gavaya, Sarabha and Gandhamādana. But I can not enumerate the rest, ten *kotis* of heroic monkeys—all

---

* Righteousness.

† Moon.

‡ Another meaning is,—"*The monkey, Vegadarçi—who is Death himself in the shape of a monkey.*" But I give the more acceptable sense.—T.

§ Fire.

sons of deities—burning for battle. And this is Daçaratha's son—this youth resembling a lion, who slew Dushana and Khara and *Triciras*. There breathes none on Earth that is like unto Râma in prowess, by whom was slain Virâdha and Kavandha, resembling the Destroyer. No person can on earth describe the virtues of Râma; by whom have been slain all those Râkshasas that had gone to Janasthâna. And here also is the virtuous Lakshmana, like unto the foremost of elephants, coming in the way of whose shafts, even Vâsava doth not live. And here are Sweta and Jyotirmukha, sprung from Vâskara's self; and the monkey Hemakuta is the son of Varuna. And the heroic Nala—best of monkeys, is the son of Viçwakarmâ. And powerful and impetuous, Durdhara is the son of Vasu. And that foremost of Râkshasas, Bibhishana, thy brother, engaged in the welfare of Râghava, hath laid seige to Lankâ. Thus have I described unto thee the entire monkey host stationed in mount Suvela. As for what remaineth to be done, thou art the master."

## SECTION XXXI.

THEN the spies of the king informed him of the forces of Râghava, incapable of being agitated, which had stationed themselves on mount Suvela. Hearing the arrival of Râma's mighty army from the spies, Râvana was a little agitated, and he spoke unto the ministers,—"Let the ministers speedily present themselves, having their wits about them,—the time forsooth hath come for counsel." Hearing his mandate, those Râkshasas, his counselors, swiftly presented themselves. And then he consulted with his Râkshasa counselors. Having deliberated duly, that resistless one, dismissing his ministers, entered his own abode. Then, taking with him the highly strong Vidyujjibha, huge-bodied and gifted with the powers of illusion, he entered where Mithilā's daughter was. And the lord of Rākshasas said unto Vidyujjibha, skilled in illusion,—"Do thou bring Janaka's daughter under the sway of illusion. And, O ranger of the night, do thou, taking an illusory head of Rāghava, as well as a mighty bow with the shaft (set), present thyself before me." Thus accosted, the night-ranger, Vidyujjibha, saying, "So be it," displayed that desired illusion unto Rāvana. Thereat, the king, eager to meet with Sitā in the Açoka woods, well-pleased, conferred an excellent ornament on him. Then the exceedingly powerful lord of the Nairitas, the younger brother of the Dispenser of riches, entered (into that place) and saw (there Sitā) distressed, albeit unworthy of distress,—with her head hung down, overwhelmed with woe,—sitting on the ground, staying at the *açoka* woods, engaged in the contemplation of her lord, conciliated by dreadful Rākshasis remaining near. Then, drawing near Sitā, Rāvana, proclaiming his exultation, said these haughty words unto the daughter of Janaka,—"O gentle one, he depending on whom thou, being soothed by (me), slightest me—that slayer of Khara, thy husband, Rāghava, hath fallen in battle. Thy roots have been competely severed, and thy pride hath been destroyed by me. In consequence of this calamity, O Sitā, thou shalt become my wife. O foolish (girl), renounce this idea. What wilt thou do with him that is dead? O meek (wench), be thou the mistress of all my wives. O thou of slender religious merit! O thou whose object hath been defeated! O thou that presumest to be wise! Hearken unto the destruction of thy lord, like the dreadful destruction of Vritra! Surrounded by a vast army gathered by the sovereign of the monkeys, Rāghava had presented himself on the shore of the sea, for compassing my destruction. And on the sun having set, Rāma stationed himself with his mighty army, oppressing the northern shore (of the sea). Then at midnight (my) spies coming to that host, thus stationed, fatigued from travel, and sleeping soundly (in consequence),—first ranged it. Then my mighty forces led by Prahasta slew his host overnight, where was present Rāma along with Lakshmana. And repeatedly upraising *pattiças* and bludgeons, swords, rods and other mighty weapons; and (discharging) showers of arrows, and darts, and daggers and maces and sticks and crows and bearded darts and discuses and clubs;—the Rākshasas discharged these among the monkeys. And while Rāma was sleeping, the furious Prahasta by means of a mighty falchion, with speed cut off his head clean. Bibhishana, who was flying at his will, was taken captive. And Lakshmana along with the monkey-army hath departed somewhere. And, O Sitā, Sugriva—lord of monkeys—hath his neck broken; and, O Sitā, with his jaw fractured, Hanumān hath been slaughtered by the Rākshasas.—And Jāmbavān, endeavouring to spring up with his thighs, was slain in the conflict; being severed by bearded darts, even as a tree cut off. And the stalwart Mainda and Dwivida—those foremost of monkeys—sighing and lamenting, bathed in blood,—destroyers of foes—were cut off with a sword. And Panaça is rolling on the earth like a (veritable) Panaça.* And mangled by many iron arrows, Darimukha lieth in a cave. And the exceedingly energetic Kumuda, dumb, is slain by shafts. And torn by innumerable (arrows) discharged on all sides by Rākshasas, Angada, vomitting blood, lieth on the ground.† And the monkeys, hard pressed by elephants, and others by networks of cars, lie low in the field, having been agitated like clouds by winds. And others afflicted with affright, flee, attacked (by the enemy) in the rear, and followed by the Rākshasas, like mighty elephants pursued by lions. And some have fallen into the

---

* The tree of that name.—T.

† This *sloka* has 'Angada' twice. One, of course, is left out.—T.

sea, and some have taken refuge in the sky; and the bears have mounted up trees along with the monkeys. And on the shore of the sea, and in mountains and woods many are the tawny-hued monkeys that have been slain by Rākshasas of frightful forms. Thus hath thy lord been slain by my forces, along with his army; and I have his head, washed in blood and besmeared with dust." Thereat, the exceedingly irrepressible lord of Rākshasas, Rāvana, spake unto a Rākshasi, in the hearing of Sitā,—"Bring (hither) the Rākshasa, Vidyujjibha of cruel deeds, who hath personally brought Rāghava's head from the field." Thereat, Vidyujjibha, taking the head along with the bow, bowing down the head (unto Rāvana), stood before him. Then spake king Rāvana unto the Rākshasa, Vidyujjibha of the long tongue, who was staying by,—"Do thou at once hold before Sitā the head of Daçaratha's son. Let her clearly behold the ultimate sad plight of her lord." Thus addressed, that Raksha, throwing that graceful head before Sitā, swiftly vanished. And Rāvana cast down the mighty blazing bow, famed through the three worlds, saying,—"This is Rāma's. This is the bow of thy Rāma with the string fixed. Slaying that man over night, Prahasta brought it hither."

## SECTION XXXII.

SEEING that head and that excellent bow, and (remembering) the union of (Rāma) and Sugriva related by Hanumān,—and (seeing) those eyes, and the complexion of that face, and that countenance like unto that of her lord,—and that hair and that forehead; and that beautiful jewel forming the crest; and recognizing (Rāma) by all these tokens combined,—

(Sitā), exceedingly aggrieved, rebuked Kaikeyi, lamenting like a female osprey,—"O Kaikeyi, have thy wishes attained. Slain hath been the son of the race; and the entire race is exterminated by thee, partial to dissension. And what evil had been done unto Kaikeyi by the revered Rāma, that along with me, he hadst been banished into the woods, with rags given him (for his covering)?" Having said this, Vaidehi, forlorn and trembling (all over), dropped to the earth, like a plantain cut off. Then, recovering after a while, and having regained her consciousness, the large-eyed one, placing the head in her front, gave way to grief. "Ah! I am undone, O mighty-armed one! O thou that didst follow stern vows! From thy (death), I have come by this final plight, having been rendered a widow. The greatest calamity (that can befall a woman), is said to be the death of her husband. And, póssessor of an excellent character, thou hast departed before me, who have ever trod the path of the righteous; but who have come by a mighty grief and am plunged in a sea of sorrow. And thou, who was engaged in delivering me, hast thyself fallen! And my mother-in-law, Kauçalyā, attached (to thee), through the death of thee, her son, at the hands of Rākshasas, hath been reduced to the condition of a cow that hath been deprived of her calf. O Rāghava, even the astrologers had predicted long life for thee. But their words are false,—thou, O Rāghava, wast short-lived. Or didst thy wisdom, wise and good as thou wert, come to naught? For God, who is the origin of all beings, maketh (every one) reap the fruit of his own acts. And why, versed in polity as thou wast, didst thou come by death, unforeseen? Thou wast acquainted with the means of warding off misfortune, and skilled in doing so. And having been brought hither by me representing the Fatal Night, fierce and fell,—after (being) embraced, and by force,—the lotus-eyed one hath met with his death. Here liest thou, O long-armed one, leaving me lone,—and embracing the Earth like thy beloved fair.

150

Ever carefully worshipped with perfumed wreaths, this bow of thine, O hero, embellished with gold, is dear unto me. O sinless one, thou hast surely gone to heaven, and (art there) in the company of thy sire and my father-in-law, Daçaratha, and all thy ancestors. Thou hast become a star of the firmament as the fruit of thy great act.* Thou hast disregarded thy righteous race of Rājarshis. O king, why dost thou not look at me? And why is it that thou dost not answer me, who am a girl, hardly arrived at youth,—and who am thy wife and companion? That thou at the time of thy espousing my hand hadst vowed—I will practise (righteousness) with thee—do thou, O Kākutstha, recollect the same, and take me, who am overwhelmed with distress. Why, O best of goers, hast thou gone from this world to that other, leaving behind me, overwhelmed with distress? That person of thine which, decked out with auspicious things, I used to embrace, beasts of prey will for certain tear the same. Having performed the Agnishtoma and other sacrifices with *Dakshinās* (dispensed),—why hadst not thou attained purity by means of the sacrificial fire? Kauçalyā, overwhelmed with sorrow, shall only behold one of the three that had gone away to distant lands,—come (back)—Lakshmana. And, on being asked by her, he shall relate thine as well as the deaths of thy friend's troops over night at the hands of the Rākshasas. And, O Rāghava, hearing thee slain while asleep, and me staying in the abode of the Raksha, she with her heart cleft (in twain), shall cease to exist. And for the sake of me, abject that I am, that sinless son of the king, Rāma, possessed of prowess, having crossed the ocean, hath been slain in the footprint of a cow. I, the befouler of my line, who had been wedded by Daçaratha's son through want of discretion, becoming the wife of the revered Rāma, was (in reality) his Death. Without doubt, in another birth I had abstained from choice gifts,—and therefore it is that I sorrow to-day,

* *The carrying out the command of thy sire.—T.*

albeit being the wife of one that was (ever dear) unto guests. Do thou, O Rāvana, speedily slay me upon Rāma; and, bringing the wife to the husband, compass my best benefit. Do thou join my head to his and my body to his body. I will, O Rāvana, follow the way of my high-souled lord." Thus, burning in grief, did that large-eyed one indulge in lamentations; and Janaka's daughter kept fast gazing at the head and bow of her lord. And as the Rākshasa was by while Sitā was thus bewailing, there appeared before his lord, with joined hands, the warder, saying,—"May the worshipful one be victorious!" And saluting and propitiating him, (Rāvana), he told him that Prahasta, general of the forces, had arrived. "Prahasta hath come to thee, surrounded by all the courtiers. And, O lord, I was despatched by him, desirous of seeing thee. O mighty monarch, surely there is—and thou art forgiving from thy regal sentiment*—some work which is momentous; and do thou see them." Hearing these words of the Rākshasa, the Ten-necked one, leaving the *açoka* wood, went to see the counselors. And, having decided his entire course of action in consultation with his competent advisers, (Rāvana), entering his court,—well knowing Rāma's prowess, set about his work. And as soon as Rāvana left that place, that head and that bow vanished. And in company with the councilors of dreadful power, (Rāvana) decided his course with reference to Rāma. And then the lord of Rākshasas, Rāvana, resembling the day of doom, addressed his generals,—all well-wishers—staying hard by, saying,—"Do ye speedily summon my forces with the beat of drums—nor do ye give out the reason (of the summons)." Then assenting to his speech with "So be it," the envoys immediately summoned that mighty force; and, when it had arrived, they informed their master, eager for conflict, of its arrival.

---

* This dislocated period insinuates that Râvana, possessed of royal nature, should forgive this untimely intrusion.—T.

## SECTION XXXIII.

Seeing Sitā overwhelmed with grief, a Rākshasi, named Saramā, who was the beloved companion (of Sitā), drew near to his dear (friend), Vaidehi. And the mild-speeched Saramā comforted the exceedingly distressed Sitā, who had been bereft of her senses by the lord of Rākshasas. Sitā, who was protected there (by Saramā), had been made a friend by her. And, protecting her at the command of Rāvana, that kind-hearted companion, firm in vows, saw Sitā, deprived of her consciousness. And she* comforted with a friend's affection that one of fair vows, who was rolling in the dust and rising up from it like a mare.† "Having come to the solitary wood for protecting thee, I, renouncing all fear of Rāvana, have, remaining hid, heard everything that he addressed unto thee, as well as what thou hadst replied unto him. For thee, O thou of expansive eyes, I have no fear of Rāvana. And, O Maithili, I, coming out, have also learnt well as to why the lord of Rākshasas hath gone out hence hurriedly. Rāma, acquainted with self, is incapable of being surprised in sleep; nor doth the slaying of that tiger-like one commend itself to me as probable. And the monkeys fighting with trees, well protected by Rāghava, like the gods protected by the foremost of the celestials, are incapable of being slain. And, possessed of arms long and rounded; graceful; broad-breasted; powerful; accoutred with the bow; and mailed; righteous; and famous over the earth; endowed with energy; and along with his brother, Lakshmana, ever protecting himself and others; of noble descent; and

---

* Saramā.—T.

† The commentator intelligently remarks: *As a mare does, to remove fatigue.*—*T.*

versed in polity; the destroyer of the hostile ranks; and of inconceivable strength and manhood,—the graceful Rāghava, O Sitā, slayer of foes, is not slain. This illusion hath been spread around thee by that fierce, illusion-creating one, whose mind ever runs upon improper acts and who opposeth himself to all creatures.—All thy sorrow hath departed, and thy good day hath dawned. Certainly Lakshmi seeketh thee. And, O lady, hearken unto what is dear to thee! Having crossed over the ocean, along with the monkey-host, Rāma hath encamped himself on the southern shore of the sea. By me hath been seen the complete Kākutstha along with Lakshmana, accompanied by the forces, stationed on the marge of the main,—protected (by his native might). Those Rākshasas of fleet vigor who had been despatched by this one, have brought the news that Rāghava hath crossed.—And, O large-eyed lady, having learnt this news, Rāvana—lord of Rākshasas—is consulting with all his counselors." As the Rākshasi, Saramā, was relating this unto Sitā, she heard the leonine roars of the army, emitted with the greatest energy. And, hearing the mighty sounds of kettledrums produced by sticks struck (thereon), the honey-tongued Saramā spoke thus unto Sitā,—"These dreadful sounds of the kettledrum, O mother, call to arms. And hark to the solemn notes of the kettledrums, resembling the rumbling of clouds! The mad elephants are caparisoned and the car-horses are yoked; and thousands (of warriors) are seen, mounted on steeds, with bearded darts in their hands. And, as waters fill up the ocean, mailed warriors of wonderful forms, vehement and roaring, by thousands rush out on all sides and fill the highways. And mark the splendour spread around by the polished arms and bucklers and mail,—and by the cars, horses and elephants of the followers of the Rākshasa-chief,—consisting of many hues shooting up,—like unto the appearance of a fire in summer, burning a forest,—and also mark the excitement of the high-spirited and fast-coursing Rakshas !* And hear the sounds of bells and the rattling of the car-wheels ! And hear the neighing of the steeds and the reports of the drums And fierce is the excitement of these Rākshasas—followers of the Raksha-chief,—with their hands bearing upraised arms,—capable of making people's hair stand on end. The sorrow removing Sree espouseth thee ; and the fear of the Rakshas is come. And as Vāsava did unto the Daityas, the lotus-eyed Rāma, thy lord—of controlled anger, and of inconceivable prowess,slaying Rāvana in battle and thus delivering thee, shall approach thee. And, as Vāsava put forth his prowess among his foes, in company with the foe-destroying Vishnu, thy lord, along with Lakshmana, shall display his prowess among the Rakshas. On the enemy having fallen, I shall behold thee, devoted to thy lord, with thy desire attained, soon lying on the lap of Rāma. And, O Jānaki, embracing (thy lord), thou shalt shed tears of joy on his mighty breast. And, O Sitā, soon shall the highly powerful Rāma loosen this braid of thine reaching unto thy hips, which thou hast been wearing for many a month. And, O exalted one, seeing his face like the full moon risen, thou shalt shed water begot of ruth, even as a she-serpent casts off her slough. And, O Mithilā's daughter, speedily slaying Rāvana in battle, that one worthy of happiness shall reap felicity in the company of thee, his beloved. And, loved by the high-souled Rāma, thou shalt be happy, even as the Earth furnished with crops brought forth by plenteous showers. Do thou, O exalted one, take refuge with him,who, going round the foremost of mountains, speedily assumeth a steed-like circular movement ; for even the maker of day is the source of people's joy and grief."

* This line of verse defies all attempts to make it fall into syntactical order with the rest of the sentence. It is a hideous hiatus in the passage.—T.

## SECTION XXXIV.

BURNING with grief on account of those words,* Saramā gladdened and cheered her, even as masses of clouds (cheer up) the burning Earth. And then, desirous of doing her good, (Sitā's) friend, conversant with season, and ever preluding her speech with a smile, spoke unto her seasonably,—"O thou having dark eyes, I can, secretly going to Rāma and communicating to him thy auspicious words, come back clandestinely. Nor, when I course the supportless sky, can even the Wind or Garura follow me." As she said this, Sitā with her grief a little lightened, said unto Saramā in sweet and smooth words,—"Thou art capable of even going to the nethermost regions. But do thou on my behalf that which is fit to be done by thee. If thou intend doing me a good turn, and if thy sense be steady, I would know what Rāvana is doing after having left this place. That guileful and wicked-minded one, Rāvana, destroyer of enemies, having powers of illusion, overwhelms me even as the Vāruni just drunk. Confining me here for ever and a day, (Rāvana) sets on dreadful Rākshasas to alike threaten and scold me constantly. And I am agitated aud alarmed, and my mind is (always) uneasy. And I, dwelling in the *açoka* wood, is ever agitated. If there is any talk (of delivering me), or keeping me confined,—thou shouldst communicate unto me the decision arrived at. This is the highest favor that I seek (at thy hands)." Thereat, the mild-speeched Saramā, wiping (Sitā's) face washed in tears, spake unto her, as she said this,—"If this is thy wish, I will go, O Jānaki. O Mithilā's daughter, having possessed myself of the intent of the enemy, I shall come back." Having said this, (Saramā),

* *i.e.* the words of Rāvana.

repairing to the Raksha, heard Rāvana's converse with his counselors. And having heard of the decision of that wicked-minded one, she, understanding decisions, swiftly retraced her steps to the fair *açoka* forest. And then, entering there, she saw Janaka's daughter, expecting (her) like a very Sri, bereft of her lotus. And, the fair-spoken Saramā, on getting back (near her), Sitā, embracing her affectionately, herself gave her a seat. "Sitting down here at ease, do thou relate to me faithfully all about the determination of the wicked-minded and guileful Rāvana." Thus accosted by the trembling Sitā, Saramā related everything that had been said by Rāvana and his counselors. "O Vaidehi, the Raksha lord was advised by his mother and the aged counselors in pregnant words informed with affection, having thy deliverance for their object. 'Do thou make over Maithili unto the king of men, paying him homage due. Thou hast in Janasthāna profusely witnessed wonderful instances (of his prowess). The crossing of the ocean, Hanumān's sight (of Sitā),—and the slaughter of the Rakshas in fight,—what person is capable of doing all this in battle?' Thus long exhorted by his counselors as well as his mother, Rāvana doth not make up his mind to emancipate thee, even as a covetuous person is loath to part with wealth (appropriated). And, O Maithili, without renouncing his life in battle, he doth not intend to liberate thee. Even this is the dermination which that cruel one hath arrived at along with his advisers. This intent is in consequence of their coveting surcease. He can not yield thee up from sheer fear; nor is he backward in battle, or shirketh his own destruction or that of all the Rākshasas. O dark-eyed lady, slaying Rāvana in battle with sharp shafts, Rāma shall take the back to Ayodhyā." In the meanwhile there was heard a mighty uproar occasioned by the whole host, and drums and conchs, —which shook the earth. Hearing that hubbub of the monkey-army, the servants of the Rākshasa monarch, ran who were in Lankā,—growing dispirited,and bereft of energy, with weakness overcoming their powers,—did not see any good, in consequence of the fault of the ruler.

## SECTION XXXV.

AND that captor of hostile capitals, the mighty-armed Rāma, was advancing (upon Lankā) with the sounds of drums mixed with the blares of conchs. Hearing this noise, Rāvana —lord of Rākshasas—reflecting for a while, cast his eyes upon his counselors. And addressing there all those counsellors, that afflictor of the world—the crooked and highly powerful lord of the Rākshasas, Rāvana, making his court resound,—running down (Rāma's) crossing the main, as well as his vigor, strength and manhood,—said to them,— "What ye have said touching Rāma's (prowess), hath been heard by me. And I also know ye to be of sterling valor in the field. Yet why, knowing Rāma's prowess, do ye silently look at each other?" Then the maternal grand sire (of Rāvana), possessed of exceeding wisdom, named Mālyavān, hearing his words, said,—"The king that is accomplished in the various kinds of learning,* and that followeth polity,ever commandeth affluence and bringeth his enemies under his subjection. He that seasonably concludes peace and carries on war with his enemies,—and who advances his own party, attaineth great affluence. A king should enter into peace, if he be an equal or inferior of his adversary, and engage in war, if be more powerful,—but an enemy should never be disregarded.

* The commentator says there are four and ten kinds of learning; but unfortunately he does not enumerate them.—T.

Therefore, O Rāvana, peace with Rāma is what commends itself to me; and do thou render unto him that for which thou hast been invaded (by him), *viz.*, Sitā. All the Devarshis and Gandharvas wish for (Rāma's) victory. Therefore, do not enter into hostilities with him; but do thou bend thy mind to the conclusion of peace with him. That possessor of the six attributes, the Great-father, hath appointed two courses, (respectively) for the Asuras and the celestials, having for their proper objects righteousness and unrighteousness. Righteousness, we hear, is the course of the high-souled celestials, as, O Rākshasa, unrighteousness is that of Rakshas and Asuras. During the Krita Yuga, righteousness swalloweth up sin; and during Tishya,* unrighteousness swalloweth up virtue. Thou, ranging the three worlds, hadst extinguished pregnant piety, and reaped unrighteousness; and it is for this that thy foes have waxed potent.† And, having grown through thy neglect, unrighteousness devoureth us, and that protector of the gods, (righteousness), is strengthening the side of the celestials. Thou, addicted to carnal pleasures and acting in defiance of duty, hadst aroused the high wrath of the saints resembling fire. The power of these possessed of souls sanctified through asceticism, and ever engaged in invoking the aid of righteousness, is incapable of being resisted and is like flaming fire. The twice-born ones engage in contemplation with intent minds, offer oblations into the fire according to the ordinance, and loudly recite the Vedas. They overpower the Rakshas, uttering the Vedas; and thereat they fly in all directions like clouds scattered in summer. And the smoke that ariseth from the Agnihotra sacrifices of saints resembling fire, enveloping the energy of the Rākshasas, spreads over the ten cardinal quarters. And the fierce austerities of vow-observing saints, performed at particular

* The Kali Yuga.—T.

† While ranging the three worlds on a career of conquest, thou didst, disturbing sacrifices, *etc*, wrong righteousness.—T.

sacred spots, try the Rākshasas sore. Thou hast obtained a boon, conferring immunity at the hands of deities, Dānavas and Yakshas. But men and monkeys, bears and Golāngulas, possessed of enormous strength and endowed with vigor, and of indomitable prowess,—coming here, are setting up roars. Witnessing various and many dire portents, I perceive the destruction of all the Rākshasas. Dreadful and terrific clouds, uttering harsh sounds, are showering blood all around Lankā. And (live) vehicles are dropping profuse tears. And all sides, covered with dust, do not appear bright as formerly. And beasts of prey, jackals and vultures, are emitting frightful cries, and, entering into the garden of Lankā, form themselves into bands. And in dreams mighty dark-hued women in front of dwellings, seizing at (the furniture) thereof, and speaking inauspiciously, laugh displaying their sable teeth. And in houses dogs are feasting on the articles of worship. And cows bring forth asses, and mungooses, mice. And cats are pairing with leopards, and swine with dogs, and Kinnaras with Rākshasas and human beings. And red-footed white sky-coursing pigeons, urged on by Doom, are going about for the destruction of the Rākshasas. And female-parrots in houses, wounded and worsted by other birds delighting in discord, are dropping down, emitting indistinct notes. And all the birds and beasts are crying (distressfully) with their faces turned towards the sun. And at dusk a frightful, withered, tawny-hued male figure, looking like Death himself, with his head shaven, peereth into the houses (of people). These and other evil omens occur. Rāma I deem as Vishnu assuming the form of a man. Rāghava of steady prowess, for certain, is no human being,—he that hath built a bridge over the deep, must be an exceedingly wonderful person. Therefore, O Rāvana, conclude peace with Rāma—king of men. Having ascertained fit course, do thou act properly." Having said this unto that vile one, and known the intention of the lord of Rakshas, that strong Mālyavān, of exceeding prowess, became silent, eying Rāvana.

---

## SECTION XXXVI.

THE Ten-necked one, come under the control of Time, did not brook the beneficial speech spoken by Mālyavān. Contracting his face into a frown, he, coming under the masterdom of passion, with his eyes rolling in wrath, addressed Mālyavān, saying,—"The words which, deeming the strength of the enemy as superior, thou hast harshly spoken, considering it as beneficial, had never before entered my ears. A (mere) man, and feeble, and alone, and having monkeys for his support, why dost thou deem Rāma, who hath (further) been cast off by his sire, and hath in consequence taken refuge in the woods,—as competent (to cope with me)? And why dost thou consider me, who am the lord of the Rakshas, and feared even by the immortals,—as weak and reft of all power? Thou, I suspect, speakest (thus) roughly either from jealousy of my heroism, or for inciting me. And who that is wise and learned, ever addresseth him roughly that is at once puissant and of (high) station, if not to spur him on? Why, having brought Sitā like a Sri shorn of her lotus, shall I give her up, from fear of Rāghava? Behold Rāghava, environed by Kotis of monkeys, with Sugriva and Lakshmana, slain one of these days! He before whom even the gods cannot stay in the field,—how can that Rāvana ever come by fear? Better that I should be riven in twain,—but bend I never will. This is my native fault; and nature is incapable of being overcome. And if Rāma hath at his pleasure constructed a bridge over the ocean, what is the wonder in this that thou hast conceived such a fear? And although Rāma hath crossed the ocean along with the monkey-army, yet I swear unto thee truly, living, he shall not back hence." When Rāvana, wrought up with passion, had spoken thus, Mālyavān, knowing him wroth, did not return a reply. And, duly tendering blessings unto the king, Mālyavān, taking his permission, went to his own abode. And the Rākshasa, Rāvana, along with his courtiers, having consulted together as to what was fit to be done, set about the defence of Lankā. And he commanded the Rākshasa Prahasta (to guard) the Eastern gate; and the exceedingly powerful Mahāpārçwa and Mahodara (to guard) the Southern gate; and he ordered his son Indrajit, possessing mighty powers of illusion, girt by innumerable Rākshasas, to guard the Western gate. And he commanded Suka and Sārana to defend the Northern gate. But he said unto the counsellors,—"I will myself go thither."* And he posted in the middle in the garrison the Rākshasa, Virupāksha, endowed with exceeding prowess and energy, backed by countless Rākshasas. Having taken these measures in Lankā, the Rākshasa-chief, urged by Fate, deemed himself as having achieved success. Having thus completely provided for the defence of the city, he dismissed the ministers; and, honored by the counsellors with blessings of victory, (then) entered his magnificent and splendid inner apartment.

## SECTION XXXVII.

THOSE kings, man and monkey, that monkey the Wind-god's son, Jāmbavān—sovereign of bears—the Rākshasa,

* *i. e.* to defend the Northern gate.—T.

Bibhishana, the son of Vāli, Angada, Sumitrā's son, the monkey, Sarabha, Sushena along with his friends, Kumuda, Nala, and Panaça, arriving at the dominions of the enemy, assembled together, began to deliberate. "Yonder is that Lankā ruled by Rāvana, invincible even unto the celestials, serpents and Gandharvas. Let us, keeping before us success in the enterprise, consult together for the purpose of arriving at a decision. We are here daily nearing Rāvana, lord of Rākshasas." As they were speaking thus, Rāvana's younger brother, Bibhishana, said in a pregnant speech free from provinicialism,—"Anala, Panaça, Sampāti and Pramāti—all courtiers of mine—having gone up to Lankā, have come back here. Wearing the forms of birds, they entered into the hostile forces; and, having seen the measures that had been adopted (by them), have come (back). O Rāma, hearken to me as I tell thee truly anent the provisions which they have related, made by the wicked-minded Rāvana. In the Eastern gate stayeth Prahasta along with his forces; in the Southern, the exceedingly powerful Mahāpārçwa and Mahodara; and in the Western, Rāvana's son, Indrajit, supported by innumerable Rākshasas, equipped with *pattiças*, swords and bows, and bearing darts and maces in their hands,—surrounded by heroes carrying various weapons. And, backed by many thousands of Rākshasas weilding weapons, and accompanied by Rākshasas conversant with counsel, Rāvana himself, his heart agitated to the height, guardeth the Northern gate of the city. And Virupāksha with a powerful force accoutred in javelins, clubs and bows, protects the garrison in the centre. Having seen these hosts thus disposed in Lankā, my counsellors have speedily come back here. There are ten thousand elephants, an Ayuta cars, two of horses, and about a *koti* of Rākshasas, powerful and strong, and equipped with arms in conflict.* These night-rangers are ever the favorites of the Rākshasa ruler. And, O king, a *koti* of

* These are, remarks the commentator, the leaders.—T.

forces accompany each of these Râkshasas in battle." Having conveyed this information concerning Lankâ, which had been communicated by his counsellors, the mighty-armed Bibhishana showed (unto Râma) those Râkshasas themselves. And in company with his counsellors, Râvana's graceful younger brother, ever striving for the welfare of Râma, by way of answer communicated everything that was going forward in Lankâ unto Râma, having eyes resembling lotus-leaves,—"O Râma, when Râvana battled with Kuvera, sixty lacs of Râkshasas marched forth (to meet him). In prowess, energy, vigor, exceeding fortitude, and hauteur, they resembled the wicked-minded Râvana himself. In this matter, thou ought not to grow wroth,—I only arouse thy wrath, and do not endeavour to frighten thee.* Thou canst subdue even the celestials by thy prowess. Therefore thou, environed by a mighty army, having arrayed the monkey-forces in order of battle, shalt thrash Râvana (in battle)." When Râvana's younger brother had spoken thus, Râghava, said these words with reference to his beating the foe,—"Let that foremost of monkeys, Nilâ, surrounded by an immense number of monkeys, cope with Prahasta at the Eastern gate of Lankâ. And, engirt by a mighty force, let Angada, son of Vâli, resist Mahâparçwa and Mahodara at the Southern gate (thereof). And let that son of the Wind-god, Hanumân, backed by innumerable monkeys, (beating the host stationed) at the Western gate, find entrance (into the city). I myself, determined to compass the destruction of the lord of Râkshasas, who, waxing powerful in consequence of the boon he hath received, hath brought about the destruction of high-souled saints resembling gods and Dânavas,—and who goeth round all regions, oppressing people,—will, along with Sumitrâ's son, smiting (the foe), occupy the Northern entrance, where Râvana with his army is stationed. And let the

* *i. e.* Thou ought not to be angry with *me* ; for I do not frighten thee, but rouse thy *wrath against Râvana.*"—*T.*

powerful king of monkeys, and the puissant sovereign of bears, and the younger brother of the Rākshasa-chief, manage the soldiery posted in the centre. And in this battle, the monkeys need not assume the forms of human being. And let this serve for a sign that the monkeys, in order to the recognition of our own forces, appear with their proper monkey-marks. We seven only shall battle with the foe in human shapes,—*viz.*, I along with my brother, the exceedingly energetic Lakshmana, and my friend Bibhishana counting for the fifth in company with his own following." Having said this unto Bibhishana for attaining success in the enterprise, that lord, the intelligent Rāma, seeing the sides of Suvela more beautiful (than other places), intended to ascend it. Then, environed by a mighty host, the high-souled and magnanimous Rāma, his features mirroring forth high exultation,—overshadowing the entire Earth (with his forces), set out for Lankā, determined upon destroying the enemy.

## SECTION XXXVIII.

HAVING been bent upon mounting Suvela, Râma, followed by Lakshmana, addressed in sweet and excellent words, Sugriva, and that righteous night-ranger, Bibhishana, versed in counsel and conversant with precepts, who was devoted to him,—saying,—"We shall all ascend this mount Suvela, bedight with metals; and pass this night even here. And (from here) will we view the abode of that Rākshasa who, foul of soul, hath carried off my spouse, to bring destruction down on himself,--who knoweth nor morality nor good conduct nor behaviour (conducive to the dignity of his descent),—and who, in consequence of his base propensity, hath committed himself to so heinous a course of action." Having decided thus, Rāma, filled with wrath at Rāvana, coming to Suvela, ascended its variegated plateau. And Lakshmana, collected, went in his wake. And, upraising bow and arrow, Sugriva, (ever) engaged in valorous acts, accompanied with Bibhishana as well as his counselors, following him, also ascended (the mountain). And all those rangers of mountains, gifted with the vehemence of the Wind in hundreds ascended mount Suvela, where Rāghava was stationed. And ascending the mountain in a short time, they all beheld from its summit the city, appearing to be built on the air. And the monkey-leaders beheld Lankā, exceedingly splendid with noble gateways; gracefully enclosed with a wall; thronging with Rākshasas; and defended by sable Rākshasas. And the foremost of monkeys saw these appearing like another wall (overtopping the one beneath). And on seeing the Rākshasas, the monkeys burning for battle set up various roars in the presence of Rāma. Then the Sun, crimsoned with Eve, ascended the Setting-hill; and Night came, illumined by the Moon at his full. Then the master of the monkey-army, Rāma, saluted and honored by Bibhishana, accompanied by Lakshmana as well as the leaders of the monkeys, sojourned happily on the breast of Suvela.

---

## SECTION XXXIX.

HAVING passed the night in Suvela, the heroic monkey-leaders surveyed woods and forests in Lankā. And seeing those extensive (woods and forests), mild, and charming, and beautiful to behold, they were seized with wonderment.

Abounding in *champakas, açokas, vakulas, çâlas,* and palms; covered with *tamâlas* and *panaças,*—and environed all around with trees,—and surrounded with Hintâlas, Aryunas, blossoming Saptaparnas, Tilakas, Karnikâras, and Pâtalas,—trees with flowering tops, entertwined with creepers,—Lankâ looked exceedingly lovely, with various sights,—resembling the Amarâvati herself of Indra. And trees there, furnished with variegated flowers having tender rosy leaves,—and blue lawns, and rows of woods; and bearing odourous and charming blossoms and fruits,—looked like men adorned with ornaments. And there a delightful and pleasant wood resembling Chaitraratha, and like unto Nandana itself—having all the seasons present,—appeared beauteous to the view, with black bees all around. And it had Dâtyuhas, and Koyasthivas, and peacocks dancing; and the strains of the coels were heard at the woodland rills. And the heroic and exhilarated monkeys, capable of wearing forms at pleasure, entered those woods and groves frequented by maddened birds and ranged by Bhramaras,—tracts overflowing with the lays of coels, and ringing with the voices of songsters,—resonant with the notes of Bhramaras—sovereigns of their species—and eloquent with the cries of ospreys. And as the exceedingly energetic monkeys entered, there blew upon them the breeze—like unto life—redolent of perfume obtained from contact with the blossoms. And others of the leaders among the heroic monkeys, coming out from the bands, ordered by Sugriva, made in the direction of Lankâ crowned with ensigns. And, terrifying the fowls and dispiriting beasts and birds and shaking Lankâ with their roars, those foremost monkeys set up shouts. And they, endowed with great impetuosity, went on, oppressing the earth with their battle-array; and clouds of dust suddenly arose from the the march of the soldiery. And bears, and lions, and buffaloes, and elephants, and deer, and birds, overwhelmed with affright, made for the ten cardinal points. The graceful and lovely summit of Trikuta was entire, elevated, sky-piercing, of golden splendour, measuring an hundred *yoyanas*, clear-shining, level, inaccessible even to fowls, and incapable of being ascended even in thought—not to say of actual ascension by people. Lankā, ruled by Rāvana, was situated on its* top,—ten *yoyanas* in width and twenty in length. And that city was graced with lofty ornamented gateways resembling pale clouds, and golden and silvern walls; and Lankā was adorned with palaces and piles; like the sky† graced with clouds on the approach of the rainy season. And that palace, which was adorned with thousands of pillars, and which, as if piercing the heavens, looked like a peak of Kailāça—was the residence of the Sovereign of the Rākshasas—the ornament of the city, (ever guarded by full hundreds of Rākshasas. And Lakshmana's auspicious and puissant elder brother, beholding that flourishing and wealthy city resembling the celestial regions,—charming to the mind, made of gold, graced with mountains, and decked out with mountains containing various metals,—resonant with the notes of various birds; abounding in various beasts,—furnished with various kinds of flowers,—and inhabited by various orders of Rākshasas,—was struck with astonishment. And Rāma, surrounded by his mighty forces, saw that palace, filled with diverse kinds of gems, adorned with rows of edifices, and having huge engines and gateways.

* Trikuta's.—T.

† *Madhyamam Vaishnavam padam*—the middle foot of Vishnu. When Vishnu in his Dwarf-form took the conceit out of Váli, the renowned Asura king,—he covered the earth with one pace, the sky with another and heaven with the last.—T.

## SECTION XL.

THEN Rāma, accompanied by the monkey-leaders, along with Sugriva, ascended the top of Suvela, measuring a circumference of two *yoyanas*. And staying there for a while and looking at the ten cardinal points, he saw Lankā finely placed on the charming summit of Trikuta,—graced with elegant groves; and (he also saw) the unconquerable lord of Rākshasas, stationed at the top of the gateway, fanned with white *châmaras*; graced with the umbrella betokening victory; smeared with red sandal; adorned in red ornaments; resembling masses of sable clouds; and apparelled in golden attire,—his breast bearing scars from the tusk-ends of Airāvata; covered with a sheet hued like the blood of hares; and appearing like clouds lighted up by the evening sun. And on seeing the Rākshasa-chief, Sugriva suddenly rose up in the sight of the lords of monkeys as well as Rāghava. And influenced by wrath, he, mustering strength and vigor, rising from the brow of the mountain, bounded to the gateway. And pausing for a while and eying the Rākshasa intrepidly, he, slighting the Raksha, addressed him in harsh speech, saying,—"O Rākshasa, I am the friend as well as the slave of Rāma—lord of men. Me, backed by the energy of that king of the Earth, shalt thou not escape to-day." Saying this, he, suddenly springing up, descended on him; and snatching away his variegated crown, let it fall on the earth. And seeing him come abruptly, the night-ranger spoke to him thus,—"Thou that wert Sugriva beyond my ken, shalt be neckless* near me." Having said this, he

* The text has *hinagriva—neckless.* There is a pun here, turning on the word *grivâ*—neck. Râvana says: "Thou wert Sugriva (good-necked) in my absence,—but now thou shalt be *hinagriva*—neckless."—T.

rose up swiftly and dragged him* down to the earth. Thereat springing like pith, the monkey pushed down his antagonist with his arms. And each having his body bathed in sweat and his person covered with blood, each choking and annuling the efforts of the other,—and resembling a *Sâlmali* or a *Kinçuka*, and dealing blows and slaps, and hitting with his arms and hands,—those exceedingly strong ones, the lord of the Rākshasas and that of the monkeys, fought wonderfully. And having for a long time encountered each other in combat on the dais belonging to the gate,—they, now lifting up their persons and now lowering them, went down, each felling the other with his legs. And smiting each other, they, their bodies fastened together, went down between the wall and the moat,—and again stood upon the ground. And heaving breath, they, resting for a space, grappled with each other; and they fast bound each other with their arms serving for ropes. And each fired with wrath, and each having both strength and skill, they now bore themselves in the lists like a tiger and a lion, furnished with teeth; or like the young of the foremost elephants engaged in encounter,—and restraining and pushing each other with their arms, they simultaneously both came down to the ground. Then starting again to their feet, they, vituperating each other, ranged the lists, displaying feats expressive of skill and strength. Nor did those heroes speedily come by fatigue. And resembling mighty elephants, they, resisting each other by means of their powerful arms like unto the trunks of elephants, fought for a long while, swiftly wheeling about the arena. And approaching each other, they strove to slay each other, like unto two cats seated, momentarily encountering each other over some food. And the lord of monkeys and Rāvana, accomplished in fight, coursed the arena, displaying wonderful *mandalas*,† various

---

* Sugriva.

† A *mandala* is of four kinds, *viz.*, *chāri*, *karana*, *khanda* and *mahāmandala*.

*sthânas,*(a) curious *gomútrakas,*(b) *gatapratyâgatas, tiraschînagatas, vakragatas, parimokshas, varjanas, paridhâvanas, abhidravanas,*(c) *âplâvanas.*(d) *savigrahâvasthânas,*(e) *parâvrittas,*(f) *apâvrittas,*(g) *apadrutas,*(h) *avaplutas,*(i) *apanyastas,*(j) and *upanyastas.*(k) In the meanwhile the Raksha attempted to put forth his power of illusion. Knowing this, the king of monkeys shot into the sky. And Rāvana, overpowered by fatigue and out of breath, thus baffled by the monkey-king, stood where he was. Thus the master of the foremost monkeys, securing fame in fight, beat the night-ranger, causing him to experience fatigue. And bounding beyond the spacious sky, the offspring of the Sun came to the side of Rāma in the midst of the monkey-forces. And having done that deed, the son of the Sun,—lord of monkeys—with his heart surcharged with rejoicing, entered that host having the speed of the wind; enhancing the martial ardour of the son of the foremost of the Raghus, and honored by the monkeys.

---

Proceeding with one leg advanced is *châri*, with two alternately advanced is *karana*; proceeding after the manner of *karana*, with some special movements, is *khanda*; and two or three *khandas* combined is a *mahâmandala*.—T.

(a) A particular adjustment of the steps successively; awry, *etc.*—It is of six kinds, *viz.*, *Vaishnava*, *Sampâda*, *Vaiçâkha*, *Mandala*, *Pratyâlirha* and *Anâlirha*.—*T.*

(b) A kind of motion resembling cow's urine flowing, as its name signifies.

(c) Swiftly fronting the antagonist.

(d) Proceeding 'like a summer's cloud.'

(e) Standing before the adversary, after making others engage in combat. What this means in the passage under notice is hard to divine.

(f) Turning away from a foe.

(g) Moving off from the side of the enemy.

(h) Movement with low posture for seizing at the thighs of the adversary.

(i) Going for a kick at the adversary.

(j) Distending the chest, so that the antagonist may not catch the arms.

(k) Stretching forth the arms for seizing those of the enemy.

## SECTION XLI.

SEEING those ominous signs, Lakshmana's elder brother, Ramā, embracing Sugriva, said,—"Without consulting with me, thou hast acted thus rashly. But kings should not act in such a rash way. Placing in suspense, me, this army and Bibhishana, thou, O hero, enamoured of daring deeds, hast put thyself to all this trouble. But, O hero, henceforth, do not act so. O subduer of enemies, if thou come by any mischance, what shall Sitā avail me; or Bharata; or my younger brother—Lakshmana; or Satrughna, O slayer of enemies; or, again, my own person? Ere thou hadst come, I had arrived at this determination; albeit, O thou that art equal to the mighty Indra or Varuna, I knew thy prowess full well. Slaying Rāvana in battle along with his sons, forces and vehicles, and installing Bibhishana in Lankā, and placing the kingdom in the hands of Bharata, I shall renounce my body, O exceedingly powerful one!" When Rāma had said this, Sugriva answered,—"Knowing my own strength, how, O Rāghava, viewing Rāvana, who had ravished away thy wife, could I forbear, O hero?" As that hero was speaking thus, Rāghava addressed Lakshmana having auspiciousness, thus,—"O Lakshmana, occupying some tract furnished with cool water and woods bearing fruits, we shall sojourn, dividing and marshalling our forces. I see a mighty fear present, destructive of people,—and boding destruction unto the foremost heroes among the bears, monkeys and Rākshasas. The winds ruffle; and the earth is tremulous. And the tops of mountains tremble, and the mountains themselves send up loud sounds. And the clouds are goblinish; and fierce; and harsh-sounding. And wearing terrific looks, they fiercely pour down showers mixed with drops of blood. And the Evening resembles the red sandal, and is fearful. And a flaming circle droppeth from the Sun. And exciting great fear, inauspicious birds and beasts, wearing cruel looks, and in distressful guise,—cry in piteous accents, facing the Sun. And at night, the ominous Moon with a black-red brim as at the time of universal wreck, burneth. And, O Lakshmana, there is a crimson, rough, slight, and graceful rim round the Sun; and a blue mark is visible on his disc. And the stars do not course as formerly. Behold, O Lakshmana, all these, prefiguring the Doom. And crows and hawks and vultures drop down. And jackals yell with loud inauspicious notes. The Earth, converted into mud with flesh and gore, shall be covered with darts and javelins and swords, discharged by Rākshasas and monkeys. This very day with all expedition shall we, surrounded on all sides by the monkeys, march towards the city governed by Rāvana." Having said this unto Lakshmana, Lakshmana's elder brother possessed of exceeding strength, hastily descended from the top of the mountain. And descending from the mountain, the righteous Rāghava surveyed his troops, incapable of being beaten by enemies. And after making the mighty host of the monkey-king equip itself, Rāghava versed in season, along with Sugriva, at the proper hour, issued orders for battle. Then in due time that one, accoutred with his bow, surrounded by a mighty army, set out, with the intention of entering the city of Lankā. And those two—Bibhishana and Sugriva—and Hanumān, and Jāmvabān, and Nala, and the bear-king Nila, and Lakshmana, followed (Rāma). Behind them, the mighty array of bears and monkeys followed Rāghava, cevering a wide surface of land. The monkeys, resembling elephants, capable of resisting foes, took mountain-peaks and tall trees by hundreds. And in a short time those repressors of foes—the brothers Rāma and Lakshmana—arrived at the city of Rāvana; with pennons streaming over her; charming; garnished with groves and woods; having variegated gateways; inaccessible; and having walls and gates. And urged on by Rāma's command, the wood-rangers,* as commanded, blocking up (Lankā) incapable of being subdued even by the gods, stationed themselves. Coming to Lankā ruled by Rāvana, that hero, Rāma, son unto Daçaratha, along with Lakshmana, remained stationed at the Northern gate, where Rāvana used to reside. None save Rāma was competent to protect that dreadful gate, where Rāvana used to reside. None save Rāma was competent to protect that dreadful gate, guarded by Rāvana himself, like the Ocean guarded by Varuna,—and protected on all sides by terrible Rākshasas equipped with weapons; capable of striking terror into the weak; like unto the nether regions guarded by Dānavas. And (Rāma) saw there many and various arms and mail of the warriors, ranged together. And coming to the Eastern gate, that leader of the monkey-army, the powerful Nila, along with Mainda and Dwivida,—took up his post there. And the exceedingly strong Angada, accompanied by Rishava, Gavāksha, Gaya, and Gavaya, occupied the Southern gate. And the mighty monkey Hanumān protected the Western entrance. And Sugriva himself, with Prajangha, Tarasa and other heroes, was quartered near the garrision in the centre. And accompanied by all the foremost monkeys resembling Suparna or the Wind, twenty *kotis* of renowned monkey-leaders, blocking up all sides, stationed themselves near the monkey, Sugriva. And at Rāma's command, Lakshmana along with Bibhishana, went from door to door, issuing instructions to *kotis* of monkeys. On the west of Rāma, Jāmbavān along with Sushena, followed by innumerable troops, remained hard by at the garrison in the middle. And those tiger-like monkeys, furnished with teeth like unto tigers, weilding trees and mountain-tops, stood ready for fight. And all had their tails curled up, and all were armed with teeth and nails, and

* Monkeys.

all had chequered bodies,and all had frightful faces. And some had the strength of ten elephants; and some had strength ten times as much; and some of the monkey-leaders there had the strength of a thousand elephants,—and some had the strength of numbers (of elephants); and some had strength hundred times as much. And others had immeasurable might. And wonderful and astonishing was their meeting. And the concourse at that place of the monkey-forces was like the concourse of locusts. And the air was filled up, and the earth was covered quite with the monkeys coursing towards Lankā and dropping down into it. And hundreds and thousands making up the army of monkeys, arrived at the gate of Lankā; while others were pouring in from all sides for encounter. And that mount was covered with monkeys. And a thousand *ayutas* were going round the city. And Lankā, blocked up everywhere with powerful monkeys bearing trees in their hands, was incapable of being entered even by the Wind. And the Rākshasas, sore pressed by thousands of monkeys resembling masses of clouds, and like unto Sakra himself in battle, were seized with amazement. And like unto the roar of water on the ocean being riven, there arose a mighty tumult in consequence of the forces surging hither and thither. And with that sound the entire Lankā, with her wall and gateways, her mountains, woods, and forests, began to shake. And that army, protected by Rāma and Lakshmana as well as Sugriva, became all the more invincible even by the Asuras and celestials. And having arranged his forces with the view of destroying the Rakshas, Rāghava, versed in the resources of war,* taking counsel of the counsellors, and deciding again and again his course of action,—intending to adopt further measures,—resolved to abide by the advice of Bibhishana†, remembering the morality regulating

* conciliation, &c.

† Which was,—" If Rávana should seek thy succour, thou shouldst confer on him his kingdom."—T.

monarchs*. And then, calling Vâli's son, Angada, (Râma) said,—"O mild one, going to the Ten-necked one, tell him in my words,—'Bounding over the deep and casting off fear and dejection, I have laid seige to the city of Lankâ; and have reft thee of thy prosperity and thy wealth; and rendered thee moribund and senseless. Thou hast, O night-ranger, through delusion and pride injured saints and celestials, and Gandharvas and Apsarâs, and Serpents, and Yakshas, and crowned heads. But, O Râkshasa, thy pride begot of the boon received from the Self-create hath gone from thee, whose destroyer,† I, afflicted in consequence of my wife having been carried off,—weilding the rod, have sat down at the door of Lankâ. O Râkshasa, thou shalt, remaining steady in fight, attain the state of celestials and Maharshis and Râjarshis. And, O worst of Râkshasas, do thou display that prowess of thine by which, aided by thy power of illusion, thou hast forcibly carried off Sitâ, disregarding me. I shall with my sharpened shafts render this world free from Râkshasas, unless rendering back Mithilâ's daughter, thou throw thyself on my mercy. And, for certain, that foremost of Râkshasas, the righteous and graceful Bibhishana, who hath joined us, shall obtain, without having a thorn in his side, all this wealth of Lankâ. For thou, foolish, wicked, ignorant of self-knowledge, and having dolts for counsellors, art not competent to unrighteously exercise kingship for a moment. Fight thou, O Râkshasa, summoning fortitude and heroism. On being slain with my shafts, thou shalt attain peace.‡ O night-ranger, if thou shouldst range the three worlds in the shape of a bird, thou, coming in my ken, shalt not be able to preserve thy life. It

* In this connection, the principle referred to is: "If a king can accomplish his purpose by conciliation, he should not employ punishment."—T.

† *Dandadhara*—lit.—rod-bearing, a name of Yama,—who is described as weilding a *rod* for chastising wrong-doers.—T.

‡ i. e. *attain heaven*.—T.

is all this for thy good ; do thou perform acts for the good of thy body surviving death ; and do thou see Lankā well ; for thy life is in my keeping.'" Thus addressed by Rāma of untiring deeds, Tārā's son went through the welkin like the embodied bearer of sacrificial offerings.* And arriving near that subduer of enemies, Rāvana, in a moment, that graceful one saw Rāvana, sitting calmly in the midst of his ministers. And dropping down in his vicinity like a flaming fire, that best of monkeys, Angada, resembling a golden bracelet,† stood there. And then introducing himself, Angada delivered unto Rāvana along with his ministers all that Rāma had excellently spoken unto him, neither extenuating nor setting down aught of himself,—"I am the envoy of the king of Koçala—Rāma of untiring deeds ; and I am the son of Vāli.—I do not know whether thou hast heard of me. And Raghu's son, Rāma—enhancer of Kauçalyā's joy—hath said unto thee,—'Do thou, O fell one, coming out, give me battle and prove thy prowess. Thee shall I slay together with thy ministers, and with thy sons and relations and friends. And thou being slain, the three worlds shall attain peace. And to-day shall I destroy the enemy of the gods and Dānavas, and Yakshas, of the Gandharvas, serpents and Rākshasas,—and the thorn (in the side of) the saints. And on thee being slain, all the wealth shall be Bibhishana's ; unless, bowing down (unto me) and paying me homage, thou render back Maithili.'" When that monkey-chief had spoken thus, the lord of the night-rangers was wrought up with wrath. And coming under the sway of passion, he commanded his counsellors, saying,—"Take this one of perverse understanding, and slay him at once".

---

* Fire.

† This simile is hardly happy; but the lure was even the name of the monkey, *Angada* suggested *kanakāngada*—golden bracelet. This typifies the tendency prevailing to this day of Hindu authors to exercise their ingenuity in *puns*.—T.

Hearing Rāvana's speech, four grim-visaged night-rangers seized (Angada) flaming in energy like fire itself. And Tārā's son suffered himself to be taken, in order that the hero might then display his prowess before the Yātudhānas.* Then Angada, taking them up, who were pressed against his arms, like insects,—leapt up on a palace resembling a hill. Thereat, in consequence of the impetuosity of his bound, the Rākshasas, slipping off, fell on to the ground in the very sight of the Rākshasa king. Then the powerful son of Vāli with his legs attacked the top of that palace, elevated like a hill,† of the lord of Rākshasas. And thereat, as formerly the summit of the Himavān had been cleft by the thunder-bolt, the palace, thus assailed, was split in the very presence of the Ten-necked one. Having reft the top of the edifice, and proclaimed his name, Angada, setting up a mighty roar, sprang into the sky. And, aggrieving the Rākshasas and rejoicing all the monkeys, he came back to the side of Rāma in the midst of the monkeys. Rāvana was transported with wrath in consequence of the breaking down of the palace. And, finding his destruction (at hand), he began to heave sighs. And Rāma, surrounded by innumerable delighted monkeys setting up shouts,—anxious for slaying his foe, prepared for battle. And at the command of Sugriva, the exceedingly powerful monkey—Sushena—resembling a mountain-summit, surrounded by a large number of monkeys capable of assuming shapes at pleasure, began to range from door to door;‡ like the Moon ranging the stars. Seeing the hundred *akshauhinis* of the wood-rangers, stationed in Lānka, extending down to the sea, some of the Rākshasas were struck with astonishment, while some

* Rákshasas.

† The commentator, however, would make *dadarça—saw*—understood. "*Angada saw that* the palace was high like a hill, *etc.*" This is unnecessary.—T.

‡ For protecting the entire army, as well as for procuring information of the movements of the enemy.—T.

came under the influence of fear; and some experienced delight from the (anticipated) delight of battle. And the space between the well and the moat all was flooded with monkeys. And the distressed Rākshasas saw the wall thronging with monkeys;* and thereat exclaiming "Alas" "Alas," the Rākshasas were extremely terrified. And on that frightful uproar arising, the warriors of the Rākshasa monarch,—Rākshasas—seizing mighty arms, began to patrol about, like unto winds blowing at the time of the universal dissolution.

## SECTION XLII.

THEN thoseRākshasas, going to that subduer of enemies, Rāvana, informed him that Rāma along with the monkeys had laid seige unto the city. Hearing the city beseiged, the night-ranger was enraged. And, hearing that double arrangements had been made (by Rāma) in guarding the gateways, (Rāvana) ascended the palace. He saw Lankā with her hills, woods, and forests, covered everywhere with innumerable monkeys eager for encounter. And he saw the entire Earth tawneyed with the monkeys; and he reflected within himself how he could destroy these. And reflecting for long, Rāvana having expansive eyes, assuming patience, gazed at Rāghava and the leader of monkeys. Rāghava with his host was fast approaching (the wall); and Rāvana saw Lankā defended on all sides by Rākshasas. And Daçaratha's son, seeing Lankā crowned with variegated ensigns and

* A translator cannot help a feeling of disappointment at the difference—to the disadvantage of English—between Sanskrit and English. The original for 'thronging with monkeys' is a verbal attributive—*vānarikrita*—lit. *monkeyed*.—*T*.

standards, mentally went to Sitā, with a sad heart. "For my sake, here that one, Janaka's daughter, having eyes resembling those of a young deer,—is undergoing affliction; and lieth down on the ground." And aggrieved at the thought of Vaidehi, the righteous Rāma speedily commanded the monkeys to compass the destruction of the enemies. As Rāma of untiring deeds said this, the monkeys, filling (the air) with leonine roars, began to press forward furiously. "We shall cleave Lankā with mountain-peaks, or with our blows"—thus thought the leaders within themselves. And the monkey-leaders stood, raising up gigantic mountain-peaks and tops of mountains, and rooting up various trees. And for doing what was dear unto Rāma, that army, divided into separate parties, in the presence of the Rākshasa-chief commenced scaling Lankā. And those copper-faced ones of golden sheen, who had consecrated their lives to the service of Rāma, equipped with trees and rocks, began to throng upon Lankā. And the monkeys with trees and hill-tops and blows crushed countless gates and tops of walls; and they filled the moat containing crystal water with dust, tops of crags, straw, and wood. Then leaders of thousands and *kotis* and hundreds of *kotis* began to scale Lankā. And the monkeys crushed golden gateways; and, breaking down gates resembling the tops of the summits of Kailāça, bounded roaring, some towards the wall and some all around. And resembling gigantic elephants, they rushed towards Lankā. "Victory to the mighty Rāma, and Victory to the exceedingly powerful Lakshmana, and Victory to king Sugriva, who is protected by Rāghava.' Thus shouting, those monkeys, wearing forms at will, sending up roars, rushed amain towards the wall of Lankā. And Viravāhu, Suvāhu, Nala and Panaça—leader of monkeys—breaking (a portion of) the wall, took up their post there. In the meantime, (they) arranged the forces in order of battle. And the strong Kumuda, surrounded by ten *kotis* of victorious monkeys, stood obstructing the Eastern gate. And for backing him, there remained the monkey, Prasabha, as also the long-armed Panaça, surrounded by monkeys. And obstructing the Southern entrance stood the strong and gallant monkey, Satavali, surrounded by twenty *kotis*. And the strong sire of Tārā, the powerful Sushena, obstructed the Western gate, backed by *kotis* upon *kotis* (of monkeys). And obstructing the Northern gate, remained the puissant Rāma himself along with Sumitrā's son, as well as the king of monkeys—Sugriva. And that huge-bodied and dreadful Golāngula—the mighty and powerful Gavāksha—surrounded by a *koti*, remained by the side of Rāma. And that destroyer of foes—the exceedingly mighty Dhumra of the bears of terrific wrath, remained by the side of Rāma—where, surrounded by vigilant counsellors, and bearing a mace in his hand, stood the exceedingly strong Bibhishana, endowed with wonderful powers, in complete panoply. And Gaya, and Gavāksha, and Gavaya, and Sarabha, and Gandhamādana, protected the monkey-army, coursing all around. And then, his soul wrought up with wrath, Rāvana—lord of Rākshasas—speedily ordered the whole host to sally out. Hearing those words, which came out from Rāvana's mouth, all of a sudden the night-rangers sent up a dreadful yell. Then awoke the kettle-drums, having moon-like pale faces,—sounded by means of golden sticks. And conchs by hundreds and by thousands, capable of producing loud blares, filled with air proceeding from the mouths of dreadful Rākshasas,—were winded. And with conchs placed in their mouths, those night-rangers, having bodies blue like those of *Cukas*, resembled masses of clouds, with lightning and cranes. And, commanded by Rāvana, the troops cheerfully issued forth like the onrushing of the mighty main filling all at the time of the universal dissolution. And then the monkey-army gave a roar, spreading all around; and it seemed as if the sound filled all Malaya with its sides and caves. And sounds of conchs, and drums, as well as the leonine shouts of the impetuous (warriors), made the earth, air, and ocean, resound ; and these mixed with the roars of elephants, the neighing of steeds, the rattle of the car-wheels, and the tread of the Rākshasas' feet. And in the meantime there commenced a mighty encounter between the Rākshasas and the monkeys, like that which took place of yore between the gods and the Asuras. And displaying their prowess, they* began to slaughter monkeys with maces, and darts, and adzes. And the vehement monkeys (on their side) slaughtered Rākshasas with trees and tops of crags as well as with their nails and teeth. And a mighty sound arose of 'Victory unto king Sugriva !' and 'Victory unto thee, O king,'—each army taking the name of its king. And then other dreadful Rākshasas that were stationed upon the wall, dropping down, pierced the monkeys with darts and *bhindipālas*. And (thereat) the monkeys, flying into fury, descending to the earth and bounding, brought down the Rākshasas with their arms. And that encounter of the Rākshasas and the monkeys was mighty and wonderful, and the ground became wet with flesh and gore.

## SECTION XLIII.

AND as the high-souled monkeys and Rākshasas faught on, their wrath vastly increased at sight of each other's forces. And furnished with steeds in golden trappings ; and elephants resembling flames of fire ; and cars appearing like (so many) suns ; and shining armour,—the valiant Rākshasas issued, making the ten cardinal points resound. The

* Rākshasas.

Râkshasas of terrific exploits were burning for victory on behalf of Râvana.—And the mighty monkey-army also, eager for victory, darted against the host of the Rakshas of dreadful deeds. And in the meanwhile, as either party assailed the other, there took place single combats between the Râkshasas and the monkeys. And as Andhaka had combated with the Three-eyed (deity),* that Râkshasa, the exceedingly energetic Indrajit, faught with Angada, son unto Vâli. Sampâti, hard to bear, engaged with Prajangha; and the monkey, Hanumân, entered into conflict with Jambumâli. And Râvana's younger brother, Bibhishana, fired with wrath, encountered Satrughna, endowed with exceeding impetuosity. And the highly powerful Nila engaged with Nikumbha. And Sugriva—lord of monkeys—undertook Praghasa, and the graceful Lakshmana was engaged with Virupâksha. And the exceedingly irrepressible Agniketu and the Râkshasa—Raçmiketu—and Mitraghna and Yajnakopa, were engaged with Râma. And Vajramushthi encountered Mainda, and Açaniprabha, Dwivida. And those foremost of monkeys faught with those dreadful Râkshasas,—the heroic and terrible Pratapana, incapable of being overcome in battle, was combating with Nala of terrific force; and that lusty son of Righteousness, well-known as Sushena,—a mighty monkey—battled with Vidyunmâli. And other fearful monkeys encountered other Râkshasas; and many were the encounters that took place. And great and fierce was the engagement that took place between the heroic Râkshasas and monkeys burning for victory, capable of making people's hair stand on end. And from the persons of the Râkshasas and the monkeys there flowed a river of gore, having hair for grass (growing on its banks), and the bodies of the warriors for pieces of planks floating (adown the current). Indrajit, growing enraged, with his mace dealt a blow at that tearer of hostile ranks, Angada,—like him of an hundred sacrifices

* Siva, fabled to have three eyes.—T.

striking with his thunderbolt. Thereat, that graceful monkey, Angada, gifted with vehemence, with his mace crushed his car decked in gold, together with the steeds and the charioteer. Sampâti was pierced with three arrows by Prajangha; and the former (in his turn) slew Prajangha on the edge of battle with an Açwakarna.* And Jambumâli, mounted on a car, possessed of prodigious strength, fired with wrath, with all the access of force derived from his car, wounded Hanumân between his paps. Thereat, getting at his car, Hanumân—son unto the Wind-god—with a slap speedily crushed his adversary's vehicle along with the Raksha. Then the terrific Pratapana, roaring, rushed at Nala; and thereat Nala, with his body pierced with sharp shafts by that swift-handed Raksha, plucked out Pratapana's eyes, and cast them to the earth. And that lord of monkeys, Sugriva, with a *Saptaparna*† swiftly slew Praghasa, who appeared to be devouring up the troops. And, tormenting the Râkshasa of dreadful form with a shower of shafts, Lakshmana slew Virupâksha with a single arrow. And the irrepressible Agniketu, the Râkshasa Raçmiketu, Mitraghna and Yajnakopa, with their arrows rendered Râma aflame. Thereat, Râma, growing wroth, in battle severed the heads of those four by means of four shafts, dreadful, and resembling the tongues of a flame. And Vajramushti was slain in conflict by Mainda with a clenched fist; and down came he to the ground along with his car and horses, like a turret toppling (headlong). And Nikumbha in fight wounded Nila resembling a mass of blue collyrium, with sharpened shafts,—as the Sun pierceth clouds with his rays. Again with an hundred arrows, that light-handed night-ranger pierced Nila in the field; and Nikumbha laughed thereat. At this, even as Vishnu did in battle, Nila with a wheel of his‡ car, cut off in

---

* A kind of tree.

† A tree.

‡ *Nikumbha's.*

conflict Nikumbha's head together with that of his charioteer. And Dwivida, possessed of the touch of the Vajra and thunder-bolt, in the presence of the entire Rākshasa host hurled a mountain-peak at him that was endowed with the splendour of the thunder-bolt. And Açaniprabha in encounter pierced that foremost of monkeys, Dwivida, with shafts resembling thunder-bolts. Thereat, beside himself with wrath, with his entire body wounded with arrows, Dwivida with a *sâla* destroyed Açaniprabha along with his car and horses. And Vidyunmāli, mounted on a car, assailed Sushena with shafts decked with gold, and began to shout momentarily. Seeing him mounted on his car, Sushena—best of monkeys—taking up a huge crag, swiftly brought his car down to the ground. Thereat, endowed with lightness, that night-ranger, Vidyunmāli, at once extricating himself from his car, stood on the ground with a mace in his hand. Thereupon, that foremost of monkeys, Sushena, growing furious, taking up a gigantic crag, rushed at the night-ranger. And as he was descending, the night-ranger, Vidyunmāli, with his mace swiftly hit at the breast of Sushena—greatest of monkeys. Thereat, without thinking at all of the terrific hit of the mace, that best of monkeys in mighty conflict brought down that* upon his† head. And, assailed with the crag, the night-ranger, Vidyunmāli, having his chest crushed, fell down to the earth, deprived of life. And, like the celestials warring against the Daityas, the heroic monkeys warred on and confounded the valiant rangers of the night. And frightful was the field of battle, with darts, and other arms; and clubs, and javelins, and lances, and other weapons; and with broken cars, and war-horses, and mad horses slain, and monkeys and Rākshasas; and wheels and *akshas*,‡ and yokes and standards,—broken and scattered over the ground; and

---

* The crag, which he had at first hit.—T.

† *Vidyunmâli's.*

‡ A part of a wheel.

swarms of jackals began to range on all sides of the monkeys and the Rākshasas; and *Kavandhas** began to rise in that terrific encounter, resembling the encounter of the gods and the Asuras. Thus destroyed by the foremost of monkeys, the rangers of night, beyond themselves with the smell of blood,—eagerly wishing for the setting of the Sun,† again made active preparations for a renewal of the fight.

## SECTION XLIV.

As the monkeys and the Rākshasas thus faught on, the sun set, and the fatal Night came. And then commenced a night-engagement between the dreadful Rākshasas and the monkeys of fixed hostility, each party burning for victory. And in that profound darknesss, the monkeys and the Rākshasas began to slay each other, exclaiming,—'Thou art a Rākshasa,' and 'Thou art a monkey.' And in that army there was heard a mighty uproar of 'slain,' 'rive!' 'come!' 'why fliest?' And, dark-hued, the Rākshasas, equipped in golden mail, in that deep darkness appeared like elevated hills clad with woods of flaming medicinal herbs. And in that limitless gloom, the Rākshasas, transported with wrath, advanced with impetuous speed, devouring monkeys. And, fired with terrible wrath, they,‡ bounding up, with their sharp teeth tore up steeds caparisoned in gold, and standards resembling venomous serpents. And the lusty monkeys in battle agitated the Rākshasa host,—and, waxing furious, with

* Spectres having bodies without heads.

† This was because, as intelligently remarks Rámánuja, night-rangers grow powerful *at night*.—T.

‡ *i. e.* the monkeys, as appears from the context.—T.

their teeth pulled and bit elephants and the riders thereof, and cars furnished with flags and standards. And Rāma and Lakshmana with shafts resembling venomous serpents, slaughtered the foremost among the Rākshasas—both those that were seen and those that were not.—And the dust of the earth arising from warring combatants, and from the hoofs of horses and the wheels of cars, choked up eye and ear. And as the mighty encounter, capable of making people's hair stand on end, went on, there flowed a fearful river of gore. And the sounds of kettle-drums and *Mridangas* and *Panavas*, mingled with those of conchs and car-wheels,—were wonderful (to hear). And the sounds of steeds neighing, and Rākshasas (roaring), and monkeys, rejoicing,—were something tremendous. And, with able monkeys slain; and darts and javelins and axes; and slaughtered Rākshasas wearing forms at pleasure, lying mountain-like,—the field of battle, seeming to have offerings of arms representing flowers,—became difficult to recognise, and inaccessible; and the earth was drenched with streams of blood. And that Night, destructive to monkeys and Rākshasas,—was dreadful, and difficult of being out-sped by all,—like unto the Fatal Night of beings. And in that profound darkness, the Rākshasas with great vivacity attacked Rāma with a shower of shafts. And the roars of those beings as they advanced, sending up shouts in anger, resembled the dashing of the Ocean at the time of the universal dissolution. And in the twinkling of an eye, Rāma by means of six shafts resembling tongues of flames, struck six of the night-rangers; *viz.*, Yajnaçatru, irrepressible (in fight),—and Mahāpārcwa, and Mahodara, and the huge-bodied Vajradanashtra,—and those two—Suka and Sārana. And, pierced in their vitals with Rāma's shafts, they, having only their lives left to them, disappeared from the field. Then in the twinkling of an eye, that Mahāratha rendered all sides clear (of all gloom) by means of arrows resembling tongues of fire; and those other heroic Rākshasas that were in front of Rāma, were destroyed on approaching the place, like insects approaching a fire. And with shafts plated with gold lying in all directions, the night resembled one in autumn decked with fire-flies. And in consequence of the uproar occasioned by the Rākshasas, and the sounds of drums, that night, already dreadful (in itself), became all the more so. And on that sound attaining dimensions on all sides, it seemed as if the mount Trikuta, containing numerous caverns, had been speaking. And huge-bodied Golāngulas of equal lustre with darkness itself,* binding fast the night-rangers with their arms, began to swallow them up. And Angada was present in the encounter, for slaying foes. And Indrajit, fairing sadly at the hands of Angada, abondoning his vehicle, and having his horses as well as his charioteer slain, vanished then and there. And that feat of Vāli's son, worthy of being honored, all the celestials with the saints and both Rāma and Lakshmana lauded to the height. All beings were acquainted with the might of Indrajit in battle; and, therefore, witnessing his discomfiture, and seeing that high-souled one, they rejoiced exceedingly. And, seeing the enemy vanquished, all the monkeys with Sugriva and Bibhishana, experiencing high delight, exclaimed, —"Excellent!" "Excellent!" And, beaten by Vāli's son of dreadful deeds, Indrajit was fired with a mighty wrath. And, being handled hard in battle, and having vanished from the field, the heroic and wicked son of Rāvana, who had received a boon from Brahmā, transported with passion,—remaining invisible, began to discharge sharpened shafts of the splendour of the thunder-bolt. And worked up into rage, he in the conflict pierced Raghu's sons, Rāma and Lakshmana all over their bodies, with terrific arrows consisting of serpents. And himself engirt with illusion, that night-ranger, given to fighting in crooked ways,—remaining

* Irony.

invisible to all creatures,—stupified the descendants of Raghu in battle ; and by means of his shafts bound the brothers, Rāma and Lakshmana. And then in the sight of the monkeys, those heroes and foremost of men were suddenly overpowered with shafts by the enraged (Indrajit). And when the son of the Rākshasa monarch felt himself incompetent to cope with them* openly, then that impious one, resorting to illusion, bound those princes (by that means).

## SECTION XLV.

THEN, anxious to ascertain his† course, the king's son possessed of prowess, and endowed with exceeding strength, Rāma, ordered ten of the monkey-leaders. And that repressor of foes ordered Vāli's son—Angada, the vigorous Sarabha, Dwivida, Hanumān, the mighty Sānuprastha, Rishabha and Rishabhaskandha. Thereat with alacrity those monkeys, weilding mighty trees, shot up into the sky, and began to scour the ten cardinal points. And Rāvana's son, skilled in arms, resisted the impetuous march of those vehement ones by means of a powerful weapon as well as arms more forceful (than the force of their rush). And the exceedingly vehement monkeys, cut and mangled with *nârâchas*, saw him in the dark like the sun enveloped in clouds. And that conquerer in battle, Rāvana's son, with shafts sorely pierced the persons of Rāma and Lakshmana. And both Rāma and Lakshmana had their bodies entirely covered by the angry Indrajit with shafts turned into serpents. And from their wounds blood began to gush out in streams ;

* Râma and Lakshmana.

† Indrajit's.

and they looked like flower-crowned *Kinçukas*. Then that one having red corners unto his eyes and resembling a mass of crushed collyrium, Râvana's son, said unto the brothers, as he vanished,—"When I fight remaining invisible, even Sakra—the lord of the celestials—cannot see or approach me,—and who are ye? And I, with my soul surcharged with wrath, shall, assailing them with showers of weapons furnished with Kanka feathers, send Raghu's sons to the abode of Yama." Having spoken thus unto the brothers—Râma and Lakshmana, cognizant of righteousness—(Indrajit)—pierced them with sharpened shafts, and shouted in joy. And stretching his large bow, that one sable like unto a mass of crushed collyrium again discharged terrific shafts in battle. And that one versed in the inner sense of things, with whetted arrows pierced the vitals of Râma and Lakshmana and shouted momentarily. And fast bound by the shackles of shafts on the edge of battle, they* could not attain respite for a moment. Then with their persons pierced with shafts and darts, and resembling the flags of the Great Indra let loose from the cords and trembling (in the air),—and with their bodies bristling with arrows,—those heroes and mighty bowmen—lords of the earth—tormented in consequence of their vitals having been pierced, dropped down to the earth. And those heroes, bathed in blood, and their persons covered with arrows,—pained and suffering terribly, lay down as became heroes. And there was not so much room unpierced in their persons as could be measured by a finger; and they were wounded with arrows up to the fore-parts of their hands.† And they being wounded by that fell one capable of assuming shapes at will, blood violently gushed out of their bodies like water from a spring. And Râma fell first, pierced in the vitals with the shafts. And the same

---

* *i. e.* Râma and Lakshmana.

† This *sloka* is rather obscure, and the Bengali translators have conveniently passed it by!—T.

Indrajit who had formerly wrathfully routed Sakra,(now) pierced (Râma) with *nârâchas* knotted with gold,and having polished heads; swift-speeding; and resembling dust carried about by the wind; and half-*nârâchas*; and darts resembling *anjalis*;* and *vatsadantas*;† and *sinhadanshtras*;‡ and razors; and, resigning his stringless bow decked in gold and curved in three places,—with its part for grasping shattered—he§ lay down like a hero. And seeing Râma—foremost of men—down within arrow-range, Lakshmana despaired of his life. And seeing his brother, Râma, having eyes resembling lotus-petals and ever delighting in battle, himself the refuge of others,—lying down in the field; (Lakshmana) began to weep. And the monkeys also, seeing him, were plunged in sorrow; and they, their eyes flooded with tears, began to cry in grief of heart. And when they had been bound and had laid themselves down as become heroes, the monkeys stood around them,—and, conversing with one another, they, headed by the son of the Wind, were seized with extreme sorrow.

## SECTION XLVI.

AND the rangers of woods, gazing at the earth and the sky, at length cast their eyes on the brothers—Râma and Lakshmana, covered all over with arrows. And after that Râkshasa had gone away having performed his work, like the God|| going away, after having showered,—there came

* The hands joined at the lower sides, with the palms hollowed.—T.

† Weapons resembling the teeth of a calf.

‡ Weapons resembling the lion's teeth

§ Râma.

|| Indra.

to that place Bibhishana with Sugriva. And, mourning Raghu's sons, there also came in all haste Nila and Dwivida and Mainda and Sushena and Kumuda and Angada in company with Hanumān. And moveless; breathing low,—covered with blood,—pierced all over with net-works of shafts; dumb; they* were lying on the field. And they were sighing like serpents; and were inert; and deprived of prowess; and washed in blood; and looking like unto golden standards. And as they lay moveless, as become heroes, the leaders of monkeys environed them with tear-charged eyes. And seeing the sons of Raghu lying, covered with showers of shafts, the monkeys, with Bibhishana, were pained (exceedingly). And the monkeys, surveying the sky as well as all directions, could not see Rāvana's son in battle enveloped with illusion. And then Bibhishana by means of illusion saw his brother's son staying before, hidden by illusion. And Bibhishana saw that hero of incomparable deeds, who had no compeer in the field and who had energy, fame and prowess,—as he remained invisible in consequence of the boon received from Brahmā. And Indrajit, seeing his own feat and them lying at length, spake in excess of joy, gladdening all the Rākshasas,—"The brothers—Rāma and Lakshmana, possessed of great strength, who had slain Khara and Dushana, are themselves slain with my shafts. And all the celestials and Asuras assembled together with the saints, are incompetent to emancipate these from the fetters of my shafts. He for whom my father was exercised with anxiety and tormented by grief, for whom my sire used to spend nights without pressing his bed,—for whom this entire Lankā had resembled a river turbulent in the rainy reason,—that same evil sticking by the root of all, hath been dispensed his quietus by me. And like clouds of autumn, the prowess of Rāma and Lakshmana as well as that of all the rangers of the woods, hath been rendered useless." Saying this in

* Rāma and Lakshmana.

the presence of all the Rākshasas, Rāvana's son—destroyer of foes—menacing the monkey-leaders, hit Nila with nine arrows, and hurt Mainda and Dwivida each with three powerful shafts. And piercing Jāmbavān with an arrow in the chest, that mighty bowman discharged ten at Hanumān. And Rāvana's son possessed of exceeding impetuosity, pierced in the conflict with two shafts each Gavāksha and Sarabha of immeasurable vigor. And Rāvana's son, summoning celerity, pierced the king of Golāngulas and Vāli's son, Angada, with innumerable arrows. And the powerful son of Rāvana, endowed with might, piercing the foremost monkeys with shafts resembling tongues of flames, set up shouts in the field of battle. And tormenting the monkeys with volleys of shafts and striking terror into them, that mighty-armed one, bursting out into a laugh, said,—"Let the Rākshasas behold these brothers, lying fast bound with dreadful arrows in front of the forces." Thus addressed, those Rākshasas—wily warriors all—resembling masses of clouds, witnessing that deed (of Indrajit), struck with wonder and rejoicing (greatly), set up tremendous roars. And thinking that Rāma was slain, they honored Rāvana's son. And seeing the brothers—Rāma and Lakshmana—motionless, and lying inert on the ground,—they took them for slain. And, experiencing excess of joy, Indrajit—conquerer in conflict—entered the city of Lankā, rejoicing all the Nairitas. Seeing the bodies as well as the limbs of Rāma and Lakshmana, covered entirely with arrows, fear took possession of Sugriva. Thereat Bibhishana said unto that lord of monkeys, staying in woe-begone guise, with a tearful countenance, and his eyes wild with wrath,—"Do not give way to fear, O Sugriva. Restrain thy rising tears! This is the way of warfare: victory is not (always) sure. But, O hero, if Fortune ultimately smile upon us, this stupor shall go off from these high-souled and exceedingly powerful ones. Therefore, O monkey, do thou cheer me, who am forlorn." Saying this, with his hand Bibhishana washed Sugriva's graceful eyes with water. And taking water, the righteous Bibhishana by means of his knowledge, washed Sugriva's eyes therewith. And washing the face of the intelligent monkey-monarch, Bibhishana spoke these words, seasonable and sedate,—"O foremost of monkey-kings, this is no time for being overcome with stupor. At this hour, even immoderate affection may lead to destruction. Therefore, casting off stupor, which tends to mar all work, do thou bethink thee how thou mayst serve this army headed by Rāma. Or do thou protect Rāma so long as he doth not regain consciousness; and when the Kākutsthas shall have regained consciousness, all our apprehension shall vanish. This is nothing to Rāma, and Rāma is not dying. And Lakshmi,* who is incapable of being attained by those that are doomed, shall not forsake this one. Therefore do thou comfort thyself, do thou also cheer up thy own forces,—while I am engaged in composing all the troops. O best of monkeys, these with distended eyes, come under the governance of terror, are, stricken with panic, whispering into each other's ears. But seeing me, let the forces rushing about, cheered up,—as well as the monkeys,—cast off all fear, like a wreath that hath been used before." Thus comforting Sugriva, Bibhishana—lord of Rākshasas—again instilled spirits into the flying forces of monkeys. And Indrajit—worker of mighty illusions—accompanied by his troops, entered the city of Lankā and presented himself before his father. And approaching Rāvana and saluting him with joined hands, he informed his sire of the welcome tidings that Rāma and Lakshmana had been slain. And hearing that his foe had fallen, Rāvana springing up in the midst of the Rākshasas, with great joy embraced his son. And scenting the crown of his head, (Rāvana) with a delighted heart, asked (Indrajit as to all that had taken place). And

* The goddess of prosperity.

on being asked, he (Indrajit) truly related unto his sire how (Rāma and Lakshmana) had been rendered senseless and lack-lustre by being fastened with shafts. Thereat, with rapture surcharging his inmost soul, Rāvana, hearing the speech of the mighty car-warrior, banished his fear of Daçaratha's son,—and rising up, honored his son with glad words.

---

## SECTION XLVII.

When Rāvana's son entered Lankā, after having accomplished his purpose, the foremost monkeys protected Rāghava, surrounding him on all sides. And Hanumān, and Angada, and Nila, and Sushena, and Kumuda, and Nala, and Gaya, and Gavāksha, and Panasa, and Samprastha—a mighty monkey—and Jāmbavān, and Rishava, and Sunda, and Rambha, and Satavali, and Prithu,—all forming themselves into array, and equipped with trees on all sides, and remaining vigilant,—the monkeys kept gazing at all sides, awry and upwards; and even when a straw stirred, they thought it to be a Rākshasa. And Rāvana, on his part, experiencing the height of exaltation, summoned the Rākshasis engaged in guarding Sitā.—And thereat the Rākshasis—Trijatā and others—presented themselves at his command. And then the lord of Rākshasas, delighted, addressed then the Rākshasis, saying,—"Tell Vaidehi that Rāma and Lakshmana have been slain in battle by Indrajit. And taking her on Pushaka, show her (Rāma and Lakshmana) lying slain on the field of battle. That one depending on whom she had proudly set her face against me,—that husband of hers, along with his brother, hath been slain in conflict. And then Mithilā's daughter, her fear gone off with her anxiety, and herself losing all support,—Sitā—daughter unto Mithilā—decked out in all ornaments, shall seek me. And today beholding Rāma with Lakshmana, come under the sway of Time, she, finding no other way, shall desist from her present course. And seeing no other resourse, that one of expansive eyes shall of herself seek me." Hearing those words of the wicked-minded Rāvana, the Rakshasis, saying,—"So be it,"—went to where Pushpaka was. Then taking Pushpaka, the Rakshasis at Rāvana's command went to Maithili staying in the *açoka* wood. Then, taking Sitā, who was overcome with grief for her lord, the Rākshasis, placed her on the car, Pushpaka. And placing Sitā on Pushpaka along with Trijatā, Rāvana took her all around (Lankā) crowded with ensigns and standards. And the lord of Rākshasas jubilantly proclaimed in Lankā,—"Rāghava as well as Lakshmana have been slain by Indrajit in battle." And going about with Trijatā, Sitā saw all the monkey-troops slain. And she found the flesh-eaters elated in spirits, and the monkeys afflicted with extreme grief at the side of Rāma and Lakshmana. Then Sitā beheld both Lakshmana and Rāma lying in the field, senseless and bound with arrows. And those heroes were lying on the earth, their mail torn, their bows cast off, their bodies mangled all over and thickly pierced with shafts. And seeing those brothers,—foremost of heroes and best of men—having eyes resembling white lotuses, and themselves like unto Kumāras,—lying in the field,*—the fire-sprung one, Sitā, striken with grief, began to weep piteously. And that black-eyed one of an excellent person, Janaka's daughter—seeing them roll in the dust, broke out into lamentation. And with her eyes shedding plentiful tears,

---

* *Virān nararshabhān—heroes and best of men*—occurs again,—left out on the score of redendancy.—T.

she seeing those brothers, endowed with god-like prowess, concluded them to be dead; and overwhelmed with grief, spoke as follows.

---

## SECTION XLVIII.

AND seeing her husband, as well as the exceedingly powerful Lakshmana,—slain, Sitā, afflicted with grief, burst into bitter lamentation. "The soothsayers had said that I should have sons, and should never be a widow. But on Rāma being slain, it seems now that those ones, possessed of knowledge, had spoken untruthfully. And those also, who having celebrated sacrifices and rites, had said that I should become the queen (of Rāma),—on Rāma being slain, seems to-day to have spoken a falsehood, although they are possessed of knowledge. And they also asserted that I should be honored of the wives of heroic kings as well as of my lord,—but on Rāma being slain, they seem to have uttered a falsehood, although possessed of knowledge. And those twice-born ones that in my hearing had said auspicious words, on Rāma being slain, seem to-day to have spoken a falsehood, although they were possessed of knowledge. These lotus-marks on the feet, betokening unto gentlewomen possessing them, that they are to be installed in the kingdom in company with their husbands—who are kings,—are on me. And those marks find I none on me by which women of rare fortune come by widowhood,—but I find that in me these good tokens are nullified. Those marks that are pronounced infallible by those versed in such knowledge, on Rāma being slain, are nullified in me. My hairs are fine, equal, and blue; my eye-brows touch each other; my hips are devoid of down and round ; and my teeth are close. My temples, and eyes, hands, feet, ankles, and thighs are equal. And my fingers are furnished with round nails, and are plump and even in the middle. And my breasts are close and firm and developed, and have their nipples sunk. And my navel is depressed, with high sides. And my chest is swelling. And my complexion is like the hue of gems,—and my down soft. And they said that I was furnished with twelve auspicious signs. And my hands in the middle parts of my fingers contain wheat-marks ; and in the spaces between the fingers, have no uneven corners. And my feet also partake of the general complexion. And my laugh is a gentle smile. And those versed in marks of women knew that I was possessed of such marks. And those Brāhmanas skilled in telling fortune said that I should be installed in the kingdom along with my husband ; but all that hath been falsified. Having purified Janasthāna (of Rākshasas),obtained tidings of me, and crossed the Ocean* incapable of being agitated, those brothers have been slain in the footprint of a cow! The descendants of Raghu had obtained Vāruna and Agneya and Aindra and Vāyava and *Brahmaçiras* weapons.† Through illusion have those lords of me, who am forlorn—Rāma and Lakshmana, resembling Vāsava himself in battle,—been slain. Coming in battle within ken of Rāghava, a foe, even if he be endowed with the fleetness of thought,—doth not go back, living. There is nothing which is too hard for Time ; and the Destroyer is incapable of being overcome ; inasmuch as Rāma along with his brother Lakshmana hath fallen in fight. And I do not so much mourn Rāma or the mighty car-warrior—Lakshmana—or, for that matter, self,—as I do the wretched Mother-in-law of mine. She ever thinketh of the period of the promise. 'When shall I behold

* The commentator assigns a metaphorical sense to *ocean*,—but this is hardly necessary.

† *And did they not remember this now* ?' completes the sense.—T.

Sitā and Lakshmana with Rāghava?'" As she was thus lamenting, the Rākshasi, Trijatā, said,—"O exalted lady, do not weep thus. Thy lord liveth. And, O dignified one, I shall unfold unto thee potent and probable reasons why the brothers Rāma and Lakshmana live. When their leader falleth, the countenances of the warriors in battle are not overspread with passion, or display cheerfulness and vivacity. And, O Vaidehi, if those had lost their lives, this celestial chariot, named Pushpaka, would not have held thee. An army that hath its heroes and chiefs slain—becoming dispirited and drooping, rangeth the field, like a vessel on water that hath lost its helmsman. But, O lorn one, these troops, betraying neither agitation nor anxiety, are guarding the Kākutsthas. This I tell thee of them out of affection. Do thou, at this conclusion bringing in joy, take comfort; and behold the Kākutsthas unslain. This I tell thee from affection. I never told thee untruths heretofore; nor, O Mithilā's daughter, will I tell them unto thee now. Thou by virtue of thy character conducive to delight, hast found an acess into my heart. These even the celestials and Asuras with Indra (at their head) are incompetent to quell. Seeing such sight, I speak to thee as to their being alive. And behold, O Maithili, this mighty wonder! These are lying insensible with arrows; but of these Grace hath not taken leave. It generally happens that the faces of persons dead and gone, are unsightly to a degree. Therefore, O Janaka's daughter, leave off grief and sorrow and stupor. For the sake of Rāma and Lakshmana thou canst not today put a period to thy existence." Hearing her words, Mithilā's daughter—Sitā—resembling the daughter of a celestial, with hands joined, said,—"May this be so!" Then turning away the car Pushpaka fleet as the mind, the distressed Sitā entered Lankā along with Trijatā. Then in company with Trijatā, alighting from Pushpaka, she along with the Rākshasis entered the *açoka* wood. And entering that sporting-ground of the Rākshasa lord abounding in woody tracts, Sitā, having beheld those princes and reflected on them, became subject to a mighty grief.

---

## SECTION XLIX.

---

BOUND up terribly with shafts, Daçaratha's sons, lying down bathed in blood, sighed hard like unto serpents. And all those foremost monkeys, along with Sugriva, possessed of exceeding strength,—overwhelmed with sorrow, remained surrounding those high-souled ones. In the meanwhile, the powerful Rāma, albeit fast bound by the shafts, awoke by virtue of the exceeding toughness of his person, as well as his might. Then, seeing his brother, having a distressful countenance, covered with blood, feeble, and fast bound by the shafts,—Rāma, greatly aggrieved, began to mourn. "Of what use unto me is the recovery of Sitā, or life either, when to-day I see my brother vanquished in fight and lying down in the field? Seeking in the world (of men), I may light upon a woman like Sitā; but never on a brother, or a helper, or a warrior like unto Lakshmana. If that enhancer of Sumitrā's joy have met with his end, my life I must renounce in the sight of the monkeys. What shall I say unto Kauçalyā: and what shall I say unto Kaikeyi? And what shall I say unto mother Sumitrā, eager for a sight of her son? And if I go (back) without him, how shall I soothe her, like unto a cow reft of her calf; and trembling; and resembling a mourning Kurari? And how shall I say unto Satrughana and the illustrious Bharata,—'He went with me to the forest; but I come (back) here without him?' I shall not be able to bear the rebuke of mother Sumitrā. Therefore even here shall I renounce my person; for certainly I dare not live. Fie on me, who am wicked and base; for me this Lakshmana, brought down, lieth in the field of battle, like one that is without life. O Lakshmana, thou ever comfortest me when I am dispirited. But to day, having lost thy life, thou canst not speak to me, who am afflicted. Thou, O hero, who hadst in battle slain innumerable Rākshasas lying around, hast (at length) thyself been slain in the field with shafts. And lying down in the battle-field, bleeding, and covered with arrows, thou appearest like the Sun when he hath gone up the Setting-hill. And in consequence of shafts piercing thy vitals, thou canst not speak; but thy visible expression, albeit thou art dumb, betokens pain. O thou endowed with exceeding splendour, even as thou didst follow me into the forest, will I follow thee unto the mansion of Yama. Thou, having dear friends, and ever following me, hast come by this plight in consequence of my reprehensible conduct. I do not remember having heard any harsh speech from the heroic Lakshmana, even when he had happened to be exceedingly wroth. He that could discharge at one shot five hundred shafts,—that Lakshmana is superior to Kārttaviryya himself in that weapon—the bow. He that with his arms could resist the arms of Sakra himself,—that one worthy of a costly couch—lieth down on the ground, slain. And that false babble shall now, without doubt, consume me; for by me hath not Bibhishana been made monarch of the Rākshasas. Do thou, O Sugriva, this very moment retrace thy steps. Bereft of thy strength through me, thou wilt be worsted by Rāvana. And, O Sugriva, placing Angada to the fore, do thou, taking thy host as well as the equipage, in company with Nila and Nala, cross over the Ocean. By thee hath been achieved a mighty feat incapable of being done by another in battle. And pleased am I with the king of bears, and the lord of Golāngulas; and Angada hath quit himself nobly, as also Mainda and Dwivida. And Keçarin and Sampâti have both faught terribly. And Gavaya, and Gavâksha, and Sarabha, and Gaja,—and other monkeys have faught as others are incapable of fighting,—determined to lay down their lives (for me). But, O Sugriva, man cannot overrule Destiny. Thou, my friend, fearing righteousness,* hast done what lay in thy power. And, Ye foremost of monkeys, ye also have acted as becometh friends. Now, with my permission, go ye whithersoever ye are minded." Hearing Râma's lament, the monkeys—those dark-eyed and others—began to shed tears from their eyes. Then Bibhishana, quieting the army, taking a mace in his hand, swiftly went to where Râghava was. And seeing him fast making his way, resembling a mass of dark collyrium, the monkeys taking him to be Râvana's son,† began to run away.

---

## SECTION L.

THEN out spake the highly energetic and exceedingly mighty king of monkeys,—"Why is this host agitated like a bark driven hither and thither by the wind?" Hearing Sugriva's speech, Vâli's son said,—"Dost thou not see both those heroes—sons of Daçaratha—Râma and that mighty car-warrior—Lakshmana—covered with arrows? And (dost thou not see) those high-sould ones lying in the field of battle, covered with blood?" Thereat, the lord of monkeys, Sugriva, spake unto his son,‡ Angada—"I do not deem it

* *Dharma-bhiru—fearing righteousness*—is the epithet generally applied to persons fearing not in fact *righteousness*, but unrighteousness. This may be taken as an *idiotism* in Sanskrit.—T.

† Indrajit. Such was the fear he had spread by his redoubtable deeds!—T.

‡ His *step-son*, for Sugriva had married Angada's father's wife, after Ráma had slain Váli in Kishkindhâ.—T.

without cause. This may have come to pass through sheer fear. These monkeys with sad faces, leaving their arms behind them, are flying in all directions, their eyes distended in affright. And they are not ashamed of each other, and they do not cast their looks back. And they hug each other, and go leaping over the fallen." In the meanwhile, that hero, Bibhishana, bearing a mace in his hand, (approaching), greeted Sugriva as well as Rāghava with blessings of victory. And Sugriva, seeing Bibhishana, capable of inspiring fear in the monkeys, spoke unto the high-souled sovereign of bears, who stood by,—"This is Bibhishana that hath come hither, seeing whom the foremost among the monkeys, from fear of Rāvana's son who, they apprehend, he is,—are fleeing away, seized with a panic. Do thou at once stay these agitated with fear and scampering all around; and proclaim,—'This is *Bibhishana*, who hath come here.'" Thus directed, Jāmbavān—king of bears—restraining those that were flying, composed the monkeys. Hearing the bear-king's words, and seeing Bibhishana, the monkeys, renouncing fear, desisted (from their flight). Then the righteous Bibhishana, viewing Rāma's as well as Lakshmana's body pierced with arrows, was exceedingly aggrieved. And washing their eyes with water, he, with his mind overpowered with grief, began to weep and broke out into lamentation,—"The Rākshasas, fighting in wily ways, have brought to this pass these ones endowed with prowess and possessed of every perfection and gifted with might (of arm). And with his guileful mind, that brother's son of mine, wicked-souled and an evil son (unto me),—hath deceived these ones of straight prowess. Pierced with innumerable shafts, and covered with blood, these are lying on the ground like Salyakas*. Those depending on whose prowess, I had sought eminence, those foremost of men, sleep here soundly for renouncing their bodies. Living, today I am in distress:

* A tree.

and my desire of dominion is annihilated; and my foe, Rāvana, hath his promise fulfilled and his aim crowned with success." As Bibhishana was thus lamenting, the lord of monkeys—Sugriva—endowed with strength, embracing him, spoke unto him,—"O thou cognisant of righteousness, thou wilt here in Lankā obtain empire: no doubt of this; and Rāvana along with his sons will be disappointed in their expectations. Both these—Rāma and Lakshmana—are under the *ægis* of Garura; and, casting off their stupor: they will in battle slay Rāvana along with his adherents." Having thus soothed and comforted the Rākshasa, Sugriva addressed his father-in-law, who was at his side, saying,—"Do thou along with numbers of heroic monkeys, taking those repressors of foes, the brothers—Rāma and Lakshmana—when they shall have regained their consciousness, repair to Kishkindhā. And I, slaying Rāvana along with his sons and friends, shall bring back Mithilā's daughter, even as Sakra recovered the lost Srî." Hearing the words of the monkey-king, Sushena said,—"I had witnessed the war of yore between the gods and the Asuras. Then the Dānavas, enveloping themselves, momentarily destroyed the deities, albeit versed in arms and accomplished in weapons. And they, their senses lost, and their lives departed, Vrihashpati treated by means of his knowledge of *mantras*, as well with medicines. Let Sampāti, Panaça, and other monkeys speedily hie to the Milky Ocean for the purpose of bringing those medicines. And the monkeys well know that mighty mountainous medicine—divine and capable of reviving the dead,—and made by the deities themselves—*viçalyâ*. There are (the mountains) named Chandra and Drona: where the ambrosia was churned, there is that supreme drug. And those mountains have been placed by the deities in the mighty deep. And, O king, let the son of the Wind-god go thither." In the meanwhile, the wind arose, and masses of clouds appeared along with lightning. And the wind blew, agitating the waters of the deep, and shaking the mountains. And mighty trees of the ocean-islands, broken down by the terrible wing-raised wind, began to topple headlong into the salt waters. And the serpents dwelling there were seized with affright ; and speedily all the aquatic animals dived deep into the salt sea. And then in a moment the monkeys saw Vinatā's son, possessed of terrific strength,—like unto a flaming fire. And seeing him come, the serpents began to dart away,—those exceedingly powerful ones that, turning into shafts, had bound those persons.* Then, touching the Kākutsthas and saluting them, Suparna rubbed with his hands their countenances furnished with the splendour of the Moon. And their wounds, on being touched by Vinatā's son, were (immediately) healed ; and the bodies of both speedily became cool and shone with an excellent complexion. And they attained immense energy and prowess ; and a double share of strength, and of rational and perceptive powers, and of memory. And then raising them up, the exceedingly energetic Garura, resembling Vāsava himself, embraced both joyfully. And then Rāma addressed (Garura), saying,—"By thy grace we have through means survived the mighty calamity that had sprung from Rāvana's son ; and we have also speedily been rendered strong. And my heart is delighted on having thee, like unto my father, Daçaratha, or my grand sire, Aja. Who art thou, furnished with beauty, and bearing wreaths and unguents (on thy person) ; clad in stainless attire ; and adorned in noble ornaments ?" Unto him spake the exceedingly energetic son of Vinatā endowed with great strength,—the lord of birds, with a pleased heart, and his eyes wild with glee,—"O Kākutstha, I am thy friend—thy life ranging externally—Garutman. I am come hither for aiding you. Neither the highly powerful Asuras, nor the exceedingly strong monkeys, nor the celestials along with the Gandharbas, having him of an hundred sacrifices at their

* Ráma and Lakshmana.

head are,—capable of delivering ( any one ) from these dreadful arrowy bonds, which had been forged by Indrajit of tortuous deeds by help of illusion. These serpents —offspring of Kadru—are sharp-fanged and venomous ; and had bound thee as arrows through the potency of illusion. O Rāma having truth for prowess, thou art fortunate,—along with that destroyer of foe in fight, Lakshmana. Hearing this, I, summoning energy, have come hither swiftly. And I, doing by thee as a friend, have from affection at once set you free from these dreadful arrowy bonds. But thou shouldst always be on thy guard. By nature the Rākshasas have cunning shifts in fight and thou, who art heroic and of a pure spirit, canst but rely on thy simplicity alone for strength. Therefore thou must not trust the Rākshasas in the field of battle. By this one instance (thou must know) that Rākshasas are ever deceitful in fight." Having said this, the wondrous mighty Suparna, embracing Rāma) tenderly (again), said,—"My friend Rāghava, O thou who even cherishest affection for thy foes, permit me thou. I shall go at pleasure. And, O Rāghava, entertain no curiosity as to our friendship.* When, O hero, thou shalt have achieved success in battle, thou shalt know all about this friendship of ours. And with the surges of thy shafts, making Lankā contain only children and aged, and slaying thy foe, Rāvana, thou shalt recover Sitā." Having spoken thus, Suparna, endowed with fleet vigor, having rendered Rāma hale in the midst of the monkeys,—having gone round them and embraced them also,—that one possessed of prowess,—set out, covering up the sky, like unto the wind. And seeing Raghu's sons rendered hale, the monkey-leaders set up leonine roars, and began to flourish their tails. And then beat the kettle-drums and the drums struck up. And conchs were cheerfully blown ; and shouts were sent. And others struck at their arms with their hands. And the

* i. e. *how it happened.*

monkeys, accustomed to battle with trees, uprooting them, stood by hundreds and thousands. And emitting tremendous roars and thereby frightening the night-rangers,the monkeys, eager for encounter, approached the gate of Lankā. And that mighty and dreadful din raised by the monkeys, resembled the terrible rumbling of the clouds at midnight about the end of Summer.

## SECTION LI.

THEN Rāvana heard the tumult raised by the highly energetic monkeys roaring in company with the Rākshasas. And hearing that low and solemn noise—that prodigious uproar—Rāvana said in the midst of his counsellors,—"From mighty roars that are heard of in innumerous delighted monkeys,—resembling the roar of clouds,—it is evident, beyond a doubt, that there is great rejoicing there. And the salt Ocean is vexed with these thundering noises. The brothers—Rāma and Lakshmana—have been fast bound with sharp shafts; and here this uproar is exciting my alarm." Having spoken thus unto his ministers, the lord of the Rākshasas addressed the Nairitas present there, saying,—"Do you speedily acquaint yourselves with the cause of rejoicing that hath arisen of these monkeys on this mournful occasion." Thus accosted, they hurriedly mounting up on the wall, surveyed the forces maintained by the high-souled Sugriva as well as those exalted ones—Raghu's sons—emancipated from their terrific arrowy fetters and arisen (now)." Thereat, with their hearts wrought up, grim-visaged Rākshasas descending from the wall, appeared before the Rākshasa-lord with pale faces. And then with woe-begone faces, those Rākshasas, skilled in speech, faithfully informed Rāvana in full of that unfortunate circumstance. "Those brothers—Rāma and Lakshmana—who had in battle been bound up in arrowy fetters by Indrajit,—and whose arms lay moveless,—having been emancipated from the arrowy bonds, are seen in the field of battle; and those ones like unto the foremost of elephants in strength, seem like elephants that have snapped their fetters." Hearing those words of theirs, the exeedingly powerful lord of the Rākshasas was wrought up with anxiety and anger, and his countenance lost its complexion. "Indrajit, having routed them in conflict, had bound them by means of irrisistible and terrible arrows, resembling venomous serpents, and like unto the Sun himself,—which had been conferred on (Indrajit) as boons. But if my enemy, having actually been bound by the weapons, can have been liberated, all this strength of mine I see placed in peril. And those shafts resembling Fire in fierceness, which had in battle deprived my foes of their lives,—have forsooth been rendered fruitless." Having said this in high rage, Rāvana, sighing like a serpent, addressed a Rākshasa, named Dhumrāksha, seated in the midst of the Rākshasas,—"O thou of dreadful prowess, surrounded by a mighty force, do thou march forth to compass the destruction of Rāma along with the monkeys." Thus accosted by the intelligent lord of the Rākshasas, Dhumrāksha, turning about, issued out of the abode of the king. And speedily sallying forth from the gate of (Rāvana's) residence, he said unto the general of the forces,—"Do thou speedily move off thy forces. Why should a warrior linger?" Hearing Dhumrāksha's words, the general of the forces, following them, at the command of Rāvana forthwith made the army ready. And those powerful and dreadful night-rangers, bursting with high spirits,—with bells tied to their arms,—set up shouts, and surrounded Dhumrāksha. And bearing various weapons in their hands, and wielding darts and clubs, and equipped with maces and bearded darts and rods and iron bludgeons and *parighas* and *bhindipālas* and lances and nooses and axes,—those terrific Rākshasas sallied out, roaring like unto clouds. And others, accoutred in armour, with cars ; adorned with banners ; furnished with golden networks, and mules having various faces, and extremely swift steeds, and lusty elephants in rut,—tiger-like Nairitas incapable of being subdued, even as tigers,—sallied out (thereafter). And then Dhumrāksha himself ascended a superb car, bearing faces of deer and lions decked with gold,—and sending forth a loud clatter. And the highly powerful Dhumrāksha, surrounded by Rākshasas, cheerfully issued out of the Western Entrance, where Hanumān was posted. And thereat, fell fowls of the air forbade that exceedingly dreadful Rākshasa of a fearful form, as he went out ascending an excellent car, yoked with mules,and sending sharp sounds. And an exceedingly terrific vulture alighted at the crest of the car ; and forming themselves into lines, vultures began to drop down about the top of the banner. And emitting a frightful cry, (a headless trunk) dropped down before Dhumrāksha. And that god* showered down blood ; and the earth shook. And the wind blew awry with a sound resembling thunder. And every side, covered with darkness, appeared dim. And witnessing those dreadful inauspicious omens at the outset, fraught with fear unto the Rākshasas, Dhumrāksha was greatly aggrieved ; and the Rākshasas marching before him, were stupified. And then as that strong and fearful one, eager for encounter, surrounded by innumerable night-rangers, issued out (of the city), he beheld that monkey-host, protected by the arm of Rāghava,—resembling the deep at the time of the universal dissolution.

---

* Indra—cloud-compeller.

## SECTION LII.

SEEING the Rākshasa—Dhumrāksha of dreadful prowess—issue out, the monkeys, rejoicing greatly, eager for encounter, set up roars. And then there took place a terrific conflict between the monkeys and the Rākshasas, charging each other with fearful trees, and darts, and maces. And the Rākshasas began to scatter the dreadful monkeys on all sides; and the monkeys (on their part) felled the Rākshasas with trees. And the Rākshasas, growing enraged, began to pierce the monkeys with straight-speeding sharp shafts winged with Kanka plumes. And riven by the Rakshas with dreadful clubs and bearded darts, daggers and maces and terrible and curious bludgeons and grasped javelins,—the exceedingly powerful (monkeys), their anger aroused, began with alacrity to perform deeds of intrepid valour. And those monkey-leaders, their bodies pierced with shafts and their persons riven with darts, took up trees and crags. And those monkeys, endowed with terrific vehemence, sending up shouts, and proclaiming their respective names, set about tossing the brave Rākshasa ranks. And that conflict between the Rākshasas and the monkeys, waged with diverse rocks and innumerable trees, waxed exceedingly furious. And some among the Rākshasas feeding on gore—on being agitated by the monkeys burning for victory,—began to vomit blood. And some were severed along their flanks; and, some, slain with trees, were heaped up; and some were crushed with crags; and some were torn with teeth. And some being broken down by means of broken standards, and some by means of fallen swords, and some crushed down by cars,—the rangers of the night suffered sorely. And (anon) the earth was covered with huge elephants measuring mountains, and mountain-tops, and steeds crushed, and the riders thereof,—all borne down by the monkeys. And bounding again and again, the vehement monkeys endowed with terrific prowess, with their finger-nails tore up the Rākshasas by the mouths. And with woe-begone faces, and with hair dishevelled, (the Rākshasas), stupified with the smell of blood, saught the earth. And other Rākshasas endowed with dreadful vigor, waxing wond rous wroth, dealt the monkeys slaps with hands having the touch of the thunder-bolt. And, gifted with greater impetuosity, the monkeys felled the impetuous (Rākshasas) with blows, and feet and teeth; and some were slain with trees. And seeing the forces fleeing away, that foremost of Rākshasas—Dhumrāksha—flying into fury, began a terrific conflict with the monkeys desirous of encounter. And some of the monkeys, sore assailed with *prâças*, began to bleed; and some, wounded with maces, dropped down to the ground. And some were beaten hard with bludgeons; and some were cleft with *bhindipâlas*. And some, on being assailed with bearded darts, became insensible and lost their lives. And some among the monkeys lay slain on the ground, drenched in blood. And some, fleeing away from the field, were slaughtered by the infuriated Rākshasas. And some, having their breasts pierced, lay on their sides. And some were riven with tridents; and the entrails of some had come out. And that mighty and dreadful encounter of the Rākshasas and the monkeys, was waged with countless weapons and rocks and trees. And that battle hecome a musical entertainment* mellifluous with bow-string for *Vinâ*,† having the neighing of chargers for its measure, and with

* The reader has already perceived that the carrying out of a simile to a number of details is a characteristic as much of Válmiki as of his rival in the epic sphere—Vyâsa. But the comparisons are never on all fours, as in the case before us.—T.

† A classical Hindu musical instrument, having metallic strings, with a pair of gourds at one end for the sounding-board. *Vide Yantra-Koça* by Sir Saurindra Mohan Tagore, *Mus-Doc.*—T.

the cries of *Maındas** for its strains. Then in the field, Dhumrāksha bow in hand, laughing, pursued the monkeys in all directions with showers of shafts. And seeing the forces hard beset by Dhumrāksha and distressed thereat, the Wind-god's offspring, waxing enraged, seizing a huge crag, approached (the Rākshasa). And with his eyes doubly reddened in wrath, that one, like unto his sire himself in prowess, brought down the crag upon Dhumrāksha's car. And seeing the crag, (Dhumrāksha) upraising his mace hurriedly, leapt down in vehemence, and stood on the ground. And having shattered his car, that crag fell down to the earth. And thereat letting go the car furnished with wheels, *Kuvaras* and a face, as well as a banner; in which Dhumrāksha had left his bow,—Hanumān—son unto the Wind-god—laid about him right lustily for destroying the Rākshasas,with trees having branches long and short. And thereat some Rākshasas with their heads shattered, lay drenched in blood; and others, struck with trees, dropped down to the earth. And then Hanumān—son unto the Wind-god—charged in full career against the Rākshasa army; and, taking a mountain-peak, he rushed against Dhumrāksha. And as Hanumān was descending, the powerful Dhumrāksha, upraising a mace, and giving out a shout, made towards him speedily. And then Dhumrāksha enraged, brought down that mace studded with innumerable pricks, on the head of Hanumān fired with wrath. And thus assailed with the mace of fearful impetuosity, the monkey endowed with the strength of the wind, without at all heeding that blow, let fall a mountain-top right against Dhumrāksha's head. And on being assailed with the mountain-peak, Dhumrāksha, having his entire body mangled, suddenly fell to the earth, like unto a toppling hill. And seeing Dhumrāksha slain, those night-rangers that survived the carnage, in extreme agitation began to pour into Lankā, attacked by the monkeys. And that high-souled

* A species of elephants.

offspring of the Wind-god, having slain his foes, and come under the influence of fatigue incident to his slaughtering his enemies,--having caused rivers of gore to flow (in the field),—experienced the excess of joy on being honored of the monkeys

## SECTION LIII.

Hearing Dhumrâksha slain, Râvana—lord of the Râkshasas—overwhelmed with a mighty rage, began to sigh like a serpent. And collied with passion, and sighing hot for a long time, he addressed a cruel Râkshasa—the exceedingly strong Vajradanshtra,*—"Go thou, O hero. Go out, environed by the Râkshasas. Slay Daçaratha's son—Râma—and Sugriva along with the monkeys." Thereupon hastily answering "So be it," that foremost of the Râkshasas skilled in illusion, marched forth surrounded by many a leader† of armies, furnished with elephants and steeds, mules and camels,—with his mind concentrated; and adorned with innumerable variegated flags and banners. And then decked out with curious *keyuras* and a tiara, and wearing armour, he rushed out with his bow in his hand. And then going round his flaming vehicle, adorned with pennons and garnished with gold, the king‡ ascended the same. And equipped with slender swords and curious *tomaras* and smooth maces and *bhindipâlas* and bows and darts and *pattiças* and scimitars and discuses and clubs and sharpened axes, the multiform infantry march bearing arms in their hands. And all those powerful and flaming Râkshasas wore variegated raiments.

* Lit.—the thunder-toothed.

† *Valai*—forces—is interpreted *leaders* by the commentator.

‡ Vajradanshtra.—T.

And heroic elephants in rut resembling mountains in motion, marched, being led by those well-skilled in battle carrying *tomaras* and hooks in their hands. And mighty steeds bearing auspicious marks, marched, ridden by heroes. And that entire Rākshasa army, as it marched forth, resembled clouds in summer roaring with lightning. And (the Rākshasas) sallied forth through the Southern Entrance, where that leader of herds—Angada—was stationed. And as they went out, evil omens appeared. From the cloudless yet fierce sky meteors began to shoot. And throwing up flames from their mouths, dreadful jackals began to emit cries. And frightful beasts betokened the destruction of the Rākshasas in battle. And warriors began to tumble down in an ominous way. Witnessing these evil omens, the exceedingly powerful and energetic Vajradanshtra, assuming patience, set out, eager for encounter. And seeing them flee away, the monkeys, burning for victory, set up tremendous shouts, filling all the ten cardinal points. And then there came on a terrific encounter of the monkeys and the Rākshasas, dreadful, of terrific deeds, and wishing for each other's death. And warriors fraught with high spirits, springing up, dropped down to the earth, their bodies and hands riven, and all their persons bathed in blood. And some approaching each other, with bludgeons in their hands, without turning away from the field, discharged various weapons at each other. And there were heard sounds of trees and rocks and weapons,—mighty and dreadful and capable of striking terror into the heart. And dreadful and mighty were the sounds of car-wheels, and conchs and trumpets and drums. And some, casting off weapons, engaged in a hand to hand combat by means of slaps, and kicks, and bones, and trees. And some Rākshasas, having their bodies broken, were killed by means of thighs. And some were crushed with crags by Dānavas invincible in battle. And Vajradanshtra, resembling the noose-handed Destroyer, frightening the monkeys, ranged in that field fatal to people. And Rākshasas, possessed of strength; equipped with various weapons, transported with passion, slew the monkey-forces. And then in the conflict the proud Wind-god's son, influenced by twofold wrath, spread havoc among the Rākshasa ranks, like the Fire at the universal dissolution. And the energetic Angada possessed of the prowess of a lion, with his eyes coppery with wrath, upraising a tree, began to spread terrible destruction among the Rākshasas, even as a lion destroyeth tiny deer. And attacked by Angada there, the Rākshasas of dreadful vigor, with their heads riven, fell down like unto trees that have been uprooted. And the earth became frightful (to behold), being covered with variegated cars and standards and steeds and the bodies of monkeys and of Rākshasas and streams of blood. And adorned with chains, and *Keyuras*, and attires, and umbrellas, the field of battle looked like an autumnal night. And agitated by Angada's impetuosity, that mighty army of Rākshasas began to shake, even as water trembleth, moved by the wind.

## SECTION LIV.

FINDING his own army destroyed by the might of Angada, the exceedingly powerful Rākshasa—Vajradanshtra—was overcome with rage. And stretching his dreadful bow of the splendour of Sakra's thunder-bolt, he began to shower shafts among the monkey-ranks. And the foremost among the heroic Rākshasas also, stationed on cars, furnished with various arms, warred on in the encounter. And the heroic monkeys also—foremost of their kind—with rocks in their hands, faught around in united strength. And in that conflict, the Rākshasas began to incessantly shower *ayutas* of arms among the flower of the monkey-army. And the monkeys,—pre-eminently valiant, and resembling mad elephants, kept showering over the Rākshasas mountain-trees and mighty rocks. And then took place a hot contest among heroic warring monkeys and Rākshasas, eager for encounter. And some, with their heads unbroken, had their arms and legs torn; and thir bodies pierced with weapons, and laved in blood. And monkeys and Rākshasas lay down in the field,—thronged with numbers of Kankas, and vultures; and swarming with flocks of jackals. And striking affright unto the timid, on the earth started up (spectral) headless trunks,—with their arms and heads torn, and their bodies riven all over. And monkeys and Rākshasas began to drop down to the earth. And the army of night-rangers, being sadly handled by the monkey-hosts, broke up at every point in the very sight of Vajradanshtra. And seeing the Rākshasas, distressed with fright and harassed by the monkeys, the powerful Vajradanshtra, with his eyes crimsoned with choler, entered the arena, bow in hand,—frightening the monkey-forces. And he began to pierce the monkeys with straight-speeding shafts winged with Kanka feathers; and he pierced simultaneously seven, eight,nine, five,monkeys (in the field). And the exceedingly powerful Vajradanshtra, transported into a towering passion, began to cleave the hostile ranks. And thereat terrified, the monkeys, with their bodies cut with arrows, rushed towards Angada, like creatures resorting to the Creator. And finding the monkey-ranks disordered, Vāli's son in a rage cast his eyes on Vajradanshtra, who also was eying|him. And Vajradanshtra and Angada faught fiercely with each other over and over again; ranging the field like a tiger and a mad elephant*. Then (Vajradanshtra) with hundreds and thousands (of shafts)

* *Harimattagajāviva—lit, like a lion and a mad elephant.* The commentator however, remarks, that the contest of a *lion* with an elephant is in-

resembling tongues of flames, pierced the powerful son of the monkey in the vitals. Thereupon Vāli's son of mighty strength and tremendous prowess, with his body covered all over with blood, hurled a tree at Vajradanshtra. And seeing the tree in full career, the Rākshasa without betraying any agitation, severed it in pieces; and the tree, thus assailed, fell to the earth. And seeing that feat of Vajradanshtra, that foremost of monkeys, taking up a huge crag, hurled it (at his foe) and sent up shouts. And seeing this descend upon him, that powerful one, calmly leaping down from his vehicle, stood on his feet on the ground. And the crag discharged by Angada, coursing on in the field, dashed to pieces the car along with the wheels and the *Kuvara* as well as the horses. And then the monkey, taking up another prodigious peak crowned with trees, let it alight on Vajradanshtra's head. Thereat vomitting blood, Vajradanshtra, deprived of his senses, for a moment overcome with stupor, stood embracing his mace, sighing. And then the night-ranger, recovering his senses, with his mace, in high rage hit at the breast Vāli's son staying in the field. And thereupon, giving up his mace, he entered into a boxing encounter (with Angada). And hitting each other there, they both—the monkey and the Rākshasa,—began to vomit blood, and were overcome with fatigue consequent on the thrashing each sustained; and they endowed richly with prowess, appeared like Angāraka and Budha.* Then the exceedingly energetic Angada—best of—monkeys—uprooting a tree, stood there, covered with flowers and leaves. And (Vajradanshtra) took a shield composed of ass's hide,† and a sword broad and sightly, covered with bells, and graced with a leathern sheath. And the monkey and the Rākshasa displayed curious and graceful movements. And

compatible in the nature of things, for even an elephant *dreaming* of a lion, gives up the ghost!—T.

* The asterisms so called.

† What could this weapon be like?—T.

attacking each other, they gave shouts, eager for victory. And with blood flowing from their wounds, they looked beautiful like blossoming Kinçukas. And warring, both, overcome with fatigue, went to the ground on their knees. Anon in the twinkling of an eye, that powerful monkey—Angada—started up, with his eyes glowing,—like unto a serpent that hath been smitten with a rod. And (at length) with his stainless and sharpened sword, Vāli's son, endeued with exceeding strength severed Vajradanshtra's huge head. And the graceful head of that one having his body covered with blood, cut off by the sword, falling to the ground with its eyes rolling, was severed in twain. Seeing Vajradanshtra slain, the Rākshasas, overwhelmed with fear and exceedingly agitated, in pitiful plight, with woe-begone faces and heads hung in shame,—fled towards Lankā, attacked (all the while) by the monkeys. Having compassed Vajradanshtra's destruction, the powerful son of Vāli, endowed with exceeding strength, in the midst of the monkey-army experienced great joy on being honored by the monkeys, like the wielder of the thunder-bolt—the thousand-eyed (Deity)—surrounded by the celestials.

## SECTION LV.

HEARING Vajradanshtra slain by the son of Vāli, Rāvana said unto the general of his forces, standing before him with joined hands,—"Let invincible Rākshasas of dreadful prowess, march forth, placing before them Akampana, skilled in all weapons and arms. He is capable of chastising foes as well as of protecting his own and leading them ; and he is excellent in warfare. And he is always desirous of my prosperity, and always loveth warfare. He will conquer the Kākutsthas, as well as Sugriva endowed with exceeding strength, and, without doubt, slay all the other dreadful monkeys." Taking Rāvana's command, that highly powerful one endowed with fleet vigor, marshalled those forces. Then equipped with various arms, the foremost of Rākshasas, having dreadful eyes (in their heads), and of dreadful forms, marched forth, urged on by their general. And, ascending a large car, adorned with burnished gold, Akampana, possessed of the splendour of clouds,* and cloud-hued, and furnished with a voice resembling the roar of clouds, went out, environed by Rākshasas of terrific forms. And Akampana, resembling the sun in power, was incapable† of being shaken in fight by the very gods, and of being beheld by them.‡ And as, burning for battle, he rushed out in wrath, the steeds drawing his car suddenly lost their energy. And the left eye of that one delighting in encounter, began to throb. And his countenance grew pale, and his voice faltered. And in a fair day, it looked foul with the wind breathing roughly. And fierce and frightful beasts and birds began to emit cries. And that lion-shouldered one like a tiger in prowess, without heeding these ominous occurences, marched forth into the field. And as that Rākshasa was setting out along with the Rākshasas, he set up mighty roars as if agitating the deep. And the mighty army of monkeys was seized with trepidation at that sound. And then there took place a mighty encounter of the Rākshasas and the monkeys equipped staying in fight with trees and rocks; who had given up all concern for their selves in behalf of Rāma and Rāvana. And each side desirous

---

* There is a pun here on the word *Akampana*—lit.—*one incapable of being shaken.*—T.

† Possessed of a person measuring, according to the commentator, a mass of clouds. I give the apparent sense, which answers.—T.

‡ Monkeys.

of slaying the other, the monkeys and the Rākshasas were exceedingly strong and heroic and like unto mountains. And each party storming at the other, in that conflict were heard loud cries emitted by those swift-speeding ones in anger. And fearful was the dust red-hued that was raised incessantly by the monkeys and the Rakshas ; and it enveloped the ten cardinal points. And in the field of battle, each enveloped with that dust raised, pale as silk, could not be discovered by the other. And in consequence of that dust arising, neither standard, nor ensign, nor shield, nor steed, nor weapon, nor car could be seen. And the fierce cries alone of those roaring and rushing were heard in that dreadful battle ; but their forms were not visible to the sight. And in that conflict in the dark then monkeys enraged slew monkeys, and Rākshasas Rākshsasas. And monkeys and Rākshasas slaying (indiscriminately) friends and foes, made the earth wet with blood, and miry. And then with showers of blood the dust was layed ; and the earth was covered with corpses. And Rākshasas and monkeys fast slew each other vigorously with trees and darts, maces and *prâcas*, rocks, bludgeons and *tomaras*, and by means of their arms resembling bludgeons, coped with their adversaries appearing like hills. And in the encounter monkeys slew Rākshasas of dreadful deeds. And in their turn Rākshasas, wrought up with passion, bearing in their hands *prâças* and *tomaras* destroyed monkeys wielding dire arms. And that leader of the force—Akampana—growing wroth, inspired with cheerfulness all the Rākshasas endowed with dreadful vigor. And the monkeys forcibly snatching away the weapons (of the Rākshasas), began to rive the Rākshasas with mighty trees and giant crags. In the meanwhile those heroes among the monkeys—Kumuda, Nila and the exceedingly exasperated Mainda, summoned the utmost impetuosity they were masters of. And those foremost of monkeys and redoubtable able warriors without much ado began to spread quite a carnage in the van of the Rākshasa army, and by means of various arms terribly beat the Rākshasas.

## SECTION LVI.

And witnessing that mighty exploit of the foremost of the monkeys, Akampana waxed furious with wrath. And transported with passion, he, twanging his mighty bow, seeing that feat of his foe, addressed his charioteer saying,—"O charioteer, swiftly conduct thou the car to that same place. These powerful ones are slaying innumerable Rākshasas in fight. And all those vigorous monkeys of dreadful deeds stay before me, armed with trees and rocks. Those, pluming themselves overmuch on their martial worth, I intended to slay in battle. And all this Rākshasa force appeared to be harassed by these." Then on a car drawn by moving steeds, Akampana from a distance attacked the monkeys with showers of arrows. And thereat the monkeys could not so much as maintain their ground in the field,—and how could they fight? And broken by the arrows of Akampana, they began to fly. And the exceedingly strong Hanumān, seeing his kindred come under the masterdom of Death and follow the course pursued by the shafts of Akampana, advanced (to the conflict). And seeing that mighty monkey, all those heroic prime monkeys together surrounded (Hanumān) in the field. And those best of monkeys, seeing Hanumān stay, grew strong by relying on that strong one. And even as the great Indra showereth down rain, Akampana showered shafts on Hanumān resembling a mountain-summit in grandeur. And without casting a thought on the showers of arrows poured on his person, that monkey gifted with exceeding strength, set his heart on compassing the death of Akampana. And laughing, that exceedingly energetic offspring of the Wind-god rushed after that Raksha, as if making the Earth herself tremble. And the form of that one roaring and flaming up in energy, was irresistible, like unto the appearance of a flaming fire. And thinking that he was unfurnished with any arms, that foremost of monkeys, waxing wroth, vehemently rooted up a hill. And taking that huge hill, the Wind-god's son endowed with prowess, sending up a tremendous roar, began to whirl it with a single arm. And as of yore Purandara had in encounter pursued Namuchi with the thunder-bolt, (Hanumān) pursued that best of Rākshasas—Akampana. And Akampana, seeing that uplifted crag, from a distance cut it off with mighty crescent-shaped shafts. And finding that mountain-top severed by the shafts of the Raksha and scattered in pieces, Hanumān was seized with a mighty wrath. And that monkey, wrought up with rage and pride, grasping an Açwakarna elevated like unto a hill, at once uprooted it. And taking that broad-shouldered Açwakarna, that one furnished with high splendour, with great glee whirled it above the ground. And thereat rushing amain vehemently, (Akampana) speedily broke the trees.* And (seeing this), Hanumān, transported with passion, rived the earth with his kicks. And Hanumān slaughtered elephants, and the riders thereof, and cars with their riders, and dreadful Rākshasas, and footmen. And seeing the enraged Hanumān resembling the Finisher armed with trees and destructive, the Rākshasas began to fly fast. And seeing that one enraged, terrific unto the Rākshasas, the heroic Akampana was agitated greatly and sent up shouts. And Akampana pierced Hanumān endowed with exceeding prowess with four and ten shafts, sharpened and capable of cleaving the bodies of people. And thus covered with iron arrows and whetted darts, that

* Why plural? So it is, however, in the text.—T.

hero—Hanumān—looked like a hill covered with trees. And that huge-bodied one endowed with wondrous prowess and great strength, appeared like a flowering Açoka or a fire without smoke. And then uprooting another tree, (Hanumān) summoning up his best impetuosity, swiftly hit Akampana—foremost of Rākshasas—on the head. And slain with that tree by that high-souled monkey-chief wrought up with passion, that Rākshasa fell down and died.* And seeing that foremost of Rākshasas—Akampana—slain (and lying) on the ground,—the Rākshasas were extremely aggrieved, and (appeared) like trees in an earthquake. And those Rākshasas defeated, leaving their arms behind, made for Lankā in fear, pursued by the monkeys. And with their hair flowing loosely, (the Rākshasas), afflicted with affright, and despirited and beaten, fled fast, with the water of fatigue running down their persons. And crushing down each other, they entered the city in a panic, momentarily casting their looks behind them. When the Rākshasas had entered Lankā, the exceedingly mighty monkeys, assembled together, paid homage unto Hanumān. And Hanumān, gifted with strength, honored the seniors each as he deserved in consideration of his lineage. And the monkeys eager for victory shouted with might and main, and began to drag the Rākshasas with the view of taking their lives. And that mighty monkey—son unto the Wind god—having destroyed the Rākshasas and arrived (in the midst of the host), attained heroic glory,—even as did Vishnu, having slain that destroyer of enemies—the mighty and dreadful Asura possessed of exceeding strength,—stationed in the van of the forces. And then the deities and Rāma himself and the highly powerful Lakshmana, and also the monkeys headed by Sugriva, and Bibhishana endowed with great strength, honored that monkey.

* This sentence, "And slain......and died" reads foolish. But the original is answerable for—in logical parlance—this identical proposition.—T.

## SECTION LVII

HEARING that Akampana had been killed, the lord of Rākshasas, overwhelmed with anger, with his face somewhat fallen, cast his eyes on his counsellors. And then pondering and reflecting for a while, in the forenoon he went round the city of Lankā for inspecting the barracks. And the king surveyed the city guarded by the Rākshasas, covered with innumerable barracks, and crowned with ensigns and standards. And seeing the city beseiged, Rāvana—lord of the Rākṣhasas—seasonably spoke words of welfare unto Prahasta skilled in fight,—"Save battle,deliverance find I none for the city suddenly beleaguered and put to straits. And this strain must be borne by these versed in warfare—me or Kumbhakarna or thee—my general—or Indrajit or Nikumbha.* And therefore do thou from this place, speedily taking this force, march to where the monkeys are, for securing victory (in the encounter). And as soon as thou settest out, the monkey-forces, hearing the roars of the foremost Rākshasas—speedily setting themselves in motion, —shall flee away. And volatile and haughty and of fickle minds, the monkeys will not be able to bear thy shouts; even as elephants are incapable of bearing the roaring of a lion. And on that monkey-army running away, Rāma in company with Sumitrā's son, deprived of his power and shorn of support, shall, O Prahasta, come under thy subjection. In this matter, thy being slain is uncertain, but victory is certain. Now do thou, as thou weighest our welfare, declare thyself for or against this course." Thus addressed by Rāvana, Prahasta—general of the forces—said unto the Rākshasa-chief; like *Uçanas* addressing the lord of Asuras,

* Grammatically faulty such is the sentence in the original.—T.

—"O king, before this we had deliberated together with wise counsellors, and then we disputed with each other in our respective views. And I had declared myself for giving up Sitā as fraught with our welfare; and we saw war involved in witholding her. I have ever been honored by thee variously with gifts and regard and soft speech. And what is thy good for which I shall not be at the pains? My life I do not care to keep,—nor yet my sons or my wife. Behold! for thee will I offer up my life into the sacrificial fire of conflict." Having said this unto his master—Rāvana—the general, Prahasta, addressed his generals staying before him, saying,—"At once bring up the mighty host of Rākshasas. To-day in the field of fight will I entertain the flesh-feeding fowls of the forest with the bodies of the foes slain with my resistless shafts." Hearing his speech, the highly powerful leaders arrayed the army in that abode of the Rākshasa. And in a moment Lankā swarmed with heroic and terrific Rākshasas equipped with various arms,—as if with elephants,—as well as with people worshipping Fire and bowing down unto Brāhmanas. And the perfumed breeze blew, laden with the incense of sacrificial offerings. And the Rākshasas, inspired with martial ardour, put on diverse garlands, consecrated with scriptural formulæ; and donned on their armour. And furnished with their bows and wearing their armour, the Rākshasas, on seeing king Rāvana, leaving (their vehicles), stood, surrounding Prahasta. Then greeting the monarch, Prahasta, furnished (with all appliances of battle),—winding his dreadful trumpet, ascended his car; having all sorts of weapons; yoked with wondrous fleet steeds; driven by a competent charioteer,—excellently furnished; sending up sounds resembling the rumbling of mighty masses of cloud,—appearing like the very Sun or Moon; invincible with a serpent-standard; having a defence as well as a portion exceedingly handsome; netted with gold all round; and seeming to be laughing in grace. And then, ascending this car, Prahasta, whom Rāvana had entrusted with authority, surrounded by a vast host, swiftly went out of Lankā. And then there were heard the sounds of kettle-drums, resembling the roars of Parjanya,—and the sounds of musical instruments, as if filling the Earth. And on that general of the forces marching, sounds of conchs were heard (all around) ; and the Rākshasas of dreadful forms and huge bodies, going before Prahasta, advanced, emitting tremendous roars. And Narāntaka,* Kambhahanu, Mahānāda,† and Samunnata,‡—Prahasta's counsellors all of them—went on, surrounding him. And he went out by the Eastern entrance, environed by this exceedingly dreadful array, resembling troops of elephants. And resembling the Destroyer—Yama himself—Prahasta in rage went out surrounded by that mighty host resembling the sea. And at the tumult raised by their exodus, as well as the roars of the Rākshasas, all creatures in Lankā began to cry in preternatural tones. And swarming under the cloudless welkin, birds feasting on flesh and gore began to gyrate at the right hand of the car. And dreadful jackals, emitting live flames from their mouths, set up cries. And stars began to shoot from the firmament ; and the winds to ruffle. And enraged at each other, the planetary bodies were shorn of their brightness. And clouds emitting sharp sounds,showered down blood upon the car, and those marching in front were washed therewith. And alighting at the topof the standard,a vulture set up cries,facing the south, and began to prick both its sides,--thereby depriving (Prahasta) of his grace. And from the hands of his charioteer and his driver conducting the steeds,never given to turning away from

---

* Lit. *destroyer of men.* Almost all the names of the Rákshasas are thus *significant* names. This assigning of names, embosoming some harmonising image, has by Sir Francis Palgrave, justly been considered as betokening a high poetical faculty.

† Lit.—*loud-throated.*

‡ Lit.—*lofty.*

the field, the goad began to drop again and again. And the auspiciousness that was bright and rare when the army set out, was clean gone in a moment,—and the steeds began to stumble on even ground. And as Prahasta of renowned worth and valor marched, the monkey-army equipped with various arms, presented themselves before him. And loud was the tumult that was raised by the monkeys. And mighty was the din that was heard of those, uprooting trees and taking up ponderous crags, of the Rākshasas roaring and the monkeys storming in both the exhilarated armies of Rakshas and wood-rangers,—of vehement and able (warriors) eager for slaying each other, and challenging each other to fight. And like an insect falling into a flame, the wicked-minded Prahasta, for obtaining victory, increasing his impetuosity entered into that host of the monkey-king.

---

## SECTION LVIII.

SEEING Prahasta sally, ready for encounter, that chastiser of foes—Rāma—with a smile said unto Bibhishana,—"Who is this huge-bodied one that armed with impetuosity, advanceth to the encounter? And what is his power and prowess like? O mighty-armed one, tell me this concerning this powerful night-ranger." Hearing Rāghava's words, Bibhishana answered, —"In Lankā this is the general of the lord of Rākshasas—the Rākshasa named Prahasta, surrounded by a third of the forces. He is possessed of prowess and is of distinguished gallantry. And that mighty army of strong monkeys, wrought up with wrath, and roaring at Prahasta, saw him dreadful and of terrific prowess and huge-bodied,—surrounded on all sides by the Rākshasas,—and setting up roars, marching. And the Rākshasas, eagerly desirous of victory, pursued the monkeys, wielding swords and darts and *rishtis*, and javelins and shafts and maces and clubs and bludgeons and *prâças* and various axes and curious bows. And the monkeys on their part, eager for encounter, took up flowering trees and hills and huge and broad crags. And each party approaching the other, great was the encounter that took place. And innumerable (monkeys and Rākshasas) kept showering rocks and arrows. And many Rākshasas in conflict slew many a powerful monkey, and the monkeys on their part slaughtered many a Rākshasa. And some were pierced with darts and with (other) powerful weapons ; and some were wounded with bludgeons ; and some were hewn with axes. And some rendered senseless, dropped down to the earth ; and some hit with weapons, had their breasts riven. And some, severed in twain with swords, dropped to the earth lifeless. And monkeys were hewn in their sides by heroic Rākshasas. And numbers of Rākshasas all around were beaten to the ground by infuriated monkeys with trees and mountain-peaks. And some smitten sore with slaps having the touch of the thunder-bolt, began to vomit blood from their mouths, with faces and eyes turned pale. And great was the uproar that arose in consequence of Rākshasas and monkeys emitting distressful cries and sending forth leonine roars. And monkeys and Rākshasas wrought up with wrath, engaged in treading the path of heroes,—looking terrific with their faces moving about,—performed deeds of intrepid courage. And Narāntaka and Kambhahanu and Mahānāda and Samunnata—all counsellors of Prahasta—set about slaughtering the rangers of the woods. Of these doing swift execution among the monkeys, Dwivida, taking up a mountain-peak, slew one—namely Narāntaka. And then the monkey, Durmukha, rising up afresh, armed with a mighty tree, killed the light-handed Rākshasa—Samunnata. And Jāmbavān endowed with energy, waxing enraged, uplifting a giant crag brought the same down on Mahānāda's breast.

And there speedily assailed by Tāra, with a mighty tree, the powerful Kumbhahanu gave up the ghost in the conflict. And not brooking that feat, Prahasta, mounted on a car, taking a bow in his hand, fell to spreading a dreadful havoc among the rangers of the woods. And then there the two hosts mingled into almost a vortex; and the sounds that arose from those infuriated ones of immeasurable might, resembled the roar of the ocean. And in terrific encounter the enraged Rākshasa irresistible in battle drove the monkeys to sore straits with showers of arrows. And the earth was covered quite with the terrible bodies of monkeys and Rākshasas; and it looked as if covered with mountains. And the earth drenched with streams of gore looked as if swarming with blossoming *palâças* in the month of spring. And as leaders of elephant-herds cross a lotus-tank covered with lotus-dust, those Rākshasas and choice monkeys crossed that river flowing in the field of conflict incapable of being crossed; having for her banks hosts of heroic warriors slain; for her mighty trees broken arms; for her volume of waters showers of blood; coursing to Yama resembling the Ocean; with livers and spleens for her vast slime; with scattered entrails for her moss; with riven bodies and heads for her fish; limbs for her lawns; swarming with vultures for her swans; with Kankas for her cranes; filled with fat representing her foam; with the roars (of warriors) for her sounds,—incapable of being crossed by cravens,—and resembling a real river swarming at the end of the rains with cranes and swans. Then all of a sudden Nila saw Prahasta stationed on his car, discharging vollies of shafts and harassing the monkeys therewith. And mounted on a sun-bright vehicle, that leader of the army—Prahasta—seeing Nila advance towards him amain in the encounter, like the wind in the sky scattering a mighty mass of clouds,—rushed towards Nila. And that leader of forces—Prahasta—foremost of bowmen, stretching his bow, began to shower arrows on Nila. And having pierced Nila sore and wounded him, those shafts sought the earth like enraged serpents. And that mighty monkey—Nila—endowed with energy,struck with those sharpened shafts resembling flames,—uprooting a tree, assailed therewith the irrepressible Prahasta—who was rushing against him. And thereat, that foremost of Rākshasas, on being attacked, flaming up into fury and uttering roars,—poured showers of arrows on the monkey-leader. And not being able to resist the arrowy vollies of that wicked-minded Rākshasa, (Nila) bore them, even as a bull beareth with closed eyes a fast-descending autumnal shower. And in the very same way did Nila with his eyes closed suddenly stand the mighty arrowy buffet of Prahasta incapable of being withstood. And wrought up with rage, the exceedingly strong and mighty Nila with a giant *Sâla* slew the steeds of Prahasta. And then his soul surcharged with wrath, Nila swiftly shattered the bow of that wicked-minded one, and then shouted again and again. On being bereft of his bow, Prahasta, general of forces, taking a terrible mace, leapt down from his car. And the redoubtable leaders endowed with activity, bearing hostility to each other, their persons bathed in blood, stood (on the ground) like two elephants (with their temples) riven. And they kept tearing each other with their teeth like a lion and a tiger, and also striving like a lion and a tiger. And endowed with victorious vigor, those heroes, never knowing to desist from fight, were eager for fame, even like Vritra and Vāsava (fighting). And then Prahasta putting forth his dearest effort, hit Nila on the temples with a mace ; and the blood began to flow. And then the mighty monkey, with his person drenched in blood, —wrought up with passion,discharged a tall tree at Prahasta's breast. And without caring for that hit, he, taking up a mighty mace, furiously rushed against the monkey—Nila. And witnessing that enraged (hero) rushing against him with exceeding impetuosity, that redoubted monkey endowed with vehemence, took up a tremendous crag. And in the encounter Nila at once let that crag alight right on the head of Prahasta, eager for encounter and fighting with the mace. And hurled by that foremost of monkeys, that huge and terrific crag then shattered Prahasta's head in pieces. And then bereft of life and shorn of nerve and devoid of sense, he suddenly dropped down to the earth like a tree whose roots have been severed. And even as fountains flow from the sides of a hill, blood flowed profusely from the person of that one, whose head had been riven. On Prahasta being slain by Nila, that mighty army of Rākshasas, never trembling (from fear),—retreated towards Lankā. And like waters rushing (through a breach in) a dyke, the Rākshasas could not stand their ground, on their leader being slain. And on that head of the hosts being killed, the Rākshasas, growing dispirited, repairing to the residence of the lord of Rakshas, remained plunged in thought, without speaking anything. And plunged in that sea of sorrow, they seemed as if they had been bereft of their senses. And then the highly powerful and victorious Nila, leader of forces, on being extolled with gracious offices, and on being joined by Rāma and Lakshmana, looked exceedingly exhilarated.

## SECTION LIX.

AND on the leader of the Rākshasa host being slain in battle by the foremost of monkeys, that army of the Rākshasa monarch, resembling the ocean in violence,—furnished with dreadful weapons, began to scamper away. And going to the lord of the Rākshasas, they apprised him of the dealth of his general at the hands of the Fire-god's offspring. And hearing those words of theirs, the Rākshasa lord was overcome with rage. And hearing that Prahasta had been killed in battle, (he), exercised with passion, with his heart influenced with grief, addressed those foremost of the Rākshasa hosts, even as Indra addresses the chiefs among the celestials, saying,—"That foe should no longer be disregarded that hath slain along with his followers and elephants that leader of my hosts that had destroyed the forces of Indra himself. Therefore, without taking thought, will I, for compassing the destruction of the foe, myself march to that marvellous field of fight. And to-day, even as a flaming fire burneth down a forest, will I with showers of shafts burn up that monkey-army, and Rāma and Lakshmana." Saying this, that enemy of the sovereign of the immortals ascended a flaming vehicle of dazzling sheen yoked to rows of excellent steeds,—displaying itself gloriously and having a glowing body. And eulogized with sacred hymns, the sovereign of the Rākshasa rulers then set out to the sounds of conchs and trumpets and *panavas ;* and in the midst of those produced by persons striking at their arms, with their hands, and of the sounds defiance, and leonine roars. And like that lord of the immortals—Rudra—surrounded by ghosts, the foremost of the Rākshsa monarchs was surrounded by bands of flesh-feeding (Rakshas) resembling cliffs and clouds,—with eyes glowing like fire. And at once issuing from the city, that one endowed with high energy saw that fierce array of monkeys, extended as the ocean or a mighty mass of clouds,—with arms upraised with rocks and stones. And seeing that terrific host of Rākshasas, that eminently auspicious one, followed by the forces, having arms resembling the lord of serpents—Rāma—spoke unto Bibhishana, foremost of those bearing arms,—"Whose is this force furnished with various ensigns and standards—and equipped with *prâcas* and swords and darts and other arms,—consisting of intrepid (Rākshasas), and having elephants resembling Mahendra* itself." Then hearing Rāma's speech,

* The mountain so named.

Bibhishana, possessed of the prowess of Sakra himself, informed Rāma anent that foremost of hosts consisting of that flower of high-souled Rākshasas, saying,—"O king, him do thou know to be Akampana, who, possessed of a high soul, is on the back of that elephant,—whose face looks like the sun new risen, and who approacheth making the head of his elephant tremble (with the splendour of his person).* And that one is named Indrajit—foremost by virtue of the boon (that he hath obtained), who ascending a car and having a lion for his ensign,—twangeth his bow like the very bow of Sakra displayed,—and who with his terrific round teeth appeareth like an elephant. And that one of a gigantic person is named Atikāya, that, like unto the Setting-hill of Vindhya, furnished with the bow and stationed on a car,—highly heroic, stretcheth his bow of unparalleled proportions. And that high-souled hero is named Mahodara that, furnished with right coppery eyes resembling the sun new risen, and ascending a car resonant with the sound of bells, shouteth shrill. And that one having the vehemence of the thunder-bolt is Piçācha, that, mounted on a steed in variegated golden trappings, and having the aspect of a mass of evening clouds, or a mountain,—(appeareth) with a *prâça* furnished with effulgence. And that one is the famed *Triçiras*,† that, grasping a whetted dart endowed with the splendour of lightning and having the speed of the thunder for its minister, approacheth, riding a bull—the best of his species—and having the appearance of the Moon himself. And that one looking like a mass of clouds, that, having a broad and beautiful breast and a banner surmounted with the king of serpents, goeth in collected carriage, stretching his bow is Kumbha. And that one is Nikumbha of wondrous valorous deeds (in

* This meaning is the commentator's.

† Some other than the celebrated hero slain by Ráma at the very outset of his sojourn in Dandaka.—T.

battle) that, grasping a flaming and smoky* bludgeon embellished with gold and diamonds,cometh—a very banner of the entire Raksha host. And that one is Narāntaka, fighting with mountain-peaks,—that appeareth before us, mounted on a car flaming like fire, furnished with pennons and equipped with bows and swords and shafts. And that crusher of the hauteur of even the celestials,—that surrounded by various spectres of dreadful forms having faces of tigers, or camels, or powerful elephants, or deer, or horses,—and with their eyes rolling,—where the white umbrella resembling the Moon,—shineth, graced with slender ribs—the high-souled sovereign of Rakshas appeareth like Rudra himself environed by spectres,—the sovereign of the Rakshas decked with a diadem, with his countenance graced with pendulous ear-rings,—with a person resembling that monarch of mountains—even Vindhya himself,—that humbler of the pride of Indra the Great and Yama,—shineth like the Sun." Then Rāma—repressor of foes—answered Bibhishana, saying,—"Alas! Rāvana—lord of the Rākshasas—is of exceeding glowing splendour; and Rāvana shineth in glory, and is incapable of being gazed at like the Sun himself. And his grace, being enshrouded in his own splendour, I cannot view plainly. And the persons of celestials appear splendid as doth the person of the Rākshasa-chief. And all the warriors of that high-souled one are like mountains and fight with crags; and all are equipped with flaming weapons. And environed by glowing ghosts of dreadful forms and fierce-looking and furnished with material tenements†,—the king of Rākshasas appeareth imposing like the Destroyer himself. And by luck it is that to-day the wickea-minded one hath come within the range of my vision; and to-day will I vent

* On account of lapises set on it.

† Having, according to the commentator, *goodly* persons. But *dehavadvi* is literally *having bodies*; and this sense, with reference to spirits, I fancy, fits in with the context.—T.

my wrath incident to the ravishment of Sitā." Having said this, Rāma endowed with prowess, ever followed by Lakshmana, stood, taking up his bow and pulling out a powerful shaft. And then that high-souled lord of Rākshasas addressed that mighty host, saying,—"Do ye casting off fear stay at ease, at the gateways, high ways, and the edifices (in Lankā). Taking note of this lapse,—*viz.*, that ye have all come hither with me, the wood-rangers in a body, subduing the empty city incapable of being withstood,—shall suddenly put (all) to straits." Then leaving those counsellors, (Rāvana), on the Rakshas having departed agreeably to his injunction, dived into that ocean of monkeys, like a mighty fish diving into the waves of over brimming deep. And seeing the lord of Rākshasas, furnished with flaming a bow and arrows,—suddenly rushing,—the king of monkeys, uprooting a mighty mountain-top, darted against the sovereign of the Rakshas. And taking up that mountain-peak having its sides covered with innumerable trees, he hurled it at the night ranger. And seeing it descend swiftly, (Rāvana) in battle severed the same by means of gold-knobbed shafts. And on that gigantic peak furnished with fair sides filled with trees, falling to the earth, severed in pieces,—the lord of Rākshasas took up an arrow, resembling a mighty serpent and having the splendour of the Destroyer himself. And taking that shaft endowed with the vehemence of the wind, flaming like a fire aglow, and having the impetuosity of the great Indra's thunder-bolt, (Rāvana) hurled it in rage to compass the destruction of Sugriva. And even as the fierce dart discharged by Guha* had pierced Krauncha,† that shaft shot by Rāvana, rushing in violence at Sugriva possessed of a person having the touch of Sakra's thunder-bolt, pierced it. Thereat, agonised by the shaft, that hero, with his senses bewildered, dropped down to the ground with shrieks. And

* The generallissimo of the celestials.

† The mountain so named.

seeing him down on the earth bereft of his senses, the Yatudhanas were filled with rejoicing. And then Gavāksha and Gavaya, Sushena, Rishabha, Jyotimukha and Nala, up-rooting crags and magnifying their bodies, rushed against the lord of Rākshasas. And the lord of Rākshasas with hundreds of shafts having sharpened heads, rendered their strokes fruitless. And then he rived those foremost of monkeys with showers of arrows having variegated golden knobs, and covered those fierce monkey-ranks with networks of arrows. And on being sore assailed and falling in consequence, those heroes, the monkeys, pierced with terrific arrows, and distressed with the shafts of Rāvana, emitting cries, sought the shelter of Rāma worthy of being sought. Then the high-souled and excellent bowman—Rāma,—taking his bow, at once sallied forth. And thereat, Lakshmana, approaching Rāma, with joined hands addressed him words couching prime import. "O noble one, I alone am fit to compass the destruction of this wicked-minded one. I will slay him. Do thou, O master, permit me." To him replied Rāma of exceeding energy, having truth for his prowess,—"Go then, O Lakshmana, and put forth thy utmost exertions in the encounter. Rāvana is forsooth endowed with mighty energy, and his prowes in battle is wonderful. Without doubt, when enraged, he is incapable of being borne by this triple world. Do thou keep an eye on his shortcomings as thou shouldst watch thine own failings. Being always on the alert, thou must with thy eyes as much as thy bow protect thyself." Hearing Rāghava's speech, Sumitrā's son, embracing Rāma, and saluting him and paying him his respects, went forth to battle. And (going unto the field), he found Rāvana, endowed with arms resembling the trunks of elephants,—wielding his dreadful and flaming bow, and covering with showers of arrows those monkeys, whose bodies had been swarming with shafts. And seeing Rāvana, the exceedingly powerful Hanumān—son unto the Wind-god—resisting that downpour of arrows,charged him vehemently. And coming at his car, the intelligent Hanumān, uplifting his right arm and terrifying Rāvana, said,—"Incapable of being slain by gods, Dānavas or Gandharvas, Yakshas or Rākshasas,—Fear hath (at last) found thee, coming even from monkeys. This my upraised right arm furnished with five fingers, shall rob thee of thy soul long resident (in thy body)." Hearing Hanumān's speech, Rāvana possessed of dreadful prowess, with his eyes reddened in wrath, said these words,—"Strike thou swift maugre fear; and acquire lasting renown. And, O monkey, having (at first) taken the measure of thy might, will I finish thee." Hearing Rāvana's words, the offspring of the Wind-god said,—"(First) remember thou thy son—Aksha—slaughtered by me!" Thus addressed, the exceedingly energetic lord of the Rākshasas possessed of prowess dealt a slap unto the offspring of the Wind-god. And struck with his slap, he shook momentarily. And staying for a moment and calling up fortitude, that magnanimous one administered a slap unto the foe of the immortals. And hit by the high souled monkey, the Ten-necked one trembled, as trembleth a mountain during an earthquake. And witnessing Rāvana struck with a slap (by Hanumān saints and Siddhas and celestials and the Asuras shouted in glee. Then attaining a little respite, Rāvana said,—"Well done, O monkey. In prowess thou art a foe I pride in." Thus addressed by Rāvana, the Wind-god's son said,—"Fie on my prowess, seeing that thou breathest yet, O Rāvana. Strike at the same time, O perverse one. Why dost thou bluster? And then my blow shall despatch thee to the mansions of Yama." And at the speech of the Wind-god's son, his ire flamed up. And then that one endowed with prowess, clenching his right fist carefully, let it alight amain on the monkey's chest. And hit at his spacious chest, Hanumān shook over and over again. And seeing the mighty Hanumān overwhelmed, that powerful car-warrior ascended on his car, approached Nila. And the powerful lord of Rākshasas—the Ten-necked one—made that general of forces —Nila—aflame with dreadful shafts entering into the vitals, resembling snakes. And assailed with shafts, Nila—leader of monkeys—with one arm took up a mountain-top and hurled it at the lord of Rakshas. And the energetic and high-minded Hanumān, attaining respite, eager for encounter, seeing (the fight between the Rākshasa and the monkey), wrought up with rage, said,—"It is not meet for me to attack Rāvana—lord of Rākshasas—engaged with Nila." And the highly powerful Rāvana, by means of seven shafts with sharpened points, hit at the mountain-top; and shivered in pieces, it fell (to the earth). And seeing that mountain peak shattered, that general of the monkey-forces—slayer of hostile heroes—flamed up in wrath like the fire at the universal wreck. And in that encounter Nila discharged Açwakarna trees, and *Sâlas*, and mangoes in full flower, and various other trees. And Rāvana, getting at the trees, severed them (by means of his arrows), and poured on the Fire-god's son terrific showers of shafts. And assailed with fearful showers of arrows as with a mass of clouds, that one endowed with eminent strength, decreasing his dimensions, dropped on the top of Rāvana's banner. And seeing the son of the Fire-god descend on the top of his banner, Rāvana was fired with ire, and Nila shouted (thereat). And seeing the monkey (now) at the top of the banner, and (now) at the end of his bow, and (now) at the crest of his tiara, Lakshmana and Hanumān and Rāma were struck with astonishment. And also Rāvana endowed with exceeding energy, astonished at the lightness of the monkey, took up a wonderful flaming fiery weapon. And the monkeys seeing Rāvana bewildered, and delighted thereat, set up shouts. And Rāvana enraged at the shouts of the monkeys, with his heart overwhelmed with agitation, could not address himself to any affort. And then taking a fiery shaft and setting the same on his bow, the night-ranger gazed at Nila. And the exceedingly energetic lord of the Rākshasas said,—"O monkey, by virtue of thy skill in illusion, thou art furnished with lightness. But, O monkey, if thou canst, preserve thy life. Thou transformest thyself into many shapes. Yet this shaft of mine discharged from my weapon, shall deprive of thy life thee that art preserving it." Having said this, the mighty-armed Rāvana—lord of the Rākshasas—fixing his shaft on his bow, shot it at the general. And Nila, struck at the chest with that arrow, which had been shot (by Rāvana), burning, suddenly fell down to the earth. And by virtue of the greatness of his sire and also of his own energy, he went to the earth on his knees, but was not utterly deprived of life. And seeing the monkey deprived of his senses, the Ten-necked one, eager for encounter, riding a car emitting a rattle resembling the rumbling of clouds, darted against Sumitrā's son. And entering into the arena of fight and posted there flaming, the powerful lord of the Rākshasas, baffling (the foe), kept stretching his bow. And as that one of immeasurable prowess kept stretching his bow, Sumitrā's son of unflagging mettle, addressed him, saying,—"O lord of night-rangers, do thou to-day try me in encounter. Thou ought not to strive with the monkeys." And hearing Saumitri's speech uttered in a full voice, as well as the terrific twangs of his bow-string, that Raksha—the king—approaching Sumitrā's son staying in the field, spoke unto him wrathfully,—"O Raghu's son, by my luck hast thou of perverse sense, finding thy fate come within the range of my ken. This very instant, tormented with the springes of my shafts, thou wilt repair to the regions of Death." Thereat, Sumitrā's son, without being overwhelmed with wonder (on witnessing Rāvana's prowess), addressed that one furnished with large and sharp teeth,—setting up roars,—"O king, those who are (really) endowed with prowess, do not storm. O prince of sinners, in vain thou vauntest. O lord of Rākshasas, I know thy prowess and strength and energy and vigor. Here am I stationed, bow and shafts in hand. Come thou. What is the use of vain-glorious self-laudation ?" Thus accosted, the Raksha monarch, growing wroth, discharged seven shafts furnished with knobs. Thereupon Lakshmana split them up with sharp-pointed arrows having variegated golden knobs. And they suddenly severed like powerful serpents cut off, Lankā's lord came under the sway of passion, and discharged other whetted arrows. And Rāma's younger brother poured showers of arrows from his bow ; and, planting himself at his post, cut off those arrows (of his adversary) by means of razors, and crescents, and excellent *karnas* and darts. And seeing his arrowy net-works rendered ineffectual, that enemy of the celestials—the king—was seized with wonderment, and again shot sharpened arrows. And Lakshmana also, resembling Indra the Great, setting on his bow sharpened, sharp-pointed, flaming, and luminous shafts, endowed with the dreadful vehement impetus of the thunder-bolt, discharged (them), to compass the destruction of the lord of Rakshas. And thereat the Rākshasa sovereign cut off those whetted arrows; and smote Lakshmana in the forehead with an arrow resembling the Fire of Dooms-day in energy,—which had been conferred on him by the Self-create. And Lakshmana, tortured with Rāvana's arrow, shook, loosely holding his bow; and then recovering his consciousness after undergoing extreme agony, he severed the bow of the foe of the foremost of celestials. And having cut off Rāvana's bow, Daçaratha's son hit (him) with three sharp-pointed arrows. And the king smarting under the shafts, with much ado regained his consciousness. And the enemy of the immortals of terrific power with his bow severed, and himself hit with shafts, and his body covered with fat, and himself washed in blood, took up a dart conferred on him by the Self-create. And the sovereign of the Rākshasas and their lord in that encounter hurled at Sumitrā's son the dart resembling smoking fire, sending up living flames, and striking terror into the monkeys. And as it coursed on, Bharata's younger brother resisted it with arrows resembling a sacrificial flame. Yet the dart pierced into the broad arm* of Daçaratha's son. And smit with the dart, that hero of the Raghu race, although possessed of strength, was aglow. And the king at once with his arms seized that one, who had been deprived of his senses. But he that could with his arms wield Himavān or Mandara or Meru or the triple world itself along with the immortals, could not (for all his strength) lift up Bharata's younger brother. And hit at his chest by the dart of Brahmā, Sumitrā's son remembered that he was verily a portion of Vishnu himself. And pressing hard Sumitrā's son—that humbler of the hauteur of the Daityas, that thorn in the sides of the celestials—could not move him (from his place). And then the Wind-god's offspring waxing wroth rushed at Rāvana, and overwhelmed with rage smote at his chest with his clenched fist resembling the thunderbolt. And boxed (by Hanumāna), Rāvana—lord of the Rākshasas—went down to the ground on his knees, and shook and dropped to the earth. And blood gushed out in streams from his mouths and eyes and arms; and staggered and senseless, he sat down on the platform of his car. And he was rendered insensible with his senses lost; and he knew not where he was. And seeing Rāvana endued with terrific prowess, rendered insensible in the encounter, saints and monkeys and gods with the Asuras set up shouts. And then the energetic Hanumān taking Lakshmana racked by Rāvana, with his arms brought him before Rāghava. And albeit incapable of being moved by the foes, (Lakshmana), on account of the friendship of the Wind-god's offspring as well as the high reverence in which he was held by Hanumān, became extremely light to the monkey. And then that dart, renouncing Sumitrā's son vanquished in fight, again sought its place in Rāvana's car. And the exceedingly powerful Rāvana, recovering his consciousness in that dread encounter,

* *Bhujāntaram* is vague. It may also mean *the chest.*—*T.*

took up whetted shafts and seized a mighty bow. And that finisher of foes—Lakshmana—recovered the exercise of his senses, and had his entire person perfectly healed,—on his recalling that he verily was a part and parcel of Vishnu himself. And witnessing the mighty army of the monkeys and the redoubted heroes brought down in the conflict, Rāghava rushed at Rāvana. Thereat drawing near to him, Hanumān said unto him,—"It behoveth thee to chastise the foe ascending my back, even as Vishnu chastiseth the enemies of the immortals, riding Garutman." Hearing the words spoken by Hanumān, Rāghava at once got up on that gigantic monkey; and that master of men beheld Rāvana in battle. And seeing him, that highly powerful one darted against Rāvana, even as the enraged Vishnu had rushed against Virochana's son,* upraising his weapons. And he sharply twanged his bow-string sounding like the terrific crash of thunder; and then in solemn tones, Rāma addressed the lord of Rākshasas, saying,—"Stay, stay, having done me such wrong. Repairing whither, shalt thou, O powerful Rākshasa, attain respite? Even if thou shouldst seek Yama or Indra or the Sun—son unto Vivaçwān—or the Self-sprung or the Fire-god or Sankara himself,—or go to the ten cardinal points in ten portions,—yet shalt thou not, so resorting, attain deliverance. And (Lakshmana), going forth to the fight, hath been wounded with the dart and hath suddenly been stupified. But, O king of the Rakshas, to-day in conflict Death shall claim for his own thee and thy sons and grandsons. By me with my shafts have been slaughtered four and ten thousand Rakshas residing in Janasthāna, wielding excellent weapons." Hearing Rāghava's words, the exceedingly strong lord of the Rākshasas, overwhelmed with a mighty wrath, recalling enmity agone, with burning shafts resembling the fire of Doom hit in encounter the exceedingly impetuous offspring of the Wind-god, who was bearing Rāghava. And although struck

* The Asura—Vali.

and resisted by the Rākshasa with arrows, the energy of that one, endowed by nature with prowess—increased greatly. And the exceedingly energetic Rāma, on seeing that foremost of the monkeys wounded by Rāvana, was mastered by wrath. And Rāma, closing with his enemy, by means of whetted arrow-points severed in pieces his car together with the wheels and the steeds, the banner, the umbrella, and the majestic streamer, as well as with the charioteer and the thunder-bolts and darts and swords. And then as the reverend Indra cleaveth Meru with his thunder-bolt, (Rāghava) swiftly smote on Rāvana's spacious and shapely chest with a shaft resembling Vajra and the thunder holt. And—that the king hero—who had not smarted nor shaken under the impetus of Vajra and the thunder-bolt,—assailed with the arrow of Rāma and agonised in consequence, shook and lost hold of his bow. And seeing him overwhelmed, Rāma took up a flaming half-moon, and with the same at once severed the sun-bright tiara of the high-souled sovereign of the Rākshasas. And Rāma in the encounter addressed the lord of Rākshasas, resembling a serpent bereft of venom, shorn of his splendour, like unto the sun shrouded (in mist),—without his wonted grace, and having his entire tiara riven—saying,—"Thou hast (in battle) performed high and dreadful deeds,—and hast also (in the conflict) slain my foremost heroes. And therefore I know thou art fatigued. And for this reason it is that I will not with my shafts bring thee to the door of Death. Go thou. I know* that thou art worn out with fight. Therefore, O king of night-rangers, enter Lankā. Having a little respite, do thou depart on thy car along with thy bowmen. Afterwards, mounted on thy car, shalt thou behold my power". And thus addressed, the king, with his pride and joy defeated, with his bow severed, and his steeds and charioteer killed, himself smarting under shafts,—and having his crown splin-

* *Jānāmi*—lit. *I know.* The commentator says that here this word means *I permit.* But the literal sense answers.—T.

tered,—speedily entered Lankā. And on that foe of the deities and the Dānavas—the puissant lord of the night-rangers—entering (into Lankā), Rāma rendered the monkeys along with Lakshmana hale in that fierce confiict. And at the break-down of that foe of the immortals, the celestials and the Asuras, the ghosts and the Cardinal points,and all the mighty serpents together with the oceans and the creatures inhabiting earth and water, felt exceedingly delighted.

## SECTION LX'

And entering the city of Lankā, the king afflicted with the fear of Rāma's arrows, with his pride humbled, was undergoing great torments. And overpowered by the high-souled Rāghava, the king resembled an elephant defeated by a lion or a serpent defeated by Garura. And remembering Rāghava's arrows resembling a comet risen at the universal wreck, and of the splendour of live lightning, the Rākshasa-chief was aggrieved. And seated on a superb golden seat, Rāma, eying the Rākshasas, spoke,—"Forsooth all the austere asceticism I have performed goeth for nothing, for although resembling the redoubtable Indra, I have been overcome by a mortal. And this dire speech of Brahmā also reverts to my remembrance,—'Know thou that thy fear cometh from a human being. Thou art incapable of being slain by deities and Danavas, Gandharvas, Yakshas, Rākshasas and serpents. But thou hast not asked for immunity from men.' And I deem even this son of Daçaratha as the occasion of my fear. And I was formerly cursed by that lord of the Ikshwāku line—Anaranya—saying,—'O worst of Rākshasas, a person shall spring in my race, who,

O wicked-minded one, shall slay thee in battle along with thy sons and courtiers and forces and horses and charioteers.' And I was also cursed by Vedavati, who was formerly outraged by me. And she is (perchance) born as the exalted daughter of Janaka. And what had also been uttered by Umā and Nandiçwara and Rambhā and Varuna's daughter,* hath come to pass.† And taking note of this, ye should strive (to the uttermost.) And let the Rākshasas be posted at the gateways, highways, and the walls. And do ye wake up that destroyer of the pride of the deities and the Dānavas—Kumbhakarna,endowed with unparalleled gravity,overwhelmed with the curse of Brahmā." And seeing himself worsted and Prahasta also slain, that Raksha endowed with dreadful power issued his orders to that fearful force. "Do ye vigilantly guard the gates and mount the wall. And do ye wake up Kumbhakarna come under the sway of slumber. And deprived of his senses through lust, he sleepeth secure. And the Rākshasa sometimes sleepeth nine, seven, ten, or eight months away. Of measureless might he hath slept for nine months. And foremost of all the Rākshasas in fight, that long-armed one shall speedily slay the monkeys as well as the princes. He is a very banner in battle, and the crown of all the Rakshas. But intent on common pleasure, Kubhakarna, with his senses stupified, sleepeth ever. I havė been worsted in fierce fight by Rāma ; but on Kumbhakarna being awakened, my grief shall go. If he doth not help me in such high peril, what shall I do with his strength resembling the

* Punjikasthalâ.

† Punjikasthalâ cursed Râvana that he should come by death if he should use violence on a woman against her inclination. Râvana had *not* been cursed by Rambhá herself, but by Nala Kuvera in *her* interest. 'Thy head shall be sundered in seven when thou forcest a female against her will.' Umâ had cursed Râvana that for a woman he should meet with death on the shaking of the peak of Kailâça.—Nandiçwara had cursed him that as he had slighted and scoffed at him, he should find his fate at the hands of the monkeys, being emanations of himself.—T.

strength of Sakra himself ?" Hearing the speech of the lord of the Rākshasas, the Rākshasas, bestirring themselves, went to the abode of Kumbhakarna. And desired by Râvana, those feeding on flesh and blood went off hurriedly, taking perfumes and wreaths and a mass of food. And entering Kumbhakarna's charming cave having a wide gateway, measuring a *yoyana* breathing around perfumes of flowers,—those highly powerful ones, pushed off by Kumbhakarna's breath, with the utmost energy they could summon up stood their ground and entered the cave. And then entering that charming cave having floors paved with gold and gems, those Nairitas endowed with great strength, saw that one of dreadful prowess, lying down. And then they together set about waking up the slumbering Kumbhakarna looking like a hill extended,—and sunk in profound slumber; with his body having its down standing on end; lying down; like a sighing serpent; rolling people* with his powerful breath,—reposing; possessed of dreadful prowess; having a huge nose; of a person vast as the nether sphere; lying stretched at length; smelling of fat and blood; decked with golden *angadas;* and waring a diadem endowed with the splendour of the Sun. And (they) saw that subduer of enemies and foremost of Nairitas—Kumbhakarna. And then they piled up Meru-like animals for conferring rare gratification, and heaps of deer and buffaloes and boars. And the Rākshasas made an astounding heap of rice. And then the enemies of the immortals put up before Kumbhakarna jars of blood and various kinds of food, and smeared that repressor of foes with excellent sandal, and made him inhale perfumes and the aroma of wreaths. And they made (the place) rife with the incense of *dhupa*, and extolled that smiter of enemies. And then the Yātudhānas roared around here and

* An instance of the material sublime unsurpassed in all literature. Kumbhakarna himself is the emblem of the material as contrasted with the spiritual typified by Ráma.—T.

there like clouds. And they winded conchs beaming moon-like. And they incapable of being beaten shouted in full chorus. And the night-rangers shouted and struck at their arms with their hands and began to pull him. And for rousing Kumbhakarna, mighty was the din that they raised. And hearing those loud sounds of conchs and drums and *panavas*; and those proceeding from persons striking at their arms with their hands; and leonine roars,—rushing on all sides and riving the very heavens,—birds suddenly dropped down. And when the high-souled Kumbhakarna sleeping soundly did not awake at that terrific tumult, the Rākshasas took up *Bhushandis** and maces. And then the Rākshasas, drawing near, smote Kumbhakarna sleeping sweetly in the chest with mountain-peaks, maces and clubs. But the Rākshasas could not stay before Kumbhakarna owing to the hurricane heaving at his breath. Then tightening their cloth† (about their waist), those Rākshasas of dreadful prowess sounded *mridangas* and *panavas*, conchs and *kumbhas*. And ten thousand Rākshasas together surrounded that one resembling a heap of dark-blue collyrium and fell to rousing him. But albeit assailed with shouts and smit with weapons, he did not wake up. And when they succeeded not in rousing him, they more than ever exerted themselves. And then they smote him with horses and camels, and mules and snakes, rods and lashes and hooks, and with might and main sounded kettledrums and conchs and *mridangas*. And they struck his body with innumerable huge blocks of wood. And summoning up their dearest energy, they dealt him blows with maces and clubs. And at that mighty uproar, entire Lankā was filled with her woods and hills; yet he did not wake up. And then they simultaneously sounded a thousand kettle-drums beaten with sticks of polished gold.

---

* A variety of the mace.

† Another reading is, *Tatah prapuritāh gārham*—then densely filling the cave.—T.

And coming under the sway of the curse,* when that one sunk in slumber did not wake up, the night-rangers were wrought up with wrath. And overcome with choler, they endowed with dreadful prowess addressed themselves vigorously to awakening him ; and others put forth their energy. And others smote the kettle-drums, and others set up loud cries. And others cut off his hair, and others bit his ears. And others poured into his ears a thousand vessels of water. But Kumbhakarna come under the spell of a mighty slumber did not wink. And others—strong ones—armed with poniards(*kutas*) and maces, made their poniards and maces alight on his person. And struck with *sataghnis* bound with cords,† that huge-bodied one did not wake up. And then when a thousand elephants rushed against his body, recovering his consciousness, he awoke. And assailed with mountain-peaks and trees descending on his body, he, without minding those tremendous blows,—on sleep having been dispelled, suddenly got up, yawning,—suffering the pangs of hunger. And then that night-ranger resembling an elephant or a serpent or a mountain-peak, casting about his arms superior in force to the thunder-bolt itself, and opening his deformed mouth like unto that of a mule, yawned (again and again). And as he yawned, his mouth resembling the subterraneous regions, looked like the Sun stationed at the summit of Meru. And that night-ranger possessed of unwieldly strength woke up, yawning. And the breath that he breathed resembled a storm raging in a mountain. And then as he sat up, Kumbhakarna's form appeared like that of the Destroyer himself at the universal wreck,—intent upon consuming all creatures. And the large eyes of that one, resembling a live flame and endowed with the splendour of lightning, appeared like a pair of glowing planets. And then they pointed unto him all those heaps of

---

* Brahmá had cursed him, as will appear afterwards.—T.

† What does this mean ?

edibles, various and profuse,—bears and buffaloes,—and that powerful (Rākshasa) fell to. And hungering, he fed on flesh and athirst, drank blood. And then that enemy of Sakra drank vesselfuls of fat and blood. And concluding that he was replete, the night-rangers came up; and bowing down their heads, stood circling him on all sides. And then with his eyes discolored and drooping from drowsiness, he casting his eyes around, addressed those night-rangers. And that foremost of Nairitas cheered all those Nairitas; and surprised at his having been roused,—spoke unto the Rākshasas,—"Why, being honored, have I been awakened by you? Is it well with the king? Or hath any fear sprung up here? Or hath a mighty fear presented itself forsooth from among others; for which I have been speedily awakened by you? This very day will I uproot quite the fear of the sovereign of the Rākshasas. I will split up the great Indra himself,—or make Fire himself give up his heat. One doth not awaken my like for a light cause. Therefore do ye give the real truth of the cause of your awakening me." Thereat a minister of the king, named Yupāksha, with joined hands said unto that humbler of foes—Kumbhakarna—wrought up with wrath, who was thus speaking,—"No fear anywise springs to us from the Deities. But, O king, a great fear doth cross us, coming from a mortal. And never fear so cometh unto us anywise from Daityas or Dānavas, as it hath arrived from a man, O king. This Lankā hath been hemmed in by monkeys resembling mountains. And terrific is the terror that cometh even from Rāma scorched with fire springing from the ravishment of Sitā. Ere this by a single monkey was this splendid city burnt down. And the prince Aksha hath been slain along with his following and elephants. And that thorn in the sides of deities, that lord of the Rākshasas—Pulasta's son himself—hath been set free in conflict by Rāghava endowed with the splendour of the Sun,—saying—'Go thou.' And what had been done unto the king by neither the gods nor the Daityas nor yet the Dānavas, hath been done by Rāma; and he hath been set free, having come to a pass imperilling his life." Hearing Yupāksha's speech and hearing of the defeat of his brother, Kumbhakarna, with his eyes whirling, spoke unto him, saying,—"To-day, O Yupāksha, after vanquishing in battle the monkey-army together with Lakshmana and Rāghava, shall I see Rāvana. And I shall regale the Rākshasas with the flesh and blood of the monkeys, and myself drink the blood of Rāma and Lakshmana." Hearing his words as he haughtily spoke thus with his spirit of insolence magnified by much, that foremost of the Nairita soldiers, Mahodara, with joined hands observed,—"O long-armed one, having at first heard Rāvana's words and considered their justice or otherwise, thou wilt afterwards defeat the foe in fight." Hearing Mahodara's words, the exceedingly energetic and mighty (Kumbhakarna) surrounded by the Rākshasas, prepared to depart. And having roused from his slumbers that one of terrific prowess having dreadful eyes,—the Rākshasas speedily arrived at the residence of the Ten-necked one. And presenting themselves before the Ten-necked one seated on a superb seat, all the night-rangers spoke with joined hands,—"O lord of the Rākshasas, thy brother, Kumbhakarna, hath been roused. Shall he march from there; or wilt thou see him come here?" Thereat, Rāvana, pleased, spoke unto those Rākshasas who had presented themselves,—"I wish to see him here, and do ye honor him fittingly." Thereat, saying 'So be it', the Rākshasas, directed by Rāvana, going back, spoke unto Kumbhakarna,—"That foremost of all the Rākshasas—the king—wisheth to see thee. So mind thou going, and gladden thy brother." And the irrepressible Kumbhakarna possessed of prodigious prowess, learning the mandate of his brother, saying,—'So be it,'—rose up from his bed. And washing his face, and having bathed, that one, feeling refreshed and enjoying exceeding exhilaration of spirit,—wishing to drink, urged (the

Rākshasas) to bring the nerve-conferring draught. And then the Rākshasas, at the command of Rāvana speedily procured wine and various kinds of viands. And having drunk two thousand vessels (of wine), he prepared to go. And slightly swolen and flushed, Kumbhakarna, attaining access of strength and fire, waxed wroth, and resembled the Doom and Destroyer —Yama himself. And striding to the residence of his brother backed by the Raksha force, Kumbhakarna shook the earth with his tread. And illuming the highway with the splendour of his person, like the thousand-rayed (Sun) discovering the earth with his rays, (Kumbhakarna) went on, engirt around by joined hands resembling wreaths,—like Satakratu* going to the abode of the Self-sprung. And suddenly seeing that slayer of foes of immeasurable prowess, resembling a mountain-summit,—walking along the highways, the wood-rangers stationed outside (the monkey-camp), along with the leaders of bands, were seized with affright. And then some sought the shelter of Rāma, worthy of being so sought; and some, stricken (with panic), dropped to the earth; and some, suffering (from fear), fled to the carindal points; and some through stress (of apprehension) lay down on the ground. And seeing that one resembling a very mountain-peak, decked with a diadem, seeming to touch the Sun himself with his energy, of colossal altitude, and wonderful to behold,—the wood-rangers, tormented with fright, began to scamper on all sides.

---

* Lit. *him of an hundred sacrifices*—an appellatiou of Indra.—T.

## SECTION LXI.

AND then the exceedingly energetic Rāma possessed of prowess, taking his bow, saw Kumbhakarna, having a huge body and decked with a diadem. And seeing that foremost of Rākshasas looking like a mountain ; filling all the heavens as formerly Nārāyana had done; resembling clouds charged with rain ; and adorned with golden *angadas*,—the mighty army of monkeys began to run away at the top of its speed. Seeing the army scamper and the Rākshasa swelling, Rāma struck with surprise, said unto Bibhishana,—"Who is that tawney-eyed one, decked with a diadem, and looking like a hill ? And in Lankā the hero appeareth like a mass of clouds embosoming lightning. And alone he seemeth like an ensign of the Earth; and seeing him the monkeys dart away hither and thither. Tell me who he is,—whether a Raksha or an Asura. The like of him mine eyes had never before lighted on." Accosted by the king's son—Rāma of untiring deeds—the exceedingly wise Bibhishana said unto Kākutstha,—"By whom in battle Vivasçwata's offspring* and Vāsava himself had been vanquished, this is he—the wondrous powerful Kumbhakarna—son unto Viçravān. No Rākshasa is there that equalleth this one in size. O Rāghava, this one in battle hath brought down Dānavas and Yakshas and Serpents† and flesh-feeders and Gandharvas and Vidyādharas and Pannagas‡ by thousands. The immortals themselves thinking the dart-handed and fierce-eyed Kumbhakarna possessed of great strength, as the Destroyer himself,—were overwhelmed with stupor and were foiled in their exertions to slay him. The exceedingly powerful Kumbhakarna is mighty by nature: the strength of other

* Yama—son of Vivaçwata or the Sun.

† *Bhujangāh* :—semi-divine serpents.

‡ Semi-divine serpents.

redoubtable Rākshasas is owing to boons obtained by them. As soon as this high-souled one was born and was a babe, he began to devour up countless creatures by the thousand. And on these having been devoured, creatures, afflicted with affright consequent on those having been eaten up, sought the shelter of Sakra and told him what had happened. And thereat the great Indra, waxing wroth, smote Kumbhakarna with the whetted levin. And hit at with Sakra's thunderbolt, that high-souled (hero) shook, and in wrath set up roars. And hearing the roars of the Rākshasa—Kumbhakarna—as he kept crying, creatures, seized with fear, were greatly agitated. And thereat, enraged with the great Indra, the mighty Kumbhakarna plucking a tusk of Airāvata, hurled it at Vāsava's chest. And with blood overflowing his person, Vāsava looked as if aflame. And thereat, all of a sudden the gods and the Brahmarshis and the Dānavas were dispirited. And then they informed the lord of creatures touching the ravages of Kumbhakarna, and informed the gods about Kumbhakarna's devouring up creatures, destroying asylums and outraging others' wives. "If this one devour creatures constantly, in a short space the world would be empty of any." Hearing Vāsava's speech, the Great-father of all called up* the Rākshasas and saw Kumbhakarna (before him). And seeing Kumbhakarna, Prajāpati† was seized with exceeding great fear. And then, pacifying Kumbhakarna, the Self-sprung addressed him, saying,—"Forsooth for compassing the destruction of creatures, hast thou been begot by Paulasta.‡ Therefore from this day forth, thou shalt lie down as one dead." Stricken with the curse of Brahmā, Kumbhakarna fell down before the Lord. Then, extremely agitated, Rāvana said,—"Thou hewest down a golden tree when about to bear fruit. O lord of creatures, thou ought not to curse

---

* *By reciting a certain scriptural formula.—T.*

† *Lit.—lord of creatures.*

‡ Viçravá.

thus thine own grandson. Thy words will never go for naught; sleep he will, without doubt. But do thou appoint a time for his sleeping and one for his awaking." Hearing Rāvana's speech, the Self-sprung said,—"Having slept for six months, he shall wake for one day. And for a single day, that hero, coming under the influence of hunger, shall range the earth, opening his mouth wide open, and devouring people like a fire that hath spread far and wide. And now king Rāvana struck with terror at thy prowess, encompassed with peril, hath waked up Kumbhakarna. And that hero possessed of dreadful prowess, wrought up with high wrath, sallying forth from his camp, rusheth about, eating up monkeys. And soon as the monkeys see Kumbhakarna, they fly away. And How can they resist in battle the enraged Kumbhakarna? Do thou tell the monkeys this is an uplifted engine. Thus assured, the monkeys shall take heart." Hearing Bibhishana's words informed with reason and tending to the good (of the monkeys), Rāghava then addressed general Nila, saying,—"Let you, monkeys, equipped with weapons and holding hill-tops in your hands,—and furnished with mountain-summits and trees and rocks, stay, occupying the highways and the bridges." Thus instructed by Rāghava, that powerful monkey, Nila—general of the forces—accordingly issued his orders to the monkey-hosts. And then Gavāksha and Sarabha and Hanumān and Angada, themselves endowed with the splendour of mountain-summits, taking up mountain-tops, drew towards the gateway. And hearing Rāma's words,* the heroic monkeys inspired with intrepidity, fiercely fell on the foe with trees. And then that dreadful army of monkeys, upraising crags and holding trees in their hands, appeared like mighty masses of scowling clouds bordering a mountain.†

* Namely, "that is an uplifted engine."

† This is apt, seeing that Lanká was situated on a hill.—T.

## SECTION LXII.

AND that tiger-like Rākshasa possessed of prowess, (still) under the influence of slumber, strode along the picturesque highway. And that exceedingly unconquerable one, surrounded by thousands of Rākshasas, went on, showered with blossoms from the houses (standing by). And then he saw the grand and graceful residence of the lord of the Rākshasas, having golden networks and sun-bright to behold. And entering the mansion of the Rākshasa sovereign, like the sun entering into a mass of clouds, he saw his elder brother seated at a distance; even as Sakra sees the Self-sprung seated. And Kumbhakarna surrounded by numbers of Rākshasas, entered his brother's abode, making the very earth tremble with his tread. And arriving at the abode and passing the entrance, he saw his superior anxiously seated on the car, Pusphaka. Seeing Kumbhakarna come, the Ten-necked one, exceedingly rejoiced, raised him up and drew him near himself. And then the exceedingly mighty Kumbhakarna saluted the feet of his brother and said,—"What dost thou say?" Thereat, delighted, Rāvana, springing up, again embraced (his brother). And embraced (by his brother), and duly greeted by him, that brother (of Rāvana)—Kumbhakarna seated himself on a shining and superb seat. And seating himself on that seat, the wondrous powerful Kumbhakarna, with his eyes reddened in wrath, addressed Rāvana, saying,—"O king, why, honoring me, hast thou awaked me? Tell me, whence springeth thy fear? And who shall be a ghost?"* Thereat, Rāvana, waxing wroth, and with his eyes rolling in rage, said unto Kumbhakarna, seated,—"O highly powerful one, thou hast slept away a long

* *Having been slain by me.*

space of time. And having been asleep, thou dost not know the great fear of mine springing from Rāma. This graceful son unto Daçaratha possessed of strength, along with Sugriva, having crossed the ocean, is destroying our race. Alack! see in own Lankā, woods and forests have been flooded with an ocean of monkeys coming without any ado by the bridge (which they have constructed). Those Rākshasas that were prime, have been slain in battle by the monkeys; but I find no destruction of the monkeys in fight. Nay, the monkeys have never been before even vanquished (by the Rākshasas) in battle. And therefore hath this fear sprung up (in my heart). Save me from this, O exceedingly powerful one. Do thou now destroy these. It is for this that I have roused thee. Do thou, favoring me, whose exchequer is empty, save this city of Lankā, having only young folks and the aged left. And, O long-armed one, do thou perform thy dearest acts in behalf of thy brother. And, O subduer of enemies, I had never before said so unto my brother. In thee is my affection and great is the probability of thy succeeding. In the wars of the celestials and Asuras, O foremost of Rākshasas, countless were the celestials that thou as an antagonist hadst beaten. Therefore, O thou of dreadful strength, summon thy entire energy. Him find I not among all beings, who is thy peer in prowess. And, O lover of battle! O dear unto friends, as thou likest, do this beloved good office, this prime benefit, unto me. By thy own energy, smite the hostile hosts, even as a mighty and strong wind (scattereth away) autumnal clouds.

## SECTION LXIII.

HEARING the lament of the king of Rākshasas, Kumbhakarna, laughing, said,—"That evil which on the occasion of the conclave we had seen, hath befallen thee, who hast passed by what was fraught with thy good. Even as a sinner reapeth perdition, verily hath the fruit of thine unrighteous act found thee. At first, O mighty king, thou didst not ponder over this course of conduct; nor, from pride of prowess, didst thou at all take note of the evil thereof. He that doeth last what should be done first, and first what should be done last, is ignorant of what is prudence and what not. Acts not performed in harmony with season and place, like unto acts performed counter to season and place, are the occasions of misery, and resemble clarified butter poured into fire that hath not been sanctified. He stayeth well in the path that, in consultation with his counsellors, ascertaineth the five ways touching the three kinds of action.* The king that aided by his own intelligence as well as his counsellors acteth after reflection in consonance with the science of polity, that distinguisheth his friends from his foes), and, O lord of the Rākshasas, that seasonably† pursueth righteousness, or profit, or desire,—or any two, or all these combined,—truly hath understanding.‡ But the king or the heir-

* The five ways are (1) the means of commencing an act (2) person, thing and wealth, (3) division of season and place, (4) providing against mischance, (5) success. The three kinds of action are treaty, war, *etc.* All this is nebulous; and the commentator is sadly reticent over this extremely important passage.—T.

† Religion is to be sought in the morning, profit in the afternoon, and desire at night,—so the commentator.—T.

‡ One is at sea in the midst of these formless generalities. The tantalized intellect makes a desperate attempt to grasp the body of the shadow seeming substance, but the empty air mocks his pains. A translator, however, is fast bound to the oar and must pull on, will be, nil he.—T

apparent, that, having heard what is prime among the three, doth not understand, hath spent his time in vain on his erudition. He that, controlling his own self, consulteth with his counsellors seasonably touching gift, forbearance, difference and prowess, as well as virtue, profiit and desire,—doth not in this world come by calamity. Perceiving the fair fruit (of a line of action) accruing to him here, a king should act in consultation with counsellors endowed with intelligence and versed in the import of things. Not understanding the sense of the scriptures, persons possessed of beastly intelligence,—entering into the heart of their counsellors,—are inspired with a desire of speaking out of sheer volubility.* Albeit uttered heedfully, the speech of those that are ignorant of learning and the knowledge of the sense of things,—and who are intent upon attaining abounding affluence,—should not be acted upon. And those—spoilers of business—who from recklessness talk of pernicious as if profitable,—should certainly be rejected as counsellors. Some counsellors—destroyers of their masters—joining intelligent enemies (of their lords), act in a way opposed to their interests in this world. Their lords, at the hour of consultation, by their behaviour should know these counsellors—enemies in the guise of friends—who have been won over (by the opposite party). Even as the fowls of the air enter the hole in the Krauncha,† enemies find an easy entrance into the shortcomings of him that is fickle‡ and that rusheth into act without heed. He that disregarding his foe, omitteth to guard himself, cometh by disasters and loseth his place. Even what had been advanced by thy beloved§ and my younger

* The sense is obscure, and the commentator does not help me.—T.

† The hole indented by Skanda the celestial generallissimo in the mountain named in the text.—T.

‡ *Chapala—fickle*. The commentator, however, reads between the lines. According to him the epithet means—*he that is pleased with speech immediately agreeable*. But the received sense answers.—T.

§ Râvana's principal queen, Mandodari.

brother, is fraught with our welfare. Do thou now what thou wishest." Hearing Kumbhakarna's words, the Ten-necked one knit up his brows, and, wrought up with wrath, said unto him,—"I am worthy of being honored by thee, like thy superior. What needs this verbal travail? Do thou what is fit. Vain is the mention now of what I did either through stupor or delusion or pride of prowess. Now bethink thee of what is proper. Do thou through thy prowess assuage the sorrow of mine springing from my impolitic conduct, if thou cherishest any feeling for me, if thy strength stayeth, and if thou deemest this business of mine as by far more momentous unto thee. He is a friend that succoureth one fallen in distress and is undergoing affliction; and he acts friendly that helpeth a person lapsing from the path of morality." As he was speaking thus in words sedate yet severe, Kumbhakarna, concluding that Rāvana was delighted, made his remarks mildly. And seeing his brother extremely sorry, Kumbhakarna, pacifying him, gently said,—"O king, intently hear my words, O repressor of foes! O lord of Rākshasas, banish this sorrow, and casting away thy wrath, return thou to nature. And, O king, so long as I live, thou must not suffer thy heart to fare thus. Him will I slay for whom thou grievest. But whatever condition thou mayst be in, I must tell what is for thy welfare; and therefore from sentiment of friendship as well as from fraternal affection I have spoken thus unto thee, O king. And what a friend from affection should do at a time like this, I shall do the same. See the havock I spread among the foes in fight. And, O long-armed one, behold, on Rāma having been slain by me on the edge of battle along with his brother, the monkey-army in headlong flight. And to-day seeing Rāma's head brought by me from the field, be thou, O long-armed one, happy; and let Sitā be overwhelmed with woe. And let those Rākshasas in Lankā who have had their kindred slain (in battle), see that dear sight—Rāma slain (in fight). And to-day shall I slaying the enemies in battle, wipe the tears of those who mourn their friends slain and are overwhelmed with grief. To-day behold the lord of monkeys—Sugriva—resembling a mountain or a mass of clouds lighted up by (the living) sun,—lying stretched on the field. But why, O sinless one, albeit comforted by these Rākshasas eager for slaying Daçaratha's son, as well as by me,—dost thou persist in thy sorrow? Rāghava forsooth shall slay thee after slaying me. But, O lord of Rākshasas, I cannot come by grief* (at Rāghava's hands). O repressor of foes, do thou now command me, O thou of unparalleled prowess, thou needst not thyself face the foe in fight. I shall abolish thy foes endowed with redoubted might. If even Sakra himself, and Yama, and the god of Fire, and the god of Wind, and Kuvera, and Varuna—shall range themselves against me, them shall I encounter in fight. Purandara himself is seized with fright at sight of me, having a body measuring a mountain,—equipped with sharpened spears,—furnished with sharp teeth,—and setting up shouts. And who wishing to save himself shall be able to stay before me as I casting away my weapons keep pounding my enemies with celerity? No need of the dart, or the mace, or the sword, or whetted arrows. I shall with my bare arms alone slay (Rāma) along with the thunderer himself. If Rāghava bear the impetus of my blows, then shall the vollies of my shafts drink his life-blood. Why, O king, while I remain, dost thou burn in anxiety? And I am ready to sally out for compassing the destruction of thine enemies. Cast off all terror of Rāma. I shall slay in battle Rāghava and Lakshmana and the exceedingly powerful Sugriva and the Raksha-destroying Hanumān, who made Lankā blaze. I shall eat up the monkeys present in the encounter. And signal is the celebrity that I shall confer on thee. And, O king, if thy fear springs from Indra

---

* *Santâpam gachchheyam—come by grief.* According to the commentator *santâpa* means *fear*; and the sense is: *I entertain no fear (on account of Râma.)*—*T.*

or the Self-create, even the immortals shall measure their lengths on the earth when I am wrought with rage. And I shall subdue Yama himself and devour the God of Fire. And I shall bring down the very welkin garnished with stars. And I shall slay Satakratu and drink up the abode itself* of Varuna. And I shall crush the mountains and rive the earth. And to-day let all creatures as they are being eaten up, witness the prowess of Kumbhakarna, after he hath slept for a long time. Even the celestial regions do not suffice for me as my fare. I go for securing felicity ushuring in pleasures plenteous flowing from the destruction of Daçaratha's son. And slaying Rāma along with Lakshmana, I shall eat up all the foremost of monkey-bands. Make merry,my king ; to-day drink Vāruni. Enjoy pleasures, banishing sorrow. And to-day on my having despatched Rāma to the mansion of Yama, Sitā shall come under thy control for good."

## SECTION LXIV.

HEARING the speech of the huge-bodied, long-armed and mighty Kumbhakarna, Mahodara said,—"O Kumbhakarna, although sprung in a noble line, thou art wondrous haughty and of a vulgar form; and thou art not everywhere competent to discern thy course. It certainly cannot well be that the king cannot distinguish between proper and improper ; but thou hast from thy youth upwards been insolent ; and thy joy is in talking perenially. But the foremost of the Rākshasas is versed in place and increase and injury,—and knoweth the duties touching season and place,—and how to advance his own party and lower that of the foe. But what

* Ocean.

person ever acteth according to what is proposed feebly* by one having strength, yet of inferior intelligence, and who hath never respected the aged? And thou art not naturally competent to understand what thou thyself sayest touching the opposed virtue, profit and desire. Verily action is the spring of all agencies of happiness or misery; and it is only those that act either well or ill that reap the results of their acts. Virtue,† and interest‡ bring about emancipation as well as heaven and prosperity. But evil cometh from unrighteousness and harms spring therefrom.§ People reap the fruit of their acts in this world or the next; but the fruit of desire is reaped readily. Therefore should a king set about attaining his desire. And this also had we advised thee with our soul. And what is the harm that one should display his prowess before a foe? Dost thou show the reasons for thy taking the field alone? But I shall point thee out what is improper and unreasonable in this (proposed) course. How shalt thou alone vanquish that Rāghava who formerly routed in Janasthāna innumerable Rākshasas possessed of exceeding strength? Dost thou not to-day in the palace behold those prowerful Rākshasas that had been beaten in Janasthāna,—cowed down in fear? Alas! thou wishest to awake Rāma,—son unto Daçaratha—knowing full well that he resembles an enraged lion or a sleeping serpent. But whom doth it behove

* *Vaktum açakyam—incapable of saying.* But what sense can be attached to—"What man acteth according to what is *not* advanced by one having strength......aged?" I therefore venture to render the passage—*feebly proposed—i.e. proposed with vascillation or half-heartedly.—T.*

† The maxims enunciated by this counsellor are hardly all of a piece. The text may have been tampered with.—T.

‡ *Artha* means sacrifices, gifts, &c., which are capable of being performed with wealth. 'Sacrifice, gift, and asceticism purify the pious.' *The Lord's word.—T.*

§ *Dharma*, remarks Rāmanuja, is here used for contemplation and recitation of scriptural formula performed without regard to happiness as the fruit of those actions. This is what hath been termed *nishkâm dharma*—disinterested piety.—T.

to confront him ever flaming in energy, difficult of being approached when enraged,—and unbearable even like Death himself? On approaching the foe, this whole host itself shall be imperilled; and therefore, my child, thy marching alone doth nowise recommend itself to me. Who is there that, albeit weak bent on renouncing his life, wisheth to bring under subjection a foe that is powerful,—as if he would act with reference to one that is inferior? O foremost of Rākshasas, why dost thou wish to fight with him whose peer there is none among men, and who is equal to Indra and Vivaçwata himself?" Having said this unto Kumbhakarna wrought up with wrath, Mahodara addressed that destroyer of creatures—Rāvana—in the midst of the Rākshasas,—"Having already obtained Vaidehi, why dost thou delay? If thou wishest it, Sitā shall come under thy control. I have perceived a way as to how Sitā may smile upon thee. Do thou listen; and should it please thee, act thou accordingly. Do thou proclaim it about that I and Dwijibha and Sanhrādi, and Kumbhakarna and Vitardana—these five—are marching for compassing the destruction of Rāma. And we, marching out, shall battle with Rāma, putting forth our uttermost. And if we succeed in securing victory, no expedient need we resort to (or bringing Sitā round). But if our foe live after fight and we also having faught the fight, then shall we do what I conceive in my mind. We shall come hither from the field, bathed in blood, and having our bodies cleft with arrows marked with the name of Rāma. And we shall give out that both Rāma and Lakshmana have been eaten up by us. And then we shall hold thy feet, saying,—'Do thou gratify us.' Then, O king, do thou through Gajaskandha publish it all round that Rāma hath been slain along with his brother and the army. And, O repressor of foes, (pretending to be) well pleased, do thou dispense—viands, and servants, and objects of enjoyments, and wealth unto thy retainers; and unto the many heroes and warriors distribute wreaths and attires and unguents. And do thou (simulating) delight, drink. And on this report—name that Rāma hath been eaten up by the Rākshasas along with his friends,—having spread round and round and entering (the açoka wood), and soothing and pacifying Sitā in solitude, allure her with corn and riches and gems. By this deceit, O king, working powerfully through Sitā's sorrow, she, albeit unwilling, shall, having lost her lord, come under thy control. Losing her charming husband, she from despair and female frailty, shall come under thy sway. Having formerly been brought up in happiness, she, although worthy of felicity, (ultimately) had come by misfortune. And now finding happiness to be in thy custody, she shall unreservedly come over to thee. In my opinion this is the properest course to follow. As soon as thou seest Rāma, evil shall befall thee. Remain here. Do not wish (to go to the field). By refraining from fight, thou shalt acquire great good. And, O lord of people, by conquering the foe without battle, thou without losing thy forces and putting thyself to peril, thou, O lord of earth, shalt attain fame and high religious merit, and prosperity and renown for ever and for ever.

## SECTION LXV.

THUS addressed, Kumbhakarna rebuking Mahodara, said unto that foremost of Rākshasa—his brother—Rāvana,—"Even I shall remove thy great fear by slaying the wicked-minded Rāma. On thy foe having been slain, attain thou ease. It is not for naught that the heroes roar, like unto clouds containing no rain.* Behold thou their roaring resulting in action in the field! Heroes do not vaunt; but

* *i. e.* autumnal clouds and which roar but do not pour.—T.

without boasting of their prowess in speech, they perform feats difficult of being achieved. O Mahodara, what thou sayest is ever acceptable only to kings that are incompetent, and foolish, pluming themselves on their knowledge. All the affairs of the monarch have been wrecked by you—cravens in fight,—sleek-tongued,—following the king (fawning) ye have made Lankā contain only the king, the treasury is lean; and the forces have been slain. By the king ye have done like foes in the guise of friends. For repairing in mighty conflict the wrong that ye have perpetrated, I am about to set out for battle for routing the enemy." Thus addressed by the intelligent Kumbhakarna, the lord of Rākshasas, laughing answered,—"Sure this Mahodara is affrighted at Rāma. And therefore, my child, O thou versed in warfare, he doth not relish battle. Like thee have I none either in friendship or strength. Therefore, O Kumbhakarna, go for destroying the foe and securing celebrity. I have waked thee up that wast lying down, in order that thou mightst destroy the enemy. O subduer of foes, perilous is the time for the Rākshasas. Go forth, grasping thy spear, like the noose-handed Destroyer himself. Do thou devour up the monkeys as well as the princes possessed of the energy of the Sun himself. On seeing thy form, the monkeys shall flee away; and the breasts of Rāma and Lakshmana shall be riven." Having spoken thus unto Kumbhakarna endowed with prodigious might, that foremost of Rākshasas—the exceedingly energetic Rāvana—felt as if he had received life over again. And well acquainted with Kumbhakarna's might, and knowing his prowess, the king felt delighted, like the cloudless Moon." Having been thus accosted, that highly powerful one, went out cheerfully.* And hearing the king's speech, he made ready for fight. And he took a whetted dart, destructive to foes on account of its impetuous

* He did not, however go yet awhile.—T.

vehemence ; entirely made of black iron ; flaming ; decorated with garniture, of shining gold ; looking like Indra's *açani* ; ponderous as the thunder-bolt ; capable of destroying gods and Dānavas, Gandharvas, Yakshas and Pannagas ; adorned with festoons of crimson flowers ; and belching forth flames. And taking that huge dart decked with the blood of foes ; the wondrous energetic Kumbhakarna spoke unto Rāvana, saying,—"I shall go alone : let this mighty host remain here. To-day hungry and enraged, I shall devour up the monkeys. Hearing Kumbhakarna's words, Rāvana said,—"Go thou, surrounded by the forces bearing darts and maces in their hands. The monkeys are high-souled, heroic and well-skilled in battle ; and if they find thee alone or unwary, they may slay thee with their teeth. Therefore do thou exceedingly irrisistible, go, environed by the forces ; and destroy the entire party of the foes, who are bent upon doing harm unto the Rakshas." Then starting up from his seat, the exceedingly energetic Rāvana hung on Kumbhakarna's neck a wreath stringed with gems in the centre. And Rāvana also decked that high-souled one with *angadas*, and finger-fences, and noble ornaments, and a chain resembling the Moon. And Rāvana adorned his person with garlands gorgeous and fragrant, and set ear-rings to his ears. And adorned with golden *angadas* and Keyuras and other ornaments of gold, the large-eared Kumbhakarna appeared like a fire fed full of sacrificial libations. And with his great dark girdle he seemed like the Mandara fastened by the serpent on the occasion of the churning of the sea. And donning on his impenetrable golden mail,splendid like lightning, and shining in its own brilliance, Kumbhakarna appeared like the monarch of mountains enveloped with evening clouds. Having all his limbs adorned with ornaments, and bearing a dart in his hand, the Rākshasa resembled Nārāyana in elation of spirits, when he covered heaven and earth and the nether regions with three paces. And then embracing his brother and going round him and bowing down the head unto him, that exceedingly powerful one went out. And Rāvana sent him with choice benedictions,—while he caused kettle-drums and conchs to be sounded and forces equipped with excellent weapons, to accompany Kumbhakarna. And high-souled mighty warriors followed that foremost of heroes with elephants and steeds and chariots sending out rattle resembling the rumbling of thunder. And mounting serpents and camels and asses and lions and leopards and deer and birds, (Rākshasas) followed the grim Kumbhakarna endowed with tremendous strength. And strewn with blossoms, and, with an umbrella held over him, that exceedingly terrible enemy of the Deities and the Dānavas, wielding a dart in his hand, —went out maddened with the smell of blood. And countless footmen wondrous powerful and mighty and dreadful and fierce-sighted Rākshasas,carrying weapons in their hands, went in his wake. The Rakshas measuring each many a *vyāma* and red, eyed, and resembling masses of dark-blue collyrium,—went out upraising darts and swords and sharpened axes and *bhindipālas* and *parighas* and maces and huge *tālaskandhas* and irrisistible *Kshapanis.* And the exceedingly energetic Kumbhakarna endowed with prodigious strength sallied forth, assuming another form terrific and dreadful to behold. And the gigantic huge-faced and fierce Kumbhakarna, measuring an hundred bows in breadth and six hundred in altitude, having eyes resembling car-wheels, and resembling a towering hill, or a mountain burnt,—marshalling the Rakshas, said with a complacent countenance, —"Like fire consuming insects, shall I to-day, wrought up with wroth, burn up one by one the bands of the flower of the monkey-forces. But the wood-ranging monkeys have not transgressed anywise unto the like of us. That species is the ornament of the gardens attached to our residences. The cause of the seige of the city is Rāghava along with Lakshmana. He being slain, all are slain. Therefore shall

I slay him in battle." As the Raksha—Kumbhakarna—was speaking thus, the Rākshasas sent up terrific shouts, as if making the very sea shake. As the intelligent Kumbhakarna sallied out speedily, dreadful were the omens that presented themselves on all sides. Clouds containing meteors and lightning looked dark like asses. And the earth shook with her oceans and woods. And fierce jackals began to cry, opening their flaming mouths. And birds began to wheel at the left. And as he marched a vulture alighted on his dart. And his left eye throbbed and his left arm shook. And a meteor dropped down with a tremendous crash. And the sun was bedimmed, and the air did not blow, enhancing pleasure. But without heeding these mighty omens that took place, capabale of making people's down stand on end, Kumbhakarna went out, urged on by the force of the Finisher. And leaping over the wall with his legs, that one resembling a mountain saw the wonderful array of the monkeys, resembling clouds. And seeing that foremost of Rākshasas resembling a hill, the monkeys began to disperse in all the ten cardinal directions like clouds driven by the wind. And seeing that terrific host of monkeys scattering in all directions, like clouds broken through (by winds), Kumbhakarna possessed of the splendour of clouds, from joy, emitted roars like clouds. Hearing those terrible shouts like unto the roaring of clouds in the welkin, innumerable monkeys dropped to the earth even as *sâla* trees that have their roots severed. And issuing forth for destroying the foe, the high-souled Kumbhakarna, equipped with a tremendous bludgeon, struck extreme terror into the monkey-ranks, like unto the Lord armed with the Fatal rod at the Universal wreck.

## SECTION LXVI.

HAVING leapt over the wall, the exceedingly powerful and gigantic Kumbhakarna resembling a mountain-summit, speedily went out of the city. And then he sent up a mighty shout making the sea resound, and as if drowning the roar of the thunder and riving mountains. And seeing that fierce-eyed one, incapable of being vanquished by Maghavān or Varuna or Yama, the monkeys began to fly away. And seeing them scamper, the king's son—Angada—said unto Nala and Nila and Gavāksha and the mighty Kumuda,—"Forgetting your lineage and prowess, whither do ye, exercised with fear, fly,—like inferior monkeys? Ye amiable ones, desist. Why should ye save yourselves? This Raksha doth not come to fight,—this is only a great phenomenon to affright. We shall by our vigor destroy this fearful phenomenon of the Rākshasas that hath presented itself. Therefore, let the monkeys desist. Cheered with much ado, the monkeys rallying, took up trees and advanced to the field of fight. And ceasing from flight, the wood-rangers waxing enraged, began to assail Kumbhakarna, like unto elephants in rut. And the exceedingly strong* Kumbhakarna, attacked with towering mountain-peaks and crags and trees with flowering top, did not shake. And countless crags descending on his person, were shattered; and trees with flowering tops, being broken, fell down to the earth. And incapable of containing himself (through rage), Kumbhakarna on his part fell to agitating the ranks of the powerful monkeys, even as a fire breaking out burneth down a forest. And many a prime monkey, crimsoned and drenched (with blood) lay down (on the ground); and many, resisted dropped to the earth, like trees bearing coppery flowers. And without looking before

* *Mahavalāh—plu*—evidently a misprint for *mahavalah*—sing.—T.

or after, the monkeys bounded and rushed. And on being attacked by the Rākshasa with ease some of those heroes dropped into the deep, and some entered the wilderness. And some ran by the same way by which they had crossed the ocean; and some with pale faces darted into downs. And some of the bears ascended up trees, and some took shelter in mountains. And others dropped* down; and some ran on. And some fell down to the earth, and some lay insensible† as if dead. Seeing the monkeys break down, Angada addressed them, saying,—"Stay we shall fight. Desist, ye monkeys. Going round this Earth place find I none where ye may rest. Stop ye all. What is the need of preserving your lives. Ye poltroons, if ye fly away leaving your arms behind, your wives shall deride you; and that is more painful to honorable persons than death itself. Born in long and noble lines, whither go ye, suffering from fear, like abject monkeys? When renouncing your prowess, ye fly away in fear, forsooth ye are base. Where now is gone that talk of yours anent your nobility and the welfare (of your king) which you had held in society. He that liveth, despised (of all), hear the reproach of being a craven. Therefore do ye follow the way frequented by the worthy, and cast off fear. We will either lie down on the earth, being slain in consequence of our shortness of days, and thus attain the region of Brahmā incapable of being attained by dastards; or achieve renown by slaying the foe in fight and slain in battle, we shall enjoy the wealth of the region of heroes. Like an insect coming to a glowing and flaming fire, Kumbhakarna, seeing Kākutstha, shall not away hence living. If we save our lives by flight, and if the many are brought down by one, we shall lose our fame utterly." As Angada decked in golden *angadas* was saying this, the monkeys, flying away spake unto that hero words not worthy of being spoken unto an

* *For fighting*, remarks the commentator.

† *Suptāh—sleeping*; but here, I presume, it means *senseless*.—T.

hero,—"Great is the havoc that the Rākshasa—Kumbhakarna—hath spread amongst us. 'Tis not the time to stay : life is dear unto us." Having said this the monkey-bands darted to the ten cardinal points ; as they saw that dreadful and grim-eyed one approach. And as those flower of the forces were on the flight, those heroes were made to desist by Angada with words of comfort and hope pointing to the future. On being cheered by the intelligent son of Vāli, all the monkey-bands stood expecting his commands.—

---

## SECTION LXVII.

And having desisted on hearing the words of Angada, those huge-bodied ones, regaining calmness, became (again) intent on fight. And attaining energy at the exhortation (of Angada), and summoning up their prowess, they stayed in the field agreeably to the words of the powerful Angada. And inspired with spirits, the monkeys, determined to face their fate, rushed into the conflict, and, casting away all care for their lives, entered into a furious fight (with the foe). And speedily upraising trees and gigantic crags, the huge-bodied monkeys charged Kumbhakarna. Thereat the mighty Kumbhakarna possessed of a prodigious person waxing wroth, taking up his mace let the same alight on the enemies. And attacked by Kumbhakarna, seven, eight hundreds and thousands of monkeys measure their lengths on the earth. And casting about his arms, he rusheth on, devouring sixteen, eight, ten, twenty or thirty. And he devoured (the monkeys) like Garura swallowing up serpents. And then cheered up with much ado, the monkeys meeting together, and taking trees and rocks in their hands, stood their ground in the van of battle. Then uprooting a crag, Dwivida—foremost of monkeys—resembling an extended mass of clouds rushed against (Kumbhakarna) having the aspect of a mountain-summit. And uprooting it, the monkey hurled it at Kumbhakarna. And without descending on him, the crag fell down amidst the army, and smashed steeds and elephants and cans and choice chargers. And then taking another mountain top, Dwivida hurled it at other Rakshas. And smit with the impetus of the peak, Kumbhakarna had his chargers and his charioteers slain; and the terrific field overflowed with the blood of Rakshas. And Rākshasa car-warriors by means of arrows resembling the Destroyer himself, cut off the heads of the foremost monkeys who had been setting up roars. And the high-souled monkeys also, uprooting giants trees, destroyed cars and horses and elephants and camels and Rākshasas.—And remaining in the sky, Hanumān discharged at Kumbhakarna's head mountain-peaks and rocks and various trees. And all those mountain-tops he cut off with his dart; and the mighty Kumbhakarna also baffled the shower of trees.—Then grasping his sharpened spear, Kumbhakarna darted against that terrific array of monkeys. And as he charged them, Hanumān armed with a mountain-peak, stood before him. And waxing enraged (Hanumān) vehemently smote Kumbhakarna with a gigantic crag. And overpowered by that, Kumbhakarna experienced great torments, and his body was covered with fat and blood. And then as Guha had pierced Krauncha with his fierce dart, Kumbhakarna the mountain-like smote the Wind-god's son in the chest with his dart resembling lightning or like a glowing mountain-summit. And having his mighty chest pierced in the mighty encounter, Hanumān, overwhelmed, and vomitting blood,—transported with wrath, set up roars resembling the roaring of the clouds at the universal disruption. And then, beholding him in torments, the Rakshas suddenly rejoiced, emitted shouts; and the monkeys aggrieved and overcome with fright, began to fly Kumbhakarna in battle. And then the powerful Nila, arranging his forces, discharged a mountain-peak at the intelligent Kumbhakarna. And seeing it descend, he dealt it a blow; and struck by the blow, the mountain-top was shattered in pieces; and dropped to the earth glowing and shooting living flames. And then Rishabha and Sarabha and Nila and Gavāksha and Gandhamâdana—these five terrific monkeys—rushed against Kumbhakarna. And in the encounter those mighty monkeys began to sorely assail the huge-bodied Kumbhakarna with crags and trees and slaps and kicks and blows. But those blows seemed to him like touches* and did not at all pain him. Then he fastened the vehement Rishabha with his arms. And agonised on being fastened with Kumbhakarna's arms, that foremost of monkeys, the dreadful Rishabha, fell down to the earth, vomitting blood by his mouth. And then the enemy of Indra smit, Sarabha with blow, and Nila, in the conflict with his thigh, struck a slap at Gavāksha. And suffering great pain in consequence of the blows (dealt by Kumbhakarna those monkeys), deprived of their senses and bathed in blood, dropped down to the earth like Kinçukas that have been cut down. And on those high-souled and mighty monkeys falling down, thousands of monkeys rushed at Kumbhakarna. And ascending a mountain-summit, those foremost of monkeys,† possessed of the splendour of a mountain-peak, sprang upon him and tore him with their teeth. And those foremost of monkeys attacked the long-armed Kumbhakarna with their claws and teeth and blows and arms. And then with thousands of monkeys on him that extraordinary one that fearful Rākshasa —resembling a hill,—looked like a mountain with trees on it. And like Garura eating up serpents, that wondrous

* *Like the feel*, remarks Râmânuja, *of wreaths, unguents, etc.—T.*

† *Plavaganshavâh*—foremost of the monkeys occurs twice—one is left out in the translation.—T.

strong one, wrought up with rage, devoured those monkeys, seizing them with his arms. And cast by Kumbhakarna into his mouth resembling the nether regions the monkeys emerged from his nose and ears. And eating up the monkeys, that foremost of Rākshasas resembling a hill, growing wroth, and fired with rage,* began to break the monkeys down.—And transported with passion, that Rākshasa, making the earth miry with flesh and blood, spread among the monkey-ranks like unto the fire at the time of the Universal dissolution. And in that encounter, Kumbhakarna armed with his dart in his hand, resembled the thunder-handed Sakra, or the noose-handed Destroyer himself. And as a conflagration† burneth up a withered forest in the summer, Kumbhakarna burnt that host of the monkeys. And thus beaten (by Kumbhakarna), those monkeys, with their ranks destroyed, the monkeys,‡ racked with anxiety, began to cry in unnatural tones. And having innumerable monkeys slain by Kumbhakarna, the monkeys, aggrieved and their hearts riven with sorrow, sought the shelter of Rāghava. Seeing the monkeys broken in the terrific encounter, the son of the thunder-handed,§ darted impetuously against Kumbhakarna. And taking up a mighty crag, he momentarily setting up roars, and thereby terroizing all the Rākshasas—followers of Kumbhakarna, he discharged the mountain-peak right against Kumbhakarna's crown.—And struck with that mountain-peak, Indra's enemy—Kumbhakarna—flamed up in fierce wrath. And the loud-throated Kumbhakarna, terrifying all the monkeys vehemently darted against the enraged son of Vāli; and then that wondrous strong one hurled his dart

---

* *Sankrudha*—infuriated, and Krudha, *angered*—this pleonasm is in the text.—T.

† The text has *pāvaka*—fire.—*T.*

‡ *Plavangamāh* and *vanarāh*—both mean *monkeys*. One is left out.—T.

§ The *thunder-handed* is Indra—his son is Vāli; and Vāli's son is Angada, who is meant in the text.—T.

at Angada. And as the dart descended, that foremost of monkeys endowed with strength,* and skilled in battle, evaded the weapon from his fleetness. And then swiftly springing up, he slapped (his antagonist) in the chest. And thereat that one resembling a hill, lost his senses. And recovering his senses, that exceedingly strong Rākshasa, dealt a blow at Angada; and the latter dropped down senseless. And on that powerful monkey falling down insensible, Kumbhakarna, taking his dart, rushed against Sugriva. And seeing the exceeding stout Kumbhakarna approach, the heroic king of monkeys—Sugriva—sprang up; and taking a mountain-top that one possessed of great strength darted against the mighty Kumbhakarna. And seeing that monkey, Kumbhakarna, stretching his limbs, stood before the lord of monkeys. And seeing Kumbhakarna, with his body laved in the blood of monkeys; and eating up mighty monkeys, Sugriva addressed him, saying,—"Thou hast felled heroes done deeds difficult of being performed, and hast devoured the warriors; and thou hast thus attained renown. But let go now the monkey-army. What shalt thou do with the ignoble? Do thou, O Rākshasa bear the descent of this mountain." Hearing those words of the monkey-king instinct with strength and fortitude, that terrible Rākshasa—Kumbhakarna—said,—"O monkey, thou stormest, because thou art the grandson of Prajāpati† and the son of the king of bears; and because as such thou art endowed with fortitude and prowess." Hearing Kumbhakarna's speech, Sugriva whirling that mountain-peak, suddenly let it go; and with that rock resembling *Vajra* or the thunder-bolt, smote Kumbhakarna in the chest. And on coming in contact with his wide breast, that mountain-peak was at once shattered in shivers. And thereat the monkeys grew

* *Valavān*—strong occurs twice.

† *Riksharajas*—the father of Sugriva, was produced from the yawning of Prajāpati or Brahmā.—T.

dispirited and the Rākshasa's ranks shouted in joy. And struck with the mountain-summit, Kumbhakarna was fired with wrath; and roared, expending his face. And then, whirling his dart resembling lightning displayed, he hurled it for compassing the destruction of the master of monkeys. Then swiftly bounding up, the Wind-god's son, resisting that whetted dart fastened with golden chains,—with his hands violently snapped it in twain. And placing the same on his thighs, (Hanumān) snapped that ponderous and terrible dart composed of black iron, and thereat the monkeys waxed delighted. And seeing the dart severed by Hanumān, the monkey-army, growing delighted, set up countless shouts and rushed in all directions. And the Rākshasa was seized with fear and turned away (from the field.) And the monkeys excessively delighted, set up loud shouts, and finding the dart broken, poured forth thanks to the Wind-god's son. Then the mighty-minded lord of Rākshasas seeing the dart thus severed, uprooted a peak from the Malaya and with it smote Sugriva. The king of monkeys struck with the mountain-peak fell senseless upon the field, and the demons finding him in this plight shouted out in great joy. Then Kumbhakarna coming to the wonderfully mighty master of monkeys, took him up and stole away from the field, as a violent gust of wind stealeth away a patch of cloud. Kumbhakarna, who resembled a mountain in loftiness of stature, while taking him away like a mass of cloud appeared like Sumeru overtopped with lofty peaks. Thus the lord of Rākshasas went on hearing thanks (from the Rākshasas) and shouts from the lords of the heavens, wondered at the capture of the foremost of monkeys. Thus taking him captive, that mighty one resembling Indra in puissance, thought his death would destroy the entire host of the opponents together with Rāghava. Then Hanumān,the shrewd son of Maruta, finding the whole host of monkeys scattered in all directions, as well as Sugriva captured by Kumbhakarna bethought himself—

"What ought to be done by me now that our king has been captured? I will doubtless do as befits me now—let me assume the shape of a mountain and kill the Râkshasas. Let me kill the mighty Kumbhakarna, splitting his body with my strong fist and thus relieve the master of monkeys—thus let the whole host of monkeys become delighted. Or, even when captured by the whole host of gods or Asuras or serpents he is mighty enough to extricate himself. Meseems, the lord of monkeys struck with dart in battle by Kumbhakarna has not yet recovered his senses. Else in a moment he would do the needful for himself as well as the monkeys. Should the relief of the mighty-minded Sugriva come from me, I should be incurring his displeasure and it would certainly lead to the loss of his reputation for ever; then I must wait a moment and see his own might displayed by himself when relieved. Meanwhile let me cheer up the monkey-host." Thinking thus within himself, Hanumân, that son of Maruta, began to stay the mighty host of monkeys. In the meantime Kumbhakarna entered Lankâ with Sugriva trembling, being honored with the showering of beautiful flowers from the sky, the buildings on the main roads and the town-gate. Then the mighty one (Sugriva) slowly recovered his senses with the shower of fried paddy and sweet scent and the sprinkling of water as well as with the coolness of the streets. Then that mighty-minded (Sugriva), caught in the arms of the powerful Râkshasa, having with difficulty come to his senses and surveying around him the streets of the town bethought himself:—"When thus within the grasp of the enemy how can I take revenge? Or let me do what will be acceptable and advantageous to our army." Then advancing all on a sudden, he with his nails and sharp teeth cut off the ears and nose of that lord of the enemies of the gods and split both his sides with the blow of his feet. And Kumbhakarna losing his ears and nose and having his sides split with nails and teeth grew angry, and becoming all covered over with blood, threw Sugriva to the ground and pressed him. Thus pressed upon the ground with main force and severely struck by the enemies of gods, he flew to the skies like a ball-rolling, and once more joined Rāma. The mighty Kumbhakarna having lost his nose and ears and drenched in blood, appeared like a mountain covered all over with streamlets. That huge-bodied Rākshasa, younger brother of Rāvana, terrible in appearance, resembling a mass of deep black collyrium, and covered all over with blood, appeared like an evening cloud; and (once more) made up his mind to appear in battle. Sugriva having thus escaped, that dreadful enemy of the king of the celestials in wrath again rushed to battle; and finding himself destitute of arms took up a fearful mace. And then that mighty-minded one, the Raksha Kumbhakarna, issuing out of the city began to devour the terrific host of monkeys, as doth the mighty fire eat up people at the end of a Yuga. On entering the mighty host of monkeys,the hungry Kumbhakarna, hankering after flesh and blood,ate up the monkeys,and with them,devoured many a Rākshasa and Pisācha by,mistake. Thus, as Death devoureth creatures at the end of a Yuga, he destroyed the mighty monkeys. And he in wrath,taking up with one hand the monkeys along with the Rākshasas, hurriedly threw them into his mouth,—one,two three,or many at a time. And blood and fat flowed copiously down his body; and though struck by the monkeys with peaks of mountains, the mighty one devoured all those monkeys. And the monkeys as they were being devoured, saught the shelter of Rāma. And Kumbhakarna wrought up with wrath, chased amain hundreds of monkeys, eating up seven, eight, twenty, or thirty. And fastening (the monkeys) with his arms, he, devouring them, rushed on. And resembling the Destroyer of prodigious dimensions at the end of a Yuga, that one furnished with extremely sharp teeth, having his body covered with fat, marrow and blood, and coiling entrails about his ears, began to discharge darts. And at this moment, that subduer of hostile hosts and captor of the capitals of foes—Sumitrā's son—Lakshmana, growing enraged, entered on an encounter with the enemy. And Lakshmana endued with prowess shot seven shafts at Kumbhakarna's body; and next, taking up other arrows also discharged them (at his antagonist). And thereat that Rākshasa, smarting under the wounds inflicted by that weapon,* cut it off (by means of a weapon). Thereupon grew enraged the powerful Lakshmana—enhancer of Sumitrā's joy. And then as the wind overspreadeth evening clouds, he with his shafts covered his† shining and graceful mail entirely made of gold. And smit with arrows dight with gold, that one resembling a mass of dark-blue collyrium appeared beautiful like the ray-furnished Sun surrounded by clouds. Then that dreadful Rākshasa voiced like masses of clouds, scornfully addressed the enhancer of Sumitrā's felicity, saying,—"By dauntlessly fighting with me, who have without ado brought down the Destroyer himself in battle, thou hast established thy heroism. Even by staying before me, who am equipped with arms in this encounter, and who in mighty conflict resemble Death himself, thou deservest to be honored. What shall I say of thy fighting? Not even that lord—Sakra himself—mounted on his Airāvata, and engirt by all the immortals,—had ever before stayed before me in the field. But to-day, O Sumitrā's son, albeit a boy, thou hast gratified me with thy prowess. Now taking thy leave, I wish to go to Rāghava. And as I have been well pleased in battle with thy vigour and strength and enthusiasm, I now wish to slay Rāma alone, who being slain, all are slain. On Rāma being here slain by me, the rest remaining in the encounter—them shall I undertake with my all-crushing vigour." When that Raksha had spoken thus,

* But Lakshmana had *not* discharged a single weapon only against Kumbhakarna.—T.

† Kumbhakarna's.

(Lakshmana), Sumitrâ's son,present in that contest, answered him laughing in terrible words,saying,—"That thy prowess is incapable of being borne by Sakra and other celestials,—is true. It is not otherwise, O hero. To-day I myself have witnessed thy prowess. Yonder is Daçaratha's son—Rāma—staying like a moveless mountain." Hearing this,that night-ranger —Kumbhakarna—possessed of immense might, disregarding Lakshmana and passing beyond Sumitrâ's son, rushed against Rāma, making the earth tremble. Thereat Daçaratha's son, Rāma, employing a terrific weapon, discharged sharpened shafts at Kumbhakarna's breast. Thereat flames mixed with live embers shot out from the mouth of that enraged one suddenly rushing (against Rāma),—as Rāma pierced him (with his arrows). And on being frightfully pierced by Rāma's weapons,that foremost of Rākshasas,roaring wrathfully darted against Rāma, and pursued the monkeys in the conflict. And those shafts adorned with peacock's plumes, alighting on ( Kumbhakarna's ) chest, his mace, escaping his hand, dropped to the earth ; and all his (other) arms also were scattered on the ground. And when that exceedingly powerful one saw himself deprived of all his arms, he began to spread a huge havoc by means of his clenched fists and hands. And with his body entirely covered with arrows and bathed in blood, he began to bleed like a hill overflowing with fountains. And fired with wrath and maddened with blood,* he rusheth on, devouring monkeys and Rakshasas and bears. And that redoubtable one possessed of dreadful prowess, resembling the Reaper himself, whirling a mighty mountain-peak, hurled it aiming at Rāma. Thereat Bharata's elder brother, the righteous Rāma, ere that prodigious peak had alighted, severed the same by means of seven straight-speeding shafts wrought with gold. Intent on finishing Kumbhakarna, the virtuous Lakshmana, revolving many a means, (at last) spoke unto Rāma,—"O king, this one

* Perhaps with the *smell* of blood.—T.

knoweth not monkeys and Rākshasas,—maddened with the smell of blood, he eateth up his own as well as his enemies. Now let the foremost monkeys, putting forth their best, mount on him; and let the leaders of bands according to their rank, stand surrounding him. And then to-day this wicked-minded Rākshasa, oppressed with a mighty weight, will no longer be able to eat up any more monkeys." Hearing the words of the intelligent prince, those exceedingly powerful monkeys with alacrity ascended Kumbhakarna. And Kumbhakarna mounted by those monkeys, waxing exceedingly enraged, shook them vehemently, even as mad elephants shake the drivers thereof. And Rāghava seeing them shaken, and concluding the Rākshasa to be wroth, furiously sprang forward, taking his bow. And with his eyes crimsoned with choler, the gentle Rāghava, as if burning up the Rākshasa with his eyes, rushed forth vehemently, summoning up all his impetuosity, thereby cheering up the leaders of bands that had been sore tried by the might of Kumbhakarna. And equipped with an excellent quiver and arrows, Rāma cheering up the monkeys sprang forward, taking a bow, resembling a serpent; terrific; having a stout string; and embellished in gold. Then surrounded by exceedingly invincible monkey-bands, that highly powerful hero, followed by Lakshmana, marched forth. And he saw the redoubtable and high-souled Kumbhakarna, with his body drenched in blood, and with blood-shot eyes; rushing against all, like unto an infuriated elephant of the cardinal points; pursuing the monkeys; wrought up with wrath; environed by Rākshasas; appearing like the Vindhya or the Mandara; decked with golden *angadas*; bleeding from his mouth; like clouds pouring showers; licking at the corners of his mouth laved with blood; smashing the monkey-ranks; and resembling Yama the Destroyer. And that best of persons, seeing that foremost of Rākshasas having the splendour of a living fire, stretched his bow to its full bent. And fired with wrath at the twang of his bow, that foremost of Rākshasas, inflamed with wrath,—not brooking that report, rushed against Rāghava. Thereat, the gentle Rāma, endowed with arms resembling the body of the sovereign of serpents, in that encounter addressed Kumbhakarna, like unto an elevated cloud and possessed of the splendour of a mountain,—as he darted forward, saying,—"Come, O king of Rakshas! Let no grief be thine! Here I stay, taking my bow in my hand. Know me for the destroyer of the race of the Rākshasas—thou who in a moment shalt be deprived of thy senses." Kowing that this was Rāma, (Kumbhakarna) laughed in frightful accents; and then, wrought up with wrath, rushed against the monkeys in the encounter. And as if riving the breasts of all the monkeys (present), the exceedingly energetic Kumbhakarna, laughing frightfully and in a terrific manner, —resembling the rumbling of clouds, addressed Rāghava, saying,—"Take me not for Virādha, or for Kavandha, or yet for Khara. I am not Vāli or Māricha. I am Kumbhakarna, that am come. Behold my dreadful and mighty mace entirely made of iron. By help of this I had formerly brought down deities and Dānavas. It doth not behove thee to scorn me in that my nose hath been severed. I do not feel any the smallest torment in consequence of my ears and nose having been cut off. O tiger of the Ikshwāku line, O sinless one, do thou witness the prowess that is in my frame. And thereafter, when thou shalt have displayed thy prowess and power, shall I devour thee up." Hearing Kumbhakarna's words, Rāma discharged (at him) shafts furnished with knobs. And smit with these having the impetus of the thunderbolt, the foe of the celestials did not feel any pain or smart. And those shafts which had severed the seven stately *sâlas*, and, to boot, had slain Vāli—best of monkeys,—they resembling the thunder itself—could not impart any pain to Kumbhakarna's body. And drinking up in his body those arrows resembling a shower, the enemy of the great Indra whirling his mace possessed of fierce vehemence, put out the arrowy discharge of Rāma. Then that Raksha whirling his mace washed in blood, capable of striking terror into the mighty hosts of gods and Dānavas, and possessed of fierce impetus,—made the monkey-army take to its heels. Then Rāma, taking a mighty *Vâyavya* weapon, used the same against the night-ranger; and cut off his arm with the mace. And having his arm cut off, he set up tremendous roars. And his arm with the mace, resembling a mountain-peak, cut off by Rāghava's arrows, fell in the midst of the army of the monkey-king, and destroyed that army,* Thereat the monkeys remaining after those broken and slain,—dispirited, and having their limbs wounded,—moving aside, looked on the dreadful encounter between the Raksha and the lord of men. And then Kumbhakarna, having his arm severed, resembling the foremost of mountains with its crest hewn away by a mighty sabre, tore up a tree with his (remaining) arm and in the conflict rushed against the monarch of men. Thereupon with a shaft plated in gold, set upon a weapon of Indra, Rāma cut off his uplifted arm with a palm tree, looking like the body of a *pannaga*. And that arm of Kumbhakarna, being severed, dropped inert on the earth, like a hill, and crushed trees and rocks and crags and monkeys and Rākshasas. And Rāma, seeing that one shorn of his arms suddenly spring up, roaring,—took up two whetted crescents, and in the contest cut off the legs of the Rākshasa. And thereupon those legs (of his), making all sides and quarters and rocks and caves and the mighty main and Lankā herself and the army of the monkeys and the Rākshasas,—resound,—dropped down (on the ground). And having his arms cut off and his legs also severed, (Kumbhakarna), opening wide his mouth resembling in sheen the mouth of a mare, roaring swiftly darted against Rāghava,—even as Rāhu pursueth the Moon in the firmament. Then Rāma stuffed his mouth full of

* This, of course, is not to be taken literally.—T.

sharpened shafts having their feathered parts furnished with gold. And having his mouth filled, he could not articulate; but with extreme effort uttered indistinct accents and swooned away. Then Rāma took an arrow of Indra,—whetted and knobbed, impetuous as the wind, resembling the effulgence of the Sun, and like unto the very banner of Brahmā, or the Destroyer himself; and fatal to foes. And then Rāma hurled it at the ranger of the night. And thereat that weapon hurled by Rāma's arm, resembling a smokeless flame, lighting up the ten cardinal points with its own glory,—saught him that was possessed of the dreadful energy of Sakra's thunder-bolt. And therewith he (Rāma) cut off the head of the lord of Rakshas resembling a mountain-summit, furnished with prominent teeth,—from which the ear-rings had fallen off,—even as formerly Purandara had cut off the head of Vritra. And then Kumbhakarna's huge head deprived of the ear-rings appeared like the Moon seated in the midst (of the heavens) on the rising of the Sun in the morning.† And struck with Rāma's arrow, the head of the Raksha resembling a hill fell down to the earth; and (in its fall) crushed edifices on the highways and gateways; and elevated walls also it bore down to the ground. And then that Raksha of gigantic proportions and vast to the view plunged into the deep; and crushing huge and mighty fishes and serpents, saught the depths. And on that enemy of the Brāhmanas and gods, endowed with immense strength,—having been slain in battle, the earth shook and the mountains also; and from excess of joy the celestials shouted aloud. And those deities and saints and Maharshis and Pannagas, and celestials and (other) beings and birds and Guhyakas, together with Yakshas and Gandharbas,—all these who had stationed themselves in the welkin,—were rejoiced at the prowess of Rāma. And at his (Kumbhakarna's) great destruction, the intelligent adherents of the king of Nairitas,—aggrieved exceedingly, began to cry at the sight

† This *sloka* is wanting in many texts.—T.

of that best of the Raghus, even as mad elephants cry at sight of a lion. And like unto the Sun emerged from the mouth of Rāhu, and destroying the darkness of the celestial fields,—shone Rāma in the midst of the monkey-army having slain Kumbhakarna in battle. And countless monkeys experienced the very height of delight ; and on (their) foe of terrific strength having been slain, they with countenances resembling awaked lotuses paid homage unto the king's son—Rāghava—the sharer of good fortune. And as the monarch of the immortals had rejoiced on slaying the mighty Asura—Vritra—Bharata's elder brother rejoiced on having in battle slain that smiter of celestial hosts, Kumbhakarna in mighty conflict, never (before) vanquished in renowned encounters.

## SECTION LXVIII.

SEEING Kumbhakarna slain by the high-souled Rāghava, the Rākshasas conveyed the tidings to the lord of the Rākshasas—Rāvana ; (and addressed him, saying),—"O king, that one resembling the Destroyer himself, urged on by Death,—having scoured the monkey-army and eaten up monkeys,—and for a while displayed his prowess, hath met with his quietus at the hands of Rāma exerting his energy. And with half his body immersed in the dreadful deep, thy brother, Kumbhakarna, with his nose and ears cut off, and blood besmearing his body,—with his head and limbs hewn away, and his body uncovered,—mountain-like blocketh up the gate of Lankā with his person,—and resembleth a tree that hath been consumed by a forest-fire." Hearing the mighty Kumbhakarna slain in battle, Rāvana burning in grief, swooned away and dropped to the earth. And hearing their uncle slain, Triçiras* and Atikāya—destroyers of gods and men,—began to weep, oppressed with sorrow. And Mahodara† and Mahāpārçwa‡ hearing of their uncle slain by Rāma of untiring deeds, were overcome with grief. Then regaining his senses with extreme exertion, that foremost of Rākshasas, distressed in consequence of the destruction of Kumbhakarna, mourned with his senses overwhelmed, saying,—"O hero! O humbler of the pride of the foe! O mighty Kumbhakarna! Leaving me, thou through Destiny, hast gone to the abode of Yama. O exceedingly powerful one, leaving me (lone) whither dost thou wend, without extracting my dart as well as that of thy friends? Now really I am not, inasmuch as my right arm hath dropped. Backed by this one, I would not fear celestials and Asuras. How to-day forsooth hath such a hero—crusher of the hauteur of gods and Dānavas—resembling the Fire arisen at the hour of universal wreck,—been slain in fight by Rāghava? He who could not be harmed by the concussion of the thunderbolt itself—how can he, smitten with Rāma's arrows, sleep soundly on the earth? These gods stationed in the sky along with the saints,—beholding thee slain in battle, are shouting in glee. Surely to-day the monkeys overjoyed,—finding occasion, will scale all the gateways and fortifications of Lankā. I have nothing to do with empire. And what shall I do with Sitā? And deprived of Kumbhakarna, I do not even wish to live. If I do not slay in encounter that slayer of my brother—Rāghava,—certainly death is even that which is good for me,—otherwise, this life is useless. This very day will I repair to that place where my younger brother is. Forsaking my brother, I forsooth dare not live for a moment; for the gods shall laugh on seeing me, who had formerly

* Three-headed.—T.

† Huge-bellied.—T.

‡ Mighty-flanked.—T.

wronged them. But, how, O Kumbhakarna, thou having been slain, shall I conquer Indra? Now the beneficial words of Bibhishana have been verified. And as through blindness I did not accept the advice of that high-souled one, Kumbhakarna and of Prahasta, this disaster arisen, shameth me sore. And as I had disgraced the virtuous and graceful Bibhishana, this peril producing grief, hath been the consequence of my conduct." Having thus piteously and long lamented Kumbhakarna, the Ten-necked one, with his inmost soul overwhelmed with sorrow, and sore distressed in consequence of grief,—fell down, knowing his brother—the enemy of Indra—slain in battle.

## SECTION LXIX.

HEARING the lamentations of the wicked-minded Rāvana, overwhelmed with grief, Triçiras addressed him, saying,—"O Sire, this second uncle unto us possessed of mighty prowess hath* forsooth been slain in fight. But, O king, heroes never indulge in grief as thou doest. O lord, thou certainly alone art competent to conquer the triple world. Wherefore then dost thou vent such sorrow like an ignoble one? Thou hast thy dart conferred on thee by Brahmā; and thy mail and thy weapon—the bow—and thy car yoked with a thousand asses, sending forth clatter resembling the rumbling of clouds. The deities and the Dānavas have by means of thy arms been terrified over and over again. And furnished with all arms, thou ought to chastise Rāghava. But stay at thy pleasure, O mighty sovereign, I will go out

* *Evameva—forsooth*, as I render it. The commentator, however, says it means *such as thou hast described him.—T.*

to battle ; and even as Garura captureth serpents, will I capture thine enemies. And as Samvara was vanquished by the lord of the immortals, or Naraka by Vishnu, will I bringing down Rāma in battle make him sleep (in the field)." Hearing Triçiras' words, Rāvana—lord of Rākshasas—urged on by Fate, considered himself as having regained his life. And hearing the speech of Triçiras, Devāntaka, and Narāntaka, and the energetic Atikāya also, were wrought up with martial enthusiasm. And then those foremost of Nairitas—the heroic sons of Rāvana—endowed with the prowess of Sakra himself—roared out, 'I will go,' 'I will go.' And all could range the sky, and all were skilled in illusion, and all were crushers of the pride of the immortals ; and all were irrisistible in encounter. And all of them were endowed with superior strength, and all had achieved wide celebrity. They had never been heard of as having been beaten in fight even by the gods along with the Gandharvas, or the mighty serpents accompanied by the Kinnaras. And all were skilled in weapons and heroic ; and all were versed in warfare. And all were possessed of the higher knowledge ; and all had obtained boons. And then the king surrounded by those sons of his,appearing like celestials,—capable of injuring the force and fortune of the foe,—looked splendid like Maghavān environed by the immortals,humblers of the hauteur of mighty Dānavas. And embracing his sons and adorning them in ornaments,—he sent them to the field with his best benedictions. And Rāvana sent the brothers—Yudhyonmatta and Matta—for protecting the princes in the field. And then, saluting the high-souled Rāvana—destroyer of creatures,—and going round him, those huge-bodied ones marched forth. And furnished with every description of medicinal herbs and perfumes, these six Nairitas—foremost of their kind—endowed with great strength,—burning for battle, marched forth,—Triçiras and Atikāya, and Devantaka and Narāntaka, and Mahodara and Mahāpārçwa went out, urged on by Fate. Then Mahodara mounted the elephant—Sudarçana—sprung in the race of Airâvata, and resembling dark-blue clouds. And accoutred in every weapon, and decked with quivers, he looked splendid on his elephant like the Sun ascending the crest of the Setting-hill. And Râvana's son—Triçiras—ascended a car yoked with excellent steeds, and furnished with every variety of arms. And having ascended the car, Triçiras bow in hand appeared beautiful like a mass of burning clouds having lightning and meteors, and crowned with Indra's bow.* And dight with three diadems, Triçiras looked splendid in that superb car, like the monarch of mountains Himavân—with the three golden hills. And then that foremost of all bowmen—the powerful Atikâya—son unto the lord of Râkshasas—ascended the best of cars, having excellent wheels and *akshas*, and yoked with excellent steeds,—and furnished with bottoms and holes; flaming with quivers and bows; and bristling with *prâças* and swords and blugdeons. And adorned with a crown plated with wrought gold and (other) ornaments, he looked like the Meru swimming in its own splendour. And that powerful son of the king surrounded by the Nairitas looked lovely on that car like the thunder-handed (Deity) engirt by the immortals. And Narântaka mounted a white steed resembling Uchchaiçravâ, caparisoned in gold, having a large frame and endowed with the velocity of the Wind. And taking a *prâça*, Narântaka appeared like the energetic Guha mounted on the peacock, grasping his dart. And taking a bludgeon decked in golden ornaments, Devântaka resembled Vishnu at the time of the churning of the ocean, holding the Darbhyâ,† and staying burthening (the earth). And the powerful Mahâpârçwa endowed with terrific energy, taking his mace, appeared like Kuvera holding in his hand a

* The rain-bow is called sometimes *Indra's bow* and at others *Râma's bow.*—T.

† The mountain Mandara which served as the churning-stick.—T.

mace in the encounter. And like immortals issuing out of Amarāvati, they marched out with elephants and steeds and cars sending out clatter resembling the rumbling of clouds. And them followed high-souled Rākshasas equipped with mighty-arms. And those sun-bright high-souled princes decked with diadems appeared splendid like burning planets in the firmament. And the various gorgeous attires which they had worn resembled rows of cranes in the sky, looking like autumnal clouds. Resolved on dying or conquering the foe in fight, those heroes sallied out seeking encounter. And those high-souled ones, incapable of being repressed in fight, roared and shouted and discharged shafts and held them. And the earth shook as they sent up leonine roars and struck at their arms with their hands; and the sky seemed riven with the leonine roars of the Rakshas. And issuing out cheerfully, those foremost of Rākshasas endowed with great strength beheld that monkey-army staying with upraised rocks and stones. And the high souled monkeys also saw that mighty host of Rākshasas thronging with elephants, horses and cars, and ringing with hundreds of bell-lets; resembling dark-blue clouds; upraising mighty arms; and environed on all sides by Nairitas resembling flaming fire. And seeing that force advance, the monkeys, finding opportunity, upraising giant crags, momentarily set up shouts. And thereat, the Rākshasas, incapable of bearing those shouts, shouted in reply unto the monkeys. And again the monkeys shouted unto the Rakshas, who were unable to put up with that cry. And hearing that loud shout of the monkey-leaders, the mighty Rakshas incapable of bearing that noise expressive of exhilaration,—shouted still more dreadfully. And then diving into that dreadful Rākshasa army, the monkey-leaders began to range it with uplifted rocks,—like unto mountains. And equipped with trees and stones, the monkeys enraged, ranged the Raksha army, now rising into the sky, and now coming down to the earth. And some among the powerful monkeys went about taking broad-shouldered trees. And the encounter that took place between the thronging Rakshas and monkeys was something terrific. And (the monkeys) began to pour a wonderful shower of trees and rocks and cliffs. And the monkeys of dread prowess were resisted with vollies of shafts. And in the contest the monkeys and Rākshasas emitted leonine roars. And monkeys crushed Yātudhānas with rocks, and, wrought with rage, (they) in the encounter slew (Rākshasas) covered with armour and ornaments; and some slew heroes mounted on cars and elephants and steeds. And the monkeys on a sudden slew heroic Yātudhānas. And smit with mountain-peaks on their persons, and with their eyes falling off, the foremost of Rākshasas moved, dropped down, or roared in the scene of conflict. And the Rākshasas (on their part) pierced the foremost of monkeys with sharpened and keen darts and clubs and scimitars; and slew them with darts and *prâcas*. And, eager for bringing down each other, the monkeys and the Rākshasas with their persons washed with the blood of their antagonists felled each other. And in a moment the earth was covered with crags and swords discharged by monkeys and Rākshasas, —and was drenched in gore. And the field was blocked up with scattered mountain-like Rakshas influenced by martial ardour,—mangled by their enemies. And the monkeys thrown down and felled by means of broken crags and monkeys* and arms and legs,—waged a wonderful war. And those foremost of Nairitas slew monkeys with (the dead bodies of monkeys); and the monkeys smote Rākshasas with (the dead bodies of) Rākshasas; and the Rākshasas slew (the monkeys), hurling rocks and crags. And snatching away their own arms by main force, the monkeys finished Rakshas; and they slaughtered them with mountain-peaks, and also wounded each other. And the monkeys and

---

* *i.e.* the carcasses thereof.

Rākshasas emitted leonine roars in the encounter. And the Rākshasas, slain by the monkeys, having their mail and defence for the body rent, bled like unto trees exuding sap. And in that encounter, some among the monkeys destroyed cars with cars, elephants with elephants, and steeds with steeds. And the Rākshasas rived the trees and rocks of the foremost monkeys by means of *Kshurapras* and crescents and sharpened *Bhallas* and arrows. And in that encounter, the earth became impassable, having been scattered with crags baffled and severed trees and (warriors) slain by monkeys and Rakshas. And those monkeys, equipped with various weapons, and with their vigor unworn, entering upon the conflict casting off fear,—cheerfully putting forth efforts springing from pride of spirit, warred on with the Rākshasas. And in that fearful conflict, which was being waged, on the monkeys having been exhilarated and the Rākshasas having been brought down, the Maharshis and the deities sent up shouts. Then mounted on a charger endued with the celerity of the Wind, and grasping a whetted dart, Narāntaka entered into that fierce army of monkeys, like a fish diving into the deep. And that hero by means of an effulgent bearded dart pierced seven hundred monkeys ; and at one time the high-souled enemy of Indra slew the army of the foremost of monkeys. And the Vidyādharas and Maharshis saw that high-souled one mounted on horseback, ranging the monkey-ranks. And his course was discovered, miry with flesh and blood and blocked up with mountain-like monkeys fallen. And when the monkeys set their hearts on displaying their prowess, Narāntaka, baffling them, pierced them with shafts. And he consumed the monkey-army, like fire burning a forest. And when the wood-rangers uprooted trees and crags, they slain by bearded darts dropped down like mountains riven by the thunder. And raising a glowing *prâça*, the powerful Narāntaka began to range about in the rear*

* *Sangrâmânte*, I presume, means *rear of the forces* ; although literally it

of the forces; dashing everywhere (against the foe) in fight, like the wind in the rainy season. And the heroes could not appear prominently, or keep their posts. And how could they then move freely? And that one endued with prowess pierced everyone, whether springing, or staying, or moving. And broken through by a single *prâça*, resembling the Reaper, and furnished with solar effulgence, the monkey-ranks began to roll on the earth. And the monkeys were ill fitted to bear the impetus of that *prâça* having the touch of thunder itself; and they raised a loud cry. And the appearances of those monkey-heroes falling were like mountains toppling, having their summits riven with the thunder-bolt. Those high-souled and powerful monkeys that formerly had been brought down by Kumbhakarna,—having recovered, were present with Sugriva in this encounter. And Sugriva, looking around, saw that monkey-army flying in all directions, agitated with the fear of Narāntaka. And after seeing the army in flight, he saw Narāntaka himself, advancing, wielding a *prâça*, and mounted on a steed. And as soon as he saw (that hero), the exceedingly energetic lord of monkeys—Sugriva—addressed the heroic prince Angada, endowed with strength equal to that of Indra, saying,—"Go against this heroic Rākshasas that is mounted on a steed; and speedily deprive of life that one who is devouring up the ranks of his foes." Hearing his master's speech, Angada descended from that host resembling clouds, like the powerful Sun himself. And resembling a mass of crags, Angada—foremost of monkeys—adorned with *Angadas*, appeared beautiful like a mountain with metals on it. And weaponless himself, and furnished only with nails and teeth, Vāli's son attacking Narāntaka, said,—"Stay! What shalt thou do with these inferior monkeys? This *prâça*, having the feel of the thunder-bolt, do thou hurl at my heart itself."

---

means, *at the conclusion of the conflict*,—because this interpretation would not be proper, the battle being now at its hottest.—T.

Hearing Angada's words, Narāntaka was fired with wrath. And knawing his upper lip with his teeth and sighing like a serpent, Narāntaka, wrought with wrath, approached Vāli's son. And then whirling his *prâça*, he suddenly discharged that flaming (weapon) against Angada. And then it was snapped on the breast of Vāli's son, resembling the thunder-bolt, and dropped to the earth. And seeing the *prâça* broken in pieces, like a powerful snake severed by Suparna, Vāli's son, raising his hand, dealt a slap at the head of his (Narāntaka's) steed. Thereat, with his legs sinking down and his eye-balls coming off and his tongue hanging down, and wearing the look of a mountain,—on being smit with that slap, Narāntaka's steed fell down to the ground, with its head lying at random. And Narāntaka seeing his charger slain and fallen, was seized with a furious wrath, and raising his clenched fist, that one endowed with exceeding great energy in that conflict hit Vāli's son on the head. Thereat Angada having his head wounded by that blow, warm blood gushed out plentifully. And momentarily burning and momentarily swooning, he, regaining his senses, was amazed. Then Vāli's son, the high-souled Angada clenching his fist into a blow resembling Death itself in energy, and like unto a mountain-peak, let it descend on the chest of Narāntaka. Thereat, with his breast riven and broken down, vomitting flames and having his body bathed in blood, Narāntaka dropped down to the earth, like a hill shattered by the impetus of the thunder-bolt. And on Narāntaka of exceeding prowess having been slain by Vāli's son in battle, there arose a tremendous uproar in the firmament from the wood-rangers and the foremost of celestials. And Angada having performed that difficult deed of prowess, capable of delighting the mind of Rāma, was seized with amazement;* and that one of terrific feats in fight was again inspired with delight in the encounter.

* Probably, *at his own prowess.*—T.

And seeing Narāntaka slain, the foremost of Nairitas —including the thre-headed Devāntaka and Pulastya's descendant, Mahodara,—began to cry (in chorus). And then the vehement Mahodara, mounted (on horseback), rushed against Vāli's son endued with energy. And aggrieved in consequence of the calamity that had befallen his brother, the strong Devāntaka grasping a dreadful bludgeon, darted against Angada. And ascending a car resembling the Sun yoked with superb steeds, the heroic Triçiras rushed against Vāli's son. Then charged by those three powerful Rākshasas —crushers of the hauteur of immortals, Angada uprooted a tree furnished with gigantic branches. And as Sakra hurleth the mighty flaming thunderbolt, that hero—Angada —at once hurled against Devāntaka that mighty tree having giant branches. And Triçiras cut off that tree in pieces by means of shafts resembling serpents. And seeing the tree severed, Angada darted up; and* then that foremost of monkeys showered crags and trees. And all those Triçiras wrought with wrath cut off by means of whetted arrows; and Mahodara snapped those trees with the end of his bludgeon. And then Triçiras rushed against that hero—Vāli's son—with shafts; and Mahodara chased him,† mounted ou an elephant; and struck Angada in thechest with *tomaras* resembling the thunder-bolt. And Devāntaka, enraged advancing, hit Angada with his bludgeon, and then, endowed with velocity, he swiftly turned away. And attacked simultaneonly by those three powerful Nairitas, the exceedingly energetic son of Vāli possessed of prowess, did not feel any pain. And that impetuous one incapable of being conquered, summoning his utmost vehemence, rushing on, pealt a slap at his‡ mighty elephant. And thereat the elephant fell down in his very sight and expired. And then

* The text has *Angada*, avoided for euphony.

† The text has Vāli's son.

‡ Mahodara's.

pulling out his tusks, the highly powerful son of Vâli, darting against Devântaka, dealt him a blow therewith in that encounter. And thereupon that strong one overwhelmed like a tree buffetted by the wind, began to discharge blood profusely, looking like the hue of lac. And then cheering him, the exceedingly energetic and powerful Narântaka, violently whirling his bludgeon with might and main, hit Angada with it. And albeit struck with the bludgeon, the son of the lord of monkeys, going down on his knees, again darted up. And as he sprang up, Triçiras hit at the temples of the son of the king of monkeys with three straight-speeding terrific shafts. And seeing Angada assailed by the three redoubtable Râkshasas, Hanumân and Nila proceeded (to his rescue). Then Nila hurled a mountain-top at Triçiras; and thereat that son of Râvana severed it with sharpened arrows. And that mountain-top on being riven, dropped down, aflame and shooting out sparks of fire. And seeing him* yawning in joy, the stalwart Devântaka in that encounter pursued the Wind-god's son with his bludgeon. And as he rushed on, that foremost of monkeys—Hanumân—dealt on the crown of his head, a blow resembling the thunder-bolt itself. And the mighty and heroic son of the Wind-god hit (at his antagonist); and that redoubted monkey also with his roars made the Râkshasas tremble (in fear). And thereat with his head crushed and cleft, and his teeth and eyes falling out, and his tongue hanging down, that son unto the sovereign of the Râkshasas suddenly dropped to the earth, deprived of life. On that fierce and mighty Râkshasa warrior—that foe of the immortals—having fallen in fight, the Three-headed one, waxing wondrous enraged began to shower terrific sharpened shafts on Nila's chest. And Mahodara, getting enraged, again swiftly mounted an elephant like the ray-furnished (Sun) mounting Mandara. Then even as a mass of roaring clouds poureth down showers enwheeled with

* Triçiras.

levin on a mountain, he showered arrows right on Nila's breast. Thereat showered with those shafts, that leader of monkeys Nila with his person pierced, had his body riven and was stupified by that exceedingly powerful one. Then that (monkey) possessed of tremendous vehemence, having regained his senses, uprooting a crag with a whole tract of trees, struck it at Mahodara's head. And struck by that mighty enemy, Mahodara, broken down by the impetus of that rock, deprived of his senses, dropped down dead on the ground, like a cliff smit with the thunder-bolt.

Seeing his uncle slain, Triçiras took up his bow; and inflamed with fury pierced Hanumân with whetted arrows. And thereat the Wind-god's son, enraged, hurled a mountain-peak (at his adversary). And Triçiras by means of keen arrows severed the same in shivers. And seeing the mountain-peak baffled, the monkey in the encounter began to shower trees on Râvana's son. And Triçiras endowed with prowess by means of sharpened shafts cut off that descending arrowy shower in the sky and shouted (in delight). Then Hanumân flying into a fury, bounding to the welkin, with his nails ript the steed of Triçiras,even as a lion cleaveth a powerful elephant. Then taking a dart even as the Destroyer employeth the Fatal Night, Râvana's son—Triçiras—discharged it at the offspring of the Wind-god. Thereat catching the dart of resistless course as it descended from the sky, the powerful monkey snapped it and then shouted. And seeing that dreadful dart broken by Hanumân, the monkeys, transported with delight, sent up shouts, even as clouds rumble. Then upraising his sword, that foremost of Râkshasas—Triçiras—brought it down on the breast of the monkey-chief. Overpowered with the sword-blow, Hanumân —son unto the Wind-god,—endowed with energy, dealt the Three-headed one a slap on the head. And smitten with that slap, the highly powerful Triçiras, with his hands and attire dropping off,fell down to the earth, deprived of consciousness.

Then that mighty monkey resembling a hill broke his sword as he fell, and roared, terrifying all the Rākshasas. But not brooking that uproar, that night-ranger sprang up; and springing up, he dealt a blow at Hanumān. And at that blow, the redoubtable monkey was wrought up with wrath; and inflamed with rage, he smote that foremost of Rākshasas about his diadem. And then with a sharp sword the Wind-god's son cut off his heads decked with diadems and furnished with ear-rings; even as Sakra had severed the heads of Tashtri's son.* Thereat even as burning stars, loosened, drop down from the course of Indra, the large organs of sense, and eyes flaming like glowing fire, and heads of that foe of Indra, dropped down to the ground. On Triçiras—enemy of the immortals—having been slain by Hanumān endowed with the prowess itself of Sakra, the monkeys shouted, the earth shook, and the Rakshas began to fly on all sides. And seeing Triçiras and Yudhyonmatta slain and seeing also the irrepressible Devāntaka and Narāntaka slain (in the encounter), that highly irascible and powerful Rākshasa—Matta—was transported with passion, and then took up a flaming mace entirely wrought with iron inlaid with gold; frothy with flesh and gore; mighty to behold; gratified with the blood of foes; with its end flaming in splendour; decked with red wreaths; and capable of striking terror into Airāvata and Mahāpadma and Sārvabhauma.† And flaming up like the Fire arisen at the end of a *Yuga*, that foremost of Rākshasas—Matta—wrought with fury,—rushed against the monkeys. Then the mighty and powerful monkey—Rishabha—springing up before Rāvana's son, stood before the hosts of Matta. And seeing that mountain-like monkey staying before (him), Matta, enraged, dealt him a blow on the breast. And smit with the mace, that foremost of monkeys, with his breast riven and trembling, began to

---

* Viçwarupa.

† Elephants of the cardinal points.—T.

bleed copiously. And regaining his senses after a long while, Rishabha—lord of monkeys—inflamed with wrath, pouting out his upper lip, gazed at Mahāpārçwa.* And then impetuously approaching the Rākshasa, that foremost of heroic monkeys resembling a hill, endowed with vehemence, clenching his fist, suddenly smote him with a blow on his breast. Thereat like a tree whose roots have been severed, he suddenly dropped on the ground, covered with blood. And thereupon, (Rishabha) swiftly snatched his dreadful mace resembling the rod of Yama himself; and shouted. Only for a moment did he† remain like one dead. Recovering his senses, the enemy of the immortals, looking like evening clouds in hue, suddenly springing up, attacked the son of the king of waters.‡ And thereat, he dropped down to the earth, senseless. In a moment regaining his consciousness, he again bounded up,—and whirling the mace resembling a peak of the foremost of mountains, in that encounter dealt (Matta) a blow therewith. And descending on the body of that dreadful one—the enemy of deities, sacrifices and Vipras—that terrific mace rived his breast; and he began to bleed profusely, even as the lord of mountains discharges minerals and water. And taking the terrific mace of the high-souled (Matta) and swinging it again and again, (Rishabha) rushed (against the Rākshasas). And that high-souled one began to slaughter Matta's forces in the field. And broken down by his own mace, Matta dropped down like a hill, with his teeth and eyes shrivelled up; and he dropped to the earth deprived of strength and life, with his eyes paling. And on that Rākshasa falling, the Rākshasa forces began to fly. And on that brother of Rāvana having been slain, that host of Nairitas appearing like the ocean in

---

* Otherwise called *Matta.—T.*

† Matta.

‡ Varuna.

grandeur, leaving its arms behind,—solely for life rushed away, like unto the deep riven (by the winds).

## SECTION LXXI.

SEEING in sore straits his own mighty forces capable of making people's down stand on end,—and seeing his brothers resembling Sakra in prowess, routed; and seeing also his uncles brought down in battle, as well as his brothers—Yudhyonmatta and Matta—foremost of Rākshasas, that crusher of the pride of deities and Dānavas—the exceedingly energetic Atikāya—resembling a hill, who had obtained from Brahmā a boon in battle, was fired with wrath. Ascending a car effulgent like a thousand suns mingling their rays into a burst of brilliance, that enemy of Sakra, charged the monkeys. And stretching his bow, (Atikāya) decked with a diadem and wearing polished ear-rings, proclaimed his name (among the monkey-ranks) and shouted in lofty tones. And with his leonine roars and the proclamation of his name, and the tremendous twang of his bow-string, he struck terror into the monkeys. Seeing the magnitude of his person, the monkeys thinking that it was Kumbhakarna who had come,—and affrighted thereat, sought the shelter of each other. And seeing his form like unto that of Vishnu when he displayed his threefold energy, the monkey-warriors seized with fear, began to scour on all sides. And on Atikāya appearing before them,the monkeys, stupified in that conflict, saught the shelter of Lakshmana's elder brother. And from a distance Kākutstha saw the mountain-like Atikāya mounted on the car and equipped with his bow, like unto roar ing clouds (seen) on the occasion of the universal disruption.

And seeing that huge-bodied one, Rāghava struck with surprise, comforting the monkeys, addressed Bibhishana, saying,—"Who is this one resembling a mountain, furnished with a bow and having leonine eyes, that is stationed on a large car yoked with a thousand steeds,—he that with effulgent sharpened darts and keen *prâças* and *tomaras,* shineth like Maheçwara environed by spectres—he that displaying his fatal tongue, appeareth splendid, surrounded with darts in his car; like a mass of clouds graced with lightning. And his bows adorned and backed with gold all over, beautify his car even as Indra's bow beautifyeth the firmament. And who is this foremost of Rākshasas and best of bowmen that embellishing the field of battle, approacheth on a car glorious as the sun; who, displaying the ten cardinal points with his shafts resembling the rays of the sun, appeareth handsome with his peak of a banner bearing the figure of Rāhu—whose bow bent in three places, emitting roars resembling the rumbling of clouds, and plated with gold, looketh like the bow itself of Satakratu? And his mighty car furnished with a banner and ensign and bottom, and having clatter resembling the roaring of clouds, hath four horsemen (attached to it). And there are on the car eight and thirty quivers and dreadful bows and yellow-golden bow-strings. And there are (in that car) two effulgent swords at his side, illumining it,—their hafts measuring four hands and their blades ten each. And that calm (warrior) wears red garlands about his neck, and resembles a mighty mountain. And a very Destroyer, he hath a mighty mouth, appearing like that of the Destroyer himself; and he looketh like the sun stationed on clouds. And with his arms adorned with golden *angadas,* he appeareth splendid like that best of mountains—the Himavān with its towering summits. And with his pair of ear-rings, his charming yet terrific countenance shineth like the full Moon entering into Punarvaçu.* O mighty-armed

* The seventh lunar asterism.—T.

one, tell me all about this foremost of Rākshasas, seeing whom the monkeys, overwhelmed with fear, fly away in all directions." Asked by the king's son—Rāma of immeasurable prowess—the exceedingly energetic Bibhishana spoke unto Rāma, informing him,—"The highly powerful king, Vaiçravana's younger brother of dreadful deeds, the high-souled Rāvana—is the sovereign of the Rākshasas. This one is his mighty son, like unto Rāvana himself in strength. He serveth the aged, is of wide celebrity and is the prime of those versed in all branches of knowledge. And he is competent to ride horses and elephants, to wield the sword or draw the bow,—or in sowing dissensions, or giving away, or in counsel,—he reposing in whose arm Lankā hath cast off fear. Know him to be Atikāya, son unto Dhānyamāli. Having adored the pure-souled Brahmā with austerities, he hath obtained weapons, and hath defeated his foes (in fight)." 'Thou shalt be incapable of being slain by celestials and Asuras'—was the boon conferred on him by the Self-sprung; and he also gave him this celestial mail and this car resembling the effulgent Sun himself. He hath vanquished (in battle) hundreds of deities and Dānavas; and he hath (always) protected the Rakshas, and destroyed Yakshas. And this intelligent one resisted the thunder-bolt itself of Indra; and in encounter baffled the very noose of the king of waters. This one is Atikāya—foremost of Rākshasas; and that son of Rāvana is the humbler of the hauteur of deities and Dānavas. Therefore, O best of persons, do thou endeavour thy best. This one with his shafts slaughtereth the monkey-hosts before (us)." And then the powerful Atikāya entering that monkey-force, stretched his bow and shouted again and again. And the high-souled principal monkeys, seeing that (hero) possessed of a dreadful person, that best of car-warriors—stationed on his car, rushed forward. And Kumuda and Dwivida and Mainda and Nila and Sarabha dashed on at one time with trees and mountain-peaks. Thereupon that foremost of those skilled in weapons, the exceedingly energetic Atikāya, severed those trees and rocks by means of shafts dight with gold. And in that encounter that powerful one possessed of a gigantic person, skilled in arms, pierced all those monkeys staying before him with arrows entirely made of iron. And agonised, having their persons pierced in that mighty conflict by that arrowy shower, they were incapable of resisting the same. And the Rākshasa terrified that host of monkey-heroes, even as an enraged lion priding in his youth terrifyeth a society of deer. And in the midst of those bands of monkeys, that lord of Rākshasas did not slay anyone without battle. And then springing up before Rāma, that one furnished with his bow and quiver, addressed him in haughty words, saying,—"Stationed in this car holding the bow and arrows in my hands, I will not fight any that is ignoble. Him that hath strength, and that also understandeth this business,—let him to-day speedily give me battle." Hearing his speech, that slayer of foes—Sumitrā's son—was fired with wrath. And not bearing him, he sprang forward disregarding his antagonist's words, and took up his bow. And flying unto fury, Sumitrā's son, darting up, took out arrows from his quiver, and stretched his mighty bow in front of Atikāya. And filling the entire earth and the sky and the ocean and all the cardinal quarters,—the terrific twang of Lakshmana's bow struck terror into the (hearts of the) night-rangers. And hearing the dreadful twang of the bow of Sumitrā's son, the exceedingly energetic and powerful son of the lord of Rākshasas was struck with surprise. Then Atikāya, enraged, seeing Lakshmana advance, taking sharpened shafts, spoke unto him,—"Thou art a boy, O Sumitrā's son ; and as such knowest not how to display prowess. Go thou. Why wishest thou to fight with me resembling Death itself. Not Himālaya itself or the firmament or the earth is capable of bearing the impetuosity of shafts shot by my arms. Thou wishest to rouse a fire slumbering sweetly. Leaving alone thy bow, do thou return. Do not lose thy life by coming in contact with me. Or it may be that thou art proud; and, therefore, hast no mind to return. Stay then. Renouncing thy life, thou shalt go to Yama's mansion. Behold my whetted arrows—crushers of the insolence of foes—resembling the weapon itself of the Lord,*—adorned with burnished gold. And even as a lion enraged sheddeth the blood of a mighty elephant, this arrow of mine resembling a serpent shall shed thy blood." Having delivered himself thus, he fired with wrath set his shaft on his bow. Hearing in that encounter Atikāya's wrathful speech fraught with hauteur, the highly powerful and intelligent son of the king possessed of exceeding grace, was transported with passion; and he said,—"Thou canst not attain pre-eminence solely by virtue of thy speech. One cannot be a worthy person simply by say. O wicked-minded one, do thou display thy strength on me equipped with the bow and holding arrows in my hands. To-day shall my shafts decked in gold, drink thy blood flowing from thy person and issuing out of wounds inflicted by my arrows resembling darts.—'This one is a boy', thinking this, thou ought not to slight me. Whether I am a boy or an old† man' —death shalt thou know in the conflict. It was as a boy that Vishnu had overpowered the triune world with his prowess." Hearing Lakshmana's words, fraught with reason and high sense, Vidyādharas and ghosts, deities, Daityas and Maharshis, and the high-souled Guhyakas then beheld that marvel.‡

Then Atikāya, enraged, setting his arrow on his bow, shot it at Lakshmana, as if devouring up the welkin. Thereat, Lakshmana—slayer of hostile heroes—with a crescent sever-

---

* *Isvara—Siva.*—His weapon is the trident.—T.

† The commentator says the passage means—"Thou knowest (me) *for death* itself'. I prefer the sense given.—T.

‡ The encounter that ensued between Lakshmana and Atikāya.—T.

ed that sharpened shaft resembling a venomous serpent, as it was descending. And seeing the shaft severed, like a serpent having its person cut off, Atikāya waxing exceedingly enraged, took up five arrows; and the night-ranger discharged them at Lakshmana. Thereat Bharata's younger brother cut off the approaching arrows with whetted shafts. And having severed them with sharpened shafts, Lakshmana—slayer of hostile heroes—took up a sharpened arrow, as if flaming in energy. And taking it, Lakshmana set it on his excellent bow; and drawing the latter, vigorously discharged the shaft. And that hero endowed with prowess hit that foremost of Rākshasas in the forehead with that shaft having bent knots, discharged from his bow drawn to its full bent.—And that arrow piercing the forehead of that dreadful Rākshasa, and smeared with blood, appeared like the lord of serpents in a mountain. And the Rākshasa, smarting under Lakshmana's shaft, showered, like the dreadful gateway of Tripurā battered by Rudra. Then recovering himself and reflecting, he said,*—"Excellent well! By this discharge of thy shaft, thou approvest thyself as a foe in whom I can well glory." Having spoken thus candidly, he, folding his hands at ease, and seated on the platform of his car, began to range in it. And then that foremost of Rākshasas began to take up, set, and shoot one, three, five, or seven shafts. And those shafts resembling Fate itself, plated with gold at the feathered parts,—and looking like the Sun himself (in splendour),—discharged from the bow of the lord of Rākshasas, lighted up the heavens. Thereat Rāghava's younger brother by means of many a sharpened shaft calmly cut off all those vollies of arrows shot by the Rākshasa. And finding all those arrows riven in the encounter, that enemy of the lord of the immortals, Rāvana's son, was fired with wrath, and took up a whetted shaft. And then aiming that arrow, that highly powerful one suddenly shot it; and with that, rushing

* *Chintayāmāsa—thought*, I apprehend, means *said* in this connection.

on, hit Sumitrā's son in the chest. And struck in the encounter by Atikāya, the son of Sumitrā began to bleed copiously, like a mad elephant discharging the temporal juice. And then that lord at once extricated the arrow; and then took up a keen shaft and fixed the same on his weapon.* And then he set a shaft (on his bow-string) reciting a formula for the Agneya† weapon; and thereat his arrow as well as bow flamed up. Then the highly powerful Atikāya took up a Raudra‡ weapon; and thereon fixed a shaft plated with gold at the feathered part, and resembling a serpent in sheen. And even as the Reaper hurleth his rod, did Lakshmana hurl that weapon inspired with divine energy, dreadful and aflame,—at Atikāya. And seeing that shaft set upon an Āgneya weapon, that night-ranger discharged a Raudra arrow set upon a Solar weapon. And there like a pair of infuriated serpents, those arrows with their heads flaming in energy, baffled each other in the sky. And burning each other, the shafts fell on the earth; and those best of arrows, shorn of brilliance and reduced to ashes, were deprived of their splendour. And having blazed in the welkin, those two fell down to the earth reft of their lustre. Then Atikāya wrought up with wrath discharged an arrow called Aishika dedicated to Tashtri. Thereat the powerful son of Sumitra severed that shaft by an Aindra§ weapon. Seeing Aishika baffled, that Prince—son unto Rāvana—fired with rage, fixed an arrow on a Yāmya|| weapon; and then the night-ranger shot that weapon at Lakshmana. And Lakshmana resisted it by a Vāyavya¶ weapon. And then as a mass of clouds poureth down showers, Lakshmana, enraged, poured volleys

---

* *i.e.* the bow.

† Belonging to the god of Fire.

‡ Relative to Rudra.

§ Belonging to Indra.

|| What could this be like? The commentator is silent over this important point.—T.

¶ Belonging to the Wind-god.

of shafts on Rāvana's son. Thereupon, hitting Atikāya, those arrows coming in contact with his mail, had their barbs broken, and fell down to the earth. And seeing them baffled, that slayer of hostile heroes—the renowned Lakshmana—began to shower shafts by thousands. And albeit showered with those arrows, that Rākshasa—the mighty Atikāya—in that encounter was not pierced by them on account of his impenetrable mail; and that best of men failed to hurt him in the contest. Then approaching him, the Wind-god spake unto him, saying,—"This one hath received a boon from Brahmā, and is covered with an impenetrable mail. Pierce him with a Brāhma* weapon. He cannot otherwise be slain. This one clad in mail and endowed with prowess is forsooth incapable of being slain by others." Hearing the words of the Wind-god, Sumitrā's son like unto Indra in prowess took an arrow endowed with fierce impetuosity, and at once set it on a Brāhma weapon. And on that sharp-headed best of arrows being fixed on that foremost of weapons, the cardinal quarters and the Moon and the Sun and the mighty planets and the sky were seized with affright; and the earth shook. And inspiring that arrow furnished with a feathered part and resembling an emissary of Yama himself, and fixing the same on his bow, Sumitrā's son in that encounter discharged that shaft like unto the thunder-bolt at the son of the enemy of Indra. And in that conflict Atikāya beheld that shaft fair-feathered and having its feathered part dight with splendid diamonds, acquiring enhanced vehemence arising from its having been discharged by Lakshmana,—and hissing and rushing on with tremendous impetuosity. And seeing it, Atikāya swiftly resisted it with countless sharpened shafts. But endowed with the energy of Suparna himself, that shaft vehemently went to him. And seeing that shaft flaming and resembling the Fatal Destroyer himself,—coming, he, exerting himself to the utmost resisted

† Belonging to Brahmā.

it with darts and *rishtis* and maces and adzes and javelins and arrows. But beating down all those weapons of wonderful forms, that arrow alive with flames, coming to the diadem-decked head of Atikāya, severed the same (in twain) And that head furnished with a corsalet, cut off by Lakshmana's arrow, suddenly dropped to the earth, like a summit of Himavān toppling (to the ground). Seeing him rolling on the earth, with his attire and ornaments scattered about, those night-rangers that survived were overwhelmed with grief. And with pāle forces and distressed, they, fatigued in consequence of the thrashing they had undergone, suddenly began to cry in frightful accents. And on their leader having been slain, those night-rangers that were about (Atikāya), without waiting any longer,—overwhelmed with panic, rushed towards the city. And on their foe endowed with terrific prowess and incapable of being confronted, having been slain, innumerable monkeys filled with excess of joy, and displaying countenances resembling blown lotuses, paid homage unto Lakshmana working out their welfare.

---

## SECTION LXIXII.

HEARING Atikāya slain by the high-souled Lakshmana, the king was filled with exceeding great anxiety and spoke thus, —"Dhumrāksha exceedingly wrathful,—best of those equipped with all arms—and Akampana and Prahasta and Kumbhakarna—all these exceedingly mighty heroes—Rākshasas ever seeking warfare, conquerers of the forces of foes, and never defeated by antagonists, have together with their hosts been slain by Rāma of untiring feats. And other Rakshasas having gigantic bodies and skilled in various arms,—countless high-souled heroes—have also been brought down. These brothers were formerly bound by my son Indrajit of renowned strength and prowess with terrific shafts, obtained as boons. And I do not know by what power or superhuman virtue or stupifying energy did those brothers—Rāma and Lakshmana—liberate themselves from those dreadful bonds, which could be loosed neither by celestials nor the highly powerful Asuras combined nor Yakyas, Gandharbas and Pannagas. And all those heroic Rākshasa warriors that marched forth at my bidding, have been destroyed by monkeys of marvellous might. Him see I not that can now slay Rāma with Lakshmana,—that hero together with his forces and Sugriva and Bibhishana. Alack! mighty must be Rāma and wondrous is his strength of weapon—he coming in contact with whose prowess, these Rākshasas have met with their deaths. Now let this palace be everywhere guarded by a vigilant garrison,—as also the *açoka* wood where Sitā is being guarded. We should always be acquainted with the ingress and egress (of every person). And do ye, surrounded by forces, remain where there are garrisons. And the night-rangers should in the evening, at midnight and in the morning always watch the movements of the monkeys. The monkeys should by no means be slighted. And ye should know whether the enemy putteth forth (fresh) efforts,—and whether they advance or remain stationed where they at present are."—Thereupon those exceeding mighty Rakshasas did as they had been desired. And having directed them, Rāvana—lord of Rākshasas—bearing the dart of ire (in his heart), in forlorn guise entered his own mansion. And with the fire of his rage blazing up, the exceedingly powerful sovereign of the night-rangers, absorbed with the danger that had befallen his son, began to sigh momentarily.

## SECTION LXXIII.

THOSE Rakshas that remained after the others had been slain, swiftly informed Rāvana that all those foremost of Rākshasas—Devantaka and the rest, Triçiras, Atikāya and others—had been slain. And suddenly hearing them slain, the king with his eyes charged with brine, thinking of the disastrous destruction of his sons and brothers, was extremely agonized. Thereupon, seeing the king afflicted, and sunk in a sea of sorrow, that foremost of car-warriors—son unto the Rākshasa king—Indrajit, addressed (his sire), saying,—"O father, it doth not behove thee to be overcome with this excessive grief, inasmuch as, O lord of Nairitas, Indrajit yet breaths. Smit by the enemy of Indra, (Rāghava) can by no means save his life in encounter. To-day behold Rāma along with Lakshmana with their bodies torn with my shafts,—lying down lifeless on the ground, having their persons covered with my sharpened arrows! Hear this vow of the foe of Indra, never swerving and instinct with prowess and divinity,—this very day will I with unfailing shafts slay Rāma along with Lakṣmana. To-day let Indra and Vaivaçwata and Vishnu and Rudra and Sādhyas and Vaiçwas and men and the Sun and the Moon, behold my immeasurable prowess, terrific like that of Vishnu at the sacrificial ground of Vāli." Having spoken thus, that foe of the lord of celestials endowed with exceeding energy, taking the king's permission, ascended a car having the velocity of the wind itself, yoked with asses, and furnished with every variety of weapons. And ascending the car, resembling the car of Hari himself, that exceedingly powerful repressor of enemies at once set out for the field of battle. And as that high-souled (hero) marched, he was followed by countless mighty (Rākshasas) breathing spirits; bearing bows in their strong hands. And some of those, resembling mountains, were mounted on elephants, and some on superb steeds, and some on bears, and some on beasts of prey, and some on lions and jackals,—and some of the Rākshasas endowed with dreadful vigor were mounted on crows, and some on swans, and some on peacocks,—they were equipped with *prâças* and maces and *nistrinças* and axes and clubs. And all sides were filled with the blares of conchs and the sounds of kettle-drums. And then that enemy of the lord of celestials marched forth with impetuosity. And with an umbrella hued like the Moon, that destroyer of enemies appeared like the full Moon stationed in the sky. And that hero garnished in golden ornaments—that foremost of all bowmen—was fanned by an excellent and graceful golden *chowri*. And with Indrajit furnished with the splendour of the Sun himself, and possessed of peerless prowess, Lankā looked beauteous even as the firmament graced with the glorious Sun.

Arriving at the scene of conflict, that highly powerful repressor of foes arrayed his forces aound the car. And then that foremost of Rākshasas with choice *mantras* duly offered libations unto Fire.* And that powerful lord of Rākshasas there worshipping Fire with fragrant wreaths and fried paddy, sacrificed unto it. And arms served for *Kâça* and *Bibhitakas* for fuel; and there were red cloths and a ladle made of black iron. And spreading Fire there, with *tomaras* representing *Kâça*, he seized the neck of a living goat. And then the kindled smokeless fire blazing up brilliantly, displayed signs betokening victory. Thereat, with his right tongue whirling, the Deity of Fire himself looking like one made of gold,—arising, accepted the offering. And then that (Rākshasa) skilled in weapons acquired a Brāhma weapon (from that Deity), and inspired his bow and car with *mantras*. On that weapon baving been

* Hutabhoktâram—*eater of sacrificial offerings*—a designation of Fire.

invoked,* and on (the god of Fire) also having been worshipped, the firmament furnished with the suns and stars and planets was afflicted with affright. Having worshipped (the god of Fire), that one endowed with the splendour of Fire itself, that one possessed of the prowess of the great Indra and gifted with inconceivable vigor, accoutred in bows and arrows and swords and having steeds and cars and darts,—disappeared in the sky. Then burning for battle, setting up roars went out the Rākshasa ranks, thronging with steeds and cars, and graced with pennons and standards. And they fell to slaughtering monkeys in the engagement with countless shafts, sharp, variegated and decorated; as also with *tomaras* and *hooks*. And Rāvana's son, fired with wrath, seeing those night-rangers, addressed them, saying,—"Do ye, burning with a desire to destroy the monkeys, fight cheerfully." Thereat all those Rākshasas, eager for victory, smitting roars, covered the dreadful monkeys with showers of shafts. And environed by Rakshas in that encounter, he† poured on the monkeys *nâlikas* and *narâchas* and maces and clubs. And trembling in the encounter, those monkeys armed with trees at once began to shower rocks and trees on Rāvana's son. Then the exceedingly powerful Indrajit, son unto Rāvana, endowed with wondrous energy, pierced the bodies of the monkeys (with arrows). And fired with wrath, that (hero) rejoicing the Rākshasas with a single shaft pierced nine and seven monkeys in that encounter. And that invincible hero in that coflict mangled the monkeys with shafts resembling the Sun, decked with gold. And their persons pierced in that contest, and the mselves pained with those arrows, they began to fall down, giving up all intention of fight, like mighty Asuras smit by the celestials. And then waxing highly enraged, those considerable monkeys in that conflict hotly pursued (Indrajit)

* *i. e.* on the *deity* presiding over that weapon, being invoked.

† Indrajit.

resembling the Sun himself and having terrific arrows for his rays. And all the monkeys, with their bodies riven and deprived of their senses, and bathed in blood and writhing in torments,—pursued (Indrajit). And putting forth their prowess in behalf of Rāma, those monkeys, equipped with rocks in the encounter, who had set apart their very lives (for him), paused,shouting up loudly. And they in that conflict showered trees and crags and mountain-tops on Rāvana's son. And that destroyer of foes—the exceedingly energetic son unto Rāvana—resisted that mighty shower of trees and stones capable of compassing destruction. Then that Lord pierced the monkey-hosts in the encounter with shafts resembling fire or venomous serpents. And piercing Gandhamādana with eight and ten sharp arrows, he wounded Nila stationed at a distance with nine shafts. And that one endowed with redoubtable prowess pierced Mainda with seven shafts capable of piercing into the pith; and he pierced Gaja with five shafts in the encounter. And he pierced Jāmbavān with ten and Nila with thirty. And then with dreadful sharp shafts obtained as boons, he rendered Sugriva and Rishabha and Angada and Dwivida (almost) lifeless. And transported with passion, and resembling the Five arisen at Doomsday, Indrajit, harassed other principal monkeys with countless arrows. And in that terrific conflict, he agitated the monkey-hosts with swift-speeding shafts, resembling the Sun himself, deftly discharged (from his bow). Then in that encounter, leaving his army, Indrajit became suddenly invisible unto the monkey-hosts,—and began to shower fierce arrows, like dark clouds pouring rain. And with their persons torn by the arrows of the conqueror of Sakra,—slain by his power of illusion,—with their teeth uprooted, those mountain-like monkeys fell down in the field, emitting frightful cries,—like a mountain smit with Indra's thunderbolt. And in the conflict they could only see sharp-pointed shafts among the monkey-ranks; but that foe of the celestial chief—the Rākshasa, hidden by virtue of illusion, they could not discover there. And then the high-souled lord of Rakshas covered all sides with sharp-pointed shafts resembling the rays of the Sun; and he rived the foremost monkeys. And whirling darts and *nistraiças* and axes, flaming and having the effulgence of Fire,—and furnished with flames shooting forth sparks,—he discharged them furiously at the forces of the sovereign of monkeys. And the monkey-leaders struck with Sakrajit's shafts resembling flames, appeared like laughing Kinçukas. And some looking at the sky were struck at their eyes. And they gradually began to hide themselves in each other and drop to the earth. And that foremost of Rākshasas—Indrajit—with *práças* and darts and whetted arrows, inspired with *mantras*, pierced all those powerful monkeys,—Hanumān and Sugriva and Angada and Gandhamādana and Jāmbavān and Sushena and Vegadarçin, and Mainda and Dwivida and Nila and Gavāksha and Gavaya and Kesari and Hariloman and the monkey Vidyutdanshtra and Suryyānana and Jyotimukha and the monkey Dadhimukha and Pāvakāksha and Nala and the monkey Kumuda. And having pierced those foremost monkeys with golden-hued maces, he showered on Rāma and Lakshmana arrows resembling the rays of the Sun. And showered with those vollies of arrows, Rāma, without heeding that discharge resembling a very downpour, —reflecting, spoke unto Lakshmāna,—"O Lakshmana, this lord of Rākshasas, this foe of the lord of celestials, having obtained the Brāhma weapon,—after having brought down the monkey-hosts, are assailing us with sharpened shafts. And that high-souled heedful one, having been given a boon by the Self-sprung, hath rendered his dreadful body invisible. How can we slay him, who is fighting with upraised weapons, but who hath hid his body. The reverend Self-sprung, I deem, is incomprehensible. And this is his weapon, embodying his energy. Therefore, O intelligent one, do thou to-day along with me calmly bear this. And let this foremost of them all—this lord of Rākshasas—cover all sides with the showers of his shafts. And in consequence of this, the army of the monkey-king with its greatest heroes fallen, doth not appear to advantage. And seeing us also fallen senseless,—and desisting from fight with our joy and anger gone off from us, for certain will the enemy of the immortals, taking the Fortune of fight seek his home." And assailed by Indrajit with networks of arrows, they were then sore distressed in the field. And having struck them with sadness, Indrajit from joy shouted in the encounter. And having thus worsted in battle that monkey-army and Rāma along with Lakshmana, he speedily entered the city ruled by the hand of the Ten-necked one. And extolled by the Yātudhānas, he, filled with, delight, related everything unto his sire.

## SECTION LXXIV.

AND they* were rendered inert in the field; and the army of the monkey-leaders was stupified, with Sugriva and Nila and Angada and Jāmbavān,—and they did not show any signs of activity. Thereupon, seeing them dispirited, that foremost of intelligent persons—Bibhishana—cheering them up with his peerless speech, said,—"Ye heroes of the king of monkeys, do not give way to fear. This is not the time to indulge in grief at this place; for the sons of that noble one,†—inactive and depressed, and seeming to be wounded with the showers of Indrajit's shafts,—are in reality

* *i. e.* Râma and Lakshmana.

† Daçaratha.

in this plight, for showing reverence unto the words* of the Self-sprung one.—On him the Self-sprung hath conferred the mighty Brahmā weapon of unfailing power; and the king's sons are doing honour to it by lying down on the field of battle. Why then do ye grieve now?" Hearing the words of Bibhishana and honoring the Brahmā weapon, Hanumān spoke as follows:—"The host of the quick-paced monkeys hath been slain by this weapon. Let us go and console them who are still living." And those two great heroes—Hanumān and that foremost of the Rākshasas, with fire-brands in their hands, began to range to and fro in the battle field. And they beheld there the earth strewn on all sides with monkeys lying down like so many hills and various shining weapons. And some of these monkeys were deprived of their tails, some of their hands, some of their thighs, some of their legs, some of their fingers, and some of their heads. And blood was gushing out from the persons of some, and others were urinating out of fear. And Bibhishana and Hanumān beheld there Sugriva, Angada, Nila, Gandhamādana, Jāmbavān, Sushena, Vegadarshin, Mainda, Nala, Jyotimukha, and the monkey, Dwivida,—almost slain. And Bibhishana and Hanumān saw in the field seven and sixty *kotis* of fleet-footing monkeys slain (in battle) at the fifth part of the day by the darling of the Self-sprung. And surveying that host worsted, dreadful like the surges of the sea, Hanumān and Bibhishana began to search for Jāmbavān. And finding that heroic son of Prajāpati, afflicted with natural decrepitude, aged, and resembling smouldering fire,—wounded with hundreds of shafts, Pulastya's son said,—"O noble one, hath not thy life been destroyed with those sharp shafts?" Hearing Bibhishana's words, Jāmbavān—best of bears—evoking utterance with extreme effort, said,—"O foremost of Nairitas, endowed with exceeding prowess, I know thee by thy voice. Having my person pierced with sharp shafts, I

---

* Mantra.

cannot see thee with my eyes. Doth he through whom Anjanā as well as Mātariçwa* are blessed with fair offspring,—doth that prince of monkeys—Hanumān—live?" Hearing Jāmbavān's speech, Bibhishana said,—"Why, passing by the son of the high and mighty,† dost thou enquire after the Wind-god's offspring? O noble one, thou dost not show that overflowing affection either for king Sugriva or Rāghava that thou showest for the son of the Wind-god." Hearing Bibhishana's words, Jāmbavān said,—"Hear, O foremost of Rākshasas, why I enquire after the Wind-god's son. While this hero is alive, this force, albeit destroyed, liveth; but if Hanumān is reft of life, although living, we are destroyed. O child, if the Wind-god's offspring, resembling his sire himself or (the deity of) Fire in prowess, is alive, there is hope for our lives." Then approaching that aged one, Hanumān—son unto the Wind-god—saluted him humbly, holding Jāmbavān's feet. Hearing Hanumān's voice, that foremost of monkeys, with his senses sorely smarting, deemed himself as having regained his life. Then that exceedingly energetic one addressed Hanumān, saying,—"Come, O powerful monkey. It behoveth thee to rescue the monkeys. There is none else. Endowed with profuse prowess, thou art the greatest friend of these. This is the hour when thou shouldst display thy might. Any other see I not. Do thou cheer up this host consisting of bears and monkeys; and do thou also heal the wounds of these two tormented by them. Bounding sheer over the main, thou, O Hanumān, shouldst repair to the Himavān—foremost of mountains. There thou wilt see that best of mountains—the golden Rishabha of terrific aspect, and, O smiter of foes, the peak also of Kailāça. Lying in the lap of these two, thou, O hero, O powerful monkey, wilt see the mountain of medicines, fraught with healing herbs of all kinds. On its summit thou wilt find four medicinal herbs

---

* The Wind-god.

† *Vide Hamlet.*

flaming and illumining the ten cardinal quarters—*viz.*, Mritasanjivani,* Viçalyakarani,† Suvarnakarani,‡ and the mighty medicine, Sandhāni. O Hanumān, providing thyself with these, thou shouldst come hither without delay. Do thou, O offspring of the Wind-god§ bringing back lives unto these monkeys, cheer them up." Thereat Hanumān filled himself with energy, even as the Ocean heaveth with the force of the winds (blowing on its breast). And ascending the summit of that mountain,|| and hurting it with his tread, that hero—Hanumān—appeared like a second mountain. And crushed under the tread of that monkey, the mountain was dispirited; and sore distressed, it could hardly contain itself. And the trees on it began to topple to the earth; and on account of the vehemence of the monkey, they flamed up. And smitten by Hanumān, its peaks were scattered around. And monkeys could no longer dwell on that foremost of mountains, which, being hard pressed (by Hanumān), was trembling all over, with its slopes covered with broken trees and rocks. And with her giant gateways shaking, and the doors of her edifices broken, that night Lankā, overwhelmed with fright, seemed to be dancing. And the offspring of the Wind-god, resembling a mountain itself, bringing that mountain to sore straits, agitated the entire earth with her Oceans. And hurting the mountain with his tread, he, opening wide his mouth resembling that of a mare, sent up loud shouts, terrifying the night-rangers. And hearing those tremendous roars as he kept emitting cries, the powerful Rākshasas were quite stupified. And bowing down unto the Ocean, that subduer of enemies, the Wind-god's son, endowed with dreadful prowess, began to ponder

---

* *Lit.* reviving the dead.

† *Lit.* healing wounds inflicted by darts.

‡ *Lit.* transmuting any thing to gold.

§ *Gandhabahātanaya*—lit., son unto the bearer of smell—a designation of the Wind in Sanskrit.—T.

|| Trikuta.

over the mighty mission with which he had been entrusted in the interests of Rāghava.—And, then upraising his tail resembling a serpent, bending his back, contracting his ears, and opening his mouth looking like that of a mare, that one possessed of terrific impetuosity, bounded into the sky. And with the vehemence of his rush,—he carried away in his wake whole tracts of trees, and rocks, and crags, and inferior monkeys ;* and after having been carried away some distance by the vehemence of his arms and thighs, they, at length losing their velocity, fell into the waters (of the Ocean.) And stretching his arms resembling serpents, the son of the Wind-god endowed with the prowess of Garura† coursed on towards the monarch of mountains, as if making all the quarters tremble. And seeing the sea with its hosts of billows rolling furiously, and with the confideracies of aquatic animals bewildered by the angry waters, he coursed on rapidly, like the discus discharged by the hand of Vishnu. And surveying hills and birds and pools and rivers and tanks and splendid cities and flourishing provinces, that one equal to his sire himself in celerity, held his way. And that hero—Hanumān—like unto his father in prowess, and incapable of being fatigued, vigorously proceeded along the orbit of the Sun. And that powerful monkey possessed of the speed of the Wind itself, and having mighty impetuosity, careered, making all sides resound with his roars. And remembering Jāmbavān's words, that redoubtable monkey, son unto the Wind-god, possessed of terrific prowess, and resembling a mountain, suddenly saw (before him) the Himavān; furnished with countless cascades and numerous caves and rivulets; with splendid summits appearing like massess of pale clouds ; and graced with various trees. And arriving at that lord of mighty mountains, furnished with excellent towering golden summits, he saw the great sacred asylums (of the

---

* Residing in the Trikuta mountain.

† The text has, *the Foe of serpents*—an appellation of Garura

ascetics), inhabited by the flower of celestial saints. And he saw Brahmakoça[a] and Rajatālaya[b] and Sakrālaya[c] and Rudraçarapramoksha[d] and Hayānana[e] and the flaming Brahmaçiras,[f] and the servants of Vaivaçwata.[g] And he saw the abode of the Fire-god, and the abode of Vaiçravana and the effulgent Suryyanivandhana,[h] and the abode of Brahmā,[i] and the bow of Sankara, and the navel of the Earth.[j] And he saw Kailaça of terrific aspect,and the stone[k] of Himavân, and that bull,[l] and the golden mountain, and that foremost of mountains furnished with all medicinal herbs, flaming, and illuminated with every kind of medicinal plants. And beholding that flaming mass of fire, the offspring of Vāsava's[m] emissary wondered. And bounding up to the lord of medicinal mountains, he fell to searching for the drugs. And that mighty monkey--the Wind-god's son—leaving behind a thousand *yoyanas*, began to range the mountain containing the divine remedies in its entrails. And those potent medicines,in that foremost of mountains, knowing (before-hand) that one was coming seeking for them, rendered themselves invisible. And not seeing them, the high-souled Hanumān was angered; and from wrath he set up roars.

---

(*a*) The place of Hiranyagarbha.

(*b*) The place of Rajatanâbha—*silver-naveled*—another form of Hiranyagarbha.

(*c*) The abode of Sakra.

(*d*) The place wherefrom Rudra discharged his arrow on the occasion of the destruction of Tripurâ.

(*e*) The place of the Horse-necked.

(*f*) The place of the deity presiding over the Brahma weapon.

(*g*) An appellation of Yama.

(*h*) The spot where the suns meet.

(*i*) The place of the four-faced Brahmâ.

(*j*) The spot of Prajâpati.

(*k*) On which Rudra sat when engaged in asceticism.

(*l*) Which had been mentioned by Jâmbavân.

(*m*) The emissary of Vâsava in his cloud-form is the Wind driving the cloud; and the passage refers to Hanumân.—T.

And not brooking that, (Hanumān) with eyes resembling glowing fire, addressed that foremost of mountains, saying,—"What is this that thou hast decided on, that thou showest no compassion for Rāghava? But, O lord of mountains, to-day witness thyself, overpowered by my arms and torn in pieces!" And (anon) on a sudden, he violently rooted up its summit with trees and elephants and gold, and furnished with thousand varieties of ore,—having its tops torn and its slopes aflame. And uprooting it, he sprang into (the bosom of the air), terrifying the worlds containing celestials and the lords thereof. And hymned by countless rangers of the air, that one endowed with the terrific impetuosity of Garura himself, taking that summit furnished with the splendour of the Sun, went along the orbit of the Sun. And near the Sun, that Sun-like one seemed to be another Sun. And with that mountain, the offspring of the bearer of perfumes appeared surpassingly grand, like very Vishnu equipped with the flaming discus having a thousand edges. And seeing him, the monkeys shouted,—and he also, seeing them, shouted in delight. And hearing their tremendous cheers, those residing in Lankā shouted still more dreadfully. And then the high-souled one dropped on that best of mountains in the midst of the monkey-forces; and, bowing down unto the principal monkeys there, he embraced Bibhishana. And then those sons of that king of men, smelling the perfume of that mighty medicine, were then and there healed of their wounds; and the heroic monkeys also sat up. And all the heroic monkeys were instantly healed and cured; and those also that were slain (in battle), through the smell of that best of drugs, sat up, like persons risen after sleep at break of day. Ever since the monkeys and Rākshasas had begun to fight, for maintaining honor, all those Rākshasas that were slain there by the mighty monkeys, were thrown into the sea. Then that monkey, the offspring of the bearer of fragrance, endowed with terrific speed, took that medicinal mountain (back) unto Himavān and again presented himself before Rāma.

---

## SECTION LXXV.

THEN the exceedingly energetic lord of monkeys, Sugriva, said unto Hanumān these words fraught with import,—"Inasmuch as Kumbhakarna hath been slain as also the princes,* Rāvana can no longer defend the city.† Now let those principal monkeys that are endowed with great strength and that are furnished with fleetness, taking fire-brands (in their hands) rapidly rush towards Lankā." Then when the Sun had set and at the terrific front of Night, those foremost of monkeys marched towards Lankā, equipped with fire-brands. And charged at all points by numbers of monkeys armed with fire-brands, those fierce-eyed (Rākshasas) that guarded the gates.‡ suddenly fled away. And thereat, (the monkeys) delighted set fire to gates and upper apartments and spacious high-ways and various by-ways and edifices. And the fire§ burnt their‖ mansions by thousands; and mountain-like superstructures toppled headlong to the earth. And there burnt *aguru*, and sweet sandal, and pearls, and sheeny gems, and diamonds and corals. And there

---

* *Nishuditāh—slain*, left out for euphony.

† *Upanirhāram* is a contested term. Kataka gives the sense adopted by me. Tirtha says it means 'Rávana cannot give battle in the open field.' According to others, it means 'He cannot offer truce to us.—T.

‡ *Arakshāh*—according to some means *gates*. According to others, a *gulma* or *division of an army.—T.*

§ *Hutabhuk—lit.* eater of sacrificial offsprings—a designation of Fire.

‖ According to the commentator this refers to the fire lighted by the monkeys. I differ.—T.

burnt linen and fine silk and *âvikas* and various kinds of woolen cloths; and vessels of gold, and weapons; divers kinds of furniture, trappings and ornaments of steeds; cords for tying elephants; burnished ornaments for cars; armour of warriors; and hides of horses and elephants. And swords and bows and bow-strings and arrows and *tomaras** and *ankuçasǂ* and darts. And blankets and *chowris* and tiger-skins and musk and other things. And pearls and excellent gems; and edifices all around. And there the fire burneth heaps of various kinds of arms. And then the fire burnt various kinds of curious structures, and the dwellings of Rākshasas and all householders. And there the fire flaming up again and again burnt down by hundreds and thousands the houses of the denizons of Lankā,—clad in curious golden mail; and wearing wreaths and ornaments and attires; having their eyes wildly moving in intoxication; reeling in drink; those whose paramours were dressed in flowing apparels; or those wroth with their foes; or bearing maces and darts and swords in their hands; or engaged in eating or drinking; or asleep with their beloved on costly couches; or who, agitated with fright, were hastily going taking their sons with them.—And that fire burnt down firm-based rich dwellings furnished with innumerable apartments, and garnished with golden Moons and crescents,—and mansions having graceful crests; and variegated windows and daises raised there, embellished with rubies and lapises, and seeming to touch the Sun; and piles resembling mountains in grandeur,—and resonant with the cries of Krannchas and peacocks and the tinklings of ornaments. And the flaming gateways all round appeared like clouds in the rainy season lighted up by lightning, or like the peaks of a mighty mountain ablaze with a forest-

* An Iron club.—T.

ǂ The hook used to drive an elephant.—T.

conflagration. And superb damsels asleep in lofty edifices,* being burnt, cast away their ornaments and shrieked. And consumed by the fire, buildings began to drop down like the summits of a mighty mountain smit with the thunder-bolt of the thunderer. And those burning, appeared from a distance like the peaks of Himālaya aglow. And in consequence of those tops of the edifices burning and of the living flames, that night Lankā looked as if swarming with flowering Kinçukas. And with elephant-riders, and elephants, and steeds let loose, Lankā appeared like the Ocean at the hour of Universal tumbling,—with its ferocious aquatic animals whirling in wild chaos. Sometimes, an elephant seeing a steed let loose,—was flying away in fear; and sometimes a horse seeing a frightened elephant,was stopping, himself seized with fear.—And on Lankā burning, the mighty main with the reflection (of the conflagration) looked like an Ocean of red waters. And in a short time that city set on fire by the monkeys, looked like the earth glowing at the time of the Universal dissolution. And the cries of the females amidst the drift of smoke, heated by the flames, could be heard from an hundred Yoyanas. And as Rākshasas having their bodies burnt came out of houses, monkeys eager for encounter on a sudden sprung upon them. And the shouts of the monkeys and the cries of the Rākshasas made the ten cardinal quarters and the ocean and the Earth resound.

And on those high souled ones—both Rāma and Lakshmana—having been cured of their wounds, possessing themselves in calmness, took up their excellent bows. And Rāma drew that best of bows. And thereat there was heard a tremendous twang striking terror into the Rākshasas. And drawing his redoubtable bow, Rāma appeared like the reverend enraged Bhava, drawing his bow having sounds and instinct with Brahma energy. And the twang of Rāma's bow, drowning the roars of both the

* *Vimána*, according to Rámânuya, is a seven-storied edifice.—T.

monkeys and the Rākshasas,—was alone heard. And the ululations of the monkeys and the cries of the Rākshasas and the rattle of Rāma's bow—these three filled the ten cardinal quarters. And with the shafts discharged from his bow, the gateway of the city resembling the summit of Kailāça was crushed in pieces, scattered around on the ground. And seeing Rāma's shafts in cars and dwellings, the preparations for conflict were pushed on with great vigor. And in consequence of the foremost Rākshasas preparing for fight, and emitting roars, that night appeared like the Fatal Night itself. And the foremost monkeys were directed by the high-souled Sugriva, saying,—"Ye monkeys, do ye fight, approaching the gate lying at hand. But he that flyeth from his ranks, should be slain by main force". As the principal monkeys stationed themselves at the gate, equipped with fire-brands, wrath took possession of Rāvana. And as he yawned, the wind (blowing) from his mouth), filled the ten cardinal regions; and his wrath resembled that appearing in the person of Rudra. And wrought up with a mighty rage, he sent forth Kumbha and Nikumbha—both sons of Kumbhakarna—in company with innumerable Rākshasas.—And in accordance with Rāvana's command, Yupāksha and Sonitāksha, and Prajangha, and Kampana went with Kumbhakarna's sons. And, setting up leonine roars, he commanded all those highly powerful Rākshasas, saying,—"Do ye go this very day for battle." Thus directed, those heroic Rākshasas, equipped with flaming weapons, went out, roaring again and again. And the firmament was illuminated with the splendour of the ornaments of the Rākshasas and the splendour of their persons and the fire kindled by the monkeys. And there the light of the Moon and that of the stars and the brilliance of their ornaments,—combined, lighted up the welkin.—And the beams of the Moon and the brilliance of the ornaments and the flaming splendour of the planets emblazoned all round the forces of the monkeys and

Rākshasas. And the light of half-burnt houses, again, falling on the restless ripples of the sea, made it wear an extremely beautiful aspect. And those dreadful Rākshasa hosts, possessed of dreadful prowess and energy, were seen,—with ensigns and banners; excellent swords and *paracwadhas*,* terrific steeds and cars and elephants rife with *paths*,† and flaming darts and clubs and scimitars and *yrâsas* and *tomaras* and bows; bearing blazing *prâsas*; ringing with the tinklings of hundreds of balls; with their arms encased in golden networks; flourishing axes; whirling their mighty weapons; fixing shafts on their bows; making the air swoon away with the perfumes of their wreaths; extremely terrific; swarming with heroes; sending out sounds like those of the sea. And seeing the army of the Rākshasas incapable of being coped with advance, the monkey-forces began to move and send up loud cheers. And thereat that array of Rākshasas vehemently sprang forward before the force of the foe, like unto insects plunging into a flame. And whirling with their arms bludgeons and *acanis*, that army of Rākshasas appeared exceedingly grand. And the monkeys, eager for encounter, darted forward like maniacs; and began to despatch the night-rangers with rocks and trees and clenched fist. And Rākshasas possessed of dreadful prowess with whetted arrows swiftly cut off the heads of falling monkeys. And the Rākshasas ranged there, with their ears torn with teeth, or their heads broken by blows, or their limbs crushed with the discharge of crags. And in the same way other grim-visaged night-rangers slew with sharpened swords the foremost of monkeys on all sides. And one about to slay another was himself slain by the latter; and one, about to bring another down, was himself brought down (by his adversary, and one that was railing at another, was in turn

* A platoon consisting of one chariot, one elephant, three horse and five foot.—T.

† A kind of sword.

rebuked by his enemy; and one who was going to bite his foe, was himself bitten by him. And one was crying 'Give,'* and his adversary anon giveth; and another, again said,—'I will give. Why puttest thyself to trouble? Stay.' Thus there did they accost each other. And there was waged a terrific encounter between the monkeys and the Râkshasas,—in which arms lay scattered about; and armour and weapons strewn around; and mighty *prâcas*† were upraised; and which was faught with blows and darts and swords and *Kuntalas.*‡ And in that conflict the Rākshasas slaughtered monkeys by tens and sevens. And then the monkeys hemmed in the Rākshasa-forces, with their apparels falling off and with their mail and standards strewn around.

---

## SECTION LXXVI.

---

ON that furious and destructive carnage proceeding, Angada, eager for encounter,approached the heroic Kampana. Thereat, challenging Angada in wrath, he assailed him with impetuosity. And Kampana dealt a blow to Angada with his mace; and thereat, wounded with it, he reeled. Then regaining his senses, that energetic one hurled a mountain-top. Borne down by the blow, Akampana dropped down to the earth. And seeing Kampana slain in the conflict, Sonitāksha mounted on a car, intrepidly rushed against Angada. And he then impetuosly pierced Angada with sharpened shafts, keen and capable of cleaving the body

---

* Battle.

† A bearded dart.

‡ What could this be like? The commentator is mute. Wilson has *Kuntalikâ*—butter-knife or scoop. *Kuntala* may, however, mean a *plough.*—*T.*

and resembling the Fatal Fire itself in appearance,—with Kshuras[(a)] and Kshurapras[(b)] and Nārāchas[(c)] and Vatsadantas[(d)] and Siliumkhas[(e)] and Karnis[(f)] and Salas[(g)] and Vipātas,[(h)] and countless (other) whetted arrows. And the powerful son of Vāli—Angada—endowed with prowess having his person pierced with arrows suddenly smashed (his adversary's) car and arrows and dreadful bow. And thereat, Sonitāksha swiftly took up his sword and shield; and without reflecting for a moment, that vigorous one sprang forward. And the powerful Angada, speedily bounding up, seized his enemy's sword and holding the same with his hands shouted. And then hitting at (Akampana's) shoulder-blade, that powerful monkey—Angada—hewed him in twain, his blow going obliquely down like the sacred thread. And taking that terrific sword, and shouting again and again, in the field, Vāli's son rushed against other enemies. And then strong and heroic Yupāksha accompanied by Prajangha,—mounted on a car, wrathfully approached the mighty son of Vāli. And taking an iron mace, that hero, Sonitāksha, adorned with a golden *angada,*—attaining a little respite, advanced against Angada. And that redoubtable hero, the powerful Prajangha, also, accompanied by Yupāksha, fired with wrath, equipped with a mace, advanced towards the son of Vāli endowed with exceeding prowess. And placed between those two—Sonitāksha and Prajangha—that foremost of monkeys appeared like the full Moon placed between the Visākhās.[(i)] And Mainda and Dwivida defending Angada,

---

(*a*) Arrows having razor-like edges.

(*b*) Crescent-shaped shafts.

(*c*) Arrows made entirely of iron.

(*d*) Arrows resembling the teeth of calves.

(*e*) Arrows resembling the feathers of the Kanka.

(*f*) Arrows furnished with two sides resembling *cars.*

(*g*) Arrows with short leads.

(*h*) Arrows resembling the tops of Karaviras—Tirtha.

(*i*) The asterisks so named.

remained beside him, desirous of witnessing the encounter between those two (combatants). And fired with fury, those huge-bodied Rākshasas endowed with dreadful prowess, equipped with swords and shafts and maces,—being on their guard, fell upon the monkeys. And the encounter that took place between these three lords of monkeys combined (on one side), and the three redoubtable Rākshasas (on the other), was dreadful and capable of making people's down stand on end. And they,* taking up trees, hurled them in the conflict (against their antagonists); and the powerful Prājangha resisted all those with his swords. And (the monkeys) in the contest showered rocks and trees on the cars (of their enemies: and the exceedingly strong Yupāksha cut them off with vollies of arrows. And the powerful Sonitāksha, endowed with prowess, with his mace severed in the middle the trees which Dwivida and Mainda had uprooted and discharged. And summoning speed, Prajangha darted against Vāli's son, upraising a huge scimitar capable of piercing into the vitals of trees. And seeing him approach, that lord of monkeys possessed of exceeding strength and great prowess struck him with an Açwakarna tree; and with a blow smote his antagonist on his arm holding a *nistringa.* And seeing the sword resembling a mace dropped to the earth, that exceedingly mighty one clenched his fist into a blow like unto the levin; and that one, endowed with wondrous energy, smote in the forehead that foremost of monkeys possessed of redoubtable prowess. And thereat he for a moment was staggered. And then recovering his senses, the energetic and powerful son of Vāli by means of his clenched fist severed Prajangha's head from his body. Thereat Yupāksha, seeing his uncle slain in battle, with his eyes filled with tears, finding his shafts exhausted, swiftly descended from his car and took a sword. And finding Yupāksha charge, Dwivida, waxing wroth, speedily smote him on the breast; and that

* The monkeys.

powerful one also seized him. And finding his brother taken, the highly energetic Sonitāksha then dealt the mighty Dwivida a blow in the chest. And overcome by that blow, that one endowed with great strength, shook; and Dwivida seized his antagonist's upraised mace. In the meanwhile Mainda came to the side of Dwivida. And Sonitāksha and Yupāksha, bestirring themselves, began to vehemently and forcibly drag and pull those (two) monkeys. And Dwivida with his nail tore Sonitāksha's face; and that powerful one violently bringing him down to the earth, pressed him with might and main. And fired with wrath, Mainda—foremost of monkeys—grasped Yupāksha with his arms; and that one dropt down dead on the earth. And thereupon the force of the lord of the Rākshasas, having its foremost heroes slain,—and aggrieved thereat, went to where Kumbhakarna's son was. And then cheering up the flying forces, that best (of Rakshas),—the energetic Kumbha—seeing that Raksha host with its mighty heroes slain by highly powerful monkeys crowned with success, began to perform difficult feats in the encounter. And heedfully taking his bow, that first of bowmen discharged shafts resembling venomous serpents capable of piercing the body. And his excellent bow with shafts shone resplendent like the very bow of Indra himself affluent with the splendour of Airāvata and lightning. And then drawing his bow to its utmost bent, he hit Dwivida with a feathered shaft knobbed with gold. And suddenly wounded with it, that best of monkeys having the splendour of Trikuta, fell down senseless to the earth, stretching his legs wide. And Mainda, seeing his brother, broken in mighty encounter, furiously rushed forward, taking a gigantic crag; and that one possessed of great strength, hurled it at the Rākshasa. And thereat Kumbha severed that crag with fire shafts discharged (from his bow). And then aiming other fair-headed arrows resembling venomous snakes, that exceedingly energetic one smote Dwivida's elder brother in the chest.

And struck (with those arrows), that leader of monkey-bands, Mainda, with his marrow pierced therewith, fell down to the earth, deprived of his senses. And Angada seeing his uncles* endowed with exceeding prowess, overpowered, darted vehemently at Kumbha staying with bow upraised. And as he descended, Kumbha pierced him with fire shafts; and as one pierceth an elephant with *tomaras*, he also pierced (Angada) with three other arrows. And the powerful Kumbha pierced Angada with a great many arrows, sharp-pointed, whetted, keen and ornamented with gold. And Vāli's son Angada, albeit pierced all over in his person, did not shake; and he kept showering on his† head stones and trees. And the graceful son of Kumbhakarna cut off and cleft all those (stone and trees) discharged by Vāli,s son. And seeing him spring up, Kumbha pierced that monkey-leader on the ground with shafts, even as one assaileth an elephant with fire-brands. And blood gushed out of his closed eyes. And then covering his eyes with his hand, Angada with another took a *sâla* that was hard by. And placing on his breast the *sâla* furnished with shoulders, and pulling its branches and bending its top, he cleared it of its foliage, in that mighty encounter. And then in the sight of all the Rakshas he violently discharged that tree resembling the very banner of Indra and appearing like Mandara itself. And thereat he‡ severed it with seven sharp shafts capable of piercing the body. And Angada experienced a sharp pang and fell down deprived of his senses. And seeing the invincible Angada down like ebbing sea, the foremost monkeys informed Rāghava of it. And Rāma, hearing that Vāli's son had come to grief in terrific fight, directed the principal monkeys, headed by Jāmbavān. And hearing Rāma's command, the monkeys, fired with wrath, charged

* Maternal uncles.

† Kumbha's.

‡ Kumbha.

Kumbha, staying with his bow upraised. And those powerful monkeys, with their eyes crimsoned with choler and bearing rocks and trees in their hands, were engaged in defending Angada. And Jāmbavān and Sushena and the monkey, Vegadarçi, wrought with wrath, darted against that hero—son unto Kumbhakarna. And seeing them spring forward; he covered up those exceedingly mighty lords of monkey, with showers of shafts, even as a crag obstructeth the course of a current. And even the great deep cannot see his own shores, those high-souled lord of monkeys, coming within the range of his arrows, could not even see. And seeing those monkeys sore distressed by the shafts, the king of the monkeys, Sugriva, in that conflict taking his brother's son on his back, rushed against the son of Kumbhakarna, even as a powerful lion rusheth at an elephant ranging on the slopes of a mountain. And that mighty monkey, uprooting many an *açwakarna* and other mighty trees of various kinds, discharged them (at the foe). And by means of his sharp arrows the graceful son of Kumbhakarna cut off that down-pour of trees covering the welkin; and incapable of being resisted. And being baffled those trees looked like *çataghnis*. And seeing that shower of trees riven by Kumbha, the graceful lord of the monkeys endowed with exceeding strength and prowess, did not feel any mortification. And suddenly attacked, he bearing those arrows, seized Kumbha's bow resembling in resplendence the very bow of Indra. And swiftly bounding up and performing that feat difficult of being achieved, he, exceedingly enraged, addressed Kumbha resembling an elephant shorn of his tusks, saying,—"O elder brother of Nikumbha, marvellous are thy might and the force of thyself as well as the modesty and prowess that are thine and Rāvana's. And, O thou equal unto Prahrada or Vāli or the slayer of Vritra or Varuna or Kuvera! thou alone walkest in the wake of thy yet mightier father. As mental anguish doth not dog one that hath controlled his senses,—the celestials cannot cope in conflict with thee alone, O repressor of foes, O of mighty arms, bearing thy dart in thy hand. O thou of high intelligence, put forth thy prowess! and do thou also witness my work. It is only by virtue of the boon he hath received, that thy uncle can bear the deities and the Dānavas. But Kumbhakarna copeth with the immortals and Asuras by means of his native might. And in the bow equal to Indrajit himself and in power equal to Rāvana, thou now in might and energy art the foremost of Rākshasas. And to-day let all creatures witness the mighty and wonderful encounter in conflict between thee and me, like unto the meeting of Sakra and Samvara. And unparalleled is the feat thou hast performed; and thou hast displayed thy skill in weapons. And heroic monkeys endowed with dreadful vigor, have been brought down by thee. And, O hero it is only because of the apprehension* of censure of the people that I do not slay thee who art fatigued in consequence of the acts that thou hast performed. And reposing from fight, do thou see my strength!" And being thus honored (by Sugriva) with fair speech, (Kumbha) flamed up like a flame into which oblations have been poured. And then Kumbha seized Sugriva by the arms. And like two elephants in rut, they sighing momentarily, fastened on each other's person, and possessed each other,—and from fatigue emitting from their mouth flames mixed with vapour. And with the stamping of their feet, the earth was rent into rivers, and the main was waxed, with its billows surging furiously. Then Sugriva lifting up Kumbha clean, violently plunged him into the salt wash, making his eyes acquainted with the locality of the deep. And in consequence of Kumbha's plunge, the waters heaving up, rolled on all sides like the Vindhya or Mandara. Then springing up, and bringing Sugriva down, Kumbha, transported with wrath

* *i.e.* Lest people should censure me, saying,—'Sugriva slew Kumbha when he was fatigued in fight.—T.

dealt a blow on his chest, like unto the levin. And thereat his skin was rent, and blood began to gush out,—and the impetus of that blow broke Sugriva's bones. And the vehemence (of the blow) caused a great fire to blaze up at that spot; even as the thunder-bolt smiting the mountain Meru, maketh place blazed. And the mighty Sugriva—foremost of monkeys—sorely handled by him, fastened his fingers into a box resembling the thunder-bolt, and furnished with all the effulgence of the solar disc having a thousand rays. And then that powerful one made that blow descend right on Kumbha's breast. And agonised with that stroke, Kumbha reft of his senses, dropped like unto a fire that hath lost its brightness. And overpowered by that blow, the Rākshasa anon dropped down, like unto the bright Lohitānga dropping from the firmament urged on by Destiny. And the aspect of the falling Kumbha with his breast broken by the blow, appeared like that of the Sun routed by Rudra. And on his being slain, in encounter, by the foremost of monkeys endowed with terrific strength, the earth with her hills and woods, shook; and a mighty fear took possession of the Rakshas.

## SECTION LXXVII.

SEEING his brother slain by Sugriva, Nikumbha, gazed at the lord of the monkeys, as if consuming him with his passion. And then that one endowed with calmness, grasped a bludgeon entwined with wreaths, and furnished with an iron ring measuring five fingers, and resembling the top of the Mahendra;* plated with gold and embellished with

* The mountain, so named.

diamonds and lapises,—and looking like the rod of Yama himself; dreadful, and capable of removing the fear of the Rakshas. And whirling this, that highly powerful one, resembling the banner itself of Sakra in energy, Nikumbha possessed of terrific strength, with his mouth wide open, set up shouts. And with gold adorning his breast, and *angadas* placed on his arms and a pair of curious and variegated ear-rings, Nikumbha, with his ornaments and that same bludgeon, appeared beautiful like a mass of roaring clouds laughing with lightning and furnished with the iris. And the head of that huge-bodied heroe's *parigha* undid the conjunction of the Seven* Winds and appeared† like a noiseless and smokeless flame. Along with the gyration of Nikumbha's *parigha* the whole welkin, together with the excellent city‡ of the Gandharbas, and the planets, stars and the moon, began to whirl. And Nikumbha was hard to approach like unto the fire of dissolution, being resplendent with the brilliance of *parigha* and other ornaments and having his anger for its fuels. And the Rākshasas and monkeys did not dare stir even out of fear. And the heroic Hanumān, spreading his breast, stood before him. And thereat the powerful (Nikumbha) having long-arms§ threw his *parigha* resembling the Sun at the breast of that powerful one. And falling on the firm and spacious breast of Hanumān it was broken into hundred pieces. And the broken portions, being scattered, appeared like hundreds of fire-brands in the sky. Like unto a mountain standing still even at the time of an earthquake that mighty monkey was not moved albeit struck with the *parigha*. Being thus hurt that highly powerful Hanumān, the foremost of the monkeys, with great velocity clenched his fist. And with this, the powerful (monkey)

---

* This indicates the length of the Parigha.

† This might refer to Kumbha as well.

‡ Some say *Vitapabati* and some say Alakā.

§ *Lit.* arms resembling *parighas.*

gifted with great impetuosity, and resembling the wind in prowess, struck Nikumbha on his breast. And with that fist, his (Nikumbha's) armour* was riven and blood gushed out. And a light rising out of his breast suddenly disappeared like unto lightning disappearing in a mass of clouds. And being struck with his (Hanumān's) fist Nikumbha was greatly moved and restoring himself attacked the mighty Hanumān and pulled him up. And beholding in conflict the terrible and powerful Hanumān pulled up by Nikumbha, the residents of Lankā began to shout with joy. Being thus put to shame by that Raksha, Hanumān the son of the Wind, struck him with his iron fist. And releasing himself from the grasp of Nikumbha, Hanumān the Wind-god's son instantly planted his foot on the earth. Inflamed with ire, he, throwing down Nikumbha, began to crush him; and gifted with vehemence, he, with great impetuosity, leaped up and sat on the breast (of the Raksha). And holding his head with two hands, he, emitting loud roars, displaced his head. Nikumbha being thus slain in conflict by the Wind-god's son, there ensued a terrible conflict between the highly enraged armies of the son of Daçaratha and the lord of Rākshasas. And Nikumbha being deprived of his life, the monkeys began to shout—as if resounding all the quarters. And with it the whole earth moved and the abode of the celestials dropped down. And the Rākshasa-hosts were greatly terrified.

---

* Some texts read *charma* (skin) in the place of *Barma*—(armour) *i. e.* his skin was rent—This equally indicates Hanumān's strength.—T.

## SECTION LXXVIII.

Beholding Kumbha and Nikumbha slain, Rāvana was excited with ire like unto flaming fire. And being beside himself, simultaneously with wrath and grief Rāvana* spoke unto Makarāksha, Khara's son, having spacious eyes, saying, —"O child, do thou proceed at my command with the army and destroy Rāghava and Lakshmana with all the monkeys." Hearing the words of Rāvana, Khara's son, Makarāksha, proud of his own prowess, delightedly spoke unto the night-ranger, saying, "Be it so." And saluting and circumambulating the Ten-necked one, that hero, at Rāvana's behest, issued out of the house. And Khara's son spoke unto the commander who was near him, saying,—"Do thou speedily bring the chariot here and all the soldiers." And hearing his words, that commanding night-ranger, soon led before him the army and the chariot. And going round the chariot and addressing the charioteer that night-ranger (Makarāksha) said,—"O charioteer, do thou soon drive the chariot." And Makarāksha addressed those Rākshasas, saying,—"O Rākshasas! do ye all fight before me. I have been commanded by the high-souled Rāvana, the lord of Rākshasas, to slay both Rāma and Lakshmana in conflict. I shall slay to-day, O night-ranger, with my excellent arrows, Rāma, Lakshmana, Sugriva and all other monkeys. Like unto fire consuming dry fuel, shall I to-day slay the host of monkeys with my darts." Hearing those words of Makarāksha, the mighty night-rangers, (addressed themselves for fight). They were armed with various weapons, cautious; assuming shapes at will, crooked, having fearful teeth, coppery eyes; roaring like elephants, having dishevelled hair and

* Nairita is another name of Rávana.

terrible. And encircling the huge-bodied son of Khara, those gigantic (Rākshasas) began to proceed, delighted and moving the earth (with the weight of their persons). There arose a terrible noise on all sides from the sound of conches, and thousands of bugles, and from the moving of the arms of the heroes. And all on a sudden the reins slipped off (the hands of) the charioteer and the flag of the Rākshasas dropped down. And the course of the steeds was thus slackend and they began to move slowly and poorly with their heads drooping down. There blew a terribly rough wind mixed with dust when the fearfully wicked-minded Makarāksha's issued out for battle. Those powerful Rākshasas neglecting those bad omens proceeded towards where Rāma and Lakshmana were. They were all black like unto clouds, elephants and buffaloes, and had marks of swords and maces on their persons. And all those night-rangers were skilled in the art of warfare and began to range to and fro (in the battle field) saying, "I shall go first."

---

## SECTION LXXIX.

BEHOLDING Makarāksha out for battle, those foremost monkeys, leaping on a sudden, addressed themselves for fight. Thereupon ensued a terrible conflict, capable of making one's down stand on end, between the night-rangers and the monkeys like unto one between the celestials and Dānavas. And those monkeys and night-rangers crushed each other down with trees, darts, maces and *parighas*. And those night-rangers began to assail those foremost of monkeys with *sakti*,* swords, maces, *kuntas*, *tomaras*, *patticas*,

---

* A short arrow thrown from the hand or shot through a tube.—T.

*Vindipalas,** arrows, nooses and clubs. Being thus assailed with fearful arrows by Khara's son, those monkeys, stricken with fear, fled away. And beholding the monkeys fly away, the victorious Rākshasas began to roar like excited lions. The monkeys thus flying away to all quarters, Rāma with a downpour of shafts assailed the Rākshasas. And beholding the Rākshasas thus overpowered, the night-ranger Makarāksha, excited with the flame of ire, said,—"Stay, O Rāma, let us both fight with each other; I shall take thy life with sharp arrows discharged off my bow. Thou didst slay my father in the forest of Dandaka. Remembering thy action and finding thee before, my ire is excited. O Rāghava! O Vicious-souled one! My limbs are being burnt (with wrath) for I did not see thee then in that mighty forest. O Rāma, by my good luck, I have got thee to-day, like unto a hungry lion desiring to have other animals. Being despatched by my arrows to the world of devils, thou shalt live with those heroes, who had been killed by thee before. What is the use of speaking more, O Rāma, do thou hear my words. Let all the people behold thy as well as my prowess in the battle-field. Either with weapon or with clubs, in whatever thou art expert, do thou fight with me in the battle-field, O Rāma." Hearing the words of Makarāksha, Rāma, Daçaratha's son, smiling, replied to the words of the babbler. "O Raksha, what is the use of idle prating? None can achieve success in a battle with idle words—but with fighting. I slew in the forest of Dandaka thy father with fourteen thousand Rākshasas, Triçira and Dushana. O vile one, thou being slain to day, with thy flesh, vultures and crows, having sharp beaks and nails, and jackals, shall be satisfied.† Being thus

* An Iron spear or dart.—T.

† Here is another sloka, which is to be found in all N. W. P. texts and in one or two texts published in Bengal—but it has been omitted by many for it conveys the same meaning as the previous sloka; the meaning is:—And the birds drinking thy blood shall fly away to various quarters.—T.

addressed by Rāghava, the mighty Makarāksha, began to dart sharp arrows towards him in the battle-field. And Rāma, with his shafts, sundered into several pieces, those arrows. And being thus rendered useless those arrows, feathered in gold, fell down on the earth. Then there arose a terrible conflict between the Rākshasa Khara's son and Daçaratha's son. And there were audible in that battle-field, the outcry of the heroes and the twang of the bows stretched by their hands, like unto the muttering of the clouds in the sky. And to beheld that wondrous conflict, the celestials, Dānavas, Gandharbas, Kinnaras and the mighty serpents stationed themselves in the sky. They were wounded with the arrows discharged by each other and their strength was doubled. And they began to fight in that battle-field one attacking and the other withstanding the attack. And in that conflict the Rākshasa sundered the shafts discharged by Rāma. And likewise Rāma severed into several pieces the arrows shot by the Rākshasa. All the quarters were covered with arrows and nothing on earth or in the sky was visible. Thereupon being excited with ire, Rāghava of long arms sundered his (Rākshasa's) bow in conflict and with eight *Nârachas* pierced the charioteer. And with arrows Rāma sundered the chariot and killing the horses brought them down. And the night-ranger Makarāksha was brought down on the earth from the chariot. He then again rose up with a dart in his hand creating terror unto all creatures and resembling the Fire of Dissolution in resplendence. It was a terribly huge dart conferred on him by Siva, shining in the sky in its native brilliance and like unto another weapon of destruction.* And beholding which dart even the celestials fly away in fear to different quarters. And taking up that huge flaming dart, the night-ranger, being excited with ire, hurled it at the high-souled Rāghava.

* This refers to the weapon used by Siva for destruction—for Siva, according to the Hindu Mythology is the God of destruction.—T.

And Rāghava, with four shafts, sundered that dart, in the sky, flaming and hurled at him by the son of Khara. And that flaming dart, feathered in gold, being splintered into several pieces by Rāma's arrows fell down on earth like a huge fire-brand. And beholding that dart baffled thus by Rāma of unwearied actions all those, stationed in the welkin began to shout, "Well done! Well done!!." And beholding his dart thus sundered, the night-ranger Makarāksha clenching his fist spoke unto Kākutstha, saying, "Stay! Stay!" And seeing him advance thus, the descendant of Raghu, smiling, fixed a fiery arrow on his bow. And with that arrow the Raksha was slain by Kākutstha in battle. And having his heart pierced he fell down and died. And beholding Makarāksha thus slain all the Rākshasas, being afraid of Rāma's arrows, proceeded towards Lankā. And seeing that night-ranger, the son of Khara, slain by Rāma's arrows, like unto a mountain clept by a thunder-bolt, the celestials were greatly delighted.

## SECTION LXXX.

HEARING of the destruction of Makarāksha, the heroic Rāvana, being excited with ire, began to grind his teeth. Being thus angered, and thinking within himself what steps to take, he ordered his son Indrajit to proceed to the battle-field. "O hero, gifted with great prowess as thou art, do thou, hidden (in clouds) or appearing before them, slay the two heroic brothers Rāma and Lakshmana. Thou didst defeat in conflict Indra of unequalled prowess. Shalt thou then neglect to slay men as they are?" Being thus addressed by the lord of the Rākshasas and obeying his father's command, Indrajit proceeded towards the sacrificial ground to satisfy Fire (with oblations). There came some she-demons with crimson turbans and waited respectfully where Rāvana's son was offering oblations unto Fire. In that sacrifice the weapons were the leaves of *sara*,* *bibhutaks*† were fuels, and there were brought crimson clothes and *sruvas*‡ made of black iron. And spreading fire on all sides with *sara* leaves and *tomaras*, (Indrajit) caught a living goat, all black, by the neck. And the fire, with oblations of *sara*, became greatly blazed and devoid of smoke. And there were visible many good omens indicating victory. The flame of the fire was like unto gold, and moving Southwards began to receive offerings of clarified butter. And thus offering oblations unto fire and unto celestials, Dānavas and Rākshasas, he ascended an excellent car and soon disappeared. It was drawn by four horses and a huge bow, set with sharp arrows, appeared beautiful on that excellent car. The chariot was brilliant with its own native resplendence, adorned with gold and painted with the figures of deer and a cresent. It was encircled on all sides with golden bracelets, adorned with flags made of *vaidurja* and was like unto the flaming fire. And being thus well protected with Brahmā weapons resembling the Sun in brilliance, the mighty son of Rāvana became invincible. And offering oblations unto Fire in accordance with demonaic incantations and thus obtaining the power of hiding himself, that hero, ever victorious in battle, issued out of the city and said,—"Slaying these two brothers in battle, who have uselessly wandered away into the forest, shall I crown my father Rāvana with victory. Destroying Rāma and Lakshmana, and clearing the monkeys off the earth, shall I satisfy my sire greatly."

* Saccharum—a reed or grass.

† Beleric myrobalan.

‡ A ladle with a double extremety or two oval collateral excavations made of wood to pour *ghee* upou the sacrificial Fire.—T.

Saying this, he disappeared from their view. Thereupon that fearful foe of the lord of celestials appeared in the battle-field, excited with wrath, armed with bow and sharp Nāraçhas and commissioned thus by the Ten-necked one. He beheld there those two heroes discharging flaming arrows and surrounded by the monkeys like unto the fearful three-hooded serpent in the midst of other serpents. And thinking "these must be Rāma and Lakshmana," and stretching his bow he began showering arrows like unto clouds. He was seated in a car in the welkin and hidden from the human gaze and began to assail Rāma and Lakshmana with sharp shafts. And being hurt with the arrows, Rāma and Lakshmana, fixing arrows on their bows, began to discharge celestial shafts. And those two highly powerful heroes could not even touch his person with their arrows resembling the Sun albeit they covered the whole welkin therewith. And clouding the whole sky with smoke that effulgent one, enveloped in frost, hid himself from their gaze. There was not audible the twang of his bow,the sound of the wheels, or the noise of the steeds. Nor was he seen by any. In that terrible darkness of clouds that one of mighty arms began to make a downpour of Nārachas and arrows like hail storms. And in that encounter, Rāvana's son, inflamed with ire, wounded Rāma, with shafts, resembling the Sun and obtained by him as a boon. And being hurt with Nārāchas, like unto mountains wet with rain, those two foremost of men, began to discharge shafts feathered in gold. And reaching the son of Rāvana in the sky and soaked in blood those golden arrows, fell down on earth. And those two best of men, hurt with his arrows, became more effulgent and baffled the shafts discharged by the Rākshasa. Thereupon Rāma and Lakshmana began to aim their sharp shafts to the direction whence the arrows came down. And stationed in his chariot that mighty car-warrior disturbed all quarters with his arrows and pierced Daçaratha's sons with sharp shafts won by him. And being greatly hurt with those sharp-pointed and terrible arrows Rāma and Lakshmana appeared like blossoming *kingsukas*. Like unto the sun hidden in clouds they could see neither his countenance and motion, nor his bow and arrows. And being wounded with those arrows hundreds of monkeys died and fell down on the earth. Thereupon Lakshmana, being excited with wrath, spoke unto his brother, saying—"To slay all the Rākshasas shall I discharge to-day Brahmā weapon." Thereupon Rāma spoke unto Lakshmana, gifted with auspicious marks, saying—"It doth not behove thee to clear all the Rākshasas off the earth for the folly of one individual. Thou shouldst not slay him,who hath retired from battle, hath hidden himself, hath sought thy shelter, hath stood before thee with joined palms, hath fled away or who is bewildered. O thou of mighty-arms, let us try to slay him (Indrajit). And to accomplish it I shall use the weapons gifted with great impetuosity and resembling the serpents. He is hidden from the public gaze so we must slay him—had he been fighting openly the leaders of the monkey hosts could have slain that Rākshasa. Truly he shall be burnt to death with my shafts and fall down on the earth albeit he entereth the regions under the earth or the abode of the celestials." Having said these words pregnant with a high significance, the high-souled and heroic descendant of Raghu, being surrounded by monkeys, began to concert various plans for the destruction of that terrible Rākshasa of wicked deeds.

## SECTION LXXXI.

Having read the intention of that high-souled Rāghava, he retired from the battle-field and entered into the city of Lankā. And remembering the destruction of many a quick-paced Rākshasa, his eyes were rendered coppery with ire; and that hero, the son of Rāvana, issued out of the city again. And that highly powerful, Indrajit, a descendant of Pulasta and an enemy of the celestials, issued out, encircled by the Rākshasas, by the western gate. And beholding the heroic brothers Rāma and Lakshmana prepared for fight, Indrajit spread illusions. And placing an illusory figure of Sitā on the car, encircled by a huge army he began to make arrangements for her destruction. And desiring to charm all with his illusions, that one of wicked intent, preparing himself to slay Sitā, proceeded towards the monkeys. And beholding him thus proceed, the monkeys, inflamed with ire, desirous of fighting and with crags in their hands, moved on. And preceded them all, Hanumān, the foremost of the monkeys, with a huge mountain-top in his hand. He beheld there, on Indrajit's car, Sitā, deprived of all joy, poorly, greatly reduced with fasts and wearing a single braid. And Rāghava's beloved spouse wore a piece of soiled cloth, and though highly beautiful, the grace of her person was greatly spoiled with dirt. That daughter of Janaka, was not seen by him for a long time. And beholding her and deciding instantly that she is the daughter of Mithilā, (he became greatly sorry). And seeing her on the car, innocent, poor, deprived of joy and brought under the influence of the son of the lord of Rākshasas that great monkey thought within himself—'What must be the intention of Indrajit?' and accompanied by heroic monkeys advanced towards the son of Rāvana. And beholding that monkey-host, Rāvana's son became beside himself with ire and unsheathing his weapon *Nistrinsha,* caught her by the hair. And that Rākshasa addressed himself to strike her in the presence of all those monkeys, and that illusory figure of Sitā began to bewail saying, "O Rāma! O Rāma!" And seeing her thus caught by the head, Hanumān, the son of Maruta, greatly sorry, began to shed tears. And beholding that beloved spouse of Rāma, having a tender and beautiful person, he addressed angrily the son of the lord of Rākshasas with harsh words. "It is for thy destruction, O Vicious-souled one! that thou hast touched her hair. Being descended from that great Brahmā ascetic thou art born as a Rākshasa. O! cursed art thou, since thou hast cherished such a desire and engaged in such a vicious deed. O vile! O wicked! O cruel and dishonorable wight! O thou having vice for thy prowess! O shameless! Art thou not ashamed of perpetrating such an inhuman deed. What hath Maithili done by thee, O cruel one! that thou art ready to slay her—She hath been banished from her home, territory and hath been separated from her lord. O thou worthy of being slain, destroying Sitā, thou shalt not live long as thou hast been brought under me. Thou shalt after the death reach the place which is occupied by those who murder women—a place which is avoided even by those who commit every sort of crime punishable by law." Saying this Hanumān, accompanied by monkeys armed with weapons, and excited with ire, proceeded towards the son of the lord of Rākshasas. Beholding the highly powerful monkeys advance thus the Rākshasas, inflamed with wrath, obstructed them. And assailing the monkey-hosts with thousands of arrows, Indrajit spoke unto that foremost of monkeys, Hanumān, saying,—"To-day I shall slay before you all Vaidehi, for whom thou, Sugriva and Rāma have come. Slaying her, O monkey, I shall afterwards kill thee, Rāma, Lakshmana and Sugriva and the dishonorable Bibhisana. And, O monkey, about not destroying women, of which thou wert speaking ( I might say ) that we must always do what pains our enemies."* Saying this, Indrajit with a sharp sword, himself killed the illusory Sitā thus bewailing. And being sundered by him obliquely in a way in which a sacred thread lies on one's own person, the innocent (Sitā) having a beautiful countenance fell down on the earth. And slaying her Indrajit spoke unto Hanumān, saying,—"Behold I have slain (before thee) with my sword Rāma's beloved. And Vaidehi being thus slain, all your labours have been rendered useless." And destroying her with his own hand by means of a huge sword, Indrajit, greatly pleased ascended his car and began to emit dreadful roars. And the monkeys stationed near heard that terrible roar and saw him enter the castle.† And slaying Sitā‡ that wicked-minded son of Rāvana became greatly pleased. And beholding him thus delighted the monkeys being greatly sorry fled away.

---

## SECTION LXXXII.

HEARING that dreadful uproar resembling the sound of Indra's thunder-bolt, the monkeys, casting their looks on all sides fled away. Thereupon Hanumān, the son of Maruta, spoke unto them, poorly, terrified and of a sorrowful countenance, saying,—" O monkeys, why do ye look so melancholy

---

* There is one *sloka* intervening according to some texts—but it has been omitted by many. The reason's for this omission are best known to them. The purport is:—"Why did Râma slay Târakâ before ? And I shall therefore slay his spouse the daughter of king Janaka." Hearin Indrajit attempts to justify himself and wants to prove that Râma is equally blameable for this.—T.

† The castle built by Indrajit by means of his illusory power in the air.—T.

‡ This refers to the figure of Sitâ made by illusion.—T.

and why are you flying away? Why have ye renounced your earnest desire for fight? And where is your heroism gone? Do ye remain behind me, I shall go first in the battle." Being thus addressed by that highly intelligent son of the Wind-god, they were greatly excited with wrath and being pleased took up trees and crags in their hands. And roaring thus the leading monkeys advanced towards the Rākshasas and stood encircling Hanumān in the battle-field. And being surrounded on all sides by leading monkeys, Hanumān began to burn down enemy's host like unto fire spreading its flames. And being encircled by monkey-hosts that mighty monkey resembling Death himself began to grind the Rākshasas. And being overwhelmed with grief and wrought up with ire, that monkey Hanumān, threw a huge crag on the car of that son of Rāvana. Beholding that crag about to fall down on the car, the charioteer moved his horses and it was speedily brought at some distance. And not reaching Indrajit stationed on the car and the charioteer, that crag, uselessly hurled, fell down on the earth. And that crag falling down many of the Rākshasas were crushed. Thereupon hundreds of huge-bodied monkeys, emitting cries and taking up crags and trees proceeded towards him (Indrajit) and hurled them at him. And the monkeys gifted with dreadful prowess began to make a downpour of crags and trees. They thus assailed the enemies and frequently emitted cries. And the grim-visaged night-rangers were thus assailed with trees in that field by the terrible monkeys. Beholding his army thus distressed by the monkeys, Indrajit, excited with wrath, and taking up his dart, proceeded towards the enemies, and encircled by his soldiers showered terrible shafts upon them. And that one of dreadful prowess slew many a leading monkey by means of darts, Açanis, swords, *pattiças* and clubs. And the highly powerful monkeys destroyed his retinue, with crags, stones and trees having strong trunks. And Hanumān thus crushed many a Rākshasa of terrible deeds. Obstructing the Rākshasas (for some time) Hanumān spoke unto monkeys, saying,—"Stay, we should not fight now. That daughter of Janaka hath been slain, for whom we have engaged in fight, renouncing all hope of life and desiring to accomplish Rāma's satisfaction. Let us now go and inform Rāma and Sugriva of it. And we shall do as we shall be commanded by them. Saying this and desisting all the monkeys from encounter that foremost of monkeys proceeded undaunted and heroically. And beholding Hanumān proceed thus where Rāghava was that wicked-minded one (Indrajit) with a view to offer oblations unto Fire entered the sacrificial altar *Nikumbhilā*. And reaching there Indrajit lighted up fire and began to pour oblations therein. And the Fire blazed up receiving oblations of blood, and being satisfied assumed the appearance of the setting sun. And Indrajit conversant with all ceremonials, offered oblations in due form for the welfare of the Rākshasas. And they all stood there watching the result and desirous of ascertaining the success of the battle.*

## SECTION LXXXIII.

HEARING the terrible war-cry of the Rākshasas and monkeys Rāghava spoke unto Jāmbavān, saying :—"O gentle one, forsooth hath Hanumān performed some mighty act—for I hear the dreadful sound of the weapons. Do thou therefore proceed speedily, O lord of bears, with all thy soldiers to assist that foremost of monkeys.

* This sloka hath been left off in some editions.—T.

Thereupon, saying, 'So be it,' that king of bears, surrounded by his forces, approached the Western gate, where the monkey, Hanumān, was stationed. And then the lord of bears saw Hanumān approach, surrounded by monkeys sighing hard, who had faught the fight. And seeing on the way that host of bears dreadful and resembling dark clouds, on the march, Hanumān made them desist. And that illustrious one along with that force, speedily presented himself (before Rāma), and with a heavy heart addressed him, saying,—"As we were fighting the field, Rāvana's son, Indrajit in our very sight slew Sitā, crying (in distress). O subduer of enemies, seeing her (in this plight), I, with my senses bewildered, have been overwhelmed with grief. Therefore I have come unto thee to inform thee of what hath befallen." Hearing these words of his, Rāghava, overwhelmed with grief, dropped down to the earth, like a tree whose roots have been severed. Seeing the god-like Rāghava down on the earth, the foremost monkeys from all sides rushed forward and came to where (he was). And with water scented with lotuses,* they fell to sprinkling that one resembling a furious fire† that hath suddenly arisen. Thereat Lakshmana, overcome with sorrow, embracing Rāma, spoke unto him words fraught with reason and import,—"Profitless‡ virtue is incapable, O noble one, of delivering from calamities thee, who hast subdued thy senses, and who ever abidest in the good path. Beings and the mobile as well as the immobile cannot have that direct perception of virtue which they have of happiness. Therefore, I ween, virtue is a non-entity. Inasmuch as the immobile (albeit devoid of any regard for

---

* *Padmotpalasugandhibhih*—water scented with *padmas*—*lotuses proper*, and *utpalas*—*blue lotuses*—(*Nymphea cerulea*).—*T.*

† 'Rāma,' remarks the commentator, 'was a' fire lighted by his grief for Sitā.'—T.

‡ 'Profitless,' although apparently an epithet of virtue, is really the predicate of the sentence. 'Virtue, incapable of delivering thee.........is *profitless*.'—*T.*

virtue) are nevertheless happy. and as the mobile also are so, this virtue cannot lead to happiness. (If it were so), one like thee would have not been placed in peril. If unrighteousness would bring unhappiness on creatures, Râvana should hence to hell, and thou possessed of virtue, shouldst not come by misfortune. And seeing that he is free from danger, and thou art in it, righteousness and its opposite are found to have tendencies the very reverse of those assigned to them respectively (by the Vedas). And if by means of virtue, one attaineth the felicity attached to it, and by means of unrighteouness, one reapeth its proper fruit, then let those that are unrighteous reap the fruit of their impiety,—nor let those that set their face against sin, be deprived of the fruit of their righteousness; and let those that walk in the way of virtue reap the fruit of their piety. But as prosperity attendeth those that are established in unrighteousness, and as those regardful of righteousness fare lamentably,—these* have not the senses assigned to them (by the scriptures). If, O Rāghava, (it is contended that)unrighteousness cutteth off the wicked,then whom shall Unrighteousness, himself slain by the act of slaughter of the destroyer,—slay in his turn ? Or if it is said that one is slain or slayeth another by ordinance, then it is Destiny, which is touched by the sinful act and not he. O chastiser of foes, incapable of meting out retribution,†—unmanifest itself, and non-existent, how can virtue, even if we grant its existence, find out the person that should be slain ? If, O foremost of the good, it had existed, thou wouldst not have come by any misfortune. But inasmuch as thou hast fallen into this plight, there is no such thing as virtue. Or itself feeble and impotent, it taketh refuge in manliness. And being powerless and bereft of dignity, it should, I deem, by no means be followed. And if virtue is a property of manliness, then carefully forsak-

* Virtue and vice.

† 'In consequence,' remarks Râmânuja, 'of their being deviod of consciousness.'

ing virtue, do thou follow strength as thou hast hitherto followed virtue. But, O subduer of enemies, if truthfulness be virtue, art thou not bound by that departing from which the king lost his life ?* And, O chastiser of foes, if virtue must be practised above all, or if prowess must have precedence,—then the thunder-handed Satakratu would not have celebrated his sacrifice, slaying the ascetic.† O Rāghava, virtue aided by prowess, destroyeth enemies. Therefore, O Kākutstha, people, for compassing their ends, resort to both virtue and prowess. This, sire, is my opinion: this, O Rāghava, is virtue. But thou, having then renounced the kingdom, hast laid the axe at the root‡ of righteousness. Like streams issuing out mountains, all acts spring from wealth flowing from various regions and attaining magnitude. Like a shrunken stream in summer, all the acts of that foolish person who hath been divorced by wealth, are annihilated.—He that renouncing riches within his reach,§ hankers after enjoyment,—being carried away by his overmastering desire, taketh to getting at wealth by sinful acts; and then he incurreth guilt. Unto him that hath wealth are friends, unto him that hath wealth are acquaintances,—he that hath wealth is an individuality in this world, and he that hath wealth is a learned person. He that hath wealth is powerful; he that hath wealth is intelligent; he that hath wealth is mighty-armed; and he that hath wealth is full of all graces. All these that I have ennumerated are the evils of forsaking fortune. (I cannot divine) what made thee, renouncing the monarchy, to adopt such a course.—

* Explains the commentator,—'King Daçaratha lost his life, because he did not observe his word of installing thee in the kingdom. Art thou not bound by his word as well ?'—T.

† The Logic is all in a jumble; but such is the text. The ascetic was Viçwarupa. The meaning, according to the commentator, is that, prowess is first and virtue next. Indra first used force, and then acquired merit.—T.

‡ 'Root', remarks Râmânuja,—'which is interest !'

§ The commentator would have '*gotten* riches.'

He that hath riches, hath virtue and desire attending on him, and hath everything auspicious. That one without wealth, that seeketh it, cannot secure the wealth of prowess, without riches and desire. And, O lord of men, cheerfulness, and desire, and pride, and piety,and anger, and self-restraint, and self-control—all these come from wealth. As the planets are not discovered on a stormy day, that wealth, the want of which renders this world naught even unto the ascetics practising righteousness,—is not visible in thee. O hero, thou having abode by the words of thy superior and having come (to the forest), thy wife dearer then life itself hath been ravished by Rakshas. But, O hero, to-day, O Rāghava, by my acts will I remove this huge sorrow that hath been heaped upon us by Indrajit. Therefore, rise thou up. Rise up, O foremost of men, O long-armed one, O thou who observest vows. Why dost thou not understand thyself as the Supreme Soul ?* And, O sinless one, urged on behalf of thy welfare, I, waxing wroth on hearing of the slaughter of Janaka's daughter, shall with my shafts entirely raze to the ground Lankā with cars and elephants and steeds and the foremost Rakshas."

## SECTION LXXXIV.

As Lakshmana devoted to his brother was comforting Rāma, Bibhishana, posting his forces at their proper quarters, came there, surrounded by four heroes accoutred in various arms, resembling masses of collyrium or leaders of elephant-herds. And approaching the high-souled Rāghava, overwhelmed with grief, he saw

* Rāma is conceived as an incarnation of Vishnu.—T.

the monkeys with tears in their eyes. And he saw that joy of the Ikshwāku race—the high-souled Rāghava—stupified with grief, lying on the lap of Lakshmana. And seeing Rāma cast down and inflamed with grief, Bibhishana, inly pained, said,—'What is this?' Thereat,gazing at Bibhishana's countenance as well as all those monkeys, Lakshmana, with his eyes flooded with tears, said these words pregnant with dire import,—"O placid one, hearing from Hanumān's lips that Sitā hath been slain by Indrajit.Rāghava hath been overcome with stupor." As Sumitrā's son was speaking thus, Bibhishana, preventing him, addressed the stupified Rāma in these pregnant words,—"O king, all that Hanumān in distressful guise had communicated unto thee I deem as improbable, like unto the drying of the deep. I know the intent of the impious Rāvana with reference to Sitā, O mighty-armed one. Her he will not slay. I, seeking his welfare, had besought him much, saying,—'Let go Vaidehi',—but he did not act up to my speech. Neither by conciliation, nor by gift, nor by dissension,—and where is war?—nor by any other means is one capable of obtaining the very sight of Sitā. Having bewildered the monkeys, the Rākshasa hath gone back; and, O mighty-armed one, know her to be the illusory daughter of Janaka. To-day, going to the sacrificial ground (called) Nikumbhilā, he will offer oblations into fire; and there the deity of fire will present himself along with Vāsava and the (other) divinities. And then Rāvana's son shall be invincible in battle. Indubitably that illusion hath been wrought by him, to deceive (the monkeys), so that they might not through their prowess disturb him there. Thither will we go before he hath furnished his (sacrifice). O foremost of men, shake off this vain sorrow that hath overcome thee! Seeing thee smitten with grief, this entire host is dispirited. Here, with thy heart composed, do thou stay, summoning thy strength. Send Lakshmana along with us and the flower of the forces.

This foremost of men by means of sharpened shafts will make Rāvana's son give up his rites; and then shall he be capable of being slain by us. These keen and sharpened shafts of his,attaining access of velocity through the feathers of birds, and themselves resembling fierce fowls, will drink his* blood. Therefore, O mighty-armed one, do thou in order to the destruction of the Rākshasa, commission Lakshmana, even as the wielder of the thunder-bolt commandeth the same. And as to-day no time should be lost, therefore do thou send Lakshmana for campassing the destruction of the foe, even as Mahendra sendeth the thunder-bolt for bringing about the destruction of the enemies of the immortals. If that foremost of Rākshasas can finish his rites, he shall be invisible to both celestials and Asuras; and, he fighting after finishing his sacrifice, the celestials themselves shall be placed in great jeopardy."

## SECTION LXXXV.

HEARING his speach, Rāghava, overwhelmed with grief, could not perfectly comprehend what was said by the Rākshasa. Then, summoning up patience, Rāma—captor of hostile capitals—spoke unto Bibhishana, seated near the monkeys,—"O lord of Nairitas, I once more wish to hear what, O Bibhishana, thou hast said." Hearing Rāghava's words,Bibhishana, skilled in speech,again spoke these words, saying,—"O mighty-armed one, I have stationed the forces, O hero, agreeably to thy directions. The entire force hath been divided around; and the leaders have also been placed properly. Further, O mighty master, listen to what I have to say. On

* Indrajit's.

thy having been causelessly aggrieved, we all of us were seized with grief. If this anxiety of thine conduceth to the joy of the enemy, do thou cast it off. And, O hero, bestir thyself,—and summon up spirits. If thou art to have Sitā, and if the night-rangers are to be slain by thee, do thou, O Raghu's son, listen to my profitable speech. Let Sumitrā's son go forth, environed by a mighty force, for slaying in battle the son of Rāvana, who hath gone to Nikumbhilā; with shafts resembling venomous serpents, discharged from the round* of his bow. By virtue of his austerities, that hero, from a boon conferred by the Self-sprung, hath obtained the Brahmaçiras weapon, together with steeds coursing at their will. Now he with his army hath gone to Nikumbhilā; and when, having finished his rites, he gets up, know that all of us are slain. 'When not reaching Nikumbhilā, and not having finished thy offerings unto fire, thou, equipped with arms, art slain by a foe,—O enemy of Indra, that is thy death.'—Thus, O mighty-armed one, did the lord of all creatures confer a boon (on Indrajit), and, O king, thus was the death of this intelligent one ordained. O Rāma, for compassing the destruction of Indrajit, do thou commission a mighty force. On his being slain, know that Rāvana along with his retainers are slain."—Hearing Bibhishana's words, Rāma said,—"O thou having truth for prowess, I know the illusion of that fierce one. Without doubt, he is skilled in the Brahma weapon, is potent in illusion and, is possessed of exceeding strength. In conflict, he depriveth of consciousness even the celestials with Varuna (at their head). And as that illustrious (one) goeth about in the welkin on his chariot, none, O hero, can perceive his course, like the course of the Sun when the sky is covered with clouds." And Rāghava, being well acquainted with the illusive energy of his wicked-minded foe, addressed the renowned Lakshmana,

* The bow drawn to its full stretch, becomes circular.—T.

saying,—"Environed by the entire host of the lord of monkeys,—accompanied by the leaders, O Lakshmana, headed by Hanumān,—with Jāmbavān—king of bears—and girt round by the forces,—do thou slay this son of the Rākshasa, possessed of the strength of illusion. And accompanied by his counsellors, this high-souled night-ranger shall follow at thy back, in this engagement with that one skilled in illusion." Hearing Rāghava's words, Lakshmana endowed with dreadful prowess, with Bibhishana,—took up another excellent bow. And donning on his mail, and putting on his armour and his sword, and furnished with arrows, and a bow in his left hand,—Sumitrā's son, touching Rāma's feet, feeling elated, addressed Rāma, saying,—"To-day the shafts discharged from my bow, piercing Rāvana's son, shall fall into Lankā, even as swans drop into a tank. This very day shall my arrows, shot from my redoubtable bow-string, rive the body of that terrific one." Having spoken thus, the effulgent Lakshmana, eager to slay Rāvana's son, went before his brother. And having saluted at the feet of his superior and went round him, Lakshmana set out for the sacrificial ground (named) Nikumbhilā, protected by the son of Rāvana. And accompanied by Bibhishana, that powerful son of the king—Lakshmana—after his brother had offered up prayers in his behalf,—set off with all speed. And surrounded by thousands of monkeys, Hanumān as well as Bibhishana together with his counsellors —speedily went in the wake of Lakshmana. And strongly encompassed by that mighty monkey-host, (Lakshmana) saw the forces of the bear-king stationed on the way. And having proceeded far, Sumitrā's son—enhancer of the delight of friends—from a distance discovered the forces of the Rākshasa-monarch, drawn up in battle-array. And that subduer of enemies—Raghu's son—bearing his bow in his hand, coming upon him whose martial might lay in illusion, —stopped (there) for conquering his foe agreeably to the ordinance* of Brahmā. And accompanied by Bibhishana, the heroic Angada, and the Wind-god's offspring, the powerful son of the king dived into the forces of the foe, various, blazing with burnished arms, dense with standards, and thronging with mighty cars,† capable of striking terror (into the hearts of the spectators), instinct with immeasurable energy, and resembling darkness.

## SECTION LXXXVI.

When things were in this condition, Rāvana's younger brother addressed Lakshmana in words fraught with evil to foes and conducing to the welfare (of his own party), saying,—"Do thou without delay bring on an engagement between this cloud-black Rākshasa army, which thou beholdest, and the monkeys having rocks for their arms. O Lakshmana, do thou exert thyself to break through his‡ mighty-army; and when the ranks are broken, the son of the Rākshasa-lord shall be visible. And scattering among the foes shafts resembling Indra's thunder-bolt, charge him while he hath not yet finished this ceremony. Slay, O hero, this wicked one, this son of Rāvana, given to illusion, and of terrific feats,—the fear of all the worlds." Hearing Bibhishana's words, Lakshmana graced with auspicious marks began to shower arrows on the son of the Rākshasa-chief. And bears and monkeys, given to fighting excellently with trees, in a body rushed towards that army (of Rakshas)

* The ordinance was that Indrajit should be slain while remaining outside Nikumbhilā, his rites not yet finished.—T.

† *Mahārathai (ab.)* may also mean with mighty car-warriors.—T.

‡ Indrajit's, that is.

drawn up there. And the Rākshasas (on their part) burning to slaughter the monkey-forces, rushed in the encounter with sharpened shafts and darts and *tomaras*. And there took place a tremendous onslaught of the monkeys and the Rākshasas. And Lankā resounded all around with that mighty tumult ; and the sky was covered with weapons of various shapes, and whetted arrows and trees and dreadful upraised mountain-tops. And Rākshasas having frightful faces and arms, plying their arms among the foremost monkeys, began to spread terror (there). And in the same way the monkeys in the conflict fell to slaying and wounding the Rākshasas with trees and hill-tops. And great was the terror that was spread among the warring Rākshasas by the flower of the bears and monkeys, possessed of gigantic persons and endowed with prodigious strength.

Hearing his own army hard beset by the enemies, and drooping,—the unconquerable one, ere yet he had finished his rites, rose up. And issuing from the gloom of the trees, Rāvana's son, fired with wrath, ascended his car, which had already been well yoked (with steeds). And accoutred in a dreadful bow and arrows,—that one resembling a mass of collyrium, having a red face and eyes, looked dreadful like the Reaper—Death. And soon as they saw him mounted on his car, that host of Rakshas possessed of dreadful impetuosity, eager to engage with Lakshmana, stood on their ground. At this time that subduer of enemies—Hanumān—resembling a mountain, uprooted a giant tree incapable of being handled. And in that encounter, the monkey, consuming (the forces) like the fire risen at Doomsday, made that army of Rākshasas insensible with innumerable trees. And finding the Wind-god's son, Hanumān, suddenly spreading devastation among the Rākshasas by thousands, (they) showered (shafts) on him. And approaching on all sides that one resembling a hill, those bearing whetted darts attacked him with darts ; those bearing swords in their hands, with swords ; those bearing javelins in their hands, with javelins; with *pattiças*, those equipped with *pattiças*; and with bludgeons, and maces and graceful *kuntas*; and with hundreds of *sataghnis*, and iron clubs; and with terrific axes; and with *bhindipâlas*; and with boxes like unto thunder-bolts; and slaps resembling the *açani*. And fired with fury, he (on his part) spread a huge havoc among them. And Indrajit saw that foremost of monkeys, resembling a hill, the offspring of the Wind-god—possessing himself in calmness, while destroying his foes. And thereat, he* addressed his charioteer, saying,—"Go where the monkey is. Being disregarded by the Rākshasas, he makes havoc among us." Thus accosted by him, the charioteer went where the Wind-god's offspring was, carrying the exceedingly invincible Indrajit seated on the car. And rushing forward, that irrepressible one—the Rākshasa—began to shower on the monkey's head arrows and swords and *pattiças* and scimitars and axes. And bearing all those dreadful arms, the Wind-god's offspring, overcome with a mighty rage said,—"O wicked-minded son of Rāvana, if thou art a hero, fight on. Combat with me with thy arms. If in the encounter, thou bearest my impetus, then, O thou of perverse sense, thou indeed art the foremost of Rākshasas." Then Bibhishana pointed out unto Lakshmana the son of Rāvana, who with his bow upraised, was eager to slay Hanumān. "This one that, mounted on his car, is eager to slay Hanumān, is the son of Rāvana that hath vanquished Vāsava himself (in battle). Do thou, O son of Sumitrā, with peerless shafts capable of resisting enemies,—dreadful, and competent to finish the lives (of foes),—slay the son of Rāvana." Thus accosted by Bibhishana terrific unto foes, that high-souled one saw (Indrajit) of dreadful prowess, difficult to get at, and resembling a hill,—stationed on his car.

* Indrajit.

## SECTION LXXXVI

HAVING spoken thus unto Sumitrā's son, Bibhishana experienced delight, and taking (Lakshmana) bearing a bow in his hand, hurriedly went off. And proceeding some way and entering the mighty wood, Bibhishana pointed out unto Lakshmana the (place of) sacrifice. And the energetic brother of Rāvana showed unto Lakshmana the Nyagrodha, dreadful to behold and resembling a mass of sable clouds. "Here offering presents unto the ghosts, the powerful son of Rāvana afterwards engages in conflict. Then the Rākshasa becomes invisible to all beings ; and he slayeth his enemies in battle and fastens them with excellent shafts. Do thou, ere he hath passed beyond the Nyagrodha, with flaming arrows destroy the powerful son of Rāvana along with his car and steeds and charioteer." Thereupon saying,—'So be it,' the exceedingly energetic son of Sumitrā—that delight of his friends—took up his post there, stretching his variegated bow. And Rāvana's son Indrajit, endowed with strength, mailed, and armed with a sword, and furnished with a banner, was seen mounted on a fire-hued chariot. And the highly powerful Lakshmana addressed Pulastya's son, never knowing defeat, saying,—"I challenge thee to the encounter. Do thou give me battle, exerting thy utmost." Thus addressed, the exceedingly energetic and intelligent son of Rāvana, seeing Bibhishana there, spoke unto him harshly, thus,—"Born and bred in this (Rākshasa race), thou art the very brother of my father. Why, O Rākshasa, being my uncle, dost thou range thyself against thy son ? But neither kinship, nor emity, nor race, O wicked-minded one, nor co-birth, can, O destroyer of righteousness, avail to make thee discern thy duty. O thou of perverse understanding, thou art indeed to be pitied ; as thou art worthy of being reproached by the virtuous; since, renouncing thine own, thou hast espoused servitude under another. Neither by thy character nor yet thy understanding dost thou perceive the mighty difference that lieth between living with one's own kindred, and taking refuge with the base. If one that is not our own, be furnished with every grace, and if one's own be void of all merit,--one's kindred, albeit unworthy, is preferable; and he that is not ours, is even always such. He that, forsaking his own party, serveth that of another, is destroyed even by the latter,when his own party is destroyed. O night-ranger, such is this thy relentlessness, that, O Rāvana's younger brother, thou being a kindred, art capable of displaying thy manliness (as no other person can do so)." Thus addressed by his brother's son, Bibhishana answered,—"O Rākshasa, why dost thou speak as if in ignorance of my character? O impious son of the Rākshasa-chief, do thou forego the roughness which thou assumest on behalf of my dignity.* Albeit born in the race of Rakshas of cruel deeds, yet having regard to the first of principles pertaining to men, my character is not that of a Rākshasa. I do not take pleasure in the terrible; nor do I revel in unrighteousness. But how can a brother, although differing from his brother in character, be renounced by the latter?† One renouncing a person, lapsing from virtue and bent on sinful acts, attaineth happiness, even as one doth by shaking off a venomous snake from his hand. The wise have called that impious one given to stealing others' goods and violating others' wives,—as worthy of being forsaken, even like a house that is aflame.—Robbing others' property, outraging the wives of others, and inspiring fear among friends,—these three vices lead to destruction. The dreadful slaughter of sages,

* Or, on account of thy heroism.

† Some read *Vishamaçilana*. Then the sense would be: 'How else could a brother bearing a difference in character, renounce his brother?' meaning Rāvana.—T.

rebellion against all the gods, overweening conceit, anger, long-continued enmity, and running amuck of counsel,—these sins are sapping the life and fortune of my brother; and they have hidden his virtues even as clouds cover a mountain. It is on account of these vices that my brother, thy sire, hath been deserted by me. And this city of Lankā will not be, nor thou, nor thy father. Thou art proud, and haughty, and a boy, O Rākshasa. Thou art fettered by the noose of Fate. Do thou say unto me whatever thou likest. To-day thou hast addressed harshly me, who have fallen on evil days; but, O worst of Rākshasas, thou canst not pass this Nyagrodha. Having smitten the Kākutstha, thou canst not live. Fight with that man-god, Lakshmana, in encounter. Being slain, thou shalt serve the deities in the abode of Yama. Displaying thy own prowess, do thou spend all thy weapons and all thy shafts. But coming within the ken of Lakshmana's arrows, thou wilt not to-day go hence, living, with thy forces."

## SECTION LXXXVIII.

Hearing Bibhishana's words, the son of Rāvana, deprived of his senses by passion, spoke harshly, and rushed forward in wrath. And with upraised weapons and scimitars, he, resembling the Destroyer himself, was mounted on a mighty car yoked with black steeds, and ornamented (on all sides). And that one endowed with terrific strength upraised a huge, gigantic, strong and powerful bow, and shafts capable of destroying foes. And that mighty bowman and slayer of foes—the powerful son of Rāvana—adorned (with ornaments) and mounted on his chariot, saw him dight (with his own splendour). And fired with wrath,(Indrajit) addressed Sumitrā's son, who, mounted on Hanumān's back, like unto the risen sun in splendour—accompanied Bibhishana; and he also addressed all those principal monkeys, saying,—"Do ye behold my prowess! To-day do ye in the conflict bear my arrowy shower shot from my bow, incapable of being approached, and resembling the down-pour in the sky. To-day my shafts discharged from my mighty bow shall mangle your limbs, even as fire burneth up a heap of cotton. To-day with your persons pierced with sharp shafts, with darts, and javelins, and *rishtis* and arrows, shall I despatch you all to the abode of Yama. Who shall stay before me, fleet-handed, creating an arrowy shower in the field, and roaring like unto clouds? Formerly in a night-engagement, with my shafts resembling the thunder-bolt and *vajra*, ye two along with your foremost adherents, were rendered insensible and laid down on the earth by me. But, perhaps, thou hast forgotten it. As thou hast presented thyself for battle before me, fired with wrath and resembling a venomous serpent, it is evident thou wilt go to the region of Yama." Hearing the vaunt of the Rākshasa-chief, Raghu's son, inflamed with rage, with an undaunted countenance, spoke unto Rāvana's son,—"O Rākshasa, hard is the achievement of the task that thou hast mentioned. He that compasseth business by act is alone intelligent.—But thou, O wicked-minded one, incompetent as thou art to bring about thy end, attaining thy arduous aim by words only, deemest thyself as crowned with success. That thou hadst rendered thyself invisible in the field of conflict, was the work of a thief,—and not the way of a hero. Coming within the range of thy shafts, I stay here,—do thou display thy prowess. What dost thou say in words?" Thus addressed, the mighty Indrajit—conquerer of enemies—stretching his dreadful bow, showered sharpened shafts. And discharged by him, those exceedingly impetuous arrows, resembling the venom of serpents, hitting Lakshmana, fell down like unto hissing snakes. And in that encounter, Rāvana's son—Indrajit—possessed of eminent impetuosity, pierced Lakshmana, graced with auspicious marks, with vehement shafts. And pierced with those arrows and bathed in blood, the graceful Lakshmana appeared like a smokeless fire. And seeing his own feat, Indrajit, coming forward, and setting up a tremendous cry, said,—"O son of Sumitrā, my feathered and sharp-edged shafts shot from my bow, capable of destroying life, will to-day finish thee up. To-day, O Lakshmana, swarms of jackals and hosts of hawks and vultures shall alight on thee lying lifeless, having been slain by me. This very day shall the exceedingly wicked Rāma behold thee, who art the friend of Kshatriyas and devoted unto thy brother,—and who ever bearest thyself ignobly,—slain by me; to-day see thee, O Sumitrā's son, slain by me, with thy armour fallen off thy person, thy bow broken, and thy head severed." As Ravana's son was speaking thus harshly, Lakshmana conversant with the import of words, replied in a reasonable speech, saying,—"Leave off thy strength of tongue, O thou of perverse sense, O Rākshasa, O thou of crooked ways! Wherefore dost thou speak thus? Bring all this to pass in worthy deed. Why, O Rākshasa, without doing (what thou sayest), dost thou simply say it? Do the deed,—so that I may have regard for thy utterances. Mark! without speaking anything harsh, without censuring thee in the least, without venting any brag, shall, I, O cannibal, slay thee." Saying this, Lakshmana drawing his bow to its full bent, hit at the Rākshasa's chest five *nārāchas*—wondrous impetuous arrows. And those arrows resembling flaming serpents, with their velocity accelerated by the feathers (with which they were furnished), blazed on the Nairita's breast like the rays of the Sun. And wounded with those shafts, Rāvana's son, fired with wrath, pierced Lakshmana with three arrows discharged (from his bow).

And exceedingly dreadful was the encounter that took place between those leonine man and Rākshasa, each eager to conquer the other. And both powerful, and both endowed with strength and possessed of prowess,—and both exceedingly invincible; and both having unparalleled might and energy,—those heroes faught like two planets in the welkin; or like Bala and Vrita, irresistible in conflict; and those high-souled ones faught like two lions. And showering countless shafts and displaying many maneuvers, that foremost of men and that of Rākshasas, faught on cheerfully.

## SECTION LXXXIX.

THEN sighing like an enraged serpent, that chastiser of foes, Daçaratha's son, setting shafts (on his bow-string) showered them on the Rakshasa-chief. And hearing the twang of his bow-string the lord of Rākshasas, with his countenance fallen, gazed at Lakshmana. And then Bibhishana spoke unto Sumitrā's son as he was fighting, "I find (inauspicious) signs in Rāvana's son. Do therefore hasten on,—broken he is, without doubt." Then fixing arrows (on his bow) resembling venomous snakes, he let go those keen shafts, like unto serpents furnished with poison. And smit by Lakshmana with arrows having the touch of the levin, (Indrajit) for a while was stupified and had his senses overwhelmed. And eying that hero—son unto Daçaratha—present in the encounter, (Indrajit) with his eyes crimsoned in choler, drew near Sumitrā's son. And coming up to him (Lakshmana), he again addressed (that hero) in a harsh speech, saying,—"Dost thou not remember my prowess at that first encounter, when thou along with thy brother was bound up,—that now thou art discharging arms (at me)? Forsooth ye two in mighty encounter, with shafts resembling the thunder-bolt and *vajra*, by me were first laid down on the ground, deprived of your lives, along with your principal adherents. Either this hath escaped thy memory or I fancy, thou plainly wishest to go to the abode of Yama,—inasmuch as thou hast set thy heart on beating me. If at the first encounter thou hast not witnessed my prowess, to-day shall I show it unto thee. Do thou now stay, summoning thy ättention." Seeing this, he pierced Lakshmana with seven shafts, and Hanumān with ten keen-edged excellent shafts. And then, fired with double fury, that powerful one pierced Bibhishana with an hundred arrows, powerfully discharged (from his weapons). Seeing this act of Indrajit, that foremost of men, Rāma's younger brother, Lakshmana, with an undaunted countenance, fired with wrath without minding the same,—and saying with a laugh,—'This is nothing',—taking dreadful arrows, in the conflict, discharged them at the son of Rāvana. "O night-rangers, heroes, coming to the field never discharge (such shafts as these). These arrows of thine are light and of slight strength, and they conduce to my comfort. Heroic warriors, eager for encounter, do not fight thus." Speaking thus, (Lakshmana) accoutred with his bow showered vollies of shafts (on his adversary). And at his arrows (hitting), (Indarjit's) mighty golden mail fell off his person, and dropped to the platform of his car like a cluster of stars dropping from the welkin. And with his armour dropping off, that hero—Indrajit—was wounded with *nârâchas*, like the Sun at dawn. That hero—Rāvana's son—endowed with dreadful prowess, in that conflict, pierced Lakshmana with a thousand shafts. And thereat Lakshmana's gorgeous and mighty mail was rent in pieces. And each rushing forward was engaged in dealing blows and harrying them. And sighing again and again, they faught furiously. And with their persons cut all over, and laved in blood, for a long while the heroes kept cleaving each other with sharpened shafts. And those high-souled ones versed in warfare, and endowed with terrific prowess exerted their utmost in securing victory. And covered with vollies of shafts, with their armour and banners rent, they drew each other's warm blood *flowing* like water from a fountain. And they discharged dreadful showers attended with tremendous sounds, like the sounds of black clouds at Dooms-day* pouring torrents in the sky. And a long time went by as they faught. Nor did they turn away from the encounter, or know fatigue. And those foremost of those acquainted with weapons repeatedly displayed their weapons; and their long and short shafts enveloped the welkin. And the skill that they displayed was perfect, and showed lightness, variety and grace; and both man and the Rākshasa carried on fearful and terrible conflict. And the dreadful and tremendous roars of each were audible (at that place); and terrific like the levin, they made the hearts of hearers tremble (in terror). And as they faught with might and main, the sounds that they sent resembled the deep rumbling of clouds in the sky. And pierced with *nârâchas* knobbed with gold, those powerful and illustrious (warriors) with their hearts set on celebrity, bled profusely. And in that engagement gold-knobbed shafts hitting each other's person, pierced the same and covered with gore, entered the earth. And other shafts were resisted in the sky by sharpened weapons; and some were snapped, and thousands of their arrows were cleft (in the sky). And in that field, the vollies of their shafts were dreadful to behold like unto a heap of Kuça aflame in a sacrifice. And the wounded frames of those high-souled ones appeared beautiful like a leafless, flowering Kinçuka and Sālmali in a wood. And each eager to vanquish the other,

* *Kalamaghuyo (gen).* The commentator says the word means (black clouds;' but I prefer the sense given.—T.

Indrajit and Lakshmana momentarily discharged tremendous and terrific showers (of arms). And Lakshmana smiting Rāvana's son, and Rāvana's son smiting Lakshmana,--they did not experience any fatigue. And with net-works of arrows deeply entering their persons, those vehement and exceedingly powerful ones resembled mountains topped (with trees). And all their limbs, drenched in blood and covered with arrows, looked like a blazing fire. And a great while did they fight; yet they neither turned away (from the fight), nor did they experience any exhaustion. Then to remove (Lakshmana's) fatigue from fight, the high-souled Bibhishana, working the weal of Lakshmana staying in front of the field, came forward in the encounter and took up his post.

---

## SECTION LXL.

SEEING the man and the Rākshasa engaged in battle, with their whole soul, each eager to beat the other,—like unto elephants with the temporal juice trickling from their temples,—desirous of beholding their encounter, Rāvana's mighty and heroic brother, bearing an excellent bow, stood in front of the arena. And taking up his post, he stretched his great bow and shot terrific sharp-pointed shafts at the Rākshasas. And even like thunder-bolt cleaving mighty mountains, those shafts furnished with peacock's plumes falling powerfully (upon the foe), rent the Rākshasas. And those foremost of Rākshasas, Bibhishana's followers, also, in the encounter discharged darts and scimitars and *pattiças* at heroic Rākshasas. And surrounded by those Rākshasas, Bibhishana, then in the midst of his followers, appeared like an elephant in the midst of young ones. Then inciting the monkeys, whose dear object was to slay Rāvana, that one versed in time, the foremost of Rākshasas, spoke seasonably thus,—"This one that stayeth (in the field) is the sole and mighty support of the Rākshasa-chief; and this is his remaining force. Why then do the monkey-chiefs remain inactive? On this wicked Rākshasa being slain on the edge of battle, the remnant of his army, with the single exception of Rāvana, is destroyed. That hero—Prahasta—hath been slain, and Nikumbha possessed of wondrous strength, and Kumbhakarna, and Kumbha, and the night-ranger Dhumrāksha, and Jāmvumāli, and Mahāmāli, and Tikshnavega and Hemaprabha, and Suptaghna, and Jajnakopa, and the Rākshasa Vajradanstra, Sankrādi, and Vikata, and Arighna, and Tapana, and Manda, and Praghasa, and Prajangha, and Jangha, and Agniketu, and Durdharsha, and the powerful Raçmiketus and Viddujjibha, and Dwijibha, and the Rākshasa—Suryyaçatru, and Akampana, and Supārçwa, and the Rākshasas—Chakramāli, and Kampana, and Satwavanta, and Devāntaka and Narāntaka. —Having slain these many powerful Rākshasas endowed with excess of might,—having crossed the sea with your arms, do ye cross this foot print of a cow. This is the remaining force which you monkeys must conquer; all those Rākshasas, that had come forward, elated with the pride of strength, have all been slain. It is not meet for me to slay the son of my brother, yet, casting off compassion will I for Rāma slay him.* Tears surcharge the eyes of me who seeketh to slay him. Let therefore Lakshmana administer him his quietus. Ye monkeys, do ye in a body (first) slaughter those that are beside him (Indrajit.)" Thus exhorted by that illustrious Rākshasa, the monkey-chiefs were exhilarated and began to flourish their tails. And then those mighty monkeys roared again and again, and sent up various shouts, even as peacocks cry on seeing

* The text has 'brother's son.'

clouds. And then Jāmbavān surrounded by his own forces, assailed the Rākshasas with rocks and with their nails and teeth. Thereat Rākshasas,endowed with exceeding strength, equipped with various weapons reproaching the lord of bears, as he was engaged in smiting (the foe),—and renouncing fear, with shafts and sharp axes and *pattiças* and *yashtis,* and *tomaras,* in the encounter assailed Jāmbavān, who was engaged in beating the Rākshasa forces. And that conflict between the monkeys and the Rakshas, waxed furious, like unto the tumultuous encounter of the immortals and the Asuras fired with wrath. And the magnanimous Hanumān incapable of being approached growing wroth,—uprooting a mountain, and putting down Lakshmana from his back, began a great carnage among the Rākshasas by thousands. And fighting a furious fight with his uncle, the powerful Indrajit—slayer of hostile heroes—again rushed against Lakshmana. And then there took place an encounter between those heroes in the field,—Lakshmana and the Rākshasa—discharging vollies of shafts and smiting each other; and those mighty and impetuous ones repeatedly covered each other with networks of arrows; like unto the sun and the moon covered by clouds at the expiration of Summer. And on account of their light-handedness, neither discharge of arrows, nor the drawing of the bow; nor the setting of the shaft on the bow-string; nor the taking of the bow; nor the selection of shafts; nor the clenching fast of their fists; nor the hitting of aims,—could be perceived as they faught on. And in consequence of the sky being covered with networks of arrows all around, discharged powerfully from their bows, the forms (of objects) could not be discovered. And Lakshmana having at Rāvana's son, and Rāvana's son having at Lakshmana, critical was the huggermugger that ensued* in the encounter between each other. And they both kept ceaselessly showering feathered

* *i. e.* in consequence of all sides being covered with arrows, neither the

and sharpened shafts, the firmament was engulphed with a deep darkness. And in consequence of countless keen arrows alighting in hundreds, all sides and all the cardinal quarters were swarming with shafts. And all being overspread with gloom, a mighty fright took possession (of creatures) when the Sun having ascended the setting-hill, and darkness environing all objects. And that day* mighty torrents of blood flowed in thousands of streams; and fierce beasts of prey set up terrific yells (all around). And at that hour the wind did not blow, and fire did not blaze; and the Maharshis said,—'Fair befell creatures.' And the Gandharvas along with the Chāranas grew exceedingly agitated. Then Sumitrā's son pierced the four black steeds of the leonine Rākshasa, caparisoned in gold. And then he hit at (Indrajit's) charioteer with another yellow and sharpened javelin splendid, furnished with feathers; and resembling the thunder-bolt of the great Indra. And through his fleet handedness the graceful son of Raghu with the thunder-bolt of his shaft, resonant with the sound of his palm, separated the (charioteer's head) from his trunk. And on his charioteer having been slain the exceedingly energetic son of Mandodari, himself began to perform the function of a charioteer, and took up his bow. And this in the encounter was wonderful to behold. And then as (Indrajit) was eagerly engaged in managing the steeds, (Lakshmana) pierced him with sharpened shafts; and when (Indrajit) was eagerly wielding his bow, (Lakshmana) discharged shafts at his steeds. And on his steeds having been torn with shafts, Sumitrā's—foremost of fleet-handed—in the encounter assailed (Indrajit) doubtlessly ranging the field. Seeing his charioteer slain in the contest, Rāvana's son forewent his martial ardour, and was cast down. And seeing the Rākshasa with his

---

Rakshas nor the monkeys could distinguish their several parties in the encounter, and the blows that each dealt were misdirected in consequence.—T.

* *Aiya to-day* in the text.

face fallen, the leaders of monkey-bands, were exceedingly delighted and rendered homage unto Lakshmana. And then those monkey-chiefs—Pramāthi, Rabhasa, Sarabha and Gandamādana, not brooking (their foe) summoned their impetuosity. And suddenly springing up, those highly powerful monkeys endowed with terrific prowess descended upon those four best of steeds. And on those chargers being assailed by those monkeys resembling mountains, blood gushed out of their mouths. And then the steeds were smashed and sent to the ground. And having slain the steeds, and smitten the mighty car-warrior,* again by a vehement bound, came to the side of Lakshmana. And springing down from his car whose steeds had been slain, Rāvana's son, his charioteer having been pounded, charged the son of Sumitrā with arrows. And then Lakshmana resembling the great Indra, on (Indrajit's) best of chargers having been despatched, in the encounter began to terribly rive with arrows discharged (his foe) footing on the earth and showering excellent sharpened shafts.

## SECTION LXLI.

HAVING his steeds slain, the night-ranger—Indrajit. standing on the ground, waxing fiercely angered, flamed up in energy. And armed with bows, they, desirous of slaying each other with shafts resembled an elephant and a bull in a forest, came out for securing victory in encounter. And

* *Maharatham* (*ac.*) may also mean *mighty car*. By the way the *samasa* or junction called *Tatpurusha* is a frequent source of obscurity in Sanskrit, specially where the gender of the word without *samâsa* is the same with that of the thing signified by the *samâsa*, as in this case.—T.

slaughtering one another, the Rākshasas and the wood-rangers, rushing this way and that, did not (for a moment) leave their lords. Then Rāvana's son, gladdening all the Rākshasas, and himself feeling cheered, addressed them in words of praise, saying,—"All sides are entirely enveloped in this gloom,—so that, O foremost of Rākshasas, here we do not know who belongeth unto us and who not.—Do ye fight fearlessly for stupifying the monkeys; and I too, mounted on a car, shall come hither into the conflict. Do ye so act that the high-souled rangers of the woods may not attack me as I enter the city." Saying this, that slayer of foes—Rāvana's son, deceiving the wood-rangers, entered the city of Lankā for providing himself with a (fresh) car. And embellishing a chariot, graceful and adorned with gold, furnished with *prâças* and swords and arrows, yoked with superb steeds, and driven by a charioteer, knowing horses and possessed of instructions (anent his art),—that victor in battle—the exceedingly energetic son of Rāvana—ascended it. And that hero, Mandodari's son, urged on by the force of the Finisher, went out of the city, surrounded by the foremost Rākshasas; and drawn by fast-speeding steeds, he presented himself before Lakshmana along with Bibhishana. And seeing Rāvana's son seated on the car, the son of Sumitrā and the exceedingly powerful monkeys and the Rākshasa—Bibhishana—were highly amazed at the lighthandedness of that intelligent one. And Rāvana's son, waxing furious, in that contest began to bring down monkeys by hundreds and by thousands. And that victor in battle—Rāvana's son—fired with wrath, summoning all his celerity, slaughtered monkeys, drawing his bow into a circle. And slaughtered by *nârâchas* of terrific impetuosity, the monkeys saught the shelter of Sumitrā's son, like creatures seeking the refuge of their Lord. Then the son of Raghu, flaming up in martial wrath, severed his* bow,

* Indrajit's.

displaying his fleethandedness. Thereat, taking another bow, (Indrajit) hurriedly fastened the string to it. And this bow also did Lakshmana cut off by means of a brace of arrows. And when (Indrajit) had his bow severed, Sumitrā's son pierced the son of Rāvana with five shafts resembling the venom of a poisonous serpent. And the shafts discharged from his* mighty bow, piercing his† person, dropped to the earth like unto powerful red serpents. And having his bow cut off, Rāvana's son, vomitting blood by his mouth, took up a superior bow powerful to a degree and having a stout string. And then aiming at Lakshmana, he, summoning his utmost celerity, showered arrows, as showereth Purandara in the season of rains. Thereat Lakshmana, subduer of enemies, retaining his calmness, resisted that powerful arrowy shower shot by Indrajit. And then that exceedingly energetic one, Raghu's son, possessing himself in calmness, displayed (his prowess) unto the son of Rāvana; and this was wonderful (to behold). And then displaying his lightness in the use of weapons, Lakshmana, growing furious, pierced the Rākshasas with three arrows each in that mighty encounter; and the lord of Rākshasas struck him with showers of shafts. And pierced sore by that powerful enemy—slayer of foes—he incessantly sent innumerable arrows after Lakshmana. And ere they reached their destination, that slayer of hostile heroes severed them with whetted arrows; and in the encounter that righteous one and foremost of car-warriors with a dart having bent joints, cut off the head of his charioteer mounted on the car. And deprived of their driver, there the steeds, retaining their calmness, began to go in rounds,—and this was wonderful. Then Sumitrā's son of steady prowess, fired with anger, in that contest, frightening all, pierced his horses with arrows. And not brooking that act (of his adversary), Rāvana's son

* Lakshmana's.

† Indrajit's

in the encounter pierced with ten shafts Sumitrā's son capable of making people's down stand on end. And his shafts resembling thunderbolts, and like unto all varieties of venom, touching (Lakshmana's) mail having a golden splendour, were reduced to naught. Thereat considering Lakshmana as clad in an impenetrable armour, Rāvana's son—Indrajit—growing furiously enraged, displaying his lighthandedness in arms, pierced Lakshmana in the temples with three well-knobbed shafts. And with those arrows lodged in his temples, Raghu's son, delighting in battle, appeared beautiful in the field like a mountain furnished with three summits. Albeit thus smitten in the contest by the Raksha with shafts, Lakshmana swiftly smote him in turn with five arrows; and in the encounter Lakshmana drawing his bow, pierced with shafts Indrajit's face graced with elegant ear-rings. And those heroes—Lakshmana and Indrajit—equipped with exceedingly powerful bows, and endowed with heroism and dreadful prowess, wounded each other with sharp arrows. And both Lakshmana and Indrajit, with their persons bathed in blood in that encounter, appeared like unto flowering Kinçukas. And approaching each other, those bowmen, each setting his heart on victory, wounded each other all over the body with terrific shafts. Then Rāvana's son, carried away by martial rage, pierced Bibhishana in his handsome face with three arrows. And piercing the lord of Rākshasas, Bibhishana, he with three iron-headed arrows, pierced the monkey-leaders each with a shaft. Thereat, enraged at him more furiously than ever, the exceedingly energetic Bibhishana with his mace despatched the steeds of the wicked-minded son of Rāvana.' Then jumping down from his chariot with its horses slain, (Indrajit), endowed with great energy, who had his charioteer pounded, discharged a dart at his uncle. And seeing it descend, the enhancer of Sumitrā's joy severed the same with whetted arrows and brought it down in ten fragments to the ground. And

Bibhishana of a tough bow, growing enraged, discharged at (Indrajit), who had his steeds slain, five speeding shafts having the touch of the thunder-bolt.—And those arrows furnished with gold at the feathered parts, riving his person, were bathed in blood, and resembled mighty red serpents. Thereat wroth with his uncle, Indrajit took up an excellent shaft—bestowed on him by Yama himself—endowed with terrific force,—the flower of shafts among all the Rakshas. And seeing that mighty shaft set by him (on the bow-string), the highly powerful Lakshmana, possessed of dreadful prowess, (in his turn) took up another arrow, bestowed by Kuvera himself of immeasurable soul in a dream,—unconquerable, and incapable of being borne even by the celestials and Asuras with Indra at their head. And on their best of bows being powerfully drawn with their arms resembling bludgeons, they set up cries like unto Kraunchas. And on those foremost of shafts set on those excellent bows of those heroes, being drawn, flamed up in exceeding splendour. And those flaming arrows, discharged from the bows, illumining the welkin, with vehemence struck at each other's head. And a concussion took place of those arrows of terrific aspects; and a furious fire sprang up thereat, with embers shooting around. And dashing against each other like unto mighty planets, they, reduced to an hundred shivers in the encounter, saught the earth. Seeing their shafts baffled, Indrajit and Lakshmana, staying on the edge of the battle, were seized with shame and wrath. Thereat Sumitrā's son, flying into a fury, took up a Vāruna weapon. And the conquerer of the great Indra intent on battle, in the encounter discharged a terrific Raudra weapon; and the exceedingly wonderful Vāruna weapon was baffled by him. Then, waxing wroth, that victor in battle—the wondrous energetic Indrajit—as if annihilating the world, discharged a flaming Agneya weapon. And the heroic Lakshmana resisted it with a Solar weapon. Seeing his weapon resisted, Rāvana's son, transported with passion, took up an Asura arrow, capable of rending foes. And from that weapon issued daggers and clubs and darts and *bhuçundis* and maces and swords and axes.* And in the conflict, seeing that dire and dreadful weapon, irrisistible to all creatures and capable of riving all arms, the effulgent Lakshmana baffled it with a Māheçwara† weapon. And the encounter that took place between them was wonderful and capable of making people's down stand on end. And beings stationed in the sky surrounded Lakshmana on all sides. And in that terrific encounter of the monkeys and the Rākshasas resounding with dreadful roars, the welkin was covered with innumerable beings seized with wonderment. And saints and *Pitris* and deities and Gandharbas and birds and serpents, placing Satakratu in their front, protected Lakshmana in the conflict. And then that hero, Rāghava's younger brother, fixed (on his bow) another superior shaft, having the feel of fire itself, and capable of riving the son of Rāvana; furnished with fair feathers; tapering; having elegant joints; symmetrical; and plated with gold,—an arrow capable of finishing the body; irrisistible; dreadful; terrific unto Rākshasas; resembling the venom of poisonous serpents; and worshipped by the celestial hosts; by which the exceedingly energetic and wonderful Lord riding the horse‡—Sakra—of old in the war between the celestials and the Asuras had defeated the Dānavas. And Sumitrā's son, Lakshmana, graced with auspiciousness, drawing on his best of bows that foremost of shafts—the Aindra weapon—invincible in conflict, spoke these words, tending to bring about his success,§—

---

* This arrow resembled somewhat the bomb-shells in modern European warfare.—T.

† *i.e.* belonging to Maheçwara or Siva.

‡ The celestial steed, Uchchaiçravā, sprung from the ocean on the occasion of the churning of the deep.—T.

§ Words addressed to the deity presiding over the weapon.

"If Daçaratha's son—Rāma—is righteous and truthful, and if in prowess he hath no rival, then slay this son of Rāvana." Saying this, the heroic Lakshmana in that conflict, drawing the straight-speeding arrow up to his ear,* discharged it at Indrajit. And shooting the Aindra weapon, that destroyer of hostile heroes—Lakshmana —severing from its trunk the head of Indrajit with its corslet, graced with burning ear-rings, brought it down to the ground. And the mighty severed head of the Rākshasa's son, resembling one made of gold, was seen covered with blood. And slain, Rāvana's son dropped to the earth, with his armour and corslet on, and his bow fallen (from his grasp). And then all the monkeys with Bibhishana set up cheers, even as the immortals cheered at the destruction of Vritra. And in the sky there arose the victorious shouts of all beings and high souled saints, and also of Gandharbas and Apsarās. And knowing (Indrajit) fallen (in fight), the mighty army of Rākshasas, attacked by monkeys burning for victory, fled in the ten cardinal directions. And assailed by the monkeys, the Rākshasas, pursued (by their foes), with their senses lost, rushed towards Lankā, leaving their arms behind. And overwhelmed with fright, Rākshasas fled in an hundred directions, all renouncing their arms—bearded darts, and swords, and axes. And harassed by the monkeys, some hurriedly entered Lankā, and some plunged into the sea, and some saught shelter in the mountains. And seeing Indrajit slain and lying down on the field of battle, thousands of Rākshasas fled away. As when the Sun sets, his rays remain no longer, on that Rākshasa having fallen, the Rākshasas dispersed in the ten cardinal quarters, like unto the Sun when his rays have been rendered mild, or fire which hath been extinguished. And the mighty-armed (Indrajit) was utterly reft of life. And on the son of the Rākshasa-chief falling, the world, having its foe slain, with its huge affliction gone off, experienced

* *i.e.* drawing the bow to its utmost stretch.

the height of joy. And on that unrighteous Rākshasa having been slain, the reverend Sakra together with the Maharshis was filled with delight. And sounds of kettle-drums were heard in the sky proceeding from the celestials. And blossoms were showered by dancing Apsarās and high-souled Gandharbas. And this was wonderful (to behold.) And on that Rākshasa of fell deeds having been slain, the dust was laid, the water became transparent, the sky looked bright, and the deities and Dānavas were filled with rejoicings. And on that Dread of all creatures having been slain, the gods, Gandharbas and Dānavas, assembled together in joy, said,—"Now let the Brāhmanas who have their sins removed, with their anxiety gone off, range about." And then the monkey-leaders, seeing that foremost of Nairitas of unparalleled prowess slain in battle, began to gladly pay homage (unto Lakshmana). And Bibhishana and Hanumān and Jāmbavān—leader of bears—saluted and hymned Lakshmana on the score of his victory. And shouting and bounding and roaring, the monkeys at this hour of high joy stood surrounding Raghu's son.* And flourishing their tails and striking the earth (with them), the monkeys shouted,—'Victory unto Lakshmana !' And embracing each other, the monkeys with delighted spirits began to converse in various ways touching Rāghava's welfare. And beholding that deed, difficult of being done, performed by their beloved friend—Lakshmana—and hearing their foe—Indrajit—slain (in battle), the celestials attained the summit of joy.

---

* Descendant, that is.

## SECTION LXLII.

Having in the conflict slain that conquerer of enemies, Lakshmana graced with auspicious marks, with his body bathed in blood, experienced delight. And then supporting himself on Bibhishana and Hanumān, the exceedingly powerful Lakshmana endowed with prowess, taking Jāmbavān, Hanumān and all the monkeys with him, speedily went to the place where Sugriva and Rāghava were. And then going round Rāma and saluted him, Sumitrā's son stood before his brother, like Indra's brother staying before Sakra. And approaching with a look which of itself was significant,* the heroic Bibhishana described unto the high-souled Rāghava the dreadful destruction of Indrajit. And then the delighted Bibhishana related unto Rāma how the high-souled Lakshmana had cut off the head of Rāvana's son. And as soon as that exceedingly powerful one heard of the destruction of Indrajit by Lakshmana, he experienced a huge accession of joy, and thus delivered himself,—"Excellent, O Lakshmana! Pleased am I (with thee). Thou hast performed a difficult feat. The son of Rāvana having been slain, know for certain that we have been victorious." And then smelling the head of the bashful Lakshmana, enhancer of fame, (Rāma) endowed with prowess, from affection forcibly hugged him into his lap. And making him seat on his lap, and overpowering him with embraces,† (Rāma) again and again tenderly eyed his brother, Lakshmana. And moved with grief, that best of persons, Rāma, smelling the head of Lakshmana, wounded with darts and having his person pierced (with arms), sighing and breathing hard,—

---

* *i. e.* of the destruction of Indrajit.

† *Avapiritam—(ao) pained.* Rāmānuya says this epithet refers to Lakshmana's having been wounded in the encounter. I differ from him.—T.

and nursing his body with his hand, addressed Lakshmana, soothing him,—"To-day his son having been slain, I deem Rāvana himself as slain in fight. On that wicked-minded enemy of mine having been destroyed, I am victorious (in encounter). By luck, O hero, hast thou in conflict severed the right arm of the fell Rāvana. Verily he (Indrajit) was his stay. Both Bibhishana and Hanumān have done mighty deeds in battle. In three days and nights, (my enemy) hath been brought down. To-day have I been made foeless. Now Rāvana will for certain march forth,—backed by a mighty phalanx. Rāvana will for certain sally out, hearing his son brought down. That unconquerable lord of Rākshasas, aggrieved for the destruction of his son, marching out,—shall I slay, environed with a mighty force. O Lakshmana, the conqueror of Sakra having in battle been slain by thee—who art my lord—Sitā and the (entire) earth are not incapable of being obtained by me." Having thus soothed and embraced his brother, Raghu's son—Rāma—highly rejoiced, calling Sushena, said,—"Do thou so act that this highly wise son of Sumitrā, devoted to his friends, may be healed and be eased. Do thou without delay heal Sumitrā's son, attached to his friends, of his wounds. And do thou also carefully relieve all those heroes in the army of bears and monkeys fighting with trees,—as well as others, who have been wounded and have got sores (in consequence)." Thus addressed by Rāma, the high-souled monkey-leader administered a potent medicine to the nose of Lakshmana. And smelling the same, he got healed; he was relieved of his pain and his outgoing vitality was shut up. And at the mandate of Rāghava he likewise treated his friends headed by Bibhishana and all the principal monkeys. And restored to his natural condition, Sumitrā's son, healed, and with his exhaustion removed, and his suffering gone off in a moment, experienced exhilaration of spirits. And Rāma and the monkey-king and Bibhishana and the powerful lord of bears along with their hosts, seeing Sumitrā's son risen hale, rejoiced greatly in delight. And the high-souled son of Daçaratha honored exceedingly that exceedingly hard feat of Lakshamana; and the monkey-king, hearing that the conquerer of Sakra had fallen in fight, was filled with joy.

---

## SECTION LXLIII.

THEN the counsellors of Pulastya's son, hearing of Indrajit having been slain, speedily conveyed the tidings unto the Ten-necked one, who was ignorant* of the same. "O mighty monarch, in our very sight thy exceedingly effulgent son hath been slain by Lakshmana with the help of Bibhishana. And that hero confronted by the (other) hero, hath been vanquished in fight. And the hero, thy son, the conquerer of the celestial chief, hath also been slain by Lakshmana. And having gratified Lakshmana with his shafts, he hath repaired to the supreme regions." Hearing of that mighty terror, *viz.*, the rueful and dreadful destruction of his son, Indrajit, in battle, he straightway swooned away. Then regaining his consciousness after a long while, that foremost of Rākshasas—the king—overwhelmed with grief for his son, and distressed, burst into lamentations, with his senses wildered,—thus,—"O foremost in the Rākshasa army! O my child endowed with high might! Having conquered Indra himself, wherefore to-day hast thou come under the sway of Lakshmana? Doubtless, thou enraged could pierce with thy arrows the Destroyer of Time himself, and the summit of Mandāra,—what shall I say

---

* *Avajudya.* Râmânuya says it means "ignorant of the same." Tirtha says it means, 'Seeing.' Then the sense would be, 'the counsellors, having first *seen* Indrajit slain, informed Râvana of it.'—T.

of Lakshmana in encounter? To-day king Viwaçwata hath raised himself immensely in my estimation, for to-day he, O mighty-armed one, hath brought thee under the law of Time. But this is the way of capable warriors as well as celestials. He that layeth down his life for his lord, repaireth to heaven. To-day seeing Indrajit slain, the deities and the guardians of the worlds, and the mighty saints, their fear gone off, shall sleep peacefully. This triple world and this entire earth with her woods, reft of one—Indrajit—appear to me as vacant. To-day shall I hear the cries of the daughters of the Nairitas in my inner apartment, like unto the roars of she-elephants in a mountain-cavern. Renouncing thy state of an heir-apparent, and Lankā and the Rakshas, O subduer of enemies, and thy mother, and me, and thy wife—whither hast thou gone, (leaving) us all? O hero, I having gone to the region of Yama, thou ought to have performed my last rites, but thou standest in a relation the very reverse of this.* And Sugriva living and Lakshmana and Rāghava, without extracting my dart, whither hast thou gone, leaving us all? And then arising from the disaster that had befallen his son, a mighty wrath overcame the lord of Rākshasas—Rāvana, as he was thus indulging in lamentations. And even as in summer, the (Solar) rays flame up the Sun, the destruction of his son flamed up all the fiercer, him, who was naturally irascible. And as he kept yawning in passion, a flaming fire with smoke darted from his mouth, even as it did from the mouth of Vritra. And burning in grief for the destruction of his son, and coming under masterdom of passion, that hero—Rāvana—reflecting (awhile) in his mind, resolved upon slaying Vaidehi. And naturally red, and reddened (still more by the fire of wrath, Rāvana's glowing eyes were dreadful (to behold). And his form, terrific by nature, in

* *i.e.* I have to perform thy last rites, thou having fallen in fight while I am alive.—T.

consequence of the fire of his wrath having possessed it entirely, resembled the form of the enraged Rudra. And from the eyes of that infuriated one fell drops of tears as drop from a flaming lamp drops of burning oil. And as he grinded his teeth, the gnashing resembled the sounds sent by the machine* drawn by the Dānavas and churning the deep. The Rākshasas durst not approach that one eying round and resembling the Destroyer himself, intent on devouring both mobile and immobile. Then exceedingly enraged, Rāvana—lord of Rākshasas—spoke in the midst of the Rākshasas, inciting them to battle,—"I practised severe austerities for thousands of years; and gratified the Self-sprung at times. Neither from Asuras nor from celestials can any fear spring to me. My mail conferred on me by Brahmā, which in effulgence resembles the Sun himself, was not broken by blows like unto thunder-bolt at the war between the deities and demons. To-day who will come forward against me in battle accoutred in that and mounted on a car in the conflict? Not even Purandara himself. Do ye, beating hundreds of drums, to-day raise that mighty and dreadful bow of mine which, with arrows, had been bestowed on one by the gratified Self-sprung at the war of the gods and Asuras,—so that I may therewith compass the destruction of Rāma and Lakshmana in mighty battle." Burning (in grief) for the destruction of his son, the fell Rāvana, coming under the influence of anger, reflecting (in his mind), resolved to slay Sitā. And eying round, that copper-eyed and dreadful one of a terrific aspect, distressed, in a piteous voice addressed all the night-rangers, saying,—"By his power of illusion, my beloved child, for deceiving the wood-rangers, slaying something (else), had shown it unto them as Sitā. Now will I do that good office myself,—Vaidehi will I slay—even her that is devoted to that friend of Kshatriyas." Having spoken thus unto his counsellors,

* Meaning the mountain Mandāra.

he swiftly took up a sword; and raising it, of excellent temper and of cerulean hue, he rushed out vehemently, surrounded by his wives and counsellors. From grief for his son, Rāvana with his consciousness wildered, taking up a sword, in rage, rushed towards the place where Mithilā's daughter was. Seeing the Rākshasa rising on, some, emitted leonine roars, and seeing the Rākshasa enraged, embracing each other, said,—"To-day those two brothers, seeing this one, will be exceedingly pained. By this one, influenced with passion were the four guardians of the worlds conquered; and many other foes were brought down in battle. Procuring gems from the three worlds, Rāvana enjoyeth them. Neither in strength nor in prowess is there any one on earth who is his compeer." As they were speaking thus, Rāvana, reft of his senses by wrath, rushed against Vaidehi, who had taken up her abode in the Açoka wood. And dissuaded by his friends endowed with good intelligence, he, wrought up with high wrath, darted (against Sitā), even as an enraged planet* rusheth against Rohini† in the firmament. And the blameless daughter of Mithilā protected by the Rākshasis, saw the infuriated Rāvana bearing that best of blades in his hand. Seeing (Rāvana) approach, sword in hand, despite the earnest entreaties of his friends, Janaka's daughter, Sitā, pained and overcome by grief, said, weeping, —"From the way in which, wrought up with wrath, this wicked-minded one is rushing on at me personally, it appears that he will slay me, who have a lord, as one who hath not. He did urge me much ever devoted to my lord, saying 'Be thou my wife;' but forsooth I disregarded him. And plainly in consequence of my refusal, he hath given way to despair. And overcome by anger and passion, he is ready to slay me. Or it may be that to-day for me those foremost of men, the brothers—Rāma and Lakshmana—have been slain in encounter by this inglorious one. I heard a furious and

* Kuja, *etc*. † Hesperus.

fearful uproar raised by countless Rākshasas rejoicing, and expressing their delight.—Alas! O fie! For me those princes have met with destruction. Or it may be that not without slaying Rāma and Lakshmana, this terrific Rākshasa, having his heart set on sin, from grief for his son, will slay me. Fool that I am, I did not then act agreeably to Hanumān's words. If I had gone away seated on his back, without waiting for the victory (of my lord), I devoted to him, placed on his lap, should not have come by this repentance. When Kauçalyā, having an only son, will hear of her son slain in battle, I fancy, her heart shall burst. And, weeping, she will remember that high-souled one's birth and boyhood, and youth and pious acts and loveliness. And that one bereft of her consciousness, filled with despair, after having performed his *srāddha*,* will doubtless enter into fire or water. Shame on the unchaste and hump-backed Mantharā, having her heart fixed in sin, for whose sake this grief shall exercise Kauçalyā!" Seeing the distressed daughter of Mithilā lament thus, like unto Rohini come under the sway of a planet in the absence of the Moon, in the meanwhile his† pure and good courtier, named Suparçwa, endowed with intelligence, albeit prevented by other courtiers, spoke unto Rāvana, foremost of Rākshasas,—"Wherefore, O Ten-necked one, O thou who art the very younger brother of Vaiçravana himself, Dost thou desire to slay Vaidehi, forsaking righteousness? Why, O hero! O lord of Rākshasas! having led the Brahmacharyya mode of life, studied the Vedas, and returned from the house of thy spiritual guide, and ever engaged in religious acts, to-day dost thou intend to slay a woman? Do thou, O king, now stay expecting Mithilā's daughter‡ endowed with loveliness;

* Funereal rites performed in accordance with the injunctions of the Hindu Scriptures.—T.

† Rāvana's.

‡ Explains the commentator: "till thou slayest Rāma in battle."—T.

and do thou along with us vent thy wrath on him.* To-day being the fourteenth day of the dark fortnight, do thou this very day prepare for conflict; at *amâvasyâ*,† environed with thy forces, do thou march for victory. Heroic, and intelligent, a mighty car-warrior and swordsman, thou, mounted on a car, slaying the redoubtable son of Daçaratha, wilt obtain Mithilā's daughter." Thus exhorted by his friend, the unrighteous Rāvana accepted his virtuous speech; and then that powerful one went (back) to his house, and, surrounded by his friends, entered the court.

## SECTION LXLIV.

ENTERING his court, the king, distressed, and exceedingly aggrieved, sat him down on the foremost seat sighing like an enraged lion. And stricken with grief in consequence of his son's death, that highly powerful Rāvana, with folded hands, addressed all the heroic Rākshasas, saying:—"Do ye all proceed to battle with elephants, horses and cars. And encircling Rāma only and discharging shafts at him, delightedly, like unto clouds, in the rainy season, pouring water, do ye slay him. Or I shall slay him to-morrow in the presence of all, wounded by you in the mighty encounter with sharpened arrows." Hearing the speech of their lord the Rākshasas, with a huge army and a host of cars, speedily issued out for battle. And they all threw at the monkeys life-destroying *Parighas, Pattiças,* arrows, daggers and *Parashwadhas.* And the monkeys too threw crags and trees at the Rākshasas. Thus on the eve of sun set there arose a terrible conflict between the Rākshasas and the monkeys.

---

* Râma.

† *i. e.* to-morrow.

And they struck each other in the conflict with clubs, *chitras*, *Prasas*, daggers and *Paraskwadhas*. The conflict being thus carried on, there arose a mighty dust which was again destroyed by the current of blood gushing out of the persons of the Rākshasas and the monkeys. Elephants and cars were like the banks of that river of blood, the arrows were like the fishes, and the flags were the trees on their banks and the corpses were like planks afloat there. Being thus wounded and assailed by the Rākshasas, those heroic monkeys leaped and broke down the flags, armours, cars, horses and other weapons. And with their sharp teeth and nails they scratched the hair, ears, foreheads and the noses of the Rākshasas. Like unto vultures falling upon a felled tree, hundreds of monkeys fell upon one Rākshasa in that encounter. And the Rākshasas resembling mountains, with huge clubs, *prâsas*, daggers and *parâshwadhas*, struck the monkeys (in their turn). Being thus assailed by the Rākshasas, the mighty host of monkeys took refuge of Rāma, the son of Daçaratha, the worthy refuge of all creatures. Thereupon the highly effulgent and powerful Rāma, taking up his bow, entered the Rākshasa host and began to make a downpour of arrows. And Rāma entering the field, those terrible Rākshasas, being burnt with the fire of his arrows, could not stand before him like unto clouds disappearing before the Sun in the welkin. And the night-rangers only espied the dreadful feats performed by Rāma and which were above the power of others. Except when guiding the huge army or driving the cars they could not see Rāma like unto the wind invisible in a forest. They all beheld the Rākshasa force scattered, wounded, burnt down with arrows, broken and assailed with weapons, by Rāma, but none could see the quick-moving Rāma. As people cannot see the soul which governs all objects of sense so they could not see Rāma, who was thus inflicting wounds on them. "It is he who is destroying the soldiers riding the elephants,it is he who is breaking down the mighty cars, and it is he who with sharp arrows is slaying the cavalry—rider and horse." Thus saying those Rākshasas, in that conflict and in the very presence of Rāma, highly enraged, began to slay each other. They were all bewildered by the huge Gandharba weapon discharged by the high-souled Rāma and so they could not see Rāma, who was thus burning down their force. And the Rākshasas sometimes beheld thousands of Rāma in the battle field and again saw one Rāma only. They at times saw the quick-moving golden end of the bow of that high-souled one, resembling a circular fire brand but they did not behold Rāghava. And he looked like *kâla chakra*, having his middle body as its navel, his own strength as its lustre, the arrow for its radius or spoke, the bow for the circumference, the twang of the bow for its sound, his power and intelligence for its brightness, and the aim of the celestial weapons for its limit. And in the eighth division of the time by Rāma alone with arrows resembling the flame of fire were destroyed ten thousands swift-coursing cars, eighteen thousand elephants fourteen thousands horses and riders and two million Rākshasa infantry assuming shapes at will. And those night-rangers, who were still left, having their horses killed, cars and flags broken, fled in fear of life to the city of Lankā. And the battle field, filled with slain horses elephants and infantry, looked like the high-souled and enraged Rudra's arena of sports. Thereupon the celestials with Gandharbas, Siddhas and the great ascetics glorified the wonderful feat of Rāma. And the virtuous-souled Rāma addressed Sugriva, Bibhishana the monkey Hanumān, the leading monkey Jāmbavān, Mainda and Divida who were near him, saying—"This is the power of my weapons and as well as that of Rudra." The high-souled Rāma, equalling Sakra in prowess, thus slaying the huge host of the lord of Rākshasas and assailing them with shafts and weapons—the celestials, delighted, sang his praises.

## SECTION LXLV.

By Rāma, of unwearied actions, with flaming arrows feathered in burning gold, were destroyed thousands of elephants—many horses with their riders, many a car crested with flaming banners; thousands of heroic Rākshasas assuming shapes at will, engaged by Rāvana, and armed with clubs and *parighās*; and golden pennons. Beholding and hearing of this the remaining night-rangers assembled and were greatly bewildered, poorly and stricken with anxiety. The widows and those who had lost their children or kinsmen approached those Rākshasas and overwhelmed with grief, bewailed piteously,—"Alas! why did the aged and grim-visaged Surpanakhā, having her belly extending downward, behold in the forest Rāma graceful like Kandarpa. And beholding him of great beauty and prowess, ever engaged in the welfare of all creatures, that ugly one, worthy of being slain by people, was excited with lust. Why did that ugly-faced she-demon, devoid of all qualities, address Rāma, having a beautiful countenance, gifted with many virtues and great effulgence? Alas for the misfortune of the Rākshasas, the aged Rākshasee brought before him such a vile proposal, hated of all and worthy of creating laughter. For the destruction of Khara, Dushana and other Rākshasas that ugly one approached Rāghava with such a vile intention. It was for her that Rāvana created enmity (with Rāma) and Sitā was carried away by the Ten-necked Rākshasa. But he could not spread his influence upon Sitā the daughter of king Janaka and deep rooted and eternal became the enmity with the highly powerful Rāghava. And beholding the Rākshasa Birādha slain by Rāma alone—(Rāvana) wishing Vaidehi should have regarded that as a sufficient proof of his prowess. And fourteen thousand Rākshasas of terrible deeds were slain by him in Janasthāna with shafts resembling the flame of fire. Khara, Dushana as well as Triçirā were slain by him in conflict with arrows resembling the Sun—this was a sufficient proof (of his power). Yoyanabāhu and Kavandha, drinking blood, were slain by him, roaring with wrath—this too was a sufficient proof of his power. Rāma slew the powerful Vāli, the son of the thousand eyed one, resembling the cloud—that too was the sufficient proof of his prowess. By him Sugriva, poorly and living in the mount Rishyamukha, having all his desires frustrated, was placed on the throne—that too even was the sufficient proof of his power. He (Rāvana) from foolishness did not like the becoming speech of Bibhishana conducive to the acquirement of piety and wealth and securing the welfare of the Rākshasas. Had the younger brother of the lord of wealth (Rāvana) observed the words of Bibhishana, Lankā would not have been overwhelmed with grief and reduced to the state of a cremation ground. Hearing of the destruction of the highly powerful Kumbhakarna by Rāma of the irrepressible Atikāya by Lakshmana as well as of his beloved son Indrajit, Rāvana did not come to his senses.* There is audible in every house of the Rākshasas, the cry,—'My son, my brother, my husband is slain in battle.' In conflict have been destroyed by the heroic Rāma, thousand cars, horses, serpents and infantry. Perhaps Rudra, Vishnu, Mahendra or the performer of hundred sacrifices, or even Death, in the shape of Rāma, is slaying us. By Rāma all the heroes have been slain—despair has taken possession of our minds—we do not behold the end of our terror and are bewailing being

---

* One *sloka* has been omitted here by some of the editors, which when translated stands thus:—When one monkey only Hanumān killed the prince Akshaya and reduced the whole city to ashes with the fire of his tail Rāvana should have come to his senses.

deprived of our lords. Does not the Ten-necked hero, who has obtained boons (from Brahmā) perceive that a mighty disaster shall befall him from Rāma? Neither the celestials, Gandharbas, Piçachas nor Rākshasas shall be able to save him from Rāma in conflict. In every battle many an accident befalls Rāvana—this bespeaks of his destruction at the hands of Rāma. The great Patriarch, being pleased, conferred upon Rāvana the boon that no fear would proceed unto him from the celestials, the Dānavas or the Rākshasas —but he did not beg of him, security from men. Forsooth, he is that fearful man who shall slay Rāvana and the Rākshasas. The celestials, being thus oppressed by Rāvana, who had obtained the boon, worshipped the great Patriarch with severe austerities. And being propitiated with them, the high-souled Patriarch, for their welfare, addressed the celestials, with the following pregnant speech. "From to-day shall the Rākshasas and Dānavas roam for ever, afraid of the celestials." Thereupon the celestials headed by Indra engaged in propitiating Mahādeva, the slayer of Tripura, and who rides upon a bull. And being pleased, Mahādeva addressed them, saying,—"For your welfare there will be born a woman who shall be the cause of the destruction of the Rākshasas." As hunger, being engaged by the celestials, did destroy in olden time, all the Dānavas, so shall she (Sitā) the root of the extinction of Rākshasa race destroy us all with Rāvana. Alas! for the foolishness of the vicious minded and insolent Rāvana destruction has faced us and we are overwhelmed with grief. We do not see any such being in the world who can afford us shelter. Rāghava has attacked us like unto the fire of dissolution. There is no refuge for us who have been stricken with fear as no help reaches the elephants in a forest beset with fire. The high-souled Bibhishana did the just thing in proper time—he took shelter of him from whom he expected danger." Thus bewailed pieteously and loudly

—the she-demons holding each other by the neck and being stricken with fear and grief.

## SECTION LXLVI.

THEREUPON Rāvana heard in every house of Lankā the piteous cries of the she-demons possessed by sorrow. And sighing hard he engaged in meditation for some time. And terrible-looking as he was, Rāvana was greatly worked up with ire. Having his eyes reddened with anger, and gnashing his teeth and biting the lips, that one, irrepressible by other Rākshasas, looked like the fire of dissolution incarnate. Thereupon the lord of Rākshasas, in anger, as if burning down everything with his look, addressed the Rakshas who were near him —Mahodara, Mahāpārsha, Birupāksha—"Do ye speedily speak to the soldiers that they should sally out for battle at my command. Hearing his speech—those Rakshas, possessed by fear, asked by the command of the king, the Rākshasa soldiers to be ready. And thereat all those grim-visaged Rākshāsas saying 'so be it' and performing benedictory ceremonies proceeded to the battle-field. And those mighty car-warriors, worshipping Rāvana, and desiring the victory of their lord, stood before them with folded hands. Thereupon Rāvana, beside himself with anger, laughing, adddressed those Rākshasas, Mahodara, Mahāpārsha, and Birupāksha, saying—"To-day shall I despatch both Rāma and Lakshmana to the abode of Death with arrows resembling the sun at the time of dissolution, discharged off my bow. And slaying the enemies I shall repair the loss of Khara, Kumbhakarna, Prahasta and Indrajit. The atmosphere, the quarters the sky and the deep being enveloped with the cloud of arrows shall become invisible. I shall slay to-day all the heroic monkeys with my winged arrows. Ascending my car gifted with the velocity of the wind shall I churn to day the monkey host with arrow-like waves coming from the ocean-like bow. I shall like an elephant distress to-day the monkey-like pools having their countenances for the blown lotuses, and the lustre of their bodies for the filaments. To-day in the encounter, the leaders of the monkey hosts, with their heads transfixed with arrows, shall cover the earth, like unto lotuses with their stalks. I shall to-day with a single arrow, cleave hundreds of heroic monkeys fighting with trees in their hands. I shall wipe to-day the tears of those whose brother or son has been slain by destroying their foe. In the encounter to-day I shall, with the monkeys deprived of their breath and clept with my arrows, so cover the earth that it may not be seen by any. I shall satisfy to-day with the flesh of the enemies slain by my shafts, the crows, vultures and others who live upon flesh. Get ready soon my car and bring my bow. And let the remaining night-rangers follow me in battle." Hearing his words Mahāpārsha addressed the leaders of the army who were near him, saying,—"Get your soldiers ready." And the commanders too quickly went round all the houses in Lankā and asked the Rākshasas to be ready soon. Thereupon began to issue out in a moment terrible-looking Rākshasas, emitting roars, having dreadful faces and with various weapons in their hands—daggers, *Pattiças,* maces, clubs, furrows, sharpened *saktis,* traps, various rods, sharpened *chakra, parashwadhas, vindipalas, satâghnis* and various other excellent weapons. Thereupon at the command of Rāvana the commanders brought one *Nijuta* (a hundred thousand) cars, three *Nijuta* elephants, sixty million horses, asses and camels and numberless infantry. They arranged the soldiers before the king and in the interval the charioteer brought the car—filled with excellent celestial weapons—richly adorned, containing many an armour, girt with a network of tinkling ornaments crested with various jewels, having jewelled pillars and a thousand golden jars. Beholding the car the Rākshasas were greatly astonished. And Rāvana, the lord of Rākshasas, rising up all on a sudden, ascended that car, brilliant like the flaming fire and the aggregate rays of a million sun, quick-coursing, having a charioteer, drawn by eight horses, huge and shining in its native lustre. Thereupon proceeded Rāvana, encircled by many a Rākshasa as if rending the earth with the excess of his prowess. There arose a huge sound of bugles accompanied with that of Mridangas, drums, conchs, and *kalâpas*. The lord of the Rakshas—wicked, the slayer of the Brahmins—the thorn of the celestials, and who hath brought away Sitā by stealth, has come with his umbrallas and chowries to fight with the foremost of Raghus—this cry was heard everywhere. And with his tremendous roar the earth shook. And hearing all on a sudden that sound, the monkeys fled away in fear. And the highly effulgent Rāvana, having huge arms and surrounded by his ministers, came there being certain of gaining victory. Being commanded by Rāvana, Mahāpārsha, Mahodara and the irrepresible Birupāksha ascended the car. They, desirous of winning victory, issued out emitting dreadful roars in delight and as if rending the earth therewith. Thereupon the highly effulgent (Rāvana) resembling Death, with uplifted bow, sallied out for battle along with the army of Rakshas. And that mighty car-warrior, went out in his chariot drawn by quick—coursing steeds by that gate which led to where Rāma and Lakshmana were. Thereat the sun lost its brilliance —the quarters were enshrouded with darkness; the birds sent forth dreadful cries and the earth shook. The celestials poured down bloody rains—the course of the horses was slackened—the vultures sat on the banners and jackals emitted inauspicious cries. His left eye and the left arm began to shake—his countenance became pale and his voice grew harsher. The Ten-necked Rākshasa thus going out for battle there appeared many bad omens indicating his destruction. From the sky fell a fire-brand accompanied with the sound of thunder; vultures and crows emitted inauspicious cries. Disregarding these dreadful omens which appeared then, Rāvana, incited by death, foolishly went out to slay his (enemies). And by the wheel-sound of the chariots of the great Rākshasas the host of monkeys calling each other, excited with anger and willing to gain victory, addressed themselves for fight. Thereupon the Ten-necked one, enraged, with his arrows feathered in gold, made a dreadful slaughter of the army of monkeys. And some of those heroic monkeys were beheaded by Rāvana—some had their hearts rent and others were shorn of their ears. Some had their breath choked, some were killed and others had their sides broken. Some had their hands cut off and others had their eyes put out. And wherever in the encounter, the Ten-headed Rākshasa, whirling his eyes in ire, went in his car—the monkey leaders could not stand the vehemence of his arrows.

## SECTION LXLVII.

THERE the earth was covered with monkeys whose bodies were rent with the arrows of the Ten-necked (Rāvana). As the flies cannot stand before the flaming fire so they could not bear the vehemence of Rāvana's shafts. Being thus assailed with pointed arrows they fled away crying, like unto elephants being burnt by fire. And Rāvana with his arrows pursued in conflict the course of clouds. Thus slaughtering the monkeys the lords of Rākshasas speedily reached in the encounter where Rāghava was. And beholding the monkeys assailed and afraid Sugriva placing Sushena in charge of a *gulma** addressed himself for the battle. And placing that heroic monkey, his equal in prowess, in that command Sugriva sallied out with a tree in his hand to meet the enemy. And followed him on all sides the leaders of the monkeys with huge crags and various trees. The heroic Sugriva emitted terrible roars in the conflict and assailed the heroic Rākshasas and many others. The huge-bodied monkey-chief crushed the Rākshasas like unto the wind uprooting the trees at the time of dissolution. He began to make a downpour of crags at the Rākshasa host like unto the cloud pouring down hailstorms at the birds in the forest. And being beheaded by the crags discharged by that monkey chief the Rākshasas fell down like unto mountains cleft. The Rākshasas being thus attacked and shattered by Sugriva and roaring and falling down on all sides, an irrepressible Rākshasa, skilled in archery, by name Birupāksha, pronouncing his own name, got down from the car and mounted an elephant. And mounted on the elephant that highly powerful Birupāksha sent forth leonine roars and dashed against the monkeys. Exciting the joy of the Rākshasas and removing their anxiety he discharged dreadful shafts at Sugriva and his army. And being assailed by the pointed arrows of that Rākshasa that lord of monkeys roared in anger and made up his mind to destroy him. Thereupon uprooting a tree the heroic monkey, skilled in warfare, leaped and struck that huge elephant down in his presence. And being assailed greatly by Sugriva that huge elephant proceeded a little within the range of the bow and roared and died. And being greatly enraged on the destruction of that elephant the highly powerful Rākshasa dashed forward to face the enemy. That one of quick movements took up

* The division of an army ; a body of troops consisting of nine platoons or nine elephants, nine chariots, twenty-seven horses and forty-five foot.

his dagger and armour and viling, approached Sugriva. And beholding his movement Sugriva took up a huge crag resembling cloud and hurled it against Birupāksha. That highly powerful leading Rākshasa, finding the crag about to fall, turned a little away and struck the monkey with his dagger. And being assailed with dagger by that powerful Rākshasa the monkey remained senseless for sometime on the ground. And rising up all on a sudden he, clenching his fist, struck that Rākshasa in the mighty encounter on his breast and got him down. Being struck with the fist the night-ranger Birupāksha greatly enraged cut down with his dagger Sugriva's armour and tumbled him down with his feet. And the monkey rising up again was about to deal him a blow, hard as a thunder-bolt, with a dreadful sound. And receding a little, he baffled its aim and returned one on Sugriva's breast. Finding his aim baffled and himself struck in return by the Rākshasa, Sugriva, the lord of monkeys, was excited with anger. And the monkey-chief was now on the look-out for an oppurtunity to strike Birupāksha. And immediately in anger he struck him down with a blow on his forehead. And being thus assailed with the fist resembling the thunder-bolt of Mahendra, he fell down on the earth bathed in a pool of blood. And blood gushed out of the person of Birupāksha like unto water issuing out of a fountain. And the monkeys beheld their enemy(Birupāksha) with his eyes disfigured in anger, bathed in a foam of blood, his whole body discoloured, trembling, rolling and crying piteously. Thereupon those too armies of the monkeys and Rākshasas, being ready to engage in the encounter, began to roar like unto two mighty oceans having their banks broken. And observing that highly powerful Rākshasa, of discoloured eyes, slain by the king of monkeys, the monkeys and Rākshasa forces engaged in fight and looked like the rising Ganges.

## SECTION LXLVIII.

LIKE unto a pond in the summer both the armies became gradually reduced. Beholding his own army and Birupāksha slain, Rāvana, the lord of Rākshasas, was doubly excited with ire. And observing his army reduced and slain by the heroic (monkeys) he perceived ill omens in the fight and was accordingly pained at heart. And he addressed Mahodara, who was near him, saying, "O thou of great arms, all my hopes of success are now centered in thee. Do thou slay the enemy's force, O hero, and display thy prowess. Now hath come the time of returning the favours of thy master. Do thou fight bravely." Being thus accosted that Rākshasa-chief Mahodara, saying "so be it" entered the enemy's army like unto a fly entering into a flame. Excited by his master's command and empowered by his own prowess that (Rākshasa) gifted with great strength, began to assail the monkeys. And the highly powerful monkeys too taking up huge crags dashed against the dreadful army of the enemies and crushed all the Rākshasas. And Mahodara, greatly angered, severed in that mighty encounter, with his arrows feathered in gold, the hands, feet and thighs of the monkeys. Then the monkeys, in fear of the Rākshasas, fled away to different quarters and some sought shelter of Sugriva. And beholding his powerful monkey force thus assailed in the conflict, Sugriva dashed forward and fronted Mahodara. And taking up a huge and dreadful crag resembling a mountain,the monkey-king hurled it with great vehemence to slay him. Thereupon finding that crag about to fall, Mahodara fearlessly severed it with his arrows. And being sundered into a thousand pieces by the arrow of that Rākshasa, it fell down on the earth like unto a band of vultures. And beholding that crag thus severed, Sugriva was beside himself with ire ; and uplifting a *sâla* tree hurled it : and the heroic Rākshasa, the slayer of enemy's force, severed it into several pieces with his arrows. Thereupon excited with wrath he saw a *parigha* on the ground. And hurling that flaming *parigha* and displaying his (light-handedness) he struck his excellent horse therewith. And having his horse slain, that hero—the Rākshasa Mahodara, ascended his car, and in great anger took up his club. Those two heroes, with club and *parigha* in their hands, engaged in battle, roaring like two bulls or clouds accompanied with lightning. Thereupon the night-ranger Mahodara, inflamed with ire, hurled at Sugriva, the club flaming like the Sun. And beholding that dreadful club about to fall the highly powerful Sugriva—the lord of monkeys, uplifting his *parigha* struck it therewith. And *parigha*, being sundered, fell quickly down on the earth. Thereupon the effulgent Sugriva picked up from the ground *musala* made of iron and ornamented with gold. Taking that *musala* up he hurled it at the Rākshasa and who again hurled a club ; and both of them being severed fell down on the earth. Having their weapons baffled thus,those two heroes, gifted with great prowess and effulgence and resembling the burning fire, were ready to interchange blows. They, emitting roars again and again, struck each other down on the earth with their clenched fists. And rising up speedily they again assailed each other. Thus those two heroes, unsubdued, struck each other with their arms. Thereupon both of them, highly proficient in fighting with arms, were greatly exhausted. Thereupon they took up daggers. And uplifting them, (those two heroes) with their persons trembling in ire, proficient in fighting and skilled in the use of weapons, dashed on roaring. And both of them enraged with each other and anxious to score success, moving in circle on each other's right side, addressed themselves for action. Thereupon the vicious-minded, heroic Mahodara, gifted with great vehemence and proud of his own heroism, flung his dagger at (the monkey's) armour. And as he was about to extricate his dagger from the armour, that foremost of monkeys severed with his dagger that Rākshasa's head with helmet and *kundalas*. And beholding the Rākshasa-chief fall down on the earth with his head off, his forces fled away from the field. And slaying him that monkey-chief, delighted, began to roar along with other monkeys. Thereupon the Ten-necked one became highly enraged and Rāghava greatly delighted. And all the Rākshasas, with their hearts broken and countenances rendered poorly and stricken with fear fled away to different quarters. Slaying and striking down on earth Mahodara like unto a portion of a mighty hill severed, that son of the Sun appeared resplendent in his own effulgence and became irrepressible like unto the Sun. And winning victory in the action that lord of monkeys was espied by the celestials, Siddhas and Yakshas along with all creatures on earth, having their eyes flushed with joy.

## SECTION LXLIX.

MAHODARA being thus slain by Sugriva, the highly powerful Mahāparshwa, having his eyes reddened with ire, looked towards him. And the Rākshasa, with his weapons, assailed the dreadful army of Angada as well as the leading monkeys. The Rākshasa severed the heads from the bodies of the monkeys like unto the wind throwing away the fruits from trees. And he cut off, with his arrows, the arms of some and some were deprived of their sides. The monkeys were thus assailed by Mahāparshwa with a shower of shafts. All the monkeys were thus stricken with grief and rendered senseless. And hearing of the anxiety of his own army thus assailed by the Rākshasa, Angada, gifted with great vehemence, taking his *parigha* made of iron and resembling the rays of the sun, dashed on like the rising deep during the lunar half of a month. And that foremost of monkeys encountered Mahāparshwa, who, thus struck by the monkey, became insensible with his charioteer and fell down on the earth. Thereupon leaped on the battle-field the highly powerful and effulgent lord of bears, having the hue of red collyrium, with his army resembling the cloud. And excited with ire, he, taking up a huge crag resembling the summit of a mountain, speedily struck down his horses and broke down his car. And regaining his senses in a moment the highly powerful Mahāparshwa, again assailed Angada with many arrows. He struck Jāmvabān, the lord of bears, on his breast with three arrows and assailed Gabāksha with many shafts. And beholding Jāmvabān and Gabāksha overwhelmed with arrows, Angada, beside himself with ire, took up a dreadful *parigha*. And holding with two hands that *parigha* made of iron and bright like the rays of the sun, Angada, the son of Vāli, with his eyes reddened in wrath, hurled it at Mahāparshwa who was stationed at a distance, to slay him. And being hurled by the highly powerful (Angada) the *parigha*, struck down from his hands the bow with arrows and the helmet of the Rākshasa. And approaching him vehemently, Vāli's son, gifted with great prowess, in anger, struck him, with clenched fist, on his ears having excellent *kundalas*. Thereupon Mahāparshwa gifted with great vehemence and effulgence, highly angered, took up in his hands a huge *parashwadha*; sharpened with oil, bright and hard as iron and discharged it at Vāli's son, and struck him therewith on his left shoulder. And Angada baffled that *parashwadha*. Thereupon that hero, powerful like his own father, clenching his fist, hard as thunder-bolt and resembling even Indra's *açani*, dealt it, in great anger, upon the Raksha's breast. And being struck with that fist the Rākshasa's breast was shattered and he fell down on earth. He falling down on earth slain, his soldiers were greatly sorry and Rāvana attained to an excess of ire in the conflict. The noise set up by the delighted monkeys like unto a dreadful leonine roar, as if rending the city of Lankā abounding in edifices and gates, resembled the great roar of the celestials along with Indra. And hearing the noise of the celestials and monkeys, the lord of Rākshasas, the enemy of the gods, in great anger, again proceeded towards the battle field.

## SECTION C.

BEHOLDING Mahodara, Mahāpārsha and the highly powerful Birupāksha slain in the encounter Rāvana attained to an excess of ire. And ordering his charioteer to hurry on he gave vent to the following words—"All my courtiers have been slain and my city is shut up—I shall remove my grief consequent on all these by slaying Rāma and Lakshmana. I shall destroy Rāma-like tree in the conflict whose flower is Sitā and whose branches are Sugriva, Jāmbavān, Kumuda, Nala, Divida, Mainda, Angada, Gandhamādana, Hanumān and all other leading monkeys." And resounding the ten quarters with the sound of his chariot wheels that mighty car-warrior proceeded quickly towards Rāghava. With that sound all quarters were filled, and the earth, with rivers, mountains and forests shook and all the lions, deer and birds were terrified. He created a dreadful darkness with the discharge of his sharp weapons and burnt down the monkeys who fled away to different directions. Dust was raised on the ground by those monkeys assailed and flying to various directions. They were unable to withstand the power of that weapon made by Brahmā himself. Beholding his own army, assailed and cut into hundred peices by the excellent weapons of Rāvana, Rāghava dashed forward. And assailing the monkey-host, that foremost of Rākshasas espied Rāma, unconquered, at a distance with his brother Lakshmana like unto Bāsava with Vishnu, holding a huge bow like one painted on the sky, having expansive eyes like lotus-petals, long arms, and always subduing the enemies. Beholding the monkeys slain in the encounter and Rāvana approach, the heroic and highly powerful Rāma, with Sumitrā's son in his company, delightedly set arrows on his bow. And as if rending the whole earth with that dreadful sound he began to draw the string of his excellent bow. With the sound of Rāvana's arrows and the twang of Rāma's bow hundreds of Rākshasas fell down on earth. And coming within the range of the arrows of those two princes, Rāvana appeared like Rāhu in presence of the sun and the moon. And desiring to fight with him first Lakshmana setting sharp arrows on his bow, discharged shafts at him resembling the flame of fire. And the highly powerful Rāvana too with his arrows stopped the course of those shafts in the sky as soon as they were discharged by Lakshmana, skilled in archery. And displaying his light-handedness, he, with one arrow, severed Lakshmana's one, with three his three and with ten his ten. Surpassing thus the son of Sumitrā, Rāvana, ever victorious in battle, confronted Rāma in the encounter, standing like another hill. And approaching Rāghava, Rāvana the lord of Rākshasas, with his eyes reddened in ire, began to make a shower of arrows. Thereupon beholding the arrows shot off Rāvana's bow fall on all sides, Rāma speedily took up a *valla*.* And Rāghava sundered with his sharp *valla* his dreadful arrows flaming and resembling poisonous serpents. With various sharpened arrows Rāghava assailed Rāvana, and he again assailed Rāma in return. And forming a circle, they passed each other by the right side. Uprooting the earth with the vehemence of their arrows, irrepressible by each other, fighting equally discharging arrows, they looked dreadful like Death himself —and created terror in all creatures. The sky was filled with their various weapons, like unto clouds in the rainy season accompanied with lightning. And the welkin appeared full of windows with that shower of arrows, sharpened, shot with great vehemence and winged like vultures. The earth was stricken with darkness caused by these arrows like unto clouds appearing after sunset. There took place a dreadful confliet between them, desiring to slay each other, having their prowess unknown and fighting like Vitra and Vāsava. Both of them were proficient in archery, skilled in the art of conflict and foremost of those conversant with the use of weapons. And they began to veer round the battle-field. And wherever they went, there appeared arrows like unto waves of the deep roused by the winds. Then that destroyer of creatures—Rāvana—with his hand engaged in discharging shafts, shot at Rāma's forehead a network of arrows. And thereat Rāma on his head bore that shower of shafts shot from his terrific bow, having the lustre of the petals of blue lotuses; nor did he experience any pain. And then reciting a formula, the exceedingly energetic Rāma endowed with prowess, wrought up with wrath, engaged in incessantly shooting his shafts, taking his Raudra weapon and again seizing his arrows, discharged them at that lord of Rākshasas. And alighting at the impenetrable mail of the Rākshasa-chief, resembling a mass of mighty clouds, those arrows did not then occasion him any pain.

* An arrow with a crescent shaped head.

Again Râma skilled in all weapons, from a powerful weapon discharged arrows at the sovereign of the Râkshasas mounted on his car. And piercing Râvana, those like unto five-hooded serpents, resisted by him, entered the earth, hissing. Having baffled Râghava's weapon, Râvana, transported with passion, took up a dreadful Âsura weapon; and discharged sharpened shafts having the faces of lions and tigers, and the faces of *kankas* and *kokas*,* and the faces of vultures and hawks, and the faces of jackals, and the faces of wolves,—with gaping mouths,—and terrific of aspect; five-mouthed and red-hued. And that highly powerful one, enraged, sighing like a snake, by his power of illusion shot at Râma other keen arrows having the faces of mules and the faces of bears, and the faces of dogs and cocks, and the faces of *makaras*† and venomous serpents,—these as well as others. Covered with that Âsura weapon, that foremost of the Raghus, himself resembling fire, discharged an exceedingly vigorous weapon informed with fire; and shot various shafts having faces filled with live flames, and faces like unto suns,—and hued like unto planets and stars,—and furnished with faces resembling mighty meteors, or resembling tongues of lightning. And those terrific shafts of Râvana, resisted by Râghava's weapon, were annihilated in the sky, and destroyed (monkeys) by thousands. And seeing that weapon (of Râvana) destroyed by Râma of untiring deeds, all those heroes, the monkeys—headed by Sugriva, capable of wearing forms at will, shouted, surrounding Râghava. And the high-souled son of Daçaratha—Râghava—having by his might destroyed that weapon discharged by Râvana's arms, was delighted; and the monkey-chiefs, filled with glee, began to emit shouts.

---

* *Koka*—a ruddy goose. It may also mean a lizard, a chamaleon, a wolf.

† A marine monster, generally confounded with the alligator and the shark : but really a fabulous animal.—T.

## SECTION CI.

On that weapon of his having been baffled, Rāvana—lord of the Rākshasas—was fired with double fury, and the highly effulgent Rāvana from wrath set about discharging at Rāghava a dreadful Raudra weapon, which had been conferred on him by Maya. And from his bow began to issue forth in large numbers darts and maces and clubs, flaming and having the might of thunder; and various kinds of sharp clubs and daggers and nooses and flaming thunder-bolts began to descend like unto the winds at the universal tumbling. And thereupon the graceful and exceedingly effulgent Rāghava—foremost of those accomplished in noble arms—resisted that weapon with a powerful Gāndharva weapon. On that weapon being baffled by the high-souled Rāghava, Rāvana, with his eyes rendered coppery with passion, took up a Solar weapon. Thereupon from the bow of the wondrous vehement and intelligent Ten-necked one rushed out discuses flaming and mighty. And the firmament all round blazed up with those impendent (arms), as blaze up the cardinal quarters on the Sun and the Moon and the planets dropping down. Thereat Rāghava in the van of that army by means of vollies of shafts cut off Rāvana's wonderful weapons and discuses. And seeing that weapon destroyed, Rāvana—lord of Rākshasas—with ten arrows pierced Rāma all through his vitals. And pierced by Rāvana with those ten shafts discharged from his mighty bow, the exceedingly powerful Rāghava did not so much shake. Then Rāghava—victor in fight—waxing wondrous wroth, with countless shafts pierced Rāvana all over his person. In the meanwhile Rāghava's younger brother, the mighty Lakshmana—destroyer of foes—growing enraged, took up seven arrows. And with those highly impetuous arrows that exceedingly effulgent one severed the human-headed standard of Rāvana. And the mighty and graceful Lakshmana with a shaft cut off the head of the Nairita's charioteer, illumined with ear-rings. And then with five sharpened arrows Lakshmana severed the bow of the Rākshasa-chief, resembling the trunk of an elephant. And Bibhishana, bounding up, with his mace despatched Rāvana's excellent steeds, resembling hills or dark-blue clouds. Thereat, leaping down from his mighty car, whose horses had been slain, Rāvana was fired with high wrath against his brother. And the powerful lord of Rākshasas endowed with immense strength, hurled at Bibhishana a dart resembling the flaming thunder-bolt. And ere the dart had reached its destination, Lakshmana severed it with three shafts; and thereat in that mighty conflict there arose a mighty uproar from the monkeys. And the dart dight with networks of gold fell down in three fragments, as droppeth a mighty meteor from the firmament, flaming and shooting out scintillations. Then (Rāvana) took up a huge dart, glowing in its own energy, celebrated as being irrisistible, and incapable of being borne by the Destroyer himself. On being whirled by the impious and strong Rāvana, the dart possessed of exceeding energy, flamed up. In the meanwhile the heroic Lakshmana swiftly came to the side of Bibhishana,* whose life was placed in peril. And in order to save him, that hero—Lakshmana—drawing his bow, covered the dart-handed Rāvana with showers of shafts. On being covered with arrows shot by that high-souled one, Rāvana, with his prowess baffled, made up his mind to let (his brother) go. And seeing his brother delivered by Lakshmana, Rāvana, facing Lakshmana, spoke these words,—"O thou proud of thy prowess! as Bibhishana hath this wise been delivered by thee, passing by the Rākshasa, this dart,

* The commentator explains: "Himself coming before the dart, Lakshmana saved Bibhishana."—T.

discharged from my bludgeon of an arm, will depart, depriving thee of thy life." Having said this, Rāvana, waxing furiously enraged, discharged at Lakshmana that dart forged by Maya with his power of illusion, furnished with eight bells, having mighty sounds,—incapable of being resisted,—competent to finish foes; and flaming in energy,—and shouted simultaneously. And hurled with terrific force, the dart sending sounds resembling that of Vajra or the thunder-bolt, vehemently alighted at Lakshmana in that encounter. Thereat, as the dart descended, Rāghava addressed* it, saying,—"Peace be to Lakshmana! Be thou fraustrated; and let thy energy go out of thee." But the dart discharged in the encounter by the enraged Rāvana, resembling a venomous serpent, dived into the dauntless and heroic Lakshmana; and (the dart) exceedingly splendid and blazing, possessed of dreadful impetuosity, and resembling the tongue of the king of serpents, smote Lakshmana in his mighty chest. And with his breast riven by the dart, driving deep through the force of Rāvana, Lakshmana fell down to the earth. And Rāghava, standing by, seeing Lakshmana in that plight, had his heart overspread with sorrow. But reflecting only for a while, he, with his eyes surcharged with tears, was filled with greater martial ardour, and resembled the fire risen at the universal dissolution. Then thinking,—'This is not the time to indulge in grief;' he, gazing at Lakshmana, entered into a terrific encounter, resolved upon slaying Rāvana, laying under contribution his dearest energies. And Rāma saw Lakshmana with his chest riven by the dart in the mighty conflict, lying drenched in blood, and resembling a hill with serpents present in it.—And in spite of all their efforts, the foremost monkeys failed to extract the dart which had been hurled by the powerful Rāvana.—And, further, they were (all the while) sore assailed with showers of shafts by the foremost

* *i. e.* as Râmânuya remarks, addressed the deity presiding over it.—T.

Rākshasa of them all. The dart, having pierced Sumitrā's son, had entered the earth. In the encounter the mighty Rāma, grasping the dreadful dart with his hands, extracted the same and wrathfully snapped it.* As he (Rāma) was engaged in pulling the dart out, the mighty Rāvana kept pouring marrow-piercing shafts all over his person. Thinking nothing of those arrows, Rāma, embracing Lakshmana, spoke unto Hanumān and the mighty monkey, Sugriva,—"Ye foremost of monkeys, do ye stay here, surrounding Lakshmana. The opportunity for putting forth my prowess which I had sought, is present. I shall slay this wicked-minded Ten-necked one, who is resolved to pursue the course of unrighteousness. Even as on the expiry of summer the Chātaka is eager for the sight of clouds, I had long been eager to obtain a sight of (Rāvana.) Ye monkeys, this, I swear unto you,—this very hour not long after ye will see this world without Rāvana or Rāma. To-day having slain Rāvana in battle, I shall renounce all sorrow arising from the loss of my kingdom, from my sojourn in the woods, from my wandering in Dandaka, from the ravishment of Vaidehi, from encounter with the Rakshas,—all the terrible evils that I have suffered, and all the troubles resembling hell. He for whom I have brought over the monkey-forces, made Sugriva king, slaying Vāli in battle, for whom I have crossed the ocean and constructed a bridge over the deep—the same hath been come at by me in conflict, and the same hath come within the range of my vision.—And having come within my ken, Rāvana will not live, even as one coming within ken of a serpent of poisonous sight, doth not live; or even as a serpent doth not live, coming within ken of Vinatā's† son. Do ye, ye irrepressible ones, ye foremost of

* The commentator has a characteristic note. 'This dart, having pierced the foe, used always to return to Rāvana. But Rāma, who was the Lord himself, having spoken to it as he did, it could not this time go back; and Rāma snapped it, which none else could do.' !—T.

† Garura.

monkeys, seated at the brow of the mountain, behold the battle between me and Rāvana. To-day let the three worlds with the Gandharvas, and the Siddhas, and the Chāranas, see that for which Rāma is Rāma. To-day I shall do a deed of which the worlds with the mobile and the immobile and the gods, shall speak as long as the Earth sustaineth (creatures.)" Having delivered himself thus, Rāma, concentrating his attention, began to charge the Ten-necked one in encounter with whetted arrows decked with burnished gold. And in the same way Rāvana showered on Rāma great *nārāchas* and clubs, even as clouds pour down showers. And there arose a tremendous uproar of mighty arrows discharged by Rāma and Rāvana, smiting one another. And the shafts shot by Rāma and Rāvana, severed and scattered, with flaming heads dropped to the Earth. And the mighty twangs of the bow-strings of both, terrifying all creatures, were wonderful to behold.* And then even as clouds disperse on being trampled by the Winds, Rāvana, covered with showers of arrowy networks by that high-souled one and reduced to sore straits by that one (Rāma) of a glowing bow, fled away in fear.

## SECTION CII.

SEEING the heroic Lakshmana brought down by the dart discharged by the powerful Rāvana, and lying drenched in blood, he (Rāma) after having fought furiously with the wicked-minded Rāvana,—and having showered vollies of shafts, addressed Sushena, saying,—"This heroic Lakshmana

* *Adbhutadarçana—wonderful to behold,—wonderful to witness* is the sense.—T.

brought down to the earth by the prowess of Rāvana, lieth like a serpent, enhancing my sorrow. Seeing this hero, dearer to me than life, what power have I, with my soul overwhelmed with dole, to fight? If this brother of mine graced with auspicious marks, delighting in battle, breathe his last, what shall life avail me or happiness? My prowess is ashamed; my bow falleth off from my hand; my arrows droop; my sight is dimmed with tears; my limbs weaken as do those of men in a dream; thought racks me; and I even desire death." Seeing his brother wounded by the wicked-minded Rāvana, crying in preternatural accents, and sore stricken in his vitals, (Rāma) overcome by a mighty sorrow, lamented with his senses wildered. "Seeing my brother, Lakshmana, wounded, and lying over the dust of the field, even victory, O hero, doth not seem to me sweet. If the Moon is hid from the sight, whom doth he then delight? What have I to do with battle? What have I to do with life? I have no more to do anything with fighting, seeing that this Lakshmana wounded, lieth in the field of battle. As this highly effulgent one had followed me into the forest, so will I in the same way follow him to the abode of Yama. Ever seeking my welfare and ever devoted to me, he hath been reduced to this pass by Rākshasas fighting in crooked ways. In land after land one meets with wives, in land after land one meets with friends, but country find I none where a uterine brother may be met with. What, O irrepressible one, shall I do with the kingdom without my Lakshmana? And what shall I say unto mother Sumitrā, fond of her son? And I shall never be able to bear the reproach Sumitrā shall cast upon me. And what shall I say unto Kauçalyā, and what unto mother Kaikeyi? And what shall I say unto Bharata, and what unto the exceedingly powerful Satrughna? 'Thou hadst gone to the woods with him. Why then dost thou come (back) without him?' 'Tis better (for me) to renounce my life here, instead of bearing the censure of friends. What a sin had I committed in another birth, seeing that my virtuous brother, staying before me, hath been slain? Ah, my brother! Thou best of men! O master, who wert the foremost of heroes! Why, forsaking me, dost thou repair to the other regions. Wherefore, brother, dost thou not speak to me, who am lamenting? Get up. See! Why dost thou lie down? Look on me with thine eyes. O mighty-armed one, in the woods and mountains thou didst ever use to cheer me, tried by grief and pining in despondency, with my mind overwhelmed (with woe)." As Rāma was speaking thus with his senses overwhelmed with emotion, Sushena, soothing him, spoke these pregnant words,—"O foremost of men, cast off this train of thought tending to overwhelm thy understanding,—this anxiety giving birth to grief, and resembling the shafts of foes in the van of the embattled forces. Lakshmana enhancer of auspiciousness is not dead. His face is not distorted or blackened. Do thou look at his countenance, which is beautifully bright and cheerful. His hands have palms resembling lotus-petals, and his eyes are pleasant. O king, one dead doth not look thus. (Therefore), O hero, do not grieve. O subduer of enemies, this one is instinct with life. As he is lying down on the ground, stretched at length, his heart, O hero, trembling momentarily, testifieth to his respiration." Having spoken thus unto Rāghava, the highly wise Sushena thus addressed the mighty monkey, Hanumān, saying,—"O placid one, hieing hence to the mountain, Mahodaya, which, O hero, had formerly been mentioned unto thee by Jāmbavān, bring hither the mighty drug sprung at its right summit—Viçalyakaraní by name, and Sāvarnyakaraní,* and Sanjívakaranî, O hero, and the potent medicine—Sandhāní. Do thou bring (these) in order that the hero—Lakshmana—may be revived." Having been thus instructed, Hanumān, repairing to the Medicinal mountain, was wrought up with anxiety, not knowing the drugs. And then

* *Lit.*—that which restores the former complexion.—T.

the thought sprang up in the mind of the Wind-god's offspring of immeasurable prowess,—'I shall go, even taking this (entire) summit of the mountain. In this very summit must that delightful drug have sprung. This I infer, inasmuch as Sushena had forsooth said so. If I fail to take Viçalyakaraní, I shall come by disgrace,—and if I spend much time (in thought), that would be fraught with evil."* Having reflected thus, the exceedingly powerful Hanumān, foremost of monkeys,—swiftly drawing up to that best of mountains, and giving three shakes to the mountain filled with various flowering trees,—raised it up with his hands. And taking that summit of the mountain resembling dark-blue clouds charged with rain, Hanumān from the earth bounded up into the sky. And arriving (at his quarters), that wondrous vehement one, putting down the mountain-peak, and reposing for a while, spoke unto Sushena,—"I did not find the drug, O best of monkeys; and therefore have I brought this entire summit of the mountain." When the Wind-god's offspring had spoken thus, that foremost of monkeys—Sushena—praising him, uprooted the herb and secured it. Seeing Hanumān's feat, incapable of being done by even the celestials, the choicest of the monkeys were amazed. Then crushing the healing herb, that best of monkeys—the exceedingly effulgent Sushena, made Lakshmana smell the same. And thereupon the wounded Lakshmana,—slayer of hostile heroes—smelling it, cured of his wound and ailments, speedily rose up from the ground. Seeing Lakshmana rise up from the earth, the monkeys, exceedingly rejoiced, honoring Lakshmana, exclaimed, "Excellent! Excellent!" "Come!" said that slayer of hostile heroes—Rāma—and with his eyes filled with tears, he deeply embraced Lakshmana. And having embraced Sumitrā's son, Rāghava then addressed him,

* Explains the commentator: 'If I take any other medicine by mistake, I shall make a fool of myself; if I spend much time in thought, Lakshmana may die.'—T.

saying,—"By good fortune it is that, O hero, I see thee returned from (the mansion of) Death.—Verily my life, or Sitā, or Victory is worthless (without thee). And thou being dead, what is my life worth?" When the high-souled Rāghava had spoken thus, Lakshmana, aggrieved on account of the words (of Rāghava) expressive of infirmity of purpose, said,—"Having bound thyself by that vow, it doth not, O thou having truth for prowess, behove thee to speak like one fickle and feeble. Those speaking the truth, never falsify their promise: the mark of a great one is even observance of vow. O sinless one, do not suffer thyself to be overcome by despair on my account. Do thou to-day by slaying Rāvana, make thy promise good. Thy foe coming within the sway of thy shafts, will not hence, living, even like a mighty elephant coming before a sharp-toothed roaring lion. I wish the speedy destruction of this impious one, ere the maker of day, having performed his work, has ascended the Setting-hill. If thou wishest to slay Rāvana in battle, if thou desirest to recover the princess, then, O noble one, O hero, to-day speedily set about what I say."

## SECTION CIII.

HEARING the words uttered by Lakshmana, that slayer of hostile heroes—Rāghava—endued with prowess, taking his bow, set shafts on it, and in the brunt of battle began to discharge dreadful arrows at Rāvana. And mounted on another car, Rāvana—lord of Rākshasas—rushed against Kākutstha, even as Swarbhānu rusheth against the Sun. And even as a mass of clouds poureth down torrents on a mighty mountain, the Ten-necked one, mounted on his car, smote Rāma with shafts resembling thunder-bolts. And in the encounter Rāma, concentrating his thoughts, showered on the Ten-necked one arrows embellished with gold and looking like living fire. And celestials and Gandharvas and Kinnaras declared that there had been no other battle like unto the encounter of Rāma stationed on the ground and the Raksha mounted on his car. Then the foremost of celestials—Sakra—hearing their ambrosial speech, summoning Mātali, said,—"Taking my car, hie to the best of the Raghus. And reaching the earth, do thou, welcoming (him), bring about great good unto the gods." Thus accosted by the sovereign of the celestials, Mātali—celestial charioteer—bending down his head, addressed that celestial, saying,—"Speedily shall I go, O lord of the celestials; and I shall also do the office of a charioteer (unto Rāghava)." Then yoking with steeds that best of cars, curiously wrought with gold; adorned with hundreds of small bells; resembling the Sun new risen; having its pole studded with lapises; yoked with excellent horses caparisoned in gold; furnished with white chowris,—drawn by steeds resembling the Sun; decked with golden net-works,—and provided with a golden standard,—the graceful car of the sovereign of the celestials,—Mātali, commanded by the king of the immortals, ascending the car, went out of the celestial regions and came to Kākutstha. And with his hand holding the reins, the charioteer of the thousand-eyed (Deity) with joined hands addressed Rāma, saying,—"O Kākutstha, in order that thou mayst obtain the victory, the thousand-eyed (god) hath sent thee this car. And, O exceedingly powerful one! O graceful (hero)! O thou that slayest thy foes! this is the redoubtable bow of Indra,—and this is the mail resembling fire,—and these are the arrows looking like the very Sun; and this is the dart shining and fraught with fair fortune. Ascend thou this car,

* This conversation between Râma and Lakshmana took place, says the commentator, on the first day of the lighted fortnight.—T.

O hero. Slay the Rākshasa—Rāvana, with me as thy charioteer, even as the lord of the celestials slayeth Dānavas." Thus addressed, Rāma, going round the car and saluting it, ascended the same, illumining the worlds with his splendour. And the encounter that took place between the two cars with the mighty-armed Rāma (on one side),and the Raksha—Rāvana—(on the other), was wonderful to behold. And Rāghava highly proficient in weapons with a Gāndharva weapon resisted the Gāndharva weapon of the Rākshasa king, and with a celestial weapon, his celestial weapon. And then that lord of Rākshasas—the night-ranger—fired with high rage, again discharged an exceedingly dreadful Rākshasa weapon. And the gold-decked shafts shot from Rāvana's bow, becoming furiously venomous serpents, covered Kākutstha. And vomitting living flames, they of terrific aspect, having flaming faces, showered over Rāma with gaping mouths. And those flaming venomous serpents, having the feel of Vāsuki himself, covered all sides and enveloped all quarters. And seeing those serpents descending in the encounter, Rāma employed a dreadful Gārura weapon. And discharged from Rāghava's bow, those arrows plated with gold at the feathered parts, and furnished with the splendour of peacocks, becoming golden birds—began to range (the field of battle) as the enemies of the serpents. And the shafts of Rāma capable of wearing forms at will, turned into birds, destroyed all the exceedingly swift-coursing arrows having the forms of serpents. On his weapon having been baffled, Rāvana—lord of Rākshasas—waxing wroth, poured tremendous showers of shafts on Rāma. And smiting Rāma of untiring deeds with thousands of shafts, (Rāvana) pierced Mātali with vollies of arrows. And with an arrow, Rāvana severed the standard; and having brought down the golden standard on the floor of the car, Rāvana wounded even Indra's steeds with a net-work of arrows. And seeing Rāma hard pressed, celestials and

Gandharvas, and Chāranas along with Dānavas, and Siddhas, and the supreme saints were overcome with sadness; and the foremost monkeys together with Bibhishana were aggrieved. And seeing a Moon of Rāma Chandra in the grasp of a Rāhu of Rāvana, that bringer of evil unto creatures—Budha—stood, assailing the Prayāpatya star—Rohini—beloved of the Moon. And the enraged Ocean, heaving with smoking surges, and flaming as it were, swelled up, seeming to the touch the Sun. And the Sun was blackened and assumed a stern aspect, with his rays dimmed. And he was seen with a headless trunk on his lap, and he was in conjunction with a comet. And that star of the Koçalas, relating to the deities—Indra and Agni—Angāraka—stood in the sky, attacking Viçākhā. And the Ten-necked one, having ten faces and twenty arms, equipped with his bow, looked like the mountain—Maināka. And Rāma reduced to sore straits by the Ten-necked Raksha, could not discharge his arrows in the conflict. And then the enraged Rāma with his eyes slightly red, flew into a tremendous passion, as if burning up the Rākshasas. Seeing the face of the enraged Rāma endued with understanding, all the creatures were overwhelmed with fear and the Earth herself shook. And mountains abounding with lions and tigers began to tremble, and trees to shiver. And even the deep—lord of streams—was wrought up wondrously. And rough and terrific clouds in the sky sent forth fierce roars. And stormy clouds rumbling went about the heavens. And seeing Rāma wrought up with a mighty passion, and the fearful disastrous omens, all creatures were possessed by fright and Rāvana was struck with dismay. And then stationed in the sky, celestials and Gandharvas and mighty serpents and saints and Dānavas and Daityas and those related to Garura—fowls—beheld that conflict like unto the universal tumbling, as the two heroes faught on with various dire arms. And as they looked on the mighty encounter, the celestials and the Asuras, who had come to the conflict, from feeling of regard,* cheerfully spoke (these words). And the Asuras staying there said unto the Ten-necked one, 'Be victorious;' and the celestials again and again said unto Rāma, 'Be victorious!' In the meantime, the impious Rāvana, desirous of slaying Rāghava, from wrath took up a mighty weapon, fraught with the essence of the thunder-bolt; sending terrible sounds; capable of destroying all foes,—furnished with forks resembling mountain-peaks; tending to strike terror unto mind and sight; sharp-pointed, resembling the smoking fire risen at the hour of universal dissolution; exceedingly terrible; irrisistible (in battle); unbearable even by the Destroyer,—the terror of all creatures—terrific; and competent to rive (all things). Flaming up with wrath, Rāvana took this dart. And fired with furious wrath, that powerful one took the dart in the encounter, surrounded in that contest by many heroic Rākshasas. And uplifting (the dart), the huge-bodied Rāvana, with his eyes reddened in passion, emitted mighty roars. And the shouts of the Rākshasa sovereign made the earth and the sky and the cardinal quarters and all sides tremble. And at the roars of that wicked-minded and huge-bodied one, all creatures were struck with terror, and the sea was vexed.† And the exceedingly energetic Rāvana, taking that mighty dart, and sending up furious shouts, addressed Rāma in a harsh speech, saying,—"O Rāma, I in wrath uplift this dart having the strength of the levin. This will utterly deprive of life thee who art assisted by thy brother. O thou that delightest in battle, to-day swiftly slaying thee, I shall make thee even with those heroic Rakshas slain in the van of the forces. Stay now. O Rāghava, thee shall I slay with this dart." Saying this, the lord of the Rākshasas hurled the dart. And discharged from Rāvana's hand, (the dart), surrounded with garlands of

* *i. e.* each party out of regard for the warrior to whom it wished well.—T.

† 'The still-*vexed* Bermoothes.'—*Tempest.*

lightning, furnished with eight bells, sending mighty roars,—rising to the sky, looked exceedingly splendid. Seeing the dart, flaming and of terrific aspect, Raghu's son—Rāma—endowed with prowess, drawing his bow, discharged arrows. And with vollies of shafts Rāghava resisted the descending (dart), even as Vāsava extinguisheth the fire of doomsday with his showers. Then even as a flame consumeth insects, the mighty dart of Rāvana burnt up those shafts shot from the bow of Rāma. Seeing those shafts reduced to ashes and crushed on coming in contact with the dart, as they were coursing in the sky, Rāghava was transported with passion. And then waxing wondrous wroth,—Raghu's son—Rāghava—took up a javelin, liked by Vāsava himself, brought by Mātali. And on being wielded by that strong one, the javelin, resonant with bells, made the welkin blaze up, like a burning meteor on the occasion of universal rack. And when hurled, it alighted on that same dart of the Rākshasa-chief. And thereat, with its splendour lost, the mighty dart, riven, dropped (to the earth.) Then Rāma, shooting straight-speeding arrows, pierced his (Rāvana's) exceedingly fleet steeds. And then he pierced Rāvana in the chest with whetted arrows. And the energetic Rāghava hit (Rāvana) in the temples with three feathered shafts. And thereat with all his limbs pierced (with arrows), and his body laved in blood, the lord of Rākshasas furnished with many limbs, looked like a flowering Açoka. And with his person pierced with the shafts of Rāma, the lord of night-rangers having his body drenched with blood, was stricken with sadness in the midst of his forces,—and was also overwhelmed with terrific wrath.

## SECTION CIV.

On being greatly harassed by Kākutstha in anger, Rāvana, delighting in battle, came under the sway of a towering passion. And with his eyes aglow, that powerful one from wrath and fury assailed Rāghava in mighty encounter. And even as clouds pour down from the sky on a pool, Rāvana showered thousands of arrows on Rāghava. And covered with vollies of shafts discharged from (Rāvana's) bow in the conflict, Kākutstha like unto a mighty mountain did not shake. And that one endowed with prowess stood in the field, resisting those networks of arrows, and took up shafts resembling the rays of the Sun. Then the fleet-handed night-ranger, fired with rage, discharged a thousand arrows at the chest of the high-souled Rāghava.—And thereat in that encounter Lakshmana's elder brother, with his body bathed in blood, appeared like a mighty Kinçuka tree in a forest. And with his ire aroused by the blows he received, the exceedingly energetic Kākutstha took up arrows resembling the Sun risen at the time of the universal dissolution. And in the darkness spread by the arrows (discharged), Rāma and Rāvana both fired with wrath could not be discovered of each other. Then that hero—Daçaratha's son—Rāma, overcome with wrath, addressed Rāvana, laughing, in a harsh speech, saying,—"Thou vilest of Rākshasas, in consequence of having through lack of sense carried off my wife from Janasthāna and brought her under thy subjection, thou hast been deprived of thy prowess. Having forcibly carried away Vaidehi staying in that mighty forest, forlorn and without me, thou thinkest—'I am a hero.' Outraging the helpless wives of others,—doing this craven deed, thou thinkest—'I am a hero.' O thou having thy dignity destroyed! O shameless wight! O thou of volatile character, having through thy violence brought destruction on thyself, thou thinkest,—'I am a hero.' A great and famous act hath been performed by thee,—a hero, and the brother of the Bestower of riches, surrounded with thy forces! To-day receive the mighty fruit of that infamous act done through pride, productive of evil.* O wicked-minded one, thou thinkest of thyself—'I am a hero;' but thou that hast taken away Sitā like a thief, hast no feeling of shame. Hadst thou forcibly outraged Sitā in my very presence, thou, slain by my shafts, wouldst have seen thy brother—Khara. By luck, O thou of an evil soul, thou hast come within the range of my vision. To-day by means of sharp shafts shall I bring thee to death's door. To-day beasts of pray will drag thy head having burning ear-rings, severed by my shafts and covered with the dust of the battle-field. O Rāvana, vultures will alight on thy breast, as thou wilt lie low on the ground; and, athirst, they will drink the blood gushing out from thy wounds. To-day fowls of the air will keep pulling at thee pierced with my shafts, and lying lifeless, as birds do serpents." Having spoken thus, that slayer of foes—Rāma—showered arrows on the lord of Rākshasas, staying before. And the prowess and strength and spirits and force of arms of Rāma burning for the destruction of his foe, were doubled. And all the Weapons† presented themselves before that one cognisant of self; and the fleet-handedness of that exceedingly powerful one increased immensely from exhilaration of spirits. Seeing all these auspicious omens coming of themselves, Rāma, finisher of Rākshasas, set about smiting his foe more energetically than ever. And assailed with stones by the monkeys and showers of shafts by Rāghava, the Ten-necked one felt his heart undergoing a

---

* Remarks Râmânuya, 'here and in the next world.'

† *i. e.* the presiding deities of them.

revolution.* And when through the stupifaction of his inner self, he could not discharge any weapon, or draw his bow, or put forth his prowess, (Rāma) did not persist in smiting him. And the shafts and various arms discharged by him betokened his death; and his last moments were present. And his charioteer, driving his car, perceiving this, calmly took the car away from the field of fight. And then, seeing the king shorn of prowess, and dropt, his charioteer, struck with fear, swiftly turned away his dreadful car having the clatter of clouds, and went away from the field of battle.

## SECTION CV.

AFTER gradually regaining his senses, Rāvana, urged on by the force of the Finisher, getting into a furious passion, with his eyes reddened in wrath, addressed the charioteer, saying,—"O thou of perverse sense, disregarding me as devoid of prowess, and incompetent, and bereft of vigor,—as cowardly, light, nerveless and shorn of energy,—and as divorced by the power of illusion and debarred by arms,—thou actest on thine own understanding. Wherefore disregarding me, and not minding my purpose, hast thou taken away my car from before the presence of the enemy? O abject one! by thee have my long-earned renown and energy and prowess and credit been brought to naught. In the very sight of an enemy of renowned prowess, and one capable of being gratified with valorous deeds, hast thou made me, burning for battle, look as if I were a coward. As, O wicked-minded one, thou dost not even through heedlessness,

* *Vighurnahridayah*: had his heart paralysed, according to the commentator. I prefer the sense given as more graphic.—T.

take the car to the field of battle, I infer for certain that thou hast been bribed by the foe. The act that thou hast done, doth not appear as that of a friend seeking our welfare; but to-day thou hast acted like an enemy. If thou hast been maintained by me, if thou rememberest my merit, do thou swiftly turn the car before my enemy has departed." Thus admonished by him of slender sense, the charioteer possessed of intelligence, humbly spake unto Rāvana words fraught with good,—"I am not afraid, nor stupified, nor have I been bribed by the foe, nor am I negligent. And I have not forgotten thy affection or thy good offices. And studious of thy welfare, I have saved thy fame; and with a mind over-flowing with affection I have done (unto thee) this unpalatable good. O mighty monarch, for this, thou shouldst not, like a frivolous and base one, criminate me that am ever engaged in what is good and dear unto thee. Listen! I shall render thee reason why I turned away from the field the car, rushing like a river when the sea is swelled up.* I knew that thou hadst been fatigued in consequence of thy mighty exertions in the fight. And I could not perceive that thy prowess then stood superior (to that of the foe).† And the steeds of my car were worn out by carrying it; and they were battered, and helpless, and perspired like kine in a shower. And bad omens fast sprang up before us. And on these occurring, I perceived that things would go against us. O thou endowed with exceeding might, a charioteer should be conversant with season and place, with omens, and the expressions of emotions; as also with depression of spirits, exhilaration, and grief. And he should have a knowledge of low, level and uneven grounds, and the time for conflict, and he should be able to perceive the shortcomings of the enemy. And a charioteer mounted on a car, should know

* On the ascension of the Moon.

† Two negatives in this verse amounting to an affirmative. This is the only instance of double negatives in Vālmiki.—T.

when to draw near an enemy, when to turn away from him; when to stay; and when to turn round from before the foe—all these (he should know). What I, for bringing respite unto thee as well as the horses of the car, have done by way of removing the terrific exhaustion, is proper. I did not, O hero, turn away the car of my own sheer will. What I have done, O lord, had been dictated by my affection for thee. Command me. What thou sayest, O destroyer of foes, I will do every way, O hero, with my whole soul." Thereat, well-pleased with the speech of the charioteer, Rāvana, eager for encounter, after praising him in various ways, said,—"O charioteer, do thou swiftly take the car towards Rāghava. Without slaying his foe in fight, Rāvana turneth not away (from the field)." Speaking thus, Rāvana—lord of Rākshasas—gave the charioteer on the car an excellent ornament for the hand. Hearing Rāvana's words, the charioteer drove the car. And urged on by the speech of Rāvana, the charioteer drove on the steeds,—and in a moment the mighty chariot of the Rākshasa-chief appeared before Rāma in the field of battle.

## SECTION CVI.

THEN the revered Agastya, who, desirous of witnessing the fight, had along with the deities come there,—seeing Rāvana spent with the toil of conflict, staying in the field plunged in thought, and stationed before Rāma for engaging in encounter,—addressed Rāma, drawing near to him, saying,—"Rāma, Rāma, O mighty-armed one, hearken to the eternal secret, whereby, my child, thou wilt conquer all foes in fight,—*Aditya-hridaya*,* sacred, capable of destroying all

* *Lit.*—The heart of the Sun.—the designation of a Vedic Hymn.

foes, bringing victory—the recitation, enduring and indestructible,—and supremely good; fraught with all welfare, removing every sin,—chasing away anxiety and grief, bringing length of days; and excellent. Do thou worship Vivaçwata's offspring—the Sun—lord of the world, furnished with rays,—who maketh people engage in work, and who is bowed down to by deities and Asuras. This effulgent one, producing rays, is instinct with the spirits of all the deities; and he with his rays ruleth all creatures—and the hosts of celestials and Asuras. This Sun is Brahmā and Vishnu and Siva and Skanda[(a)] and Prajāpati,[(b)] and Mahendra and Dhanada[(c)] and the Destroyer—Yama—and Soma[(d)] and the Lord of waters; and the Pitris,[(e)] and the Vasus, and the Sādhyas[(f)] and the two Açwinis[(g)] and the Maruts and Manu,[(h)] and the Wind-god and the God of fire and the creatures and the Creator of life and the seasons. And he is Āditya[(i)] and Savitā[(j)] and Suryya[(k)] and Khaga[(l)] and Pushā[(m)] and

(a) The celestial generallissimo. The commentator gives a spiritual interpretation. 'He that by means of his rays openeth up the five organs of perception.'

(b) The lord of all creatures, by virtue of his bringing forth all beings through his energy.

(c) Dispenser of riches, a name of Kuvera.

(d) Furnished with splendour, a name of the Moon. According to some 'endowed with energy.'

(e) *Lit.* the ancestral manes. Here the generator of everything.

(f) An order of semi-divine beings. Here, 'He who is adored by the spiritual.'

(g) In virtue of his omnipresence and his being the healer of all ailments.

(h) All-knowing and being the primæval sovereign.

(i) 'He from whom all derive sustenance.'

(j) 'The producer of heart and the spiritual faculties by heat, and corn, *etc.* by showers'

(k) 'Coursing alone, according to the commentator. It may also means—'He that sets people to work.'

(l) 'Coursing the highest heavens,' or says the commentator 'the heavens of the heart.'

(m) 'The maintainer.'

Gavastimān,(a) and the Golden-looking and Bhānu(b) and Hiranyaretā(c) and Divākara.(d) And he is Haridaçwa(e) and Sahasrārchi(f) and Saptasapti(g) and Marichimān.(h) And he subdueth darkness, and he is Sambhu(i) and Tashtā(j) and Mārtandaka(k) and Ançumān.(l) And he is Hiranyagarbha,(m) Sicira,(n) and Tapana,(o) and Ahaskara(p) and Ravi,(q) and Agnigarbha,(r) and Aditi's son,(s) and Sankha,(t) and Siciranāçana,(u) Byomanātha,(v) and Tamabheda,(w) the one proficient in Rik, Yajus and Sāma; and Ghanavrishti,(x) and

---

(a) *Gavastimán*—'Ray-furnished, or having the all-permeating Spirit of Auspiciousness.'

(b) *Bhánu*—'having brightness.'

(c) *Hiranyaretá*—'instinct with the cosmic energy.'

(d) *Divákara*—'maker of day.'

(e) *Haridaçwa*—'pervading all sides,' or 'having black steeds.'

(f) *Sahasrárchi*—'thousand-rayed. The commentator explains spiritually, He whose cognition points in infinite directions.'

(g) 'He from whom proceed the seven organs of sense of people.' Or 'he who has seven steeds.'

(h) 'Having rays.'

(i) 'He from whom proceed the several sorts of happiness.'

(j) 'He who removes the misfortunes of his votaries.'

(k) 'He that infuses life into the lifeless mundane egg.'

(l) 'Having rays.'

(m) The cause of the creation, preservation and destruction of the Universe.

(n) 'Good-natured.'

(o) *Tapa*—means 'wealth.' *Tapana—the possessor of all riches.*

(p) *Ahas*—day and *Kara—maker.*

(q) *Rauti—teacheth*—Ravi—*he that teacheth.*

(r) *Lit. fire-wombed.* He that carries the fire of doom within himself.

(s) Aditi—'without destruction'—means 'Brahma knowledge.'

(t) Supreme happiness.

(u) The remover of intellectual stupor or evil-mindedness.

(v) Lord of the welkin.

(w) Dispeller of darkness.

(x) He from whom floweth the fruit of acts: or he from whom come downpours. The latter epithet is justified on grounds of Physical Geography, *rain being ultimately dependant on solar heat.*

the friend of the Apas,(a) and he that swiftly courseth in the Vindhya way. And he is Ātapi(b) andMandali(c) and Mrityu.(d) And he is Pingala,(e) and the destroyer of everything, and the Omniscient, and he having the universe for his form,(f) and the exceedingly energetic one,and the beloved of all,and that one lording it over all kinds of actions. And he is the lord(g) of stars and planets and constallations, and the origin of everything, and the one powerful pre-eminently of powerful things,(h)—and the one having twelve forms.(i) I bow unto thee (having these forms and functions). Salutation unto the Eastern mount and the mount of the West. Salutation unto the lord of the stellar bodies and salutation also unto the lord of day. Salutation and salutation unto him that bringeth victory, and the joy that springeth up from victory ; and unto him of yellow steeds. Salutation,salutation,O thousand-rayed one ! Salutation and salutation unto Āditya. Salutation unto him that keepeth his senses under subjection ; Salutation and salutation unto the Hero,(j) and unto Sāranga(k) and unto him that awakenest the Lotus.(l) And (salutation) nnto thee, O fierce one. Salutation unto the Lord himself of Brahmā, Içāna(m) and Achchyuta,(n) and unto Sura(o) and unto him

---

(a) Apas may mean either 'the good,' or 'water.' Vindhya way mean either the way known as Brahmanári or the orbit of the Sun.

(b) He that is intent on creating the cosmos.

(c) Ray-crowned or adorned with gems.

(d) The bringer of death.

(e) The motive force of the blood-tube called Pingalá.

(f) Or the ornament of the Universe.

(g) *i. e.* the controller of them, remarks Rámánuja.

(h) Such as, observes the commentator, as fire.

(i) *i. e.* the months of the year.

(j) Him that leadeth the senses, and that is endowed with the prowess of slaying Tripurá *etc.*

(k) Him that deservest the *pranaba,* the holiest formula in all Hindu Scripture.

(l) That awakenest the external lotus as well as the lotus of the heart.—

(m) Siva. (n) Vishnu. (o) The sun.

that constitutes the knowledge of Āditya, and unto him that unfoldeth me and not-me ; and unto the devourer of all, and unto the form of the destroyer of the darkness of ignorance. Salutation unto the destroyer of darkness, and unto the destroyer of enemies, and unto him of immeasurable Soul, and unto the destroyer of the ingrate, and unto the deity, and unto the lord of all stellar bodies. And salutation unto him that boasteth of the splendour of burning gold, unto the destroyer of all mental obscurity,—and unto the maker of the universe. Salutation unto the remover of darkness ; unto the illuminator of the Soul ; unto the all-beholding one of all the worlds. The lord createth everything and verily destroyeth it. And with his rays he sucketh up, and destroyeth and createth (everything). When all are asleep, this one waketh, and he is resident in the hearts of all creatures. This one is both Agnihotra as well as the fruit reaped by the sacrifices thereof. And he constitutes the gods and the sacrifices and the fruit also thereof ; and he is the lord of all acts that are performed by creatures. If a person recites this (hymn), he, O Rāghava, doth not come by misfortune, when he is in peril of his life, or is ill, or in a lonely place, or in fear. Do thou, with concentration, worship this god of gods, this lord of the universe. By reciting (this hymn) instinct with the three virtues, thou wilt obtain victory in battle. This very instant, O mighty-armed one, thou wilt conquer Rāvana." Having said this, Agastya went whither from he had come. Hearing this, that exceedingly energetic one had his grief gone. Then, well pleased, Rāghava, exerting himself, contemplated (the hymn). And reciting this, he beholding the Sun, attained excess of joy. And sipping water again and again, and becoming purified, that powerful one, taking up his bow, and viewing Rāvana, advanced with a delighted heart, to obtain victory. And he became intent on his death with his dearest energies. Then exceedingly delighted, and filled with rejoicings, the Sun, in the midst of the celestial hosts knowing that the destruction of the Sovereign of the night-rangers was at hand,—spoke unto Rāma "Bestir thyself."

## SECTION CVII.

Then the charioteer fully drove with speed Rāvana's car, capable of bringing down the hosts of foes, resembling in form a city of the Gandharvas, having elevated streamers, yoked with surpassingly superb steeds, engarlanded in gold; stocked with war-like implements; furnished with ensigns and standards; appearing to devour the welkin; making the earth herself resound; destructive to hostile hosts; and filling its own party with delight. And as it speedily descended, the monarch of men beheld that Rākshasa-king's resounding car, having huge standards, yoked with black chargers, and endowed with fierce splendour; as if flaming in the firmament; having the resplendance of the Sun himself; with thronging lightning pennons; displaying the glow of Indra's weapon;* showering arms; and resembling rain-charged clouds. Seeing the enemy's car resembling a mass of clouds having a chatter resembling the sounds sent by a cleaving mountain rived by the thunder, Rāma, vehemently drawing his bow curved like the infant moon, addressed Mātali—charioteer unto the thousand-eyed (deity),† saying,—"O Mātali, behold the enraged chariot of my foe as it courseth on. From the furious speed with which he is again wheeling at my right, it appeareth that he hath set his heart on slaying me in encounter. Do

* The rain-bow.

† Indra.

thou therefore heedfully drive the car right against the vehicle of my foe. I wish to destroy this one even as the wind scattereth clouds that have appeared. Do thou with all thy wits about thee, without trepidation, and holding thy heart as well as thy eye in calmness, swiftly drive the chariot ruled by the reins. Worthy of Purandara's car, thou ought not to be taught by me. Desirous of encounter and my whole soul bent on fight, I simply remind thee—not teach thee." Pleased with these words of Rāma, the excellent celestial charioteer—Mātali—drove the car. Then leaving Rāvana's mighty car on the right, he enveloped Rāvana with the dust raised by the wheels. Thereat the Ten-necked one, enraged, with his eyes coppery and dilated (in passion), covered with arrows Rāma staying in front of his car. Enraged at the smiting, Rāma, with his ire aroused, but summoning up patience, took up in the encounter the bow of Indra endowed with exceeding vehemence; as well as highly impetuous shafts having the resplendance of the solar rays. And then there began a furious encounter between those (two) eager for slaying each other; confronting each other like unto flaming lions. And then desirous of destruction of Rāvana,—celestials with Gandharvas, and Siddhas and supersaints assembled to go to behold the encounter taking place between the two cars. And for the destruction of Rāvana and the success of Rāghava, there occurred round about the cars terrible bodements capable of making people's down stand on end. The god poured down showers of blood on the car of Rāvana; and a violent tornado eddied on his right. And a mighty swarm of vultures, wheeling in the heavens, pursued the car wherever it moved. And Lankā was enveloped with evening resembling the red *javâ* flowers and even in day appeared ablaze. Lightnings and firebrands accompanied by a terrible sound began to fall down on all sides. And beholding these omens inauspicious unto Rāvana all the Rākshasas were greatly sorry. And wherever Rāvana moved the earth shook and the hands of all the Rākshasas fighting were as if paralysed. The copper coloured, the yellow, the red, and the white rays of the sun falling before Rāvana appeared like melted metals of a mountain. And the jackals followed by vultures, vomitting forth fire and casting their looks at him, began to emit inauspicious cries. And in that battle-field the unfavourable wind began to blow raising dust and obstructing the vision of the king of Rākshasas. On the Rākshasa host on all sides dreadful lightnings were showered without the sound of the clouds. All the quarters were enshrouded with darkness and the welkin became invisible being covered with darkness. And setting up a dreadful quarrel hundreds of terrible *Sharikas** began to fall down on his chariot. The horses emitted forth sparks of fire from their hips and tears from their eyes. These and various other dreadful omens arose there announcing the destruction of Rāvana. And there appeared on all sides many an auspicious and good sign intimating the approach of Rāma's victory. And beholding all those auspicious marks announcing Rāma's success, Lakshmana was greatly delighted and considered Rāvana as slain. Thereupon beholding all those auspicious signs, Rāghava, well qualified to decipher them attained an excess of delight and became anxious to display a greater prowess.

---

* A kind of bird (Turdus Salica, Buch).

## SECTION CVIII.

THEREUPON there ensued a mighty and dreadful encounter of two cars between Rāma and Rāvana, creating terror unto all people. And the army of Rākshasas and the mighty host of the monkeys, although they had weapons in their hands, became stupified (for the time being). And beholding them (Rāma and Rāvana) fight, all the Rākshasas and monkeys, having their minds agitated,were greatly surprised. With various weapons and hands uplifted for fight, they, greatly wondered, stood there beholding them and did not address themselves to fight with each other. The Rākshasas beholding Rāvana, and the monkeys beholding Rāma with wonder-stricken eyes, the whole army appeared like a picture. And espieing all omens Rāghava and Rāvana began to fight, undaunted, firm, resolute and unagitated by anger. And determining that Kākutstha would win victory and Rāvana would die, they began to display their own prowess. Thereupon the highly powerful Rāvana, setting his arrows in anger, discharged them at the pennon stationed on Rāghava's car. Those arrows reaching the flag staff of the Purandara chariot and perceiving its might fell down on the earth. Thereupon the highly powerful Rāma, wroth, stretching his bow, made up his mind to return the blow. And aiming at Rāvana's flag staff he discharged a sharpened shaft flaming unbearably by its own lustre like a huge serpent. And the effulgent Rāma discharged a shaft aiming at (Rāvana's) banner which, piercing the Ten-necked demon's flag fell, down on the earth. And beholding his flag staff thus broken down the highly powerful Rāvana became ablaze as if burning down every thing with his unbearable ire. And being possessed by wrath he began to make a downpour of shafts. Rāvana then, with flaming arrows, pierced Rāma's steeds. The celestial horses were not bewildered thereby nor their course was slackened. And they remained thoroughly unagitated as if they were stricken with lotus stalks. Beholding the steeds thus unmoved Rāvana was again exercised with wrath and began to discharge afresh his various weapons—*gadâs, parighas, chakras* and *musalas,* mountain tops, trees, darts and *parashus* and thousands of other shafts by virtue of his illusive powers. And unmoved was his energy. And that downpour of various weapons became huge and terrible in the conflict creating terror and making a dreadful noise. Thereupon leaving aside Rāghava's car he began to assail the monkey-host and enveloped the sky with a continual discharge of arrows. The Ten-necked demon let loose many a weapon even at the risk of his own life. And beholding Rāvana in the encounter thus actively engaged in the discharge of arrows, Kākuthstha, smiling, set up pointed shafts, and discharged them by hundreds and thousands. Beholding them Rāvana again filled the welkin with arrows—and thus with shafts discharged by them both another flaming sky was created. None (of the arrows) missed the aim, none of them failed to pierce another and none of them was fruitless. And the arrows discharged by Rāma and Rāvana stricking each other fell down on the earth. And they standing on their right and left began to make a continued downpour of arrows and enveloped the sky entirely. And they opposing each other, Rāvana slew Rāma's steeds and Rāma in his turn slew Rāvanan's. They, thus enraged fought with each other and for sometime there ensued a terrible encounter capable of making ones down stand on end. And the highly powerful Rāvana and Rāma* fighting with each other in the conflict by means of sharpened arrows, the lord of Rākshasas beholding his

* The epithet in the text is Lakshmana's elder brother.

flag staff broken down became enraged with the foremost of Raghus.

---

## SECTION CIX.

RAMA and Rāvana thus opposing each other in battle, all the animals beheld them, stricken with astonishment. And those two great heroes, highly angered, began to dash towards and assail each other; and being determined to slay each other they looked greatly dreadful. And their charioteers drove the cars on, displaying their skill by moving in circles, in rows and diverse other ways. And those two excellent heroes, discharging their shafts and influenced by illusions, assailed each other proceeding and receding, Rāma attacking Rāvana and Rāvana withstanding him. And these two cars coursed the earth for sometime like clouds accompanied by showers. And displaying many a movement in the conflict they again stood facing each other, the forepart of one car touching that of the other and the heads of the steeds touching each other; and the pennons, stationed on one touched those of the other. Rāma, with four sharpened arrows shot off his bow, removed the flaming horses of Rāvana to some distance. And finding his steeds thus removed he was exercised with wrath. And the Ten-necked one discharged sharpened arrows at Rāghava. And he was pierced by those arrows coming from the powerful Ten-necked demon. He was neither overwhelmed nor pained therewith and he again discharged arrows resembling the thunder-bolts. And the Ten-necked demon again discharged arrows at the charioteer, which fell with great vehemence on the person of Mātali. Mātali was not the least pained or overwhelmed in that encounter. And beholding his charioteer thus assailed Rāma was excited with wrath and overwhelmed his foe with a net of arrows. And the heroic Rāghava showered on his enemy's chariot shafts by twentys, thirtys, sixtys, hundreds and thousands. And the lord of Rākshasas, Rāvana, who was stationed on the car, wroth, attacked Rāma in the conflict with maces and *Musalas.* And there again ensued a terrible conflict capable of making one's down stand on end. And the seven oceans were overwhelmed with the sound of maces, *musalas, Parighas* and gold-feathered arrows. And those inhabiting the regions under the agitated oceans, all the Dānavas and thousands of *Pannagas* were greatly pained. And greatly shook the earth with her mountains, forests and gardens. The Sun was shorn of its resplendance and the wind blew very rough. Thereupon the celestials, with *Gandharbas, Siddhas,* great saints, *Kinnaras* and serpents, were all worked up with anxiety. And beholding the dreadful encounter between Rāma and Rāvana capable of making people's down stand on end, the celestials with ascetics began to pray,—"May good betide the Brahmins and cows, may people live in peace and may Rāghava defeat Rāvana, the lord of Rākshasas, in the conflict." And the crowd of *Gandharbas* and *Apsaras* beholding that wonderful battle between Rāma and Rāvana, said,—"The ocean resembleth the sky and the sky resembleth the ocean—forsooth this encounter between Rāma and Rāvana befits them only." Thereupon Rāma of long-arms, the enhancer of the glory of Raghu's race, enraged, set his arrow, resembling a serpent, on his bow, and cut assunder Rāvana's head wearing shinning *Kundalas.* And that head in the presence of the inhabitants of the three regions fell down on the earth. Instantly there arose another head resembling the former; and it was speedily cut off by the light-handed Rāma. As soon as the second head was clopped off in the encounter by means of shafts another appeared again. And that was again severed by Rāma's shafts resembling thunder-bolts. And thus were severed hundred heads all equal in brilliance. But the end of Rāvana's life was not seen by him. Thereupon the heroic Rāghava, conversant with the use of all weapons, the enhancer of Kauçalyā's joy, began to reason within himself in various ways,—"Verily these are the arrows by which Māricha was killed, and Khara with Dushana was slain—Viradha was destroyed in the forest of Krauncha—the headless demon in the forest of Dandaka—Salas and mountains were broken —the ocean was agitated—and Vāli was killed ;—I do not perceive the reason, why they are becoming fruitless when discharged at Rāvana." Thinking thus Rāghava made himself ready in the conflict and began to shower arrows on Rāvana's breast. Thereupon Rāvana too, the lord of Rākshasas, seated in a car and highly enraged, assailed Rāma in the conflict with a downpour of maces and *Musalas*. That dreadful and huge conflict, capable of making hairs stand on end, continued for seven nights before the eyes of the celestials, Dānavas, Yakshas, Pisāchas, Uragas and serpents stationed in the sky, on the earth or on the mountain-tops. Neither for the night nor for the day, nor for a moment did the fight between Rāma and Rāvana cease. And beholding the conflict between Daçaratha's son and the lord of Rākshasas, and Rāghava's victory, the high-souled charioteer of the lord of the celestials spake speedily unto Rāma engaged in the conflict.

---

## SECTION CX.

THEREUPON Mātali, reminding him, spake unto Rāghava—"Why dost thou, O hero, as if not knowing, fear him? Do thou, O lord, discharge at him the weapon obtained from the great Patriarch. The time for (his) destruction, as described by the celestials, hath arrived." Being reminded by those words of Mātali, Rāma took up the flaming shaft, breathing as if like a serpent. The great Rishi Agastya first conferred this upon him. This is a huge and dreadful shaft given by Brahmā and highly useful in battle. It was made by Brahmā of undecaying prowess for Indra and conferred by him upon the Lord of celestials desirous of acquiring victory. In its wings there is wind, in its head there is fire and the Sun, in its body there is the sky and in its weight there are the (hill) Meru and Mandara. It is resplendent by its own lustre, well feathered and adorned with gold—made of the essence of all objects and bright as the rays of the Sun. It is like the fire of dissolution enveloped in smoke—like the flaming serpent, capable of piercing men, serpents and horses and was swift-coursing. (It can) rend the gateways, *Parighas* and hills—is soaked in blood, dipped in marrow, and extremely dreadful. It is hard as the lightning—producing a dreadful sound, assailing various (divisions of the) army, creating terror unto all, dreadful and (as if) breathing like a serpent. It is terrible as the Death in the conflict and provides food always for the herons, vultures, cranes, jackals and the Rākshasas. It is the enhancer of the monkey-leaders' joy and the repressor of the Rākshasas and is feathered like unto a bird with many a picturesque wing. And the highly powerful Rāma, consecrating in accordance with the *mantras* laid down in the Vedas, that huge shaft—the foremost of all in the world, removing the fear of the

Ikshwāku race, destroying the fame of the enemies and conducing to the joy of its own party, set it on his bow. And that excellent arrow being mounted on his bow by Rāghava all the animals were stricken with fear and the earth shook. And (Rāma) highly enraged, and greatly wary, suppressing (his breath) discharged that shaft at Rāvana—piercing to the vitals. (That Brahmā weapon) irrepressible as the thunder, dreadful as the Death and discharged by Rāma, fell down on Rāvana's breast. And that shaft, capable of bringing about death and gifted with velocity, when discharged, cleft the breast of the vicious-souled Rāvana. And that body-ending arrow, bathed in blood, stealing away the life of Rāvana, entered the earth. That shaft, slaying Rāvana, soaked in blood and successful, again entered the quiver* humbly. And from his hand, who was deprived of his life, fell down instantly on earth his shafts and bow. And fell down on the earth from the chariot, the highly effulgent Rāvana, gifted with dreadful velocity and shorn of his life. And beholding him thus fallen down, the remaining night-rangers, deprived of their lord and stricken with terror fled away to various quarters. And beholding the destruction of the Ten-necked (demon) and the victory of Rāghava, the monkeys, fighting with trees, pursued them on all sides. And being assailed by the monkeys and having their countenances full of tears in consequence of their lord being slain they fled away to Lankā in fear. Thereupon the monkeys being greatly delighted roared out the victory of Rāma. The celestial bugle was sounded in the sky and there blew the excellent air carrying the celestial fragrance. Flowers were showered upon Rāma's car which was covered therewith. The celestials in the sky began to chaunt the glory of Rāma and praise him. And Rāvana, the dread of all people, being slain, the celestials with the

---

* In some texts there is "*napunarabishat*" *i. e.* did not enter the quiver.—T.

*Charanas* were greatly delighted. And slaying that foremost of the Rākshasas, Rāma satisfied the desire of Sugriva, Angada and Bibhishana. Thereupon the celestials attained their peace, the quarters were delighted, the atmosphere was clear, calm air began to prevail all over the earth, and the Sun appeared in its full rays. Thereupon Sugriva, Bibhishana and Lakshmana, welcomed Rāma, of unmitigated prowess, singing his glory. And there appeared beautiful at the battle-field Rāma of firm promise, slaying his enemy and encircled by his army and friends, like unto the Lord of the celestials surrounded by the gods.

## SECTION CXI.

BEHOLDING his brother defeated, slain and lying down on the battle-field, Bibhishana, overpowered with the weight of his grief, began to lament—"O hero, well-known for thy prowess, wise and conversant with polity, thou wert used to excellent beds, why dost thou lie down on the earth, spreading (on the earth) thy long and actionless arms, always adorned with *Angadas* and being shorn of thy helmet having the resplendance of the Sun? O hero, thou hast come by what I had anticipated and what did not please thee who wert possessed by delusions. Prahasta, Indrajit, Kumbhakarna, Atikāya, Atiratha, Narāntaka, yourself and others—none of you paid heed, out of haughtines, to what I had said which hath now been brought about. Oh! the bridge of the pious hath been broken, the figure of the virtue hath been spoiled, the refuge of the strong and powerful hath disappeared and thou hast attained to the state of the heroes! The sun hath fallen down on the earth, the moon hath been shorn of its lustre, the fire hath been extinguished and virtue hath desisted from its action, this heroe, the foremost of those using weapons, falling down on the earth. O thou the foremost of the Rākshasas lying down in the dust on the battle field like one asleep, whom else have these remaining (Rākshasas) deprived of their power and energy, got? The huge tree, of the lord of Rākshasas, having patience for its leaves, velocity for its flowers, the power of asceticism and heroism for its firm roots, hath been uprooted by the *Ràghava* wind. Mad-elephant-like Rāvana, having prowess for its tusk, family rank for its back bone, anger for its legs, and delightedness for its trunk, hath been laid low on the ground by the lion of the Ikshwāku race. The powerful Rākshasa-fire, having prowess and energy for its rays, angry breath for its smoke, own strength for its power of burning, hath been extinguished in battle by *Ráma*-like cloud. The Rākshasa bull ever defeating others and powerful as the wind, having Rākshasas for its tail, hump and horns, and fickleness for its ears and eyes, hath been slain to-day by *Ráma*-tiger." Hearing these words, pregnant with sound reasonings from Bibhishana and beholding him overwhelmed with grief Rāma said,—"(This lord of Rākshasas) of dreadful prowess hath not been slain in battle disabled. He is gifted with great prowess and energy and devoid of the fear of death.* The heroes abiding by the virtues of the Kshatriyas, who fall at the battle field for enhancing their glory, when dead, should not be mourned for. This is not the time to mourn for him although possessed by death, by whom gifted with intellect, Indra with the three worlds was terrified in conflict. Besides success in battle is not perpetual; either one slays his enemy or meets with his destruction at his hands in the conflict. This procedure of the Kshatryas was laid down by the

---

* *i. e.* he has accidentally met with death.

ancient preceptors that a Kshatrya, when slain in battle should not be mourned for. Beholding this to be certain and attaining calmness, do thou be freed from thy sorrow and think what should be done now. Thereupon Bibhishana stricken with grief addressed the powerful son of the king speaking thus with words tending to his brother's well-being. "Thou hast, like the ocean breaking down its banks, broken him down, who had not been ere this even defeated by Bāsava and the celestials. By him were conferred many a gift on those who wanted them, were enjoyed many a luxury, were maintained many a servant, distributed wealth unto friends and slain the enemies. He propitiated fire, performed great austerities, was conversant with the Vedas and the great performer of sacrifices. I desire to perform, by thy instructions, his becoming obsequies." Being thus addressed by Bibhishana with piteous accents, the high-souled son of the lord of men, gifted with great energy, ordered him to perform his obsequies and said. "With death our enmity hath terminated and our object hath been accomplished: he is as dear unto me as unto thee: perform (therefore) his funeral rites."

## SECTION CXII.

BEHOLDING Rāvana slain by the high-souled Rāghava Rākshasees, stricken with grief, issued out of the inner appartments. Stricken with grief and with dishevelled hairs they rolled in the dust albeit prevented again and again like unto cows separated from their calves. And coming out by the northern gate along with the Rākshasas, entering the dreadful arena of battle and searching their slain lord the she-demons cried piteously—"O lord, O husband, O our all" and moved along the battle field soaked in blood and filled with headless corpses. With eyes full of tears and overwhelmed with the grief of their husband they began to move about like she-elephants without the lord of their herd. Thereupon they beheld there on the earth the huge-bodied and the highly powerful and effulgent Rāvana slain like red collyrium. And beholding their lord lying down on the battle-field they all fell on his body like creepers torn assunder. Some wept embracing him respectfully—some holding his feet and some placing themselves around his neck. And some taking up his hand rolled on the ground and some were beside themselves (with grief) beholding the slain (Rāvana's) countenance. And some placing her head on his lap, and beholding his face, wept, bathing it with tears like a lotus enveloped with snow. Seeing their husband Rāvana thus slain on the earth, they stricken with grief, bewailing again and again in sorrow, wept profusely. He by whom the king Vaisrābana was deprived of his flower car, who terrified the high-souled Gandharbas, ascetics and the celestials in battle field, who did not know of any fear from the Asuras, celestials and the Pannagas, hath now been overpowered by a man. He, whom the celestials, the Dānavas and the Rakshas could not slay, hath been slain in conflict by a man walking on foot. He, who was incapable of being killed by the celestials, Yakshas and Asuras, hath met with death like one devoid of prowess at the hands of a mortal." Speaking in this wise, the she-demons, overpowered with sorrow, wept and bewailed again and again (saying),—"Not hearing (the counsels) of thy friends, always pointing out thy welfare, thou didst bring Sitā for thy destruction as well as that of the Rākshasas. Although thy brother Bibhishana addressed thee with words pregnant with thy welfare—thou, for thy own destruction, out of thy misgivings, didst excite his anger and hast (now) seen (the result thereof). Hadst thou returned Sitā the daughter of the king of Mithilā to Rāma, this mighty and dreadful disaster, destroying the very root, would not have befallen us. Rāma's desire would have been encompassed—his friends would have been successful (through Bibhishana)—we would not been widowed and our enemies would not have got their desires fulfilled. By thee, Sitā was kept by force in captivity in a ruthless manner, and the Rākshasas, ourselves and thyself—all three equally have been slain. O foremost of the Rākshasas, forsooth this is not thy own folly—it is Accident that uniteth all things and it is Accident again that bringeth about destruction. O thou of huge arms—the destruction of the monkeys and the Rākshasas as well as that of thyself hath been brought about by Accident. When the course of accident is about to bring about result—wealth, desire, prowess or command—nothing is capable of withstanding it." Thus wept piteously the wives of the lord of Rākshasas like unto so many she-elephants—rendered poorly, stricken with grief and with tears in their eyes.

---

## SECTION CXIII.

THE foremost of the wives of the Rākshasa (king) bewailing piteously cast her looks poorly towards her husband. And beholding her Ten-necked husband slain by Rāma of inconcievable actions Mandodari bewailed there piteously,—"O thou of huge arms! O younger brother of Baishravana! Even Purandara feared to stand before thee when enraged. The great Rishis—the far-famed Gandharbas and the *Cháranas*, fled away to different quarters in thy fear.

And then (how) hast thou been overpowered in battle by Rāma who is a mere man ? Why is it that thou art not ashamed of it, O king, O lord of the Rākshasas ? Conquering the three worlds with thy prowess thou didst attain thy glory; and it is unbearable, that a man, ranging in the forest, hath slain thee. Thou, who art capable of assuming shapes at will, hast been slain in conflict by Rāma, in the city of Lankā unapproachable by men. I do not believe that thy destruction,—who hadst always been crowned with success, before the forces, is work of Rāma. (Methinks) Death (himself) came there in the shape of Rāma and spread illusions unconsciously for thy destruction, O thou of great strength. Or thou hast been slain by Vāsava—(no) what power has he got to face thee in the conflict gifted with great strength, prowess and energy and an enemy of the celestials as thou art ? It is evident that the great ascetic Vishnu, having truth for his prowess—the soul of all beings, ever existing, without beginning, middle or end, greater than the great, the Preserver of the Nature, holding conch, discus and club, having *Sribatsa** on his breast, always beautiful, incapable of being conquered, without destruction, devoid of end, and the lord of all men, assuming this shape of a man and encircled by the celestials, assuming monkey shapes, hath for the behoof of mankind, slain (thee) the dreadful enemy of the gods with all (thy) family and Rākshasas. Subduing all thy passions, thou didst conquer the three worlds—remembering their grudge they have now overpowered thee. Rāma is not a man since he slew at Janasthāna thy brother Khara encircled by many a Rākshasa. We were sore-distressed when Hanuman, by his own prowess, entered the city of Lankā incapable of being approached even by the celestials. And I prevented thee from creating enmity with

* A particular mark usually said to be a curl of hair on the breast of *Vishnu*. The emblem of the tenth *jina* or the mark above ascribed to *Vishnu* or *Krishna*.

Rāghava, but thou didst not pay heed to my words and this is the result (thereof). O foremost of Rākshasas—O thou of a vicious understanding, for the destruction of thy wealth, thyself and thy relatives, thou didst suddenly cherish amour for Sitā, greater than (even) Arundhuti and Rohini. Forsooth thou didst perpetrate an unbecoming deed by distressing the adorable Sitā ever devoted unto her lord, an earth* even unto Earth herself and a Sree† even unto Sree herself. And having brought in a false guise from the solitary forest the sorrowful and chaste Sitā, having a blameless person, thou didst bring on the destruction of thy family. Thou didst fail to encompass thy desire for the company of Sitā. But now, forsooth, O my lord, thou hast been burnt down by her devotion who is devoted unto her husband.‡ Thou wert not burnt down when thou didst captivate that middle-statured (damsel) whom fear all the celestials headed by Indra and *Agni.*§ O husband, (proper) time appearing the perpetrator gets the result of his vicious deeds: there is not the least doubt in this. The performer of the good receives good (result)—the perpetrator of the vicious (deeds) meets with bad (result). Bibhishana hath attained to happiness and thou hast met with this thy end. There are damsels in your seraglio far more beautiful than she but thou possessed by cupid couldst not perceive this. Maithilee is not my equal nor superior either in birth,beauty or accomplishments, but thou didst not perceive this by thy misgivings. Death doth not always visit all men without any cause—and Maithilee is the cause of thy death. And death, in consequence of Maithilee, hath taken thee far away. And she, shorn of

---

* The Earth is an emblem of patience but Sitā is more patient than the Earth.—T.

† Sree is the goddess of wealth and good fortune—but Sitā is more fortunate than fortune herself.—T.

‡ *i.e.* that thou wert not burnt down there and then shows her greatness of mind.—T. § The god of Fire.

all sorrow, shall enjoy in the company of Rāma, and I, of limited piety, am now sunk in the the ocean of grief. Roaming at large with thee in a car unequalled in beauty on the hill Kailāça, Mandara, Maru, in the garden of Chaitraratha and all other celestial gardens, beholding many a country, wearing variegated clothes and garlands, I have been deprived of all pleasures and enjoyments, O hero, by thy death. And I am a widow now. O fie on fickle fortune! O king, in lustre of countenance thou art like the Sun, in grace like the Moon, in beauty like the lotus; thou art graceful, O thou having excellent brows; thou hast got excellent skin, high nose and thy countenance is graced with a brilliant crown and *Kundalas*. Oh how beautiful, thou didst look with various garlands when thy eye whirled with intoxication on the drinking ground and how beautiful were thy smiles, O lord. Thy countenance doth not shine now—being severed with Rāma's shafts, bathed in a pool of blood, having thy back-bone and brain deranged and covered with the dust raised by the wheels of the chariots. Alas! by my ill-luck I have attained to that after state making me a widow which I did never think of. My father is the king of Danavas, my husband the lord of Rakshasas, and my son the subduer of Sakra. I was greatly proud of this and always confident that my protectors were undaunted, dreadful, repressors of the enemies and famous for their strength and manliness. O ye foremost of the Rakshasas, how could this fear from man overwhelm you all who were so powerful? (This thy body) is cool, green like *Indraneela*, high like a huge mountain, and adorned with *Keyura*, *Angada*, jewels and garlands of flowers. It was graceful in places of enjoyments and incapable of being looked at in the field of battle. It was brilliant, being decked with ornaments like unto clouds accompanied by lightnings. And this thy person hath been pierced with shafts to-day; (and knowing) that it is not easy of attainment for me I am incapable of embracing (it), covered with shafts piercing through the very vitals. O king (this thy body) green-hued (but now) blood-red is now lying on the ground like unto a mountain shattered with thunder-bolts. That thou wouldst be slain by Rāma was like a dream, but it hath proved true! Thou wert like death unto Death himself, why hast thou been possessed by him then? Thou wert the enjoyer of the three worlds' wealth and dread unto them; thou wert the conqueror of the deities presiding over various quarters; thou didst shake Sankara (himself)—thou wert the subduer of the proud and thy prowess was well-known; thou didst repress the people and slay many a pious man—thou didst, by thy prowess, use to give vent to haughty words before the enemies; thou wert the maintainer of thy kinsmen and servants and the slayer of many perpetrating dreadful deeds; thou wert the destroyer of thousands of celestials, Dānavas and Yakshas; thou wert the subbuer of *Nivata Kavachas* in the encounter; thou didst hinder the performance of many sacrifices and wert the protector of thy relatives; thou wert the obstructer of pious observances, creator of illusions in conflict and thou didst bring away from hither and thither the daughters of the celestials, demons and men; thou didst aggrieve the wives of thy enemies; thou wert the leader of thy own men, the protector of the island of Lankā and the performer of many a dreadful deed; thou didst confer upon us the enjoyment of many a pleasure—and wert the foremost of car-warriors. Beholding such a husband slain by Rāma, I am, deprived of my dear lord, still maintaining my being; (forsooth) my heart is very hard. O lord of Rākshasas, used ere to many a valuable bed, why art thou sleeping on earth covered with dust? When my son Indrajit was slain by Lakshmana in conflict I was greatly pained—but to-day I am slain. Deprived of my friends and relatives, separated from thee O my lord, deprived from the enjoyment of many pleasures I shall lament for thee perpetually. Thou hast, O king, reached the way, long and hard to be treaded—do thou take me, who am stricken with grief and who shall not be able to live without thee. Why dost thou wish to go leaving me behind who have been rendered poorly? Why dost thou not welcome me, unfortunate and poor, who am bewailing? Why art thou not angry, O lord, beholding me, having put off my veil, walk out on foot by the city-gate? O beloved of thy wives, do thou behold thy wives—who have thrown off their veils. Why art thou not angry seeing them all come out (of the city)? I was thy companion in sports, O my lord; I long for having thee; why art thou not consoling and welcoming me? O king, being imprecated by those damsels, not one, devoted to their husbands, pious and ever engaged in attending upon their superiors, who had been widowed by thee, thou hast been overpowered by thy enemy. The curse, proceeding from them who had been ill-treated by thee, hath borne fruit. O king, the saying, that the tears of chaste damsels do not uselessly fall on the ground, hath been verified (here) forsooth. O king, conquering the worlds with thy prowess, how couldst thou, always honored by the king, cherish the vile desire of stealing away women? Taking away Rāma and Lakshmana from the hermitage by an illusionary deer, thou didst steal away Rāma's spouse. I remember to have never heard thee lament in battle. Forsooth, it is our misfortune and the sign of impending death (that thou didst do this) conversant as thou art with the past, present and future. Beholding the daughter of the king of Mithilā brought (in the city of Lankā) what, thy younger brother Bibhishana, thinking and sighing, said, hath now proved true, O thou of long-arms. This destruction of the leading Rākshasas hath proceeded from the disaster arising from thy anger and lust. For thy (vicious) deeds all our good fortune is lost—(and from them) hath proceeded the great disaster exterminating the race. And by thee all the Rākshasa families have been deprived of their lords. Thou, well-known for thy strength and manliness, art not worthy of being grieved by me. On account of my effeminate nature my understanding is possessed by sorrow. Carrying thy pious and iniquitous deeds thou hast attained to thy own state—I am only lamenting for me who have been sorry for thy destruction. O Ten-necked one, thou didst not hear the words of thy friends and brothers, who spoke those well meaning words out of affection. Thou didst not obey the words uttered by Bibhisana, duly and mildly, pregnant with meaning and reasoning and tending to thy welfare. Maddened with thy own prowess thou didst not hear the words of Māricha, Kumbhakarna as well as those of my father—and this is the result thereof. O thou resembling the red clouds, O thou wearing yellow cloth and excellent *Angada*, stretching thy person on the gronnd why art thou in the long run bathed in blood? Why dost thou not, like one asleep, welcome me who am stricken with grief? I am the grand-daughter of the highly powerful Rākshasa Sumāli who never flies away from the field of battle: why dost thou not welcome me? Rise up! rise up! why dost thou lie down (on this occasion of) new discomfiture? To-day have the rays of the Sun entered fearlessly the city of Lankā. The Parigha, by which, brilliant as the rays of the Sun, thou didst distress the enemies in conflict, which was always adored by thee like the thunder of the wielder of thunder-bolt, which slew many in battle, and which was adorned with golden nets, now lieth shattered into thousand pieces by arrows. Why dost thou lie on the battle-field embracing her like your beloved spouse? Why dost thou not wish to welcome me like one not beloved unto thee? Oh fie on this heart of mine which is not sundered into thousand (pieces) albeit distressed with the grief of thy death!" Bewailing thus, she, with profuse tears in her eyes, and with her heart overflowing with affection, became senseless. And being beside herself she flung herself on Rāvana's breast, like unto the bright lightning appearing on red evening clouds. Thereupon the other wives, of Rāvana, greatly distressed and weeping, and rasing her up who was greatly weeping, began to console her saying :--"Dost thou not know, O worshipful dame, that the life of beings is very uncertain, and with adverse circumstances even the royal fortune becometh fickle?" Being thus accosted she again wept aloud, bathing with tears her breast and beautiful countenance. In the meantime Rāma said to Bibhisana,—"Do thou perform the funeral ceremonies of thy brother and console his wives." Whereto the intelligent Bibhisana replied with the following words—pointing out wealth and piety, and judging by his understanding what is proper. "I do not think it proper to perform his cremation ceremony who had renounced all pious deeds, was wicked, cruel, liar and who had ravished others' wives. He is my enemy in the shape of a brother ever engaged in doing injury unto others—and Rāvana is not worthy of my adoration albeit he is adorable by virtue of his being my elder brother. O Rāma, perhaps people of this earth will call me cruel but they will again recognise my act as good when they will hear of his vicious deeds." Hearing those words, Rāma, the foremost of the pious and conversant with the skill of speech, greatly delighted, spoke unto Bibhishana (equally) skilled in speech,—"It behoveth me to encompass thy welfare since by thy help I have gained the victory. O lord of Rākshasas, forsooth, thou shouldst hear my well-meaning words. Although this night-ranger perpetrated many vicious and impious deeds still he was ever powerful, heroic and strong in warfare. I have heard that this high-souled Rāvana, gifted with strength and a dread unto all people, was not defeated (even) by the celestials headed by the performer of hundred sacrifices. Enmity extendeth up to death—so it hath ended; there is no necessity (of carrying it on). Do thou (therefore) perform his cremation ceremony—he is unto thee as he is unto me. O thou of long-arms it behoveth thee to perform, speedily with due rites and religious ceremonies, his funeral ceremony—thou shalt be the object of praise (unto people)." Hearing the words of Rāghava, Bibhishana hastened on and began to make arrangements for the cremation of his slain brother Rāvana. And entering the city of Lankā, Bibhishana, the lord of Rākshasas, speedily got out Rāvana's *Agnihotra*,* carts, brass utensils, fire, (and brought) *Jajakas*,† sandal-wood, other woods, essences, *Agura*, other fragrant substances, precious stones, pearls and corals. Thereupon arriving immediately accompanied by Rākshasas and Malyavāna he engaged in the performance of cremation ceremony. Thereupon the twice-born ones, with tears in their eyes, covered the Rākshasa-king Rāvana's body, with a silken cloth and placed it on a golden celestial litter. With the sound of various bugles they began to chaunt his praise. And taking up this litter adorned with various charming paintings and flags and carrying fire woods, all the Rākshasas headed by Bibhishana proceeded towards the South.‡ The Brahmins, versed in *Yayur Veda* and with burning fire in their hands, proceeded and were followed by the attendants. And the damsels of the seraglio followed speedily leaping (being ever unused to walking). And placing Rāvana on the cremation ground, they, greatly stricken with grief, prepared the funeral pyre according to due rites with sandal-woods, *Padmakas*,§ *Ushiras*‖ and sandal and spread an antelope-skin thereon. They (then) performed the excellent obsequies of the manes of the lord of Rākshasas. And raising an altar at the south-east corner they placed fire at the proper place. They then poured curd and clarified butter upon (Rāvana's) shoulders. And placing

* A pot for preserving sacred fire.

† The Brahmins who perform obsequies.

‡ Cremation-place.

§ A sort of drug commonly called *Padmakas*.

‖ The root of a fragrant grass.

*Sakata* on his legs, *Ulukhala** on his thighs, and the brass untensils, Arunis and Musals in their proper places, they celebrated (the obsequies of his manes). Thereupon slaying beasts according to the rites laid down in *Sástras* and pointed out by the great saints, the Rākshasas (made a coverlet dipped in their marrow and clarified butter) and placed it on the face of the lord of Rākshasas. And decking Rāvana with fragrant garlands and various clothes, the friends, of Bibhishana, with depressed heart and tears in their eyes, showered dried paddy (on his person). And Bibhishana according to due rites put fire to his (funeral pyre). Bathing and with wetted cloth, offering duly linseed and sacrificial grass mixed with water and consoling (Rāvana's) wives again and again, he entreated them to go back. They then entered the city. And those damsels having entered the city, Bibhishana, the lord of Rākshasas, approaching Rāma, stood by his side gently. And Rāma too, along with his army, Sugriva and Lakshmana, was greatly delighted after slaying his enemy like unto the wielder of thunder-bolt after slaying (the demon) Vitra. Thereupon leaving aside his bow with arrows, and the huge armour conferred by Mahendra and renouncing ire after the destruction of his enemy Rāma assumed gentle mein.

## SECTION CXIV.

BEHOLDING the destruction of Rāvana the celestials, Gandharbas and Dānavas ascending their respective cars went away chanting this excellent theme. And talking of Rāvana's dreadful destruction, Rāghava's prowess, the

* A wooden mortar used for cleaning rice.

excellent warfare of the monkeys, the counsels of Sugriva, the devotion and prowess of the Wind-God's son and Lakshmana and Sita's devotion unto her husband, those high souled ones, delighted, repaired to their respective quarters. And Rāghava, having long arms, permitting the charioteer to take back the celestial car bright as the sky sent by Indra, honoured him greatly. And being commanded by Rāghava Mātali, the charioteer of Sakra taking the celestial car, rose up in the welkin. And that charioteer rising up into the celestial region, Rāghava, the foremost of car-warriors, greatly delighted, embraced Sugriva. And embracing Sugriva, bowed unto by Lakshmana and worshipped by the monkey he repaired to the camp of his soldiers. Thereupon Kākuthsha spoke unto Lakshmana—the son of Sumitrā gifted with auspicious marks who was near him—"O gentle one, take this Bibhishana to the city of Lankā ever devoted and attached unto us, and who had done us good. This is my great desire that I may behold Bibhishana the younger brother of Ravana installed on the throne of Lankā." Being thus addressed by the high-souled Rāghava, the son of Sumitrā, saying—"So be it" and greatly delighted, brought a golden jar. And placing that jar at the hands of the lord of monkeys, that one, gifted with great energy, ordered them to bring water from the Ocean. And repairing speedily those excellent monkeys came back with water from the ocean. And taking that jar and placing him on an excellent seat Saumitri with that water sprinkled Bibhishana as king of Lankā in the presence of all the Rakshasas, at Rāma's command. And (Lakshmana) encircled by friends sprinkling him according to rites laid down in the Vedas, all the Rākshasas, devoted unto him, his counsellors and the monkeys attaining incomparable delight, sang the glory of Rama. And beholding Bibhishana the lord of Rakshasas installed in the city of Lankā, Raghava along with Lakshmana attained to an excess of delight. And consoling his subjects he went to Rama. And the monkey citizens, delighted, brought him curd, fried grain, sweetmeats, fried paddy and flowers. And taking all those things indicating auspiciousness, he, irrepressible and gifted with energy, conferred them upon Rāghava and Lakshmana. And beholding Bibhishana crowned with prosperity and success, Rama accepted them all for his satisfaction. Thereupon Rāma spoke unto the heroic monkey Hanumān, resembling a a mountain and standing before him humbly with folded hands, saying—"O gentle one, obtaining permission from the king Bibhishana, do thou enter the city of Lankā and enquire after Maithili's welfare. Do thou, O foremost of monkeys, inform Vaidehi of the destruction of Rāvana in conflict after communicating unto her mine health as well as that of Lakshmana and Sugriva. O lord of monkeys, it behoveth thee to return with the tidings of Vaidehi after informing her of this pleasant news.

## SECTION CXV.

Being thus commanded, Hanumān, the son of Maruta, worshipped of the night-rangers, entered the city of Lankā. Entering the city with Bibishana's permissiom, Hanumān, again permitted, entered the Briksha Vatika.* And entering there duly, the monkey, who was already known to Sitā,, espied her, having her person not cleansed, like Rohini, oppressed by Rāhu, sitting at the foot of a tree, devoid of joy and encircled by she-demons. And approaching her and bowing unto her, he stood there humbly and unmoved. And beholding the highly powerful Hanumān arrived there the

* A garden in the city of Lanká.—T.

worshipful dame stood silent for sometime and then recognising him became greatly delighted. And beholding her gentle countenance, Hanumān, the best of monkeys, began to relate unto her what Rāma had said—"O Vaidehi, it is all well with Rāma Sugriva and Lakshmana. He hath enquired after thy welfare. He hath accomplished his end subduing his enemies—and his enemy is slain. O worshipful dame, the powerful Rāvana hath been slain by Rāma, helped by Bibhishana and accompanied by the monkeys and Lakshmana. I do relate unto thee this pleasant news, O worshipful dame; I do again delight thee; it is by thy grace, O thou conversant with piety, O Sitā, victory hath been gained. Do thou be consoled and relieved of thy anxiety. The enemy Rāvana hath been slain and the city of Lankā hath been brought under submission. (Rāma said),—'For discomfitting thy enemy a bridge was constructed over the sea by me who was determined and who did not sleep (for days) and thus my promise hath been fulfilled. Do thou not be afraid for living in Rāvana's abode for I have placed at Bibhishana's hands the sovereignty of Lankā. Do thou be consoled thinking as if that thou art living in thy own house. To behold thee, Bibhishana, delighted, shall soon proceed." Being thus accosted the worshipful Sitā, having a moon-like countenance, and her voice choked in delight, could not utter any thing. And beholding Sitā incapable of replying the foremost of monkeys said,—"What art thou thinking of, O worshipful dame? Why art thou not welcoming me?" Being thus addressed by Hanumān Sitā, ever treading the paths of morality, greatly delighted, replied with words suppressed by tears. "Hearing this pleasant news concerning the victory of my husband—and being brought under the control of joy I am speechless for sometime. O monkey, I do not perceive any such thing which I can confer upon thee, in return, for this pleasant news. I do dot see any such thing on this earth which can match thy pleasant tidings and bestowing which upon thee I may be happy. Silver, gold, or diverse jewels or the kingdom of the three worlds—nothing is a becoming return for thy speech." Being thus addressed by Vaidehi the monkey replied—folding his hands with delight and stationed before Sita,—"O blameless damsel, forsooth this excellent speech becometh thee, who is ever engaged in the welfare of thy husband and ever desirous of his victory. I do consider, O worshipful dame, these words of thine, far greater than the wealth, jewels or even the sovereignty over the celestials. Forsooth I have gained the kingdom of the celestials and other things since I have beheld Rāma, slay his enemy, victorious and peaceful. Hearing those words of (Hanumān) Maithili the daughter of king Janaka spoke unto the Wind-god's son far more excellent words—"Thou art capable of speaking words, chaste, pleasant and significant of eight sorts of knowledge. Thou art the praise-worthy son of the Wind-god and greatly virtuous; strength, prowess, heroism, knowledge of *Sâstras*, noble-mindedness, energy, forgiveness, patience, endurance, humility and many other excellent qualities crown thee." Thereupon not being elated the least, he again, humbly folding his hands with delight and stationed before Sitā, said—"If dost thou permit me I may slay all these she-demons who had tortured thee before, distressed thee in the forest of Açoka, stricken with grief of thy lord, and who are cruel, have grim eyes and who perpetrate always dreadful deeds. O worshipful dame, I have heard that these grim-visaged she-demons distressed thee greatly with harsh words at the command of Rāvana. I desire to slay all these dreadful, crooked, ugly (she-demons) having fearful eyes, meting out unto them various punishments. I wish to slay all these she-demons, who had used harsh words and had always offended thee, stricking them with fists, fingers, arms, dreadful knee-joints, teeth, chopping off their ears and noses, and pulling them by their hairs: do thou confer upon me this permission. O far famed lady, I shall slay them by these various means, by whom, dreadful as they are, thou hadst been distressed before." Being thus addressed by Hanumān, she, ever kind unto the poor, thinking and meditating, said to him—"O foremost of monkeys, why art thou angry with these she-slaves, who subject as they are to the command of their lord, have done this in accordance with another's order. For my adverse fortune and vicious deeds perpetrated in another birth I have been subject to such a plight and been suffering the consequence thereof. Do thou not speak thus, O thou of huge arms. Such is the course of Fortune. Forsooth by my ill-luck I have met with (this misfortune). I forgive, out of pity, all these she-servants of Rāvana; they used to torture me at the command of that Rākshasa. And he being slain they shall not repress me any longer, O son of the Wind-god. Do thou, O monkey, hear of a *Sloka*, related in a *Purāna* and pregnant with religious import, which was uttered by a boar to a tiger. 'No one taketh upon himself the iniquity of a perpetrator of vicious deeds. So it behoveth the pious crowned with an excellent character to observe the rules (of piety). So it is proper to show compassion even upon those who perpetrate crimes and are worthy of being slain. Who is there who doth not commit a crime? It is not proper to act cruelly even by them who take delight in killing men, although they commit various iniquitous deeds." Being thus addressed by Sitā, Hanumān, skilled in speech, spoke unto the blameless Rāma's spouse, saying—"Thou art the worthy spouse of Rāma, religiously wedded and crowned with many qualities. Permit me, O worshipful dame, to proceed where Rāghava is." Being thus accosted by Hanumān, Vaidehi, the daughter of king Janaka, said,—"I wish to see my lord, ever fond of those who are devoted unto him." Hearing these words, the high-minded Hanumān, the son of Maruta, pleasing Maithili said—"Thou shalt behold Rāma, having a countenance like the full moon, with Lakshmana, surrounded by his friends and having his enemies slain as Sachi beholdeth Indra the king of the celestials." Addressing these words unto Sitā appearing like Sree herself the highly effulgent Hanumān returned where Rāghava was. Thereupon Hanuman, the foremost of monkeys, related duly all what did the daughter of king Janaka say unto Rāghava resembling the lord of the celestials.

## SECTION CXVI.

THEREUPON bowing unto Rāma, the foremost of bowmen, having eyes, resembling lotus-petals, the highly wise monkey said,—"It behoveth thee now to see Maithilee, stricken with grief for whom thou didst initiate all these works and the fruit whereof hath now been attained. Hearing of thy victory Maithilee, possessed by grief and having eyes full of tears, expressed her desire to see thee. And I was told by her, confident of her previous trust, with profuse tears in her eyes,—"I wish to see my husband." Being addressed by Hanumān, Rāma the foremost of the pious being bathed in tears, engaged instantly in meditation. Thereupon sighing hard and casting his looks upon the ground he spoke unto Bibhishana resembling clouds, who was near him. "Do thou speedily bring Sitā here —the daughter of the king of Mithilā—bathed, sprinkled with celestial paste and adorned with celestial ornaments." Being thus addressed by Rāma, Bibhishana hastened on and entering the inner appartment sent information unto Sitā through the female attendants. And beholding the great Sitā, the graceful lord of Rākshasas—Bibhishana, humbly and placing his joined palms on his crown, said,—"O Vaidehi, may good betide thee; sprinkled with celestial paste and adorned with celestials ornaments do thou ascend this car; thy husband wisheth to see thee." Being thus addressed Vaidehi replied unto Bibhishana,—"O lord of Rākshasas, without bathing even I wish to see my husband." Hearing those words Bibhishana replied,—"It behoveth thee to do what thy lord Rāma hath said." Whereto the chaste Maithilee, regarding her husband as God and filled with devotion unto her husband, replied saying "So be it." Thereupon placing Sitā, bathed, performing the due rites wearing valuable clothes and adorned with valuable ornaments, on a palanquin, carried by many a capable Rākshasa,brought her (unto Rāma). Thereupon approaching the high-souled Rāma, who, being informed of (Bibhishana's approach) was engaged in meditation, Bibhishana bowing down and delighted communicated unto him the arrival of Sitā. And hearing of her arrival who had lived long in the abode of the Rākshasa Rāghava, the slayer of enemies attained (simultaneously) to anger, delight and depression. And considering Sitā, who was in the palanquin, overwhelmed with grief, Rāghava delighted addressed Bibhishana with the following words. "O lord of Rākshasas, O gentle (king), O thou ever engaged in encompassing my success, do thou speedily bring Vaidehi nearer to me." Hearing these words of Rāghava, Bibhishana, conversant with piety speedily cleared (the people out of that place). And attendants with armours and head-dresses on and with cane and drums in their hands began to move about driving away the crowd thereform. And the crowds of bears, monkeys and Rākshasas being driven on all sides began to fly at a distance. And they being thus driven there arose a huge noise resembling that of the ocean when agitated by the wind. Beholding the monkeys driven on all sides and troubled, Rāghava out of anger and compassion prevented him. And thereupon as if burning (every thing) with his angry eyes Rāma addressed the highly intelligent Bibhishana with the following angry words—"Why dost thou insult me by destroying all these? Do thou remove their anxiety—they are all my own men. Neither the houses, clothes, walls nor reception like these are the veils of women. There is no sin consequent upon seeing women in danger, difficulty, war, *Svyambara** sacrifice and marriage. She is now in great danger and difficulty—there is no sin in seeing her specially in my presence. Therefore leaving behind the palanquin let her come here on foot and let the monkeys behold Vaidehi in my presence." Being thus addressed by Rāma, Bibhishana, being sorry, humbly brought Sitā near him. Thereupon hearing Rāma's accents, Lakshmana, Sugriva and the monkey Hanumān were greatly sorry. As if hiding herself in her own person in shame Maithili, following Bibhishana, approached her husband. And she, having a gentle countenance and always regarding her husband as her god, fixed her looks upon her lord's face out of surprise, joy and love. And beholding the gentle countenance of her dearest lord, resembling the full moon she removed her mental distress. Thereupon she appeared (beautiful) having the countenance of the clear moon.

* It is a form of marriage in which the bride selects a bridegroom for herself.

## SECTION CXVII.

Beholding Maithili standing humbly by him, Rāma began to give vent to his pent-up feelings—"O gentle one, destroying all the enemies in the arena of battle I have subdued thy enemy—I have done all that can be accomplished by manliness. I have reached the other end of my anger, rubbed off (the insult) for my spouse being taken away by the enemy and have killed simultaneously my disgrace and enemy. My manliness hath been displayed to-day, my labour hath been crowned with success and to-day I have fulfilled my promise by my own prowess. That accidental misfortune, under the influence whereof thou wert carried away by the fickle-minded Rākshasa in my absence, hath been subdued to-day by me, a man. What is the use of his manliness, who when insulted, cannot remove it? Even if he be a great man he may be called mean. The praise-worthy works of Hanumān—the crossing of the deep and the devastation of Lankā, have been crowned with success to-day. The labour of Sugriva with his army, who displayed valour in the encounter and gave me good counsels, hath borne fruit to-day. To-day also the labour of Bibhishana hath borne fruit—who renouncing his brother, devoid of all good qualities, came to my side." Hearing those words of Rāma, Sitā began to look wistfully like a hind,with eyes full of tears. And beholding his beloved spouse near him and afraid of popular ignominy his heart was broken into two. Thereupon he spoke unto the exquisitely beautiful Sitā, in the midst of the monkeys and Rākshasas, having eyes resembling lotus-petals and black and curling hairs, saying,—"As the southern quarter, incapable of being got at by the people, was conquered by the self-controlled great ascetic Agastya, so for thee slaying Rāvana, I, (always) anxious to have honour, have removed my insult—as is the duty of a man. May good betide thee—do thou know that all my labour, in the battle-field, backed by the prowess of my friends, is for thee. To uphold the dignity of my well-known family, to remove the ignominy consequent upon thy being stolen away as well as to wipe off my own insult I have encompassed this. I have suspected thy character; thou, (therefore) standing before me,art distressing me like unto a lamp before one who is subject to an eye-desease. Do thou therefore proceed, O daughter of king Janaka, wherever thou likest to one of these ten quarters. I permit thee, O gentle one. I have nothing to do with thee. What powerful man, born in a high family, take back his wife considering her as friend out of lust, who hath lived long in another's house? Thou wert taken by Rāvana on his lap, beheld by him with sinful eyes; how can I, taking thee back, bring disgrace upon my great family? The object, with which I have gained thee back, hath been accomplished. I have got no attachment for thee—do thou go wherever thou wishest, O gentle one. I speak these unto thee impelled by my sense of duty. If thou wishest thou mayest live with Lakshmana, Bharata or Satrughna or with Sugriva or Rākshasa Bibhishana. Do thou settle, O Sitā, where you may find thy own pleasure. O Sitā, (I do not think) Rāvana hath overlooked thee, who lived in his house, beholding thee so graceful and beautiful." Thereupon hearing those unpleasant words from her beloved (husband) Sitā, always sensitive and who had never heard such unpleasant words, trembling like a creeper torn by the trunk of an elephant,began to weep shedding tears profusely.

## SECTION CXVIII.

BEING thus addressed by Rāghava, enraged, with those harsh words Sitā was greatly pained. And hearing those words of her lord, unheard of, before the great assembly Maithili was greatly humiliated with shame. As if entering unto her own person (with shame) and greatly pained with these arrow-like words the daughter of king Janaka began to shed tears. Thereupon wiping the tears off her countenance, she with sorrowful words, addressed her husband—"Why dost thou, O hero, like a common man addressing an ordinary woman, make me hear these harsh and unbecoming words painful unto ears? O thou of long arms, I am not what thou hast taken me to be. Do thou believe me—I do swear by my own character. Seeing the ordinary women thou art distrusting the whole sex. Do thou renounce this suspicion since thou hast tried me. O lord, though my person was touched by another—but it was not in my power; nor was it an wilful act (of mine); accident is to blame in this. My heart is under my control and that is in thee;—and what could I do of my body which was subject to another and of which I was not the mistress. O thou the conferrer of honour—our affection towards one another was increased by our living continually for a long time; even then if thou hast not been able to understand me I am ruined for ever. O king, when the great hero Hanumān was despatched by thee to Lankā to see me why didst thou not renounce me then? Hadst thou deputed the monkey with that message I would have renounced my life there and then, O hero. Thou wouldst not have been required to undergo this toil at the risk of thy own life and giving unnecessary trouble to thy friends. O foremost of kings, being subject to ire—thou dost not perceive anything but womanhood in me, like an ordinary man. Although I am known to have a father but in fact I am born of the earth. Thou dost not sufficiently honour my character, O thou conversant with characters. Thy marriage with me in boyhood shall be disproved and thou art not sufficiently considering all my devotion and good conduct unto thee." Saying thus with accents choked in tears and weeping Sitā spoke unto Lakshmana, poorly and engaged in meditation. "Make a funeral pyre for me, O Saumitri, that is the only remedy for this disaster. Being thus branded with an unfounded stigma I do not like to keep my life. To adopt the proper course for me who had been renounced before this assembly by my disaffected husband I shall enter this." Being thus addressed by Vaidehi, Lakshmana, the slayer of enemies, being possessed by anger, looked towards Rāghava. And understanding Rāma's intention by gestures and at his command the powerful Saumitri prepared a funeral pyre. None dared there request, speak with or even look at Rāma like unto Death at the time of dissolution. Thereupon circumambulating Rāma, standing with his head down, Vaidehi approached the burning fire. And bowing unto the celestials and Brāhmanas, Maithili, with folded hands, spoke before the fire :—"As my heart hath never gone away from Rāghava, may thou protect me, O fire, the witness of the people. As Rāghava considereth me vile, who have got a pure character, may fire, the witness of the people, protect me on all sides." Saying this and going round the fire, Vaidehi, with undaunted heart, entered the flaming fire. The great assembly there, young and old, overwhelmed with grief, saw Maithili enter the flaming fire. And (Sitā) resembling the burning gold entered the flaming fire in the presence of all people. All beheld Sitā, having expansive eyes, enter fire like unto a golden altar. The ascetics, celestials and Gandharbas saw that great damsel enter fire like unto a full oblation in the sacrifice.

And beholding her fallen into the fire like unto *Vasudhárá,* sanctified by Mantras in a sacrifice, all the females began to weep. And the three worlds—the celestials, Gandharbas and Dānavas saw her fallen like unto a celestial from the heaven when imprecated. She having entered the fire, lamentations, unheard of before, rose from all sides from the Rākshasas and monkeys.

## SECTION CXIX.

HEARING the lamentations (of the Rākshasas and monkeys) the virtuous-souled Rāma, with a poor heart and having his eyes full of tears, engaged in meditation for some time. Thereupon the king Vaisrāvana, Yama with his progenitors, the thousand-eyed lord of the celestials, Varuna, the lord of water, the three-eyed graceful Mahādeva—the rider of bull, Brahmā the creator of the world and the foremost of those conversant with the knowledge of Brahma—all these arriving at the city of Lankā in their cars bright as the rays of the sun, approached Rāghava. Thereupon raising up their huge hands, decked with various ornaments and folding them, those foremost of the celestials said unto Rāghava—"O lord, thou art the preserver of all the worlds and the foremost of the wise, why dost thou neglect Sitā entering into fire ? Why dost thou not understand thyself the foremost of the celestials ? Thou wert before the Patriarch of all *Vasus,** by the name of Kratadhāma. And thou art thyself, O lord, the creator of the three worlds. Thou art the eighth of the *Rudras*† and the fifth of the

* A kind of demi-god of whom eight are enumerated.

† A demi-god—an inferior manifestation of Siva : they are eleven in number.

*Sâdhyas* ;* the Açwinis are thy two ears and the sun and the moon are thy eyes. O slayer of enemies, thou appearest at the begining and the end of the creation. Why dost thou neglect Vaidehi like an ordinary man ?" Being thus addressed by the deities presiding over quarters, Rāghava, the lord of people and the foremost of the pious, spoke unto those leading celestials, saying :—"I know myself to be man—Rāma, the son of Daçaratha. Let the great Patriarch tell me, who I am and whence I have come." Thereupon Brahmā, the foremost of those conversant with the knowledge of Brahma, spoke unto Kākutstha, who had spoken thus, saying,—"Do thou hear my true words, O thou having truth for thy prowess. O lord, thou art the great and effulgent, Nārāyana holding discus and mace ; thou art the boar having one tusk ; thou hast conquered the past, present and future ; thou art undecaying and without end, O Rāghava ; thou art the great virtue of the pious—thou art the propounder of all laws and art four-armed ; thou art the holder of bow of time—the subduer of senses—the execllent Purusha (person), unconquerable by sins ; thou art Vishnu holding dagger, Krishna and of incomparable strength ; thou art the army, the minister—the universe—the understanding, forgiveness and control of passions ; thou art the creation and destruction ; Upendra and the slayer of ( demon ) Madhu ; thou art the creator of Indra ; thou art Mahendra ; thou hast a lotus-like navel and thou art the slayer of enemies. The celestials and the great saints style thee as the refuge of those who seek for shelter. Thou art the foremost of *Vedas* with its thousand branches and hundred regulations. Thou art thyself the creator of the three worlds, O lord. Thou art the refuge of the *Siddhas*† and *Sâdhyas*, thou art the *Purvaja*,‡ the

---

* An inferior deity or demi-god, one of a class of twelve.

† Saints of accomplished piety.

‡ Produced or appearing before creation.

sacrifice, *Vaskatkar*,* *Om*† and *Parátpara*.‡ No one is conversant with thy birth and destruction—thou art manifest in all creatures—cows and Brahmins—in all quarters, in the sky, in the mountain, and in the river. Thou art gifted with thousand legs, thousand heads and thousand eyes. Thou dost uphold all creatures, the earth and all the mountains. Thou appearest like the great serpent in the water underneath the earth. O Rāma, thou dost uphold three creations—the celestials, the Gandharbas and the Dānavas. O Rāma—I am thy heart, the worshipful Swaraswati (Goddess of learning) is thy tongue and all other celestials, O lord, created by Brahmā are thy down. The closing of thy eye is the night and the opening is the day. The *Vedas* are significant of thy desire and the control thereof—none hath got independent existence but thee. The whole universe is thy body, the earth is thy patience, the fire is thy anger—the sun and the moon are thy delight; thou hast got *Sreebatsha* (a peculiar curl of hair); thou didst before tread the three worlds with thy three foot steps; thou didst get the dreadful Bāli bound and make Mahendra king; Sitā is Lakshmi and thou art Krishna and Vishnu the Preserver of people. For Rāvana's destruction thou hast assumed the human shape. Thou hast accomplished that work of ours, O thou the foremost of the pious. O Rāma, Rāvana hath been slain. Do thou go up to heaven delighted. Sure is thy godly energy and never goes for nothing thy prowess. O Rāma, never is fruitless thy view and the chanting of thy glory. And always successful shall be these persons on earth who shall be devoted unto thee. Those

---

* Burnt offering, oblation with fire—from the exclamation used on the occasion.

† *Om*—the first term of the *Mantra*, *Om* or *Omkára* is well-known as a combination of letters invested by Hindu mysticism with peculiar sanctity.

‡ Greatest of the great.

who shall be devoted unto thee at one with *Purána** and the excellent *Purasha*,† shall attain all their desires both in this world and the next. Those persons shall never be unsuccessful both in this world and the next who shall chant this theme—excellent, instinct with the knowledge of Brahma and describing the old history.

---

## SECTION CXX.

---

HEARING those excellent words uttered by the great Patriarch rose up *Bibhábasu*‡ with Vaidehi on his lap shaking the funeral pyre. With the daughter of the king Janaka, the receiver§ of sacrificial offerings, being incarnate, rose up. And carrying on his lap Vaidehi, wearing a red cloth, resembling the newly risen sun, adorned with ornaments of burning gold—having black curling hairs and decked with fresh garments, *Bibhábasu* gave her unto Rāma. Thereupon the Deity of Fire, the witness of the people, spoke unto Rāma, saying—"O Rāma, here is thy Vaidehi—no sin hath visited her. Neither by words,mind,understanding nor eyes, she, good-natured and beautiful—hath deviated from thee who hath got a good character and is heroic. She was in the solitary forest separated from thee, poorly and having no control over herself and hence she was carried away by the Rākshasa Rāvana having enough prowess in him. Although shut up in the inner appartment—well protected and guarded by the dreadful she-demons she had

---

* A class of writings considered saered by the Hindus.

† Great or supreme spirit—*Purasha* meaning that which abides or is quiesent in body.

‡ The Deity of Fire.

§ Fire.

always her mind in thee and was devoted unto thee. Although tempted in many a way and remonstrated with she did not think of that Rākshasa in her inner mind. Her heart is pure and she is not spoiled with sin—do thou therefore take back Maithili. Do thou not speak otherwise—I do command thee." Thereupon hearing those words—the virtuous-souled Rāma, the foremost of those skilled in speech, with his eyes agitated with delight, meditated for sometime. Being thus addressed, the highly effulgent and intelligent Rāma, of unmitigated prowess—the foremost of the pious, spoke unto that best of celestials saying—"Beautiful (Sitā) lived in the inner appartment of Rāvana for a long time so she needs this purification in the presence of all people. If I would take the daughter of Janaka without purifying her, people would say that Rāma the son of king Daçaratha is lustful and ignorant of the morality of the people. I know it full well that Maithili, the daughter of king Janaka, hath her mind devoted unto me and hath not given it to any one (else). As the ocean cannot go beyond its banks so Rāvana could not approach her having expansive eyes protected by virtue of her own chastity. The greatly vicious-souled one could not even by his mind get Maithili, who was beyond his reach like unto the burning flame of fire. Her mind could not have been moved although she lived in the inner appartment of Rāvana—she belongs to none else ; Sitā is mine as the rays belong to the Sun. Maithili—the daughter of Janaka hath been purified before the three worlds—So I am incapable of renouncing her as a self-controlled person cannot forsake his (own) reputation. It behoveth me to carry out the well-meaning words of you all—the lords of people who have spoken them out of affection." Saying this, the victorious, highly powerful, well renowned Rāghava, worthy of enjoying happiness, and having his praise chanted in consequence of his noble action, regaining his spouse, attained to happiness.

## SECTION CXXI.

HEARING those excellent words uttered by Rāghava, Maheswara (Siva) spoke far more important words—"O thou having lotus-eyes, O thou having huge arms and a spacious breast, O thou the slayer of enemies, O thou the foremost of the pious—it is a good fortune that this hath been done by thee. It is by good fortune, O Rāma, the dreadful and increasing darkness—the fear of all people—Rāvana, hath been removed by thee in the encounter. Consoling the poor Bharata and the famed Kauçalyā, beholding Kaikeyi and Sumitrā the mother of Lakshmana, obtaining the kingdom of Ayodhyā, pleasing all thy friends, establishing the prestige of thy family, O thou of great strength, performing horse-sacrifices, attaining fair fame and conferring riches upon the Brahmins do thou repair to heaven. This king Daçaratha stationed on the car is thy father. He was thy superior on this earth, O Kākutstha. Obtaining thee as his son, that graceful (king) hath repaired to the region of Indra. Do thou bow unto him with thy brother Lakshmana." Hearing the words of Mahādeva, Rāghava, along with Lakshmana, bowed unto their father who was seated on the top of the car. He with Lakshmana beheld their father shining in his own effulgence and wearing an unsullied cloth. Thereupon beholding his son dearer than his life, attaining great delight (in consequence thereof) placing him on his lap and embracing him with his arms, the great king Daçaratha, having long arms and seated on an excellent seat in the car, said—"I am now in heaven and am equal with the celestials, but without thee, O Rāma, I do not like it—this is true—I do swear by thee. O thou the foremost of those skilled in speech, I have still in my mind the words which were uttered by Kaikeyi for sending thee away to the woods. Beholding thee all well and embracing thee with Lakshmana I am now shorn of grief like unto the sun, devoid of dues. I have been emancipated, O my son, through thee—a good and high-souled son, as the virtuous-souled Brahmana Kapāla was by Asthabakra. O gentle one, I have heard from the celestials, (that thou art) the excellent Purusha in the guise (of a man) for the destruction of Rāvana. Blessed is Kauçalyā, O Rāma, who shall be greatly delighted, on beholding thee, the slayer of enemies, gone home from the forest. Blessed are those men, O Rāma, who shall behold thee installed in the city as the king of the world. I wish to behold thee reconciled with Bharata, devoted powerful, pure and performing pious observances. O gentle one, thou hast spent fourteen years in the forest with Sitā and Lakshmana. The term of thy exile is over—thy promise hath been fulfilled ; and slaying Rāvana, in the conflict thou hast pleased the celestials. Thou hast performed a mighty deed and attained to excellent fame, O slayer of enemies ; and placed in charge of thy kingdom do thou with thy brothers attain a long life." The king speaking thus Rāma spoke unto him with folded hands saying,—"O thou conversant with piety, do thou be propitiated with Bharata and Kaikeyī. Thou didst imprecate Kaikeyi, saying,—"I renounce thee with thy son"—may not that dreadful curse visit her and her son." Saying "so be it" unto Rāma with folded hands and embracing Lakshmana the great king said to him :—"O thou conversant with piety and fame on this earth, thou shalt attain to heaven and excellent state there. O thou the enhancer of Sumitrā's joy—do thou attend upon Rāma ; may good betide thee ; Rāma is ever engaged in the welfare of all beings. All these celestials headed by Indra, Siddhas and Great saints, bowing unto this high-souled and excellent Purusha, worship him. Rāma, the subduer of foes, is the indescribable and undecaying letter *Brahma*, which has been described (in the Vedas) as the heart and secret of the celestials. For serving him along with Sitā, the daughter of king of Videha, thou hast attained piety and excellent fame." Addressing Lakshmana thus, the king spoke unto his daughter-in-law, who was standing before him with folded hands, saying :—"It doth not behove thee, O Vaidehi, to be enraged (with Rāma) for renouncing thee; for purifying thee this was done by him ever wishing thy welfare. What thou hast performed, O daughter, to establish the purity of thy character, is hard to perform. What thou hast done, shall glorify all other females. Though there is no necessity for giving thee any instruction as regards thy duty towards thy husband-still I should say that he is thy great god." Having thus instructed his two sons and Sitā, he repaired, in his car, to the region of Indra. Having advised his two sons along with Sitā, ascending the car, and shining in his effulgence, that excellent king, greatly delighted, repaired to the region of the king of celestials.

## SECTION CXXII.

DASARATHA having repaired, Mahendra greatly delighted spoke unto Rāghava, stationed there with folded hands, saying :—"O Rāma, O foremost of men, this our presence here, must not be fruitless, we are pleased—do thou ask for what thou wishest." Being thus accosted by the high-souled Mahendra—delighted, Rāghava spoke, with a pleased heart—"O lord of the celestials, O thou the foremost of those skilled in speech, if thou art propitiated with me, I shall pray for (my wished-for-object); do thou grant it. Let all these highly powerful monkeys, who have been despatched to the abode of Death, on my account, regaining their life, stand up. O thou the conferror of honour, I wish to see all those delighted monkeys, who were separated from their wives and children on my account. O Purandara, do thou revive all these heroic and powerful (monkeys) who did not care for death, and who worked hard and were distressed (for me). May all those, by thy favour, who were ever devoted unto me and did not care for death (even) regain their life—this is the boon I pray for. O conferror of honour, I wish to see all these monkeys, *Golangulas* and bears, pale and hurt, unheart and gifted with strength and prowess like before. Let there be flowers, fruits and roots, even out of season wherever these monkeys shall live—and let rivers there be full of clear water." Hearing those words of the high-souled Rāghava Mahendra replied with words instinct with delight—"O my boy, O foremost of the Raghus, mighty is the boon thou hast prayed for—my words shall never be falsified, so let them be be fulfilled. Let all those bears and *Golângulas* rise up who were slain in the conflict by Rākshasas and had their heads and arms severed. Let the monkeys gifted with their pristine strength and prowess rise up unhurt and healthy as if after the end of sleep. And being reconciled with their friends, relatives and kinsmen let them attain to excellent joy. O thou the weilder of a huge bow, all the trees shall be filled with flowers and fruits and all the rivers shall be filled with water even out of season (wherever they shall live)." Thereupon all these leading moekeys who had their persons wounded but now healed up, rose up like those asleep. And all those monkeys were greatly wondered, saying, "What is it?" And beholding Kākutstha of accomplished end and eulogizing Rāma and Lakshmana, all the celestials, greatly delighted, said,—"Do thou, O king, repair to Ayodhyā—despatch all the monkeys—console the famed Maithilee, ever devoted unto thee—behold thy brother Bharata observing ascetic vows in consequence of thy grief—and the high-souled Satrughna and all thy mothers, O slayer of foes. And being installed on the throne do thou conduce to the joy of all citizens." Having thus addressed Rāma along with Lakshmana, the thousand-eyed Deity, delighted, went away along with the celestials, in their cars resembling the Sun (in brilliance). And saluting all the celestials, Kākutstha, with his brother Lakshmana, ordered the encampment of the army. Thereupon that famous and well-pleased huge army of the monkys protected by Rāma and Lakshmana, appeared resplendant on all sides like unto a night beautified with the rays of the Moon.

## SECTION CXXIII.

RAMA having spent that night happily and risen up the next morning, Bibhishana, chanting his victory, spoke unto that slayer of foes, with folded hands, saying:——"Here are various articles for bathing, pastes, clothes, ornaments, sandal and various excellent garlands. And here are present women having eyes like lotuses and conversant with the art of decking. Let them perform their duty, O Rāghava." Being thus accosted Kākutstha replied unto Bibhishana, saying:—"Do thou invite all these monkeys headed by Sugriva to bathe. The virtuous-souled Bharata, having huge arms and ever used to comforts, is greatly distressed on my account. Without Bharata the son of Kaikeyi, ever performing pious rites, I do not value bathing or these clothes and ornaments. Do thou so manage that we may go to the city of Ayodhyā speedity. For difficult is the way leading to Ayodhyā." Being thus accosted

Bibhishana relied unto Kākutstha,—"O son of the lord of earth, may good betide thee, I shall soon take thee to that city. The car *Pushpaka* resembling the Sun, belonging to my brother Kuvera, was brought by the powerful Rāvana. O thou of unequalled prowess, that celestial and excellent car, going everywhere at will, since the destruction of Rāvana in battle, is ready for thee. And that car resembling the cloud is in the city of Lankā, in which thou shalt, relieved of thy anxiety, repair to Ayodhyā. If I am worthy of being favoured by thee, if dost thou remember any accomplishment of mine—if thou hast any friendship for me, do thou, O wise one, wait here with thy brother Lakshmana and spouse Vaidehi till I accomplish all my desires by worshiping thee. And then thou shalt go (to Ayodhyā) O Rāma. I shall worship thee with great delight and do thou, O Rāma, with thy friends and army, accept that adoration. O Rāma, out of love, honor, and brotherly feeling, I do crave thy permissinn. I am a servant I cannot command thee." Being thus addressed, Rāma replied unto Bibhishana in the presence of all the Rākshasas and monkeys, saying:—"I have been worshipyed by thee, O hero, with thy excellent counsels,with thy earnest endeavours and with thy great friendship. Do not think, O lord of Rākshasas, that I do not comply with thy request—my heart hastens me to behold my brother Bharata, who, to take me back, did come to the mount Chitrakuta, who laid low his crown at my feet and whose words I did not keep. (I am anxious to see) Kauçalyā, Sumitrā, Kaikeyi, with my friends, citizens and villagers. Do thou regard me, O Bibhishana, O gentle one, as worshipped. O friend do thou be not angry—I request thee. Do thou speedily being the car for me, O lord of Rākshasas—my work is done—how can I wish to live here long." Being thus addressed by Rāma, Bishishana the lord of Rākshasas, speedily brought the car resembling the Sun.

Thereupon arrived there the car adorned all over with gold paintings, altars crested with *Baidurja* jewels, having upper rooms, silvered all over, adorned with white flags and flagstaffs, beautified with gilt lotuses, adorned with golden houses, covered with a network of girdles, having windows made of pearls and jems, girt on all sides with a net of bells, giving forth melodious sound, resembling the summit of the mount Meru, constructed by *Viçwakarmá* (the architect of the celestials) adorned with huge apartments beautified with silver and pearls—having its base crested with crystal, containing excellent seats made of *Baidurja*, abounding in valuable coverlets and immense wealth, incapable of being broken down and coursing at will. And communicating unto Rāma (the arrival of that car) Bibhishana waited there. Beholding that flowery car, coursing at will and resembling a huge mountain, Rāma, of a generous spirit, along with Saumitri, attained to an excess of astonishment.

## SECTION CXXIV.

HAVING brought that car *Pushpaka*, adorned with flowers and having stationed himself at a distance, Bibhishana the lord of Rākshasas, being incited to hurry on, humbly and with folded hands, spoke unto Rāma, saying, "What shall I do, O Rāghava ?" Hearing those words the highly powerful Rāghava, in the presence of Lakshmana, gave vent to the following accents out of affection—"All these monkeys and bears have brought about the accomplishment of my work with great care. Do thou, satisfy them, O Bibhishana, with diverse jewels and riches. With these and thee, I conquered the city of Lankā, O lord of Rākshasas. They all fought with a delighted heart, having renounced all fear of life and who did never go away from the battle-field. Do thou, with a gift of riches and jewel, make good the work of these monkeys and bears who encompassed the accomplishment (of my end). Being honoured and delighted by thee grateful, all these leading monkeys shall repair (to their respective quarters). (If thou art found to be) sacrificing, self-controlled, compassionate and (the just) collector of revenues, all shall be attached unto thee. For this I do address you (thus). O lord of men, the soldiers, disgusted, renounce that king who is void of all royal accomplishments, and who uselessly slays soldiers in the conflict." Being thus accosted by Rāma, Bibhishana, with a distribution of jewels and riches, honoured all those monkeys. And beholding all those leading monkeys worshipped with jewels and riches Rāma ascended that excellent car, taking the bashful, and high-minded Vaidehi on his lap and accompanied, by his powerful brother Lakshmana, a skilled bowman. And being stationed on the car Kākutstha honouring all the monkeys, the highly powerful Sugriva and Bibhishana, said—"O foremost of monkeys, ye have performed a friendly service—it hath been appreciated by me—do ye repair to your wished-for quarters. O Sugriva, thou, ever afraid of impiety, hast performed all that a loving and well-wishing friend should do. Do thou, encircled by thy army, proceed towards Kishkindhā. Do thou, O Bibhishana, live in thy kingdom, Lankā, conferred upon thee, by me. Not even the celestials, headed by Indra shall be able to assail thee. I wish to return to Ayodhyā, the capital of my father's (kingdom). I wish to obtain your permission (and for this) I have invited you all." Being thus addressed by Rāma, all the leading monkeys bears as well as the Rākshasa Bibhishana said with folded hands—"We wish all to go to Ayodhyā. Do thou take us.

We shall all range with delight at forests and gardens. Beholding thee installed and bowing unto Kauçalyā, we shall soon return to our respective homes, O foremost of kings." Being thus accosted by the monkeys with Bibhishana, the virtuous-souled Rāma, spoke unto them and Sugriva and Bibhishana, saying—"Dearer than the dear, I shall attain to, when returning my city, along with you all, I shall enjoy in the company of all my friends and relatives. O Sugriva, do thou soon ascend the car along with the monkeys. Do thou ascend too, O Bibhishana, lord of Rākshasas, with all thy courtiers." Thereupon ascended that celestial car *Pushpaka*, Sugriva, greatly delighted with the monkeys and Bibhishana, with his courtiers. And they all having got up, the excellent car, of Kuvera at the command of Rāghava, rose up in the welkin. And in that car coursing at will and drawn by effulgent ganders, Rāma greatly delighted appeared like Kuvera (himself). And all the monkeys, bears and the highly powerful Rākshasas sat in that celestial car unobstructed and at their pleasure.

---

## SECTION CXXV.

BEING commanded by Rāma, that excellent car, drawn by ganders, with a huge noise, rose high up in the welkin. And casting his looks on all sides, Rāma, the descendant of Raghus, spake unto Sitā, the daughter of the king of Mithilā, having a moon-like countenance, saying,—"O Vaidehi, do thou behold Lankā, situate on the summit of the mount Chitrakuta, resembling that of Kailāça and constructed by *Viçwakarmā*. And behold, O Sitā, that huge arena of battle, bathed in the blood and flesh of the monkeys and Rākshasas. Do thou behold, O thou having expansive eyes, Rāvana, the lord of Rākshasas, the repressor of people and who obtained a boon, lying there, slain by me on thy account. Kumbhakarna was slain there, the night-ranger Prahasta, as well, and Dumrāksha, were slain by the monkey Hanumān. Bidyutmāli was slain there by the high-souled Sushena—and Indrajit, the son of Rāvana, was slain there in the encounter, by Lakshmana. The Rākshasa named Bikata was slain there by Angada—and Birupāksha, hard to look at and Mahaparsha and Mahodara. And the powerful Akampana was slain (there) and all other Rākshasas—Trishirā, Atikāya, Devantaka and Narantaka—and the two leading and powerful Rākshasas, mad after conflict—the sons of Kumbhakarna—Nikumbha and Kumbha, Bajradanstra, Danstra and many other Rākshasas were slain and the irrepressible Makarāksha was slain (there) by me in the conflict. Akampana was slain—and the powerful Sonitāksha. And Yupāksha and Prajangha were destroyed (there) in the great conflict. The grim-visaged Rākshasa Viddutsjmha was slain there—and Yajnāsatru and the highly powerful Suptaghna. (And there was slain) Suryāsatru and Brahmasatru. (And there bewailed for Rāvana) his spouse Mandodari, surrounded by his thousand other wives. O thou having an excellent countenance, do thou behold the descending place of the ocean, where I spent the night after crossing the deep for thee. O thou having expansive eyes, for thee, this difficult construction of the bridge was made by me over the deep by the help of Nala. Do thou, O Vaidehi, behold the unagitated deep—the abode of Varuna, appearing as if without the other end, roaring and abounding in conchs and pearl oysters. O Maithili, do thou behold the golden mount, which rose above the deep for affording a resting place unto Hanumān. And on the bank of this ocean I halted with my soldiers. And here Mahādeva, the lord of the celestials, was propitiated with me. It behoveth thee to behold this descending place of the high-souled Ocean, known as *Setubandha,** worshipped of the three worlds, highly sacred and destroying even the worst sin. There, Bibhishana, the king of Rākshasas first came to me. Do thou behold,O Sitā, Kishkindhā, having beautiful gardens, the pleasant city of Sugriva, where Vāli was slain by me." And beholding the city of Kishkindhā, ruled over by Vāli, Sitā, incited by her love, addressed Rāma, with worthy words, saying—"O king, I wish to repair to Ayodhyā thy capital with thee, in the company of Tārā, the dear wife of Sugriva,as well as of the wives of other leading monkeys." Being thus addressed by Vaidehi Rāghava replied—saying, "this shall be done" and getting at Kishkindhā he stopped the car. And having beheld the car stationed he spoke unto Sugriva, saying—"O foremost of monkeys, do thou speak unto all the leading monkeys that they may go to Ayodhyā accompanied by their wives. O thou of great strength—they may all go with Sitā. Do thou hurry them on, O Sugriva. We shall (soon) go, O thou the lord of monkeys." Being thus addressed by Rāma, of unmitigated prowess—the beautiful lord of monkeys, encircled by them, entered speedily the inner apartment and beholding Tārā there, said—"O dear, at the command of Rāghava and the kind desire of Sitā, do thou soon go, taking with thee the wives of all the high-souled monkeys. We shall see Ayodhyā and the wives of Daçaratha." Hearing the words of Sugriva, Tārā, having a pecfectly beautiful person, assembling all the wives of the monkeys, said—"You have been ordered by Sugriva to repair (to Ayodhyā)with the monkeys ;—to behold Ayodhyā, is also a dear object of mine. ("I shall behold)

* This is still to be seen in the shape of a delapidated bridge near *Rámeswar* a place of pilgrimage. Pilgrims go there Via Madura, a district in South Madras. The Raja of Ramnud in whose Zemindari it is situate is called Setupati.—T.

Rāma enter the city with the citizens and villagers and the wealth and riches of the wives of Daçaratha." Being thus commanded by Tārā,the wives of the monkeys, putting on all their ornaments and circumambulating (her) ascended the car, with a view to behold Sitā. And beholding the car going up with them all, Rāghava again spoke unto Sitā, near the mount Rishyamuka, saying,—"Do thou behold there, O Sitā, the huge and foremost mount Rishyamuka abounding in gold and various metals, like unto clouds accompanied with lightnings. There I was joined by Sugriva, the lord of monkeys. And there I entered into an agreement, O Sitā, for the destruction of Vāli. And there is (the lake) Pampā abounding in lilies and skirted by picturesque forest where separated from thee, I bewailed piteously. And on its bank I beheld the pious *Savari.* And there I slew *Kavandha* and *Yoyanavāhu.* Behold there, O Sitā, a beautiful tree, in Janasthāna, where, O thou ever used to luxuries, for thee, the highly powerful and energetic Yatāyu, the foremost of birds, was slain by Rāvana. Do thou behold there, O thou of a beautiful person, O thou of auspicious looks, our hermitage and the beautiful cottage of leaves, wherefrom thou hadst been carried away by force by the lord of Rākshasas. Do thou behold there the beautiful and sacred river Godāveri having clear water and the hermitage of Agastya, surrounded by plantain trees. Do thou behold there, O Vaidehi, the great hermitage of *Sarabhanga*, where came the thousand-eyed, Sakra, the subduer of enemies' cities. O worshipful dame, O thou having a middle stature—amongst all those ascetics, thou beholdest, there lived Atri, the lord of our family—resembling the fire of the Sun. There was slain the huge-bodied Birādha by me. There thou didst behold, O Sitā, the female astectic (the wife of Attri) ever performing pious observances. There cometh in view, O thou having a beautiful person, the king of mountains, Chitrakuta, where to propitiate me, came the son of Sumitrā. Behold the beautiful Yamunā, having picturesque forest on its bank and the pleasant hermitage of Varadwāya. Behold there the sacred river Ganges, dividing itself into three branches. Behold there the city of Sringabera, where I made friendship with Guha. Behold there, O Sitā, the capital of my father. Do thou bow unto Ayodhyā, O Vaidehi." Thereupon all the monkeys and Rākshasas along with Bibhishana rose up delightedly and saw the city. Thereupon the monkeys and Rākshasas beheld the city abounding in white houses having spacious compartments, filled with elephants and horses and looking like Amarāvati, the capital of Mahendra.

## SECTION CXXVI.

HAVING completed the fourteen years (of exile), the self-controlled elder brother of Lakshmana, arriving at the hermitage of Varadwāya on the fifth day, saluted the ascetic. And bowing unto Varadwaya, having asceticism for his wealth, he said,—"O thou gifted with six sorts of wealth, hast thou heard of the prosperity and well being (of my city)? Is Bharata still engaged (in guarding the people)? Are my mothers living?" Being thus addressed by Rāma the great ascetic Varadwāya replied, delighted, and smiling, unto that foremost of Raghus,—"Abiding by thy command and with matted locks, Bharata is waiting for thee, always honoring thy sandals. And all others are well in thy house. O subduer of thy enemies, I was greatly pained, when I saw thee before entering the huge forest, wearing bark, three with thy wife,* deprived of thy kingdom for piety only,

* *i.e.* thyself, Lakshmana and Sitá.

walking on foot, renouncing every thing, obeying the command of thy sire, deprived of all comforts, like a celestial banished from heaven, deprived of thy kingdom at the words of Kaikeyi, and living on wild roots and fruits; but beholding thee now of accomplished end, with all thy friends having vanquished the enemy, I have attained to highest delight. O Rāghava, I am apprised of immense griefs and happinesses which befell thee when thou didst live in Janasthāna. Thy blameless spouse was carried away stealthily by Rāvana engaged as thou wert in the behoof of the Brāhmanas,and in the protection of all the ascetics. The view of Māricha—the carrying away of Sitā,—the beholding of the headless demon,—thy going to (the lake) Pampā,—thy friendship with Sugriva, where Vāli was slain by thee,—the enquiry of Vaidehi undertaken by the son of Wind-god,—the construction of the bridge by Nala after the whereabouts of Vaidehi had been known—the conflagration of Lankā by the delighted and the leading monkeys—the destruction,in the conflict, of Rāvana proud of his own strength, along with his sons, friends, courtiers, army and steeds—the arrival of the celestials on the destruction of Rāvana, the thorn of gods and the grant of boon by them—I have known all these by virtue of my asceticism, O thou fond of virtue. My disciples used to go hence to that city to bring tidings. I shall even now grant thee a boon, O foremost of those using weapons. Do thou accept my *Arghya** and then repair to Ayodhyā to-morrow." And respectfully abiding by his words, that effulgent son of the king, delighted, begged of him the boon. "O thou gifted with six qualities, on my way while proceeding to Ayodhyā, let all the trees, bearing fruits out of season,and producing honey,bear many a nectar-smelling fruit." No sooner he replied saying,—"Thy promise shall be fulfilled" than all the trees there became like those of heaven.

* A respectful oblation to gods or venerable men of rice, *durva* grass, flowers &c with water in a small boat-shaped vessel.

Trees without fruits were filled therewithal and trees without flowers were covered with them. All the trees, whose leaves were dried up, were enveloped with foliage and all of them began to pour honey. The way to Ayodhyā for three *Yoyanas* was thus filled all over (with trees). Thereupon thousands of monkeys, living, at pleasure and delightedly, on various celestial fruits, thought as if they were in heaven.

## SECTION CXXVII.

THEREUPON beholding Ajodhyā, Rāma, the descendant of Raghu, of light movements and desirous of affording delight unto others, thought of welcoming (them). Thinking thus the intelligent and effulgent (Rāma) cast his looks towards the monkeys and spoke unto Hanumān, saying,—"O foremost of monkeys, speedily reparing to Ayodhyā do thou learn of the welfare of all people in the palace of the king. Arriving at the city of Sringavera, do thou communicate unto Guha, the king of *Nishadhas** having the forest as his kingdon, my well-being, at my command. Hearing that I am hale and hearty and relieved of all troubles, Guha, my friend like my own self, shall attain to delight. And Guha, the lord of *Nishadhas*, delighted, shall inform thee of the way to Ayodhyā and the well being of Bharata. Do thou ask of Bharata his well-being at my words, and communicate unto him my (arrival) with Lakshmana and my spouse after having made good the vow

* A low caste aboriginal Hindu corresponding to our *Chandālas* always living in the forest. The Raja of Ramnud in the district of Madurá in Madras traces his descent from this Guha.

(of my sire)—the carrying away of Sitā by the powerful Rāvana—the friendship with Sugriva and the destruction of Vāli in the conflict—the search of Maithili instituted by thee having got over the huge lord of rivers—the advance (of the monkeys) to the banks of the deep—the view of the ocean, the construction of the bridge—the destruction of Rāvana,—the grant of boon by Mahendra, Brahmā and Varuna—my meeting with my father by the favour of Mahādeva. Do thou, O gentle one, communicate unto Bharata, my arrival here with the lord of Rākshasas and king of monkeys. (Tell him) 'vanquishing his foes and attaining to excellent fame Rāma hath arrived at the gate of the city with his valiant friends, having satisfied the vow (of his sire).' Thou shouldst read the signs expressive of joy or sorrow that Bharata shall display on hearing this and infer therefrom his attitude towards me. Thou shouldst know, from the colour of his countenance, his looks and his words, all the movements and actions of Bharata. Whose mind doth not change obtaining such an ancestral kingdom, filled with all prosperity and abounding in elephants, horses and chariots? If the effulgent Bharata, the descendant of Raghu, ruling over it, wisheth the kingdom for himself, let him lord over the entire earth. Therefore, O monkey, it behoveth thee to come back speedily apprised of his intention and movements, before we proceed further." Being thus commanded, Hanumān, the son of Wind-god, assuming a human shape speedily proceeded towards Ayodhyā. Hanumān the son of Māruta rose up in the welkin with velocity like unto Garuda ready to fall upon a huge serpent. Then crossing the Wind-path and the abode of the birds, getting over the terrible confluence of the Ganges and Yamunā, reaching the city of *Sringavera* and meeting Guha, the energetic Hanumān, delighted, (addressed him) with the following excellent words—"Thy friend Rāma, the descendant of Kākutstha, having truth for his prowess, with Sitā and son of Sumitrā, hath enquired of thy welfare. Having spent five nights* till to-day, he, having obtained permission from the ascetic *Varadwâja*, shall proceed to-morrow." Having said this the highly energetic monkey, not caring for the exhaustion of travel, greatly delighted and with hairs erect, rose up with great velocity. Beholding the holy river sanctified with the name of Parasurāma, the rivers—Bālukini, Baruthi, Gomati, the huge forest of *Sála* trees, the various countries populated with thousands of people, and proceeding a great distance speedily, that foremost of monkeys got at the trees near *Nandigrâm*† like unto those of Chaitraratha, the garden of the lord of celestials the flowers whereof were being plucked off by many a damsel accompanied by their children decked in various ornaments. He saw at a distance of one *crosa* from Ayodhyā Bharata wearing the skin of an antelope, poorly, greatly reduced, living in a hermitage, wearing matted hairs, having his body covered with dirt, greatly pulled down in consequence of his brother's disaster, living on roots and fruits, self-controlled, living the life of an ascetic, observing pious observances, with a bundle of clotted hairs on his head, wearing bark and deer skin, having control over his passions and senses, effulgent like *Brahmarshis,* ruling the earth always placing the sandals before him, protecting people of four *Varnas* against all fear, with courtiers, priests leading a holy life and soldiers all wearing red clothes around him. All those citizens, fond of piety, did not like to use good clothes beholding the prince use bark and deer skin. Thereupon Hanumān, the son of Maruta spake with folded hands unto him, conversant with piety like virtue incarnate, saying—"Kākutstha, living in the forest of Dandaka with bark and matted hairs, for whom thou art lamenting, hath

---

* Having spent five nights after the expiry of fourteen years of exile he is living at the hermitage of Varadwája. He shall leave that place to-morrow.—T.

† The country of Bharata's maternal uncle.—T.

enquired after thy welfare. Do thou, O worshipful sire, speak out thy welfare and renounce the dreadful grief. Thou shalt in this moment be reconciled to thy brother Rāma. Slaying Rāvana, and regaining Maithili, Rāma, having accomplished his end, hath arrived here with his valiant friends. The highly effulgent Lakshmana and the famed Vaidehi (have also come). Sitā fareth well with Rāma like unto Sachi in the company of Mahendra." Being thus addressed by Hanumān, Bharata, the son of Kaikeyi, delighted, fell down all on a sudden in a swoon of joy. Thereupon rising up in no time, and welcoming him, Bharata, the descendant of Raghu, spake unto Hanumān communicating the pleasant tidings, the following words. And embracing the monkey respectfully the graceful Bharata sprinkled him with profuse tears not out of grief but of joy. He said,—"Art thou a man or god who hast kindly come here? O gentle one, I shall confer upon thee, who hast communicated unto me this pleasant tidings, hundreds and thousands of kine, hundreds of prosperous villages, sixten young wives, pious, wearing excellent *Kundalas*, golden-hued, having beautiful noses and breast, having moon-like countenances, decked with all ornaments and born of respectable families." And hearing from that leading monkey of that wonderful return of Rāma, the son of the king, delighted became anxious to behold him and again addressed joyously Hanumān with the following words.

## SECTION CXXVIII.

"I HEAR the tidings of my brother affording me great delight who hath been living in the huge forest for many a year. The saying of the people appeareth to me as instinct with well meaning that a man, if alive, may attain to joy even after a century. Do thou relate truly unto me, how and in what country the union between Rāghava and the monkeys was brought about." Being thus accosted by the prince and seated on Kuça, he, thereupon, began to describe Rāma's life in the forest. "How Rāma was exiled, the two boons conferred upon thy mother, how king Daçaratha died in consequence of (his) son's grief, how by emissaries, O lord, thou wert brought up from the house of thy maternal uucle, how thou didst not wish for the kingdom having entered Ayodhyā, how thy brother, the repressor of enemies, was solicited by thee for accepting the kingdom, reparing to the mount Chitrakuta, who hast ever wended the track of the pious, the renouncement of kingdom (by him) abiding by the words of the king, thy return after taking the sandals of thy revered (brother)—all these, O thou of long-arms, are known to thee. I shall relate unto thee all that happened after thy return. Thyself having returned thence, all the birds and animals were overwhelmed with terror and that forest appeared as if distressed. Thereupon he entered the solitary and huge and dreadful forest Dandaka distressed by the elephants and abounding in lions, tigers and deer. And they entering the dense forest there appeared before them the powerful Birādha* emitting a dreadful sound. And taking him up roaring aloud like an elephant Rāma threw him with his arms upwards and face downwards into a pit.

* A demon of that name.

Having accomplished that difficult work the two brothers Rāma and Lakshmana, arrived in the evening at the pleasant hermitage of *Sarabhanga*. And *Sarabhanga* having attained to heaven, Rāma, having truth for his prowess, saluting all the ascetics, repaired to Janasthāna. And by the high-souled Rāghava, living there, fourteen thousand inhabitants of Janasthāna were slain. In the company of one person only and at the commencement of the fight, by Rāma, within the one fourth part of a day, were exterminated all the highly powerful and valiant inhabitants of the forest of Dandaka always putting obstructions in the way of the ascetics. All the Rākshasas were grinded (to death) by Rāghava. Khara was slain in the conflict; Dushana being slain first Trishirā was slain thereafter by him. Thereafter (a she-demon) named Surpanakhā, came to the side of Rāma. Thereupon being commanded by Rāma, the highly powerful Lakshmana rose up all on a sudden and taking a dagger chopped off her ears and nose. Being thus insulted by him that she-demon came to Rāvana. Thereupon a dreadful Rākshasa named Māricha—an attendant of Rāvana, assuming the shape of a jewelled deer, allured Vaidehi. And beholding it, Vaidehi spake unto Rāma, saying,—'Do thou catch it; with it when caught our hermitage shall be more charming.' Thereupon Rāma, with bow in his hand, pursued that deer and with one shaft destroyed it. O gentle one, Rāghava going out on hunting, and Lakshmana having issued out of the hermitage, the Ten-necked (demon) entered therein. And he speedily got hold of Sitā, like unto Rohini possessed by the planet in the sky. Thereupon slaying the vulture Yatāyu in the conflict desirous of rescuing her and getting hold of Sitā that Rākshasa speedily repaired (to his capital). Thereupon some monkeys resembling mountains, stationed on the summit of a mountain, stricken with wondrous fear and astonishment, beheld Rāvana, the lord of Rākshasas proceed with Sitā. Ascending the car

*Pushpaka*, going at will, with Vaidehi and hastening his course that highly powerful Rāvana, the lord of Rākshasas entered Lankā. And entering the huge and excellent golden palace Rāvana consoled Maithili with ( diverse ) words. But she regarded that foremost of Rākshasas and his words as straw. And Vaidehi was placed in the forest of Asoka. Thereupon returned Rāma after having slain the deer in the forest. Having returned and seen the vulture, dearer than his father,slain, Rāma, the descendant of Kākutstha was pained. And searching Vaidehi and ranging at the banks of Godāveri and forest-lands covered with flowers, Rāma with Lakshmana, met in that huge forest a Rākshasa named Kavandha. Thereupon at the words of Kavandha, Rāma, having truth for his prowess, repairing to the mount Rishyamuka, was united with Sugriva. There had grown mutual love in them before they were known to each other. Sugriva was driven away by his angry brother Vāli. And informed of each other's affairs their friendship grew closer. Thereupon slaying the huge-bodied and highly powerful Vāli in the conflict by virtue of the strength of his own arms Rāma obtained (for Sugriva) his own kingdom. And being placed on the throne with all the monkeys, Sugriva promised unto Rāma the enquiry of the Princess (Sitā). Being commanded by the high-souled Sugriva, the lord of monkeys, ten *kotis* of monkeys repaired to ( various ) quarters. Among them some of us lost our way in a cavity of the Vindhya mountain, and were striken with great terror—and accordingly much time was lost. The powerful brother of the king of vultures named Sampāti communicated unto us the residence of Sitā in the palace of Rāvana. Thereupon removing the grief of my relatives stricken with sorrow and resorting to my own prowess, I jumped over hundred *yoyanas* and beheld her placed in the forest of Asoka, wearing a red cloth, pale, deprived of all joy and observing strict penances. And then nearing her and beholding her of a perfectly blameless person I bestowed upon her an ensign a ring with Rāma's name engraven on it. And obtaining a jewel as an ensign, I, with my object accomplished, returned. And having returned I presented Rāma of unwearied actions with that ensign of a brilliant gem. And hearing (of the news of Vaidehi) Rāma regained his life like one on the verge of death regaining his being after drinking nectar. And exciting (his soldiers) for making preparations like unto Fire about to destroy all people he made up his mind for the devastation of Lankā. Thereupon arriving at the banks of the ocean he had a bridge constructed by Nala by which the army of monkey-heroes crossed (the deep). Nala destroyed Prahasta, Rāghava slew Kumbhakarna, Lakshmana killed the son of Rāvana and Rāma himself slew Rāvana. He was then met by Sakra, Yama, Varuna, Siva, Brahmā and Daçaratha. And that graceful descendant of Kākutstha, the slayer of foes, obtained the boon from them as well as from the saints assembled there—(celestial and otherwise). Having obtained the boon he, delighted, met the monkeys and in the car *Pushpaka* reached Kishkindhā. Again reaching the Ganges he is living with the ascetic; it becometh thee to behold him to-morrow under the auspices of of *Pushya*,* without any hindrance." Thereupon being delighted with the sweet accents of Hanumān, Bharata addressed him, with folded hands, with words affording delight, saying,—"After a long time my desire hath been fulfilled."

* The lunar asterism comprising three stars of which one is the Cancer.

## SECTION CXXIX.

HEARING those words affording great delight, Bharata, the slayer of enemies, having truth for his prowess, delighted, ordered Satrughna, (saying),—"Let all people being purified worship all the deities and altars of the city with fragrant garlands and diverse music. Let all the bards conversant with the chanting of the pedigree, the flatterers, all those conversant with music, the dancing girls, the queens, the courtiers, the soldiers with their wives, Brāhmanas, Kshatryas, and people of all other castes, issue out to behold the moon-like countenance of Rāma." Hearing the words of Bharata, Satrughna, the slayer of enemies, divided the work amongst the servants, (saying),—"Do ye level the high and low ground from Nandigrām to (Ayodhyā). Do ye perfectly water the ground with cold water. Thereafter sprinkle all the places with flowers and dried paddy; hoist up flags all over the city; decorate all the houses, before the rising of the moon with garlands, jewels, flowers of gold and things of five other colours. Let hundreds of men watch the thoroughfares." Hearing the command of Satrughna, issued out with delight Dhristi, Jayanta, Vijaya, Siddartha, Arthasadhaka, Asoka, Mantrapāla and Sumantra. Thereupon issued out men on horse back and in cars with thousands of mad elephants well-decked with pennons and she-elephants with golden seats (on their back). And some heroes proceeded encircled by thousand excellent steeds and persons carrying *Sakti, Risthi*, maces and pennons and thousands of infantry. Thereupon proceeded Sumitrā and all other wives of Daçaratha placing Kauçalya before them and seated in excellent conveyances. And hearing of the return of his brother and attaining to delight, the high-souled and pious Bharata, reduced with fasting, poorly, wearing bark and skin of an antelope and conversant with religion, issued out to receive back Rāma in the company of his counsellors and encircled by the twice-born ones, the people of diverse castes, his own relations and kinsmen and ministers with garlands and *Modaka** in their hands, eulogized by the bards, having his arrival announced with the sound of conchs and bugles and placing the sandals of his worshipful brother on his head and taking white umbrella adorned with white garlands and white *Chowries* decked with gold and worthy of being used by the kings. Thereupon with the sound of the horses' hoofs and cars, conchs and bugles the earth shook. And the whole city went to Nandigrām. And beholding the Wind-god's son, Bharata said,—"Didst thou not resort to the usual fickleness of the monkeys? We do not behold the worshipful Rāma, the descendant of Kākutstha--the slayer of foes. Nor do we behold the monkeys assuming shapes at will." Having been addressed with those words, Hanumān replied, communicating unto Bharata, having truth for his prowess, the truth, —"Having reached the trees, covered by the favour of Varadwaja, with fruits and flowers and pouring honey, the monkeys are emitting noise like maddened black bees. O slayer of foes, this boon was granted him ( Rāma ) by Vāsava. (Varadwaya) is treating him with his army with all hospitality. Hear the dreadful noise of the delighted monkeys. Methinks the monkey host hath crossed the river Gomati. Behold the huge upheaval of dust towards the *Sála* forest. Methinks the monkeys are agitating the graceful *Sála* forest. Behold there at the distance the car resembling the Sun. This celestial car *Pashpaka*, constructed by Brahma's mind, was obtained by the high-souled (Rāma) after having slain Rāvana with his friends. This celestial car, resembling the newly risen Sun, coursing at will and carrying Rāma (was

* A kind of sweet meat.

gained) by the favour of the Giver of wealth. (There are) the two heroic borthers—the descendants of Raghu with Vaidehi, the highly effulgent Sugriva and the Rākshasa Bibhishana. Thereupon with the sound of "there is Rāma" there arose a joyous noise reaching the abode of the celestials from among women, children, the young and the old. Thereupon descending upon the earth from chariots, elephants and horses all people beheld him (Rāma) stationed on the car like unto the moon in the sky. And facing Rāghava and with folded hands Bharata delightedly worshipped him with agreeable words, *Arghya* and water to wash his feet. There appeared in the car constructed by Brahmā's mind the elder brother of Bharata having expansive eyes like the immortal weilder of thunder-bolt. Thereupon Bharata humbly saluted his brother Rāma seated on the top of the car like unto the Sun on the summit (of the mount Meru). And commanded by Rāma that excellent car drawn by ganders got down on the earth with great velocity. And ascending that car, Bharata, having truth for his prowess, reaching Rāma, delighted, again bowed unto him. And raising Bharata up who had been seen after a long time and placing him on his lap Kākutstha, delighted, embraced him. Thereupon Bharata, the slayer of foes, bowed unto Vaidehi and welcomed Lakshmana. And the son of Kaikeyi (then in turn) embraced Sugriva, Jāmbabana, Angada, Mainda, Dwivida, Nila and Rishava. And he then embraced Sushena, Nala, Gabāksha, Gandhamādana, Sarabha, and Panasa. And assuming human shapes, those monkeys, assuming shapes at will, delightedly enquired after Bharata's well-being. And embracing Sugriva, the foremost of monkeys, the highly effulgent prince Bharata, the foremost of the pious, said—" O Sugriva, thou art our fifth brother. From brotherliness groweth friendship and doing injury is the sign of an enemy." And Bharata then addressed Bibhishana with soothing words—"It is by fortune that through your help he hath accomplished such a difficult work." Thereupon the heroic Satrughna saluting Rāma and Lakshmana, respectfully bowed unto Sitā. And having approached his mother, pale and pulled down with grief, Rāma humbly touched her feet and enhanced her delight. And thereupon saluting Sumitrā, famed Kaikeyi and all his mothers he approached the priests. Thereupon all the citizens with folded hands welcomed him saying—"Welcome art thou, O thou of long arms! O thou the enhancer of Kauçalya's joy!" And the elder brother of Bharata observed the folded hands of the citizens like so many blown lotuses. And himself taking the sandals of Rāma, Bharata, conversant with piety, placed them at the feet of that lord of men. Thereupon Bharata with folded hands spoke unto Rāma, saying—"This all thy kingdom, which thou didst leave to my care, I return thee. Blessed is my birth to-day and accomplished is my desire, since I behold thee again as king in Ayodhyā after thy return. Do thou examine thy wealth treasury, palace and army. By thy favour I have increased all these ten fold." Hearing Bharata speak in that wise and beholding him devoted to his brother all the monkeys and the Rākshasa Bibhishana shed tears. Thereupon placing Bharata, in delight, on his lap, Rāghava, with his army in that car, proceeded towards Bharata's abode. And reaching Bharata's palace Rāghava with his army descended upon the earth. Thereupon Rāma said to the excellent car—"Do thou (now) go to *Vaisrâvana*—I do permit thee." Thereupon being thus commanded by Rāma, that excellent car, proceeding towards the north, reached the abode of the Giver of wealth. That celestial car *Pushpaka* had been taken away by the Rākshasa (Rāvana); but now at the words Rāma it reached (again) the Giver of wealth. And touching the feet of his priest the powerful Rāghava sat on a separate and excellent seat like unto Sakra, the lord of immortals (by the side of) *Vrihashpati*.

## SECTION CXXX.

THEREUPON having placed her palms on his head Bharata, the enhancer of Kaikeyi's joy, spoke unto his elder brother Rāma, having truth for his prowess, saying,—"Abiding by my mother's request thou didst confer this kingdom upon me; I do return thee the kingdiom thou didst give me. Like unto a young one unable to carry a heavy burden thrown off by a powerful bull I am unable to carry this huge burden (of the kingdom). I do consider this kingdom infested with thieves, difficult to govern, as it is difficult to re-construct a bridge broken down by a powerful current of water. As an ass cannot follow the course of a horse and a crow cannot follow that of a gander, so I am unable, O hero, O slayer of foes, to follow thy footsteps. If a tree, planted in the inner appartment of a house, growing huge with a big trunk and many branches, is dried up as soon it blossoms without bearing fruits, his object for whom it is planted, becomes fruitless. And this simili, O thou of long-arms, shall prove good in thee, if dost thou not, our master, govern us, O lord of men, who are thy servants. Let the world, O Rāghava, behold thee installed (to-day) like unto the powerful mid-day Sun burning in effulgence. Do thou sleep and rise up with the sound of stringed instruments, womens' girdles and *Nupuras* and charming songs. Do thou govern the people as long as the solar system exists and as far as the earth extends." Hearing the words of Bharata, Rāma the conqueror of enemies' cities, saying,—"So be it" sat on an excellent seat. Thereupon at the command of Satrughna, expert, skilful and quick-handed barbers gathered round Rāghava. At first, Bharata, the highly powerful Lakshmana, Sugriva the lord of monkeys, and Bibhishana the lord of Rākshasas bathed. Thereupon shorn of his matted hairs, bathed, with paste excellent garlands and precious clothes on, he appeared there shining in grace. The valiant and graceful Satrughna, the upholder of the dignity of Ikshwaku race, himself got ready the dresses for Rāma and Lakshmana. And all the high-minded wives of Daçaratha with their own hands decked Sitā with various charming (ornaments). Thereupon Kauçalyā, delighted and fond of her son, herself with great care, decorated the wives of monkeys. Thereupon at the words of Satrughna, the charioteer by name Sumantra got ready the perfectly beautiful car. And beholding that celestial car, bright as the fire of the sun, stationed before him, Rāma, having long-arms, the conqueror of enemies' cities, ascended it. Sugriva and Hanumān, graceful like Mahendra, bathed, dressed in celestial clothes and wearing excellent *Kundalas*, proceeded (to view the city). And then went Sitā and all the wives of Sugriva decorated with all ornaments and wearing excellent *Kundalas*, anxious to behold the city. All the ministers of king Daçaratha in Ayodhya began to hold consultation respectfully with the priest. Asoka, Vijaya and Siddhartha, with undivided mind, consulted with each other about the welfare of Rāma as well as that of the city. (Thereupon they ordered the servants) saying,—"Do ye collect materials necessary for the auspicious installation of the high-souled (Rāma) worthy of being crowned with victory". The priest and the ministers having ordered thus all speedily issued out of the city to behold Rāma. Like unto the thousand-eyed Indra in his car drawn by horses the blameless Rāma, seated in his car, proceeded towards the excellent city. Bharata took up the reins, Satrughna held the umbrella and Lakshmana began to fan him on the head with *Chowries*. And Bibhishana, the lord of Rākshasas standing on one side, took up the white *Chowrie* shining like the second moon. There was audible the sweet encomium of Rāma chanted by the crowd of ascetics in the sky, the celestials and the Marutas. Thereupon the highly effulgent Sugriva, the foremost of monkeys, got up upon an elephant named *Satrunyaya* resembling a mountain. And riding nine thousand elephants proceeded the monkeys assuming human shapes and adorned with various ornaments. And with the music of conches and bugles that foremost of men entered the city abounding in houses. (And the citizens) beheld Rāghava enter the city with a graceful person and seated in the car. And they having bowed unto that descendant of Kākutstha were welcomed by him. And they followed that high-souled one encircled by his brothers. And surrounded by his courtiers, Brāhmanas and subjects Rāma appeared beautiful like unto the Moon encircled by stars. And he went preceeded by men who play on stringed instruments, by people with *Karatal* and Sustika in their hands and by men chanting delightedly auspicious songs. Persons with *Akshata* and gold in their hands, kine, girls, Brāhmanas and persons with *Modaka* in their hands went before Rāma. Thereupon before the ministers Rāma began to describe the friendship of Sugriva, the prowess of the Wind-god's son and the works accomplished by the monkeys. And hearing of the works of the monkeys and the prowess of the Rākshasas, the inhabitants of the city of Ayodhyā attained to astonishment. Having related thus (the works of the monkeys) the graceful Rāma encircled by the monkeys entered (the city of) Ayodhyā abounding in delighted and plump persons. Thereupon the citizens hoisted up flags upon every house and he reached the picturesque abode of his ancestors inhabited by the descendants of Ikshwaku. And having reached and entered his ancestral palace and bowed unto Kauçalyā, Sumitrā and Kaikeyi, the high-souled prince, the enhancer of the joy of the descendants of Raghu, addressed Bharata the foremost of the pious, with sweet words instinct with meaning, saying,

—"Do thou set apart for Sugriva my huge and excellent palace abounding in pearls and *Vaidurjas.*" Hearing those words, Bharata, having truth for his prowess, taking Sugriva by the hand, conducted him to the palace. And commanded by Satrughna, (servants) speedily entered (that palace) with oil, lamps, bedsteads and beddings. Thereupon the highly effulgent younger brother of Rāghava spoke unto Sugriva, saying,—"Do thou, O lord, order some (to bring water) for Rāma's installation." And Sugriva conferred upon four leading monkeys four golden jars crested with diverse jewels and said to them,—"Do ye so conduct, O monkeys,that ye may return by the dawn with the jars filled with the water of the four oceans." Being thus addressed by the high-souled (Sugriva) the monkeys resembling the elephants speedily rose up in the welkin like unto quick-coursing vultures. Jāmbavana, Hanumān, the monkey Vegadarshi and Rishabha brought the jars filled with water from five hundred rivers. Sushena, gifted with prowess, brought that jar crested with gems, filled with water from the Eastern Ocean. And Rishabha speedily brought water from the Southern Ocean. And Gabaya brought, from the great Western Ocean in that golden jar, water perfumed with the fragrance of red sandal and camphor. And the virtuous-souled Wind-god's son, gifted with all accomplishments and the prowess of Garuda and Wind-god, brought, speedily from the Northern Ocean, water in that jewelled jar. And beholding water thus brought by the leading monkeys for the installation of Rāma, Satrughna, with his ministers, communicated that unto the leading priests and friends. Thereupon the self-controlled Vasishtha, striken in years, along with other Brāhmanas placed Rāma with Sitā on a jewelled seat. Vasishtha, Vijayā, Jāvāli, Kātyāyana, Goutama and Bāmadeva, sprinkled that foremost of men, with clear and fragrant water as Vasus did the thousand eyed Vāsava. (He was then sprinkled by) the *Rittigas,* Brāhmanas, maidens ministers, soldiers and the merchants all delighted. (Thereupon) with the juice of *Oshadhis** (he was sprinkled by) the celestials stationed in the sky, the deities presiding over four quarters and all other celestials collected. And having placed him on a seat crested with various jewels in the arena decorated with gold, various jewels and rich parapharnalia, (he placed on his head) the jewelled crown made by Brahmā, brilliant and with which in the days of yore Manu and other kings, born in his race, were installed. And being decked by the high-souled Vasishtha with that crown, Rāghava was afterwards dressed with the celestial garments by the *Rittigas.*† And Satrughna held the white and excellent umbrella and Sugriva the lord of monkeys took the white *Chowrie.* And Bibhishana the lord of Rākshasas took up another *Chowrie* resembling the moon. And the wind commanded by Vāsava conferred upon Rāghava, a garland of hundred golden lotuses, shining in their native lustre. And the wind commanded by Sakra conferred upon that lord of men a jewelled garland crested with diverse gems. The intelligent and worthy Rāma being installed the celestials and the Gandharvas sang and the Apsarās danced. The earth was filled with crops, the trees with fruits and the flowers were fragrant on the occassion of Rāghava's installation. And that foremost of men conferred upon the twice-born ones one million of horses, hundred thousand cows and hundred thousand bulls. And Rāghava again conferred upon the Brāhmanas thirty *crores* of golden coins and diverse costly ornaments and clothes. Thereupon that lord of men conferred upon Sugriva a celestial garland brilliant like the rays of the Sun and crested with gold and jewels. And he, gifted with intelligence, conferred upon Angada, Vali's son, two *Angadas*‡ brilliant as the rays of the moon and made of

---

* An annual plant or herb—one that dies after becoming ripe.

† A domestic chaplain—a family priest.

‡ A kind of ornament worn on upper arms.

*Baidurja*. And Rāma conferred upon Sitā an excellent pearl necklace crested with precious jems, celestial clothes and various excellent ornaments. And taking off the necklace from her person Vaidehi, the daughter of king Janaka, conferred it upon the Wind-god's son remembering the services (rendered by him) and cast her looks again and again upon her lord and the monkeys. And beholding that (Rāma) capable of reading the gestures, spoke unto the daughter of king Janaka, saying—"O fortunate and beautiful lady, do thou confer this necklace upon him with whom thou art pleased." Thereupon the lotus-eyed (Sitā) conferred that upon the Wind god's son. And Hanumān, the foremost of monkeys, in whom perpetually exist, energy, forgiveness, fame, skillfullness, prowess, humility, tactics, manliness, valiance and intellect, appeared with that necklace like a mountain beautified with the rays of the moon and white clouds. And all other elderly and leading monkeys were respectively honoured with clothes and ornaments. And being honoured by Rāma of unwearied actions with enough of jewels and other wished-for objects, Bibhishana, Sugriva, Hanumān, Jāmbhabān and other leading monkeys, delighted, returned to their respective habitations. Thereupon, the lord of earth and the slayer of foes conferred,all wished-for things, upon Dwivida, Mainda and Nila. And beholding (the installation of Rāma) the high-souled monkeys, taking leave of the lord of earth, went to Kishkindhā. And beholding the inauguration of Rāma, Sugriva, the foremost of monkeys, honored by Rāma, repaired to the city of Kishkindhā. And having obtained his own kingdom, the greatly famous and virtuous-souled Bibhishana, with all the Rākshasas, repaired to the city of Lankā. Having slain his foes, the highly generous and glorious Rāma, ruled in great delight, the kingdom extending all over the earth. And Rāma, fond of the pious, spoke unto Lakshmana, conversant with piety,saying—"O thou conversant with piety, do thou with me and four-fold forces, govern this kingdom, ruled by our predecessors. Like unto our ancestors do thou now carry the burden of an associate in the throne." When the son of Sumitrā did not accept the heir apparentship albeit solicited earnestly again and again, the high-souled (Rāma) conferred upon Bharata that dignity. And that son of king performed various sacrifices such as *Paundarika,** *Aswamedha*†, *Bājimedha* and others. And governing the kingdon for ten thousand years Rāghava performed ten horse-sacrifices with excellent horses and profuse presents. And that highly powerful Rāma, having his arms extended up to the knee-joint, having a spacious breast and Lakshmana as his attendant, ruled the earth (in this wise). And obtaining that excellent kingdom, the virtuous-souled Rāghava performed many sacrifices with his sons, brothers and friends. And Rāma governing the kingdom, the widows were not distressed and there was no fear from voracious animals or from diseases. The people were saved from the thieves and there was no other trouble. And the old were not constrained to perform the funeral ceremonies of the children. All were delighted and devoted to pious observances. And beholding Rāma they did not envy one another. And Rāma governing the kingdom, (people) lived for thousand years and had thousand children,—they were freed from diseases and sorrow. And the trees bore fruits and flowers perpetually—there were showers at will and the wind blew pleasant. And the people delighted engaged in their respective works and the subjects grew pious and truthful, under Rāma's regeme, and were devoted to the observance of all pious works and gifted with all auspicious marks. And Rāma ruled the kingdom for ten thousand years. And this sacred Epic, the first of its kind, affording piety, fame, and long life, and describing the conquest of the kings, was composed by Vālmiki in the days of yore.

---

* A kind of sacrifice.

† A kind of sacrifice in which a horse is slain.

He, who on this earth, shall hear (this story) shall be divested of sins. People, wishing for children, shall obtain the same and those, wishing for riches, shall get by them. Thus people on this earth shall attain to their wished-for objects hearing of this Rāma's installation—the king may conquer the earth and subdue his foes. Females may obtain sons (in the same way) as Kauçalyā gave birth to Rāma, Sumitrā to Lakshmana and Kaikeyi to Bharata. Hearing the story of this work describing the victory of Rāma of unwearied actions one may attain to a long life. He, who with devotion and having his anger subdued, shall hear the story of this epic written by Vālmiki in the days of yore shall get over all troubles. And hearing the story of the Epic composed by Vālmiki in the days of yore, one living in foreign countries, shall return home and enjoy in the company of his friends. Hearing this people shall secure all their wished-for objects from Rāghava and the celestials shall be greatly delighted. When this book is kept in a house it becomes free from the disturbance of evil spirits. Hearing this a king may conquer the earth, and one living in a foreign country fareth well. If a female, during her monthly course, hears the story, she shall give birth to an excellent son. By reading and worshipping this ancient history people are freed from all sins and attain to a long life. The Kshatryas, bending low their heads, should hear this daily from the Brāhmanas. Hearing or reading the whole of Rāmāyana, forsooth shall people get sons and riches. Rāma is ever pleased with him. He is the ever-existing Vishnu—the first God, the huge-armed Hari, Nārāyana and Lord. This ancient work produceth such fruits. May good betide ye. Do ye openly declare that Vishnu's prowess may increase. The celestials shall be greatly delighted for reading or hearing this story of Rāma and the progenitors shall be always pleased. Those, who shall write this story of Rāma first recorded by the Rishi (Vālmiki) shall reach the region of Brahmā. Hearing this people attain to, on this earth, multiplied relations, increased wealth and crops, beautiful wives, excellent happiness, and the accomplishment of all desires. They attain to long life, health, fame, intellect, prowess, and good brothers. Therefore it behoveth those good men, who wish for prosperity, to hear this story perpetually.

THE END OF YUDDHAKANDAM.